Anthology of World Religions

Anthology of World Religions

Sacred Texts and Contemporary Perspectives

Lewis Vaughn

New York Oxford
OXFORD UNIVERSITY PRESS

Oxford University Press is a department of the University of Oxford.
It furthers the University's objective of excellence in research, scholarship, and education by publishing worldwide. Oxford is a registered trade mark of Oxford University Press in the UK and certain other countries.

Published in the United States of America by Oxford University Press
198 Madison Avenue, New York, NY 10016, United States of America.

For titles covered by Section 112 of the US Higher Education Opportunity Act, please visit www.oup.com/us/he for the latest information about pricing and alternate formats.

Library of Congress Cataloging-in-Publication Data

Names: Vaughn, Lewis, author.
Title: Anthology of world religions : sacred texts and contemporary perspectives / Lewis Vaughn.
Description: New York : Oxford University Press, 2017.
Identifiers: LCCN 2016015267 (print) | LCCN 2016021363 (ebook) | ISBN 9780195332360 | ISBN 9780190248758
Subjects: LCSH: Religions.
Classification: LCC BL80.3 .V38 2017 (print) | LCC BL80.3 (ebook) | DDC 200--dc23
LC record available at https://lccn.loc.gov/2016015267

9 8 7 6 5 4 3 2 1
Printed by LSC Communications, United States of America

Brief Contents

Contents

3 Hinduism 83

5 Buddhism 155

14 New Religious Movements 481

Preface

Why should you try to acquire a deeper understanding of religions that are not your own? That is, why study the world's religions? *Anthology of World Religions* is one answer to that question. You need not read very far into it before seeing that religions are deeply interwoven into societies, cultures, governments, history, literature, philosophy, ethics, and the arts—and that to study religions is to learn a great deal about the world and how it works. Many of the great moral, political, and social issues of our times are deeply enmeshed in religious traditions—and it is unlikely that we can completely resolve or fully understand these matters without at least knowing the basics of the traditions involved.

Anthology of World Religions introduces and explains religious traditions by coupling objective explorations of their history, beliefs, and practices with annotated selections from their texts and scriptures and from contemporary commentary by adherents and knowledgeable observers.

This text covers each major religion's history, teachings, founder, leaders, and the factors that are now challenging and changing it—secularism, modernism, pluralism, science, the status of women, and sectarian or factional conflicts.

A few of the elements that help this text stand out among some of its competitors include:

- The coverage of women and the inclusion of several readings by or about women within a particular tradition
- A substantial introduction to each tradition
- A carefully selected mix of readings that includes both sacred texts and modern commentary by practitioners and scholars
- Clear and concise writing that explains difficult concepts without oversimplifying
- An introductory chapter that reviews various approaches to the study of religion, defines religious terms and concepts, discusses theories of religion, and distinguishes between the insider and outsider perspectives on religious traditions

The pedagogy in each chapter includes:

- Timelines and maps
- Text boxes providing background information or more details on relevant topics
- Explanatory notes before each reading
- A list of key terms
- End-of-chapter study/discussion questions
- A list of further reading, including books, articles, and online sources

Ancillaries

The Oxford University Press Ancillary Resource Center (ARC) at http://oup-arc.com/vaughn-anthology-world-religions houses an Instructor's Manual with Test Bank and PowerPoint Lecture Outlines for instructor use. Student Resources are available on the Companion Website at www.oup.com/us/vaughn and include self-quizzes, flashcards, and helpful web links.

Acknowledgements

This text would not have been possible without the efforts of my talented and hard-working editors at Oxford University Press—especially Robert Miller, Meg Botteon, and Alyssa Palazzo—and the conscientious labors of the following scholarly reviewers:

Asad Ahmed, University of California at Berkley
Sujan Burgeson, Yuba College
Derek Daschke, Truman State University
Peter Gardella, Manhattanville College
John Goulde, Sweet Briar College
Joseph Gouverneur, University of North Carolina at Wilmington
Ravi Gupta, Utah State University
Cathy Gutierrez, Sweet Briar College
Jennifer Jesse, Truman State University
James Joiner, Northern Arizona University
Dennis Kelley, University of Missouri at Columbia
Kate Kelley, University of Missouri at Columbia
Kenneth Lee, California State University at Northridge
James Lochtefeld, Carthage College
Henry Munson, University of Maine
Paul Schneider, University of South Florida
Robert Stephens, Clemson University
Mari Stuart, University of South Carolina
Paul Thomas, Radford University
Mark Toole, High Point University
Christopher Van Gorder, Baylor University
Gretel VanWieren, Michigan State University
Catherine Wessinger, Loyola University at New Orleans

1 The Beginning of Understanding

With all the changes that have been wrought in the world by religion in the opening years of the twenty-first century, asking why we should bother to study world religions may seem peculiar, like asking why pedestrians should know the meaning of traffic signals at a busy intersection. In either case, the answer at its most basic level appears obvious: ignorance is risky, blinding, diminishing—and sometimes tragic. Yet far too many people—including some who wield enormous influence in governments, politics, business, the media, education, popular culture, and religions themselves—still fail to see any point in acquiring a deeper understanding of religions or of any religion not their own. This failure should worry the rest of the world, and—increasingly—it does.

The answer to our query is that there are many reasons for a closer, more thoughtful examination of world religions. First, studying world religions is like studying any other academic subject: a legitimate goal is knowledge for its own sake. For countless reflective people—both great minds and serious students of every level—the truth is its own reward, and the searching requires no other justification. Neither does the searching require you to embrace the particular view under study. You need not be a believer to examine sacred beliefs, no more than you must be a romanticist to explore romantic literature or a Stoic to investigate Stoic philosophy.

Second, for many, the study of world religions is part of an even larger project—the ongoing development of a coherent worldview. A worldview is a philosophy of life, a set of beliefs and principles that helps us make sense of our lives, the cosmos, and our place in it. We all have a worldview, and we will likely spend our lifetimes shaping it or being shaped by it. A fully developed worldview must encompass many of the very issues that religions address. What are we? Why are we here? What is real and what is not? What can we know? What is the meaning of life? How should we live? The study of religion broadens and deepens our worldview, just as the study of literature, art, philosophy, and history does. A thoughtful expedition through the world's religions will not necessarily detour the course of our lives, as some may fear, but it will surely deepen our understanding of whatever path we take.

Third, perhaps more than at any other time in history, fully fathoming how the world works requires some understanding of world religions. World religions are part of the mosaic of ideas and phenomena that constitute modern life. This fact alone makes them worth studying. History, archeology, art, music, philosophy, mathematics, anthropology, politics—these and other disciplines also investigate pieces of the mosaic. If they are valuable pursuits because of the understanding they can produce for humankind, then so is the study of world religions. But even this claim is, in a sense, understated. In many disciplines (art, music, and history, for example), plumbing the depths of the subject is not possible without also following its broad waters back into the tributaries of religious traditions.

Fourth, a knowledge of world religions can help us understand and perhaps even douse some of the flames of conflict that now rage on the planet. The world is dotted with flashpoints of violence and discord—much of it inspired or begotten by religions. In the name of faith, peace has too often given way to war, coexistence to confrontation, and respect to wrath. But an objective understanding of religions can help engender tolerance and an acceptance of differences. Mutual respect can be the ruling principle of social interaction—even while people disagree vigorously about religious ideas and articles of faith. The nonreligious can learn respect for the religious, and the religious can learn respect for the nonreligious and for those of other faiths. And peace may follow. There is no guarantee that understanding will lead to tolerance and that tolerance will then ease conflict, but a lack of understanding is sure to make tolerance less likely.

With a solid grounding in world religions also comes the realization that some strains of religion are fervently intolerant, fanatical, or violent, just as some secular worldviews are. They have no desire for mutual respect or compromise or peace. Only by understanding them can we hope to deal effectively with their threat to the rest of the world. Since the terrorist attacks of September 11, 2001, people everywhere have debated how to respond to

FIGURE 1.1 On September 11, 2001, terrorists associated with the Islamic extremist group al-Qaeda flew two airliners into the towers of the World Trade Center in New York City, killing nearly 3,000 people and leaving two burning, gaping holes in the towers. Both towers collapsed.

those who wield terror and death in the name of religion. Some commentators have argued that the response thus far has been dangerously misguided because of a colossal ignorance of the world's religions. Some have leaped to untenable conclusions that are themselves harmful: that religions are the root of all violence or, just as blinkered, that violence is a rare anomaly in religious traditions. The best corrective for such views is study of, and reflection on, world religions—measures that seem increasingly important for informed and meaningful life in the pluralistic, globalized twenty-first century.

Finally, countless political, social, and moral issues of our times are entwined with religions of the world—and it is unlikely that we can completely resolve or fully understand the former without comprehending the latter. Frequently these issues are the sparks that arise when there is a clash between religion and secular society, or two or more religious traditions, or religion and modern life, or competing ideas within a single religion. Often the fire of controversy has a secular source, and religion joins the debate because it, like other segments of society, has a stake in the outcome. In any case, the questions in contention are both serious and varied: democracy, gay marriage, abortion, capital punishment, euthanasia, women's rights, religion in schools, contraception, religious expression in public life, government funding of religion, discrimination against religious groups, censorship of secular mass media, racism, religious extremism, pornography, offensive speech, biological evolution, government support of art deemed sacrilegious, aid for the poor, population control, civil rights, homosexuality, gender roles, capitalism, sexuality, reproductive technologies (such as in vitro fertilization), animal rights, blasphemy. . . . The list goes on, and so does the need for a thorough knowledge of the religious traditions that help shape the beliefs defining our lives.

FIRST LOOK

In most fields of study, the first step in exploring the subject is defining what the subject is. But in world religions, defining *religion*—identifying what makes religion religion—is notoriously difficult to do. There are many proposed definitions of the term, but none seem to capture the social, experiential, and conceptual diversity of religions. Some attempted definitions include:

"the belief in Spiritual Beings" (Edward Tylor)

"what the individual does with his own solitariness" (A. N. Whitehead)

"that which is of ultimate concern" (Paul Tillich)

"a unified system of beliefs and practices relative to sacred things, that is to say, things set apart and forbidden—beliefs and practices which unite in one single moral community called a Church, all those who adhere to them" (Émile Durkheim)

"the human attitude towards a sacred order that includes within it all being—human or otherwise—i.e., belief in a cosmos, the meaning of which both includes and transcends man" (Peter Berger)

Each of these refers to important aspects of some religions but seems to leave something out of account, and none of them can comfortably apply to all the religions of the world. Not

FIGURE 1.2 The Po Lin Monastery on Lantau Island in Hong Kong features the giant Tian Tan Buddha, or Big Buddha, a large bronze statue of Buddha Shakyamuni.

all religions emphasize relationships with deities, ethical systems, institutional structures, the interior life of individuals, scriptures, faith, or beliefs. But although definitions are problematic, it is possible to examine some of the common features of what we would consider unambiguous examples of religions. A religion would need not have all these features, but it would exhibit many of them. Some scholars have sorted these features into several categories: for example, rituals and practices, experiences and feelings, stories and myths, doctrines and philosophies, ethical and legal concerns, social and institutional structures, and material expressions (art, architecture, icons, and sacred objects and places).

One question that scholars have tried to answer is: What is the source of religion—that is, how did religion originate or what function does it serve? Those who have studied religions in the past have provided several answers, many of which are discussed in the following readings. Their answers include the following:

- Nature worship—Religion began as early humans responded to the forces of nature (the sun, moon, tides, winds, etc.) by personifying them and attaching myths and rituals to them (Max Muller, 1823–1900).
- Imagination—People have imagined religion by projecting human desires, needs, or attributes onto imaginary deities (Ludwig Feuerbach, 1804–1872).
- **Animism**—Religion originated in the belief that everything (both living and inanimate) is animated by spirits (Edward Tylor, 1832–1917).
- Magic—Religion arose from early humans' attempts to control nature through magic (James George Frazer, 1854–1941).
- Utility—Religion performs an important function or satisfies particular needs by either (1) promoting social cohesion and harmony (Émile Durkheim, 1858–1917), (2) easing

the pain of oppression (Karl Marx, 1818–1883), (3) reflecting and contending with internal psychological conflicts (Sigmund Freud, 1856–1939), or (4) helping to ensure human survival by preserving gene replication (John Bowker, b. 1935).

Like the proposed definitions of religion, these theories about the sources of religion are thought by most experts to be incomplete. Religion is more complex, and its sources are more diverse, than any one of these views suggests. But these theories are still considered important starting points for the study of religion. (Some of the views are represented in the readings that follow.)

RELIGIOUS QUESTIONS AND ANSWERS

Either explicitly or implicitly, religions provide answers to questions—often the most important questions we can think to ask. One way to express the most general form of these questions is: What exists? What is good (or right)? and What can we know?

To ask *What exists?* is to ask What is real? or What is the nature of reality? This is to ask what entities, objects, or forces exist in the universe, which includes both material or natural objects and nonphysical, divine, supernatural, or spiritual things. The latter may refer to gods, God, other supernatural beings (e.g., angels and demons), or mysterious or impersonal forces.

Making sense of religious concepts of reality requires specific terminology. Belief in one God (as in Christianity, Judaism, and Islam) is called **monotheism**. The more general term for belief in God or gods is **theism**, and we refer to such belief as *theistic. Nontheistic* describes a lack of belief in God or gods. It can apply to **atheism** (a denial of the existence of any kind of divinity), or to the view that the divine is not a person but a mysterious force or energy (e.g., Brahman in Hinduism). A belief in several gods or goddesses is known as **polytheism**. The word may also refer to belief in several gods or goddesses that are all manifestations of one divine entity. To neither believe nor disbelieve in God is to adopt the position of **agnosticism**. The word also pertains to the view that it is not possible to know whether or not God exists.

To ask what is good or right is to ask about moral values, about how we should live our lives. Many religions express such values in moral codes that prescribe proper behavior and proscribe violations of the code. Prime examples are the Ten Commandments (plus over six hundred rules of behavior and religious practice) in Judaism; the Law or *shari'a* in Islam; the *Laws of Manu* in Hinduism; and the *Five Precepts* in Buddhism. Some religions don't offer a code; they instead provide a guiding moral principle, a prevailing attitude, or a story or myth to live by. The Christian faith emphasizes an attitude of love and the story of Christ's life to shape moral behavior. Confucianism teaches the supreme importance of harmony in the family, community, and state.

To ask what we can know is to ask what truths about the world or a particular religion we can be sure of and how we can go about attaining that assurance. This is a question about the source of religious knowledge, and among world religions there are several possible answers. In some religions, revelation—the supernatural imparting of knowledge or wisdom to

FIGURE 1.3 **In Bodhgaya, Bihar, India, a group of pilgrim Buddhist monks read prayers beneath a tree decorated with prayer flags.**

believers—is the key source. Through revelation, adherents are thought to obtain moral codes, prophecies, instructions, or the texts of holy books. In other religions the source of religious knowledge is faith, conscience, tradition, reason, or all of the above.

STUDYING RELIGIONS

Religious studies is the academic discipline that tries to understand religions from a unique perspective. It seeks to understand religions, but it remains neutral regarding the truth or justification of religious claims. It is *descriptive*, not evaluative. It is scientific, scholarly, and investigative, not religious. Its ideal is an unbiased and accurate examination of the teachings, practices, experiences, history, and culture of a particular religion or several religions.

The academic study of religions is not the discipline known as the *philosophy of religion*, whose primary task is to understand, analyze, and evaluate the truth of religious claims. The philosophy of religion asks, What does this claim mean, and is it justified? Neither is religious studies *theology*, the study of issues and themes relating to one's own religion. Generally, theologians try to understand their own religious tradition, not to dismantle it. Theology is a religious endeavor.

There are many ways to view the workings of a religious tradition, but two especially need to be distinguished. The academic discipline of religious studies looks at a religion from an *outsider's* perspective, from the viewpoint of someone who is not a practitioner of the religion. But there is also the *insider's* perspective, the viewpoint of an adherent of the religion. The best work in religious studies tries to incorporate both perspectives—to investigate impartially using the outsider's view and to strive, with empathy and imagination, to view the religion as an insider would.

The academic study of world religions is multidisciplinary. Many disciplines are put to work in investigating religions—sociology, mythology, archeology, philosophy, theology, anthropology, history, psychology, linguistics, and others. The point of it all is to try to discover how religions have influenced multiple aspects of human lives and how these aspects have affected religions.

The following readings will help you better understand the world's religions through a study of scriptures and an exploration of important ideas, origins, history, development, and influence throughout the world.

KEY TERMS

agnosticism The position of neither believing nor disbelieving in God. The word also pertains to the view that it is not possible to know whether or not God exists.

animism The view that objects in the natural world—rocks, trees, fire, rivers, mountains, animals, stars—are, or have, spirits or consciousness.

atheism A denial of the existence of any kind of divinity, or the view that the divine is not a person but a mysterious force or energy.

monotheism Belief in one God (as in Christianity, Judaism, and Islam).

polytheism Belief in several gods or goddesses. The term may also refer to belief in several gods or goddesses that are all manifestations of one divine entity.

profane Whatever is deemed nonreligious or secular; the converse of sacred.

socialism The political and economic doctrine that the means of production (property, factories, businesses) should be owned or controlled by the people, either communally or through the state.

theism Belief in God or gods.

READINGS

IDENTIFYING RELIGIONS

The Nature of Religion

NINIAN SMART

Ninian Smart (1927–2001) is known for his groundbreaking work in world religions at several universities throughout the world. He established the first department of religious studies in the United Kingdom at the University of Lancaster. For this achievement and others he has been called the "father of religious studies" in Britain. In this excerpt he details his well-known seven dimensions of religion.

In thinking about religion, it is easy to be confused about what it is. Is there some essence which is common to all religions? And cannot a person be religious without belonging to any of the religions? The search for an essence ends up in vagueness—for instance in the statement that a religion is some system of worship or other practice recognizing a transcendent Being or goal. Our problems break out again in trying to define the key term "transcendent." And in answer to the second question, why yes: there are plenty of people with deep spiritual concerns who do not ally themselves to any formal religious movement, and who may not themselves recognize anything as transcendent. They may see ultimate spiritual meaning in unity with nature or in relationships to other persons. . . .

Despite all this, it is possible to make sense of the variety and to discern some patterns in the luxurious vegetation of the world's religions and subtraditions. One approach is to look at the different aspects or dimensions of religion.

THE PRACTICAL AND RITUAL DIMENSION

Every tradition has some practices to which it adheres—for instance regular worship, preaching, prayers, and so on. They are often known as rituals (though they

Ninian Smart, "Introduction," *The World's Religions*, 2nd ed. (Cambridge: Cambridge University Press, 1998), 11–22.

may well be more informal than this word implies). This *practical* and *ritual* dimension is especially important with faiths of a strongly sacramental kind, such as Eastern Orthodox Christianity with its long and elaborate service known as the Liturgy. The ancient Jewish tradition of the Temple, before it was destroyed in 70 CE, was preoccupied with the rituals of sacrifice, and thereafter with the study of such rites seen as equivalent to their performance, so that study itself becomes almost a ritual activity. Again, sacrificial rituals are important among Brahmin forms of the Hindu tradition.

Also important are other patterns of behavior which, while they may not strictly count as rituals, fulfill a function in developing spiritual awareness or ethical insight: practices such as yoga in the Buddhist and Hindu traditions, methods of stilling the self in Eastern Orthodox mysticism, meditations which can help to increase compassion and love, and so on. Such practices can be combined with rituals of worship, where meditation is directed toward union with God. They can count as a form of prayer. In such ways they overlap with the more formal or explicit rites of religion.

THE EXPERIENTIAL AND EMOTIONAL DIMENSION

We only have to glance at religious history to see the enormous vitality and significance of experience in the formation and development of religious traditions. Consider the visions of the Prophet Muhammad, the conversion of Paul, the enlightenment of the Buddha. These were seminal events in human history. And it is obvious that the *emotions* and *experiences* of men and women are the food on which the other dimensions of religion feed: ritual without feeling is cold, doctrines without awe or compassion are dry, and myths which do not move hearers are feeble. So it is important in understanding a tradition to try to enter into the feelings which it generates—to feel the sacred awe, the calm peace, the rousing inner dynamism, the perception of a brilliant emptiness within, the outpouring of love, the sensations of hope, the gratitude for favors which have been received. One of the main reasons why music is so potent in religion is that it has mysterious powers to express and engender emotions. . . .

THE NARRATIVE OR MYTHIC DIMENSION

Often experience is channeled and expressed not only by ritual but also by sacred narrative or myth. This is the third dimension—the *mythic* or *narrative*. It is the story side of religion. It is typical of all faiths to hand down vital stories: some historical; some about that mysterious primordial time when the world was in its timeless dawn; some about things to come at the end of time; some about great heroes and saints; some about great founders, such as Moses, the Buddha, Jesus, and Muhammad; some about assaults by the Evil One; some parables and edifying tales; some about the adventures of the gods; and so on. These stories often are called myths. The term may be a bit misleading, for in the modern study of religion there is no implication that a myth is false.

The seminal stories of a religion may be rooted in history or they may not. Stories of creation are before history, as are myths which indicate how death and suffering came into the world. Others are about historical events—for instance the life of the Prophet Muhammad, or the execution of Jesus, and the enlightenment of the Buddha. Historians have sometimes cast doubt on some aspects of these historical stories, but from the standpoint of the student of religion this question is secondary to the meaning and function of the myth; and to the believer, very often, these narratives *are* history.

This belief is strengthened by the fact that many faiths look upon certain documents, originally maybe based upon long oral traditions, as true scriptures. They are canonical or recognized by the relevant body of the faithful (the Church, the community,

Brahmins and others in India, the Buddhist Sangha or Order). They are often treated as inspired directly by God or as records of the very words of the Founder. They have authority, and they contain many stories and myths which are taken to be divinely or otherwise guaranteed. But other documents and oral traditions may also be important—the lives of the saints, the chronicles of Ceylon as a Buddhist nation, the stories of famous holy men of Eastern Europe in the Hasidic tradition, traditions concerning the life of the Prophet (hadith), and so forth. These stories may have lesser authority but they can still be inspiring to the followers. . . .

THE DOCTRINAL AND PHILOSOPHICAL DIMENSION

Underpinning the narrative dimension is the *doctrinal* dimension. Thus, in the Christian tradition, the story of Jesus' life and the ritual of the communion service led to attempts to provide an analysis of the nature of the Divine Being which would preserve both the idea of the Incarnation (Jesus as God) and the belief in one God. The result was the doctrine of the Trinity, which sees God as three persons in one substance. Similarly, with the meeting between early Christianity and the great Graeco-Roman philosophical and intellectual heritage it became necessary to face questions about the ultimate meaning of creation, the inner nature of God, the notion of grace, the analysis of how Christ could be both God and human being, and so on. These concerns led to the elaboration of Christian doctrine. In the case of Buddhism, to take another example, doctrinal ideas were more crucial right from the start, for the Buddha presented a philosophical vision of the world which itself was an aid to salvation.

In any event, doctrines come to play a significant part in all the major religions, partly because sooner or later a faith has to adapt to social reality and so to the fact that much of the leadership is well educated and seeks some kind of intellectual statement of the basis of the faith. . . .

THE ETHICAL AND LEGAL DIMENSION

Both narrative and doctrine affect the values of a tradition by laying out the shape of a worldview and addressing the question of ultimate liberation or salvation. The law which a tradition or subtradition incorporates into its fabric can be called the *ethical* dimension of religion. In Buddhism, for instance, there are certain universally binding precepts, known as the five precepts or virtues, together with a set of further regulations controlling the lives of monks and nuns and monastic communities. In Judaism we have not merely the Ten Commandments but a complex of over six hundred rules imposed upon the community by the Divine Being. All this Law or Torah is a framework for living for the Orthodox Jew. It also is part of the ritual dimension, because, for instance, the injunction to keep the Sabbath as a day of rest is also the injunction to perform certain sacred practices and rituals, such as attending the synagogue and maintaining purity.

Similarly, Islamic life has traditionally been controlled by the Law or *shari'a,* which shapes society as both a religious and a political society, as well as shaping the moral life of the individual—prescribing that he should pray daily, give alms to the poor, and so on, and that society should have various institutions, such as marriage, modes of banking, etc. . . .

THE SOCIAL AND INSTITUTIONAL DIMENSION

The dimensions outlined so far—the experiential, the ritual, the mythic, the doctrinal, and the ethical—can be considered in abstract terms, without being embodied in external form. The last two dimensions have to do with the incarnation of religion. First, every religious movement is embodied in a group of people, and that is very often rather formally organized—as Church, or Sangha, or *umma.* The sixth dimension therefore is what may be called the social or *institutional* aspect of religion. To understand a faith we need to see how it works among people. This is one reason why such an important tool of the investigator of religion is that subdiscipline which is known as the sociology of religion. Sometimes the social aspect of a worldview is simply identical with society itself, as in small-scale groups such as tribes. But there is a variety of relations between organized religions and society at large: a faith may be the official religion, or it may be just one denomination among many, or it may be somewhat cut off from social life, as a sect. Within the organization of one religion, moreover, there are many models—from the relative democratic governance of a radical Protestant congregation to the hierarchical and monarchical system of the Church of Rome.

It is not, however, the formal officials of a religion who may in the long run turn out to be the most important persons in a tradition. For there are charismatic or sacred personages, whose spiritual power glows through their demeanor and actions, and who vivify the faith of more ordinary folk—saintly people, gurus, mystics, and prophets, whose words and example stir up the spiritual enthusiasm of the masses, and who lend depth and meaning to the rituals and values of a tradition. They can also be revolutionaries and set religion on new courses. They can, like John Wesley, become leaders of a new denomination, almost against their will; or they can be founders of new groups which may in due course emerge as separate religions—an example is Joseph Smith II, Prophet of the new faith of Mormonism. In short, the social dimension of religion includes not only the mass of persons but also the outstanding individuals through whose features glimmer old and new thoughts of the heaven toward which they aspire.

THE MATERIAL DIMENSION

This social or institutional dimension of religion almost inevitably becomes incarnate in a different way, in *material* form, as buildings, works of art, and other creations. Some movements—such as Calvinist Christianity, especially in the time before the present century—eschew external symbols as being potentially idolatrous; their buildings are often beautiful in their simplicity, but their intention is to be without artistic or other images which might seduce people from the thought that God is a spirit who transcends all representations. However, the material expressions of religion are more often elaborate, moving, and highly important for believers in their approach to the divine. How indeed could we understand Eastern Orthodox Christianity without seeing what ikons are like and knowing that they are regarded as windows onto heaven? How could we get inside the feel of Hinduism without attending to the varied statues of God and the gods?

Also important material expressions of a religion are those natural features of the world which are singled out as being of special sacredness and meaning—the river Ganges, the Jordan, the sacred mountains of China, Mount Fuji in Japan, Ayers Rock in Australia, the Mount of Olives, Mount Sinai, and so forth. Sometimes of course these sacred landmarks combine with more direct human creations, such as the holy city of Jerusalem, the sacred shrines of Banaras, or the temple at Bodh Gaya which commemorates the Buddha's Enlightenment.

USES OF THE SEVEN DIMENSIONS

To sum up: we have surveyed briefly the seven dimensions of religion which help to characterize religions as they exist in the world. The point of the list is so that we can give a balanced description of the movements which have animated the human spirit and taken a place in the shaping of society, without neglecting either ideas or practices.

Naturally, there are religious movements or manifestations where one or other of the dimensions is so weak as to be virtually absent: nonliterate small-scale societies do not have much means of expressing the doctrinal dimension; Buddhist modernists, concentrating on meditation, ethics, and philosophy, pay scant regard to the narrative dimension of Buddhism; some newly formed groups may not have evolved anything much in the way of the material dimension. Also there are so many people who are not formally part of any social religious grouping, but have their own particular worldviews and practices, that we can observe in society atoms of religion which do not possess any well-formed social dimension. But of course in forming a phenomenon within society they reflect certain trends which in a sense form a shadow of the social dimension (just as those who have not yet got themselves a material dimension are nevertheless implicitly storing one up, for with success come buildings and with rituals ikons, most likely).

COMPARATIVE STUDIES

Comparing Religions

WILL DEMING

Will Deming is associate professor of theology at the University of Portland. He stresses the importance of comparing religions to learn more about them, and he explains how to avoid making comparisons that are biased, arbitrary, and otherwise uninformative. For example, it will not do, he says, to compare elements that are only superficially similar. Two religious traditions may use water as a symbol, but they may interpret it differently and employ it in dissimilar ways. It's better to compare what he calls "dynamic equivalents"—elements that play equivalent roles within the religious traditions.

The comparison of religions explores meaningful similarities and differences between religions. Unlike the *evaluation* of religions, it is undertaken for the purpose of learning more about religion and religions, whether or not one plans to use this knowledge to judge a religion's worth. Just as other fields of study have recognized the importance of a comparative subdiscipline—comparative government in political science, comparative anatomy in biology—so, too, the comparison of religions is an essential aspect of studying religion. As we noted earlier, familiarity with only one specimen of a thing, be it wine, business management models, or religions, courts intellectual myopia.

The starting point for comparison is the recognition that each religion is a coherent system and that

Will Deming, *Rethinking Religion: A Concise Introduction* (New York: Oxford University Press, 2005), 109–112.

its elements derive their meaning as parts of that system. Just as a word has no meaning when it is isolated from its proper system of language, the elements of a religion become opaque if we ignore their native context. When this happens, comparisons become arbitrary and biased, moving from neutral exploration to misunderstanding and condemnation.

For example, we might be tempted to compare the Christian Trinity of Father, Son, and Holy Spirit with the Hindu Trinity of Brahma, Vishnu, and Shiva. A simple listing of the characteristics of each Trinity would be easy enough. But if we overlook the fact that the former is central to the religion of most Christians, whereas the latter is an intellectual formulation of limited practical significance for most Hindus, this is like comparing the mathematical abilities of Albert Einstein and Mark Twain. The differences are marked and real, but not of any great value for understanding either figure.

Or again, we could compare the Jain promotion of non-violence (*ahimsa*) with the sacrificial practices of ancient Judaism. In the one, priests go to great lengths to avoid harming any sentient creature, even gnats and slugs. In the other, priests butchered and roasted birds and beasts on the altar of God. Unless we take into account the larger systems of these religions, which include, respectively, a belief in *karma* and rebirth into nonhuman forms and a belief in God as Creator of the natural world and guardian of a chosen people, we not only venture into a pointless comparison, as in the previous example, but also risk coming to foregone conclusions based on *our* sensibilities about the sanctity of life. In neither case will we have addressed the subject on its own terms, on the basis of its own inner-logic.

Some comparisons of this sort are particularly tempting, as when the same symbol is used by more than one religion. Water, as we have noted, is one of these. Because so many religious traditions understand the profane world as "impure" and ultimate reality as "pure," orientation to the latter often takes the form of washing oneself "clean." This observation has encouraged a few scholars to speak of "universal symbols" or "patterns" of symbols.

Yet washing rituals can vary greatly between traditions. Hindu ablutions at sunrise are not the same as Christian baptism or a Shinto priest sprinkling an adherent with a wet evergreen sprig. It is also true that religions use water for ends other than purification. In Taoism and Zen Buddhism water orients adherents to a divine flow or Way, in agrarian religions water can connect adherents with the powers of life and regeneration, and in religions that rely on mythologies of sea gods and primal floods water orients adherents to such higher-order realities as chaos and evil. Thus, to the extent that there is no generic religion or universally held vision of ultimate reality, we must use considerable caution when speaking of common or universal symbols.

Fortunately, most of these pitfalls can be avoided if, in setting up a comparison, we take into account the larger systems of religions by identifying "dynamic equivalents." Instead of beginning with "obvious" similarities or "reasonable" points of comparison, which often have more to do with our worldviews than those of the religions in question, we need to locate elements that play "equivalent" roles within the "dynamics" of their respective religious systems. In this way, we can determine which comparisons are superficial and arbitrary, and which will lead us into a fuller understanding of the religions being compared. Sometimes elements that initially appear to have nothing in common emerge as informative dynamic equivalents. For instance, an Episcopalian walking through a stylized labyrinth or singing Taize songs, an evangelical Protestant observing "quiet time," a Vaishnava Hindu chanting from the Vedas, and a Zen monk raking leaves are all "equivalent" symbolic acts within the dynamics of each religion. All are routine, "intentionless" activities that inhibit one's thoughts from focusing on profane reality. Each prepares the adherent's mind for interaction with ultimate reality, based on the manner in which each tradition envisions that reality.

This procedure of locating dynamic equivalents also allows the student of religion to postulate larger, comparative categories, such as "worship," "mysticism," and "initiation rite," *from within the religions themselves,* establishing a basis for comparing religions that is both "organic" and "reciprocal." In this way we avoid comparisons based on our own preconceptions and minimize the risk of understanding one religion in terms of another. Of course, in adopting this procedure, we must also reckon with another eventuality. If we confine our comparisons to elements that are dynamic equivalents, we will encounter instances in which no comparison is possible. We have no guarantee that every element in one religion will be matched by a dynamic equivalent in another. But this, too, is valuable information for the student of religion.

Finally, it needs to be said that the comparison of religions is more than just the intellectual pursuit of academics. Beyond informing the academic study of religion, it has a practical side, too. Amid the pluralism of American society, the comparison of religions enables us to "cope"—to fathom, to adjust to, and to enter into dialogue with those whose mores and lifestyles diverge from our own. Americans still struggle with racial and ethnic difference. Some attention to "comparative religious ethics" will prevent similar impasses over religious difference.

Furthermore, the comparison of religions can give people perspective on their place in their own religious tradition. Few religions are monolithic, and the diversity *within* religions becomes increasingly apparent as our world becomes more interconnected. Formerly separated by distance and time, different forms of the same religions now come into contact with each other on a regular basis: first- and third-world evangelicals, high- and low-church Methodists, Orthodox and Conservative Jews, Italian and Irish Catholics, and Southern, Independent, and Free-Will Baptists. By knowing that each of these manifestations of a tradition differs from its cousins by virtue of different symbols and visions of realities, we may analyze and compare the various forms of a single denomination in the same way that one analyzes and compares Hinduism and Confucianism.

In fact, one need not venture outside of his or her own personal religious worldview to appreciate the value of comparing religions. Since all religions change over time, every religion has a history. Even persons who isolate themselves from every tradition but their own must, in some manner, reckon with past versions of that tradition. Present-day Mormonism is not what it was in the days of its founder, Joseph Smith, nor is early twentieth-century Catholicism the same as post-Vatican II Catholicism. If one sees oneself as standing in a particular tradition, as a modern representative of a historical faith (and most do), then one must adopt some identification vis-à-vis his or her forerunners.

This becomes especially urgent when a tradition defines itself with reference to a golden era—the first-century church, the first Buddhist *sangha*, the lifetime of Muhammad—or a sacred scripture. For example, the Bible has been scripture for ancient and modern Christians—as well as patristic, late antique, early medieval, high medieval, and Renaissance Christians—but not in the same way. Since the Bible is an ancient document, the oldest aspects of which are now several millennia old, using it to define the religion of the modern church requires a process of interpretation. Yet the question this interpretation must answer is not so much, How does the Bible speak to Christians (or Southern Baptists, or third-world evangelicals, or post-Vatican II Catholics) today?, for that has the potential of severing ties with the past. Rather, the question is, How *should* the Bible speak to Christians today, in light of how it *once* spoke to Christians in the past? This type of interpretation, therefore, is really a matter of comparison. It compares past systems with present systems: how the Bible functioned as a symbol in the religious system of, say, medieval Christianity, as compared with the possibilities for it functioning as a symbol in the religious systems of Christianity today.

To shift to the language of theology, what we are speaking of here is "hermeneutics." This is the attempt, common to all religions, to keep a tradition viable and coherent by reappropriating past practices and beliefs. It is through hermeneutics that the example of Jesus, or the Buddha, or Muhammad, and the pronouncements of the Bible, or the *Pitakas*, or the Quran, remain relevant in today's world. Likewise, it is hermeneutics that determines whether a tradition will address this or that modern issue—stem-cell research, the "greenhouse" effect—or advance this or that modern cause—environmental justice, nuclear disarmament. Thus, understood as hermeneutics, the comparison of religions is far from an intellectual luxury. If a religion cannot justify the relevance of its tradition to each succeeding generation, it goes the way of "dead religions"—Mithraism, Gnosticism, and the religions of classical Greece and Rome and Egypt. It is swallowed up by a more viable tradition or becomes extinct.

THE SACRED AND THE PROFANE

The Sacredness of Nature and Cosmic Religion

MIRCEA ELIADE

Mircea Eliade (1907–1986) was a professor at the University of Chicago, where he encouraged universities in several countries to focus on the study of religion. Other eminent scholars studied religions by determining how a belief or ritual functions within the tradition to meet particular needs. This approach is a *reductionist* method because it tries to explain religion by reducing it to something exterior to religion, such as particular psychological or social factors. Eliade, however, rejected the reductionist view. He argued that religion is an independent variable in the minds of religious people: religion must be explained "on its own terms." The idea is to uncover the heart of religion by examining how it handles certain archetypal notions such as the **profane** and sacred. In this excerpt, we see an example of Eliade's method.

For religious man, nature is never only "natural"; it is always fraught with a religious value. This is easy to understand, for the cosmos is a divine creation; coming from the hands of the gods, the world is impregnated with sacredness. It is not simply a sacrality *communicated* by the gods, as is the case, for example, with a place or an object consecrated by the divine presence. The gods did more; *they manifested the different modalities of the sacred in the very structure of the world and of cosmic phenomena.*

The world stands displayed in such a manner that, in contemplating it, religious man discovers the many modalities of the sacred, and hence of being. Above all, the world exists, it is there, and it has a structure; it is not a chaos but a cosmos, hence it presents itself as creation, as work of the gods. This divine work always preserves its quality of transparency, that is, it spontaneously reveals the many aspects of the sacred. The sky directly, "naturally," reveals the infinite distance, the transcendence of the deity. The earth too is transparent; it presents itself as universal mother and nurse. The cosmic rhythms manifest order, harmony, permanence, fecundity. The cosmos as a whole is an organism at once *real*, *living*, and *sacred*; it simultaneously reveals the modalities of being and of sacrality. Ontophany [a manifestation of the sacred in an unlimited, ultimate form] and hierophany [a manifestation of the sacred in a limited object or time] meet.

. . . [W]e shall try to understand how the world presents itself to the eyes of religious man—or, more precisely, how sacrality is revealed through the

Mircea Eliade, *The Sacred and the Profane: The Nature of Religion*, trans. W. R. Trask (New York: Harcourt Brace Jovanovich, 1959), 116–120.

structures of the world. We must not forget that for religious man the supernatural is indissolubly connected with the natural, that nature always expresses something that transcends it. As we said earlier: a sacred stone is venerated because it is *sacred*, not because it is a *stone*; it is the sacrality *manifested through the mode of being of the stone* that reveals its true essence. This is why we cannot speak of naturism or of natural religion in the sense that the nineteenth century gave to those terms; for it is "supernature" that the religious man apprehends through the natural aspects of the world.

THE CELESTIAL SACRED AND THE URANIAN GODS

Simple contemplation of the celestial vault already provokes a religious experience. The sky shows itself to be infinite, transcendent. It is pre-eminently the "wholly other" than the little represented by man and his environment. Transcendence is revealed by simple awareness of infinite height. "Most high" spontaneously becomes an attribute of divinity. The higher regions inaccessible to man, the sidereal zones, acquire the momentousness of the transcendent, of absolute reality, of eternity. There dwell the gods; there a few privileged mortals make their way by rites of ascent; there, in the conception of certain religions, mount the souls of the dead. The "most high" is a dimension inaccessible to man as man; it belongs to superhuman forces and beings. He who ascends by mounting the steps of a sanctuary or the ritual ladder that leads to the sky ceases to be a man; in one way or another, he shares in the divine condition.

All this is not arrived at by a logical, rational operation. The transcendental category of height, of the superterrestrial, of the infinite, is revealed to the whole man, to his intelligence and his soul. It is a total awareness on man's part; beholding the sky, he simultaneously discovers the divine incommensurability and his own situation in the cosmos. For the sky, *by its own mode of being*, reveals transcendence, force, eternity. It *exists absolutely* because it is *high, infinite, eternal, powerful.*

This is the true significance of the statement made above that the gods manifested the different modalities of the sacred in the very structure of the world. In other words, the cosmos—paradigmatic work of the gods—is so constructed that a religious sense of the divine transcendence is aroused by the very existence of the sky. And since the sky exists absolutely, many of the supreme gods of primitive peoples are called by names designating height, the celestial vault, meteorological phenomena, or simply Owner of the Sky or Sky Dweller.

The supreme divinity of the Maori is named Iho; *iho* means elevated, high up. Uwoluwu, the supreme god of the Akposo Negroes, signifies what is on high, the upper regions. Among the Selk'nam of Tierra del Fuego God is called Dweller in the Sky or He Who is in the Sky. Puluga, the supreme being of the Andaman Islanders, dwells in the sky; the thunder is his voice, wind his breath, the storm is the sign of his anger, for with his lightning he punishes those who break his commandments. The Sky God of the Yoruba of the Slave Coast is named Olorun, literally owner of the Sky. The Samoyed worship Num, a god who dwells in the highest sky and whose name means sky. Among the Koryak, the supreme divinity is called the One on High, the Master of the High, He Who Exists. The Ainu know him as the Divine Chief of the Sky, the Sky God, the Divine Creator of the Worlds, but also as *Kamui*, that is, Sky. The list could easily be extended.

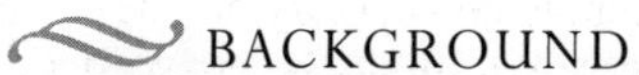
BACKGROUND

Importance of Religion, by Country

Country	Percentage of People for Whom Religion Is Important
Bangladesh	99%
Niger	99%
Indonesia	99%
Sri Lanka	99%
United States	65%
Belarus	34%
Russia	34%
France	30%
United Kingdom	27%
Japan	24%
Denmark	19%
Sweden	17%
Estonia	16%

Gallup World, "Religiosity Highest in World's Poorest Nation," August 2010, Gallup.com. Results are based on telephone and face-to-face interviews conducted in 2009 with approximately 1,000 adults in each country. Survey question: "Is religion an important part of your daily life?" For results based on the total sample of national adults, one can say with 95% confidence that the maximum margin of sampling error ranges from ±5.3 percentage points in Lithuania to ±2.6 percentage points in India. In addition to sampling error, question wording and practical difficulties in conducting surveys can introduce error or bias into the findings of public opinion polls.

SUBJECTIVE BELIEF

Religious Experience: The Root of Religion

WILLIAM JAMES

William James (1842–1910) was one of America's most influential philosophers, leaving a lasting impression on debates in epistemology, philosophy of religion, ethics, and free will. He was born in New York City and grew up in an intellectually stimulating family. His father was a philosopher of religion, and his brother Henry was the famous novelist. His reputation as the greatest psychologist of America and Europe was ensured by the publication of his voluminous work *The Principles of Psychology* (1890). After that came numerous philosophical essays and books, including *The Will to Believe and Other Essays in Popular Philosophy* (1897) and *The Varieties of Religious Experience* (1902). In this excerpt from *Varieties*, James details four characteristics of mystical states, which he views as the heart of religious experience. For him, such subjective feelings are the "deeper source of religion," but nonmystical, rational scrutiny is necessary to make sense of these private feelings.

One may say truly, I think, that personal religious experience has its root and centre in mystical states of consciousness; so for us, who in these lectures are treating personal experience as the exclusive subject of our study, such states of consciousness ought to form the vital chapter from which the other chapters get their light. . . .

First of all, then, I ask, What does the expression "mystical states of consciousness" mean? How do we part off mystical states from other states? . . . I propose to you four marks which, when an experience has them, may justify us in calling it mystical for the purpose of the present lectures.

1. *Ineffability.* The handiest of the marks by which I classify a state of mind as mystical is negative. The subject of it immediately says that it defies expression, that no adequate report of its contents can be given in words. It follows from this that its quality must be directly experienced; it cannot be imparted or transferred to others. In this peculiarity mystical states are more like states of feeling than like states of intellect. No one can make clear to another who has never had a certain feeling, in what the quality or worth of it consists. . . .

2. *Noetic quality.* Although so similar to states of feeling, mystical states seem to those who experience them to be also states of knowledge. They are states of insight into depths of truth unplumbed by the discursive intellect. They are illuminations, revelations, full of significance and importance, all inarticulate though they remain; and as a rule they carry with them a curious sense of authority for after-time.

William James, *The Varieties of Religious Experience* (New York: Longmans, Green, and Co., 1923), 36–37, 40–44.

These two characters will entitle any state to be called mystical, in the sense in which I use the word. Two other qualities are less sharply marked, but are usually found. These are:

3. *Transiency.* Mystical states cannot be sustained for long. Except in rare instances, half an hour, or at most an hour or two, seems to be the limit beyond which they fade into the light of common day. Often, when faded, their quality can but imperfectly be reproduced in memory; but when they recur it is recognized; and from one recurrence to another it is susceptible of continuous development in what is felt as inner richness and importance.

4. *Passivity.* Although the oncoming of mystical states may be facilitated by preliminary voluntary operations, as by fixing the attention, or going through certain bodily performances, or in other ways which manuals of mysticism prescribe; yet when the characteristic sort of consciousness once has set in, the mystic feels as if his own will were in abeyance, and indeed sometimes as if he were grasped and held by a superior power. This latter peculiarity connects mystical states with certain definite phenomena of secondary or alternative personality, such as prophetic speech, automatic writing, or the mediumistic trance. When these latter conditions are well pronounced, however, there may be no recollection whatever of the phenomenon, and it may have no significance for the subject's usual inner life, to which, as it were, it makes a mere interruption. Mystical states, strictly so called, are never merely interruptive. Some memory of their content always remains, and a profound sense of their importance. They modify the inner life of the subject between the times of their recurrence. Sharp divisions in this region are, however, difficult to make, and we find all sorts of gradations and mixtures.

These four characteristics are sufficient to mark out a group of states of consciousness peculiar enough to deserve a special name and to call for careful study. Let it then be called the mystical group.

Our next step should be to gain acceptance with some typical examples. Professional mystics at the height of their development have often elaborately organized experiences and a philosophy based thereupon. . . .

The simplest rudiment of mystical experience would seem to be that deepened sense of the significance of a maxim or formula which occasionally sweeps over one. "I've heard that said all my life," we exclaim, "but I never realized its full meaning until now." "When a fellow-monk," said Luther, "one day repeated the words of the Creed: 'I believe in the forgiveness of sins,' I saw the Scripture in an entirely new light; and straightway I felt as if I were born anew. It was as if I had found the door of paradise thrown wide open." This sense of deeper significance is not confined to rational propositions. Single words, and conjunctions of words, effects of light on land and sea, odors and musical sounds, all bring it when the mind is tuned aright. Most of us can remember the strangely moving power of passages in certain poems read when we were young, irrational doorways as they were through which the mystery of fact, the wildness and the pang of life, stole into our hearts and thrilled them. The words have now perhaps become mere polished surfaces for us; but lyric poetry and music are alive and significant only in proportion as they fetch these vague vistas of a life continuous with our own, beckoning and inviting, yet ever eluding our pursuit. We are alive or dead to the eternal inner message of the arts according as we have kept or lost this mystical susceptibility. . . .

I have now sketched with extreme brevity and insufficiency, but as fairly as I am able in the time allowed, the general traits of the mystic range of consciousness. *It is on the whole pantheistic and optimistic, or at least the opposite of pessimistic. It is anti-naturalistic, and harmonizes best with twice-bornness and so-called otherworldly states of mind.*

My next task is to inquire whether we can invoke it as authoritative. Does it furnish any *warrant for the truth* of the twice-bornness and supernaturality and pantheism which it favors? I must give my answer to this question as concisely as I can.

In brief my answer is this, and I will divide it into three parts:

1. Mystical states, when well developed, usually are, and have the right to be, absolutely authoritative over the individuals to whom they come.

2. No authority emanates from them which should make it a duty for those who stand outside of them to accept their revelations uncritically.
3. They break down the authority of the non-mystical or rationalistic consciousness, based upon the understanding and the senses alone. They show it to be only one kind of consciousness. They open out the possibility of other orders of truth, in which, so far as anything in us vitally responds to them, we may freely continue to have faith.

I will take up these points one by one.

1

As a matter of psychological fact, mystical states of a well-pronounced and emphatic sort *are* usually authoritative over those who have them. They have been "there," and know. It is vain for rationalism to grumble about this. If the mystical truth that comes to a man proves to be a force that he can live by, what mandate have we of the majority to order him to live in another way? We can throw him into a prison or a madhouse, but we cannot change his mind—we commonly attach it only the more stubbornly to its beliefs. It mocks our utmost efforts, as a matter of fact, and in point of logic it absolutely escapes our jurisdiction. Our own more "rational" beliefs are based on evidence exactly similar in nature to that which mystics quote for theirs. Our senses, namely, have assured us of certain states of fact; but mystical experiences are as direct perceptions of fact for those who have them as any sensations ever were for us. The records show that even though the five senses be in abeyance in them, they are absolutely sensational in their epistemological quality, if I may be pardoned the barbarous expression—that is, they are face to face presentations of what seems immediately to exist.

The mystic is, in short, *invulnerable*, and must be left, whether we relish it or not, in undisturbed enjoyment of his creed. Faith, says Tolstoy, is that by which men live. And faith state and mystic state are practically convertible terms.

2

But I now proceed to add that mystics have no right to claim that we ought to accept the deliverance of their peculiar experiences, if we are ourselves outsiders and feel no private call thereto. The utmost they can ever ask of us in this life is to admit that they establish a presumption. They form a consensus and have an unequivocal outcome; and it would be odd, mystics might say, if such a unanimous type of experience should prove to be altogether wrong. At bottom, however, this would only be an appeal to numbers, like the appeal of rationalism the other way; and the appeal to numbers has no logical force. If we acknowledge it, it is for "suggestive," not for logical reasons: we follow the majority because to do so suits our life.

But even this presumption from the unanimity of mystics is far from being strong. In characterizing mystic states as pantheistic, optimistic, etc., I am afraid I over-simplified the truth. I did so for expository reasons, and to keep the closer to the classic mystical tradition. The classic religious mysticism, it now must be confessed, is only a "privileged case." It is an *extract,* kept true to type by the selection of the fittest specimens and their preservation in "schools." It is carved out from a much larger mass; and if we take the larger mass as seriously as religious mysticism has historically taken itself, we find that the supposed unanimity largely disappears. To begin with, even religious mysticism itself, the kind that accumulates traditions and makes schools, is much less unanimous than I have allowed. It has been both ascetic and antinomianly self-indulgent within the Christian church. It is dualistic in Sankhya, and monistic in Vedanta philosophy. I called it pantheistic; but the great Spanish mystics are anything but pantheists. They are with few exceptions non-metaphysical minds, for whom "the category of personality" is absolute. The "union" of man with God is for them much more like an occasional miracle than like an original identity. . . . The fact is that the mystical feeling of enlargement, union, and emancipation has no specific intellectual content whatever of its own. It is capable of forming matrimonial alliances with material furnished by the most diverse philosophies and theologies, provided only they can find a place in their framework for its peculiar emotional mood. We have no right, therefore, to invoke its prestige as distinctively in favor of any special belief, such as that in absolute idealism, or in the absolute monistic identity, or in the absolute goodness, of the world. It is only relatively in favor of all these things—it passes out of common human consciousness in the direction in which they lie.

So much for religious mysticism proper. But more remains to be told, for religious mysticism is only one half of mysticism. The other half has no accumulated traditions except those which the text-books on insanity supply. Open any one of these, and you will find abundant cases in which "mystical ideas" are cited as characteristic symptoms of enfeebled or deluded states of mind. In delusional insanity, as they sometimes call it, we may have a *diabolical* mysticism, a sort of religious mysticism turned upside down. The same sense of ineffable importance in the smallest events, the same texts and words coming with new meanings, the same voices and visions and leadings and missions, the same controlling by extraneous powers; only this time the emotion is pessimistic: instead of consolations we have desolations; the meanings are dreadful; and the powers are enemies to life. It is evident that from the point of view of their psychological mechanism, the classic mysticism and these lower mysticisms spring from the same mental level, from that great subliminal or transmarginal region of which science is beginning to admit the existence, but of which so little is really known. That region contains every kind of matter: "seraph and snake" abide there side by side. To come from thence is no infallible credential. What comes must be sifted and tested, and run the gauntlet of confrontation with the total context of experience, just like what comes from the outer world of sense. Its value must be ascertained by empirical methods, so long as we are not mystics ourselves.

3

Yet, I repeat once more, the existence of mystical states absolutely overthrows the pretension of non-mystical states to be the sole and ultimate dictators of what we may believe. As a rule, mystical states merely add a supersensuous meaning to the ordinary outward data of consciousness. They are excitements like the emotions of love or ambition, gifts to our spirit by means of which facts already objectively before us fall into a new expressiveness and make a new connection with our active life. They do not contradict these facts as such, or deny anything that our senses have immediately seized. It is the rationalistic critic rather who plays the part of denier in the controversy, and his denials have no strength, for there never can be a state of facts to which new meaning may not truthfully be added, provided the mind ascend to a more enveloping point of view. It must always remain an open question whether mystical states may not possibly be such superior points of view, windows through which the mind looks out upon a more extensive and inclusive world. The difference of the views seen from the different mystical windows need not prevent us from entertaining this supposition. The wider world would in that case prove to have a mixed constitution like that of this world, that is all. . . . The counting in of that wider world of meanings, and the serious dealing with it, might, in spite of all the perplexity, be indispensable stages in our approach to the final fullness of the truth.

In this shape, I think, we have to leave the subject. Mystical states indeed wield no authority due simply to their being mystical states. But the higher ones among them point in directions to which the religious sentiments even of non-mystical men incline. They tell of the supremacy of the ideal, of vastness, of union, of safety, and of rest. They offer us *hypotheses*, hypotheses which we may voluntarily ignore, but which as thinkers we cannot possibly upset. The supernaturalism and optimism to which they would persuade us may, interpreted in one way or another, be after all the truest of insights into the meaning of this life. . . .

I do believe that feeling is the deeper source of religion, and that philosophic and theological formulas are secondary products, like translations of a text into another tongue. But all such statements are misleading from their brevity, and it will take the whole hour for me to explain to you exactly what I mean.

When I call theological formulas secondary products, I mean that in a world in which no religious feeling had ever existed, I doubt whether any philosophic theology could ever have been framed. I doubt if dispassionate intellectual contemplation of the universe, apart from inner unhappiness and need of deliverance on the one hand and mystical emotion on the other, would ever have resulted in religious philosophies such as we now possess. Men would have begun with animistic explanations of natural fact, and criticised these away into scientific ones, as they actually have done. In the science they would have left a certain amount of "psychical research," even as they now will probably have to re-admit a certain amount. But high-flying speculations like those of either dogmatic or idealistic theology, these they would have had no motive to venture on, feeling no need of commerce with such deities. These speculations must, it seems to me, be classed as over-beliefs, buildings-out performed by the intellect into directions of which feeling originally supplied the hint.

But even if religious philosophy had to have its first hint supplied by feeling, may it not have dealt in a superior way with the matter which feeling suggested? Feeling is private and dumb, and unable to give an account of itself. It allows that its results are mysteries and enigmas, declines to justify them rationally, and on occasion is willing that they should even pass for paradoxical and absurd. Philosophy takes just the opposite attitude. Her aspiration is to reclaim from mystery and paradox whatever territory she touches. To find an escape from obscure and wayward personal persuasion to truth objectively valid for all thinking men has ever been the intellect's most cherished ideal. To redeem religion from unwholesome privacy, and to give public status and universal right of way to its deliverances, has been reason's task.

I believe that philosophy will always have opportunity to labor at this task. We are thinking beings, and we cannot exclude the intellect from participating in any of our functions. Even in soliloquizing with ourselves, we construe our feelings intellectually. Both our personal ideals and our religious and mystical experiences must be interpreted congruously with the kind of scenery which our thinking mind inhabits. The philosophic climate of our time inevitably forces its own clothing on us. Moreover, we must exchange our feelings with one another, and in doing so we have to speak, and to use general and abstract verbal formulas. Conceptions and constructions are thus a necessary part of our religion; and as moderator amid the clash of hypotheses, and mediator among the criticisms of one man's constructions by another, philosophy will always have much to do. It would be strange if I disputed this, when these very lectures which I am giving are (as you will see more clearly from now onwards) a laborious attempt to extract from the privacies of religious experience some general facts which can be defined in formulas upon which everybody may agree.

Religious experience, in other words, spontaneously and inevitably engenders myths, superstitions, dogmas, creeds, and metaphysical theologies, and criticisms of one set of these by the adherents of another.

RELIGION AS HUMAN INVENTION

Religion Is "the Opium of the People"

KARL MARX

Few philosophers have had as much influence on the world as Karl Marx (1818–1883)—who, ironically, did not consider himself a philosopher and did not believe that ideas alone could have much of an impact on history. He thinks that what drives philosophy, history, society, law, government, and morality is economics. It is the dominant system of economics in every age, he says, that determines how society is structured and how history will go. And the best, most just system is **socialism**, the political and economic doctrine that the means of production (property, factories, businesses) should be owned or controlled by the people, either communally or through the state. The guiding principle of the socialist view is equality: the wealth of society should be shared by all. The ideal distribution of goods usually follows the classic formula laid down by Marx, the father of modern socialism: "From each according to his ability, to each according to his needs." But for Marx, the social force that works against this just system, that lulls people into a slave mentality and a blinding illusion, is religion.

For Germany, the *criticism of religion* has been essentially completed, and the criticism of religion is the prerequisite of all criticism.

The *profane* existence of error is compromised as soon as its speech for the altars and hearths has been refuted. Man, who has found only the *reflection* of himself in the fantastic reality of heaven, where he sought a superman, will no longer feel disposed to find the *mere appearance* of himself, the non-man, where he seeks and must seek his true reality.

The foundation of irreligious criticism is: *Man makes religion*, religion does not make man. Religion is, indeed, the self-consciousness and self-esteem of man who has either not yet won through to himself, or has already lost himself again. But *man* is no abstract being squatting outside the world. Man is *the world of man*—state, society. This state and this society produce religion, which is an *inverted consciousness of the world*, because they are an *inverted world*. Religion is the general theory of this world, its encyclopaedic compendium, its logic in popular form, its spiritual *point d'honneur*, its enthusiasm, its moral sanction, its solemn complement, and its universal basis of consolation and justification. It is the *fantastic realization* of the human essence since the *human essence* has not acquired any true reality. The

Karl Marx, *A Contribution to the Critique of Hegel's Philosophy of Right* (Paris: Deutsch-Französische Jahrbücher, 1844); marxists.org.

struggle against religion is, therefore, indirectly the struggle *against that world* whose spiritual *aroma* is religion.

Religious suffering is, at one and the same time, the *expression* of real suffering and a *protest* against real suffering. Religion is the sigh of the oppressed creature, the heart of a heartless world, and the soul of soulless conditions. It is the *opium* of the people.

The abolition of religion as the *illusory* happiness of the people is the demand for their *real* happiness. To call on them to give up their illusions about their condition is to call on them to *give up a condition that requires illusions.* The criticism of religion is, therefore, *in embryo, the criticism of that vale of tears* of which religion is the *halo.*

Criticism has plucked the imaginary flowers on the chain not in order that man shall continue to bear that chain without fantasy or consolation, but so that he shall throw off the chain and pluck the living flower. The criticism of religion disillusions man, so that he will think, act, and fashion his reality like a man who has discarded his illusions and regained his senses, so that he will move around himself as his own true Sun. Religion is only the illusory Sun which revolves around man as long as he does not revolve around himself.

A CLOSER LOOK

Religiosity of Americans by Age (2014)

% of U.S. adults who say . . .

Religious Behaviors	**Baby Boomers (born 1946–1964)**	**Older Millennials (born 1981–1989)**	**Younger Millennials (born 1990–1996)**
They pray daily	61	46	39
They attend services at least weekly	38	27	28
Religious Beliefs			
They believe in God	92	84	80
. . . with absolute certainty	69	54	50
They believe in heaven	74	67	68
They believe scripture is word of God	64	50	52
They believe in hell	59	55	56

Pew Research Center, 2014 Religious Landscape Study, conducted June 4–Sept. 30, 2014, nationally representative telephone survey of 35,071 adults; margins of error of less than 1 percentage point.

RELIGION AS ILLUSION

The Future of an Illusion

SIGMUND FREUD

Sigmund Freud (1856–1939) is the father of psychoanalysis, which is an extremely influential theory of the mind's dynamics and structure as well as a form of psychological therapy. Religion, he says, is an illusion. It is the mind's way of dealing with the feelings of fear and helplessness that first arise in childhood and continue throughout adult life. These experiences prompt people to seek protection from them through religion, which assures them of a protective divinity, a moral order, and a guaranteed future.

I think we have prepared the way sufficiently for an answer to both these questions. It will be found if we turn our attention to the psychical origin of religious ideas. These, which are given out as teachings, are not precipitates of experience or end-results of thinking: they are illusions, fulfilments of the oldest, strongest and most urgent wishes of mankind. The secret of their strength lies in the strength of those wishes. As we already know, the terrifying impression of helplessness in childhood aroused the need for protection—for protection through love—which was provided by the father; and the recognition that this helplessness lasts throughout life made it necessary to cling to the existence of a father, but this time a more powerful one. Thus the benevolent rule of a divine Providence allays our fear of the dangers of life; the establishment of a moral world-order ensures the fulfilment of the demands of justice, which have so often remained unfulfilled in human civilization; and the prolongation of earthly existence in a future life provides the local and temporal framework in which these wish-fulfilments shall take place. Answers to the riddles that tempt the curiosity of man, such as how the universe began or what the relation is between body and mind, are developed in conformity with the underlying assumptions of this system. It is an enormous relief to the individual psyche if the conflicts of its childhood arising from the father-complex—conflicts which it has never wholly overcome—are removed from it and brought to a solution which is universally accepted.

When I say that these things are all illusions, I must define the meaning of the word. An illusion is not the same thing as an error; nor is it necessarily an error. Aristotle's belief that vermin are developed out of dung (a belief to which ignorant people still cling) was an error; so was the belief of a former generation of doctors that tabes dorsalis [loss of coordination of movement] is the result of sexual excess. It would be incorrect to call these errors illusions. On the other

Sigmund Freud, *The Future of an Illusion,* in *The Standard Edition of the Complete Psychological Works of Sigmund Freud* (1927), Volume XXI (1927–1931): *The Future of an Illusion, Civilization and Its Discontents, and Other Works,* 29–30.

hand, it was an illusion of Columbus's that he had discovered a new sea-route to the Indies. The part played by his wish in this error is very clear. One may describe as an illusion the assertion made by certain nationalists that the Indo-Germanic race is the only one capable of civilization; or the belief, which was only destroyed by psycho-analysis, that children are creatures without sexuality. What is characteristic of illusions is that they are derived from human wishes. In this respect they come near to psychiatric delusions. But they differ from them, too, apart from the more complicated structure of delusions. In the case of delusions, we emphasize as essential their being in contradiction with reality. Illusions need not necessarily be false—that is to say, unrealizable or in contradiction to reality. For instance, a middle-class girl may have the illusion that a prince will come and marry her. This is possible; and a few such cases have occurred. That the Messiah will come and found a golden age is much less likely. Whether one classifies this belief as an illusion or as something analogous to a delusion will depend on one's personal attitude. Examples of illusions which have proved true are not easy to find, but the illusion of the alchemists that all metals can be turned into gold might be one of them. The wish to have a great deal of gold, as much gold as possible, has, it is true, been a good deal damped by our present-day knowledge of the determinants of wealth, but chemistry no longer regards the transmutation of metals into gold as impossible. Thus we call a belief an illusion when a wish-fulfilment is a prominent factor in its motivation, and in doing so we disregard its relations to reality, just as the illusion itself sets no store by verification.

THE GODDESS

When God Was a Woman

MERLIN STONE

Merlin Stone (1931–2011) was a sculptor and professor of art and art history. Through her art she was led to a study of archeology and ancient religion. She explains that the goddess—known by such names as Isis and Ishtar—was the dominant deity in the ancient Near and Middle East. She argues that the goddess was not just a fertility symbol but was regarded as the wise creator and the provider of order in the universe. The goddess, Stone maintains, presided over matriarchal societies that gave women a much higher status than the one allowed in patriarchal societies and Judeo-Christian teachings.

Merlin Stone, *When God Was a Woman* (New York: Harcourt, 1976), 1–8.

Though we live amid high-rise steel buildings, Formica countertops and electronic television screens, there is something in all of us, women and men alike, that makes us feel deeply connected with the past. Perhaps the sudden dampness of a beach cave or the lines of sunlight piercing through the intricate lace patterns of the leaves in a darkened grove of tall trees will awaken from the hidden recesses of our minds the distant echoes of a remote and ancient time, taking us back to the early stirrings of human life on the planet. For people raised and programmed on the patriarchal religions of today, religions that affect us in even the most secular aspects of our society, perhaps there remains a lingering, almost innate memory of sacred shrines and temples tended by priestesses who served in the religion of the original supreme deity. In the beginning, people prayed to the Creatress of Life, the Mistress of Heaven. At the very dawn of religion, God was a woman. Do you remember?

For years something has magnetically lured me into exploring the legends, the temple sites, the statues and the ancient rituals of the female deities, drawing me back in time to an age when the Goddess was omnipotent, and women acted as Her clergy, controlling the form and rites of religion.

Perhaps it was my training and work as a sculptor that first exposed me to the sculptures of the Goddess found in the ruins of prehistoric sanctuaries and the earliest dwellings of human beings. Perhaps it was a certain romantic mysticism, which once embarrassed me, but to which I now happily confess, that led me over the years into the habit of collecting information about the early female religions and the veneration of female deities. Occasionally I tried to dismiss my fascination with this subject as overly fanciful and certainly disconnected from my work (I was building electronic sculptural environments at the time). Nevertheless, I would find myself continually perusing archaeology journals and poring over texts in museum or university library stacks.

As I read, I recalled that somewhere along the pathway of my life I had been told—and accepted the idea—that the sun, great and powerful, was naturally worshiped as male, while the moon, hazy, delicate symbol of sentiment and love, had always been revered as female. Much to my surprise I discovered accounts of Sun Goddesses in the lands of Canaan, Anatolia, Arabia and Australia, while Sun Goddesses among the Eskimos, the Japanese and the Khasis of India were accompanied by subordinate brothers who were symbolized as the moon.

I had somewhere assimilated the idea that the earth was invariably identified as female, Mother Earth, the one who passively accepts the seed, while heaven was naturally and inherently male, its intangibility symbolic of the supposedly exclusive male ability to think in abstract concepts. This too I had accepted without question—until I learned that nearly all the female deities of the Near and Middle East were titled Queen of Heaven, and in Egypt not only was the ancient Goddess Nut known as the heavens, but her brother-husband Geb was symbolized as the earth.

Most astonishing of all was the discovery of numerous accounts of the female Creators of all existence, divinities who were credited with bringing forth not only the first people but the entire earth and the heavens above. There were records of such Goddesses in Sumer, Babylon, Egypt, Africa, Australia and China.

In India the Goddess Sarasvati was honored as the inventor of the original alphabet, while in Celtic Ireland the Goddess Brigit was esteemed as the patron deity of language. Texts revealed that it was the Goddess Nidaba in Sumer who was paid honor as the one who initially invented clay tablets and the art of writing. She appeared in that position earlier than any of the male deities who later replaced Her. The official scribe of the Sumerian heaven was a woman. But most significant was the archaeological evidence of the earliest examples of written language so far discovered; these were also located in Sumer, at the temple of the Queen of Heaven in Erech, written there over five thousand years ago. Though writing is most often said to have been invented by *man*, however that may be defined, the combination of the above factors presents a most convincing argument that it may have actually been woman who pressed those first meaningful marks into wet clay.

In agreement with the generally accepted theory that women were responsible for the development of agriculture, as an extension of their food-gathering activities, there were female deities everywhere who were credited with this gift to civilization. In Mesopotamia, where some of the earliest evidences of agricultural development have been found, the Goddess Ninlil was revered for having provided Her people with an understanding of planting and harvesting methods. In nearly all areas of the world, female deities were extolled as healers, dispensers of curative herbs, roots, plants and other medical aids, casting the priestesses who attended the shrines into the role of physicians of those who worshiped there.

Some legends described the Goddess as a powerful, courageous warrior, a leader in battle. The worship of the Goddess as valiant warrior seems to have been responsible for the numerous reports of female soldiers, later referred to by the classical Greeks as the Amazons. More thoroughly examining the accounts of the esteem the Amazons paid to the female deity, it became evident that women who worshiped a warrior Goddess hunted and fought in the lands of Libya, Anatolia, Bulgaria, Greece, Armenia and Russia and were far from the mythical fantasy so many writers of today would have us believe.

I could not help noticing how far removed from contemporary images were the prehistoric and most ancient historic attitudes toward the thinking capacities and intellect of woman, for nearly everywhere the Goddess was revered as wise counselor and prophetess. The Celtic Cerridwen was the Goddess of Intelligence and Knowledge in the pre-Christian legends of Ireland, the priestesses of the Goddess Gaia provided the wisdom of divine revelation at pre-Greek sanctuaries, while the Greek Demeter and the Egyptian Isis were both invoked as law-givers and sage dispensers of righteous wisdom, counsel and justice. The Egyptian Goddess Maat represented the very order, rhythm and truth of the Universe. Ishtar of Mesopotamia was referred to as the Directress of People, the Prophetess, the Lady of Vision, while the archaeological records of the city of Nimrud, where Ishtar was worshiped, revealed that women served as judges and magistrates in the courts of law.

The more I read, the more I discovered. The worship of female deities appeared in every area of the world, presenting an image of woman that I had never before encountered. As a result, I began to ponder upon the power of myth and eventually to perceive these legends as more than the innocent childlike fables they first appeared to be. They were tales with a most specific point of view.

Myths present ideas that guide perception, conditioning us to think and even perceive in a particular way, especially when we are young and impressionable. Often they portray the actions of people who are rewarded or punished for their behavior, and we are encouraged to view these as examples to emulate or avoid. So many of the stories told to us from the time we are just old enough to understand deeply affect our attitudes and comprehension of the world about us and ourselves. Our ethics, morals, conduct, values, sense of duty and even sense of humor are often developed from simple childhood parables and fables. From them we learn what is socially acceptable in the society from which they come. They define good and bad, right and wrong, what is natural and what is unnatural among the people who hold the myths as meaningful. It was quite apparent that the myths and legends that grew from, and were propagated by, a religion in which the deity was female, and revered as wise, valiant, powerful and just, provided very different images of womanhood from those which we are offered by the male-oriented religions of today.

"A FORTNIGHT AFTER THE CREATION OF THE UNIVERSE"

As I considered the power of myth, it became increasingly difficult to avoid questioning the influential effects that the myths accompanying the religions that worship male deities had upon my own image of what it meant to be born a female, another Eve, progenitress of my childhood faith. As a child, I was told that Eve had been made from Adam's rib, brought into being to be his companion and helpmate, to keep him from being lonely. As if this assignment of permanent second mate, never to be captain, was not oppressive enough to my future plans as a developing member of society, I next learned that Eve was considered to be foolishly gullible. My elders explained that she had been easily tricked by the promises of the perfidious serpent. She defied God and provoked Adam to do the same, thus ruining a good thing—the previously blissful life in the Garden of Eden. Why Adam himself was never thought to be equally as foolish was apparently never worth discussing. But identifying with Eve, who was presented as the symbol of all women, the blame was in some mysterious way mine—and God, viewing the whole affair as my fault, chose to punish *me* by decreeing: "I will greatly multiply your pain in childbearing; in pain you shall bring forth children, yet your desire shall be for your husband and he shall rule over you" (Gen. 3:16).

So even as a young girl I was taught that, because of Eve, when I grew up I was to bear my children in pain and suffering. As if this was not a sufficient penalty, instead of receiving compassion, sympathy or admiring respect for my courage, I was to experience this pain with guilt, the sin of my wrongdoing laid heavily upon me as punishment for simply being a woman, a daughter of Eve. To make matters worse, I was also supposed to accept the idea that men, as symbolized by Adam, in order to prevent any further foolishness on my part, were presented with the right to control me—to rule over me. According to the omnipotent male deity, whose righteousness and wisdom I was expected to admire and respect with a reverent awe, men were far wiser than women. Thus my penitent, submissive position as a female was firmly established by page three of the nearly one thousand pages of the Judeo-Christian Bible.

But this original decree of male supremacy was only the beginning. The myth describing Eve's folly was not to be forgotten or ignored. We then studied the words of the prophets of the New Testament, who repeatedly utilized the legend of the loss of Paradise to explain and even prove the natural inferiority of women. The lessons learned in the Garden of Eden were impressed upon us over and over again. Man was created first. Woman was made for man. Only man was made in God's image. According to the Bible, and those who accepted it as the divine word, the male god favored men and had indeed designed them as naturally superior. Even now I cannot help wondering how many times those passages from the New Testament were read from the authoritative position of a Sunday pulpit or from the family Bible that had been pulled down from the shelf by father or husband—and a pious woman listened to:

> Let the woman learn in silence with all subjection. But I suffer not a woman to teach or to usurp authority over the man, but to be in silence. For Adam was first formed and then Eve, and Adam was not deceived, but the woman being deceived was in the transgression. . . . (I Timothy 2:11–14)

> For the man is not of the woman, but the woman of the man. Let the women keep silence in the churches, for it is not permitted unto them to speak; but they are commanded to be under obedience, so saith the law. And if they learn anything, let them ask their husbands at home; for it is a shame for women to speak in the church. (I Corinthians 11:3, 7, 9)

Strangely enough, I never did become very religious, despite the continual efforts of Sunday School teachers. In fact, by the time I reached adolescence I had rejected most of what the organized religions had to offer. But there was still something about the myth of Adam and Eve that lingered, seeming to pervade the culture at some deeper level. It appeared and reappeared as the symbolic foundation of poems and novels. It was visually interpreted in oils by the great masters whose paintings glowed from the slide projectors in my art history courses. Products were advertised in high fashion magazines suggesting that, if a woman wore the right perfume, she might be able to pull the whole disaster off all over again. It was even the basis of dull jokes in the Sunday comics. It seemed that everywhere woman was tempting man to do wrong. Our entire society agreed; Adam and Eve defined the images of men and women. Women were inherently conniving, contriving and dangerously sexy, while gullible and somewhat simple-minded at the same time. They were in obvious need of a foreman to keep them in line—and thus divinely appointed, many men seemed quite willing.

As I began to read other myths that explained the creation of life, stories that attributed the event to Nut or Hathor in Egypt, Nammu or Ninhursag in Sumer, Mami, Tiamat or Aruru in other parts of Mesopotamia and Mawu in Africa, I began to view the legend of Adam and Eve as just another fable, an innocent attempt to explain what happened at the very beginning of existence. But it was not long afterward that I began to understand how specifically contrived the details of this particular myth were.

In 1960, mythologist Joseph Campbell commented on the Adam and Eve myth, writing:

> This curious mythological idea, and the still more curious fact that for two thousand years it was accepted throughout the Western World as the absolutely dependable account of an event that was supposed to have taken place about a fortnight after the creation of the universe, poses forcefully the highly interesting question of the influence of conspicuously contrived, counterfeit mythologies and the inflections of mythology upon the structure of human belief and the consequent course of civilization.

Professor Chiera points out that "The Bible does not give us one creation story but several of them; the one which happens to be featured in chapter one of Genesis appears to be the one which had the least vogue among the common people . . . It was evidently produced in scholarly circles." He then discusses the differences between the religions of today and the ancient worship, saying:

> Just a few years ago we succeeded in piecing together from a large number of tablets the complete story of an ancient Sumerian myth. I used to call it the Darwinian theory of the Sumerians. The myth must have been widely circulated for many copies of it have already come to light. In common with the biblical story, a woman plays the dominant role, just as Eve did. But the resemblance ends there. Poor Eve has been damned by all subsequent generations for her deed, while the Babylonians thought so much of their woman ancestress that they deified her.

Now as I read these other myths, it was apparent that the archetypal woman in ancient religions, as represented by the Goddess, was quite different, in many respects, from the woman Eve. I then observed that many of these origin and creation legends came from the lands of Canaan, Egypt and Babylon, the very same lands in which the Adam and Eve myth had been developed. The other legends of creation were from the mythical religious literature of the people who did not worship the Hebrew Yahweh (Jehovah), but were in fact the closest neighbors of those early Hebrews.

STUDY QUESTIONS

1. State three reasons for studying world religions. Which reason seems most important? Why?
2. How can a better understanding of religions engender tolerance and prevent sectarian conflicts?
3. What are the elements of religion discussed by Ninian Smart? Using these elements as a guide, would you conclude that a political party or interest group (such as the National Association of Manufacturers or the Environmental Defense Fund) is a religion? Why or why not?
4. According to Will Deming, what method can be used to study religion? What are the advantages of this method?
5. What is Freud's view of religion? What is his explanation of how the need for religion arises?
6. What is Stone's explanation for why the goddess does not play a more dominant role in Western religions?
7. What does Marx mean by "religion is the opium of the people"?
8. What does Eliade say about the presence of the sacred in nature?

9. Theorize about the reason that religiosity in the United States seems to increase with age—and decrease with youth.
10. In James's view, what is the role that subjective feelings play in the existence of religion?
11. What is the relationship between religion-inspiring private feelings and the nonmystical, rational examination of these feelings?

FURTHER READING

Karen Armstrong, *The Great Transformation: The Beginning of Our Religious Traditions* (New York: Knopf, 2006).

John Bowker, ed., *The Oxford Dictionary of World Religions* (New York: Oxford University Press, 1997).

Mircea Eliade, ed., *The Encyclopedia of Religion* (New York: MacMillan, 1987).

John R. Hinnells, *A New Handbook of Living Religions* (London: Penguin, 1997).

Darlene Juschka, ed., *Feminism in the Study of Religion: A Reader* (New York: Continuum, 2001).

Seth D. Kunin, *Religion: The Modern Theories* (Baltimore: Johns Hopkins University Press, 2003).

James R. Lewis, ed., *The Oxford Handbook of New Religious Movements* (New York: Oxford University Press, 2004).

Daniel L. Pals, *Eight Theories of Religion* (New York: Oxford University Press, 2006).

Ninian Smart, *Worldviews: Crosscultural Explanations of Human Belief* (New York: Scribner's, 1983).

ONLINE

American Academy of Religion, https://www.aarweb.org/.

New York Times, "Resources: World Religions," http://learning.blogs.nytimes.com/2010/09/10/resources-world-religions/.

Adherents, http://www.adherents.com/.

2 Indigenous Religions

North America and Africa

Indigenous, or native, religions exist in every corner of the world, in nearly every time zone, wherever **indigenous people** have had substantial influence. They are local, numerous, and smaller than the major religious traditions. They have ancient roots, in many cases stretching back to the first glimmers of history before the major religions were founded. They have been passed down from distant ancestors and altered by encounters with the modern world, the cultural and political realities, and the nonindigenous religions. The differences among their beliefs and practices are striking, and their contrasts with nonindigenous traditions are just as remarkable.

Indigenous religions have been accused of being simple, primitive, basic, or archaic, but researchers and scholars say these preconceptions are mistaken. A closer look at native religions would find them elaborate and sophisticated, distinguished by intricate metaphysics, mature moral theories, complicated rituals, or inspiring spiritual narratives. It would be difficult to make a convincing case that they are more primitive than the more familiar traditions such as Buddhism, Christianity, Islam, Daoism, and Confucianism. In some of their ideas and cosmologies, indigenous traditions resemble ancient Greek speculations about the world. And at least in outline, some of their metaphysical views bring to mind concepts developed in many Eastern religions. Most or all the basic types of beliefs in indigenous religions are also found to some degree in the major religions of the East and West.

Indigenous traditions are incredibly diverse. Two traditions—even if they are geographically close—can have very different beliefs or attitudes about the world and distinctive ways of expressing them. Fortunately many traditions share at least some features that can help define them and aid our understanding of them.

Many, perhaps most, indigenous religions have used (and continue to use) stories to transmit values, beliefs, and attitudes. Most of the stories have been conveyed through speech (and written down only in recent times), passed on from one generation to the next. A few traditions preserved their stories in writing, but most did not. The purpose of many stories is to explain the origin of the world, teach the standards of proper behavior, or answer questions about things like the afterlife or spirits.

In many native traditions, the world is thought to be filled with entities that have consciousness and can interact with humans—spirits, souls of dead ancestors, or demons. **Animism**, the view that objects in the natural world are, or have, spirits or consciousness is strong in indigenous religions. If everything is spirit, everything can be revered or worshipped: a river, a mountain, the sun, the moon, a stone, or a tree can be the object of devotion.

In many native religions, everything is also connected. The world, nature, human beings, and animals all form a single web of life, connected by sacred processes, a supreme being, or spiritual power—and are sensitive in every part to every other part. Such interconnectedness requires proper balance throughout the system, and every person bears some responsibility for ensuring balance between humans and nature or some other part of the cosmos.

Indigenous traditions do not have a common conception of a supreme being or ultimate power. Rather, they posit a variety of such things—for example, a supreme impersonal force or energy pervading nature, a pantheon of minor spirits with or without a dominant sovereign god, or a single Great Spirit (similar to the Christian God) who may interact with humans or generally ignore them.

In Christianity, Judaism, and Islam, there is a clear distinction between the sacred and the profane. The mundane activities and things that fill up our day-to-day lives—eating, walking, working, studying—are generally regarded as secular, nonspiritual, or material. The sacred aspects of life are said to be distinct from the ordinary, and we can alternate between them. In many indigenous religions, however, there is no such distinction. Carrying firewood, bathing, preparing food, and hunting could be sacred acts.

In some indigenous traditions, particular humans—priests, medicine men, "wonder workers," or others—are supposed to have extraordinary abilities. One such ability is the use of **magic**, the power to control events through supernatural or mysterious means. Magicians believe they can use their magic to manipulate natural processes—to make the buffalo hunt successful, limit the winter's snowfall, heal a sick friend, or harm a rival or enemy. Another

FIGURE 2.1 Arikara Native Americans, "four night men," dance in a medicine ceremony.
Photograph by Edward S. Curtis, 1908.

ability is **divination**, the power to predict the future. To arrive at their predictions, priests may try to read the future in patterns found in nature—in formations of birds in flight, quartz crystals, or animal entrails.

INDIGENOUS NORTH AMERICAN RELIGIONS

Some scholars estimate that at the time of Columbus's arrival in the New World, 40 to 50 million indigenous people lived in the Americas, representing hundreds of tribes and perhaps as many as two thousand distinct languages. Today there are 2 to 5 million Native Americans living in the continental United States and Alaska, asserting membership in over five hundred tribal groups. And in this multitude of tribes and tongues, there has always been a multitude of distinctive religious traditions. But these religions are mostly unknown among non-Native Americans and are often deemed too crude or too simplistic to be worthy of serious study. Such assessments, however, would themselves be crude and simplistic.

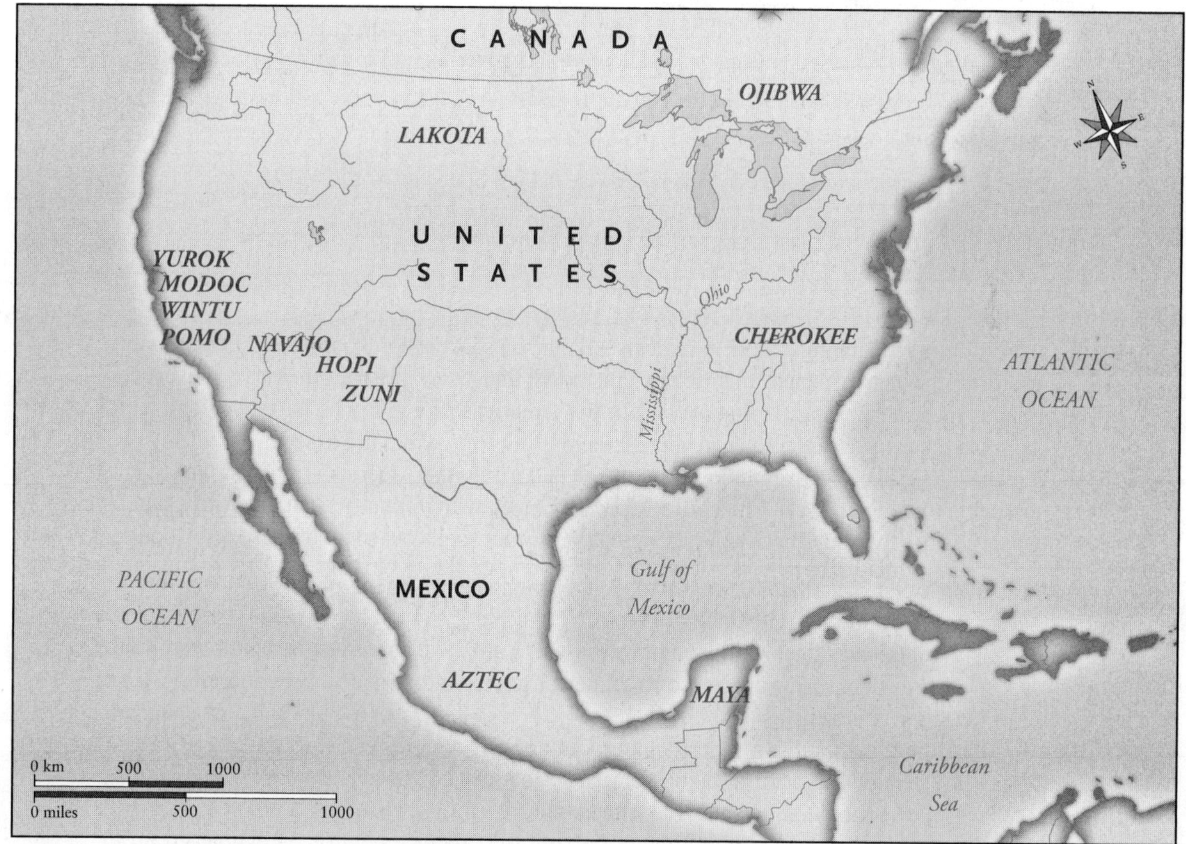

MAP 2.1 Indigenous peoples of North America.

NATIVE NORTH AMERICAN TIMELINE

BCE

15,000–20,000 People now called Native Americans arrive in North America.

CE

300–900 Mayan culture flourishes.

1100–1519 Aztec culture flourishes.

1492 Columbus lands in the Americas.

1513 The Spanish land in Florida.

1565 The Spanish found the city of St. Augustine in Florida.

1607 The English found the settlement of Jamestown.

1845–1911 Life of Quanah Parker

1863–1950 Life of Black Elk

1863–1864 U.S. forces kill thousands of Navajo.

1876 Indian Act is passed in Canada, disallowing self-government for natives.

1890 Massacre at Wounded Knee; the end of "Indian Wars"

1890 Ghost Dance religion

1941–1945 Navajo work as "code talkers" for the United States in World War II.

1960 Natives in Canada are given the right to vote in federal elections.

Part of understanding Native American religions is separating popular myths from reality regarding the native people themselves. Distorted images of Native Americans have been around since the Europeans first arrived in the Americas. Some myths have been spread to denigrate the native people; some, to glorify them. Both approaches fail to see them as fully real human beings. The negative stereotype of the bigot portrays the American Indian as the violent, inhuman, illiterate "savage" who can be killed and caged with impunity. But the positive stereotype is equally twisted. The scholar Frederick W. Turner spells out some of these distortions:

1. The Indian was the original ecologist, killing only what he needed, caring for the natural world through which he moved.
2. The Indian was the original communist with a small "c"; he lived in a highly communal atmosphere in which not only material goods and services were shared but also love and affection.
3. The Indian, although a superb fighter, did not wage aggressive warfare. . . .
4. The Indian was a natural democrat, easily tolerating differences between individuals within the tribe and between the tribes themselves.
5. The Indian was noncompetitive, preferring the advancement of the whole group to his own.[1]

A CLOSER LOOK

The Ghost Dance Movement

In about 1870 in the American West, a religious movement known as the **Ghost Dance** sprang up among Native North Americans in Nevada. It was inspired by a Paiute man claiming to be a Ghost Dance prophet. He preached that a new era was dawning in which white people would vanish, Native ancestors would return from the dead, and a utopian life would begin. He declared that doing the ceremonial Ghost Dance would help bring the utopia into existence. The movement spread and then faded but was revived in 1889 by another prophet named Wovoka. He claimed to have had a vision of the Supreme Being who told him that through religious rites such as the Ghost Dance and ritual singing, Indians could raise the dead and free the land of whites. This time the Ghost Dance was embraced by Indians in the upper Midwest, Nevada, Idaho, Utah, Wyoming, Oregon, and elsewhere.

The Ghost Dance movement, however, was to end in tragedy:

> The Ghost Dance provided a hopeful message to all Indians, but it proved particularly enticing to Lakotas suffering poor conditions on reservations and to Lakota leaders such as Sitting Bull (Tantanka Iyotanka), who had resisted U.S. Indian policy. Lakota participants added vestments known as ghost shirts to the ceremonies and songs. . . . They believed these white muslin shirts, decorated with a variety of symbols, protected them from danger, including bullets. The Lakotas' white neighbors and reservation officials viewed the movement as a threat to U.S. Indian policy and believed the Ghost Dance ceremonies and ghost shirts indicated that the Lakotas intended to start a war. Reservation officials called on the U.S. government to stop the dancing. The government dispatched the U.S. Army and called for the arrest of key leaders such as Sitting Bull and Big Foot (Si Tanka). Indian police killed Sitting Bull while arresting him. Two weeks later, on December 29, 1890, members of the Seventh Cavalry killed Big Foot and at least 145 of his followers (casualty estimates range to higher than 300) in the Wounded Knee Massacre, thus eliminating key leaders most opposed to the United States and its Indian policy. Many historians have pointed to Wounded Knee as the closing episode in the West's Indian wars.

Figure 2.2 A photograph of Wovoka (seated), a.k.a. John Wilson, the Paiute religious leader who helped spread the Ghost Dance movement among tribes in the American West.

Todd M. Kerstetter, "Ghost Dance," *Encyclopedia of the Great Plains*, http://plainshumanities.unl.edu/encyclopedia/about.html (September 12, 2014).

According to Turner, these are half-truths. He points out that although Indians did have reverence for the natural world, there is also evidence of their environmental plunder. Although Native Americans were indeed communal, the extended-family arrangement often led to "brutal treatment" of elderly members of the group. In Indian cultures, success in warfare was given great emphasis. "Every bit of evidence we have," says Turner, "suggests that intertribal warfare was a condition of aboriginal life before the coming of the Europeans, though there is no doubt that this was greatly exacerbated by the intrusion of the hairy men from the East." As for tolerance, Indians did have this virtue, but "it existed side by side with the weapon and fear of ridicule," which led in some cases to the suicide of those ridiculed for deviation from certain tribal norms. Native American cultures did emphasize sharing, Turner says, but "competition, rivalry, and intense individualism were also aspects of tribal cultures, even among those groups generally characterized as cooperative."

Compared to the many volumes of sacred writings found in the major world religions, written materials by or about Native North Americans are limited. The Aztec and Mayan civilizations of Central America developed systems of writing and wrote about their religions, so we have their account of beliefs and practices. Native North American people, however, mostly conveyed their religious views orally and left few if any writings, sacred or not. Most of what we know about their religions comes from written sources acquired in the last century and a half—either reports from missionaries, soldiers, and explorers, or oral histories, stories, and descriptions by Native Americans written down by social scientists. These materials at least give us an idea of the complexity, subtlety, and intelligence found in a range of religious mythologies—some of which reveal the heart of traditions still very much alive.

INDIGENOUS AFRICAN RELIGIONS

Like the indigenous traditions of North America, African indigenous religions are numerous and varied. There is no such thing as "the African religion"; there are instead many indigenous traditions that have arisen from a plethora of cultural and language groups on the African continent. These religions, some of which have been around for thousands of years, have been strongly influenced by Christianity and Islam, the two dominant world religions there, and the indigenous religions in turn have in many cases been incorporated into the fabric of the larger faiths.

Many African religions are polytheistic: they accept many deities. Non-Africans have focused on this aspect of the traditions, but a large proportion of African religions also assume the existence of a supreme deity, or High God, the creator of the universe and all the beings that inhabit it. This God is thought to be omniscient, omnipotent, eternal, and transcendent. This latter characteristic refers to the High God's absence from the day-to-day affairs of human beings. The High God created everything but now lets subordinate deities tend to the day-to-day workings of the world. African devotees are likely to have far more dealings with these lesser gods than with the supreme being.

INDIGENOUS AFRICAN RELIGIONS TIMELINE

BCE

190,000 Earliest evidence of indigenous Africans

CE

First and second century Christianity arrives in North Africa.

Sixth century Christianity comes to Nubia.

630s Islam arrives in North Africa.

640–750 Umayyad Caliphate

600–1100 Ghana empire flourishes.

1500–1800s Atlantic slave trade

1807 British abolish slave trade.

1800–1900s European colonization

1914 Mourimi movement arises in Mozambique.

1947 Mcapi cult is founded in Zambia and Malawi.

1950s–1990s End of colonial rule; sub-Saharan countries become independent.

2007 United Nations adopts Declaration on the Rights of Indigenous Peoples.

Many indigenous traditions also emphasize the existence of spirits, disembodied or nonmaterial entities. The source of spirits may be either dead humans (usually ancestors) or natural objects such as mountains, the moon, wind, and rivers. The spirits of the dead (whether ancestors or not) provide a connection to the spirit world; they are essentially still active members of the living community. Ancestors are to be venerated and appeased through ceremony, for they can help or harm the living, depending on the latter's behavior and commitments.

Like other indigenous religions, African traditions make no hard distinction between the sacred and the profane. Life is a fusion of the spiritual and the ordinary. Through magic, divination, and witchcraft, for example, a devotee may appeal to the supernatural, but these practices would be regarded as just another facet of everyday life.

Also like Native North American religions, African traditions use stories to transmit spiritual lore and moral values, and most of this material has been conveyed orally. Some of it, however, has now been written down.

The three major Western religions (Christianity, Judaism, and Islam) are doctrinal or creedal. They emphasize the importance of correct beliefs. African religions generally are less interested in creeds and doctrines and more attuned to lived religion—to the rituals, practices, and attitudes that make up the spiritual life. They may fully accept some religious doctrines, but their main focus is on *being* religious.

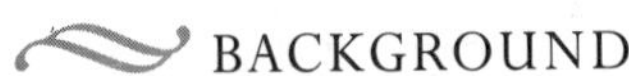 BACKGROUND

The United Nations Declaration on the Rights of Indigenous Peoples

In 2007 the United Nations General Assembly adopted the *Declaration on the Rights of Indigenous Peoples*. The introduction to the document says, "Colonial conquest and the more subtle but sustained impact of the modern-day lodestar of scientific and technological progress have pushed indigenous peoples and their cultures to the brink of extinction. Nation states often adopted policies of assimilation and integration . . . that left First Nations fundamentally uprooted, marginalized and dispossessed. Still, many indigenous peoples . . . overcame their cultural and political isolation and joined together to reclaim their essential identity as well as their role on the global stage of decision making."

Article 1. Indigenous peoples have the right to the full enjoyment, as a collective or as individuals, of all human rights and fundamental freedoms as recognized in the Charter of the United Nations, the Universal Declaration of Human Rights, and international human rights law.

Article 2. Indigenous peoples and individuals are free and equal to all other peoples and individuals and have the right to be free from any kind of discrimination, in the exercise of their rights, in particular that based on their indigenous origin or identity.

Article 3. Indigenous peoples have the right to self-determination. By virtue of that right they freely determine their political status and freely pursue their economic, social and cultural development.

Article 4. Indigenous peoples, in exercising their right to self-determination, have the right to autonomy or self-government in matters relating to their internal and local affairs, as well as ways and means for financing their autonomous functions.

Article 5. Indigenous peoples have the right to maintain and strengthen their distinct political, legal, economic, social and cultural institutions, while retaining their right to participate fully, if they so choose, in the political, economic, social and cultural life of the State.

Article 6. Every indigenous individual has the right to a nationality.

Article 7. 1. Indigenous individuals have the rights to life, physical and mental integrity, liberty and security of person. 2. Indigenous peoples have the collective right to live in freedom, peace and security as distinct peoples and shall not be subjected to any act of genocide or any other act of violence, including forcibly removing children of the group to another group. . . .

Article 10. Indigenous peoples shall not be forcibly removed from their lands or territories. No relocation shall take place without the free, prior and informed consent of the indigenous peoples concerned and after agreement on just and fair compensation and, where possible, with the option of return.

United Nations, *Declaration on the Rights of Indigenous Peoples*, September 13, 2007 (20 December 2015).

KEY TERMS

animism The view that objects in the natural world—rocks, trees, rivers, mountains, animals, stars—are, or have, spirits or consciousness.

divination The power to predict the future.

Ghost Dance A religious movement beginning in 1870 involving Native North Americans who believed that by doing the Ghost Dance, they would be liberated from white oppression.

indigenous people The original or native inhabitants of a region.

magic The attempt to control events through supernatural or mysterious means.

NOTE

1. Frederick W. Turner, ed., *The Portable North American Indian Reader* (New York: Penguin, 1973), 10.

READINGS

INDIGENOUS NORTH AMERICAN RELIGIONS

Thunder Rides a Black Horse

CLAIRE R. FARRER

Claire Farrer is an anthropologist, Native Americanist, and folklorist. In this excerpt from her classic book *Thunder Rides a Black Horse* she explores some of the beliefs and folkways of Mescalero Apaches living on a contemporary Indian reservation, where she too lived for a while and did research for many years.

Claire R. Farrer, *Thunder Rides a Black Horse* (Long Grove, IL: Waveland Press, 2011), 1–13.

Apache! The very word conjures visions of half-naked, tall, slender men with long, straight, black hair streaming in the wind behind them—hair held in place only with headbands that function as much to keep sweat from eyes as to confine stray locks—men whose sinewy legs caress the sides of sleek horses that have hooves virtually flying along the ground, raising occasional sparks as the units of horse and rider dart into and out of sight, disappearing into mountain vastness or the tall grasses of the plains. Hollywood and western novels have given us such visions of Apache men, ignoring the women or portraying them as only nubile maidens who are the objects of white men's lust and who are invariably chiefs' daughters. Perhaps there may be a few—a very few—Apache people who could step into the Hollywood and novelists' stereotypes and find the fit a comfortable one, but I do not know them; they are not among the more than 200 Apaches with whom I am well acquainted and who give the lie to the stereotypes.

Apaches, especially those of the Mescalero Apache Indian Reservation in south-central New Mexico and who are the ones I know the best, are like any other ethnic group of people: some are skinny and some chubby; some are short and some tall; there are good ones, some of whom are friends for life, and there are some on whom it is best not to turn one's back for their lying and backstabbing ways. In sum, they are like people everywhere. But they are different, too, as I have learned from my three decades of experience with the people of the Mescalero Apache Indian Reservation.

Contemporary reservations are in mainstream American culture. Sometimes they are of that culture as well, but not always. The reservations with which I am familiar, all in the Southwestern or Western states, have buckskin and Ultrasuede™; finely bred horses and 4 × 4 Broncos; TV, often with satellite dishes, and older relatives with the *real* stories; Teenage Mutant Ninja Turtles and Warrior Twins; California ranch-style houses and sweat houses; strollers and cradleboards; Wonder bread and fly bread. Reservation Indians attend to each other, to TV "stories," and to the people in narrative, whether those people are the stuff of what mainstream Americans call everyday life or label as legend, folklore, or mythology.

The Native American people on contemporary reservations live in concert with those who have gone before as they do with those who are here now; perhaps this is true for urban Indians, as well—I know few of them and do not feel qualified to comment. For the Indians I know on several reservations in the American West and Southwest, life is lived in what I term the "mythic present." What mainstream Americans consider to have happened long ago, if it happened at all, is real and present during everyday life on reservations. There is a co-presence of events in which the Warrior Twins engaged and those taking place around a dinner table; this is the mythic present. Both the Long Ago and the Now are present together in thought, song, narrative, everyday life, and certainly in religious and ritual life.

The mythic present includes those who have gone before and who are remembered today. Sometimes they are culture heroes and heroines; sometimes they are tricksters, like the irascible Coyote, who has frailties as do all people but who, like each of Creator's children, also has worthy attributes. Regardless of who they are, the reality of those from the mythic present is as tangible to most Indian people as is that of the person sitting next to you at the ceremonial or the baby you tuck into bed at night, or your spouse or lover. It is the oscillating movement between the mythic present and the lived present, as I call what we perceive as reality, that gives contemporary Indian reservations their special character, their sense of depth, their roots, their rationale and exemplar. And it is the mythic present in concert with the lived present that are my concerns in this book. . . .

The "ethnographic present" is the term that anthropologists use for such a collapsing of time. All events are related in the present tense, even when they happened some time ago. The ethnographic present is also the mode of discourse that Indians themselves use when speaking of events from myth or the long ago. It is as though those events were happening in concert with the events in which people who are alive today participate. This commingling of long-ago time, place, character, and activity with the present constitutes the mythic present. Thus, time has a different character, a different dimension, on Indian reservations than it does in mainstream American life. . . .

Mescalero Apache people are fully aware of the mainstream American clock and calendar times and, indeed, function by them in much of their daily lives. However, they also have their own "Indian time." Indian time is not precisely linked to Anglo time. The business of time, when considered cross-culturally, can be very confusing.

Often Anglos complain because things "don't happen on time" on Indian reservations. They most certainly do happen on time; it is just that "on time" takes on different connotations in the two separate cultures. Indian time, as it is called by Native people themselves, is governed by participants rather than a clock; it is when things and participants are all present and ready. That time may be ahead of or behind clock time.

Edward T. Hall . . . has discussed this issue of time in several books. His terms "polychronic time" (several things occurring at the same time) and "monochronic time" (when one thing happens at a time in sequence) are useful. Native American people operate on polychronic time; when all the swirl of preparatory activities coalesce with the necessary participants and ingredients, the event occurs. Obviously, one cannot have a dance if the dancers are not present or if the musicians are not ready. So, on most Indian reservations, saying a dance begins at 8:00 PM is to say that sometime after dinner, when the musicians are ready and when the stage is set and when the dancers are present, we will dance: this is a typically polychronic attitude. An astute observer might well see some of the preparations as they occur—perhaps musicians tightening drumheads, or a person going from camp to camp to announce that the dancers are painted—and, through such observations, realize that the dance is not yet quite ready. But Anglos, being firmly ensconced in monochromic time, have a tendency to ignore the polychronic events and to consider the dancing as being forty-five minutes late when the first dancer does not appear until 8:45. Anglos are equally appalled when they arrive promptly at eight only to find that the dancing has been going on for half an hour or more. Time is indeed perplexing when one is operating in a cross-cultural context, as Anglos or other non-Indians are when on Indian reservations or as reservation Indians are when operating in mainstream American culture.

People's names can also be a problem area between mainstream Americans and reservation Indians. Most Mescalero Apache people do not like to have their names mentioned in books. Some of the people I write about did give permission for their actual names to be used, but others did not. Therefore, almost all of the names in this book are pseudonyms. But they represent very real people, some of whom are or were well-known off the Reservation.

For example, Wendell Chino is the real name of the president of the Mescalero Apache Tribe. Through the more than twenty-five years of his tenure as tribal president, there have been many successful law cases brought under his name and that of the Tribe as a corporate entity; his name can be found in law books and often in newspaper articles.

And Bernard (BERN-ard; rhymes with Leonard) Second, whose name appears often in the chapters that follow, was a real person and was the man from whom I learned much of what I understand about Mescalero Apache people. He died in 1988, still a young man, and I miss him—especially as I write this book—for it was he who was responsible for my family connections at Mescalero. Bernard was active in the National Indian Youth Council and in various ecumenical councils; he was the narrator for films and television programs on his people or, on one occasion, on Central American people. He was highly regarded among Native Americans. He lives still in my memory, as I trust he will for you in the other chapters of this book.

The two well-known names of Chino and Second are used here, as are those of my daughter and myself; but no other real names are used, even when people gave permission to me to do so. People deserve their privacy. Being an anthropologist is intrusive enough without also subjecting the people to possibly unwanted attentions from strangers.

The purpose of this book is to allow non-Indians some insight into what it is like to live on a contemporary Indian reservation. There are moments of joy and incredible beauty, just as there are moments of sorrow and horridness; in these aspects, life on a reservation is like life anywhere in the United States—or anywhere else in the world. Yet there are some differences that can be difficult to comprehend.

Most Native North American people live simultaneously in two cultures: their own, Native one and the one of the larger, mainstream American society. They are enriched by having two traditions upon which to draw while also being impoverished by sometimes feeling they are not fully accepted into either one.

Many non-Indian Americans feel the same way when they have strong family or ethnic traditions; this is especially true of first- and second-generation immigrants to this country, as can be seen today among Hmong or Mien people who want to learn quickly to become proper Americans while still feeling that particular aspects of their own home culture are important. Often people cling to the old culture's festivals, ceremonies, food, and items of belief; these become valued markers of ethnic identification to help define who, for example, is Hmong-American and who is not.

Native American people have similar pulls on their loyalties and beliefs. In some ways theirs is an easier problem in that there are reservations. When one lives on a reservation, the vast majority of other residents are also of one's own tribe who know, even if not all believe in and follow, the same traditions and who share the same history. Members of each household on the reservation will feature the same foods prepared in similar ways for particular occasions. Just about everyone on a reservation has heard the same stories, even if they are told in slightly different ways. Everyone knows the same rules for politeness and decorum, who can marry whom and why, who is forbidden to marry whom and why, and how the world came into being. All of these things, and others as well, make ethnic identity easier to define when people live on reservations.

But reservations can as easily be perceived as prisons. Reservations have boundaries that often seem more permeable for outsiders than for the Indians themselves. Reservations are places where the United States government and its agents are a daily presence. Often job opportunities are limited on reservations, and there is depressing poverty. Many reservations are the shrunken enclaves that remain after treaties were broken and land, once promised, has been confiscated by the U.S. government. Customs learned on the reservations often differ from those of mainstream Americans, making Native people feel out of place and the object of curiosity when they are off-reservation. Most Native people I know view reservations as a mixed blessing while adamantly maintaining their aboriginal rights to more land than they have.

And not all Native Americans live on reservations. That is important to keep in mind. I write of reservation Mescalero Apaches; yet, there are many Mescalero people who live in other parts of the United States, in Mexico, or in other foreign countries. What they all share in common is the sense that the reservation is home, even if they have had little life experience there. . . .

Many of the [Native American] living areas are visible from Highway 70, but others are hidden away on those narrow roads. Most houses are set into the terrain with as little modification of the land as is possible. Lawns are rare, and generally considered unnecessary. Most people keep the areas around their homes immaculately clean. Still they sometimes seem cluttered with corrals (horses are still important, although almost everyone relies on pickup trucks or cars), sometimes sheds for tack and hay, vehicles, tipi poles (for summer encampments or to be used when houses overflow and it becomes necessary to erect a "guest house"—a tipi), and often a camper shell. Despite these additions, the general impression is of a series of clean and tidy mini-communities meandering up the sides of mountains.

Between 1976 and 1988, I visited the Reservation each year for varying periods of time. In some years I stayed for only a few days, and in other years I stayed much longer. I almost always was there for the major religious and ritual event, the public girls' puberty ceremony that takes place each July. This is a time of homecoming, not just for members of the Mescalero Apache Tribe but also for their friends and those Anglos who used to live on the reservation whether they were school teachers, Bureau of Indian Affairs (BIA) employees, other government employees, tribal employees, those attached to the Indian Health Service (IHS) hospital on the Reservation as health care professionals, or even anthropologists-folklorists. On these return visits, I rarely stayed in motels; usually, I stayed with a fictive family member, most often in Bernard's house.

In November of 1988 Bernard Second died. He had been gutaal/singer (a ritual specialist and holy man) for the Mescalero Apache Tribe as well as my primary consultant and fictive brother from 1975 until his death. Bernard's family became our fictive family as our family became fictive relatives to them; for example, Bernard called my mother "Mom" while she always affectionately referred to him as "that dear boy," much to his amusement. The fictive family relationships continue through to the present, even though Bernard, who initiated them, has died. . . .

The girls' puberty ceremonial is vitally important for the Mescalero Apache people, and that four-day, four-night event forms the structure of this book.

Each year around the Fourth of July holiday, the Tribe as a whole stops to celebrate the attainment of womanhood by its girls. In a matrilineal society, where kinship and descent are traced through one's mother, it is truly joyous to have new young women who will become the future mothers of the tribe. In July, the ceremonial lasts for four days and four nights, in the manner described in the following chapters. Some parents or guardians of girls-women who have reached initial menses (and therefore, by definition, *are* women) choose to have a private ceremonial rather than the public one. Private ceremonials may be only a day long, but the majority of them are held for two days. In increasing numbers of families lately, private ceremonies are also being performed for the full four days.

A ceremonial is a very expensive affair, for which families prepare literally for years. Through the three decades that I have been going to or living at Mescalero, I have witnessed, and often photographed, dozens of puberty ceremonials as a portion of the fieldwork that has allowed me to come to know the Apache people of the Mescalero Reservation.

Basic Call to Consciousness

IROQUOIS NATION

This passage is a formal statement of the beliefs of the northeastern (Hau De No Sau Nee) Iroquois Nation, submitted to a United Nations conference and published in 1978. It declares that all living things are spiritual beings, including all humankind, and this fact leads to the insight that all living beings are interconnected and thus deserving of humanity's respect and support.

The Haudenosaunee, or the Six Nations Iroquois Confederacy, has existed on this land since the beginning of human memory. Our culture is among the most ancient, continuously existing cultures in the world. We still remember the earliest doings of human beings. We remember the original instructions of the Creators of Life on this place we call Ionkhi'nistenha onhwentsia—Mother Earth. We are

Iroquois Nation, in Akwesasne Notes, ed., *Basic Call to Consciousness* (Summertown, TN: Native Voices, 1978), 85–86.

the spiritual guardians of this place. We are the Onkwehon:we—the Real People.

In the beginning, we were told that the human beings who walk about the Earth have been provided with all the things necessary for life. We were instructed to carry a love for one another, and to show a great respect for all the beings of this Earth. We are shown that our life exists with the tree life, that our well-being depends on the well-being of the vegetable life, that we are close relatives of the four-legged beings. In our ways, spiritual consciousness is the highest form of politics.

Ours is a Way of Life. We believe that all living things are spiritual beings. Spirits can be expressed as energy forms manifested in matter. A blade of grass is an energy form manifested in matter—grass matter. The spirit of the grass is that unseen force that produces the species of grass, and it is manifest to us in the form of real grass.

All things of the world are real, material things. The Creation is a true, material phenomenon, and the Creation manifests itself to us through reality. The spiritual universe, then, is manifest to man as the Creation, the Creation that supports life. We believe that man is real, a part of the Creation, and that his duty is to support life in conjunction with the other beings. That is why we call ourselves Onkwehon:we—Real People.

The original instructions direct that we who walk about on the Earth are to express a great respect, an affection, and a gratitude toward all the spirits that create and support life. We give a greeting and thanksgiving to the many supporters of our own lives—the corn, beans, squash, the winds, the sun. When people cease to respect and express gratitude for these many things, then all life will be destroyed, and human life on this planet will come to an end.

Our roots are deep in the lands where we live. We have a great love for our country, for our birthplace is there. The soil is rich from the bones of thousands of our generations. Each of us was created in those lands, and it is our duty to take great care of them, because from these lands will spring the future generations of the Onkwehon:we. We walk about with a great respect, for the Earth is a very sacred place.

We are not a people who demand or ask anything of the Creators of Life; instead, we give greetings and thanksgiving that all the forces of life are still at work. We deeply understand our relationship to all living things. To this day, the territories we still hold are filled with trees, animals, and the other gifts of the Creation. In these places we still receive our nourishment from our Mother Earth.

We have seen that not all people of the Earth show the same kind of respect for this world and its beings. The Indo-European people who have colonized our lands have shown little respect for the things that create and support life. We believe that these people ceased their respect for the world a long time ago. Many thousands of years ago, all the people of the world believed in the same Way of Life, that of harmony with the universe. All lived according to the Natural Ways.

Iroquois Myth: The Creation

A common element in Native American beliefs is the creation myth, an explanation of the origins of human beings, the earth, or a specific people. This Iroquois version begins with the story of how the whole earth grew from a bit of soil placed on the back of a giant turtle, the Earth Bearer. It then relates the origins of the moon, sun, stars, animals, birds, and wind.

Frederick W. Turner, ed., *The Portable North American Indian Reader* (New York: Penguin, 1973), 36–42.

THE COUNCIL TREE

In the faraway days of this floating island there grew one stately tree that branched beyond the range of vision. Perpetually laden with fruit and blossoms, the air was fragrant with its perfume, and the people gathered to its shade where councils were held.

One day the Great Ruler said to his people: "We will make a new place where another people may grow. Under our council tree is a great cloud sea which calls for our help. It is lonesome. It knows no rest and calls for light. We will talk to it. The roots of our council tree point to it and will show the way."

Having commanded that the tree be uprooted, the Great Ruler peered into the depths where the roots had guided, and summoning Ata-en-sic, who was with child, bade her look down. Ata-en-sic saw nothing, but the Great Ruler knew that the sea voice was calling, and bidding her carry its life, wrapped around her a great ray of light and sent her down to the cloud sea.

HAH-NU-NAH, THE TURTLE

Dazzled by the descending light enveloping Ata-en-sic, there was great consternation among the animals and birds inhabiting the cloud sea, and they counseled in alarm.

"If it falls it may destroy us," they cried.

"Where can it rest?" asked the Duck.

"Only the oeh-da (earth) can hold it," said the Beaver, "the oeh-da which lies at the bottom of our waters, and I will bring it." The Beaver went down but never returned. Then the Duck ventured, but soon its dead body floated to the surface.

Many of the divers had tried and failed when the Muskrat, knowing the way, volunteered to obtain it and soon returned bearing a small portion in his paw. "But it is heavy," said he, "and will grow fast. Who will bear it?"

The Turtle was willing, and the oeh-da was placed on his hard shell.

Having received a resting place for the light, the water birds, guided by its glow, flew upward, and receiving the woman on their widespread wings, bore her down to the Turtle's back.

And Hah-nu-nah, the Turtle, became the Earth Bearer. When he stirs, the seas rise in great waves, and when restless and violent, earthquakes yawn and devour.

ATA-EN-SIC, THE SKY WOMAN

The *oeh-da* grew rapidly and had become an island when Ata-en-sic, hearing voices under her heart, one soft and soothing, the other loud and contentious, knew that her mission to people the island was nearing.

To her solitude two lives were coming, one peaceful and patient, the other restless and vicious. The latter, discovering light under his mother's arm, thrust himself through, to contentions and strife, the right born entered life for freedom and peace.

These were the Do-ya-da-no, the twin brothers, Spirits of Good and Evil. Foreknowing their powers, each claimed dominion, and a struggle between them began, Hah-gweh-di-yu claiming the right to beautify the island, while Hah-gweh-da-et-gah determined to destroy. Each went his way, and where peace had reigned discord and strife prevailed.

THE SUN, MOON, AND STARS

At the birth of Hah-gweh-di-yu his Sky Mother, Ata-en-sic, had died, and the island was still dim in the dawn of its new life when, grieving at his mother's death, he shaped the sky with the palm of his hand, and creating the Sun from her face, lifted it there, saying, "You shall rule here where your face will shine forever." But Hah-gweh-da-et-gah set Darkness in the west sky, to drive the Sun down behind it.

Hah-gweh-di-yu then drew forth from the breast of his Mother, the Moon and the Stars, and led them to the Sun as his sisters who would guard his night sky. He gave to the Earth her body, its Great Mother, from whom was to spring all life.

All over the land Hah-gweh-di-yu planted towering mountains, and in the valleys set high hills to protect the straight rivers as they ran to the sea. But Hah-gweh-da-et-gah wrathfully sundered the mountains, hurling them far apart, and drove the high hills into the wavering valleys, bending the rivers as he hunted them down.

Hah-gweh-di-yu set forests on the high hills, and on the low plains fruit-bearing trees and vines to wing their seeds to the scattering winds. But Hah-gweh-da-et-gah gnarled the forests besetting the earth, and led monsters to dwell in the sea, and herded hurricanes in the sky which frowned with mad tempests that chased the Sun and the Stars.

THE ANIMALS AND BIRDS

Hah-gweh-di-yu went across a great sea where he met a Being who told him he was his father. Said the Being, "How high can you reach?" Hah-gweh-di-yu touched the sky. Again he asked, "How much can you lift?" and Hah-gweh-di-yu grasped a stone mountain and tossed it far into space. Then said the Being, "You are worthy to be my son"; and lashing upon his back two burdens, bade him return to the earth. Hah-gweh-di-yu swam for many days, and the Sun did not leave the sky until he had neared the earth. The burdens had grown heavy but Hah-gweh-di-yu was strong, and when he reached the shore they fell apart and opened.

From one of the burdens flew an eagle guiding the birds which followed, filling the skies with their song to the Sun as they winged to the forest. From the other there came animals led by the deer, and they sped quickly to the mountains. But Hah-gweh-da-et-gah followed with wild beasts that devour, and grim flying creatures that steal life without sign, and creeping reptiles to poison the way.

DUEL OF HAH-GWEH-DI-YU AND HAH-GWEH-DA-ET-GAH

When the earth was completed and Hah-gweh-di-yu had bestowed a protecting Spirit upon each of his creation, he besought Hah-gweh-da-et-gah to reconcile his vicious existence to the peacefulness of his own, but Hah-gweh-da-et-gah refused, and challenged Hah-gweh-di-yu to combat, the victor to become the ruler of the earth.

Hah-gweh-da-et-gah proposed weapons which he could control, poisonous roots strong as flint, monsters' teeth, and fangs of serpents. But these Hah-gweh-di-yu refused, selecting the thorns of the giant crab-apple tree, which were arrow pointed and strong.

With the thorns they fought. The battle continued many days, ending in the overthrow of Hah-gweh-da-et-gah.

Hah-gweh-di-yu, having now become the ruler, banished his brother to a pit under the earth, whence he cannot return. But he still retains Servers, half human and half beasts, whom he sends to continue his destructive work. These Servers can assume any form Hah-gweh-da-et-gah may command, and they wander all over the earth.

Hah-gweh-di-yu, faithful to the prophesy of the Great Ruler of the floating island, that the earth should be peopled, is continually creating and protecting.

GA-OH, SPIRIT OF THE WINDS

Though of giant proportions, Ga-oh, who governs the winds, is confined in the broad north sky. Were Ga-oh free, he would tear the heavens into fragments.

In the ages of his solitary confinement, he does not forget his strength, and punishes the winds to subjection when they suddenly rear for flight.

At the entrance of his abode and reined to his hands are four watchers: the Bear (north wind), Panther (west wind), Moose (east wind), and Fawn (south wind).

When Ga-oh unbinds Bear, it leads its hurricane winter winds to Earth; when he loosens Panther, its stealthy west winds creep down and follow Earth with their snarling blasts; when Moose is released, its east wind meets the Sun and its misty breath floats over the Sun's path blinding it with rains; and when Ga-oh unlocks his reins from Fawn, its soothing south winds whisper to Earth and she summons her Spring, who comes planting the seeds for the summer sunglow.

Though in his subjugation of the winds it is Ga-oh's duty to pacify them, frequently they are influenced by his varying moods. When Ga-oh is contented and happy, gentle and invigorating breezes fan Earth; when he is irritated by his confinement and restless, strong winds agitate the waters and bend the forest trees; and when, frenzied to mighty throes, Ga-oh becomes vehement, ugly blasts go forth, uprooting trees, dashing the streams into leaping furies, lifting the sea waters to mountainous waves, and devastating the earth.

Notwithstanding these outbursts, Ga-oh is faithful in disciplining the winds to their proper seasons, and guarding Earth from the rage of the elements.

When the north wind blows strong, the Iroquois say, "The Bear is prowling in the sky"; if the west wind is violent, "The Panther is whining." When the east wind chills with its rain, "The Moose is spreading his breath"; and when the south wind wafts soft breezes, "The Fawn is returning to its Doe."

NAMING THE WINDS

When, in the creation of the earth, Hah-gweh-di-yu limited the duties of the powerful Ga-oh to the sky, assigning to him the governing of the tempests, he blew a strong blast that shook the whole earth to trembling, and summoned his assistants to a council.

Ga-oh chose his aides from the terrestrial because of their knowledge of the earth; and when his reverberating call had ceased its thunderous echoes, he opened his north gate wide across the sky and called Ya-o-gah, the Bear.

Lumbering over the mountains as he pushed them from his path, Ya-o-gah, the bulky bear, who had battled the boisterous winds as he came, took his place at Ga-oh's gate and waited the mission of his call. Said Ga-oh, "Ya-o-gah, you are strong, you can freeze the waters with your cold breath; in your broad arms you can carry the wild tempest, and clasp the whole earth when I bid you destroy. I will place you in my far north, there to watch the herd of my winter winds when I loose them in the sky. You shall be North Wind. Enter your home." And the bear lowered his head for the leash with which Ga-oh bound him, and submissively took his place in the north sky.

In a gentler voice Ga-oh called Ne-o-ga, the Fawn, and a soft breeze as of the summer crept over the sky; the air grew fragrant with the odor of flowers, and there were voices as of babbling brooks telling the secrets of the summer to the tune of birds, as Ne-o-ga came proudly lifting her head.

Said Ga-oh, "You walk with the summer sun, and know all its paths; you are gentle, and kind as the sunbeam, and will rule my flock of the summer winds in peace. You shall be the South Wind. Bend your head while I leash you to the sky, for you are swift, and might return from me to the earth." And the gentle fawn followed Ga-oh to his great gate which opens the south sky.

Again Ga-oh trumpeted a shrill blast, and all the sky seemed threatening; an ugly darkness crept into the clouds that sent them whirling in circles of confusion; a quarrelsome, shrieking voice snarled through the air, and with a sound as of great claws tearing the heavens into rifts, Da-jo-ji, the Panther. sprang to the gate.

Said Ga-oh, "You are ugly, and fierce, and can fight the strong storms; you can climb the high mountains, and tear down the forests; you can carry the whirlwind on your strong back, and toss the great sea waves high in the air, and snarl at the tempests if they stray from my gate. You shall be the West Wind. Go to the west sky, where even the Sun will hurry to hide when you howl your warning to the night." And Da-jo-ji, dragging his leash as he stealthily crept along, followed Ga-oh to the farthermost west sky.

Yet Ga-oh rested not. The earth was flat, and in each of its four corners he must have an assistant.

One corner yet remained, and again Ga-oh's strong blast shook the earth. And there arose a moan like the calling of a lost mate, the sky shivered in a cold rain, the whole earth clouded in mist, a crackling sound as of great horns crashing through the forest trees dinned the air, and O-yan-do-ne, the Moose, stood stamping his hoofs at the gate.

Said Ga-oh, as he strung a strong leash around his neck, "Your breath blows the mist, and can lead the cold rains; your horns spread wide, and can push back the forests to widen the path for my storms as with your swift hoofs you race with my winds. You shall be the East Wind, and blow your breath to chill the young clouds as they float through the sky." And, said Ga-oh, as he led him to the east sky, "Here you shall dwell forevermore."

Thus, with his assistants, does Ga-oh control his storms. And although he must ever remain in his sky lodge, his will is supreme, and his faithful assistants will obey!

Cherokee Myth: How the World Was Made

This Cherokee narrative explains how the earth got to be the way it is now—a great island floating in a vast sea, suspended by four cords hanging down from the "sky vault," a world inhabited by men, animals, and plants.

The earth is a great island floating in a sea of water, and suspended at each of the four cardinal points by a cord hanging down from the sky vault, which is of solid rock. When the world grows old and worn out, the people will die and the cords will break and let the earth sink down into the ocean, and all will be water again. The Indians are afraid of this.

When all was water, the animals were above in Galun'lati, beyond the arch; but it was very much crowded, and they were wanting more room. They wondered what was below the water, and at last Dayu-ni'si, "Beaver's Grandchild," the little Water-beetle, offered to go and see if it could learn. It darted in every direction over the surface of the water, but could find no firm place to rest. Then it dived to the bottom and came up with some soft mud, which began to grow and spread on every side until it became the island which we call the earth. It was afterward fastened to the sky with four cords, but no one remembers who did this.

At first the earth was flat and very soft and wet. The animals were anxious to get down, and sent out different birds to see if it was yet dry, but they found no place to alight and came back again to Galun'lati. At last it seemed to be time, and they sent out the Buzzard and told him to go and make ready for them. This was the Great Buzzard, the father of all the buzzards we see now. He flew all over the earth, low down near the ground, and it was still soft. When he reached the Cherokee country, he was very tired, and his wings began to flap and strike the ground, and wherever they struck the earth there was a valley, and where they turned up again there was a mountain. When the animals above saw this, they were

James Mooney, *Myths of the Cherokee*, in *Nineteenth Annual Report of the Bureau of American Ethnology* (Washington, DC: U.S. Government Printing Office, 1900).

afraid that the whole world would be mountains, so they called him back, but the Cherokee country remains full of mountains to this day.

When the earth was dry and the animals came down, it was still dark, so they got the sun and set it in a track to go every day across the island from east to west, just overhead. It was too hot this way, and Tsiska'gili', the Red Crawfish, had his shell scorched a bright red, so that his meat was spoiled; and the Cherokee do not eat it. The conjurers put the sun another hand-breadth higher in the air, but it was still too hot. They raised it another time, and another, until it was seven handbreadths high and just under the sky arch. Then it was right, and they left it so. This is why the conjurers call the highest place Gulkwa'gine Di'galun'latiyun', "the seventh height," because it is seven hand-breadths above the earth. Every day the sun goes along under this arch, and returns at night on the upper side to the starting place.

There is another world under this, and it is like ours in everything—animals, plants, and people—save that the seasons are different. The streams that come down from the mountains are the trails by which we reach this underworld, and the springs at their heads are the doorways by which we enter it, but to do this one must fast and go to water and have one of the underground people for a guide. We know that the seasons in the underworld are different from ours, because the water in the springs is always warmer in winter and cooler in summer than the outer air.

When the animals and plants were first made—we do not know by whom—they were told to watch and keep awake for seven nights, just as young men now fast and keep awake when they pray to their medicine. They tried to do this, and nearly all were awake through the first night, but the next night several dropped off to sleep, and the third night others were asleep, and then others, until, on the seventh night, of all the animals only the owl, the panther, and one or two more were still awake. To these were given the power to see and to go about in the dark, and to make prey of the birds and animals which must sleep at night. Of the trees only the cedar, the pine, the spruce, the holly, and the laurel were awake to the end, and to them it was given to be always green and to be greatest for medicine, but to the others it was said: "Because you have not endured to the end you shall lose your hair every winter."

Men came after the animals and plants. At first there were only a brother and sister until he struck her with a fish and told her to multiply, and so it was. In seven days a child was born to her, and thereafter every seven days another, and they increased very fast until there was danger that the world could not keep them. Then it was made that a woman should have only one child in a year, and it has been so ever since.

Cherokee Myth: Origin of Disease and Medicine

This story proposes that the world began as an Eden-like paradise in which all living creatures—from bugs to beasts—could talk, and they and the people lived together peacefully as friends. But the humans eventually overran the earth, slaughtering and trampling the other forms of life. The animals held a council at which they decided to give man a multitude of diseases and conditions (rheumatism and nightmares among them) to slow or deter his cruelty. The plants, however, sided with man, giving him cures for some of the maladies inflicted by the animals.

James Mooney, *Myths of the Cherokee*, in *Nineteenth Annual Report of the Bureau of American Ethnology* (Washington, DC: U.S. Government Printing Office, 1900).

In the old days the beasts, birds, fishes, insects, and plants could all talk, and they and the people lived together in peace and friendship. But as time went on the people increased so rapidly that their settlements spread over the whole earth, and the poor animals found themselves beginning to be cramped for room. This was bad enough, but to make it worse Man invented bows, knives, blowguns, spears, and hooks, and began to slaughter the larger animals, birds, and fishes for their flesh or their skins, while the smaller creatures, such as the frogs and worms, were crushed and trodden upon without thought, out of pure carelessness or contempt. So the animals resolved to consult upon measures for their common safety.

The Bears were the first to meet in council in their townhouse under Kuwa'hi mountain, the "Mulberry place," and the old White Bear chief presided. After each in turn had complained of the way in which Man killed their friends, ate their flesh, and used their skins for his own purposes, it was decided to begin war at once against him. Some one asked what weapons Man used to destroy them. "Bows and arrows, of course," cried all the Bears in chorus. "And what are they made of?" was the next question. "The bow of wood, and the string of our entrails," replied one of the Bears. It was then proposed that they make a bow and some arrows and see if they could not use the same weapons against Man himself. So one Bear got a nice piece of locust wood and another sacrificed himself for the good of the rest in order to furnish a piece of his entrails for the string. But when everything was ready and the first Bear stepped up to make the trial, it was found that in letting the arrow fly after drawing back the bow, his long claws caught the string and spoiled the shot. This was annoying, but some one suggested that they might trim his claws, which was accordingly done, and on a second trial it was found that the arrow went straight to the mark. But here the chief, the old White Bear, objected, saying it was necessary that they should have long claws in order to be able to climb trees. "One of us has already died to furnish the bowstring, and if we now cut off our claws we must all starve together. It is better to trust to the teeth and claws that nature gave us, for it is plain that man's weapons were not intended for us."

No one could think of any better plan, so the old chief dismissed the council and the Bears dispersed to the woods and thickets without having concerted any way to prevent the increase of the human race. Had the result of the council been otherwise, we should now be at war with the Bears, but as it is, the hunter does not even ask the Bear's pardon when he kills one.

The Deer next held a council under their chief, the Little Deer, and after some talk decided to send rheumatism to every hunter who should kill one of them unless he took care to ask their pardon for the offense. They sent notice of their decision to the nearest settlement of Indians and told them at the same time what to do when necessity forced them to kill one of the Deer tribe. Now, whenever the hunter shoots a Deer, the Little Deer, who is swift as the wind and can not be wounded, runs quickly up to the spot and, bending over the blood-stains, asks the spirit of the Deer if it has heard the prayer of the hunter for pardon. If the reply be "Yes," all is well, and the Little Deer goes on his way; but if the reply be "No," he follows on the trail of the hunter, guided by the drops of blood on the ground, until he arrives at his cabin in the settlement, when the Little Deer enters invisibly and strikes the hunter with rheumatism, so that he becomes at once a helpless cripple. No hunter who has regard for his health ever fails to ask pardon of the Deer for killing it, although some hunters who have not learned the prayer may try to turn aside the Little Deer from his pursuit by building a fire behind them in the trail.

Next came the Fishes and Reptiles, who had their own complaints against Man. They held their council together and determined to make their victims dream of snakes twining about them in slimy folds and blowing foul breath in their faces, or to make them dream of eating raw or decaying fish, so that they would lose appetite, sicken, and die. This is why people dream about snakes and fish.

Finally the Birds, Insects, and smaller animals came together for the same purpose, and the Grubworm was chief of the council. It was decided that each in turn should give an opinion, and then they would vote on the question as to whether or not Man was guilty. Seven votes should be enough to condemn him. One after another denounced Man's cruelty and injustice toward the other animals and voted in favor of his death. The Frog spoke first, saying: "We must do something to check the increase of the race, or people will become so numerous that we shall be crowded from off the earth. See how they have kicked me about because I'm ugly, as they say, until my back is covered with sores;" and here he showed the spots on his skin. Next came the Bird—no one remembers now which one it was—who condemned Man "because he burns my feet off," meaning the way in which the hunter barbecues birds by impaling them on a stick set over the fire, so that their feathers and tender feet are singed off. Others followed in the same strain. The Ground-squirrel alone ventured to say a good word for Man, who seldom hurt him because he was so small, but this made the others so angry that they fell upon the Ground-squirrel and tore him with their claws, and the stripes are on his back to this day.

They began then to devise and name so many new diseases, one after another, that had not their invention at last failed them, no one of the human race would have been able to survive. The Grubworm grew constantly more pleased as the name of each disease was called off, until at last they reached the end of the list, when some one proposed to make menstruation sometimes fatal to women. On this he rose up in his place and cried: "*Wadan'!* [Thanks!] I'm glad some more of them will die, for they are getting so thick that they tread on me." The thought fairly made him shake with joy, so that he fell over backward and could not get on his feet again, but had to wriggle off on his back, as the Grubworm has done ever since.

When the Plants, who were friendly to Man, heard what had been done by the animals, they determined to defeat the latters' evil designs. Each Tree, Shrub, and Herb, down even to the Grasses and Mosses, agreed to furnish a cure for some one of the diseases named, and each said: "I shall appear to help Man when he calls upon me in his need." Thus came medicine; and the plants, every one of which has its use if we only knew it, furnish the remedy to counteract the evil wrought by the revengeful animals. Even weeds were made for some good purpose, which we must find out for ourselves. When the doctor does not know what medicine to use for a sick man the spirit of the plant tells him.

Sioux Genesis

This Sioux narrative relates how the first man arose from the mud of the Great Plains. From this man came the Lakota Sioux nation. The moral to be drawn is that "the great plains is claimed by the Lakotas as their very own. We are of the soil and the soil is of us."

. . . Our legends tell us that it was hundreds and perhaps thousands of years ago since the first man sprang from the soil in the midst of the great plains. The story says that one morning long ago a lone man awoke, face to the sun, emerging from the soil. Only his head was visible, the rest of his body not yet being fashioned. The man looked about, but saw no mountains, no rivers, no forests. There was nothing but soft and quaking mud,

From Chief Luther Standing Bear, *Land of the Spotted Eagle* (Boston and New York: Houghton Mifflin Company, 1933; reprint Ann Arbor, MI: University Microfilms, 1969).

for the earth itself was still young. Up and up the man drew himself until he freed his body from the clinging soil. At last he stood upon the earth, but it was not solid, and his first few steps were slow and halting. But the sun shone and ever the man kept his face turned toward it. In time the rays of the sun hardened the face of the earth and strengthened the man and he bounded and leaped about, a free and joyous creature. From this man sprang the Lakota nation and, so far as we know, our people have been born and have died upon this plain; and no people have shared it with us until the coming of the European. So this land of the great plains is claimed by the Lakotas as their very own. We are of the soil and the soil is of us.

Native American Spirituality

EVAN T. PRITCHARD

Evan T. Pritchard laments the huge spiritual gap between Native Americans and most other Americans, a gap that separates "ourselves and nature, between ourselves and our true spiritual self, and between ourselves and God." Understanding Native American spirituality is not like understanding Christianity or some other major religion. Native Americans do not have a unified, definitive set of religious beliefs; they are instead more interested in a way of life that fosters meaningful religious experiences.

It has always struck me as odd that so many Americans know much more about the beliefs of Taoists in Taiwan and Taipei, Buddhists in Sri Lanka, and Hindus in Srinigar than they do about comparable Native American beliefs and enlightenment traditions that were brought to fruition literally in their own backyards. When I speak of how important it is for Algonquin and Siouian pipe carriers to grow their hair long, some people will be puzzled; they will ask, "What does growing your hair have to do with God?" But if I compare it to the beliefs of the Nazirites in the Bible, of whom it is said, "The crown of his God is upon his head" (Samson was a Nazirite), they might say, "Oh, sure, that makes sense!"

There are countless similarities between the early ceremonial practices mentioned in the Hebrew scriptures and those of Native Americans. It doesn't mean that any Native American tribe is "the lost tribe of Israel." Native American nations generally predate even the ancient Hebrew tribal nations of pre-Mosaic times and, according to recent discoveries, the pre-Clovis ancestors of the Algonquins date back at least to 16,000 B.C.E., if not earlier. We can't always explain why such similarities exist, except that we all are related, as the saying goes. While ceremonies may differ from place to place, the truths embraced in Native American traditions are powerful, sacred, universal, and eternal. So it stands to reason they

Evan T. Pritchard, ed., *Native American Stories of the Sacred* (Woodstock, VT: SkyLight Paths Publishing, 2005), xviii–xxi.

would have parallels in all times and all places around the world.

The gap that exists today between ourselves and the essence of Native American spiritual traditions is probably larger than we tend to think, but it is the same gap that stands between ourselves and nature, between ourselves and our true spiritual self, and between ourselves and God. The gap exists not between one ancient sacred path and another, but between ourselves and the sacred, between our media-saturated lives and the lives of our own ancestors, between our artificial lives and the mysterious forces of nature. If we really understood the heart of Judaism as Moses did, the heart of Christianity as Jesus did, the heart of Islam as Muhammad did, the heart of Jainism as Mahavira did, and the heart of Buddhism as Buddha did, our understanding of Native American traditions would deepen to a comparable degree. These great teachers were close to the earth and to their own indigenous roots, as were the Lakota man Black Elk, the enlightened Lenape Delaware men Neoline and Oneeum, Chief Seattle, Chief Joseph of the Nez Perce, Sweet Medicine of the Cheyenne, the Peacemaker who came to the Iroquois/Haudenosaunee, and Wovoka of the Paiute, to name a few. If we sat under a Bodhi tree for a while and waited for enlightenment, we would, at the very least, feel a lot closer to the rhythms of nature, and that alone would help us understand these "strange" Native American spiritual tales.

So, if Native American spirituality has so much in common with other traditions, why can't we just add "Native American" to the list of world religions and proclaim them equal? Because it is not a unified religion. Native Americans have no dogma, other than "thou shalt have no dogma," and no central unifying creed, other than "take care of Mother Earth, and Father Sky, and they will take care of you." There are numerous other common beliefs that we can presume most traditional native people lean toward: the sacredness of the circle; the belief in a spirit world; the importance of ritual and of making offerings; and the importance of purification, of prayer, of healing, of honesty, of community, of seeking visions, and of communication with animals. However, Native American communities developed in different places and at different times and have diverged greatly since the fifteenth century, influenced by different European encroachments. Today the differences between tribes and nations are as significant as the similarities. Tribes and nations have become proud of their own individual and local insights and won't easily give them up to jump into someone else's game bag in the name of religion. It is said, "God is too big for one religion," and the Great Spirit is too big for one Native American view to dominate.

The Jewish and Christian traditions have always been celebrated for presenting a single, unified, and definitive picture of the cosmos, most aspects of which can be clearly visualized, verbalized, and written down. But the decentralized yet all-inclusive tradition of the Native Americans, most of which cannot be written down, has always defied definitions and final answers. It has no one center and therefore is organic, not cosmic, at least not in the conventional sense. It is oriented toward seeing the way things are rather than the way we think they should be, and it does not assume the universe is designed in a way that the mind can understand—hence the term *Great Mystery.* Not surprisingly, there are certain traditions within Christianity that echo the Native American. The *docta ignorantia* of Catholic theology states that God can only be known by what God is not, a teaching completely in agreement with the Vedic view of Brahma and with the Native American view of the Great Mystery.

Native traditions are no less God-filled for insisting on these maddening absences of linear theological structure, and they are no less simple to live by just because they allow for such complexity in the real world. The Native American ancestors seem to have understood the craving of the human mind to explain everything and to tie it all up in one neat package, right or wrong, and long ago decided to sabotage that possibility at every turn so that no one could create a religion out of it. Instead, what was created was a way of life that nurtures deeply religious experiences, which is a different thing.

The simplest explanation I have ever heard of Native American theology is this: We human beings stand halfway between heaven and earth. Father Sky (or Sun) is distant but wise, and keeps the stars and planets on their rightful paths. Mother Earth is always under our feet, always trying to keep us from getting sick with all her helpful medicines and herbs, always loving us. And we are the baby—when we stand in sacred space and when we are in ceremony. We have a right to be here. We are part of all that is holy, part of a holy trinity. That's it. If you are looking for a central point from which to begin your exploration of Native American spirituality, start here, but then abandon it as soon as you outgrow it.

Teaching tales are often like parables, but, unlike the parables in the Christian Bible that comprise a large percentage of Jesus's teachings, the Native American stories are usually left unexplained. This is done out of respect for both the intelligence of the listener and the Great Mystery. However, stories are also as three-dimensional as the objects and creatures that inhabit them, and so no matter how much you explain them, there is always a great deal left over to wonder at and ponder over, becoming clear to us later, when we are ready, each according to his or her own capacity. Everyone gets what they can from them, and the rest is left to dawn on you later.

Sacred Ways of a Lakota

WALLACE BLACK ELK

In this excerpt Wallace Black Elk, the last of the Sioux holy men, describes his shaman journey to spiritual understanding and awareness. He speaks of visions, encounters with spirits, the acquisition of sacred powers, and mystical connections to the Sacred Pipe, a ritual object that he believes is the world's most holy instrument.

You know, straight across the board, hardly anyone really knows what is Indian. The word *Indian* in itself really doesn't mean anything. That's how come nobody knows anything about Indians. So I want to tell you how I grew up and who I am. I've never read books. I wasn't educated that way. What I am saying here is based on my life. That's what I am telling you. I grew up with this *Chanunpa*, this "*Sacred Pipe*" [a ritual object sometimes used by Native Americans], and I have a spirit guide with me all the time. He leads me in and out of all the difficulties, all the obstacles I have to go through. The spirit always finds a pathway. The Chanunpa [Sacred Pipe] finds a pathway. It's like a deer trail. If you find a deer trail and follow that trail, it's going to lead you to medicines and waterholes and a shelter.

I began when I was five years old. That sacred power was given to me. It belonged to my forefathers and foremothers. My grandfather and grandmother decided they wanted to leave something with our people so that in future times there would be little guys behind me. So it was for the unborn to come, and we had a prophecy about that nineteen generations before. We can't remember back any further

Wallace Black Elk and William S. Lyon, *Black Elk: The Sacred Ways of a Lakota* (New York: Harper and Row, 1990), 3–15.

than that. Every seven generations we have a family reunion. You call our family the Sioux, but we call ourselves *Lakota*. We are Earth People because we live close to our mother, the Earth. At first we all spoke the same language and the same mind. At the end of seven generations we had a big family reunion, and we spoke many different languages. Then everybody went off again. They went in all directions. At the end of that seven generations we had a family reunion, and we spoke even more languages. Each time our people came together they had to unanimously understand where we came from. They had to understand that we are a part of the fire and a part of the rock, or earth, and a part of the water and a part of the green, or living. That way we were able to communicate with all the living. And so we spoke many different languages, but we still spoke the same mind. So we know where we came from. We still know our roots.

At that time we were warned that an unknown power would come to us and would cause in us that little shadow of a doubt. That shadow of a doubt would lead to nothing but hurt and destruction and even to death. For us, death means you are gone forever. For the white man, death means physical death, but to us that is a sleep. In the real death, the spirit is gone forever.

So I learned all this little bitty, kindergarten stuff when I was five years old. We have a biological father and mother, but our real Father is *Tunkashila* [Creator], and our real Mother is the Earth. They give birth and life to all the living, so we know we're all interrelated. We all have the same Father and Mother. That is why you hear us always saying *mitakuye oyasin*. We say those words as we enter the sacred *stone-people-lodge* [sweat lodge] and also at the end of every prayer. It means "all my relations." It helps to remind us that we are related to everything that exists.

So I was educated that way, and it was prophesied nineteen generations ago that that gift would be given to me at the age of five. The old people were waiting and ready for me. So when I was five years old, I became an adult. I was just a little guy, but in my mind I was an adult.

When my old people talked, I always sat right in the middle. I was just a little guy, you know, but I listened to them. It's really hard to hear an old man talk. You have to have a lot of patience to hear those people talk, because when they talk, they talk about the motivation, the feeling, the unsound that is around in the universe. They explain everything to one understanding. They bring it all together, and when they finish, just one word comes out. Just one word. They might talk all day, and just one word comes out. The next day they'll talk again, and then another word comes out. So for three or four days of talking, there might be just three or four words that come out. But once you hear that one word, you hear it and understand it. You'll never forget it because your subconscious mind will see and understand it. That silent communication will come in, and you will receive it. One side of the hemisphere will receive it, and the other side will record it. It will remain with you for the rest of your life. It will go even further to your generation, and generation after generation. It will even go to four generations. So that is really hard for this society here to really understand.

So you have a little tape recorder back there in the mind. I call it color TV, and it records. So if you turn up the volume, the electrical power will come in and hit those little water bubbles or molecules and make a sound. If you turn it down, you could have silence. So that's the way my mind works. So I used to sit there with the old people and turn on my video. Then I would go to sleep, and it would record. So while I was sleeping, the electrical power would come in. It records, runs my heart, pumps my breathing, keeps me living. So when I went there and turned on my video and went to sleep, I could still hear, because this was a spiritual power that came from the wisdom given to us by the Creator and *Grandmother* the Earth.

That power is here all the time. It is continuous, and nobody controls it. The government doesn't control it, and the *BIA* [Bureau of Indian Affairs] doesn't control it. It's continuous, and it just goes on. So that's the way it was with me. I sat there and listened as the old people brought all these powers around. And when you understood, just one word came out—a sacred word. Then I gathered this and the definition, the motivation, the feeling, the unsound came in. I could close my eyes, but I could see little moving pictures. I could see molecules that are like little soap bubbles, and I could see those genes and organics. Then a word comes out. Then that is recorded. So I don't have to write it down here and then file it over here, see? At the same time, I never discovered anything. I don't like that word *discover.* My people—I call them Earth People—never discovered anything, because we are part of the fire, and we're part of the rock, and we're part of the water and green, see? So we never discovered anything or created anything, because we are a part of it. We know we are a part of it, because we are still connected to our roots.

So when I was a little boy, I loved listening to my old people. The other little guys would go out and play around together, but I would go sit with the old people and listen to them. My grandmother and grandpa, they noticed this, so they prayed for me. When they were getting ready for a ceremony, they would give me a little *tobacco tie* [prayer offering] or a piece of sage or cedar. "Here, you could have that." So they made those little offerings to me. So that is the way of the spirit. My forefathers saw it a long time ago. So now, here they picked me, this little guy, this little shrimp, this little rascal. "You could have that." So I'm just a little tobacco tie. I'm just an offering. But my brothers and sisters, they're all good looking. They are all the first-born daughters and first-born sons, so they already have the star place. They are the first ones to eat at the table. What's left over, I eat. When I come home, there's a woodpile. So that's where I sleep. But when I visit my grandma and grandpa, they get up early, so I crawl in their bed. I lie there, and it's warm. Go to sleep. When it's time to eat, they are cooking. "Get up, you're going to eat." So I was the first one to eat. So when I stayed there, I was the first one to eat.

Then, when I was five years old, my grandparents prayed to Tunkashila that I would be given something to hang onto that would help the people behind me, the little ones and the unborn to come. So they put up a ceremony for me and prayed. I was sitting there between Grandma and Mom, and Grandpa was performing this ceremony. When we turned out the lights, those spirits started coming right through the ceiling, and I could see lightning. They came dancing around the room, and each time they hit, there's a lightning, lights. When those spirits came dancing by in front of me, I was pretending like trying to catch them. I wasn't going to catch them, just kind of grabbing at them in the darkness. Then one of them hit me on the forehead. So I tried to catch that one. About that time another one came and hit me on the shoulder, so I tried to catch that one, too. Then another one hit me on the back, but there's a wall there, and I'm leaning against it. Still it hit me on the back like there wasn't anything there.

Those spirits also came as gourds. Those gourds were going around the room rattling. Then one of those gourds came up my pant leg and went out through my shirt sleeve. I tried to catch him also. They were playing with me that way. They were demonstrating to me what they could do. Then two separate gourds came over, and a pair of hands grabbed my wrists, and another pair of hands grabbed my ankles. I thought they were gourds, but they were hands. They lifted me up and started swinging me, and at the same time another pair of hands started tickling me. You know, they call me a dumb Indian, and I must be dumb, because if I had had any sense I would have been screaming, "Mama! Mama!" like that. Instead, I was laughing and kicking around.

Then those spirits started swinging me back and forth and threw me across the room in the dark. Another pair of hands caught me. They tickled me and threw me back. They kept doing that, and on the fourth throw they threw me right through the ceiling. I sailed through that ceiling right out into the solar system. Now that's scary! I could see all those stars around me, and they were showing me the powers of the universe. There was the Creator with his wisdom, and below was the knowledge [of Grandmother the Earth]. So there was a man standing there, and there was a fire there. There was some water there, and this eagle was standing there on this *altar.* Each time it lifted its wing there was a fire underneath it. When he pushed his wing down, there was a tremendous force of wind, like a jet flying through the stratosphere. Hot and cold air hit and vapor. It was something like that. Then it spiraled clockwise, and at the center the sun was sitting right in the middle. And right on the edge, this rock, this Earth, was sitting there. And there were seven stones [planets], like a little race track, going around.

Then the spirit said, "When you return to Earth, tell your people to love each other and stay behind this sacred Chanunpa for there is something moving up there now." That's what he said. So then they brought me back. It was like a jet with rushing and whistling sounds. When they brought me back to the altar there was a wind. There were low clouds and a storm. All my people were there. There was like a moonlight and like a shadow there. The house and floor were gone, and I was standing out in the open. All around me tall grass and weeds were blowing. My people were still there, and I was able to talk to them, but they were all like shadows, little shadows of my ancestors. So I knew they will eventually die. They will lay down their *robe,* and their body will be earth again. There will be weeds, grass, and flowers growing there. But I knew that I would still be able to communicate with my grandma, grandpa, dad, mom, and relatives. So I was really fortunate that I lost nothing.

Then I knew that that altar was the universe, the Earth; that little patch of dirt was the Earth; that little patch of dirt I had seen from out in the universe was this Earth; and that when I left I would still be able to talk to my people, but they would be like shadows. Also, I realized that this power was not something to be toyed around with. So after I came back, I told my people what I had learned from the spirits.

So I'm happy that that vision was given to us when I was just a little guy. After that my grandpa and grandma kept telling me to stay right there where the lodge was. "Don't go away. Don't go away. Stay here. Stay here." For ordinary people there's nothing there, you know, but there was something that I saw that was there all the time. My grandpa told me, "Don't go away. We might go away, but we'll come back. We'll help you. The powers of *Four Winds,* they'll be here. So be firm, be steadfast. You pray and don't feel sad. Don't feel emptiness. Don't feel loneliness." But when they left, I really felt bad.

There is an old story we have about that feeling after someone you love leaves this life. There was this puppy playing around in the woods, tall weeds, and grass near the camp. Then the camp crier comes, and he tells everybody to pack because the camp is moving. So everybody starts getting ready, but this little boy can't find his puppy. So everyone starts helping him look for that puppy, but it can't be found. So they leave the camp, and that little boy is looking back still crying for his puppy. And all the other kids are yelling and crying for that puppy, but they keep on moving.

So when I prayed, my grandpa and grandma were gone. I was like that little lost puppy. When I came back out of the woods to the camp it was dark, and I didn't know which way they went. So here I sat at the old campsite crying. It's empty, and it's lonely. [Black Elk continues the story about the lost puppy.] Then a scout came into the camp and called for this puppy. When the puppy saw this scout he was happy and started jumping around. So the scout picked up this puppy and took him, because he knew in what direction the people had gone. He traveled through the night on horseback, and at daybreak he caught up with the other people. So that scout brought that puppy home. That family and the kids were really happy. Nobody knew who that scout was. So it was a *two-legged* spirit that had brought that puppy back.

So when I pray now, my grandpa and grandma, everybody, is gone. The whole camp has moved out. This whole Western Hemisphere has moved out. So I'm just a little lost puppy sitting out in an old campsite, crying. Here some place I heard a horse, and I heard a voice. That scout came, and I recognized him and that horse. I was happy. So he comforted me and carried me back to my people.

Anyway, my grandparents had prayed to Tunkashila to bless me through this sacred Chanunpa, and the spirits gave me that power. They gave me at least one drop of wisdom and one drop of knowledge. I was given something that I could hold onto for our little ones and the unborn behind me. It was something they could rely on. It was something I could use to help lead them back to Tunkashila and Grandma. It was the power of the Four Winds, and it covered a huge distance. It was a good thing I didn't get educated in school; otherwise I would have lost this gift. I might have even gone against it.

So that happened to me when I was only five years old. I became an adult and learned about these sacred powers. From that age until I was nine, I caught all the terminology used in the universities today. In those four years everything was like a little moving picture. Everything that I see, hear, smell, taste—I have a little color TV back there that records it. That's how I came to know what I know. Everything I saw and everything I heard was recorded in there, and I could rewind it and replay that little picture. So there was always something new coming in. New pictures were being recorded all the time. So I was given that understanding that way. And in the spiritual power I could see my people, my grandpa, my grandpa's father, and their fathers and mothers, and it goes on and on. I could see the whole camp, and I knew they were my relatives.

At the age of nine I held the sacred Chanunpa and went before Tunkashila and Grandmother. When darkness approached, clouds started forming all the way around me, and there was lightning underneath. Then the powers of the Four Winds came. At first I experienced someone walking up behind me. I could hear heavy footsteps coming—boom, boom, boom. With each step the whole Earth trembled. The whole mountain started to shake, and that gave me a spooky feeling. So I tried to shake it off. "Okay, Black Elk, what's wrong with you? You come from an intelligent, respectable family. Are you going to chicken out?" I tried to give myself hell that way.

Pretty soon I heard a hooting in the distance. "HOOO. HOOO." Like an owl, but it was real deep and real loud. So I knew they were coming to me, and my heart started pounding. So that also gave me a spooky feeling like somebody pouring cold water down my back, and my ribs are sticking out, and water is trickling down the ribs. At the same time I was trying to pray and trying to listen to see what was going on. All three things were going at once in my head, and my mind was running wild. It was kind of funny how I observed all these things going through my head at once, you know. I could hear my heart pounding loudly. So I was standing there holding this Chanunpa and trying to give myself hell and trying to give myself encouragement and trying to listen and trying to pray all at the same time.

So I prayed, but I had to pray from my heart. All of my concentration and thoughts went from my head to my heart. All of my senses—hearing, smell, taste, and feeling—were connected to my heart. So my spirit tried to understand the power that was coming from behind me. "Hey, try to shake it off. Try to pray." So I prayed, and now I was calm, but the footsteps were still coming. Another hoot again, and this time it's a little louder. As it gets closer, it gets louder. Then it was like my whole body became hollow, and that sound echoed up and down inside. It vibrated my whole body.

So I was standing there praying, and my mind was saying, "Gee, I must really be crazy. If I had a little sense, I should take off." But there was no sense in me, you know. As I was praying, I heard this hooting for the third time, and I heard that spirit say loud and clear, "I am coming. I am coming." It was like the hooting was on the outside, and his voice was on the inside. Then he hooted for a fourth time, and I felt a finger poking me in the top of my back, kind of pushing me. I almost flew off from there without wings! My head was going that way, but I stood firm and began to pray again. I was practically glued to the ground. So I was holding this Chanunpa and listening, and this voice said, "I am here. I am here." That's what he said. Again, "Hoo. Hoo," is what I heard on the outside, but his voice I heard on the inside.

Hey, I got company. I feel good now. Then that shadow of fear melted from me. It felt like someone comforting me by putting his hand on my head. Then he came around and stood in front of me and sat down. So I sat down. Now we could shoot the breeze. It really felt good! Then we conversed, and I could say anything I wanted. He answered all my prayers. He even revealed every word I had said, and he answered every word I said. (So when you go out there to pray, you'd better memorize what you are going to say. Sometimes words just come out of your mouth and go away.) Then he left. After he left there was a little stone lying there. So the stone people talk. So I learned a lot from that spirit.

So I learned about this sacred Chanunpa when I was nine years old. After I went back, one day I was holding this piece of wood and piece of stone [Sacred Pipe], and this little dog goes by. First time I saw him go by. So I said, "Hey, little guy, what's your name?" So he stopped and looked up. Then he answered me. All of a sudden I realized, "Hey, with this thing you could talk to this little guy here." So I was really excited. I was like a kid with a new toy. "Hey, with this Chanunpa you could talk to trees and talk to rocks and talk to buffaloes." I thought everybody knew about this little walkie-talkie. I thought everybody knew how to hear those little creatures. Also, I thought I was the last person to find this out, but soon I found out that nobody knew anything about it. So when I told people, they thought I was crazy or just talking through my hat. I was just a little guy, but my brain was big.

So my brothers and cousins were older than me. They'd go to school, and when they came back they'd call for me.

"Hey, little shrimp, come here. The teacher asked us these questions, and we don't know how to answer them. How shall we answer?"

Then I'd tell them. Then they would tell me to keep my mouth shut and go play with the kids my own age or go play with my bone horses. Then these big guys would go to school and tell their teacher the answers I had given them. When they brought their report cards home, they had straight As. But they never told who gave them those answers, and they told me to keep my mouth shut. So I would go crawl in and play with [children] my own age, but at the same time my head was real big.

So Tunkashila gave me those powers, and they also gave me a command. Instead of promoting and elevating me over everyone, they put me back to earth. They put me under the feet of everything that exists. Even that little ant has feet, and I'm underneath his feet. So I'm under the feet of all life. That's why my name is "Welcome." I'm just a little throw rug with *welcome* written on it. So you wipe your feet and go in the sacred arbor. That's how come people with sickness, worries, and sadness come to me. They wipe their feet and go on in to get to that good life. I was told to use this sacred Chanunpa as a cane and that would lead me to Tunkashila and Grandmother, where there is no end. It's everlasting life there.

So this Chanunpa is a cane. It has no end. So the old people, they called it a horse. It has a lot of strength and patience. The horse thinks real slow. But when he's finished thinking, his action is lightning fast. He does things lightning fast, but man is totally opposite. We think lightning fast, but we're real slow, real poky. We're a lot slower than a turtle. So those old people tell really simple stories—like kid stories.

So I learned a lot from my grandpas and grandmas. Actually, in the Lakota way, I had eleven grandpas and grandmas that taught me these sacred ways. Sometimes they told stories, and sometimes they just said it real short. When it's short, you call them *sayings*. For example, they used to tell us that our days would be long for giving food to old people and little ones. So you should remember that. Always look for old people and orphans, because Tunkashila is then going to bless you for that. Your days will be long, and you're going to have wrinkles. Your buckskin is going to outlast all these modern materials. I wore out a lot of blue jeans, but I still wear my birthday suit.

So I could say that I was the first Indian boy that went all the way up through these powers. I went inside this communication [English language] to study the white man. It was like walking up to the Statue of Liberty. You go inside and walk up to her arms or go inside her head and look out through the crown. It was something like that. I went inside everywhere. I went into the heart. I went into the head and even looked out through his eyes to see what he sees, how he observes things. What I learned was that the white man, we call him *wasichu* [waa-she'-chew], has a real keen sense of eyes. They see values, so I give them credit for that. But what they don't see is the spirit.

I went into the ear, and I heard all this rock and roll music, radios, and televisions. When I went to the sense of smell, there were a lot of camouflages there. I smelled a lot of perfumes, but they were mostly based on alcohol. It didn't cure anything; it only camouflaged. So I saw that. Then the taste, there again everything was camouflaged. But what I saw there was mostly alcohol, like beer, wine, and whiskey. They like that taste, so they become alcoholics. It is a disease. You can't think straight, you can't walk straight, and it always drives you to madness. So they have to numb themselves, and they call it "relaxation."

Then I went to the feeling and the senses. All I saw were those little gadgets like temperature gauges that tell you how hot it is or cold it is. So they have all those little machines, because they don't know how hot or cold it is. So the whole structure was mechanized machines. So that's what I saw. Then I came back.

So you might say that I'm a scout for my people. It's tough to be a scout, really tough. To be a lone scout like me is even tougher, because you might run into a whole bunch of enemies. Then the odds would be against you, and you have to maneuver around to escape from many enemies. I'm not talking about just physical enemies. There are sicknesses and all kinds of death you have to maneuver around. But then there are the powers of the Four Winds. They come to your rescue. And when those buffaloes come, they stomp and tromp everything in their path. If cancer is in their way, they'll just tromp it to nothing. Anything—sadness, sorrow, sickness—they'll tromp it to nothing, to dirt. So they have those powers to destroy. Then they make things good again. They never bring anything bad. They only bring health and help.

So like this coyote, it has the same power. If troubled times come, you call on this little coyote, and he'll maneuver you out from the danger. He also has sacred powers. People use everything on him to get rid of him, like poisons, traps, guns, helicopters, and airplanes, but he still survives. So he has that power. So we have that power.

So I don't speak English, but I speak Lakota fluently, very fluently. If you understood Lakota, you'd be surprised, because I would tell you the answers to some of the mysteries your scientists are now probing. But when it comes to English, the funny part is I hear it loud and clear. I understand everything that is said. So I pray for you that you obtain the same power I have. You and I are no different. It's just that understanding. You just drifted away from it, just walked away from it for thousands and thousands of years. That's how come you have lost contact. So now you're trying to find your roots. They are still here. So I am able to communicate with you and help you that way. So I'm just a little tool, just a little instrument.

So I started with these powers when I was five years old, and now I'm sixty-eight. So that Ph.D. was built inside me. I was built with it. So I'm part of the *fire, rock, water,* and *green.* I am a product of Tunkashila's handwork, and Grandmother, she gave me birth. She gave me all these gifts free of charge. I never discovered anything. I never formed or shaped anything. [Black Elk refers to the use of the fire in metallurgy, chemistry, etc.] Maybe that's how come they call me a dumb Indian. I'm trying to trace down why they call me dumb. Maybe they're right, you know, or maybe I'm just having a mad dream. Then I pinch myself. "Hey, wake up." It's like that, so sometimes it's tough to be an Indian.

My people say that there were times it was tough to be a Lakota, or Earth Man. The way the spirit translated it, there is this immense body of water, and in the midst lay a long island. They call it *Turtle Island,* but in modern terminology it is known as "Western Hemisphere." The spirits told us that this is where peace lives. It is the home of peace, and *Lakota* means "peace." We're Lakotas. We're living legends. We're living evidence of peace. So there are times it's kind of hard to be a man of peace, but I'm still thankful to my grandfathers and grandmothers.

The Gift of the Sacred Pipe

WALLACE BLACK ELK

Black Elk tells the story of how the Sacred Pipe came to the Sioux and explains how it relates to spiritual living and sacredness in the world.

Early one morning, very many winters ago, two Lakota were out hunting with their bows and arrows, and as they were standing on a hill looking for game, they saw in the distance something coming towards them in a very strange and wonderful manner. When this mysterious thing came nearer to them, they saw that it was a very beautiful woman, dressed in white buckskin, and bearing a bundle on her back. Now this woman was so good to look at that one of the Lakota had bad intentions and told his friend of his desire, but this good man said that he must not have such thoughts, for surely this is a *wakan* [holy] woman. The mysterious person was now very close to the men, and then putting down her bundle, she asked the one with bad intentions to come over to her. As the young man approached the mysterious woman, they were both covered by a great cloud, and soon when it lifted the sacred woman was standing there, and at her feet was the man with the bad thoughts who was now nothing but bones, and terrible snakes were eating him.

"Behold what you see!" the strange woman said to the good man. "I am coming to your people and wish to talk with your chief *Hehlokecha Najin* [Standing Hollow Horn]. Return to him, and tell him to prepare a large tipi in which he should gather all his people, and make ready for my coming. I wish to tell you something of great importance!"

The young man then returned to the tipi of his chief, and told him all that had happened: that this *wakan* woman was coming to visit them and that they must all prepare. The chief, Standing Hollow Horn, then had several tipis taken down, and from them a great lodge was made as the sacred woman had instructed. He sent out a crier to tell the people to put on their best buckskin clothes and to gather immediately in the lodge. The people were, of course, all very excited as they waited in the great lodge for the coming of the holy woman, and everybody was wondering where this mysterious woman came from and what it was that she wished to say.

Soon the young men who were watching for the coming of the *wakan* person announced that they saw something in the distance approaching them in a beautiful manner, and then suddenly she entered the lodge, walked around sun-wise, and stood in front of Standing Hollow Horn. She took from her back the bundle, and holding it with both hands in front of the chief, said: "Behold this and always love it! It is *lela wakan* [very sacred], and you must treat it as such. No impure man should ever be allowed to see it, for within this bundle there is a sacred pipe. With this you will, during the winters to come, send your voices to *Wakan-Tanka,* your Father and Grandfather."

After the mysterious woman said this, she took from the bundle a pipe, and also a small round stone which she placed upon the ground. Holding the pipe up with its stem to the heavens, she said: "With this sacred pipe you will walk upon the Earth; for the Earth is your Grandmother and Mother, and She is sacred. Every step that is taken upon Her should be

Joseph Epes Brown, ed., *The Gift of the Sacred Pipe: Black Elk's Account of the Seven Rites of the Oglala Sioux* (Norman: University of Oklahoma Press, 1953, 1989), 3–8.

as a prayer. The bowl of this pipe is of red stone; it is the Earth. Carved in the stone and facing the center is this buffalo calf who represents all the four-leggeds who live upon your Mother. The stem of the pipe is of wood, and this represents all that grows upon the Earth. And these twelve feathers which hang here where the stem fits into the bowl are from *Wanbli Galeshka,* the Spotted Eagle, and they represent the eagle and all the wingeds of the air. All these peoples, and all the things of the universe, are joined to you who smoke the pipe—all send their voices to *Wakan-Tanka,* the Great Spirit. When you pray with this pipe, you pray for and with everything."

The *wakan* woman then touched the foot of the pipe to the round stone which lay upon the ground, and said: "With this pipe you will be bound to all your relatives: your Grandfather and Father, your Grandmother and Mother. This round rock, which is made of the same red stone as the bowl of the pipe, your Father *Wakan-Tanka* has also given to you. It is the Earth, your Grandmother and Mother, and it is where you will live and increase. This Earth which He has given to you is red, and the two-leggeds who live upon the Earth are red; and the Great Spirit has also given to you a red day, and a red road. All of this is sacred and so do not forget! Every dawn as it comes is a holy event, and every day is holy, for the light comes from your Father *Wakan-Tanka;* and also you must always remember that the two-leggeds and all the other peoples who stand upon this earth are sacred and should be treated as such.

"From this time on, the holy pipe will stand upon this red Earth, and the two-leggeds will take the pipe and will send their voices to *Wakan-Tanka.* These seven circles which you see on the stone have much meaning, for they represent the seven rites in which the pipe will be used. The first large circle represents the first rite which I shall give to you, and the other six circles represent the rites which will in time be revealed to you directly. Standing Hollow Horn, be good to these gifts and to your people, for they are *wakan!* With this pipe the two-leggeds will increase, and there will come to them all that is good. From above *Wakan-Tanka* has given to you this sacred pipe, so that through it you may have knowledge. For this great gift you should always be grateful! But now before I leave I wish to give to you instructions for the first rite in which your people will use this pipe.

"It should be for you a sacred day when one of your people dies. You must then keep his soul as I shall teach you, and through this you will gain much power; for if this soul is kept, it will increase in you your concern and love for your neighbor. So long as the person, in his soul, is kept with your people, through him you will be able to send your voice to *Wakan-Tanka.*

"It should also be a sacred day when a soul is released and returns to its home, *Wakan-Tanka,* for on this day four women will be made holy, and they will in time bear children who will walk the path of life in a sacred manner, setting an example to your people. Behold Me, for it is I that they will take in their mouths, and it is through this that they will become *wakan.*

"He who keeps the soul of a person must be a good and pure man, and he should use the pipe so that all the people, with the soul, will together send their voices to *Wakan-Tanka.* The fruit of your Mother the Earth and the fruit of all that bears will be blessed in this manner, and your people will then walk the path of life in a sacred way. Do not forget that *Wakan-Tanka* has given you seven days in which to send your voices to Him. So long as you remember this you will live; the rest you will know from *Wakan-Tanka* directly."

The sacred woman then started to leave the lodge, but turning again to Standing Hollow Horn, she said: "Behold this pipe! Always remember how sacred it is, and treat it as such, for it will take you to the end. Remember, in me there are four ages. I am leaving now, but I shall look back upon your people in every age and at the end I shall return."

Moving around the lodge in a sun-wise manner, the mysterious woman left, but after walking a short distance she looked back towards the people and sat down. When she rose the people were amazed to see that she had become a young red and brown buffalo calf. Then this calf walked farther, lay down, and rolled, looking back at the people, and when she got up she was a white buffalo. Again the white buffalo walked farther and rolled on the ground, becoming now a black buffalo. This buffalo then walked farther away from the people, stopped, and after bowing to each of the four quarters of the universe, disappeared over the hill.

Misunderstanding Native Americans

FREDERICK W. TURNER

Frederick W. Turner decries most Americans' continuing ignorance and fear of the original Americans—the Native Americans who for hundreds of years have lived on this continent and endured all manner of ill treatment and neglect. In part because of early attitudes toward the American Indians, most of us have gaps in our historical and cultural understanding of them. But we have a duty to try to fill in the gaps as best we can.

If we think about it for a moment, it will appear odd that after more than four centuries on this continent it should seem necessary to introduce anyone to what must have been the first and most engaging fact of the New World itself: the people who lived here. And yet, to judge from the evidence of American history past and present, this is precisely our need. The American government is still pursuing an Indian policy that alternates between brutal neglect and racist paternalism; private enterprise and state and local governments are still raping the natives' remaining natural resources; at the broadest levels of our popular culture we still find redactions of that most cherished myth of how we won the country from the skulking savages; and deep in the hearts of too many of us there resides the notion that all that is significant in American culture has been the achievement of the Anglo-Saxon white. What all this points to, of course, is our ignorance concerning the North American Indian and the part he has played in the shaping of the American experience. Nor is this an isolated phenomenon, but rather another illustration of our general refusal to face up to our past and its meanings. Here as in so many other instances the majority of Americans have refused to confront the continuing, fundamental challenge and contradiction which the American Indian is and represents to our republican democracy. Our strategies of avoidance have ranged from attempted genocide to the creation of various racist stereotypes, but even after two hundred years of this the challenge, the contradiction remains. After two hundred years of sovereignty the newer Americans still have neither understood the original ones nor solved the predicament presented by the existence of a people with a prior claim to territory and the dignity and endurance to voice that claim through all the intervening years of defeat, diseases, blasphemous treaties, and the building up around them of an enormously complicated and impersonal federal bureaucracy. Yet the voices of the tribes are heard, however faintly, disturbing us like the dripping of a broken faucet in a far-away room.

It is our sense of this coupled with our inability to initiate reformative changes that makes so many of our collective responses oddly poignant. We seem rather like some benign, blinded Polyphemus who gropes in utter darkness toward expressions of good will. And let none mistake this: American good will is a reality, whatever the rest of the world may call it, whatever we ourselves may call it—racism, genocide, callous economic opportunism. These are the ghastly blunders of the giant doomed to commit them out of historical ignorance and fear. This is indeed tragic, for the truth is that the average white American, whether Newark hardhat or California grape-grower, genuinely wants everybody to be happy

Frederick W. Turner, ed., *The Portable North American Indian Reader* (New York: Penguin, 1973), 3–7.

in this sprawling country; wants, for example, the Indian to have his share of the national pie—except that there is the way the country developed, the way Western Europeans first came to it, what they did here, the very names by which we know ourselves. All this militates constantly, silently, against everything that in our hearts we want for all men. And all this the average American either knows nothing about or avoids.

Once, on a dusty back country road in Wyoming I met this agonized condition of my country in the muzzle of a gun held in the glare of a pickup truck's headlights: our car's generator had gone out, and I was guiding us by flashlight when I was confronted by a motorized cowboy, his finger on the trigger of a pistol, a shotgun racked up behind him and a canister of Mace on the seat. It seems we had passed through a portion of his spread, and the dim spot of my flashlight had awakened his sense of territory and individualism. Just weeks before thieves had taken off with a pair of his skis, and so now he was ready to confront this potential marauder. In that little moment which he has undoubtedly forgotten, something larger than both of us was abroad in the country darkness; it was something of the past with all its gnarled realities—call it cultural history if you like—a powerful, subterranean force whose existence he would have vehemently denied. Like too many of us the cowboy had no real belief in the past and its ability to shape actions and events in the present. More precisely, his sense of the past was rigorously selective and thus almost wholly fictional.

Somewhat later I learned in conversation with the cowboy that he was a decent and essentially well-intentioned man. Yet in that summer night in a territory barely wrested from the first dwellers I had been transmogrified by ignorance into the Indian as these men had been taught to see him—a ruthless and casual depredator who threatened what good men had put together. In the darkness of our antihistorical civilization the cowboy had only been acting out his second nature. As were those other cowboys who a few days later in nearby Casper captured a roving hippie and pulled his long hair out by the roots.

In view of these situations one is forced to the conclusion that many of the actions that have made up the American experience have been misguided and uninformed.

We could begin, for convenience, with Columbus, who, as Albert Murray reminds us, "set out for destinations east on compass bearings west." Driving toward the fabulous riches of the Indies, Columbus found a tropical island, the original name of which was never even recorded before it was rechristened San Salvador. The name of the first tribe to greet this white man in unsuspecting amazement was the Arawak, but little else remains of them or their history, so quickly and completely were they engulfed by the events that followed in the wake of the Spanish ships. But because Columbus was a man with a dream, a dream that had haunted men of his world for centuries, the tribe became . . . just Indians, a generic designation which prevented the whites from ever *seeing* them for what they truly were.

This was only the second mistake. Others followed with the rapidity which only the loosing of long-pent-up desires can bring: Mexico became New Spain, the Southwest became the locale of the Seven Cities of Gold, the southeastern peninsula became Florida, the Island of Flowers, and somewhere in its recesses nestled the Fountain of Youth. And all the while the tribes were losing their several identities and becoming just Indians. They still are, and the misnomer should serve as a continual reminder to us of how ignorant we remain of the realities of this land we live in.

The consequences of this ignorance are so vast and tangled that to attempt to explore them is to become another De Soto, lost and sweating in a jungle of lianas and palmetto groves. Still, if we are to free ourselves, if we are to find ourselves and so escape the heavy oppression that ignorance always entails, we must begin somewhere and what better place than with the original inhabitants themselves? But here at the very outset of our exploration one meets with a consequence of our ignorance and of the mad haste and greed with which we swarmed over the continent: the aboriginal past of the American tribes in something of its full and accurate detail is forever lost to us. No whites in those early days thought it worth the effort to record the histories, traditions, customs of nonliterate and often hostile "savages." What we now have is what archaeologists and anthropologists have been able to piece together; the spare, bleak accounts of some old soldiers and explorers; fragmentary tribal legends all but obliterated by the destruction of the tribal cultures. The picture we have of the tribes in the first moments of contact is thus like some ruined hieroglyphic, legible only in parts and then only to specialists, with other areas a mute and unforgiving blankness. Nor can we escape the blame for this great loss by reminding ourselves that the social sciences, which would have made possible the preservation of all this precious material, had not even been invented, for what does it say about a civilization that it can develop the science and the technology to get to distant lands but not the intellectual equipment to understand these lands and their peoples when it does arrive? I say nothing here of the justifications for colonization or of the spiritual equipment necessary for such tasks.

And so there are these gaps, these blanknesses, and they are there because they are in us as well, in the civilization we have made. What, for example, were the conditions of the tribes of the interior in 1600? What was the culture of the Pequots like before King Philip's War? What of the Cherokee before 1830? We can supply fragmentary answers at best but the worst is that so few Americans still can care whether these questions might have answers. They will only see and lament our present-day condition—a divided and deeply troubled nation, streaked with racial, sectional, and class antagonisms, uncertain of its global position, morally enfeebled. The roots of all this lie buried in our past, and despite the disheartening losses of which I speak, it is our first imperative to try to trace what we can.

INDIGENOUS AFRICAN RELIGIONS

Women in African Traditional Religions

JOSEPH AKINYELE OMOYAJOWO

Omoyajowo examines the possibility of an increased emphasis on feminine elements in African indigenous religions, which have traditionally been dominated by male deities and male-oriented worship. A few traditions do contain some devotional roles for women. A notable case is the Yoruba of Nigeria, whose progenitor god was likely female, and whose pantheon included female deities.

Joseph Akinyele Omoyajowo, "The Role of Women in African Traditional Religion," in Jacob K. Olupona, ed., *African Traditional Religions in Contemporary Society* (New York: Paragon House, 1991), 73–80.

INTRODUCTION

This paper will mainly focus on the possibility of a feminine image of deity in our traditional religion and the functions of women in the religious system of the Yoruba race in a world that is so fundamentally masculine and in which women are not accorded any visibly prominent status in religious matters.

Generally and globally, the superiority of men over women has always been taken for granted. Women themselves seem to have internalized this image of female inferiority (a situation in which I have seen the women's liberation or feminist movements as no more than apologetic) and have therefore somehow taken male domination as the natural order of things.

The Oriental world keeps women behind the veil, and they continue to be denied the right to think for themselves. Jewish thought did not regard women as a necessity but merely as helpers to men. In this regard, Professor Omosade Awolalu's conclusion is that the woman surrenders to the standard of a man-made world in which she finds herself, and her husband becomes her keeper in every sense. According to him, the woman hardly decides anything on her own, even the small details of her daily life are settled by her husband.[1]

The Jews had a strictly masculine concept of God: We read of the God of Abraham, of Isaac, and of Jacob and not of Sarah, Rebecca, Leah, or Rachael.[2] In their synagogue assemblies, they never counted women to make a quorum. This prejudice was crystallized in the miracle of feeding performed by Jesus. The figure of five thousand was said not to include women and children. To Paul, it was an anathema for a woman to speak in the church; if there was anything she wanted to know, she should ask her husband at home. In Islam, women could only lead prayers for a congregation of women. In the mosque women are not to stand in the same row with men but separately behind the rows of men.

AFRICAN CONCEPT OF GOD

The African concept of God is not altogether masculine. In many parts of Africa, God is conceived as male, but in some other parts, he is conceived as female; the Ndebele and Shona ethnic groups of former Rhodesia have a triad made up of God the Father, God the Mother, and God the Son. The Nuba of the Sudan regard God as "Great Mother" and speak of him in feminine pronouns. The Ovabo of South West Africa say that "the mother of pots is a hole in the ground, and the mother of people is God."[3] Although called the queen of Lovedu in South Africa, the mysterious 'She' is not primarily a ruler but a rain-maker; she is regarded as a changer of seasons and the guarantor of their cyclic regularity.[4]

There may be more cases of a feminine image of God than we can easily identify here because of the difficulty created by the fact that most African languages have identical male and female pronouns. Be that as it may, we can safely conclude that African traditional religion is, generally speaking, less sexist in its masculine image of God than other religions. This may be the factor that makes it possible for men and women to perform sacerdotal functions in the worship of the deity and of his functionaries, the divinities, who are also in both sexes.[5]

The Akan of Ghana and the Igbo of Nigeria have a feminine image of the Earth Spirit. Although the Akan did not regard Asase Yaa (the Earth Spirit) as a goddess, they nevertheless rank the spirit after the Supreme God and pour libations and sacrifice fowls to her. The Igbo accord worship to Ani (or Ala or Ale) as Mother goddess, or Queen of the under-world, who is responsible for public morality.[6] Ani is the most-loved deity and the one who is closest to the people. She helps them if they are troubled by other divinities, but punishes hardened criminals.[7]

THE YORUBA CONCEPT

Among the Yoruba of Nigeria, Oduduwa, its progenitor, is believed by certain traditions to be a female orisa (divinity). J.O. Lucas asserts that there is hardly any doubt that Oduduwa was originally a female deity. With her adoption as the progenitor of the

Yoruba race, there seemed to have arisen a tendency to regard her as a leader and a hero in consequence of which later stories transforming her as a male deity, were invented.[8] This male-divinity tradition has become very strong in Ile-Ife, where originally the myth that Oduduwa was a female divinity (she was called Iya, male-mother of divinities) was well known. However, today, the popular tradition is that Oduduwa was the strong and powerful leader under whom the nucleus of a strand of the present Yoruba race migrated into the land from their original home. The import of all this is that the powerful progenitor of the Yoruba race was believed to be originally a female divinity; and it can therefore be argued that the Yoruba society was at one time based on a matriarchal system.[9]

Yemoja (literally Yeye-omo-eja; mother of fishes) was also a female Yoruba divinity representing water. The myth was that she had a good-for-nothing son who committed incest against her. The mother fled, and the wicked son pursued her until she fell backward as a result of exhaustion. Streams of water poured from her body and eventually united to form a lagoon. The divinities that emanated from her include: Olosa (lagoon goddess) Olokun (God of sea) Oya (goddess of River Niger) Osun (River Osun goddess) oba (goddess of River Oba) Orisa-oko (fertility god) etc., etc. The priesthood of Orisa-Oko is open to both male and female, but he actually has more priestesses than priests. His priestesses form a secret society of their own, and no man dare injure or offend any of them.

Among the Owe people of Kwara state the traditional religion, like in many other Nigerian communities, is an affair completely controlled by the adult male section. As Bishop John Onaiyekan pleads, Owe traditional society is very much patriarchal.[10] But there is the phenomenon of "Ofosi," women who are initiated into an esoteric and deeply religious society involving periodic and authentic spirit-possession. They are considered as wives of the divinity. Specifically, their part consists mainly in singing and dancing in honor of the "Ebora" divinity on the appropriate occasions. On such occasions they sing and dance round the town visiting the houses of elders and of their own leaders.

The progenitor of my home village Isarun, known as Oluasarun (literally, the lord of Isarun), was originally a powerful hunter, who like most founders of Yoruba towns and settlements, was believed to have come from Ile-Ife. He stopped over in many places including Benin, Oba-Ile, Ilaramokin, and Igbara-Oke and became deified after he sank into the earth while dancing during a festival.

What is relevant to our subject here is the fact that the divinity has always been manifested in a priestess commonly referred to be as "Aya Olua" (Olua's spouse). During special festivals (especially the Annual Yam Festival), the priestess would bring messages from the divinity to the entire community or to individuals within and outside the community. When possessed, the priestess would speak as if she is the divinity himself and has to be addressed in masculine pronouns.[11]

This pattern is common throughout Yorubaland. We did highlight it elsewhere when we said that the manifestation of possession by the spirit of a divinity occurs when the priestess has been seized with frenzy and thrown into a state of ecstasy for many days. She would not be referred to by her own name but by the name of the divinity manifested in her.[12]

Also of relevance to us is the phenomenon of singing and dancing by well-dressed women during celebrations (one example is in respect of Olua-Isarun). While the songs and dancing add glee to the celebrations, they have a veiled, but more significant effect of curbing recalcitrant and criminally minded members of the community, who during the year had broken the norms, conventions, and customs prevalent in that community. The songs are usually deliberately composed to highlight the crimes committed and expose the criminals. The singing groups, protected by the community's traditions, perform the "role of the people's court" to whose verdict the culprits and their relations cannot pretend to be indifferent and against which they have no appeal.

The popular Omojao festival (in honor of Obalufon divinity) in Akure shares the same features with Oluasarun but is more aggressive. The gaily dressed young women, armed with well-rehearsed abusive songs, move from house to house, naming names and coming down heavily on the social-miscreants within the community. One such song will suffice as an illustration:

In merun sodo, In merun sodo
Omode mee bu ye re
O gbideregbe, o gbideregbe
O gbideregbe lokelisa
Omo re ki in meesukun
Ebi re ki in meesunkun
In mee sunkun ekun debe.
Bow your heads and speak in whispers.[13]
It is forbidden for the youth
to abuse elders (or their mother)
She stole a goat, she stole a goat,
She stole a goat from Okeisa Street,
Her children stop crying,
Her relations weep no more.
Weep no more, your weeping can no
longer avail anything.

While Omojao festival is celebrated in daylight, Ogun Obinrin (female celebration of Ogun festival) is common to every community within Akure Division and is celebrated during the night. Under the cover of darkness and the immunity graciously conferred by tradition, the women boldly call out in songs the names of the offenders in front of their respective houses and contemptuously pour opprobrious condemnation on them. In all this, women act as messengers of the deity to the community. Some of them act as cultic-functionaries who are set apart for the services of certain divinities. As such they are in categories of priestesses, diviners, mediums and medicine women. Like Orisa-Oko, some of them may even become deified and so attract worship (e.g., Oya).

SIGNIFICANCE

It may not be a wild assumption to conclude that in the traditional Yoruba society, with all its prejudices against women, religion, more than any other factor, plays a major role in ascribing status to women. Even with the prohibitions and restrictions[14] that are strongly supported (if not actually motivated) by the male-chauvinist attitude, that a woman should not aspire to tasks which would challenge the male authority at home and despite the thought that it is unsuitable for a woman to speak in public meetings, since such public roles belong to the man,[15] women cannot possibly remain passive in a society in which they have to come to terms with the tutelary spirits, if they must live a successful and peaceful life. Their special contribution to the general welfare and cohesion of the society can really be indispensable to the deity.

In every Yoruba community, there is an elaborate code of manners and etiquette, the observance of which helps to reduce the strains and frustrations of interpersonal relationships.[16] A breach of this code tragically disturbs the rhythm of the society and undermines the authority of the gods whose duty it is to ensure, if not enforce, strict obedience to the norms. With their ritual dances and singing, women warm the hearts of the gods and with their invectives, especially in the homes of the social non-conformists, they contribute a very significant and effective mechanism of social control. Disarmed by the traditional immunity enjoyed by the women, the victim is either compelled to mend his ways or take the easier way out—flee from that society. It is also the duty of the traditional ruler and chiefs to offer sacrifices to purify the community to remove the evil effect of the women's action.

CONCLUSION

We feel scandalized today by the brazen prevalence in our society of the most heinous crimes like ritual killing, cold-hearted murder, kidnapping, drug trafficking, armed robbery, witchcraft, embezzlement, bribery and corruption, to mention just a few, on scales unknown in history. Heightened by the undermining of such controlling factors as we have discussed, and other related effective measures, and with the superimposition on our culture of ill-acquired alien habits in the name of religions, modernity, and civilization, the worst may not have been seen yet.

One's advocacy is not for a return to the "primitive" features of our traditional religions, but for a resuscitation of those noble aspects of our enviable culture which among other things, promoted cohesion within the society and for an amelioration of those traditional measures of social control whose strict enforcement might infringe upon the inalienable and fundamental human rights of the citizens.

Our conclusion, therefore, is that the Yoruba woman, in addition to her having an intimate experience of the deity, plays within the religious milieu a very functionally significant and dynamically relevant role in the social life of the Yoruba society. Firmly believing, like Professor Kofe Asare Opoku, that religion (which as cement, holds our societies together) binds man to the unseen powers helping him to form the right relationships with these nonhuman powers and to his fellow human beings,[17] I am persuaded that our patriarchal image of God and the globally low view of women in religious matters can only lead to a disparagement of the efforts of women in the achievement of those objectives.

But beyond the dynamic role already acknowledged, women would need to heed the challenge thrown by one of their number, Rose Zoe-Obianga, that women must be willing to fight against their own alienation (in whatever area—religious, political, social, or economic) and timidity. They must be willing to fight at the side of their own brothers, whose struggle could then become efficacious as they recognize their own true worth.[18]

NOTES

1. J.O. Awolalu, "Women from the Perspective of Religion," in *ORITA: Ibadan Journal of Religious Studies* x/2 Dec. 1976, 95.

2. W.T. Davis, "Our Image of God and Our Image of Women," *ORITA, op.cit.*, 123–4.

3. J.S. Mbiti, *Concepts of God in Africa* (London: S.P.C.K., 1982), Impression, 92.

4. E.G. Parrinder, *African T*
Sheldon Press, 1962), 79.

5. Awolalu, "Women from t

6. Kofi Asare Opoku, *We*
gion (Singapore: Feb, 1978),

7. Parrinder, *African Trad*

8. J.O. Lucas, *The Religio*
shop (Lagos 1948), 92–94.

9. E.G. Idowu, *Olodumare: God in Yoruba Belief* (Longman, 1962), 23–25.

10. John Onaiyekan, "The Priesthood in Owe Traditional Religion," in *Traditional Religion in West Africa*, (ed.) A.A. Adegbola (Ibadan: Daystar Press, 1983), 26.

11. The current Priestess made history a couple of years ago when she sent messages about sacrifices prescribed by the divinity to the writer, a very senior church minister. The embarrassed, most spiritually ambivalent citizens of the community strongly protested against such a frivolous message and threatened to discredit and depose the alien priestess.

12. J.A. Omoyajowo, "Women's Experience of God and the Ultimate-the African's Experience." Paper presented to the *Conference on God: The Contemporary Discussion*. Seoul, South Korea, August 1984, 3.

13. Heads are bowed while the leader of the group raises the song in order to conceal her identity.

14. There are many rituals women are not allowed to watch or witness, just as there are secret societies, the membership of which is reserved exclusively for men. Where both sexes share membership of a society, the women so allowed must have passed child-bearing age and are therefore ritually acceptable to the gods. Similarly, women, from the impurity associated with menstruation, are not usually "called" by the gods.

15. Marja-Liisa Swantz, "The Changing Role of Women in Tanzania," in *Christianity in Independent Africa,* (eds.) Fashole-Luke, Gray, Hadrian and Tasie (London 1978), 141.

16. N. Fadipe, *The Sociology of the Yoruba* (Ibadan University Press, 1970), 301.

17. Opoku, *West African Traditional Religion, op.cit.,* 11.

18. Rose Zoe-Obianya, "The Role of Women in Present-Day Africa," in *African Theology en Route*, (eds.) Kofi Appia-Kubi and Sergio Torres (Maryknoll, N.Y.: Orbis Books, 1979), 148.

…aditional Religions in Contemporary Africa

WANDE ABIMBOLA

Abimbola assesses the impact of Islam, Christianity, and modernism on the traditional religion of Yoruba. His conclusion is that despite these pressures, the traditional religion is still influential and still meaningful to many of the Yoruba.

INTRODUCTION

[This] paper is motivated by the need to investigate how much of the traditional religion is left with the access gained by Islam, Christianity, and modern trends into the traditional religious situation in Africa. It is to be noted and appreciated here that despite the devastating effects of Islam and Christianity on the autochthonous religion of the Yoruba, the religion continues to hold its own and is regarded in modern Nigeria as one of the three major religions in the country. It is in this connection that one can talk of the place of Yoruba traditional religion in contemporary Yorubaland and Africa at large. In this study we will concentrate on the place and significance of Yoruba traditional religion in the Nigerian plural religious situation. It should however be noted that the situation in Nigeria is similar to what obtains in many other black African countries.

THE BEGINNING OF ISLAM AND CHRISTIANITY IN YORUBALAND: CONFLICT AND THE DECLINE OF TRADITIONAL RELIGION

Islam reached Yorubaland several centuries before the Jihad of Uthman dan Fodio, but Christianity gained access much later in 1842 through Badagry. The following Yoruba saying explains the situation.

> Aye la ba'Fa Aye la ba 'Mole
> Osan gangan nigbagbo wole de.
> We met Ifa in the world
> We met Islam in the world
> It was late in the day that Christianity arrived.

THE DECLINE OF YORUBA RELIGION: ILE-IFE AS A CASE STUDY

In order to gain a thorough understanding of our subject matter, we have made an in-depth study of the religious situation in Ile-Ife, a sizeable Yoruba community believed by the Yoruba to be their ancestral home. It is obvious from the study that the decline of Yoruba religion as a formal entity in Ile-Ife and its environs has been very rapid during the last generation. It is estimated that Yoruba religion has lost about 40 percent of its adherents during the last half century, and that at present it can claim but 60 percent of the total population. However, it would be erroneous to conclude from this that traditional religion plays no significant part in the life of the Ile-Ife community. To a striking degree, traditional practices have been

Wande Abimbola, "The Place of African Traditional Religion in Contemporary Africa," in Jacob K. Olupona, ed., *African Traditional Religions in Contemporary Society* (New York: Paragon House, 1991), 51–58.

retained by those who have embraced Christianity and Islam, and they still play an important role in the community generally. Four aspects of Yoruba religion are selected for examination: the retention of the cults, the observance of the festivals in honor of the *orisa*, the place of Ifa divination, and the role which traditional medicine still plays among the Muslims and Christians in Ile-Ife and its environs.

It was estimated that about 34 percent of all Muslims and a slightly higher percentage of all Christians attended one or other of the festivals in honor of the local deities. A slightly lower proportion of members of the established Mission churches participate in the traditional festivals.

Some of the cults are already only imperfectly understood, and it was evident that the significance of others is fast being forgotten. In other cases, there was some indication of a confusion between two or more cults. A bewildering number of deities are worshipped in Ile-Ife. To make some order out of such a complex pantheon of divinities is by no means easy. However, a broad division can be made between those deities of national significance to all the Yoruba, and those which have special relevance only to the ancient city of Ile-Ife.

It was noticeable that the national deities were not widely worshipped. As in most cultures, the "high god," *Olodumare* or *Olorun* as he is known among the Yoruba, is not given any image and does not have shrines. The gods of the Yoruba myths are not venerated to any significant degree either by the Muslims or the Christians. It is true that many of these deities have temples often like that of *orisanla*, which are quite imposing in structure. But these cults seem generally to be in the hands of particular families which act as priests and guardians of the shrines.

TRADITIONAL CULTS THAT PERSIST TO DATE IN ILE-IFE AND ITS ENVIRONS

Despite the decline, it is to be noted that a good number of cults exist to date in Yorubaland. First, the cults which concern the ancestors, the so-called living dead, play a role of considerable importance. One writer on Yoruba religion has declared that the "great annual appearances of the *Egungun* are the chief communal ancestral rites of the Yoruba." This is largely true. In addition, there are many family ancestral cults of varying importance.

A second national cult widely observed is that in connection with the oracle divinity known as Ifa. Ifa is also used to designate a method of divination and has been described in detail by the present investigator. Ifa is frequently resorted to in times of stress and crisis by the Christians. The festival of Ifa is still popular in many areas. Another widely venerated of the national deities, however, is the *ogun*, the iron god whose devotees are considerable in number and for whom many families maintain a household shrine. *Ogun* has become the patron of those professions that have to do with iron, such as farming, hunting, blacksmithing, and driving. Most families therefore, can be, to some extent, connected with activities over which *Ogun* exercises patronage.

Our second group of festivals—those which were connected with Ile-Ife itself—supported the theory that the sociological, rather than the religious, significance is uppermost. There are a good number of festivals which are in honor of mythical or historical figures who had played an important part in the historical traditions of the town. It is sometimes difficult to be sure whether we are dealing with myth, legend, or history, as for example, in the story of *Oduduwa,* the traditional founder of Ile-Ife and the great ancestor of the Yoruba. Here, it seems probable that the myth enshrines some genuine historical event, namely the advent of a victorious warrior-leader who was eventually deified after his death. There is a tradition which has it that we are dealing with the displacement of an ancient culture by that of new conquerors represented by *Oduduwa*.

A second popular group of festivals centers around *Moremi*, who by the virtue of her beauty, wisdom, and courage is said to have saved the people of Ife from the troublesome and intractable *Igbo* invaders. Others are the cults of *Oluorogbo* and *Ela*. The oral traditions have it that *Oluorogbo* was the son of *Moremi,* the great heroine of Ile-Ife, who offered her son as a sacrifice in payment of a vow. In this connection, it is interesting that in Ile-Ife the festival of *Oluorogbo* is independent of that of *Moremi*. In point of truth, as maintained by Idowu, *Oluorogbo* and *Moremi* have no cultic connection.

It may be argued with some degree of plausibility that the observance of some of the traditional festivals and, to a lesser extent, of the cults by the Yoruba in general is largely a sociological phenomenon rather than a religious one. This would not, perhaps, be the case with the adherents of the traditional cults. But among the Muslims and Christians, the basic reason for the worship of the deities and the veneration of the ancestors is economic. In which case some patron deity such as *Ogun* is worshipped to ensure professional success. There is also a sociological reason. The observance of these cults and festivals in connection with the past is a pointer to the national desire on the part of the Christians and Muslims to be associated with the wider social group and its past heritage. Such group loyalty is even stronger in the case of the cult of the ancestors in which the family nexus is extremely pronounced. The traditional elements which are retained by the Yoruba Christians and Muslims in Ile-Ife and its environs may thus well be of more significance to the sociologist than to the investigator into the phenomenology of religions.

It is interesting to note that what is left of the followership and practice of the traditional religion in Yorubaland is recognized by the Nigerian government. It is also important to note that African traditional religion is given a prominent place in the higher institutions in the country. It is taught up to university level in order to maintain the religio-cultural identity of Africans in the face of the world.

THE SIGNIFICANCE OF YORUBA TRADITIONAL RELIGION IN CONTEMPORARY NIGERIAN TRADITIONAL FESTIVALS

A lot of festivals abound in Yoruba traditional religion. A good number of them are in honor of the most important divinities of the Yoruba such as *Obatala*, *Orunmila*, *Sango*, *Esu*, *Oya*, *Orisa-oko*, *Sonponna*, and a countless number of others. The significance of the festivals is seen as pointed out earlier, in terms of local trade and the phenomenon of religious co-fraternity generated by the festivals. The devotees of these divinities, as well as the Christians and Muslims, trade in some items needed for the celebrations irrespective of their religious leanings. What matters here is not the issue of religious differences, but how to effect sales of commodities and make profits. Here it is to be noted that, in consequence of these festivals and other items, the issue of religious solidarity has become a phenomenon to be reckoned with in Yoruba religious history.

Moreover, it is to be noted that during the festivals and in consequence of family solidarity, which existed before religious differences came into the show, Muslims and Christians usually join in the celebrations. Interviews conducted show that a good number of those who celebrate festivals such as *Egungun* and *Oro* in most parts of Yorubaland are either Muslims or Christians. Thus the traditional festivals serve as instruments to weld together the deities and their devotees, the *oba* and his subjects.

THE SIGNIFICANCE OF THE CULT OF THE ANCESTORS: DEATH AND BURIAL RITES

Here we shall have a specific look at the significance of burial and funeral rites in contemporary Yorubaland. The phenomena of death and burial rites usually bring people of diverse beliefs together since people come from various walks of life irrespective of their religious leanings as sympathizers, mourners, friends, and relations. Thus, regardless of religio-social differences, people troop together to sympathize with the bereaved and to mourn the dead by showing a kind of solidarity. The Yoruba shed all religio-social differences in mourning the dead and regardless of the religious leanings of the deceased and his survivors. These phenomena serve, at least, to effect some kind of interim peaceful co-existence or inter-faith fraternity during the mourning period, burial, and funeral ceremony. Traditional and modern singers, drummers, and choral groups are invited from various places, regardless of their religious leanings, to add flavor and gaiety to the ceremony. In this connection, it is not entirely religion that dictates which singers or drummers to invite. What is important here is the question of skill in the work and the choice of the children and relations of the deceased. Funeral ceremonies as occasions of religio-social differences, transcend religious camp or particularity. It is an occasion that usually serves as a sure locus of contact in a heterogeneous or pluralistic religious community.

On such occasions, children, relations, and friends come in groups, in uniform regalia to celebrate the occasion. What takes priority now is social integration rather than religious differentiation and disintegration. The occasion is usually one of religio-social interaction and equilibrium, mutualization, and socialization. On such occasions, people of diverse religious convictions talk together, dance together, sing together, trade together, move together, and exchange pleasantries and gifts. Thus the occasion of a funeral celebration can be regarded as one of the best times to effect inter and intra religious fraternity in Yorubaland.

The significance of grandiose funerals in the Yoruba pluralistic society should not be left out here. The Yoruba, regardless of their conversion to either Islam or Christianity, still attach importance to grandeur during burial and funeral ceremony. The importance attached to the ceremony is one of the reasons why they lay high premium on plurality of wives and multiplication of children who they think would be able to support them when they grow old and feeble and accord them decent and grandiose burial when they die. Christianity, in particular, had acted as a check to the Yoruba inclination for multiplicity of wives through the practice of one man, one wife, but it has not been able to achieve a serious success. A good number of Yoruba Christians still marry more than one wife. Here, the issue of tradition is rated higher than adherence to Christian practices.

MAGIC AND MEDICINE

Magic and medicine are features of Yoruba traditional religion which are still influencing Yoruba contemporary society, despite the incursion of foreign religions and the Western system of therapeutics. The Muslims, Christians, and others patronize local herbalists in Yorubaland for one problem or the other. The issue of religious difference is not considered important when it comes to solving a problem—physical, mental, spiritual, and mystical. In this connection Dopamu observes:

> But in view of improved medical conditions and accelerating technological progress, beliefs in Yoruba magic and medicine have persisted. Observations have shown that there are many Yoruba, literate and non-literate, who still hold tenaciously to the beliefs in magic and medicine, especially those that are relevant to their present-day needs. Although they may rely on the English medicine or spiritual healing, they still augment this by the use of Yoruba magic or medicine.

Magic that helps in this regard includes the following: *madarikan* magic that protects one against one's enemies; *ajepo* magic that enables one to vomit any poison taken; *ajera* magic that renders poison taken harmless. Then we have *oogun awon agba* magic that neutralizes the effect of the witches; *awure* magic that effects good luck; *ataja* magic that helps sales; *iferan* magic that makes everyone love one another; and *awijare* magic that enables one to win a case.

Another category of traditional medicine relates to the cure of the various diseases and ailments. A good number of the traditional medicinal items have been found to be very effective in Yorubaland. Thus the government of the Federation of Nigeria has been called upon in recent times to give official recognition to the traditional systems of healing, such that both the traditional and the Western practices can co-exist in hospitals and health centers. It is interesting to note that many diseases especially related to mental and psychological disorders which cannot be cured in the modern hospitals are being treated in the herbal homes of the Yoruba traditional healers.

Today in contemporary Yorubaland and Nigeria at large, there is always the sustained and insatiable demand for magical benefits, the elimination of evil agents, a sense of access to power, protection, the enhancement of status, health, increase in prosperity, and relief from both physical and mental anguish in day-to-day life. These are the various worldly activities which require the reassurance of supernatural goodwill and favor. As long as these activities and functions variously appeared to be fulfilled through the application of Yoruba traditional magic, and as long as people continue to show anxiety with regard to their future, Yoruba religion through the agency of its traditional magic and medicine would continue to be relevant to the contemporary African society.

CONCLUDING REMARKS

In the preceding pages we have been able to demonstrate that, despite the competition between Yoruba traditional religion and foreign religions, the former has not been relegated to the background. It should be accepted that Yoruba traditional religion no longer holds sway over the entire population in terms of cultic activities, yet it influences the society in various ways as itemized above. It is a statement of fact that traditional religion, despite the entry of foreign faiths, has been the *sine qua non* of the existence of the Yoruba. Foreign religions and modern trends have not been able to relegate traditional religion to the status of a thing of the past. The religion is as relevant and meaningful to a good number of the Yoruba, Muslims, and Christians alike in contemporary Yorubaland as it was in the pre-Islamic and Christian era.

African Traditional Religions: Worldviews and Cosmology

JACOB K. OLUPONA

Jacob K. Olupona is professor of African Religious Traditions at Harvard Divinity School. He highlights some of the ways that African native religious worldviews and cosmologies (explanations for the origins and structure of the universe) differ from the views on these matters common in Western countries. From the former perspective, the world is a mix of the sacred and secular, a blend that cannot be easily separated, and time is both linear and cyclic.

African religions are as diverse as the African continent itself. Africa is home to more than fifty countries, nearly every form of ecological niche found on Earth, and hundreds of ethnic groups who together speak more than a thousand languages. It is not surprising, then, that this enormous range of peoples, cultures, and modes of living would also be reflected in a diverse range of religious expressions. Religious

Jacob K. Olupona, *African Religions: A Very Short Introduction* (Oxford: Oxford University Press, 2014), 1–8.

worldviews, often unique to distinct ethnic groups, reflect people's identities and lie at the heart of how they relate to one another, to other people, and to the world at large. These religious worldviews encode, as well as influence, ethical practices, taboos, and the knowledge particular to each group.

WORLDVIEWS

The integration of religion into all aspects of daily life poses a sharp contrast to the church–state dichotomy upheld in Euro-American societies; African religious worldviews permeate economics and politics on the continent, where the sacred and secular realms influence one another. In fact, the use of the term "religion" is problematic when speaking of African traditional religions if one approaches the topic without questioning assumptions about what religion is, means, and does. The separation between religion and government, championed in one form or another in nearly all Western democracies, is predicated upon a particular vision of religion as something that can be extracted from public life and quarantined in its own sphere.

While the separation of church and state has, in many cases, proven more theoretical than actual, the fact that it is even believed to be possible—or desirable—reveals important Western assumptions about the nature of religion, especially as it pertains to communal life. For adherents of African traditional religions, such a separation is neither desirable nor possible, because religious beliefs inform every aspect of life—including birthing and death, marriage, family dynamics, diet, dress and grooming, health care (including mental health), the spending and saving of money, interactions with one's friends and neighbors, and of course, governance. In many traditional African governments, civic authorities were—and in some cases still are—not only arbiters of divinely appointed laws and religious leaders but are also believed to be semidivine. It would be a mistake, however, to view this suffusion of daily life with religion as evidence of religious theocracy or fundamentalism. On the contrary, it is quite normal and balanced when one begins with the assumption that religion is not a separate mode unto itself but is instead a varied and diverse set of components touching upon every aspect of life.

Indeed, religion in Africa remains the pulse of the private and public spheres, placing a strong emphasis on moral and social order in families, clans, lineages, and intraethnic interactions. As such, it pervades the daily affairs and conduct of African societies. Most traditional African societies employ two classes of morals: those pertaining to individual conduct, and those governing social and community relations. Community morals also dictate codes of conduct at the family level. These complex mandates aim to maintain balance among maternal and paternal relatives, clans, and lineages.

Religious Africans, like religious people everywhere, often ascribe supernatural origin to codes of conduct, believing that they derive from spirits, gods, and ancestors. Usually, communities maintain these edicts through the observance of taboos and ritual practices guided by priests, kings, and chiefs. African traditional religions typically strive for a this-worldly salvation—measured in terms of health, wealth, and offspring—while at the same time maintaining close contact with the otherworldly realm of the ancestors, spirits, and gods who are seen as having strong influence on the events and people in the here and now. Human and agricultural prosperity, longevity, vitality, and fertility are the central objectives of the spiritual life. Yet life's adversities also inform African conceptions of the universe.

The tribulations impeding one's successes may stem from negative spirits or malevolent practices such as witchcraft. Or they may be the result of neglect of one's mandatory secular or religious obligations to the deceased ancestory, the elderly, or to family shrines. Among the Ndembu of Zambia, a Bantu people from southern Africa, illness is seen primarily not as something that resides within the body of the patient but rather is a communal condition caused by imbalances in relationships with spirits, kinfolk, and members of one's community. In order to heal the person's body, what must actually be addressed by the healer is the underlying social and spiritual disruptions. Although Victor Turner specifically studied the Ndembu, subsequent generations of scholars have shown that Turner's findings have resonances in many traditional African societies and indeed in modern life in which, as has been medically proven, stress can lead to certain forms of illness.

Such practices warrant the prominent role of medicine men and women who are qualified to navigate the delicate moral and social balance between the good and evil forces exerted on the human realm. Similarly, diviners and priests use dreams and various divinatory techniques to ascertain revelations pertinent to the community. That traditional African religious worldviews continue to shape events in contemporary Africa is not in dispute.

The suffusion of daily life with religion happens in numerous ways. Leading up to the 2010 FIFA World Cup tournament in South Africa, there were popular assertions that the South African *sangomas*, the traditional healers and diviners, would magically impact the outcome of the games. By employing their supernatural aid, some believed they could influence the game in favor of their national team. Similarly, in a traditional wrestling contest that has metamorphosized into a spectacular professional sport in modern Senegal called *laamb*, participants deploy magical and religious substances provided by their spiritual leaders called *marabouts* to insure their victory in the wrestling match. In a case of higher stakes, a no-nonsense traditional ruler, Oba Akenzua, in Benin, Nigeria, ordered his chiefs and priests to perform a ritual against incessant kidnapping in the city. Sensing that the problem would not dissipate and would continue to evade the state security forces, he requested that the ritual be performed as a prophylaxis against kidnapping.

Although it is difficult to generalize about African traditional worldviews, a common denominator among them is a three-tiered model in which the human world exists sandwiched between the sky and the earth (including the underworld)—a schema that is not unique to Africa but found in many of the world's religious systems. A porous border exists between the human realm and the sky, which belongs to the gods. Similarly, although ancestors dwell inside of the earth, their activities also interject into human space. African cosmologies portray the universe as fluid, active, and impressionable, with agents from each realm constantly interacting with one another. This integrated worldview leads many practitioners of African religions to speak about the visible in tandem with the invisible. Each living and inanimate object is potentially sacred on some level. Many practitioners, for instance, revere animals for the wisdom they hold or for their potency as sacrificial offerings. Similarly, certain herbs are sacred, and pharmacological teachings remain embedded in priests' and diviners' knowledge.

COSMOLOGY AND MYTHS

The flexibility characterizing African religious traditions stems, in part, from the reliance on oral as opposed to written narratives, whose purported timelessness grants them authority. African traditional religions are communally maintained and routinely change in response to people's lived experiences and needs. The emphasis is on the core beliefs—ancestors, deities, divination, and sacred myths—rather than uniform doctrinal teachings. Sacred myths, especially those pertaining to the creation of the universe (cosmogonic) or to nature and the structure of the world (cosmological), describe significant events and noteworthy actors central to a particular people's worldview. These sacred stories are not static but rather undergo reinterpretation as one generation passes down the oral narratives to the next generation.

History and myths are each seen as containing truth. In many African communities, myths and history are effectively indistinguishable; both belong to the same genre. Among the Yoruba of Nigeria, the word *itan*, from the verb *tan* (to spread), is used for legends, myths, history, and folktales. This suggests that stories are narratives that spread, pointing to their oral transmission. *Tan* also references "to light," as in lighting a candle, thereby connoting enlightened meanings within the narratives.

Significantly, creation myths sometimes overlap with myths about a culture or social institution's origins. A myth among the people of Northern Yatenga in Burkina Faso demonstrates this. Two groups comprise the Yatenga people: the Foulse and the Nioniosse. According to this myth, the Foulse descended from the sky and the Nioniosse emerged from the earth. For this reason, ruling personnel, chiefs, and kings often arise from the first group while leaders in rites relating to the earth's fertility originate from the latter. The complementarity between earth and sky parallels the equally necessary functions both groups perform in Yatenga society. Many Western religious traditions, when pressed, would identify the sky as the home of divinity and the space under the earth as unpleasant, bad, or outright evil. By contrast, many African cosmologies posit that the sky and the earth are both divine abodes in which creation and divine action take place.

What is the definition of "myth" itself? As a comparative term, it is not typically one used by people to describe their own beliefs and stories. For our purposes, "myth" refers to narratives that are regarded by a people as sacred, describe a portion of the worldview of that people, and provide significant insight into the people's rationale for their customs, traditions, beliefs, and practices. There are varieties of myths in African societies that display the diverse motifs, meanings, and functions of African oral traditions. There are stories about the origin of various African peoples; myths about how rituals came into practice; myths of migration; and stories about human mortality and the origins of death. More specifically, there are different varieties of cosmogonic myths and how they define the created world, people, the physical environment, and social and cultural institutions. Primordial myths continue to hold sway on contemporary societies that regard them as sources of knowledge and as the basis of their existence and moral standards.

Central to an understanding of the dynamic of myth is an awareness of the competing modes of linear and cyclical time. Linear time refers to what most readers will recognize as their default sense of time—namely, of minutes, hours, and years passing inexorably, with an unceasing movement from the past into the future. Linear time is an arrow that travels in one direction at a constant speed. By contrast, cyclical time is like a wheel, with a set amount of time and events in time that repeat indefinitely. It is like the calendar, with its finite number of names for things (Sunday to Saturday, January to December) that follow a predictable pattern from start to finish before beginning again from the top. Much has been made of the seeming emphasis on linear time in the West versus cyclical time in Africa and other places that are often caricatured as less modern. In point of fact, linear and cyclical time are found everywhere.

In Europe and America, the emphasis may be placed more heavily on linear time. Not only does it order the day but also most festivals—both secular and sacred—which are commemorations of events that happened once, at a specific time in the past. However, there are some events that still operate on cyclical time. In Christian theology, all Christians are said to be present at the moment of the Crucifixion, making the Paschal celebration not merely a reenactment or commemoration but a taking part in the original event itself that repeats every year. In the African Anglican tradition, the wedding ceremonies in cathedrals and churches begin with a popular song that references the primordial wedding in the garden of Eden, a ritual invocation of a famous song, "the Blessings said in the Garden of Eden in the first human marriage remain forever true." The song is a ritual invocation of Adam and Eve's archetypal wedding. Many traditional African festivals are kin to this, closely tied to agricultural and natural cycles.

Less focus has been given to the fact that many African festivals are of a linear sort, celebrating historical events such as the acts of kings and famous conquests. And of course, Islam has brought with it a host of celebrations tied to historical events, in particular those commemorating the lives and acts of Prophet Muhammad and his immediate deputies and successors called the Rashidun Caliphs. That is, they were perceived by Muslims as divinely chosen and guided by God to rule the community after the death of the prophet Muhammed.

Ceremonial events and ritual activities typically take place on special occasions or at times determined by a religious leader through divination or following a ritual calendar. It is particularly significant to note that many of these ceremonies and rituals depend on a cyclical notion of time, coinciding with a cosmic renewal of time. At these occasions, the cosmos is believed to have undergone a full circle and requires a reactivation or recharging in order to continue anew through a new turn of the cycle. In several African countries, the end of the year marks an important time for such renewal, a time when life is at its lowest ebb and requires rejuvenation. It is interesting that when I was growing up in a Nigerian town, the people, who were mainly converts to Christianity, referred to Christmas as *odun kekere* (little festival) and to the New Year as *odun nla* (big festival), illustrating the significance they ascribed to the end of the year. Both notions of time and ritual cycles are embedded in African religious life and practices.

STUDY QUESTIONS

1. Explain why the terms *primitive* and *simple* do not apply to indigenous religions.
2. What are three common features of indigenous religions?
3. Explain how indigenous religions differ from the three major world religions.
4. For many native religions, the spiritual world connects with the physical world. In what way are they thought to connect?
5. Are all native religions polytheistic? Do some native traditions posit a supreme being? If so, what are some of the attributes of this being?
6. According to some native traditions, what extraordinary powers can humans possess?
7. Examine four myths that have been invented about native Americans by non-natives.
8. What is the attitude of many indigenous religions toward religious doctrines and creeds?
9. Describe the Ghost Dance movement. What beliefs were associated with it?
10. Why are writings by native Americans and Africans so scarce?

FURTHER READING

Indigenous North American Religions

Wallace Black Elk and William S. Lyon, *Black Elk: The Sacred Ways of a Lakota* (San Francisco: Harper & Row, 1990).

Joseph Epes Brown, ed., *The Sacred Pipe* (Norman: University of Oklahoma Press, 1989).

George A. Dorsey, *The Mythology of the Wichita* (Norman: University of Oklahoma Press, 1995).

Claire R. Farrer, *Thunder Rides a Black Horse* (Long Grove, IL: Waveland Press, 2011).

James Mooney, *The Ghost Dance Religion and Wounded Knee* (New York: Dover, 1973).

James Mooney, *History, Myths, and Sacred Formulas of the Cherokees* (Asheville, NC: Bright Mountain, 1992).

Akwesasne Notes, ed., *Basic Call to Consciousness* (Summertown, TN: Native Voices, 1978).

Evan T. Pritchard, *Native American Stories of the Sacred* (Woodstock, VT: Skylight Paths, 2005).

Frederick W. Turner, ed., *The Portable North American Indian Reader* (New York: Penguin, 1973).

Indigenous African Religions

John Bowker, ed., "African Religion," in *The Oxford Dictionary of World Religions* (New York: Oxford University Press, 1997).

Karen McCarthy Brown, *Mama Lola: A Vodou Priestess in Brooklyn* (Oakland: University of California Press, 1998).

Macel Griaule, *Conversations with Ogotemmeli* (New York: Oxford University Press, 1965).

John S. Mbiti, *An Introduction to African Religion*, 2nd ed. (Long Grove, IL: Waveland Press, 2015).

Jacob Olupona, ed., *African Traditional Religions in Contemporary Society* (New York: Paragon House, 1991).

Dominique Zahan, *The Religion, Spirituality, and Thought of Traditional Africa* (Chicago: University of Chicago Press, 1979).

ONLINE

Encyclopaedia Britannica, "Native American Religions," http://www.britannica.com/topic/Native-American-religion (December 21, 2015).

Indians.org, "Native American Religion," http://www.indians.org/articles/native-american-religion.html (December 21, 2015).

Internet Sacred Text Archive, "African Religion," http://www.sacred-texts.com/afr/ (December 21, 2015).

3 Hinduism

Hinduism can claim to be one of the world's oldest living religions (some say the oldest) and the third largest (with about 1 billion adherents). Hindus are spread throughout the world—most of them in India, but many others in South Asia, Africa, Europe, Canada, and the United States. Many observers are amazed that Hinduism boasts of no single creed, ruling body, founder, founding narrative, or sacred text. It comprises an astonishing array of philosophies, sects, and cosmologies, and it has accumulated these gradually through nearly four thousand years of history. It encompasses not one mode of devotion but many. Offerings to deity images, the chanting of mantras, temple worship, sensual rites, mystical experiences, ascetic privations—such practices may be embraced by some Hindus and ignored by others, but the broad tent of Hinduism accommodates them all.

So how can the term "Hinduism" be applied to such diversity, as if Hinduism were a monolith of ideas and observances? The answer is that Hinduism is not a monolith; it is not a unified whole. It is a family of traditions with some important characteristics in common. To be a Hindu, you need not adopt every characteristic but should embrace at least some of them. To fully understand Hinduism, then, you need to understand the commonalities as well as the ways that the religion has incorporated significant variations over time.

HINDU BELIEFS

Hinduism is so complex and varied that it is easily misunderstood. Part of the difficulty is that even widely accepted beliefs and practices may be interpreted differently among Hindus. Also, to adherents of other religious traditions or to those familiar only with Western perspectives on religion, Hinduism can seem profoundly alien and difficult to relate to their own religious experience. They may wonder how Hinduism can have so many gods, or why devotees pay homage to statues, or how people can seriously believe that natural objects (such as mountains or rivers) are sacred, or how God can take physical form as divine beings who can intervene in human affairs.

First, understand that for the majority of Hindus, God is both one and many. God is the impersonal, all-pervading Spirit known by many Hindus as **Brahman**. Brahman is the universe, yet Brahman transcends all space and time. As Hindu scripture, the Maitri *Upanishad*, says,

> Verily, in the beginning this world was Brahman, the limitless One—limitless to the east, limitless to the north . . . limitless in every direction. . . . Incomprehensible is that supreme Soul, unlimited, unborn not to be reasoned about, unthinkable—He whose soul is space.[1]

Brahman is one thing yet pervades everything, so everything is a manifestation of God. The many gods of Hinduism, then, are expressions of God. This means that for Hindus there is no contradiction in worshiping many deities while asserting the oneness of God. Each god is an embodiment (not just a representation) of Brahman, Absolute Reality. Such devotion is therefore polytheistic in the sense that the gods are manifestations of the one great all-pervading Spirit.

The *Upanishads* stress that Brahman is ineffable—Brahman cannot be described in words and must therefore be experienced directly through several means: meditation, various forms of yoga (both mental and physical disciplines), and **asceticism** (the denial of physical comfort or pleasures for religious ends). The aim of these practices is to look inward and discern the true nature of Brahman.

For most Hindus, life's central aim is liberation from **samsara**, one's repeating cycle of death and rebirth. The Hindu belief is that at death, one's eternal soul or self (**atman**) departs

FIGURE 3.1 A statue of Ganesha, the elephant-headed god, son of Shiva.

from the lifeless body and is reborn into a new body, residing for a time until death, then being reborn in yet another physical form—a sequence that may repeat for many lifetimes. (Westerners call this the doctrine of *reincarnation.*) For Hindus, *samsara* is a journey of happiness and suffering, a revolving merry-go-round that Hindus hope to exit.

The force that regulates *samsara* is **karma**, the universal principle of cause and effect: a person's actions cause particular effects, and the particular effects govern the characteristics and quality of each rebirth, or future life. Good actions (those reflecting moral and religious norms) earn merit; bad actions earn demerit. A lifetime accumulation of merit leads to desirable rebirths; an accumulation of demerit doesn't. Desirable rebirths increase the likelihood of escaping *samsara*.

Ultimate liberation from *samsara* is known as **moksha**. The repeating pattern of rebirth–death–rebirth continues because humans are ignorant of the true nature of reality, of what is real and what is merely appearance. This ignorance and its painful consequences can only be ended, and release from *samsara* can only be won, through the freeing power of an ultimate, transcendent wisdom.

For many Hindus, this wisdom comes when an *atman* realizes that he or she is not separate from the world or from other souls but is one with the impersonal, all-pervading Brahman. The essential realization, then, is the oneness of God and *atman*. This view is decidedly non-dualistic (monistic), maintaining that the universe consists of only one kind of thing. Once an individual fully understands this ultimate unity, *moksha* occurs, *samsara* stops, and the *atman* attains full union with Brahman. For many other Hindus, however, *moksha* is attained by realizing that the universe is dualistic, that there is a distinction between an *atman* and God. Liberation occurs, then, when there is a proper relationship between the two. In both approaches, attaining *moksha* involves defeating egotistical desires and detaching from materialistic concerns.

Achieving *moksha* may be difficult, requiring great effort and involving many lifetimes through long expanses of time. Or it can occur in a single lifetime through intense study or rigorous practice. In any case, it is the focus of Hindu life and the subject of Hindu teachings and scriptures.

In Hinduism there is a general appreciation of both the demands of the spiritual life and the pressures of earthly concerns, and Hindu teachings have tried to take both into account. Hindu writings affirm four goals in life: *kama* (pleasure of several kinds, including sensory, sexual, and aesthetic); *artha* (material wealth and worldly success); **dharma** (fulfillment of social, moral, and religious duty); and *moksha* (release from *samsara*, the highest goal). There is general agreement that *moksha* is the most important aim and that there must be balance among the four, but adherents have disagreed about how the first three should be weighted or ranked.

HINDU RITUAL

Hinduism is rich in devotional practice. Hindus usually worship in temples and in private homes (although almost any place can be a place of worship), celebrate religious holidays and festivals, visit pilgrimage sites, conduct sacred performances in dance and drama, participate in rites of passage, and more. The most common form of worship, however, is **bhakti**, devotion to a particular deity.

Although Hinduism has many gods, most adherents devote themselves to just one god or goddess. They may regard the deity as one of the many manifestations of God or as the most important manifestation. The focus of worship, whether in temples or at home altars, is an image or icon of the deity. But the image is thought to be much more than a representation; it is regarded as God or filled with God. And although God is present in the image, this does not diminish God's oneness or immanence. In a temple, the icon may be treated as a distinguished guest and be honored, bathed, dressed, fanned, anointed, ornamented, and serenaded.

The typical form of worship is an offering to the deity in which a priest or worshipper presents incense, fruit, flowers, fire, or coconut to the image. The ritual can be simple and brief or elaborate and long. The food may be returned to the devotee and thus be considered a spiritually elevated gift from the god.

One very prevalent form of worship is **arati**—honoring the deity with an offering of light from a flame. The usual procedure is for a devotee or priest to wave a five-wick oil lamp or

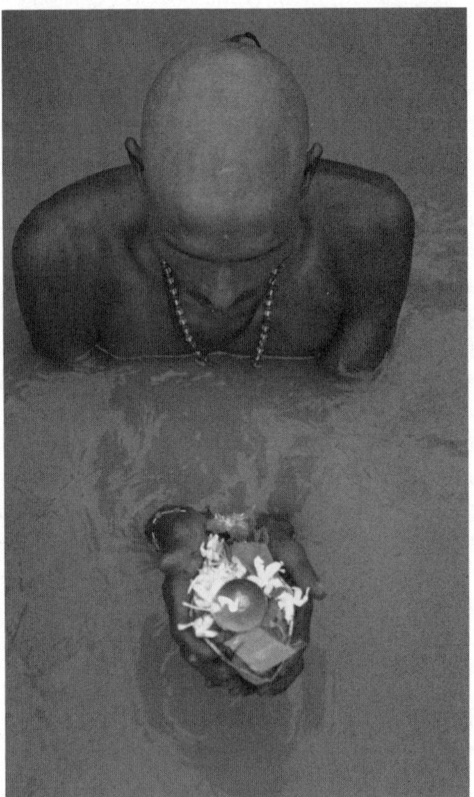

FIGURE 3.2 In Allahabad, India, where the Ganges and Yamuna meet, a Hindu takes a ceremonial dip.

a single-flame camphor lamp in a clockwise motion in the presence of the deity's image. Some Hindus say that the single camphor flame symbolizes the oneness of the devotee and deity and that the deity's protection is granted to devotees as they place their hands near the flame and then touch their head or eyes. The waving of the five flames (symbols of the five elements—earth, water, fire, air, and aether or void) is also thought to benefit the worshipper. In temples, several *aratis* may be performed each day.

HINDU PHILOSOPHIES

Hinduism is more than a religion of devotional practice and religious belief. It also contains complex systems, or schools (*darshana*), of philosophical reflection offered by ancient sages and commentators. To immerse yourself in one of these is to follow the path of knowledge (*jnana-marga*). The schools include six major orthodox ones, some of which appeared as far back as 500 BCE: *Samkhya* (probably the oldest), *Yoga*, *Nyaya*, *Vaisesika*, *Mimamsa*, and *Vedanta*. They all differ in important ways but presuppose the authority of the *Vedas*, accept the doctrines of *samsara* (the cycle of birth and death) and *moksha* (liberation), and set forth their doctrines in discourses, or books (*sutras*). They are not, however, exclusively philosophical or aloof from the lives of most Hindus. *Vedanta*, *Yoga*, and *Samkhya*, for example, have devotional sides to them, and their views have had a strong influence on everyday Hindu practice. Let's look at three of them:

Samkhya. The *Samkhya* school sees the world as dualistic—that is, consisting of two kinds of stuff or essences: spirit and matter. Although some early forms of *Samkhya* may have been theistic, it is essentially atheistic in that it rejects the notion of a personal or impersonal God. The central concern is that myriad souls are lodged in matter, and to be dislodged is to attain blissful liberation.

Yoga. The Yoga school accepts the philosophical outlook of *Samkhya* regarding spirit, matter, and liberation but goes farther in emphasizing meditative and physical techniques for binding the spirit to Brahman and thus achieving *moksha*. It also makes room for a qualified theism.

Many forms of yoga exist, the classic one being *raja* yoga, which involves working through several stages of physical, spiritual, and meditative discipline to reach a liberating state of consciousness. The adepts in *raja* yoga are said to be capable of extraordinary physical and mental feats. Most Westerners, however, understand yoga as *hatha* yoga, the use of physical techniques and postures for mastering the body. But this physical discipline is just one facet of liberation-oriented yoga.

Vedanta. The term *Vedanta* means "the end of the Vedas" or the "culmination of the Vedas," suggesting that this philosophical system is based heavily on the last part of the *Vedas*, the *Upanishads*. An influential outlook in this school is known as *Advaita Vedanta*. It maintains a thoroughgoing **monism** (non-dualism, *advaita*), claiming that reality consists not of two kinds of essential stuff (as the dualistic *Samkhya* school holds), but only one kind, and this kind is Brahman, who alone is real. Brahman is all, and the self is identical to Brahman. The most influential proponent of this view is Shankara (788–820 CE). He argues that people persist in believing they are separate from Brahman because of *maya*—illusion. Only by shattering this ignorance with knowledge of true reality can they escape the tortuous cycle of death and rebirth.

Other early *Vedanta* philosophers departed from Shankara's perspective. Ramanuja says, for example, that individual selves and Brahman are not exactly one, as Shankara teaches. Individuals and material reality are distinct but are aspects of Brahman. Madhva departs even farther from Shankara's monism, declaring that there is an irreducible difference in kind between Brahman and the universe.

HINDU BEGINNINGS

Hinduism began in northwest India, emerging from a blend of native religions and the religious traditions of an Indo-European people who migrated there from central Asia. The indigenous populace established an advanced civilization that flourished in the Indus River region and beyond as early as 2600 BCE. This Indus Valley civilization, as it is called, rivaled

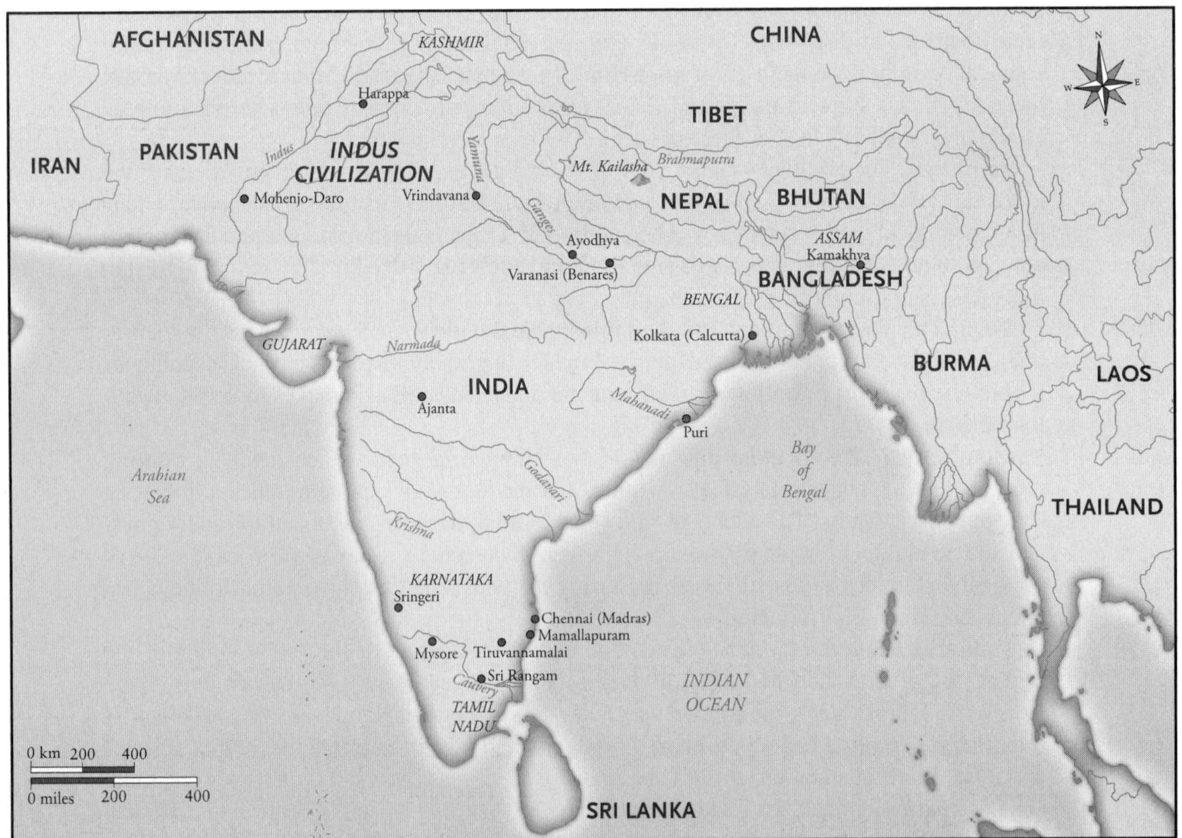

MAP 3.1 Significant sites in the history of Hinduism.

in many ways the Roman Empire, which was to come later. It devised a writing system, erected planned cities, and built impressive structures small and large—two-story houses, civic centers, porticos, baths, bathrooms, stairways, drainage systems, and worship halls.

Based on artifacts found in the region, scholars have hypothesized that the people were polytheistic and that some of their gods may have been forerunners of present-day Hindu deities. Many sculptures seem to have been used in worship of both gods and goddesses, and a few of these were depicted as half-human and half-animal. Evidence suggests that the inhabitants made animal sacrifices, performed ritual ablutions with water, and conducted rites where fire was the central element.

Around 1500 BCE, the migrating Indo-Europeans, called *Aryans*, moved into northwest India, carrying their distinctive culture with them. Most importantly, they brought their speech, from which was derived the ancient language of Sanskrit, the medium of Hindu scripture. They too were polytheistic, worshiping gods that were thought to embody powerful elements of nature such as the sun, moon, and fire. And they sacrificed animals (including horses) and animal byproducts (such as butter and milk) as offerings to these gods.

HINDUISM TIMELINE

BCE

2600–1700 Indus Valley civilization

1500–900 The *Vedas* composed

900–600 Early *Upanishads*

563–483 Life of the Buddha

400 BCE–400 CE *Mahabharata* composed

c. 272 Accession of King Ashoka

200 BCE–200 CE *Ramayana composed*

CE

First century *Bhagavad-Gita* composed

c. 200 Compilation of *Laws of Manu*

300–900 *Puranas* composed

700 Flourishing of *bhakti* in southern India

788–820 Life of Shankara, influential philosopher and proponent of *Advaita Vedanta*

800–1200 Six schools of elite philosophical Hinduism established.

1526–1757 Moghul rule of India

1869–1948 Life of M. K. Gandhi, leader of civil disobedience campaigns and Hindu reform

1947 India wins independence from Britain.

1948 Gandhi assassinated

Aryan culture was partitioned into four social classes called *varnas*. From these, the hereditary caste system was developed in Hindu society and is still holding sway in modern India, although it has been refined into thousands of subdivisions based on social and occupational criteria. Traditionally the dominant class consisted of **brahmins**, the priests and teachers who alone could study and teach scripture. Brahmins still play a priestly role and are prevalent among India's professionals and civil servants.

HINDU SCRIPTURES: THE VEDIC PERIOD

For Hinduism, the most important result of the melding of Aryan and Indus River cultures was a set of sacred compositions known as the **Vedas** ("knowledge"), regarded by almost all Hindus as eternal scripture and the essential reference point for all forms of Hinduism. They were produced by the Aryans between 1500 and 600 BCE (what has been called the Vedic era), which makes these compositions India's oldest existing literature. For thousands of years the *Vedas* were transmitted orally from brahmin to brahmin until they were finally put into writing. They are said to be *shruti* ("that which was heard")—revealed directly to Hindu seers (*rishis*) and presumed to be without human or divine authorship. Later scriptures are mostly thought to be *smriti* ("what is remembered")—of human authorship. These consist of commentaries and elaborations on the *shruti*. Hindus revere the *Vedas*, even though the majority of adherents are ignorant of their content, and their meanings are studied mostly by the educated. In fact, most Hindu devotional practices are derived not from the *Vedas*, but from the sacred texts that came later.

The *Vedas* consist of four collections, or books, of writings, each made up of four sections. The four books are the *Rig-Veda*, the *Yajur-Veda*, the *Sama-Veda*, and the *Atharva-Veda*. The sections are (1) *samhitas*: hymns, or chants, of praise or invocation to the gods (including many Aryan deities), mostly to be uttered publicly during sacrifices; (2) *brahmanas*: treatises on, and how-to instructions for, rituals; (3) *Aranyakas*: "forest treatises" for those who seek a reclusive religious life; and (4) the **Upanishads:** philosophical and religious speculations.

The oldest book is the *Rig-Veda*, which contains a section of over one thousand ancient hymns, each one invoking a particular god or goddess—for example, Indra (the ruler of heaven, Agni (the god of fire), and Varuna (the god of moral order in the universe). Most of the hymns in the other books are taken from the *Rig-Veda*.

The hymns in the *Atharva-Veda* are intended not for use in public sacrifices but for rites in the household. Most of these compositions contain charms, spells, and prayers to solicit healing or good fortune, as well as curses and incantations to ward off evil or to harm others.

There are dozens of *Upanishads*, but only thirteen or fourteen (called the principal *Upanishads*) are revered by all Hindus. The *Upanishads* were added to the *Vedas* last, composed primarily from about 900 to 600 BCE during a time of intellectual and religious unease. The ancient certainties—the authority of the brahmins, the status of the *Vedas*, the caste system, the sacrificial rites, and the nature of the deities—were being called into question. The *Upanishads* put these issues in a different light and worked out some philosophical doctrines that became fundamental to Hinduism right up to the twenty-first century.

In the early *Vedas*, there is an emphasis on improving one's lot in life through religious practice and faith in the gods. But in the *Upanishads*, the central aim is release from this world. Specifically, the goal is liberation from *samsara*.

HINDU SCRIPTURES: AFTER THE VEDAS

As noted earlier, the *shruti* scriptures of the Vedic period (roughly 1500 to 900 BCE) are thought to be of divine origin, revealed to the *rishis* (ancient seer-poets) who received them via an intuitive or mystical experience. Hindus regard these (the *Vedas*) as authoritative, eternal, and fixed. This canon remains as it was written, without further revelations or later emendations. But after the Vedic period, the *smriti* scriptures appeared. They too are venerated and generally considered by most Hindus to be more authoritative than the *Vedas*. Over the centuries revered figures have added to them and continue to do so. But these facts have not diminished the influence of the *smriti* scriptures, which have probably had a greater impact on Hindu life than the *Vedas* have.

In Hindu scripture, newer writings generally do not supersede the old; they are added to the ever-expanding canon. Thus many ideas and practices found in both the *Vedas* and the post-Vedic scriptures are still relevant to contemporary Hinduism. Likewise, the ancient Vedic gods and goddesses were never entirely discarded. They were reduced to the status of mortal divinities and absorbed into the monotheistic traditions that came later in history. Today many of the old gods are ignored or deemphasized, while some of them are still revered.

The *smriti* material is voluminous and wide-ranging. It consists mainly of (1) the epics (the *Mahabharata* and the *Ramayana*); (2) traditional histories (the *Puranas*); and (3) legal and moral treatises (for example, *The Laws of Manu*).

The Epics

The great epics have served Indian and Hindu civilization much as Homer's *Iliad* and *Odyssey* served the ancient Greek and Hellenistic world: the stories express the culture's virtues, heroes, philosophy, and spiritual lessons. With eighteen voluminous chapters (or books) and 100,000 verses, the *Mahabharata* is the longest poem in existence, many times more extensive than the Christian Bible. Composed between 400 BCE and 400 CE, the epic recounts the ancient conflict between two great families, both of which are descendants of the ruler of Bharata (northern India). Their struggle culminates in a fateful battle at Kurukshetra. Among the warriors who are to fight there is the war hero Arjuna, who has serious misgivings about a battle that will pit cousin against cousin. Before the fight begins, as Arjuna contemplates the bloody fratricide to come, he throws down his bow in anguish and despair. He turns to his charioteer, Krishna—who in fact is God incarnate—and asks whether it is right to fight against his own kin in such a massive bloodletting. The conversation that then takes place between Krishna and Arjuna constitutes the most famous part of the *Mahabharata*: the *Bhagavad-Gita*, the most highly venerated and influential book in Hinduism.

The seven-hundred-verse **Bhagavad-Gita** (Song of the Lord) is no mere war story. In dramatic fashion, it confronts the moral questions and conflicts that arise in the human condition, as seen by Hindus—devotion to the gods, the caste system, obligations to family, duties in time of war, the nature of the soul, the concept of Brahman, and the correct paths toward *moksha*.

Krishna tells Arjuna to join the battle, for it is Arjuna's duty (*dharma*) as a warrior to fight. But duty must be performed "without attachment," without a desire for the results of the action. A person must act out of devotion to duty only, to simply do what is right without motivation to bring about particular consequences.

Krishna tries to ease Arjuna's grief over the deaths of his kinsmen by explaining the true nature of the soul. The soul cannot die; it enters a body at birth and leaves it at death, repeating death and rebirth many times until it is liberated.

In the *Gita*, we get a new account of the nature of God. In the *Upanishads*, Brahman is the impersonal Ultimate Reality, or World-Soul, pervading and constituting the universe but aloof from humans and their concerns. But Krishna turns out to be the ultimate God, a personal deity who loves and cares for humans and who often takes human form to help them.

In the *Gita*, Krishna insists that several paths (*marga*) can lead to *moksha*, a view that fits well with modern Hinduism. (Since these paths amount to spiritual disciplines, they are also referred to as forms of *yoga*.) Today there is a general awareness of multiple paths to liberation, each appropriate for a particular kind of person.

Krishna teaches Arjuna that one path to salvation is the way of unselfish action done for duty's sake (*karma-marga*). As human beings, we cannot avoid acting. But when we do, only actions done without regard to rewards, punishments, praise, or blame can lead to liberation and union with God. We must act with detachment from these motives. Our deeds should be done with the right intention—the intention to do our duty only because it is our duty.

The path to liberation that Krishna speaks of most often is devotion to a personal god (*bhakti-marga*), the path chosen by most Hindus. *Bhakti-marga* entails overwhelming love and adoration of a deity. The candidates for adoration are many—Krishna, Vishnu, Shiva, Varuna, Indra, Ganesha, Kali, and many other deities. The Hindu view of *bhakti* is that to love one of these finite manifestations of God is to love the infinite God of everything. Thus a Hindu may bring an offering of flowers to an image of Krishna and pray for help or healing, expecting that Krishna himself will be pleased and perhaps answer the plea.

The *Ramayana*, the second great epic of Hinduism, has been read, cherished, and dramatized by Hindus for centuries. Like the stories in the Christian Bible, the *Ramayana* has been told and retold by generations of devotees who looked to it for spiritual lessons and moral guidance. The main characters are moral exemplars, role models who behave with integrity and moral courage, even in the worst situations. Throughout India the story is celebrated and reenacted every year, and Indian television serialized it for an appreciative mass audience.

The epic is about Prince Rama of the kingdom of Kosala. By rights, the prince is to inherit the throne of his father, Dasaratha. But Dasaratha is duty-bound to deny Rama his prize. To keep a promise made earlier to one of his wives (who wants her own son on the throne), Dasaratha reluctantly banishes Rama from the kingdom for fourteen years. Rama is a virtuous and dutiful son, so he obeys his father's edict and leaves Ayodhya, the capital city, and retreats into the forest to live as an ascetic. His beautiful and noble wife, Sita, and one of his half-brothers, Lakshman, remain loyal and choose to accompany him, even though they could live in luxury in Ayodhya. Deeply saddened over Rama's banishment, Dasaratha dies, and the brother who is to be king pleads with Rama to come home and take his rightful place on the throne. But unwilling to disobey his father's order of exile, Rama refuses.

In the forest, Ravana, the king of the demons, kidnaps Sita, and Rama sets out to get her back. In his quest, Rama is befriended by a troop of monkeys. After the divine monkey Hanuman finds Sita, the monkeys fight alongside Rama in a horrendous war against Ravana. Eventually Prince Rama slays Ravana and rescues Sita. (In modern India, the defeat of Ravana is celebrated every year in the festival of Dussehra.) The prince and his wife return to Ayodhya, where they ascend to the throne as king and queen.

In some versions of the story, Rama is the incarnation of the god Vishnu. And in a well-known addition to the epic, Rama banishes Sita after questions are raised about her fidelity during captivity, but she is eventually vindicated.

The Puranas

As suggested earlier, *bhakti* is the most widely practiced form of Hinduism, thanks in large measure to the *smriti* scriptures known as the *Puranas*, "Ancient Lore" (composed around 300 BCE to 900 CE). Through myths and legends expressed in poetic verse, these Sanskrit texts praise the divine powers and miraculous exploits of a pantheon of gods and goddesses.

A CLOSER LOOK

Hindu–Muslim Violence

In 1528 CE a Mughal emperor built a mosque—the Babri Masjid—in Ayodhya, India. In 1992 a dispute between Hindus and Muslims exploded into communal violence over the ownership of the plot of ground upon which the mosque stood. Muslims claimed the site because of the mosque's long history; Hindus claimed it because they believed it to be the birthplace of Rama, the Hindu hero and god. Hindu nationalists rushed the mosque and razed it to the ground. Fighting broke out between Hindus and Muslims in several Indian cities, and as a result two thousand people died.

In 2002, Hindu–Muslim violence also flared, with horrendous results. As *Time Magazine* reports,

> Seventy people were killed in Gujarat province on Thursday, as Hindu mobs attacked Muslims and torched a mosque and other Islamic facilities. The violence came as retaliation for Wednesday's firebombing by Muslims of a train carrying Hindu activists returning from Ayodhya. Fifty-eight people, many of them women and children, died in that attack, fueling outrage that threatens to spark a new wave of communal bloodletting throughout India.[2]

In 2012, Hindu–Muslim conflict flared up again near Ayodhya. Two people were killed after a rumor spread that a statue of the Hindu goddess Durga had been defaced. Rioters destroyed shops and vehicles, and a day-long curfew was imposed.

These examples run contrary to Hinduism's reputation for religious tolerance and to the instances of Hindu–Muslim civility in other areas of India.

The *Puranas* also pay tribute to the ancient devotees and provide instructions in the proper methods of worship. The principal deities are Brahma (not to be confused with Brahman), Vishnu, Shiva, and the goddess Parvati, the consort of Shiva. In whatever form, the deity is considered a manifestation of the Divine; the deity is the Supreme Deity.

Sincere devotion to a favorite god is also a way to petition the deity for a demonstration of divine grace. In the *Puranas*, deities are portrayed as intimately involved in the affairs of humans, sometimes appearing to devotees to deliver rewards, punishments, or warnings. In the *Bhagavata Purana*, the god Krishna declares that of all the ways of approaching the divine (including chanting, asceticism, and the various yogas), he is most pleased with simple, heartfelt devotion.

The Legal and Moral Codes

Much of the social and religious landscape of modern India has been influenced by two-thousand-year-old Hindu treatises on religious, legal, and moral duty (*dharma*), the most famous being *The Laws of Manu.* (In legend, all humans are descended from Manu, the original man.) Completed by around the first century of the Common Era, *The Laws of Manu* provided the basic outlines of India's caste system, laid down a code of conduct for each social class, and marked out the four stages of life for upper-class Indian men. *The Laws of Manu*, in effect, defined the ideal Hindu society, which served as a reference point for laws and social rules in India today.

As noted earlier, Aryan culture was divided into four hierarchical classes called *varnas*, which became the basis of the four main classes of Hinduism. In later eras these divisions were refined into a myriad of subdivisions or castes (*jati*) and hardened to forbid social movement in one's lifetime from one caste to another. In modern India the castes are based on occupation, kinship, geography, even sectarian affiliation, and they are especially influential in rural areas. In general, caste protocol forbids members of one caste to marry members of another, and interactions with people from another caste are often restricted.

The highest *varna* (class) was occupied by *brahmins* (priests and teachers) only. They had the exclusive authority to study and teach the *Vedas*. Next came the *kshatriyas*, the kings, rulers, and warriors. The *vaishyas* made up the next caste. They primarily worked in agriculture but also handled commercial transactions and artistry. The lowest of the four castes (*shudras*) consisted of workers and servants who served the upper classes. In *The Laws*, the top three classes are called the "twice born," meaning that they were born into the world and then spiritually born again through an initiation rite.

In ancient India the concepts of *dharma* and karma were central to the **caste system**, and the same is true today. Each caste is prescribed a *dharma*, a set of duties mandated for that caste. Theoretically no upward movement is possible during one's lifetime, but diligently performing one's *dharma* could lead to better karma and a higher-level rebirth in the next life. So the caste system implies that being dutiful in this life would be rewarded only in later incarnations. It also insists that caste members must not jump to another caste but confine themselves to their caste-designated lots in life. As the *Laws* declare, "Better to do one's own *dharma* badly than another caste's *dharma* well."[3]

Eventually the caste system was modified to include a fifth group—the "untouchables," or *Dalits* ("oppressed ones"), who are thought to be "too polluting" to be included in any of the higher castes. This group comprises those who do "polluting" work such as sweeping streets, cleaning toilets, and handling leather, human waste, or dead bodies. The term "untouchables" comes from the traditional Hindu idea that upper-class persons who touch someone from the lowest class will be polluted and must therefore perform rituals to cleanse themselves. For generations *Dalits* have been subjected to violence and discrimination—and they still are even in modern India and even though the untouchable class has been officially outlawed. Mohandas Gandhi called the *Dalits* "the children of God" and advocated for their rights and their equal status in society.

The caste system has been criticized by Hindus and non-Hindus throughout India's history. In recent years the main complaint is that the system is inherently unfair. The plight of the *Dalits* is just one example. *The Laws of Manu* mandate a lower status for the lowest class, and caste hierarchy itself implies that some people are inherently less worthy than others, or that some deserve better treatment under the law than others, or that the highest classes are privileged and therefore should get special treatment. In practice, the influence of caste in people's daily lives is weak in urban areas and much stronger in the countryside.

For "twice-born" males, *The Laws of Manu* require passage through four stages of life, each one of which calls for the completion of important social or spiritual tasks. In contemporary India, working through all four stages is still considered a laudable achievement, although few upper-class males go beyond the second stage. The first stage is *student*, in which a young man studies the *Vedas* and other subjects under the supervision of a teacher. After marrying within his caste, the student enters the stage of *householder*, a time to raise children, acquire wealth, and remain faithful to his wife. The third stage is that of the *forest dweller*, begun after a man's children are grown. The householder retires to the forest to study the *Vedas*, meditate, perform rituals, give up the physical comforts of society, and renounce sexual pleasures. After spiritual development in the forest, the fourth stage begins: a man becomes a homeless, wandering ascetic, cultivating detachment from the world and seeking ultimate liberation.

 BACKGROUND

Forehead Marks

At least once in a while, most Hindus wear forehead marks, or *tilaka*. But what do these signs mean? They don't have a uniform meaning but can be interpreted in many ways, depending on the context and the attributes of the wearer. The marks (which can be many different colors and take the shape of dots, lines, and other configurations) can be used to indicate the wearer's social status (marital status, caste, etc.), sectarian affiliation, chosen god, community, and participation in particular rites. On many women, *tilaka* can be purely decorative, fashion accessories like earrings or mascara. A red dot on a woman's forehead can indicate that she is married; black, white, red, and yellow lines can announce one's sect; vertical or horizontal lines can signify adherents of Vishnu, Krishna, Shiva, and Parvati; and lines of ash are signs of male ascetics.

MAJOR MONOTHEISMS

Hinduism has a multiplicity of deities, but over the centuries three in particular have attracted so many devotees and engendered so much interest that each one has become associated with a major religious tradition. The three deities are *Shiva* (devotees are called *Shaivas*); *Vishnu* (*Vaishnavas*); and the Goddess *Devi* (*Shaktas*). Each tradition has its own form of worship, favored scriptures, doctrines, and stories about the deity.

Shiva is a complex god, having multiple aspects, some of them seeming to exist in opposition to one another. He is destructive and creative, menacing and benign, sensual and ascetic, male and female, solitary and familial. He is depicted in many different ways, sometimes alone and sometimes with his divine consort, Parvati. In one well-known sculpture he is the "Lord of the Dance," shown dancing within a flaming halo, his four arms outstretched. The objects and gestures portrayed symbolize his powers: a drum in his upper right hand represents creation; a gesture made by his lower right hand means "Be not afraid"; a flame in his upper left hand signifies destruction; his right foot crushing a demon symbolizes the defeat of illusion; and his front left hand pointing to his raised foot means he is a refuge for devotees.

Shiva is often symbolized abstractly by the *linga*, a phallus-shaped column inserted into a base or pedestal representing the vulva. Together these two items represent Shiva's infinitely creative and generative energy.

To Vaishnavas, Vishnu is the ultimate deity, supreme above all, cause and preserver of the universe. His devotees see him as the epitome of loving kindness, mercy, and goodness, for his avatars (incarnations) have often intervened in the affairs of men and women in times of crisis. Among his better-known avatars are Rama and Krishna; some devotees believe Buddha was also one of the avatars.

Like Shiva, Vishnu is variously depicted. Often he is portrayed as a great four-armed monarch wearing a tall, ornate crown and royal clothes, his four hands holding symbols of his divinity. He is usually accompanied by his consort Lakshmi, a goddess strongly devoted to him.

Shaivas and Vaishnavas revere their respective masculine gods as supreme, and they relegate feminine deities to subordinate roles. But to Shaktas, the Great Goddess is the supreme deity—omnipotent, omnipresent, the great creator and destroyer of the universe, the Supreme Being. She is known by the name of Devi, Mahadevi, and many others, and she has had—and still has—many followers.

CHALLENGES TO HINDUISM

No major religion can long remain unchanged against the pressures of cultural and religious diversity, modernity, and reform. Hinduism is no exception.

In the eighth century, conquering Muslim leaders brought Islam to India, and from 1526 to 1707 CE the emperors of the Mughal Empire ruled northern and central India, encouraging converts to Islam and reinforcing a permanent Muslim presence on the subcontinent. This uneasy coexistence of Islam and Hinduism evolved into the tense and sometimes violent relationship that we see in India today.

By far, the culture that has had the greatest impact on Indian Hinduism is Britain. In the seventeenth century, the British formed the East India Company, which marked the beginning of their three-century rule in India. (The British reign ended in 1947 when India won its independence.) During this era, Hinduism was strongly influenced by Christian missionaries (British, European, and American) as well as by Hindu reformers. At various times, both groups sought to eliminate practices and beliefs they found morally objectionable or contrary to true Hinduism. Their main targets were the caste system, polytheism, widows' marriage (remarriage after the death of their husbands), child marriage, superstition, and **sati** (*suttee*), the self-immolation of a widow on her husband's funeral pyre. Some Hindus responded by discarding these practices, but many did not. In fact, some reacted by returning to a more orthodox form of Hinduism that fully embraced such practices.

Like other religions, Hinduism has had to contend with the forces of modernity—secularism, religious liberalism, modern values (including human rights, women's rights, free inquiry, and individual freedom), scientific progress, modern technology (including mass media), urbanization, and religious and cultural pluralism. These trends are powerful, and they have influenced Hinduism in countless ways.

For example, a slow slide toward secularism is evident in the lives of some Hindus in India (especially in the large cities), but the fundamental attitudes and core values of most Hindus are probably unaffected by it. One general definition of secularism is this: the tendency of people to see their lives as not completely defined or consumed by otherworldly or supernatural concerns. Westerners generally assume that religion is only part of their lives, that important endeavors and interests exist outside the purview of religion. But to millions of Hindus, this seems wrong. Their lives and their identity are defined by their religion.

One issue that has vigorously challenged orthodox Hinduism in modern society is the role and standing of women. Hindu attitudes toward them are complicated and contradictory, and this was the case hundreds of years ago as well as today. *The Laws of Manu* say women are to be honored as spiritually powerful and auspicious goddesses who bring divine blessings to husband and home. Yet traditionally a wife's duty, or *dharma*, has been to be faithful to her husband whom she is to worship as a god, even if he an unfaithful lout. She must obey him, endure abuse, bear him sons, and never remarry even if she is widowed. She is to be entirely dependent on him. As the *Laws* put it,

> By a girl, by a young woman or even by an aged one, nothing must be done independently, even in her own house. In childhood a female must be subject to her father, in youth to her husband, when her lord is dead, to her sons; a woman must never be independent.[4]

The rules laid down in the *Laws* were directed toward upper-caste women and were taken less seriously by the lower castes. Even among the former, some women did not adhere to Manu's decrees, choosing instead to exercise artistic, literary, religious, and financial freedom. Today many women in India have bypassed the rules to achieve extraordinary political and professional success or to chart a different understanding of their social and religious obligations.

NOTES

1. Maitri, *Upanishad*, VI. 17.
2. Tony Karon, "Hindu-Muslim Violence Imperils India," *Time Magazine*, February 28, 2002.
3. *The Laws of Manu*, 10:97.
4. *The Laws of Manu*, 5:147–148.

KEY TERMS

arati Honoring a deity with an offering of light.

asceticism The denial of physical comfort or pleasures for religious ends.

atman Soul or self.

bhakti Devotion to a particular deity.

Bhagavad-Gita The most highly venerated and influential scriptures in Hinduism.

Brahman The impersonal, all-pervading spirit that is the universe yet transcends all space and time.

brahmin A priest or teacher; a man of the priestly caste.

caste system The idealized social hierarchy of Indian society. *Caste* refers to one of the divisions or classes in Hindu society.

dharma Religious and moral duty or teaching; cosmic and social truth or order.

karma The universal principle that governs the characteristics and quality of each rebirth, or future life.

moksha Ultimate liberation from *samsara*.

samsara One's cycle of repeated deaths and rebirths.

sati (suttee) The self-immolation of a widow on her husband's funeral pyre.

Upanishads Vedic literature concerning the self, Brahman, *samsara*, and liberation.

Vedas Early Hindu scriptures, developed between 1500 and 600 BCE.

READINGS

TEACHINGS

Selections from the *Rig Veda*

In the Beginning: The Dawn of the Gods

This hymn offers an explanation of creation and the origin of the gods. In the very beginning, "existence was born from non-existence." Later the earth and the gods were born of a crouching goddess "with legs spread."

1 Let us now speak with wonder of the births of the gods—so that some one may see them when the hymns are chanted in this later age.

2 The lord of sacred speech, like a smith, fanned them together. In the earliest age of the gods, existence was born from non-existence.

3 In the first age of the gods, existence was born from non-existence. After this the quarters of the sky were born from her who crouched with legs spread.

4 The earth was born from her who crouched with legs spread, and from the earth the quarters of the sky were born. From Aditi, Daksa was born, and from Daksa Aditi was born.

5 For Aditi was born as your daughter, O Daksa, and after her were born the blessed gods, the kinsmen of immortality.

6 When you gods took your places there in the water with your hands joined together, a thick cloud of mist arose from you like dust from dancers.

7 When you gods like magicians caused the worlds to swell, you drew forth the sun that was hidden in the ocean.

8 Eight sons are there of Aditi, who were born of her body. With seven she went forth among the gods, but she threw Martanda, the sun, aside.

9 With seven sons Aditi went forth into the earliest age. But she bore Martanda so that he would in turn beget offspring and then soon die.

Rig Veda, 10.72, from the *Rig Veda*, Wendy Doniger, trans. (New York: Penguin Books, 1981), 38–39.

Hymn of the Primeval Man

This Vedic hymn tells the story of the world's creation. In it the gods sacrifice the primeval man, Purusha, a gargantuan male in the cosmos who comes to symbolize the male gender of any being. The gods dismember him, and the parts become the stars, the planets, living things, and all the liturgical components of a Vedic ritual sacrifice. Strangely enough, he is the thing to be sacrificed as well as the deity to whom the sacrifice is made.

1 The Man has a thousand heads, a thousand eyes, a thousand feet. He pervaded the earth on all sides and extended beyond it as far as ten fingers.

2 It is the Man who is all this, whatever has been and whatever is to be. He is the ruler of immortality, when he grows beyond everything through food.

3 Such is his greatness, and the Man is yet more than this. All creatures are a quarter of him; three quarters are what is immortal in heaven.

4 With three quarters the Man rose upwards, and one quarter of him still remains here. From this[1] he spread out in all directions, into that which eats and that which does not eat.

5 From him Viraj was born, and from Viraj came the Man. When he was born, he ranged beyond the earth behind and before.

6 When the gods spread the sacrifice with the Man as the offering, spring was the clarified butter, summer the fuel, autumn the oblation.

7 They anointed[2] the Man, the sacrifice born at the beginning, upon the sacred grass.[3] With him the gods, Sadhyas,[4] and sages sacrificed.

8 From that sacrifice in which everything was offered, the melted fat[5] was collected, and he[6] made it into those beasts who live in the air, in the forest, and in villages.

9 From that sacrifice in which everything was offered, the verses and chants were born, the meters were born from it, and from it the formulas were born.

10 Horses were born from it, and those other animals that have two rows of teeth;[7] cows were born from it, and from it goats and sheep were born.

11 When they divided the Man, into how many parts did they apportion him? What do they call his mouth, his two arms and thighs and feet?

12 His mouth became the Brahmin; his arms were made into the King, his thighs the People, and from his feet the Servants were born.

13 The moon was born from his mind; from his eye the sun was born. Indra and Agni came from his mouth, and from his vital breath the Wind was born.

14 From his navel the middle realm of space arose; from his head the sky evolved. From his two feet came the earth, and the quarters of the sky from his ear. Thus they[8] set the worlds in order.

15 There were seven enclosing-sticks[9] for him, and thrice seven fuel-sticks, when the gods, spreading the sacrifice, bound the Man as the sacrificial beast.

16 With the sacrifice the gods sacrificed to the sacrifice. These were the first ritual laws. These very powers reached the dome of the sky where dwell the Sadhyas, the ancient gods.

NOTES

1. That is, from the quarter still remaining on earth, or perhaps from the condition in which he had already spread out from the earth with three quarters of his form.

2. The word actually means "sprinkle" with consecrated water, but it indicates the consecration of an initiate or a king.

3. A mixture of special grasses was strewn on the ground for the gods to sit upon.

4. A class of demigods or saints, whose name literally means "Those who are yet to be fulfilled."

5. Literally, a mixture of butter and sour milk used in the sacrifice; figuratively, the fat that drained from the sacrificial victim.

6. Probably the Creator, though possibly the Man himself.

7. Incisors above and below, such as dogs and cats have.

8. The gods.

9. Green twigs that keep the fire from spreading; the fuel sticks are seasoned wood used for kindling.

The Rig-Veda, 10.90, Wendy Doniger O'Flaherty, trans., in *The Norton Anthology of World Religions* (New York: W. W. Norton, 2015), 93–94.

Creation of the Universe

This hymn is a piece of philosophical speculation on the earliest of times when there was neither "non-existence nor existence." Perhaps the cosmos formed itself, or maybe it did not. Maybe a supreme power in the highest heaven knows how things really began—or maybe he doesn't know. Questions are raised, but no firm answers are given.

1 There was neither non-existence nor existence then; there was neither the realm of space nor the sky which is beyond. What stirred? Where? In whose protection? Was there water, bottomlessly deep?

2 There was neither death nor immortality then. There was no distinguishing sign of night nor of day. That one breathed, windless, by its own impulse. Other than that there was nothing beyond.

3 Darkness was hidden by darkness in the beginning; with no distinguishing sign, all this was water. The life force that was covered with emptiness, that one arose through the power of heat.

4 Desire came upon that one in the beginning; that was the first seed of mind. Poets seeking in their heart with wisdom found the bond of existence in non-existence.

5 Their cord was extended across. Was there below? Was there above? There were seed-placers; there were powers. There was impulse beneath; there was giving-forth above.

6 Who really knows? Who will here proclaim it? Whence was it produced? Whence is this creation? The gods came afterwards, with the creation of this universe. Who then knows whence it has arisen?

7 Whence this creation has arisen—perhaps it formed itself, or perhaps it did not—the one who looks down on it, in the highest heaven, only he knows—or perhaps he does not know.

Rig Veda, 10.129, from the *Rig Veda,* Wendy Doniger, trans. (New York: Penguin Books, 1981), 25–26.

Indra, King of the Gods

Indra is the king of the gods, a great warrior who destroys his enemies with his powerful thunderbolts. This hymn celebrates his most famous feat—the slaying of Vrtra, a dragon that spread disorder and calamity throughout the cosmos. Indra shattered him, establishing his supremacy over all adversaries.

1 Let me now sing the heroic deeds of Indra, the first that the thunderbolt-wielder performed. He killed the dragon and pierced an opening for the waters; he split open the bellies of mountains.

2 He killed the dragon who lay upon the mountain; Tvastr fashioned the roaring thunderbolt for him. Like lowing cows, the flowing waters rushed straight down to the sea.

3 Wildly excited like a bull, he took the Soma for himself and drank the extract from the three bowls in the three-day Soma ceremony. Indra the Generous seized his thunderbolt to hurl it as a weapon; he killed the first-born of dragons.

4 Indra, when you killed the first-born of dragons and overcame by your own magic the magic of the magicians, at that very moment you brought forth the sun, the sky, and dawn. Since then you have found no enemy to conquer you.

5 With this great weapon, the thunderbolt, Indra killed the shoulderless Vrtra, his greatest enemy. Like the trunk of a tree whose branches have been lopped off by an axe, the dragon lies flat upon the ground.

6 For, muddled by drunkenness like one who is no soldier, Vrtra challenged the great hero who had overcome the mighty and who drank Soma to the dregs. Unable to withstand the onslaught of his weapons, he found Indra an enemy to conquer him and was shattered, his nose crushed.

7 Without feet or hands he fought against Indra, who struck him on the nape of the neck with his thunderbolt. The steer who wished to become the equal of the bull bursting with seed, Vrtra lay broken in many places.

8 Over him as he lay there like a broken reed the swelling waters flowed for man. Those waters that Vrtra had enclosed with his power—the dragon now lay at their feet.

9 The vital energy of Vrtra's mother ebbed away, for Indra had hurled his deadly weapon at her. Above was the mother, below was the son; Danu lay down like a cow with her calf.

10 In the midst of the channels of the waters which never stood still or rested, the body was hidden. The waters flow over Vrtra's secret place; he who found Indra an enemy to conquer him sank into long darkness.

11 The waters who had the Dasa for their husband, the dragon for their protector, were imprisoned like the cows imprisoned by the Panis. When he killed Vrtra he split open the outlet of the waters that had been closed.

12 Indra, you became a hair of a horse's tail when Vrtra struck you on the corner of the mouth. You, the one god, the brave one, you won the cows; you won the Soma; you released the seven streams so that they could flow.

13 No use was the lightning and thunder, fog and hail that he had scattered about, when the dragon and Indra fought. Indra the Generous remained victorious for all time to come.

14 What avenger of the dragon did you see, Indra, that fear entered your heart when you had killed him? Then you crossed the ninety-nine streams like the frightened eagle crossing the realms of earth and air.

15 Indra, who wields the thunderbolt in his hand, is the king of that which moves and that which rests, of the tame and of the horned. He rules the people as their king, encircling all this as a rim encircles spokes.

Rig Veda, 1.32, from the *Rig Veda*, Wendy Doniger, trans. (New York: Penguin Books, 1981), 149–151.

A Prayer to the God Agni

Agni is the god of fire, a prominent figure in the Vedas. His most important function is to convey sacrificial offerings from devotee to the other gods.

1 I pray to Agni, the household priest who is the god of the sacrifice, the one who chants and invokes and brings most treasure.
2 Agni earned the prayers of the ancient sages, and of those of the present, too; he will bring the gods here.
3 Through Agni one may win wealth, and growth from day to day, glorious and most abounding in heroic sons.
4 Agni, the sacrificial ritual that you encompass on all sides—only that one goes to the gods.
5 Agni, the priest with the sharp sight of a poet, the true and most brilliant, the god will come with the gods.
6 Whatever good you wish to do for the one who worships you, Agni, through you, O Angiras, that comes true.
7 To you, Agni, who shine upon darkness, we come day after day, bringing our thoughts and homage.
8 To you, the king over sacrifices, the shining guardian of the Order, growing in your own house.
9 Be easy for us to reach, like a father to his son. Abide with us, Agni, for our happiness.

Rig Veda, 1.1, from the *Rig Veda*, Wendy Doniger, trans. (New York: Penguin Books, 1981), 99.

Selections from the *Upanishads*

Chandogya Upanishad

The *Upanishads* are thought to be evocative meditations on great truths. In the following two excerpts, a father explains to an arrogant son important concepts of spiritual wisdom.

CHAPTER 6: 1

1 There was one Śvetaketu, the son of Āruni. One day his father told him: 'Śvetaketu, take up the celibate life of a student, for there is no one in our family, my son, who has not studied and is the kind of Brahmin who is so only because of birth.'

2 So he went away to become a student at the age of 12 and, after learning all the Vedas, returned when he was 24, swell-headed, thinking himself to be learned, and arrogant.

3 His father then said to him: 'Śvetaketu, here you are, my son, swell-headed, thinking yourself to be learned, and arrogant; so you must have surely asked about that rule of substitution by which one hears what has not been heard of before, thinks of what has not been thought of before, and perceives what has not been perceived before?'

'How indeed does that rule of substitution work, sir?'

4 It is like this, son. By means of just one lump of clay one would perceive everything made of clay—the transformation is a verbal handle, a name—while the reality is just this: "It's clay."

Upanishads, Patrick Olivelle, trans., *Chandogya Upanishad*, 6.1, 12; *Brihadaranyaka Upanishad*, 2.4 (Oxford: Oxford University Press, 1996).

5 'It is like this, son. By means of just one copper trinket one would perceive everything made of copper—the transformation is a verbal handle, a name—while the reality is just this: "It's copper."

6 'It is like this, son. By means of just one nail-cutter one would perceive everything made of iron—the transformation is a verbal handle, a name—while the reality is just this: "It's iron." That, son, is how this rule of substitution works.'

7 'Surely, those illustrious men did not know this, for had they known, how could they have not told it to me? So, why don't you, sir, tell me yourself?'

'All right, son,' he replied.

CHAPTER 6: 12

1 'Bring a banyan fruit.'

'Here it is, sir.'

'Cut it up.'

'I've cut it up, sir.'

'What do you see there?'

'These quite tiny seeds, sir.'

'Now, take one of them and cut it up.'

'I've cut one up, sir.'

'What do you see there?'

'Nothing, sir.'

2 Then he told him: 'This finest essence here, son, that you can't even see—look how on account of that finest essence this huge banyan tree stands here.

'Believe, my son:

3 The finest essence here—that constitutes the self of this whole world; that is the truth; that is the self (*atman*). And that's how you are, Śvetaketu.'

'Sir. teach me more.'

'Very well, son.'

A teacher of spiritual wisdom explains the counterintuitive notion of one's soul becoming one with Brahman.

Brihadaranyaka Upanishad

CHAPTER 2: 4

12 'It is like this. When a chunk of salt is thrown in water, it dissolves into that very water, and it cannot be picked up in any way. Yet, from whichever place one may take a sip, the salt is there! In the same way this Immense Being has no limit or boundary and is a single mass of perception. It arises out of and together with these beings and disappears after them—so I say, after death there is no awareness.'

After Yajnavalkya said this,

13 Maitreyi exclaimed: 'Now, sir, you have totally confused me by saying "after death there is no awareness."' He replied:

'Look, I haven't said anything confusing; this body, you see, has the capacity to perceive.'

14 For when there is a duality of some kind, then the one can smell the other, the one can see the other, the one can hear the other, the one can greet the other, the one can think of the other, and the one can perceive the other. When, however, the Whole has become one's very self (*atman*), then who is there for one to smell and by what means? Who is there for one to see and by what means? Who is there for one to hear and by what means? Who is there for one to greet and by what means? Who is there for one to think of and by what means? Who is there for one to perceive and by what means?

'By what means can one perceive him by means of whom one perceives this whole world? Look—by what means can one perceive the perceiver?'

Selections from the *Bhagavad-Gita*

In this story of war and death, the *Bhagavad-Gita* confronts the moral questions and conflicts that arise in Hindu concepts and practice. Here Krishna (who is God masquerading as a charioteer) instructs Arjuna in morality, duty, and metaphysics. Krishna tells Arjuna to join the battle, for it is Arjuna's dharma as a warrior to fight. But duty must be performed "without attachment," without a desire for the results of the action. Krishna tries to ease Arjuna's grief over the deaths of his kinsmen by explaining the true nature of the soul. Krishna insists that several paths (marga) can lead to moksha, but the path to liberation that he speaks of most often is devotion to a personal god (bhakti-marga).

FIRST TEACHING: ARJUNA'S DEJECTION

Arjuna saw them standing there:
fathers, grandfathers, teachers,
uncles, brothers, sons,
26 grandsons, and friends.
He surveyed his elders
and companions in both armies,
all his kinsmen
27 assembled together.
Dejected, filled with strange pity,
he said this:
"Krishna, I see my kinsmen
28 gathered here, wanting war.
My limbs sink,
my mouth is parched,
my body trembles,
29 the hair bristles on my flesh.
I see omens of chaos,
Krishna; I see no good
in killing my kinsmen
31 in battle.
I do not want to kill them
even if I am killed, Krishna;
not for kingship of all three worlds,
35 much less for the earth!
Honor forbids us to kill
our cousins, Dhritarashtra's sons;
how can we know happiness
37 if we kill our own kinsmen?
How can we ignore the wisdom
of turning from this evil
when we see the sin
39 of family destruction, Krishna?
When the family is ruined,
the timeless laws of family duty
perish; and when duty is lost,
40 chaos overwhelms the family.
In overwhelming chaos, Krishna,
women of the family are corrupted;
and when women are corrupted,
41 disorder is born in society."
Saying this in the time of war,
Arjuna slumped into the chariot
and laid down his bow and arrows,
47 his mind tormented by grief.

The Bhagavad Gita, selections from Teachings 1, 2, 4, 15, Barbara Stoller Miller, trans. (New York: Bantam Books, 1986), 24–27, 31–34, 36–38, 49–50, 54–55, 130.

SECOND TEACHING: PHILOSOPHY AND SPIRITUAL DISCIPLINE

LORD KRISHNA

You grieve for those beyond grief,
and you speak words of insight;
but learned men do not grieve
11 for the dead or the living.
Never have I not existed,
nor you, nor these kings;
and never in the future
12 shall we cease to exist.
Just as the embodied self
enters childhood, youth, and old age,
so does it enter another body;
13 this does not confound a steadfast man.
Nothing of nonbeing comes to be,
nor does being cease to exist;
the boundary between these two
16 is seen by men who see reality.
Our bodies are known to end,
but the embodied self is enduring,
indestructible, and immeasurable;
18 therefore, Arjuna, fight the battle!
He who thinks this self a killer
and he who thinks it killed,
both fail to understand;
19 it does not kill, nor is it killed.
It is not born,
it does not die;
having been,
it will never not be;
unborn, enduring,
constant, and primordial,
it is not killed
20 when the body is killed.
Arjuna, when a man knows the self
to be indestructible, enduring, unborn,
unchanging, how does he kill
21 or cause anyone to kill?
Death is certain for anyone born,
and birth is certain for the dead;
since the cycle is inevitable,
27 you have no cause to grieve!
If you are killed, you win heaven;
if you triumph, you enjoy the earth;
therefore, Arjuna, stand up
37 and resolve to fight the battle!
Be intent on action,
not on the fruits of action;
avoid attraction to the fruits
47 and attachment to inaction!
Perform actions, firm in discipline,
relinquishing attachment;
be impartial to failure and success—
48 this equanimity is called discipline.
Even when a man of wisdom
tries to control them, Arjuna,
the bewildering senses
60 attack his mind with violence.
Controlling them all,
with discipline he should focus on me;
when his senses are under control,
61 his insight is sure.
Brooding about sensuous objects
makes attachment to them grow;
from attachment desire arises,
62 from desire anger is born.
From anger comes confusion;
from confusion memory lapses;
from broken memory understanding is lost;
63 from loss of understanding, he is ruined.
But a man of inner strength
whose senses experience objects
without attraction and hatred,
64 in self-control, finds serenity.
In serenity, all his sorrows
dissolve;
his reason becomes serene,
65 his understanding sure.
Without discipline,
he has no understanding or inner power;
without inner power, he has no peace;
66 and without peace where is joy?
As the mountainous depths
of the ocean

are unmoved when waters
rush into it,
so the man unmoved
when desires enter him
attains a peace that eludes
70 the man of many desires.

FOURTH TEACHING: KNOWLEDGE

LORD KRISHNA

I have passed through many births
and so have you;
I know them all,
5 but you do not, Arjuna.
Though myself unborn, undying,
the lord of creatures, I fashion nature,
which is mine, and I come into being
6 through my own magic.
Whenever sacred duty decays
and chaos prevails,
then, I create
7 myself, Arjuna.
To protect men of virtue
and destroy men who do evil,
to set the standard of sacred duty,
8 I appear in age after age.
He who really knows my divine
birth and my action, escapes rebirth
when he abandons the body—
9 and he comes to me, Arjuna.
As they seek refuge in me,
I devote myself to them;
Arjuna, men retrace
11 my path in every way.
Desiring success in their actions,
men sacrifice here to the gods;
in the world of man
12 success comes quickly from action.
No purifier equals knowledge,
and in time
the man of perfect discipline
38 discovers this in his own spirit.
Faithful, intent, his senses
subdued, he gains knowledge;
gaining knowledge,
39 he soon finds perfect peace.
An ignorant man is lost, faithless,
and filled with self-doubt;
a soul that harbors doubt has no joy,
40 not in this world or the next.
Arjuna, actions do not bind
a man in possession of himself,
who renounces action through discipline
41 and severs doubt with knowledge.
So sever the ignorant doubt
in your heart with the sword
of self-knowledge, Arjuna!
42 Observe your discipline! Arise!

FIFTEENTH TEACHING: THE TRUE SPIRIT OF MAN

LORD KRISHNA

I penetrate the earth
and sustain creatures by my strength;
becoming Soma, the liquid of moonlight,
13 I nurture all healing herbs.
I am the universal fire
within the body of living beings;
I work with the flow of vital breath
14 to digest the foods that men consume.
I dwell deep
in the heart of everyone;
memory, knowledge,
and reasoning come from me;
I am the object to be known
through all sacred lore;
and I am its knower,
15 the creator of its final truth.

Selections from the *Crest-Jewel of Discrimination*

ADVAITA VEDANTA

In this excerpt Shankara preaches the core concepts of his school of Hindu philosophy known as Advaita Vedanta. He insists that there is only one kind of stuff in the cosmos—Brahman, who alone is real. Brahman is all, and the self is identical to Brahman. And only by freeing ourselves from the delusion that we are separate from Brahman can we achieve liberation.

The Master speaks:

You are blessed indeed! You are drawing near to the goal. Through you, your whole family has become purified, because you long to get free from the bondage of ignorance and reach Brahman.

Children may free their father from his debts, but no other person can free a man from his bondage: he must do it himself.

Others may relieve the suffering caused by a burden that weighs upon the head; but the suffering which comes from hunger and the like can only be relieved by one's self.

The sick man who takes medicine and follows the rules of diet is seen to be restored to health—but not through the efforts of another.

A clear vision of the Reality may be obtained only through our own eyes, when they have been opened by spiritual insight—never through the eyes of some other seer. Through our own eyes we learn what the moon looks like: how could we learn this through the eyes of others?

Those cords that bind us, because of our ignorance, our lustful desires and the fruits of our karma—how could anybody but ourselves untie them, even in the course of innumerable ages?

Neither by the practice of Yoga or of Sankhya philosophy, nor by good works, nor by learning, does liberation come; but only through a realization that Atman and Brahman are one—in no other way.

It is the duty of a king to please his people, but not everybody who pleases the people is fit to be a king. For the people can be pleased by the beauty of a vina's form, and the skill with which its strings are plucked.

Erudition, well-articulated speech, a wealth of words, and skill in expounding the scriptures—these things give pleasure to the learned, but they do not bring liberation.

Study of the scriptures is fruitless as long as Brahman has not been experienced. And when Brahman has been experienced, it is useless to read the scriptures.

A network of words is like a dense forest which causes the mind to wander hither and thither. Therefore, those who know this truth should struggle hard to experience Brahman.

When a man has been bitten by the snake of ignorance he can only be cured by the realization of Brahman. What use are Vedas or scriptures, charms or herbs?

A sickness is not cured by saying the word "medicine." You must take the medicine. Liberation does not come by merely saying the word "Brahman." Brahman must be actually experienced.

Shankara's Crest-Jewel of Discrimination, Swami Prabhavananda and Christopher Isherwood, trans. (Hollywood: Vedanta Press, 1975), 40–41 and 72–74.

Until you allow this apparent universe to dissolve from your consciousness—until you have experienced Brahman—how can you find liberation just by saying the word "Brahman"? The result is merely a noise.

THAT ART THOU

The scriptures establish the absolute identity of Atman and Brahman by declaring repeatedly: "That art Thou." The terms "Brahman" and "Atman," in their true meaning, refer to "That" and "Thou" respectively.

In their literal, superficial meaning, "Brahman" and "Atman" have opposite attributes, like the sun and the glow-worm, the king and his servant, the ocean and the well, or Mount Meru and the atom. Their identity is established only when they are understood in their true significance, and not in a superficial sense.

"Brahman" may refer to God, the ruler of Maya and creator of the universe. The "Atman" may refer to the individual soul, associated with the five coverings which are effects of Maya. Thus regarded, they possess opposite attributes. But this apparent opposition is caused by Maya and her effects. It is not real, therefore, but superimposed.

These attributes caused by Maya and her effects are superimposed upon God and upon the individual soul. When they have been completely eliminated, neither soul nor God remains. If you take the kingdom from a king and the weapons from a soldier, there is neither soldier nor king.

The scriptures repudiate any idea of a duality in Brahman. Let a man seek illumination in the knowledge of Brahman, as the scriptures direct. Then those attributes, which our ignorance has superimposed upon Brahman, will disappear.

"Brahman is neither the gross nor the subtle universe. The apparent world is caused by our imagination, in its ignorance. It is not real. It is like seeing the snake in the rope. It is like a passing dream"—that is how a man should practice spiritual discrimination, and free himself from his consciousness of this objective world. Then let him meditate upon the identity of Brahman and Atman, and so realize the truth.

Through spiritual discrimination, let him understand the true inner meaning of the terms "Brahman" and "Atman," thus realizing their absolute identity. See the reality in both, and you will find that there is but one.

When we say: "This man is that same Devadatta whom I have previously met," we establish a person's identity by disregarding those attributes superimposed upon him by the circumstances of our former meeting. In just the same way, when we consider the scriptural teaching "That art Thou," we must disregard those attributes which have been superimposed upon "That" and "Thou."

The wise men of true discrimination understand that the essence of both Brahman and Atman is Pure Consciousness, and thus realize their absolute identity. The identity of Brahman and Atman is declared in hundreds of holy texts.

Give up the false notion that the Atman is this body, this phantom. Meditate upon the truth that the "Atman" is "neither gross nor subtle, neither short nor tall," that it is self-existent, free as the sky, beyond the grasp of thought. Purify the heart until you know that "I am Brahman." Realize your own Atman, the pure and infinite consciousness.

Just as a clay jar or vessel is understood to be nothing but clay, so this whole universe, born of Brahmin, essentially Brahman, is Brahman only—for there is nothing else but Brahman, nothing beyond That. That is the reality. That is our Atman. Therefore, "That art Thou"—pure, blissful, supreme Brahman, the one without a second.

The Path of Devotion: *Bhagavata Purana*

In this passage from the *Bhagavata Purana* (the most popular of the Puranas), the sage Kapila is actually Vishnu incarnate. He teaches his mother (Devahuti) the proper form of devotion (bhakti) and distinguishes between worship that is empty and that which reveals the true presence of the Lord in all things.

[The Lord, Sage Kapila, tells His mother Devahuti:] Blessed lady! The path of devotion is conceived in various ways according to different approaches; for by reason of nature, qualities, and approach, the minds of men differ.

That devotee who, in a harmful manner, with vanity and intolerance, goes about ostentatiously making distinctions between one being and another, and practices devotion, is of the lowest type, impelled by ignorance.

Contemplating material enjoyment, fame, or riches, he who, still making distinctions, worships Me in images, etc., is of the middling type, impelled by desire.

He who adores Me with a view to put an end to all actions [good or bad] or offering up all his actions to Me, the Supreme Being, or worships Me because I must be worshiped, he is of the superior type, though he has yet the sense of difference. . . .

The characteristic of pure devotion to the Supreme Being is that it has no motive and is incessant. . . .

That devotion is described as absolute by which one transcends the three dispositions [purity, passion, and darkness] and renders himself fit to become one with Me. . . .

I am always present in all beings as their soul and yet, ignoring Me, mortal man conducts the mockery of image-worship. He who ignores Me resident in all beings as the Soul and Master, and, in his ignorance, takes to images, verily pours oblations on ash [i.e., worships in vain]. The mind of that man who hates Me abiding in another's body, who, in his pride, sees invidious distinctions and is inimically disposed to all beings, never attains tranquility. Blessed lady! when the worshiper is one who insults living beings, I am not satisfied with his worship in My image, however elaborate the rites and manifold the materials of his worship. Doing one's appointed duty, one should adore Me, the Master, in images and the like, only so long as one is not able to realize in one's own heart Me who am established in every being. That man of invidious perception who draws the line between himself and another, him Death pursues with his dangerous fear.

Therefore, with charity and honor and with friendship toward all and a nondifferentiating outlook, one should worship Me, the Soul of all beings, as enshrined in all beings. . . .

Honoring them, one should mentally bow to all the beings, realizing that the Lord the Master has entered them with an aspect of His own being.

Bhagavata Purana, R. N. Dandekar, trans., in *Sources of Indian Tradition* (New York: Columbia University Press, 1988), 323–324.

Shiva Purana

This Purana dramatizes an unorthodox view of how people may achieve release from samsara through bhakti. The story is that a bad man who had been wicked all his life was able to achieve release by performing one causal, accidental act of devotion to Shiva just before dying.

Once upon a time, in the city of the Kiratas,[1] there was a Brahmin who was not at all strong when it came to sacred knowledge. He was a poor man, a seller of liquors, and he turned away from the gods and from dharma. He had ceased to perform the ritual of bathing at twilight and he devoted himself instead to making a living like a Vaishya; he was called Devaraja ("King of the Gods"), and he used to deceive people who trusted him. He took as his prey various sorts of people—Brahmins, Kshatriyas, Vaishyas, Shudras, and even people lower than that—and he would kill them and take their money. Through this violation of dharma he eventually accumulated great wealth, but he was such an evil man that he didn't use even a small part of his money for dharma.

One day, that god upon the earth went to a pond to bathe, and there he saw a whore named "Gorgeous" who excited him wildly. The beautiful woman was delighted when she realized that a rich Brahmin was in her power; and she satisfied his mind with her professional banter. He decided to make her his wife, and she to make him her husband; thus overpowered by lust, they made love for a long time. Sitting, lying, drinking, eating, and playing, the two of them constantly seduced one another, like newlyweds. Though his mother and father and (first) wife kept trying to stop him, he paid no attention to their words, so intent was he on his evil ways.

One day he became so impatient that he completely lost control, and in the night he killed his mother, father, and wife as they slept; and then that wretch took their money. He was so out of his mind with lust that he gave that whore all his own money as well as the money that he had taken from his father and the others. Then that sinner, the lowest of Brahmins, took to eating what should not be eaten, and he became addicted to drinking wine; he always ate out of the same plate as his whore.

Now, as fate would have it, one day he came to the town of Pratisthanam, and there he saw a Shiva temple filled with good people. While he stayed there, constantly hearing the *Shiva Purana* recited from the mouths of the Brahmins, that Brahmin was laid low by a fever. At the end of a month, Devaraja was dead of that fever; the minions of Yama (god of the dead) bound him with nooses and led him by force to the city of Yama. At the same time, the hosts of Shiva, shining with their tridents in their hands, smeared with white ashes all over their bodies, wearing the rosaries of Shiva, set out from the world of Shiva and came in fury to the city of Yama. They beat up the messengers of Yama and reviled them over and over; they set Devaraja free, put him up on their marvelous celestial chariot, and got ready to go to Kailasa (the mountain of Shiva).

Then a great tumult arose in the middle of the city of Yama, and (Yama) the King of Dharma heard it and came out of his palace. There he saw the four messengers like four more Rudras before his eyes, and as he knew dharma, the King of Dharma honored them with the proper ritual. Then, through his eye of knowledge, Yama realized all that had happened, but he was too frightened to ask a single question of the noble messengers of Shiva. When they had been honored and asked for their blessings, they went to Kailasa and gave (Devaraja) to Shiva,

Shiva Purana, 1.2.15–40, Wendy Doniger O'Flaherty, trans., in *The Norton Anthology of World Religions* (New York: W. W. Norton, 2015), 236–238.

the ocean of compassion, and to Amba (the wife of Shiva).

Precious is the reciting of the *Shiva Purana,* the highest purification, by the mere hearing of which even a very evil person attains Release. It is the great place of the eternal Shiva, the highest dwelling, the high spot; those who know the Vedas say that it stands above all worlds. That evil man who, in his greed for money, injured many Brahmins, Kshatriyas, Vaishyas, Shudras, and even other creatures that breathe, the man who killed his mother and father and wife, who slept with a whore and drank wine, the Brahmin Devaraja went there and in a moment became released.

NOTE

1. A tribal people, on the borders of Hinduism. For Devaraja to live among such polluting, low-caste people in the first place would be sufficient to seal his doom, *under normal conditions.*

The Goddess Durga

DAVID R. KINSLEY

In his treatise on Hindu goddesses, the scholar David Kinsley describes the attributes, powers, and history of the warrior goddess and demon-slayer Durga.

One of the most impressive and formidable goddesses of the Hindu pantheon—and one of the most popular—is the goddess Durga. Her primary mythological function is to combat demons who threaten the stability of the cosmos. In this role she is depicted as a great battle queen with many arms, each of which wields a weapon. She rides a fierce lion and is described as irresistible in battle. The demon she is most famous for defeating is Mahisa, the buffalo demon. Her most popular epithet is Mahisamardini, the slayer of Mahisa, and her most common iconographic representation shows her defeating Mahisa.

At a certain point in her history Durga becomes associated with the god Siva as his wife. In this role Durga assumes domestic characteristics and is often identified with the goddess Parvati. She also takes on the role of mother in her later history. At her most important festival, Durga Puja, she is shown flanked by four deities identified as her children: Karttikeya, Ganesa, Sarasvati, and Laksmi.

It also seems clear that Durga has, or at least at some point in her history had, a close connection with the crops or with the fertility of vegetation. Her festival, which is held at harvest time, associates her with plants, and she also receives blood offerings, which may suggest the renourishment of her powers of fertility. . . .

The best-known account of Durga's origin, however, is told in connection with her defeat of the demon Mahisa. After performing heroic austerities, Mahisa was granted the boon that he would be invincible to all opponents except a woman. He subsequently defeated the gods in battle and usurped their positions. The gods then assembled and, angry at the thought of Mahisa's triumph and their apparent

David R. Kinsley, *Hindu Goddesses* (Berkeley: University of California Press, 1986), 95–97.

inability to do anything about it, emitted their fiery energies. This great mass of light and strength congealed into the body of a beautiful woman, whose splendor spread through the universe. The parts of her body were formed from the male gods. Her face was formed from Siva, her hair from Yama, her arms from Visnu, and so on. Similarly, each of the male deities from whom she had been created gave her a weapon. Siva gave her his trident, Visnu gave her his *cakra* (a discus-like weapon), Vayu his bow and arrows, and so on. Equipped by the gods and supplied by the god Himalaya with a lion as her vehicle, Durga, the embodied strength of the gods, then roared mightily, causing the earth to shake.

The Spirit of Indian Philosophy

SARVEPALLI RADHAKRISHNAN

In this brief discussion of Indian philosophy, Radhakrishnan examines the attitudes that have been characteristically stressed by the many Indian philosophies. In general, Indian philosophy, he says, emphasizes (1) the spiritual, (2) a belief in the close relationship between philosophy and life, (3) introspection, (4) philosophical idealism, (5) the belief that intuition is the only method for knowing the ultimate, (6) acceptance of authority, and (7) an overall synthesizing tradition.

Indian philosophy, it has been noted, is extremely complex. Through the ages the Indian philosophical mind has probed deeply into many aspects of human experience and the external world. Although some methods, such as the experimental method of modern science, have been relatively less prominent than others, not only the problems of Indian philosophy but also the methods used and the conclusions reached in the pursuit of truth have certainly been as far-reaching in their extent, variety, and depth as those of other philosophical traditions. The six basic systems and the many sub-systems of Hinduism, the four chief schools of Buddhism, the two schools of Jainism, and the materialism of the Carvaka are evidence enough of the diversity of views in Indian philosophy. The variety of the Indian perspective is unquestionable. Accordingly, it is very difficult to cite any specific doctrines or methods as characteristic of Indian philosophy as a whole and applicable to all the multitudinous systems and subsystems developed through nearly four millenniums of Indian philosophical speculation.

Nevertheless, in certain respects there is what might be called a distinct spirit of Indian philosophy. This is exemplified by certain attitudes which are fairly characteristic of the Indian philosophical mind or which stand as points of view that have been emphasized characteristically by Indians in their philosophies.

1. The chief mark of Indian philosophy in general is its concentration upon the spiritual. Both in life and in philosophy the spiritual motive is predominant in India. Except for the relatively minor materialistic school of the Carvaka and related doctrines,

Sarvepalli Radhakrishnan, *A Sourcebook in Indian Philosophy* (Princeton, NJ: Princeton University Press, 1957), xxii–xxviii.

philosophy in India conceives man to be spiritual in nature, is interested primarily in his spiritual destiny, and relates him in one way or another to a universe which is also spiritual in essential character. Neither man nor the universe is looked upon as physical in essence, and material welfare is never recognized as the goal of human life, except by the Carvaka. Philosophy and religion are intimately related because philosophy itself is regarded as a spiritual adventure, and also because the motivation both in philosophy and in religion concerns the spiritual way of life in the here-and-now and the eventual spiritual salvation of man in relation to the universe. Practically all of Indian philosophy, from its beginning in the Vedas to the present day, has striven to bring about a socio-spiritual reform in the country, and philosophical literature has taken many forms, mythological, popular, or technical, as the circumstances required, in order to promote such spiritual life. The problems of religion have always given depth and power and purpose to the Indian philosophical mind and spirit.

2. Another characteristic view of Indian philosophy is the belief in the intimate relationship of philosophy and life. This attitude of the practical application of philosophy to life is found in every school of Indian philosophy. While natural abundance and material prosperity paved the way for the rise of philosophical speculation, philosophy has never been considered a mere intellectual exercise. The close relationship between theory and practice, doctrine and life, has always been outstanding in Indian thought. Every Indian system seeks the truth, not as academic "knowledge for its own sake," but to learn the truth which shall make men free. This is not, as it has been called, the modern pragmatic attitude. It is much larger and much deeper than that. It is not the view that truth is measured in terms of the practical, but rather that the truth is the only sound guide for practice, that truth alone has efficacy as a guide for man in his search for salvation. Every major system of Indian philosophy takes its beginning from the practical and tragic problems of life and searches for the truth in order to solve the problem of man's distress in the world in which he finds himself. There has been no teaching which remained a mere word of mouth or dogma of schools. Every doctrine has been turned into a passionate conviction, stirring the heart of man and quickening his breath, and completely transforming his personal nature. In India, philosophy is for life; it is to be lived. It is not enough to *know* the truth; the truth must be *lived*. The goal of the Indian is not to know the ultimate truth but to *realize* it, to become one with it.

Another aspect of the intimate inseparability of theory and practice, philosophy and life, in Indian philosophy is to be found in the universally prevalent demand for moral purification as an imperative preliminary for the would-be student of philosophy or searcher after truth. Samkara's classic statement of this demand calls for a knowledge of the distinction between the eternal and the noneternal, that is, a questioning tendency in the inquirer; the subjugation of all desire for the fruits of action either in this life or in a hereafter, a renunciation of all petty desire, personal motive, and practical interest; tranquility, self-control, renunciation, patience, peace of mind, and faith; and a desire for release (*moksa*) as the supreme goal of life.

3. Indian philosophy is characterized by the introspective attitude and the introspective approach to reality. Philosophy is thought of as *atmavidya*, knowledge of the self. Philosophy can start either with the external world or with the internal world of man's inner nature, the self of man. In its pursuit of the truth, Indian philosophy has always been strongly dominated by concern with the inner life and self of man rather than the external world of physical nature. Physical science, though developed extensively in the Golden Age of Indian culture, was never considered the road to ultimate truth; truth is to be sought and found within. The subjective, then, rather than the objective, becomes the focus of interest in Indian philosophy, and, therefore, psychology and ethics are considered more important as aspects or branches of philosophy than the sciences which study physical nature. This is not to say that the Indian mind has not studied the physical world; in fact, on the contrary, India's achievements in the realm of positive science were at one time truly outstanding, especially in the mathematical sciences such as algebra, astronomy, and geometry, and in the applications of these basic sciences to numerous phases of human activity.

Zoology, botany, medicine, and related sciences have also been extremely prominent in Indian thought. Be this as it may, the Indian, from time immemorial, has felt that the inner spirit of man is the most significant clue to his reality and to that of the universe, more significant by far than the physical or the external.

4. This introspective interest is highly conducive to idealism, of course, and consequently most Indian philosophy is idealistic in one form or another. The tendency of Indian philosophy, especially Hinduism, has been in the direction of monistic idealism. Almost all Indian philosophy believes that reality is *ultimately* one and *ultimately* spiritual. Some systems have seemed to espouse dualism or pluralism, but even these have been deeply permeated by a strong monistic character. If we concentrate our attention upon the underlying spirit of Indian philosophy rather than its variety of opinions, we shall find that this spirit is embodied in the tendency to interpret life and reality in the way of monistic idealism. This rather unusual attitude is attributable to the nonrigidity of the Indian mind and to the fact that the attitude of monistic idealism is so plastic and dynamic that it takes many forms and expresses itself even in seemingly conflicting doctrines. These are not conflicting doctrines in fact, however, but merely different expressions of an underlying conviction which provides basic unity to Indian philosophy as a whole.

Materialism undoubtedly had its day in India, and, according to sporadic records and constant and determined efforts on the part of other systems to denounce it, the doctrine apparently enjoyed widespread acceptance at one time. Nevertheless, materialism could not hold its own; its adherents have been few in number, and its positive influence has been negligible. Indian philosophy has not been oblivious to materialism; rather, it has known it, has overcome it, and has accepted idealism as the only tenable view, whatever specific form that idealism might take.

5. Indian philosophy makes unquestioned and extensive use of reason, but intuition is accepted as the only method through which the ultimate can be known. Reason, intellectual knowledge, is not enough. Reason is not useless or fallacious, but it is insufficient. To know reality one must have an actual experience of it. One does not merely *know* the truth in Indian philosophy; one *realizes* it. The word which most aptly describes philosophy in India is *darsana*, which comes from the verbal root *drs*, meaning "to see." "To see" is to have a direct intuitive experience of the object, or, rather, to realize it in the sense of becoming one with it. No complete knowledge is possible as long as there is the relationship of the subject on one hand and the object on the other. Later developments in Indian philosophy, from the time of the beginning of the systems, have all depended in large part upon reason for the systematic formulation of doctrines and systems, for rational demonstration or justification, and in polemical conflicts of system against system. Nevertheless, all the systems, except the Carvaka, agree that there is a higher way of knowing reality, beyond the reach of reason, namely, the direct perception or experience of the ultimate reality, which cannot be known by reason in any of its forms. Reason can demonstrate the truth, but reason cannot discover or reach the truth. While reason may be the method of philosophy in its more intellectualistic sense, intuition is the only method of comprehending the ultimate. Indian philosophy is thus characterized by an ultimate dependence upon intuition, along with the recognition of the efficacy of reason and intellect when applied in their limited capacity and with their proper function.

6. Another characteristic of Indian philosophy, one which is closely related to the preceding one, is its so-called acceptance of authority. Although the systems of Indian philosophy vary in the degree to which they are specifically related to the ancient *shruti*, not one of the systems—orthodox or unorthodox, except the Carvaka—openly stands in violation of the accepted intuitive insights of its ancient seers, whether it be the Hindu seers of the *Upanishads*, the intuitive experience of the Buddha, or the similarly intuitive wisdom of Mahavira, the founder of Jainism, as we have it today. Indian philosophers have always been conscious of tradition and, as has been indicated before, the great system-builders of later periods claimed to be merely commentators, explaining the traditional wisdom of the past. While the specific doctrines of the past may be changed by interpretation, the general spirit and frequently the basic concepts are

retained from age to age. Reverence for authority does not militate against progress, but it does lend a unity of spirit by providing a continuity of thought which has rendered philosophy especially significant in Indian life and solidly unified against any philosophical attitude contradicting its basic characteristics of spirituality, inwardness, intuition, and the strong belief that the truth is to be lived, not merely known.

The charge of indulging in an exaggerated respect for authority may be legitimately leveled against some of Indian philosophy, but this respect for the past is rooted in the deep conviction that those who really know reality are those who have *realized* the truth and that it is to them that we must turn ultimately, beyond all our power of reasoning, if we are to attain any comprehension of the truth which they saw and realized. As has been said, India has produced a great variety of philosophical doctrines and systems. This has been true despite universal reverence for and acceptance of the authority of the ancient seers as the true discoverers of wisdom. The variety of the systems, even in their basic conceptions, looked at in the light of the prevalent acceptance of authority, reveals the fact that this reverence has not made Indian philosophy a dogmatic religious creed, as is often alleged, but rather a single tone or trend of thought on basic issues. How completely free from traditional bias the systems are is seen, for example, by the fact that the original Samkhya says nothing about the possible existence of God, although it is emphatic in its doctrine of the theoretical undemonstrability of his existence; the Vaisesika and the Yoga, especially the latter, admit the existence of God, but do not consider him to be the creator of the universe; the Mimamsa speaks of God but denies his importance and efficacy in the moral ordering of the world. To emphasize the point further, reference should be made also to the early Buddhist systems, which reject God, and to the Carvakas, who deny God without qualification.

7. Finally, there is the overall synthetic tradition which is essential to the spirit and method of Indian philosophy. This is as old as the *Rg Veda*, where the seers realized that true religion comprehends all religions, so that "God is one but men call him by many names." Indian philosophy is clearly characterized by the synthetic approach to the various aspects of experience and reality. Religion and philosophy, knowledge and conduct, intuition and reason, man and nature, God and man, noumenon and phenomena, are all brought into harmony by the synthesizing tendency of the Indian mind. The Hindu is prone to believe even that all the six systems, as well as their varieties of subsystems, are in harmony with one another, in fact, that they complement one another in the total vision, which is one. As contrasted with Western philosophy, with its analytic approach to reality and experience, Indian philosophy is fundamentally synthetic. The basic texts of Indian philosophy treat not only one phase of experience and reality, but of the full content of the philosophic sphere. Metaphysics, epistemology, ethics, religion, psychology, facts, and value are not cut off one from the other but are treated in their natural unity as aspects of one life and experience or of a single comprehensive reality.

It is this synthetic vision of Indian philosophy which has made possible the intellectual and religious tolerance which has become so pronounced in Indian thought and in the Indian mind throughout the ages. Recent squabbles between religious communities, bred of new political factionalism, are not outgrowths of the Indian mind but, instead, are antagonistic to its unique genius for adaptability and tolerance, which takes all groups and all communities into its one truth and one life.

Selections from *The Secret Garland*

The "secret garland" refers to the sumptuous lines of poetry by the ninth-century poet Antal, a woman Hindu mystic with a gift for capturing in verse her experiences of the divine. She writes that the great and powerful god Vishnu is her lover—ironic since Antal is herself now revered as a goddess.

1. Markali Tinkal

It is the month of Markali
the moon is full and the day auspicious.
Come to bathe
you precious girls, richly adorned
    dear to Ayarpati,
        land of abounding prosperity.
The son of Nandagopa
    fierce with his sharp spear,
the youthful lion-cub of Yasoda
    woman of matchless eyes,
dark-hued and lotus eyed
his face, is both the sun and the moon
that Narayana alone can give us the *parai*-drum.
Undertake this vow
And the whole world will rejoice.

2. Vaiyattu Valvirkal

All you people of this world,
consider the rituals of our *pavai*-vow:
We sing the praises of the supreme one
who rests silently
upon the ocean of milk.
We eat no ghee and drink no milk
and daily, we bathe before the dawn.
Kohl does not darken our eyes
and flowers do not adorn our hair.
We do nothing that is wrong
and speak nothing that is evil
Instead, we give freely
and offer alms to those in need
    We live joyously,
    trusting that all this will liberate us.

3. Oriki Ulakalanta

Singing the names
    of the perfect one who
    spanned the worlds with his feet
    and measured them
we bathe at the break of dawn
and proclaim:
If we undertake this vow
    our land will be free from evil
    rains will fall three times a month
    and the *kayal* will leap agilely
    amidst the thick, tall, red grain
    the spotted bee will sleep
    nestled in the *kuvalai* bloom.
    and when we clasp their heavy udders,
    the great, generous cows
    will fill our pots ceaselessly.
limitless wealth is certain to abound.

4. Ali Malai Kanna

Beloved rain, withhold nothing from us.
You scoop up the ocean and rise up replete and full:
your body dark
    as the form of the primordial lord:
    supreme in the final deluge.
Flash like the flaming discus
Resound like the *valampuri*
    held aloft in the hands of Padmanabha,
    whose shoulders are broad and beautiful.
Rain without delay
    like a shower of arrows
        released from his *sarnga*.
Rain, so we may bathe in the month of Markali

Archand VenKatesan, trans., *The Secret Garland* (Oxford: Oxford University Press, 2010), verses 1–10.

so we may live in this world
and rejoice.

5. Mayanai Mannu

O enigmatic Mayan
king of eternal Mathura of the North
lord who plays
by the great unsullied waters of the Yamuna
radiant beacon
of the cowherd clan,
Damodara
who brightened his mother's womb—
We are pure and
come to you
with these fresh flowers.
we sing of you.
we think of you.
So let all our past misdeeds
and even those still to come
burn
and turn to ash.
O, sing of him!

6. Pullum Cilampina Kan

Listen: even the birds are chirping.
Can you not hear
the vibrant sound of the white conch
from the temple of Garuda's lord?
Wake up, child!
The one
who sucked poison
from the breast
of the demoness
The one
who raised his foot
and destroyed
cunning Sakata
That primordial lord
who rests on his serpent
upon the ocean of milk . . .
Sages and ascetics rise gently
and place *him* in their hearts.
The immense sound
"Hari"
is everywhere
It enters our minds
and we are cooled.

7. Kicu Kicu

Can you not hear
the pervasive
screech and chatter
of the *anaiccattan*?
Witless ghost of a girl
do you not hear
the clink of long necklaces
and the jangle of ornaments,
as the women of Ayarpati
whose hair is fragrant,
swish and turn their churning rods
in the curd?
O you who are our leader
how can you just lie there
even as we sing of Kesava
the essence of Narayana?
O beautiful maiden
come now—open your door.

8. Kilvanam Velenru

As the eastern sky brightens into dawn
the buffaloes let loose for a short while
spread out to graze.
All the girls eager to go, have not gone
but wait for you.
We have come to rouse you
spirited girl
Wake up now.
If we sing of him
and we attain the *parai*-drum
If we go to him,
who ripped open the beak of the bird
who destroyed the terrible wrestlers
that god of gods
he will listen intently and grant us grace.

9. Tamani Matattu

In your mansion,
studded with immaculate gems
surrounded by glowing lamps
and filled with fragrant frankincense
You continue to sleep upon your soft bed
O cousin
won't you unlock your jeweled door?

Mami, wake her!
Is your daughter mute or deaf?
Perhaps, she is simply weary
or entranced into a deep sleep.
We are here singing
"O great, elusive Madhava!"
"Great lord of Vaikuntha!"
Join us and sing his many names.

10. Norruccuvarkam

Dear friend, who wishes to enter heaven
through rituals and vows
Why won't you answer us?
Open your door now.
We praise Narayana
whose dark curls are fragrant with *tulasi*
the immaculate one
who will give us the *parai*-drum
A very long time ago
Kumbhakarna defeated
fell
into the gaping jaws of death.
Did he then gift
his great undisturbed sleep to you?
O listless maiden, rarest of gems
Shake off your sleep
and open this door.

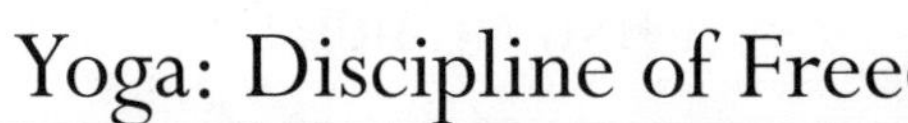

PRACTICES

Yoga: Discipline of Freedom

BARBARA STOLER MILLER

Barbara Miller discusses the ancient practice of yoga and translates the sage Patanjali's discourse on the subject in his *Yoga Sutra*. She says that "yoga is a way to control the physical part of a person to achieve inner spiritual perfection," and Patanjali declares, "Yoga is the cessation of the turnings of thought."

The aim of yoga is to eliminate the control that material nature exerts over the human spirit, to rediscover through introspective practice what the poet T. S. Eliot called the "still point of the turning world." This is a state of perfect equilibrium and absolute spiritual calm, an interior refuge in the chaos of worldly existence. In the view of Patanjali, yogic practice can break habitual ways of thinking and acting that bind one to the corruptions of everyday life. Although the practice of yoga is much more ancient than the *Yoga Sutra,* this brief text represents the earliest known systematic statement of the

Patanjali's Yoga: Discipline of Freedom, Barbara Stoler Miller, trans. (New York: Bantam Books, 1998), 1–2, 29, 31, 33, 34, 38.

philosophical insights and practical psychology that define yoga. Through the centuries since its composition, it has been reinterpreted to meet the needs of widely divergent schools of Indian yoga, for which it remains an essential text.

More broadly, yoga refers to the complex system of physical and spiritual disciplines that is fundamental to Buddhist, Jain, and Hindu religious practice throughout Asia. The meditating figures of the Buddha and the Hindu god Shiva are familiar images in Asian religion. Sculptures show the Buddha seated in calm repose teaching his doctrine of universal compassion and the ascetic god Shiva in postures of perfect discipline. Hindu poets also evoke Shiva in his Himalayan retreat seated cross-legged and completely motionless, absorbed in pure contemplation, like an ocean without waves, the gates of his mind closed to outside intrusion as he meditates on the self within himself.

These descriptions suggest the physical and psychological state of an adept who follows the path prescribed in the *Yoga Sutra.* For Patanjali, physical control is only a precondition of inner spiritual perfection, which is cultivated by confronting the paradoxical nature of memory and thought itself. His analysis exposes the mechanisms whereby we construct false identities and enslave ourselves to a world of pain.

THE NATURE OF YOGA

This is the teaching of yoga. (1)
Yoga is the cessation of the turnings of thought. (2)
When thought ceases, the spirit stands in its true identity as observer to the world. (3)
Otherwise, the observer identifies with the turnings of thought. (4)

THE TURNINGS OF THOUGHT

The turnings of thought, whether corrupted or immune to the forces of corruption, are of five kinds. (5)
They are valid judgment, error, conceptualization, sleep, and memory. (6)
The valid means of judgment are direct perception, inference, and verbal testimony. (7)
Error is false knowledge with no objective basis. (8)
Conceptualization comes from words devoid of substance. (9)
Sleep is the turning of thought abstracted from existence. (10)
Memory is the recollection of objects one has experienced. (11)

PRACTICE AND DISPASSION

Cessation of the turnings of thought comes through dispassion. (12)
Practice is the effort to maintain the cessation of thought. (13)
This practice is firmly grounded when it is performed for a long time without interruption and with zeal. (14)
Dispassion is the sign of mastery over the craving for sensuous objects. (15)
Higher dispassion is a total absence of craving for anything material, which comes by discriminating between spirit and material nature. (16)

WAYS OF STOPPING THOUGHT

Conscious cessation of thought can arise from various forms of conjecture, reflection, enjoyment, and egoism. (17)
Beyond this is a state where only subliminal impressions remain from the practice of stopping thought. (18)
For gods and men unencumbered by physical bodies, but still enmeshed in material nature, the cessation of thought is limited by reliance on the phenomenal world. (19)
For others cessation of thought follows from faith, heroic energy, mindfulness, contemplative calm, and wisdom. (20)
For those who possess a sharp intensity, it is immediate. (21)
Higher than this is cessation beyond distinctions of mild, moderate, or extreme. (22)

TRANQUILITY OF THOUGHT

Tranquility of thought comes through the cultivation of friendship, compassion, joy, and impartiality in spheres of pleasure or pain, virtue or vice. (33)

Or through the measured exhalation and retention of breath. (34)
Or when the mind's activity, arisen in the sense world, is held still. (35)
Or when thought is luminous, free from sorrow. (36)
Or when thought is without passion in the sphere of the senses. (37)
Or when its foundation is knowledge from dreams and sleep. (38)
Or through meditation on a suitable object. (39)
For one whose thought is tranquil, mastery extends from the most minute particle to the vast expanse.

Chanting the Sacred Syllable Om

In Hinduism, Om (or Aum) is the most sacred syllable, a sound said to contain all mantras, all the Vedas, and all essences—perhaps even Brahman itself. By chanting Om, devotees hope to gain this knowledge and to attain liberation. In this excerpt from the *Upanishads*, the meaning and use of Om is explained.

1 OM—one should venerate the High Chant as this syllable, for one begins the High Chant with OM. Here is a further explanation of that syllable.

2 The essence of these beings here is the earth; the essence of the earth is the waters; the essence of the waters is plants; the essence of plants is man; the essence of man is speech; the essence of speech is the Rg verse; the essence of the Rg verse is the Saman chant; the essence of the Saman chant is the High Chant.

3 This High Chant is the quintessence of all essences; it is the highest, the ultimate, the eighth.

4 What ultimately is the Rg verse? What ultimately is the Saman chant? What ultimately is the High Chant? These questions have been the subject of critical enquiry.

5 The Rg is nothing but speech; the Saman is breath; and the High Chant is this syllable OM. Speech and breath, the Rg and the Saman—each of these sets, clearly, is a pair in coitus.

6 This pair in coitus unites in the syllable OM, and when a pair unites in coitus, they satisfy each other's desire.

7 So, when someone knows this and venerates the High Chant as this syllable, he will surely become a man who satisfies desires.

8 Clearly, this syllable signifies assent, for one says "OM" when one assents to something. And assent is nothing but fulfilment. So, when someone knows this and venerates the High Chant as this syllable, he will surely become a man who fulfils desires.

9 It is by means of this syllable that the triple Veda continues—the Adhvaryu priest says "OM" before he issues a call; the Hotr says "OM" before he makes an invocation; and the Udgatr says "OM'" before he sings the High Chant. They do so to honour this very syllable, because of its greatness and because it is the essence.

10 Those who know this and those who do not both perform these rites using this syllable. But knowledge and ignorance are two very different things. Only what is performed with knowledge, with faith, and with an awareness of the hidden connections (*upanishad*) becomes truly potent.

Now, then—that was a further explanation of this very syllable.

Chandogya Upanishad, 1.1.10, in *Upanishads*, Patrick Olivelle, trans. (Oxford: Oxford University Press, 1996).

Bhakti Yoga

This passage is from the *Bhagavad-Gita* where Krishna declares to Arjuna that the best way to achieve a union with Brahman (enlightenment) is not through the rigors of asceticism but through sincere devotion (bhakti) to God.

Arjuna
Who best knows discipline:
men who worship you with devotion,
ever disciplined, or men who worship
1 the imperishable, unmanifest?
Lord Krishna
I deem most disciplined
men of enduring discipline
who worship me with true faith,
2 entrusting their minds to me.
Men reach me too who worship
what is imperishable, ineffable, unmanifest,
omnipresent, inconceivable,
3 immutable at the summit of existence.
Mastering their senses,
with equanimity toward everything,
they reach me, rejoicing
4 in the welfare of all creatures.
It is more arduous when their reason
clings to my unmanifest nature;
for men constrained by bodies,
5 the unmanifest way is hard to attain.
But men intent on me
renounce all actions to me
and worship me, meditating
6 with singular discipline.
When they entrust reason to me,
Arjuna, I soon arise
to rescue them from the ocean
7 of death and rebirth.
Focus your mind on me,
let your understanding enter me;
then you will dwell
8 in me without doubt.
If you cannot concentrate
your thought firmly on me,
then seek to reach me, Arjuna,
9 by discipline in practice.
Even if you fail in practice,
dedicate yourself to action;
performing actions for my sake,
10 you will achieve success.
If you are powerless to do
even this, rely on my discipline,
be self-controlled,
11 and reject all fruit of action.
Knowledge is better than practice,
meditation better than knowledge,
rejecting fruits of action
12 is better still—it brings peace.
One who bears hate for no creature
is friendly, compassionate, unselfish,
free of individuality, patient,
13 the same in suffering and joy.
Content always, disciplined,
self-controlled, firm in his resolve,
his mind and understanding dedicated to me,
14 devoted to me, he is dear to me.
The world does not flee from him,
nor does he flee from the world;
free of delight, rage, fear,
15 and disgust, he is dear to me.
Disinterested, pure, skilled,
indifferent, untroubled,
relinquishing all involvements,
16 devoted to me, he is dear to me.

The Bhagavad Gita, Barbara Stoler Miller, trans. (New York: Bantam Books, 1986), 111–113.

He does not rejoice or hate,
grieve or feel desire;
relinquishing fortune and misfortune,
17 the man of devotion is dear to me.
Impartial to foe and friend,
honor and contempt,
cold and heat, joy and suffering,
18 he is free from attachment.

Neutral to blame and praise,
silent, content with his fate,
unsheltered, firm in thought,
19 the man of devotion is dear to me.
Even more dear to me are devotees
who cherish this elixir of sacred duty
as I have taught it,
20 intent on me in their faith.

Hindu Ritual: Cremation

This passage from the *Rig Veda* consists of instructions on how to correctly conduct the ritual of cremation so the deceased can journey to his ancestors. There is a prayer to Agni, the god of fire, to beg him for a proper cremation of the body ("a good cooking") and a plea to the dead man to prepare himself for the sacrificial burning.

1 Do not burn him entirely, Agni, or engulf him in your flames. Do not consume his skin or his flesh. When you have cooked him perfectly, O knower of creatures, only then send him forth to the fathers.

2 When you cook him perfectly, O knower of creatures, then give him over to the fathers. When he goes on the path that leads away from the breath of life, then he will be led by the will of the gods.

3 [*To the dead man*:] May your eye go to the sun, your life's breath to the wind. Go to the sky or to earth, as is your nature; or go to the waters, if that is your fate. Take root in the plants with your limbs.

4 [*To Agni*:] The goat is your share; burn him with your heat. Let your brilliant light and flame burn him. With your gentle forms, O knower of creatures, carry this man to the world of those who have done good deeds.

5 Set him free again to go to the fathers, Agni, when he has been offered as an oblation in you and wanders with the sacrificial drink. Let him reach his own descendants, dressing himself in a life-span. O knower of creatures, let him join with a body.

6 [*To the dead man*:] Whatever the black bird has pecked out of you, or the ant, the snake, or even a beast of prey, may Agni who eats all things make it whole, and Soma who has entered the Brahmins.

7 Gird yourself with the limbs of the cow as an armour against Agni, and cover yourself with fat and suet, so that he will not embrace you with his impetuous heat in his passionate desire to burn you up.

8 [*To Agni*:] O Agni, do not overturn this cup that is dear to the gods and to those who love Soma, fit for the gods to drink from, a cup in which the immortal gods carouse.

9 I send the flesh-eating fire far away. Let him go to those whose king is Yama, carrying away all impurities. But let that other, the knower of creatures, come here and carry the oblation to the gods, since he knows the way in advance.

The Rig Veda, 10.16, Wendy Doniger, trans. (New York: Penguin, 1981), 49–50.

10 The flesh-eating fire has entered your house, though he sees there the other, the knower of creatures; I take that god away to the sacrifice of the fathers. Let him carry the heated drink to the farthest dwelling-place.

11 Agni who carries away the corpse, who gives sacrifice to the fathers who are strengthened by truth—let him proclaim the oblation to the gods and to the fathers.

12 [*To the new fire*:] Joyously would we put you in place, joyously would we kindle you. Joyously carry the joyous fathers here to eat the oblation.

13 Now, Agni, quench and revive the very one you have burnt up. Let Kiyamba, Pakadurva, and Vyalkasa plants grow in this place.

14 O cool one, bringer of coolness; O fresh one, bringer of freshness; unite with the female frog. Delight and inspire this Agni.

Domestic Worship

VASUDHA NARAYANAN

Hinduism scholar Vasudha Narayanan explains the nature and purpose of Hindu worship in private homes.

Rituals performed in the home are generally called *puja* ("worship"). Worship of the deity or a spiritual teacher at a home shrine is one of the most significant ways in which Hindus express their devotion. Many Hindu households set aside some space in the home (such as a cabinet shelf or an entire room) where pictures or small images of the lord are enshrined. *Puja* may involve simple acts of daily devotion like the lighting of oil lamps and incense sticks, recitation of prayers, or the offering of food to the deity. Usually all members of the family can participate in daily raja, but more elaborate or specialized rituals of worship, like the ones to Satyanarayana (a manifestation of Visnu) on full-moon days, may involve the participation of a priest or special personnel.

In home worship, simpler versions of some temple rituals take place. In daily worship the rites are led by family members, instead of an initiated priest. The concept of appropriate hospitality guides home worship. The image of the deity receives the hospitality accorded to an honoured guest in the home: ritual bathing, anointing with ghee (clarified butter), offerings of food and drink, lighted lamps, and garlands of flowers such as marigold or jasmine.

Some domestic rituals do not involve prayers to a deity but to dead women, or strictly speaking, to women who died when their husbands were alive; that is, they died when they were *sumangalis* or "auspicious women." Even in death such women are said to have immense power to bring to fruition or to

Vasudha Narayanan, "The Hindu Tradition," in Willard G. Oxtoby, ed., *World Religions: Eastern Traditions* (Oxford: Oxford University Press, 2002), 81–82.

hinder the progress of any ritual. In some Hindu communities, principally in the south, before a major family celebration such as a wedding, the women may gather together to petition the *sumangali* women ancestors to bless the oncoming event. Rituals such as these are found in certain geographic regions and in some communities, and may not be recognized by Hindus from other regions. Thus the veneration of a young virgin girl by other women (who believe she is a temporary manifestation of the Goddess) may take place in some northern communities, but may not even be heard of in the south.

More widespread are the "auspiciousness" rituals that women conduct in many parts of India. On certain days of the year, women gather together to celebrate the goddess by fasting and feasting, and then perform rites (*vratas*) for the happiness of the entire family.

In the home as well as in the temple, the worshipper participates in the mythic structures associated with the deity. When a prayer is enunciated or sung, the worshipper participates in the passion of the devotee who composed the hymn. Thus, in Srivaisnava worship, when a devotee recites verses by the woman poet Antal, to some extent he or she is participating in her devotion. Temple liturgies at home and in the temple are based on participation by the devotee in the myths of the many saints and the many acts of redemption that Visnu, Siva, or the goddess engaged in. The devotees participate in the passion and surrender of the saints whose verses they utter, and through this identification, they link themselves with the devotional community extending through time. The passion of the saints and the composers of the prayers are appropriated by the devotee who recites or sings the songs.

Darsan: Seeing the Sacred

DIANA L. ECK

Diana Eck explores the meaning of the popular Hindu rite of *darsana*—seeing, and being seen by, a deity or holy person. This is "religious seeing," which is more than a mere visual experience; it is a way to directly apprehend the divine and to gain its blessings.

A common sight in India is a crowd of people gathered in the courtyard of a temple or at the doorway of a streetside shrine for the *darsan* of the deity. *Darsan* means "seeing." In the Hindu ritual tradition it refers especially to religious seeing, or the visual perception of the sacred. When Hindus go to a temple, they do not commonly say, "I am going to worship," but rather, "I am going for *darsan*." They go to "see" the image of the deity—be it Krsna or Durga, Siva or Visnu—present in the sanctum of the temple, and they go especially at those times of day when the image is most beautifully adorned with fresh flowers and when the curtain is drawn back so that the image is fully visible. The central act of Hindu worship, from the point of

Diana L. Eck, "Seeing the Sacred," in *Darsan: Seeing the Divine Image in India*, 3rd ed. (New York: Columbia University Press, 1998), 3–6.

view of the lay person, is to stand in the presence of the deity and to behold the image with one's own eyes, to see and be seen by the deity. *Darsan* is sometimes translated as the "auspicious sight" of the divine, and its importance in the Hindu ritual complex reminds us that for Hindus "worship" is not only a matter of prayers and offerings and the devotional disposition of the heart. Since, in the Hindu understanding, the deity is present in the image, the visual apprehension of the image is charged with religious meaning. Beholding the image is an act of worship, and through the eyes one gains the blessings of the divine.

Similarly, when Hindus travel on pilgrimage, as they do by the millions each month of the year, it is for the *darsan* of the place of pilgrimage or for the *darsan* of its famous deities. They travel to Siva's sacred city of Banaras for the *darsan* of Lord Visvanath. They trek high into the Himalayas for the *darsan* of Visnu at Badrinath. Or they climb to the top of a hill in their own district for the *darsan* of a well-known local goddess. The pilgrims who take to the road on foot, or who crowd into buses and trains, are not merely sightseers, but "sacred sightseers" whose interest is not in the picturesque place, but in the powerful place where *darsan* may be had. These powerful places are called *tirthas* (sacred "fords" or "crossings"), *dhams* (divine "abodes"), or *pithas* (the "benches" or "seats" of the divine). There are thousands of such places in India. Some, like Banaras (Varanasi), which is also called Kasi, are sought by pilgrims from their immediate locales.

Often such places of pilgrimage are famous for particular divine images, and so it is for the *darsan* of the image that pilgrims come. The close relationship between the symbolic importance of the image and the symbolic act of pilgrimage has been explored in a Western context by Victor and Edith Turner in *Image and Pilgrimage in Christian Culture*. In the West, of course, such traditions of pilgrimage were often attacked by those who did not "see" the symbolic significance of images and who, like Erasmus, denounced the undertaking of pilgrimages as a waste of time. In the Hindu tradition, however, there has never been the confusion of "image" with "idol," and in India, pilgrimage is the natural extension of the desire for the *darsan* of the divine image, which is at the heart of all temple worship.

It is not only for the *darsan* of renowned images that Hindus have traveled as pilgrims. They also seek the *darsan* of the places themselves which are said to be the natural epiphanies of the divine: the peaks of the Himalayas, which are said to be the abode of the gods; the river Ganga, which is said to fall from heaven to earth; or the many places which are associated with the mythic deeds of gods and goddesses, heroes and saints.

In addition to the *darsan* of temple images and sacred places, Hindus also value the *darsan* of holy persons, such as *sants* ("saints"), *sadhus* ("holy men"), and *sannyasins* ("renouncers"). When Mahatma Gandhi traveled through India, tens of thousands of people would gather wherever he stopped in order to "take his *darsan*." Even if he did not stop, they would throng the train stations for a passing glimpse of the Mahatma in his compartment. Similarly, when Swami Karpatri, a well-known *sannyasin* who is also a writer and political leader, would come to Varanasi to spend the rainy season "retreat" period, people would flock to his daily lectures not only to hear him, but to see him. However, even an ordinary *sannyasin* or *sadhu* is held in esteem in traditional Hindu culture. He is a living symbol of the value placed upon renunciation, and he is a perpetual pilgrim who has left home and family for a homeless life. Villagers are eager for the *darsan* of such a person, approaching him with reverence and giving him food and hospitality. In *The Ochre Robe,* Agehananda Bharati writes, "There is absolutely no parallel to the conception of *darsan* in any religious act in the West. . . ."

In popular terminology, Hindus say that the deity or the *sadhu* "gives *darsan*" (*darsan dens* is the Hindi expression), and the people "take *darsan*" (*darsan lena*). What does this mean? What is given and what is taken? The very expression is arresting, for "seeing" in this religious sense is not an act which is initiated by the worshiper. Rather, the deity presents itself to be seen in its image, or the *sadhu* gives himself to be seen by the villagers. And the people "receive" their *darsan*. One might say that this "sacred perception," which is the ability truly to see the divine image, is given to the devotee, just as Arjuna is given the eyes with which to see Krsna in the theophany described in the Bhagavad Gita.

CONTEMPORARY CHALLENGES

The Case of Uma Bharati

KATHERINE K. YOUNG

The treatment of women in India, a country with a majority Hindu population, is controversial. Activists, male and female, have called for equality and rights for women, and many defer to tradition and reject these pleas. One well-known female activist does not easily fit in either category. She is Uma Bharati, former member of parliament, social worker, and devout Hindu.

A different style of activism on women's issues is represented by Ms. Uma Bharati. She has been a BJP member of Parliament from Khajuraho. When she was interviewed in December, 1989, for *Times of India News*, she described her life in the style of a sacred biography. She recalled, for instance, her early, extraordinary religious experiences:

> I began having unusual experiences. At the age of six, I found myself giving discourses on the scriptures to the villagers. As far back as I can remember I have had this feeling of two existences within me—dual voices—one of a philosopher-scholar, the other of a child. It was almost an organic phenomenon; I can't explain it. It was as natural as breathing, to orate on religious matters or on the need for a spiritual revolution.

The interviewer then asked how she was discovered as a religious prodigy. Bharati answered:

> Well, one day some professors from a Tikamgarh degree college came to the village as part of a *baraat* (marriage party). When they heard me, they were so amazed, they did not even wait for the *bidaai* (nuptials). They bundled me into a car and I was admitted to a school in the town. Then followed years of participation at religious *sammelans*. I travelled abroad, toured in private planes, was feted and banqueted, nearly drowned in flowers from admirers. When the initial glamour of the adulation wore off, I began to feel caged in the worship. I wanted to appear ordinary, not the image of a *devi* or *avatar*, or live up to a created image.

Bharati remarks that she was once engaged but broke off the relationship because of her "religious commitments." She thought of becoming a *brahmacarini* until her mentor told her that being a *brahmacarini* meant total renunciation—that is, complete withdrawal from the world. Because she wanted to serve the people and work for the welfare of the world (*lokasangraha*), she decided against total renunciation (hence her sporadic wearing of the ochre robe). Working for the "welfare of the world" has meant working with outcastes and women in her native village and in Khajuraho. Of women, she said:

> Women are inherently superior as a created species. Men are not such noble beings that women should fight for equality. Instead they should fight to be treated with respect. . . .

Katherine K. Young, "Women in Hinduism," *Today's Woman in World Religions* (Albany: State University of New York Press, 1994), 97–100.

> If Indian women combine the *madhurya* (sweetness), their femininity, with self-pride and political awareness, they can teach the whole world the path of liberation. . . .
>
> You cannot sacrifice either aspect—sword in the hand and child on the back. Our women have to combine the heroism of Draupadi, Gargi, Savitri, Jabala, and Kunti. It is self-respect that will free us, not legislation. I don't eat in houses where, as per the tradition, women eat after men and observe *purdah* . . . for crimes like rape, I feel there should be [the] death sentence.

When the interviewer asked her whether she has ever experienced sexual discrimination in political life, she replied, "No, because I am well known in my area. And in the BJP we give the woman a very exalted status." Then, with a twinkle in her eye, she told the reporter, "my religious image has helped women overcome their prejudices." Folding her ochre robes, she added "I have faith in myself. . . . And may God give me some of the reformist energy of my idols—Rani Laxmi Bai and Swami Vivekananda."

Uma Bharati sees no contradiction between working for the cause of women and being a member of the BJP Party, usually portrayed in the press as the Hindu fundamentalist or militant party, and stereotyped as a regressive force on women's issues. Bharati is a Hindu liberal, at least on women's issues. But like many other Hindus she is disturbed at the loss of Hindu values and perceives secularism under leaders such as Rajiv Gandhi negatively. When defending Indian voters, she remarks: "maybe they didn't like Rajiv's foreign wife . . . or his elite coterie of friends . . . or his mania for computerisation and breakneck modernisation in certain sectors when so many lakhs [100,000] were denied basic amenities."

Her remedy for conflict brought on by communalism and religious extremism is to make room for moderate religion in the public square:

> The fact is the Indians can only understand religion. We are an instinctively religious people. The police, law, science—these are external controls; even our communists are "astiks" (theists) in their heart of hearts. The best methods of controlling communalism is to get moderate religious leaders on public forums to address the masses, spiced with examples from the scriptures. Those who are inflamed by religion can only be calmed down by religion, not by a slick or rational explanation.

Bharati told the interviewer that all parties exploit religious sentiment: "But the BJP believe in Hindutva ("Hinduness") and are proud of it and just because of this we are branded communal." More recently, Bharati has become much more militant and vociferous against the Muslims. Prior to the projected showdown (regarding the rebuilding of a Hindu temple to Lord Rama at the site of a mosque) at Ayodhya on October 30, 1990, she made speeches in Hindi that were later made into cassettes and sold. The message was virulent:

> On October 30, by beginning the construction of the temple, our holy men will be laying the foundations of making Hindustan a Hindu [state]. Bharat Mata Ki Jai . . . Glory to Mahadev [the Great Deity]. Destroy the tyrant in the same way that Ravana was vanquished. Do not display any love (nij preet). This is the order of Ram. Announce it boldly to the world that anyone who opposes Ram cannot be an Indian. Muslims, remember Rahim who longed for the dust of Lord Ram's feet. . . . Songs of Hindu Muslim brotherhood were sung by Mahatma Gandhi. We got ready to hear the Azaan along with the temple bells, but they can't do this, nor does their heritage permit them to do so. . . . The two cultures are polar opposites. But still we preached brotherhood. . . . We could not teach them with words, now let us teach them with kicks. . . . Let there be bloodshed once and for all. . . . Leftists and communists ask me if we desire to turn this land into a Hindu rashtra. I say it was declared one at the time of Partition in 1947—Hindustan, a nation of Hindus and Pakistan, a nation of the Muslims. Those Muslims who stayed behind could do so because of the tolerance and large-heartedness of the Hindus. . . . Declare without hesitation that this is a Hindu rashtra, a nation of Hindus.

Uma Bharati finally took samnyasa (formal renunciation) in 1992. It was prompted, some say, to clear her reputation after she was accused by the opposition parties of having an affair. Be that as it may, she shaved her head, was renamed Uma Shri Bharati, and began to wear only ochre robes. As the opposition was quick to point out, she did not give up her status as a member of parliament. She also continued to support the cause of rebuilding the Ram Janmabhoomi temple.

Untouchability

MOHANDAS GANDHI

Here is Mahatma Gandhi, the champion of nonviolent protest, arguing for equal rights and equal status for the untouchables, the low caste that he calls "the children of God."

It is a tragedy that religion for us means today nothing more than restrictions on food and drink, nothing more than adherence to a sense of superiority and inferiority. Let me tell you that there cannot be any grosser ignorance than this. Birth and observance of forms cannot determine one's superiority and inferiority. Character is the only determining factor. God did not create men with the badge of superiority or inferiority; no scripture which labels a human being as inferior or untouchable because of his or her birth can command our allegiance; it is a denial of God and Truth which is God.

There is an ineffaceable blot that Hinduism today carries with it. I have declined to believe that it has been handed down to us from immemorial times. I think that this miserable, wretched, enslaving spirit of "untouchableness" must have come to us when we were at our lowest ebb. This evil has stuck to us and still remains with us. . . .

Untouchability as it is practised in Hinduism today is, in my opinion, a sin against God and man and is, therefore, like a poison slowly eating into the very vitals of Hinduism. In my opinion, it has no sanction whatsoever in the Hindu *Shastras* taken as a whole. . . . It has degraded both the untouchables and the touchables. It has stunted the growth of nearly 40 million human beings. They are denied even the ordinary amenities of life. The sooner, therefore, it is ended, the better for Hinduism, the better for India, and perhaps better for mankind in general.

So far as I am concerned with the untouchability question it is one of life and death for Hinduism. As I have said repeatedly, if untouchability lives, Hinduism perishes, and even India perishes; but if untouchability is eradicated from the Hindu heart, root and branch, then Hinduism has a definite message for the world. I have said the first thing to hundreds of audiences but not the latter part. Now that is the utterance of a man who accepts Truth as God. It is therefore no exaggeration. If untouchability is an integral part of Hinduism, the latter is a spent bullet. But untouchability is a hideous untruth. My motive in launching the anti-untouchability campaign is clear. What I am aiming at is not every Hindu touching an "untouchable," but every touchable Hindu driving untouchability from his heart, going through a complete change of heart.

It is bad enough when dictated by selfish motives to consider ourselves high and other people low. But it is not only worse but a double wrong when we tack religion to an evil like untouchability. It, therefore, grieves me when learned pundits come forward and invoke the authority of *Shastras* for a patent evil like untouchability. I have said, and I repeat today, that we, Hindus, are undergoing a period of probation. Whether we desire it or not, untouchability is going. But if during this period of probation we repent for

Mahatma Gandhi, "Untouchability," *The Message of Mahatma Gandhi* (New Delhi: Government of India, Publications Division, 1968), 90–95.

the sin, if we reform and purify ourselves, history will record that one act as a supreme act of purification on the part of the Hindus. But if, through the working of the time spirit, we are compelled to do things against our will and Harijans come into their own, it will be no credit to the Hindus or to Hinduism. But I go a step further and say that if we fail in this trial, Hinduism and Hindus will perish.

Harijan means "a man of God." All the religions of the world describe God preeminently as the Friend of the friendless, Help of the helpless and Protector of the weak. The rest of the world apart, in India who can be more friendless, helpless or weaker than the forty million or more Hindus of India who are classified as "untouchables"? If, therefore, any body of people can be fitly described as men of God, they are surely these helpless, friendless and despised people. Hence, in the pages of *Navajivan,* I have always adopted Harijan as the name signifying "untouchables." Not that the change of name brings about any change of status, but one may at least be spared the use of a term which is itself one of reproach. When caste Hindus have of their own inner conviction and, therefore, voluntarily, got rid of the present-day untouchability we shall all be called Harijans, for, according to my humble opinion, caste Hindus will then have found favour with God and may, therefore, be fitly described as His men.

Harijan service is a religious obligation. There is no room in it for cunning. It has to be absolutely truthful and non-violent. It can be accomplished only by sacrifice and penance. I very much fear that we shall not be able to win the trust of Harijans without self-purification. It should not surprise us if today they look upon all we do with suspicion and distrust. Hitherto we had been riding their shoulders. We must dismount if we would do justice to them, and regard them as we regard other Hindus.

Economic and educational uplift is no doubt an essential part of true repentance by caste Hindus. It is a test of the sincerity of their professions. But the uplift will not be complete without the throwing open of temples. The throwing open of temples will be an admission of the religious equality of Harijans. It will be the surest sign of their ceasing to be the outcastes of Hinduism, which they are today.

And when temples are thrown open to Harijans, schools, wells and many similar facilities will be automatically open to Harijans.

A vigorous campaign with a definite time limit for the complete removal of all the disabilities under which the Harijans suffer ought to be launched. Emancipation of the Harijans can no longer be postponed to an indefinite distant date. It has to be realised here and now even like Independence. Independence itself will turn into bitter ashes in our mouth if the most useful section of the community is baulked of its essential rights.

There will be under *Swaraj* no such scandal as that of the use of public temples being denied to untouchables when it is allowed to all other Hindus. The authority of the *Vedas* and the other *Shastras* will not be denied but their interpretation will not rest with individuals but will depend upon the course of law in so far as these religious books will be used to regulate public conduct. Conscientious scruples will be respected, but not at the expense of public morals or the right of others. Those who will have extraordinary scruples will have themselves to suffer inconvenience and pay for the luxury. The law will not tolerate any arrogation of superiority by any person or class whether in the name of custom or religion.

The real hunger of the Harijans which needs to be satisfied is for decent living as self-respecting, equal citizens, for a square deal as human beings, for freedom from fear, inculcation of clean and sanitary habits, thrift, industry, education. This requires perseverance, self-sacrifice and patient, intelligent labouring on our part. If you give me money to feed Harijans, I shall refuse to accept it. For I do not want to make beggars and idlers of them.

One experience stands quite distinctly in my memory. It relates to my 21 days' fast for the removal of untouchability. I had gone to sleep the night before without the slightest idea of having to declare a fast the next morning. At about 12 o'clock in the night something wakes me up suddenly, and some voice—within or without, I cannot say—whispers, "Thou must go on a fast." How many days? I ask. This voice again says, "Twenty-one days." When does it begin? I ask. It says, "You begin tomorrow." I went quietly off to sleep after making the decision. I did not tell anything to my companions until after the morning prayer. I placed into their hands a slip of paper announcing my decision and asking them not to argue with me, as the decision was irrevocable. Well, the doctors thought I would not survive this fast. But something within me said that I would, and that I must go forward. That kind of experience has never in my life happened before or after that date.

STUDY QUESTIONS

1. Define *Brahman*, *asceticism*, *atman*, and *dharma*.
2. Explain the relationships among *samara*, *moksha*, and *karma*.
3. What are the *Upanishads*?
4. What is the Hindu attitude toward images of deities? Do Hindus worship idols—that is, mere representations of gods? Why or why not?
5. Describe the chief differences between the *Samkhya* and *Advaita Vedanta* schools.
6. What is the story told in the *Bhagavad Gita*? What lessons have Hindus derived from it?
7. What is the story told in the *Ramayana*?
8. Describe the main differences between Shaivas, Vaishnavas, and Shaktas.
9. What is the caste system? What are the prescribed roles for the original four classes? What are the *Dalits*?
10. Distinguish between *shruti* and *smriti*.
11. Describe some of the rituals encompassed in *bhakti*.

FURTHER READING

Diana L. Eck, *Darsan: Seeing the Divine Image in India*, 3rd ed. (New York: Columbia University Press, 1998).

Ainslee T. Embree, ed., *Sources of Indian Tradition* (New York: Columbia University Press, 1988).

Gavin Flood, ed., *The Blackwell Companion to Hinduism* (Oxford: Blackwell Publishing, 2003).

Lex Hixon, *Great Swan: Meetings with Ramakrishna* (Burdett, NY: Larson Publications, 1992).

W. J. Johnson, trans., *The Bhagavad Gita* (Oxford: Oxford University Press, 1994).

W. J. Johnson, *The Oxford Dictionary of Hinduism* (Oxford: Oxford University Press, 2009).

Patrick Olivelle, trans., *Upanishads* (Oxford: Oxford University Press, 1996).

Vasudha Narayanan, "The Hindu Tradition," Willard G. Oxtoby, ed., *World Religions: Eastern Traditions* (Oxford: Oxford University Press, 2002).

Vasudha Narayanan, *Hinduism* (Oxford: Oxford University Press, 2004).

Arvind Sharma, ed., *Today's Woman in World Religions* (Albany: State University of New York Press, 1994).

ONLINE

Hinduism Today Magazine, "What Is Hinduism?" hinduismtoday.com (October 9, 2012).

Hinduism website, hinduwebsite.com (December 10, 2015).

Internet Sacred Text Archive, "Hinduism," http://www.sacred-texts.com/hin/ (December 10, 2015).

Religion Facts, "Hinduism," http://www.religionfacts.com/hinduism (December 10, 2015).

4 Jainism

Jainism is a religious and philosophical tradition that arose in ancient India as Buddhism was also beginning to flourish. The two systems, however, evolved more or less separately, with Jainism embracing a distinctive set of core doctrines that have remained substantially unchanged for 2,500 years. Through the centuries, the basic tenets of other traditions underwent significant revision, but not those of the Jains. Today only a tiny minority of Indians are Jains (probably less than 0.5 percent of the population), the rest being mostly Hindus, Muslims, and Sikhs. Worldwide, Jainism has about 5 million adherents, the vast majority living in India, with relatively few residing elsewhere (up to 30,000 in Britain and about 45,000 in North America). Yet Jains, although few in number, have had an outsized impact on Indian culture. They have excelled in art, architecture, and literature. Their temples rank among the finest examples of architecture in India. They are known for their high levels of education, preeminence in business, charitable giving, environmental concerns, and low levels of crime. Most of all, they have helped to change society through their unshakeable commitment to nonviolence, vegetarianism, religious tolerance, piety, and honesty.

From its outward manifestations, Jainism may seem to be a simple religious tradition with a single-minded focus on devotional practice, but it is much more than that. A Jain scholar explains:

> [Jainism] is a complete system with all the necessary branches, such as dogma or ontology, metaphysics, philosophy, epistemology, mythology, ethics, ritual, and the rest, and is divided into several sects and subsects indicative of a long process of development. It has its own deities, gurus and scriptures, its own temples, places of worship and pilgrimage, and its own festivals and fairs.[1]

JAIN HISTORY

According to Jain tradition, the religion has had a series of great teachers, or founders, throughout the current cosmic era, a period that is to last 21,000 years. Jains look back to these twenty-four teachers and revere them because they conquered **samsara**, the painful cycle of one's repeated deaths and rebirths. Each one is therefore known as a **jina**, a "conqueror," from which we derive *Jainism*. They are also called **tirthankaras**, "bridge-builders" or "makers of

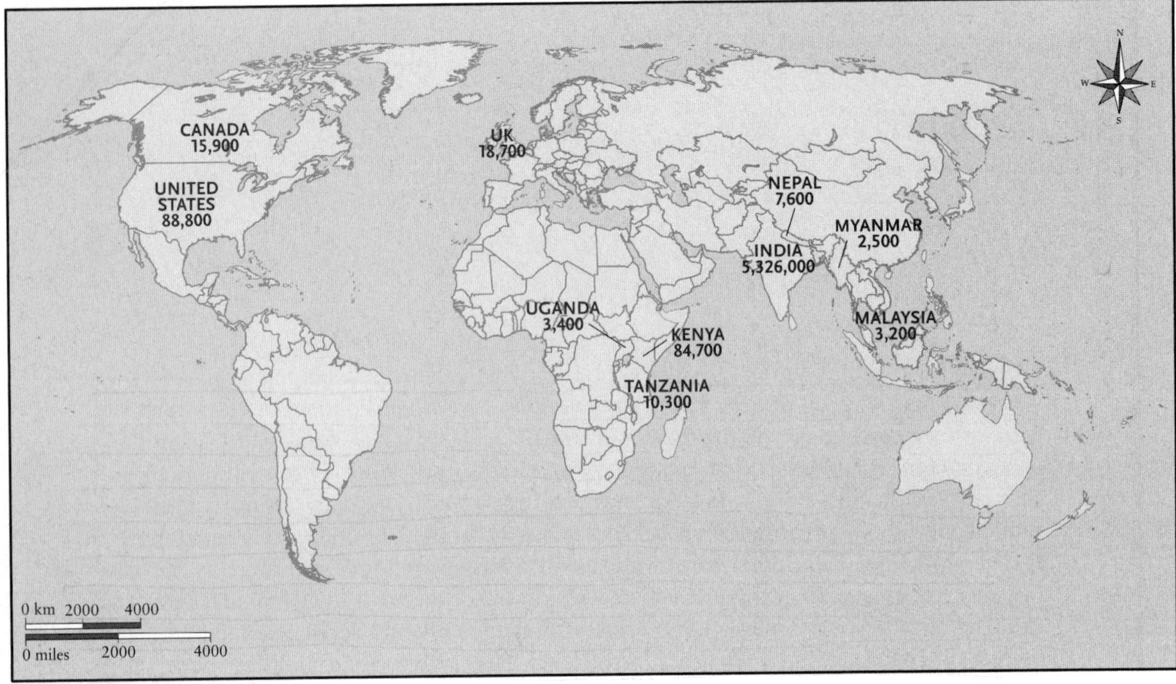

MAP 4.1 World Jain population.

the ford," because they crossed over from their captivity in *samsara* to the world of enlightenment and freedom from rebirth.

The *tirthankara* that Jains revere most is the last one, the twenty-fourth, known by the title Mahavira. Rival Jain sects give different dates for his life, some saying he lived from 599 to 527 BCE, with others insisting that the true dates are 599 to 510. In any case, he is said to have been a contemporary (or almost a contemporary) of the Buddha, and his life story in its main features resembles that of the Buddha. According to most scholars, he was born of an aristocratic family in northern India and renounced his comfortable position at age thirty to seek salvation as a wandering ascetic. He chose to follow in the spiritual footsteps of Parshva, the twenty-third *tirthankara*. His asceticism was extreme, consisting of severe fasting, meditation, and nakedness, which exposed him to the elements and to insects, which he refused to harm. His diet, lack of clothing, mode of travel, postures, and regard for even the smallest life forms all derived from the cardinal Jain principle of **ahimsa**, or nonviolence: Do not harm any living thing.

Jain texts say that after twelve years of this harsh asceticism, at age forty-two, Mahavira attained **kevala**, or omniscience—absolute knowledge that destroys *samsara*. After his physical death, he would no longer be subject to the endless rounds of birth and rebirth. This enlightenment experience is what made Mahavira a *jina* (or a *kevalin*, a "completed soul"). In the ensuing thirty years, he roamed northeast India as a naked monk and founded a community of such monks, teaching by word and example the doctrine of *ahimsa* and the

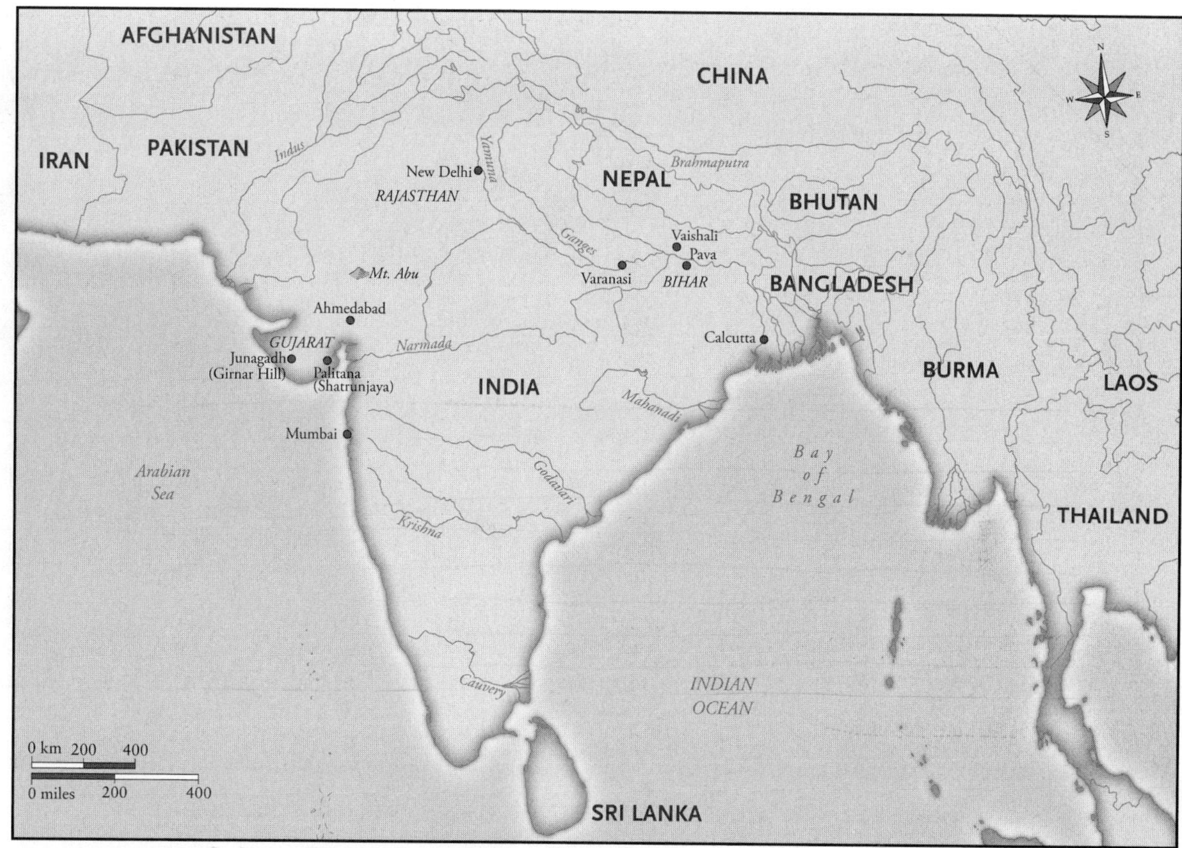

MAP 4.2 Significant sites in the history of Jainism.

importance of renunciation of physical attachments and comforts. At the age of seventy-two, he died in a village called Pava, near Patna in northern India. According to tradition, he left behind thousands of Jain monks, nuns, and laypeople.

Like any major religion, Jainism from the beginning has been subject to dissents and disagreements among adherents. Eventually two main sects came to dominate the tradition, mostly differing not on fundamental Jain principles but on the details of devotional practices and the status of scripture. The *Digambara* sect holds that (1) their monks (but not nuns) should always be unclothed (thus they are called "Sky-clad" or "Space-clad," suggesting that they wear only the air), (2) they should use only their hands for begging and eating food, (3) women cannot attain enlightenment until they are reborn as men, and (4) the most important Jain scriptures have been lost. The *Shvetambara* sect, the largest Jain faction, insists that (1) both monks and nuns should wear clothes (specifically white clothes, which is why the sect's adherents are called "White-clad"), (2) they should use a begging bowl instead of bare hands, (3) women can achieve enlightenment, and (4) ancient writings (called the *Limbs*) are bona fide Jain scripture.

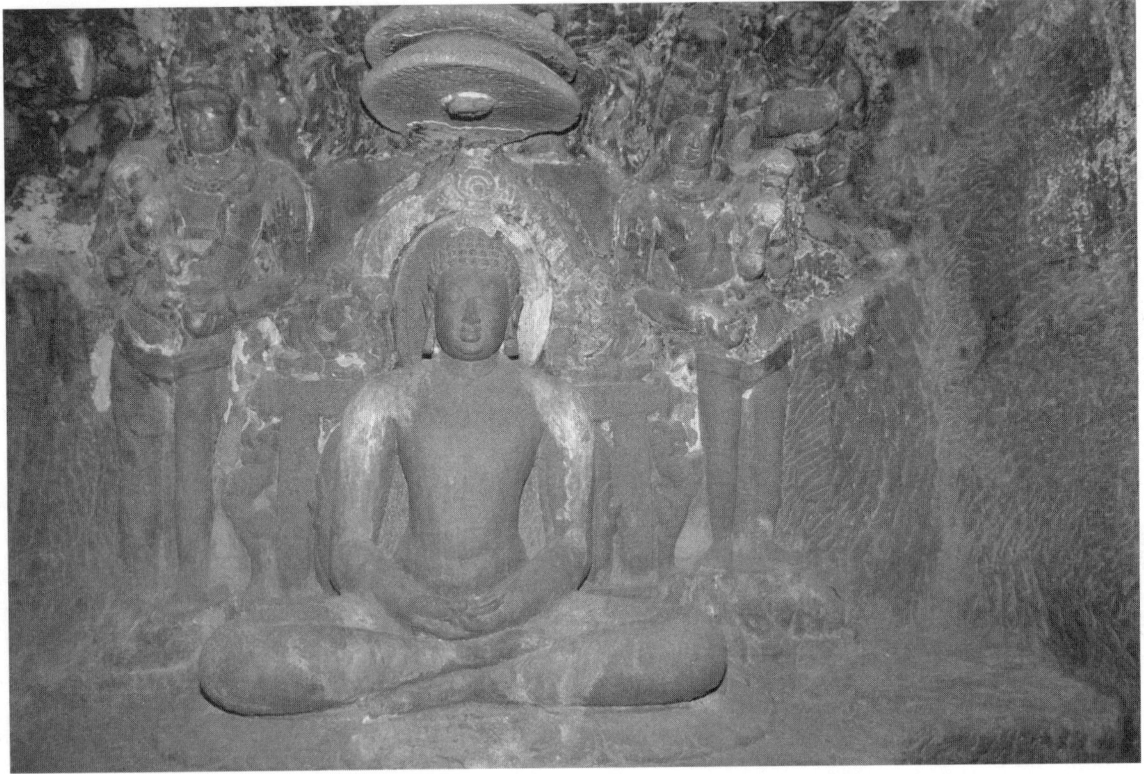

FIGURE 4.1 In a section of the cave temples of Ellora, Maharashtra, India, sits a sculpture of Mahavira, the founder of Jainism.

TEACHINGS AND PRACTICES

A respected Jain scholar sums up the basic teachings of Jainism like this:

> The phenomenal individual consists of a soul closely enmeshed in matter, and his salvation is to be found by freeing the soul from matter so that it may regain its pristine purity and enjoy omniscient self-sufficient bliss for all eternity.[2]

Our understanding of Jainism depends on our grasping the Jain notion of **jiva**, or soul, the essence of every living thing. *Jivas* are conscious and eternal; they are distinct from each other and independent of the body, though capable of controlling the body. When a *jiva* attains a perfected state (when, for example, a monk attains *kevala*), it becomes omniscient, bright, pure, and infinitely blissful. But the *jiva* can become dimmed, dirtied, and weighed down by particles of lifeless matter deposited by **karma** (the universal principle that governs the characteristics and quality of each rebirth, or future life), and the impurities adhere the soul to the tortuous workings of *samsara*, causing dreadful rebirths. Misdeeds, especially

JAIN TIMELINE

BCE

800–700 (?) Era of Parshva, the twenty-third *tirthankara*

1500–600 The *Vedas* composed

900–600 Early *Upanishads*

563–483 Life of the Buddha

599–527 (or possibly 599–510) Life of Mahavira

CE

First century *Bhagavad Gita* composed

c. 79 (or 82) Jain sects of Shvetambara and Digambara established

c. 200–400 Period of flourishing of Kundakunda, teacher of the Jain sect of Digambara

788–820 Life of Shankara, influential Hindu philosopher and proponent of Advaita Vedanta

1200–1757 Muslim rule of North India

1469–1539 Life of Nanak, founder of Sikhism

Seventeenth century Founding of the *Sthanakvasi* sect

1726–1803 Life of Acarya Bhikshu, founder of *Terapanthi* sect

1757 British rule established in India

1869–1948 Life of M. K. Gandhi, leader of civil disobedience campaigns and Hindu reform

1947 India wins independence from Britain.

acts of violence, cause bad karma and the accumulation of impurities. But right actions and ascetic discipline can erase the layers of impurities. Jain ascetics therefore fast, do penance, and refrain from inflicting harm on even the tiniest creatures (for they are souls too), doing nothing and acquiring nothing that involves violence. To avoid killing insects, for example, they may strain drinking water, wear masks over their mouths, practice vegetarianism, and sweep the ground in front of them as they walk. They refuse to eat potatoes, radishes, and other root vegetables because they contain many microscopic lives. They—and Jains generally—shun occupations and activities that entail the killing or mistreatment of animals and plants, such as meat processing, hunting, fishing, earthmoving, and clear-cutting (destroying trees). Jain ascetics cannot live without doing violence to at least some lives, but they try their utmost to minimize the harm.

To strive toward liberation of the soul, Jains conduct themselves according to Five Great Vows, which mandate a rigorous asceticism. Monks and nuns commit to following them,

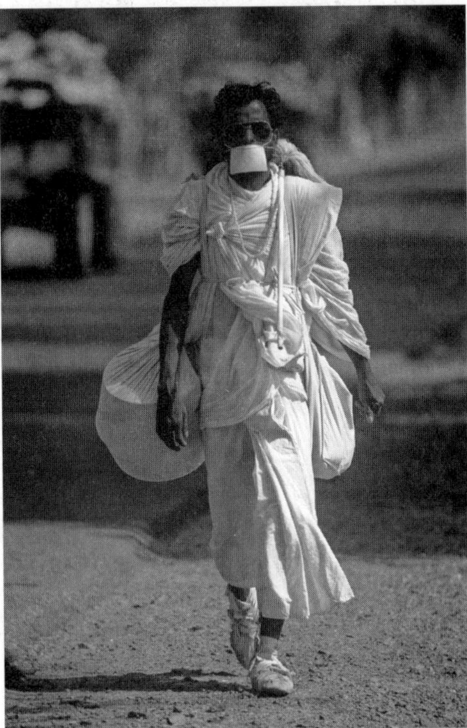

FIGURE 4.2 While walking on a road, a Jain monk wears the *muhpatti* to prevent unnecessary harm to airborne insects.

and laypersons adhere to them as best they can. The vows are easy to understand but difficult to fulfill:

1. *Do not harm any living thing* (*ahimsa*). As mentioned earlier, this directive is at the heart of Jainism. Almost all Jain practices and attitudes can be traced to this prohibition. *Ahimsa* is also woven into the other four vows.
2. *Speak the truth.* This vow entails both not lying and not concealing the truth. It must be followed in all situations, except when adhering to it would cause violence.
3. *Do not steal*, or as Jains express it, Do not take what has not been given to you.
4. *Be chaste.* This admonition is a call for sexual purity. Monks and nuns should refrain from all sexual activity. Laypersons are expected to abstain from sexual relations with anyone except their spouses.
5. *Renounce all possessions.* This vow includes a prohibition of covetous thinking. It is a warning against attachments, for they can distract from the goal of enlightenment and incite violence. Laypersons are expected to greatly minimize possessions; monks pledge to own little or nothing.

It should be clear by now that for Jains, salvation depends solely on their own efforts. Unlike many other traditions, Jainism holds that mere belief in God or gods is not enough to secure the blessings of enlightenment. Jains reject the notion of a supreme creator god, and in this sense they can be characterized as atheistic. They believe in multiple gods (they borrow some of them from Hinduism), but these are finite deities that ultimately cannot help anyone achieve *kevala* or alter the cycles of *samsara*.

Devotional practices among the Jain laity are not as austere as those of the Jain ascetics, but they are nonetheless arduous. Jains traditionally have practiced many forms of worship, including devotion to *jinas*, *tirthankaras* (especially Mahavira), and gods (mostly Hindu deities). They may direct their worship toward a mental image of these persons, or they may worship them by focusing on physical images of them in ornate temples (there are thousands in India) or around home shrines. They sing hymns, utter praise, or consecrate the statues by anointing them with perfumed or colored liquids. Some statues are small, suitable for home

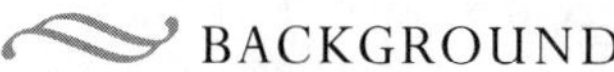
BACKGROUND

Women in Jainism

What is the status of women in Jainism? Here is an answer given by Nalini Balbir for JAINpedia, an online project of the Institute of Jainology.

Historically, Jainism's attitude towards women has shared a view common amongst other Indian and Asian traditions, which see women as innately unequal to men. Counter to these long-established attitudes, Jainism gives women a central role in its ethical and spiritual patterns. For example, the fourfold community that is the foundation of Jain daily life includes lay women as well as lay men, nuns as well as monks. Among Śvetāmbara sects, there tends to be more female mendicants than male. Traditional sources name several distinguished women who play important roles in the tales of the Jinas, while goddesses are significant cultural and religious figures. . . .

Women lead the key Jain religious activities surrounding food, especially fasting, and often have principal roles in the performance of worship, particularly singing hymns. Jain women are also often the keenest participants in religious festivals.

Despite the vital importance of female activity in Jain religious life and the high proportion of female mendicants, nuns must defer to male colleagues. Frequently, senior nuns have limited authority and are not allowed to preach like monks. One of the most basic Jain beliefs is that each individual is responsible for his or her spiritual condition and thus anyone may read the scriptures, which guide spiritual progress. It is very likely, however, that female Jains generally had lower educational levels than their male counterparts, which must have hindered their scriptural knowledge. Nowadays female education for both nuns and lay women is a focus of disagreement among the sects.

This is partly connected to the main philosophical distinction between the Digambaras and Śvetāmbaras. The capacity of women to achieve liberation from the cycle of rebirth has been hotly debated for around two thousand years, and relates to whether nudity is necessary for salvation. The sectarian dispute over whether the 19th Jina, Mallī, was male or female symbolises disagreements about female liberation.

JAINpedia, "Women in the Jain Tradition," http://www.jainpedia.org/themes/people/women-in-the-jain-tradition.html (21 December 2015).

shrines; others are towering works of stone. In either case, Jains consider these physical images helpful reminders of the goal of liberation; they generally do not deem physical representations of revered entities alive, as many Hindus do.

Jain devotional practices also include pilgrimages to holy sites (sacred caves, mountains, and shrines), festivals and fasts on specific dates throughout the year, gifts of food to Jain ascetics, and ritual donations of money to sponsor formal rites and underwrite the erection of new statues.

JAIN SCRIPTURES

There is no single, extensive collection of texts that all Jains recognize as the official Jain canon. Jainism's two main sects—the Digambaras and Shvetambaras—consider different sets of writings, or books, to be true scripture. They both recognize the oldest texts, the *purvas*, as authoritative, but they also recognize that these vanished centuries ago. The Digambaras insist that the essence of some of the *purvas* was recovered by later writers; the Shvetambaras deny this. So basically the two schools claim separate, distinct canons.

The Digambaras claim as the primary part of their canon the books called the *prakaranas* (treatises). All these texts were written in the first century CE and include the *Doctrine* (*Samayasara*), the *Conduct* (*Mulacara*), and the *Accomplishment* (*Aradhana*). Both factions revere large collections of commentaries on the scriptures called *Supplements* (*anuyoga*), and both acknowledge the *Treatise on Attaining the Meaning of Principles* (*Tattvarthadhigama Sutra*).

The main compilation of Shvetambara scripture is called the *Agama* (tradition), which comprises forty-five books organized into six parts: *Angas* (Limbs), *Upangas* (sub-limbs, or ancillary material), *Prakirnakas* (miscellaneous writings), *Chedasutras* (mostly about discipline), *Culikasutras* (appendices), and *Mulasutras* (fundamental texts).

As in most other traditions, Jains often recite scripture during rituals. A section of the *Chedasutras* called the *Kalpasutra* is a Jain favorite and is a prime candidate for recitation at festivals. Laypersons study sacred books, but usually only with the help of a knowledgeable teacher. Jain scriptures themselves are venerated. Temples are dedicated to particular books, and sacred sites are used as scripture depositories.

NOTES

1. Jyoti Prasad Jain, *Religion and Culture of the Jains* (New Delhi: Bharatiya Jnanpith, 1982), 2.
2. A. L. Basham, "The Basic Doctrines of Jainism," in *Sources of Indian Tradition*, vol. 1, 2nd ed. (New York: Columbia University Press, 1988), 52.

KEY TERMS

ahimsa The principle of not harming living beings (often referred to as the "non-harm" or "nonviolence" principle).

jina "Conqueror"; one who has overcome *samsara*.

jiva Soul, the essence of every living thing.

karma The universal principle that governs the characteristics and quality of each rebirth, or future life.

kevala Omniscience, absolute knowledge of reality; enlightenment that terminates *samsara*.

samsara The painful cycle of one's repeated deaths and rebirths.

tirthankara A "bridge-builder" or "maker of the ford"; one who has crossed over from the captivity of *samsara* to the world of enlightenment and freedom from rebirth.

READINGS

Nonviolence

This sutra elaborates on Jainism's central tenet, *ahimsa*: Do not harm any living thing. Almost all Jain practices and attitudes are based on this prohibition.

Non-violence, and kindness to living beings is kindness to oneself, for thereby one's own self is saved from various kinds of sins and the consequent suffering, and is thus able to secure its own welfare.

Venerable is he who vieweth all creatures as his own self and seeth them all alike.

He who looketh on creatures, big and small, of the earth, as his own self, comprehendeth this immense universe.

To do harm to others is to do harm to one-self: "Thou art he whom thou intendest to kill. Thou art he whom thou intendest to tyrannise over!"

Know other creatures' love for life, for they are alike unto you. Kill them not: Save their life from fear and enmity.

All living beings desire happiness, and have revulsion from pain and suffering. They are fond of life, they love to live, long to live, and they feel

Jain Sutras, Jyoti Prasad Jain, trans. *Religion and Culture of the Jains*, 3rd ed. (New Delhi: Bharatiya Jnanpith, 1983), 187–188.

repulsed at the idea of hurt and injury to or destruction of their life. Hence, no living being should be hurt, injured, or killed.

All things breathing, all things existing, all things living, all beings whatsoever, should not be slain, or treated with violence, or insulted, or tortured, or driven away.

*He who hurts living beings himself, or gets them hurt by others, or approves of hurt caused by others, augments the world's hostility towards himself.

He who vieweth all living beings as his own self, and seeth them all alike, hath stopped all influx of the karma; he is self-restrained, and incurreth no sin.

Wise and Foolish Men

In this sutra the wise and foolish are distinguished: the wise practice asceticism and moderation in pursuit of liberation; the foolish strive for luxuries and end up dirtying their souls.

Who will boast of family or glory, who will desire anything, when he thinks that he has often been born noble, often lowly, and that his soul, [his true self] is neither humble nor high-born, and wants nothing?

Thus a wise man is neither pleased nor annoyed. . . . A man should be circumspect and remember that through carelessness he experiences many unpleasantnesses and is born in many wombs, becoming blind, deaf, dumb, one-eyed, hunchbacked, or of dark or patchy complexion. Unenlightened, he is afflicted, and is forever rolled on the wheel of birth and death.

To those who make fields and houses their own, life is dear; they want clothes dyed and colored, jewels, earrings, gold, and women, and they delight in them. The fool, whose only desire is for the fullness of life, thinks that penance, self-control, and restraint are pointless, and thus he comes to grief. . . .

There is nothing that time will not overtake. All beings love themselves, seek pleasure, and turn from pain; they shun destruction, love life, and desire to live. To all things life is dear. They crave for riches and gather them together, . . . using the labor of servants both two-footed and four-footed; and whatever a man's share may be, whether small or great, he wants to enjoy it. At one time he has a great treasure, . . . while at another his heirs divide it, or workless men steal it, or kings loot it, or it is spoiled or vanishes, or is burned up with his house. The fool in order to get riches does cruel deeds, which in the end are only of benefit to others, and stupidly comes to grief on account of the pain that he causes.

This the Sage [Mahavira] has declared—such men cannot and do not cross the flood; they cannot, they do not reach the other shore; they cannot, they do not get to the other side.

Though he hears the doctrine such a man never stands in the right place,

But he who adopts it stands in the right place indeed.

There is no need to tell a man who sees for himself,

But the wretched fool, delighting in pleasure, has no end to his miseries, but spins in a whirlpool of pain.

Acaranga Sutra, 1.2, 3, from A. L. Basham, trans., in *Sources of Indian Tradition*, 2nd ed. (New York: Columbia University Press, 1988), 68–69.

Moral Verses

These passages are taken from *The Quatrains*, an assemblage of verses on morality. *The Quatrains* contain no reference to gods, but they do exhibit the characteristically pessimistic Jain outlook on life. Adherents are urged to combine their devotion to correct behavior with a sense of community and a cultivation of noble feelings such as love.

There is no passing the fixed day [of death]. No one
On earth has escaped death, and fled, and gone free
You who hoard up wealth, give it away! Tomorrow
The funeral drum will beat. [6]

My mother gave me birth, left me, and went
To seek her mother, who had gone on the same quest.
And so goes on the search of each man for his mother.
This is the way of the world. [15]

Men come uninvited, join the family as kinsmen,
And silently depart. As silently the bird
Flies far from the tree where its old nest remains,
Men leave their empty bodies to their kin. [30]

The skulls of dead men, with deep caves for eyes,
Horrid to see, grinning, address the living—
"Take heed, and keep to the path of virtue.
That is the blessing that makes the body worth having." [49]

When men rise up in enmity and wish to fight,
It is not cowardice, say the wise, to refuse the challenge.
Even when your enemies do the utmost evil,
It is right to do no evil in return. [67]

If you send a little calf into a herd of cows
It will find its mother with unfailing skill.
So past deeds search out the man who did them,
And who must surely reap their fruit. [107]

Cows are of many different forms and colors;
Their milk is always white.
The path of virtue, like milk, is one;
The sects that teach it are manifold. [118]

Those who snare and keep encaged the partridge or the quail,
Which dwell in the wilds where beetles hum around the flowers,
Shall [in a later life] till black and hungry soil,
Their legs in fetters, as slaves to alien lords. [122]

Learning is a treasure that needs no safeguard;
Nowhere can fire destroy it or proud kings take it.
Learning's the best legacy a man can leave his children.
Other things are not true wealth. [134].

In the city of the gods, in the after-life,
We shall learn if there is any greater joy
Than that when wise men, with minds as keen as steel,
Meet together in smiling fellowship. [137]

You may bite the sugar-cane, break its joints,
Crush out its juice, and still it is sweet.
Well-born men, though others abuse or hurt them
Never lose their self-respect in words of anger. [156]

The greatness of the great is humility.
The gain of the gainer is self-control.
Only those rich men are truly wealthy
Who relieve the need of their neighbors. [170]

People speak of high birth and low—
Mere words, with no real meaning!
Not property or ancient glory makes a man noble,
But self-denial, wisdom and energy. [195]

Naladiyar, from A. L. Basham, trans., in *Sources of Indian Tradition* 2nd ed. (New York: Columbia University Press, 1988), 72–75.

This is the duty of a true man—
To shelter all, as a tree from the fierce sun,
And to labor that many may enjoy what he earns,
As the fruit of a fertile tree. [202]

Better hatred than the friendship of fools.
Better death than chronic illness.
Better to be killed than soul-destroying contempt.
Better abuse than praise undeserved. [219]

If I do not stretch out my hand and risk my life
For a friend in need,
May I reap the reward of one who seduces the wife of a friend,
While the wide world mocks me in scorn. [238]

Best is a life passed in penance,
Middling, that spent with those one loves,
Worst, the life of one never satisfied,
Cringing to rich men who care nothing for him. [365]

As a scroll read by one who well understands it,
As wealth to the men of generous spirit,
As a sharp sword in the warrior's hand,
Is the beauty of a faithful wife.

There Is No Creator God

Jains are atheistic in the sense that they deny the existence of a creator God. They don't reject the notion of lesser gods, but neither do they elevate supernatural beings to an honored place in their belief system. For Jains, belief in a deity or deities is not sufficient to win salvation. The following excerpt from Jain scripture presents several sophisticated arguments against theistic beliefs.

Some foolish men declare that Creator made the world.
The doctrine that the world was created is ill-advised, and should be rejected.

If God created the world, where was he before creation?
If you say he was transcendent then, and needed no support, where is he now?

No single being had the skill to make this world—
For how can an immaterial god create that which is material?

How could God have made the world without any raw material?
If you say he made this first, and then the world, you are faced with an endless regression.

If you declare that this raw material arose naturally you fall into another fallacy,
For the whole universe might thus have been its own creator, and have arisen equally naturally.

If God created the world by an act of his own will, without any raw material,
Then it is just his will and nothing else—and who will believe this silly stuff?
If he is ever perfect and complete, how could the will to create have arisen in him?
If, on the other hand, he is not perfect, he could no more create the universe than a potter could.

If he is formless, actionless, and all-embracing, how could he have created the world?
Such a soul, devoid of all modality, would have no desire to create anything.

If he is perfect, he does not strive for the three aims of man,

Mahapurana, 4.16–31, 38–40, from A. L. Basham, trans., in *Sources of Indian Tradition* 2nd ed. (New York: Columbia University Press, 1988), 80–82.

So what advantage would be gain by creating the universe?

If you say that he created to no purpose, because it was his nature to do so, then God is pointless.
If he created in some kind of sport, it was the sport of a foolish child, leading to trouble.

If he created because of the karma of embodied beings [acquired in a previous creation]
He is not the Almighty Lord, but subordinate to something else. . . .

If out of love for living things and need of them he made the world,
Why did he not make creation wholly blissful, free from misfortune?

If he were transcendent he would not create, for he would be free;
Nor if involved in transmigration, for then he would not be almighty.

Thus the doctrine that the world was created by God
Makes no sense at all.

And God commits great sin in slaying the children whom he himself created.
If you say that he slays only to destroy evil beings, why did he create such beings in the first place? . . . .

Good men should combat the believer in divine creation, maddened by an evil doctrine.

Know that the world is uncreated, as time itself is, without beginning and end,
And is based on the principles, life and the rest.

Uncreated and indestructible, it endures under the compulsion of its own nature,
Divided into three sections—hell, earth, and heaven.

Be Watchful

In this sutra we find more exhortations to adhere to Jain moral principles. These words are said to have been spoken by Mahavira to one of his followers called Gautama (not the Buddha).

"As the dead leaf when its time is up
falls from the tree to the ground,
so is the life of man.
Gautama, always be watchful!

"As the dewdrop that sways on a blade of grass
lasts but a moment,
so is the life of man.
Gautama, always be watchful!

"For the soul which suffers for its carelessness
is whirled about in the universe,
through good and evil karma.
Gautama, always be watchful!

"When the body grows old and the hair turns white,
and all the vital powers decrease . . .
despondency and disease befall, and the flesh wastes and decays.
Gautama, always be watchful!

"So cast away all attachments,
and be pure as a lotus, or as water in autumn.
Free from every attachment,
Gautama, always be watchful!

Uttaradhyayana Sutra, A. L. Basham, trans., in *The Wonder That Was India* 2nd ed. (New York: Grove Press, 1954), 293–294.

PRACTICES

The Eternal Law

This sutra, taken from the *Book of Good Conduct*, urges Jains to follow the eternal law—that is, the supreme moral teaching of nonviolence, *ahimsa*.

Thus say all the perfect souls and blessed ones, whether past, present, or to come—thus they speak, thus they declare, thus they proclaim: All things breathing, all things existing, all things living, all beings whatever, should not be slain or treated with violence, or insulted, or tortured, or driven away.

This is the pure unchanging eternal law, which the wise ones who know the world have proclaimed, among the earnest and the non-earnest, among the loyal and the not-loyal, among those who have given up punishing others and those who have not done so, among those who are weak and those who are not, among those who delight in worldly ties and those who do not. This is the truth. So it is. Thus it is declared in this religion.

When he adopts this Law a man should never conceal or reject it. When he understands the Law he should grow indifferent to what he sees, and not act for worldly motives. . . .

What is here declared has been seen, heard, approved, and understood. Those who give way and indulge in pleasure will be born again and again. The heedless are outside [the hope of salvation]. But if you are mindful, day and night steadfastly striving, always with ready vision, in the end you will conquer.

Acaranga Sutra, 1.4.1, from A. L. Basham, trans., in *Sources of Indian Tradition* (New York: Columbia University Press, 1988), 64–65.

Sinning Against the Earth

This passage argues for a strong respect for life—that is, an abhorrence of harm to other creatures, a wrong characterized as "sinning against the earth." It explores in detail all the ways that living things can be destroyed.

Earth is afflicted and wretched, it is hard to teach, it has no discrimination. Unenlightened men, who suffer from the effects of past deeds, cause great pain in a world full of pain already, for in earth souls are individually embodied. If, thinking to gain praise, honor, or respect, . . . or to achieve a good rebirth, . . .

Acaranga Sutra, 1.1, from A. L. Basham, trans., in *Sources of Indian Tradition* 2nd ed. (New York: Columbia University Press, 1988), 65–66.

or to win salvation, or to escape pain, a man sins against earth or causes or permits others to do so, . . . he will not gain joy or wisdom. . . . Injury to the earth is like striking, cutting, maiming, or killing a blind man. . . . Knowing this a man should not sin against earth or cause or permit others to do so. He who understands the nature of sin against earth is called a true sage who understands karma. . . .

And there are many souls embodied in water. Truly water . . . is alive. . . . He who injures the lives in water does not understand the nature of sin or renounce it. . . . Knowing this, a man should not sin against water, or cause or permit others to do so. He who understands the nature of sin against water is called a true sage who understands karma. . . .

By wicked or careless acts one may destroy fire-beings and, moreover, harm other beings by means of fire. . . . . For there are creatures living in earth, grass, leaves, wood, cowdung, or dustheaps, and jumping creatures which . . . fall into a fire if they come near it. If touched by fire, they shrivel up, . . . lose their senses, and die. . . . He who understands the nature of sin in respect of fire is called a true sage who understands karma.

And just as it is the nature of a man to be born and grow old, so is it the nature of a plant to be born and grow old. . . . One is endowed with reason, and so is the other; one is sick, if injured, and so is the other; one grows larger, and so does the other; one changes with time, and so does the other. . . . He who understands the nature of sin against plants is called a true sage who understands karma. . . .

All beings with two, three, four, or five senses, . . . in fact all creation, know individually pleasure and displeasure, pain, terror, and sorrow. All are full of fears which come from all directions. And yet there exist people who would cause greater pain to them. . . . Some kill animals for sacrifice, some for their skin, flesh, blood, . . . feathers, teeth, or tusks; . . . some kill them intentionally and some unintentionally; some kill because they have been previously injured by them, . . . and some because they expect to be injured. He who harms animals has not understood or renounced deeds of sin. . . . He who understands the nature of sin against animals is called a true sage who understands karma. . . .

A man who is averse from harming even the wind knows the sorrow of all things living. . . . He who knows what is bad for himself knows what is bad for others, and he who knows what is bad for others knows what is bad for himself. This reciprocity should always be borne in mind. Those whose minds are at peace and who are free from passions do not desire to live [at the expense of others]. . . . He who understands the nature of sin against wind is called a true sage who understands karma.

In short he who understands the nature of sin in respect of all the six types of living beings is called a true sage who understands karma.

The Five Great Vows

Here are the Five Great Vows of Jainism articulated in the *Akaranga [Acaranga] Sutra*. The first and foremost pledge is to respect all life, to do no violence to any creature. The other commitments are to forswear lying, stealing, being unchaste, and having attachments. Consistently keeping these vows, which is hard to do, is supposed to cleanse the soul *(jiva)* of moral grime accumulated through bad karma and worldly attachments.

Akaranga Sutra, Book II, Lecture 15, Hermann Jacobi, trans., in *Sacred Books of the East*, vol. XXII (Delhi: Motilal Banarsidass, 1964, 1884), 202–210.

The first great vow, Sir, runs thus:

I renounce all killing of living beings, whether subtle or gross, whether movable or immovable. Nor shall I myself kill living beings (nor cause others to do it, nor consent to it). As long as I live, I confess and blame, repent and exempt myself of these sins, in the thrice threefold way, in mind, speech, and body.

There are five clauses.

A Nirgrantha [someone without attachments or impurities] is careful in his walk, not careless. The Kevalin [an enlightened one] assigns as the reason, that a Nirgrantha, careless in his walk, might (with his feet) hurt or displace or injure or kill living beings.

A Nirgrantha searches into his mind (i.e. thoughts and intentions). If his mind is sinful, blamable, intent on works, acting on impulses, produces cutting and splitting (or division and dissension), quarrels, faults, and pains, injures living beings, or kills creatures, he should not employ such a mind in action.

A Nirgrantha searches into his speech; if his speech is sinful, blamable, intent on works, acting on impulses, produces division and dissension, quarrels, faults, and pains, injures living beings, or kills creatures.

A Nirgrantha is careful in laying down his utensils of begging, he is not careless in it. The Kevalin says: A Nirgrantha who is careless in laying down his utensils of begging, might hurt or displace or injure or kill all sorts of living beings.

A Nirgrantha eats and drinks after inspecting his food and drink; he does not eat and drink without inspecting his food and drink. The Kevalin says: If a Nirgrantha would eat and drink without inspecting his food and drink, he might hurt and displace or injure or kill all sorts of living beings.

The second great vow runs thus:

I renounce all vices of lying speech (arising) from anger or greed or fear or mirth. I shall neither myself speak lies, nor cause others to speak lies, nor consent to the speaking of lies by others. I confess and blame, repent and exempt myself of these sins in the thrice threefold way, in mind, speech, and body. . . .

The third great vow runs thus:

I renounce all taking of anything not given, either in a village or a town or a wood, either of little or much, of small or great, of living or lifeless things. I shall neither take myself what is not given, nor cause others to take it, nor consent to their taking it. . . .

The fourth great vow runs thus:

I renounce all sexual pleasures, either with gods or men or animals. I shall not give way to sensuality. . .

The fifth great vow runs thus:

I renounce all attachments, whether little or much, small or great, living or lifeless; neither shall I myself form such attachments, nor cause others to do so, nor consent to their doing so. . . .

If a creature with ears hears agreeable and disagreeable sounds, it should not be attached to, nor delighted with, nor desiring of, nor infatuated by, nor covetous of, nor disturbed by the agreeable or disagreeable sounds. . . .

If a creature with eyes sees agreeable and disagreeable forms (or colours), it should not be attached, nor delighted with, nor desiring of, nor infatuated by, nor covetous of, nor disturbed by them.

If a creature with an organ of smell smells agreeable or disagreeable smells, it should not be attached to them. . . .

If a creature with a tongue tastes agreeable or disagreeable tastes, it should not be attached to them. . . .

If a creature with an organ of feeling feels agreeable or disagreeable touches, it should not be attached to them. . . .

He who is well provided with these great vows and their twenty-five clauses is really Houseless, if he, according to the sacred lore, the precepts, and the way correctly practises, follows, executes, explains, establishes, and, according to the precept, effects them.

Life of a Jain Nun

N. SHANTA

This is a biographical sketch covering the spiritual journey of the influential Jain nun Sadhvi Vicaksana. She was known for her keen mind, powers of expression, and uplifting effect on those around her. She preached harmony, universal friendship, and the need to banish sectarianism among Jains.

Jethi Bai was born at Amaravati, a town of Maharastra, into a family whose origins were in the district of Jodhapura. Like the majority of Maravadis settled in other regions or overseas for business or professional reasons, the parents of Jethi Bai had family members in their native village to which they frequently returned. The horoscope of the child revealed, so it was said, an unusual degree of courage and predicted that she would become an ascetic of great renown. In the meantime, she was an affectionate, friendly and intelligent child. They called her Dakhi, from *draksa*, bunch of grapes. In accordance with the custom of the day, she was affianced in childhood and up to the age of eight she knew the life of a happy family. The sudden death of her father was a terrible shock for her, for not only did she now lack his parental affection, but she began to ask the reason for her father's being so abruptly snatched from her. Life changed for her. Having neither brothers nor sisters, she remained alone with her mother, a young widow who was obliged to yield to the customs of her community. After many enquiries, this latter managed to trace the whereabouts of her cousin Sadhvi Suvarana and, taking Dakhi with her, stayed with her several times. Thus Dakhi came into contact with the sadhvis whom she proceeded to astonish by the liveliness of her intelligence. The mother of Dakhi had decided to receive *diksa* when her daughter married the young man to whom she had been betrothed. This, however, was not Dakhi's desire. She felt an attraction for the ascetic life and to fulfil this aspiration, she carried on a tenacious struggle with her paternal grandfather, who loved her dearly and refused to give his consent to the *diksa*. The young man's family, perturbed and unhappy, also applied pressure. Dakhi struggled alone with a grandfather whom, at the same time, she loved—alone, for neither could her mother or the sadhvis help her in any way, for the grandfather would have accused them of bringing influence to bear upon the child. The story of this struggle follows. . . .

Now started the second phase: Dakhi was kept at home and forbidden to go out to visit the temple or the *upasraya*. Dakhi replied that she would obey, that, as she was being forbidden to go to the temple, she would fast. This, then, is what she did. In the evening of the first day of the fast, her grandfather, softened at heart, offered her a cup of milk, but Dakhi refused. Softened still further, the grandfather gave her permission to attend the temple, but re-affirmed stoutly that he would never give his consent to her receiving *diksa* and that Dakhi must needs get married. To this she replied that she would not disobey, so, said she, she would wait for *diksa* but would never on any account marry! Confrontations of this sort continued for one week. The grandfather, realising his powerlessness to persuade Dakhi and despairing of the affair, lodged an

N. Shanta, *The Unknown Pilgrims*, Mary Rogers, trans. (Delhi: Sri Satgguru, 1997), 585–587, 589–593.

appeal with the civil authorities. He informed them that the sadhvis had brought pressure to bear upon his thirteen-year-old grand-daughter and were desirous of admitting her to *diksa* against the will of her guardian (himself); that they should be so good as to help him prevent Dakhi from joining the sadhvis. A *thakura*, a type of magistrate of the district, was appointed to study the case and administer justice. He sent for Dakhi and questioned her at length, even threatening her with his rifle. She did not allow herself to be intimidated and responded to everything with astonishing clarity and determination. Meanwhile, the grandfather was sending telegrams to two of his grandsons to come at once to his aid. While the magistrate, highly embarrassed by this difficult case, was considering what verdict he should give to the grandfather, everybody was trying to dissuade Dakhi, but all to no avail. . . .

Here, now, are her chief replies in her dialogue with the magistrate:

Thakura: "Do you really, my child, desire to embrace the ascetic life?"

Dakhi: "Yes, sir."

Thakura: "Why?"

Dakhi: "It is an inner call."

Thakura: "Why do you not wish to marry?"

Dakhi: "I have no desire for it."

Thakura: "Do you know what the ascetic life means?"

Dakhi: "Without a knowledge of the ascetic life it is not possible to experience its attraction. I do know what is meant by both life in the world and by asceticism."

Thakura: "Is not obedience to one's parents also part of the *dharma*?"

Dakhi: "Yes, indeed, but if it is clear that one's parents' demands are an obstacle to the full realisation of human life and of the *atman*, respectfully to oppose these demands is not contrary to the *dharma*."

Thakura: "Do you see, my child, what is in front of you?"

Dakhi: "Yes, it is a rifle."

Thakura: (to test her) "Leave aside all these arguments of yours and do as your grandfather tells you. If not, I'm going to use this rifle."—and with that he grasped the rifle. . . .

Dakhi: "If it is your duty to do so, use the rifle. I have no fear of death, one must die some day. It's all the same, whether I die today from a gunshot or tomorrow from some illness. It is a great thing to die for one's ideal."

THE FORMATIVE YEARS WITH SADHVI SUVARNA

After the *diksa*, the young Sadhvi Vicaksana became a disciple of Sadhvi Jatana Sri. Her two first *caturmasyas* were spent in Rajasthana, at Badalu and at Jayapura where she gave evidence of her capacity for study. Then, to her great joy, she was summoned to Dilli to the side of the *pravartini*, Sadhvi Suvarana. She stayed there until the latter's Great Departure, that is to say, about seven years. These years of training were thus passed under the direction of a remarkable guruni. Sadhvi Suvarana continued in the same line as Sadhvi Punya. She inherited all that the great pioneer had brought into being and was able to discern wisely how, at one and the same time, both to consolidate and deepen the inheritance and also to make further advances. She attached prime importance to *dhydna*, *svadhyaya* and *adhyayana*. She was herself the example and also the inspiration of her disciples. For her, *dhyana* did not consist solely in a technique that one followed for a limited time; *dhyana* was, as it were, the breathing of her whole being. Her depth of contemplation, people say, was most striking. She habitually remained for six to seven hours in deep concentration, in which *japa* alternated with long moments of silence. Whoever her interlocutor might be, she brooked no idle talk. During the last years of her life, her concentration intensified and she was used to remain thus silent and absorbed for about twelve hours. Her favourite, because very short, *mantra* was *arham* (*arhat*). . . .

VISVAMITRA: THE UNIVERSAL FRIEND

After the years of training in Dilli, Sadhvi Vicaksana began her *viharas* up and down the country. We find her in the North, in the West, in the Centre and in the South. Her ardour is diminished by no obstacle or difficulty. She has, however, a delicate constitution and suffers from malaria and, after a while, from a heart condition that obliges her to remain stationary for two years; later on, on account of a fall, she hurt her ribs and must receive attention. Each time, with simplicity of heart, she agrees to see the doctor and follow the prescribed treatment. She accepts also, temporarily, the hospitality of the sravakas.

They have called her: *jaina kokila*, the Jaina cuckoo, on account of her melodious voice, the sincerity and convincingness of her words, which, like the cuckoo's song, have enchanted all hearts. Of what does Sadhvi Vicaksana speak? Why do the crowds flock to hear her? The answer is simple: her language is direct, without pomposity or the slightest affectation; she goes straight to the essentials. It is her deep sincerity, her love for all living beings and the clarity with which she expresses herself that not only captivate all hearts, but transforms them, removing both barriers and prejudices and lessening or even completely obliterating all enmities. On reading her biography, one is struck by the way in which, simultaneously, she resembles a fresh breeze and a blazing fire. A fresh breeze, for in her presence one feels uplifted; a blazing fire, for her ardent words act like a purifying fire. . . .

She addresses herself first and foremost to the Jainas, so little united among themselves; when she arrives in some place, her presence constitutes a unifying factor between the several communities, of which one may be affecting indifference, another being positively hostile, towards the rest. Her *pravacanas,* furthermore, are for all human beings without exception; here and there Hindus and Musulmans alike come to listen to her; through her they come to know the Jaina *dharma* for the first time or to see it in a fresh light. Let us consider a few particular passages or actual happenings that may help us to grasp her influence. In the presence of Digambaras, Sadhvi Vicaksana, herself a Svetambara, attacks neither party, but rather seeks that which may unite them. At Hastinapura, a pilgrimage-place venerated by both traditions, but where the Digambaras are more numerous and more firmly entrenched, she broached the subject of the principal causes of dispute between them: can women attain *moksa*? Do the *kevalins* take nourishment or not? The Digambaras answer both questions in the negative, the Svetambaras in the affirmative. Addressing the whole assembly, she told them: "Brethren, a man all of whose *karmas* were destroyed would not even so attain *moksa*, is not this what nowadays you and I believe? Then, why this question on the subject of women? It is surely stupid to vitiate the present on account of differences void of substance (for today) . . ." Then she went on to say: "Do we not believe, you and I, that the *atman* is neither male nor female, that it is subject to no change and that maleness and femaleness are due to the mode of *karman* relative to the body? But is *moksa* attained in the *atman* or in the body? . . ." In the same vein, she said: "Do the *kevalins* take nourishment or not? Does that really affect the state of *kevalajnana*? *Jnana* appertains to the *atman;* nourishment is for the body. It is of little concern to us whether the *kevalins* take nourishment or not. Our aim is to believe in the state of being of the *kevalin* and to strive towards it. These useless quarrels are damaging and lead nowhere." Thus she exhorts them all, as disciples of Mahavira, to drop these scholastic disputes inherited from the past, to come to a brotherly understanding and demonstrate *visvamaitri*, instead of reviling one another and becoming thus the laughing-stock of all.

CONTEMPORARY CHALLENGES

Jains Today

VASUDHA NARAYANAN

Vasudha Narayanan discusses the relationship between Jains and Hindus in modern India. Their history reveals times of cordial relations as well as seasons of conflict, intolerance, and suspicion. Although Hinduism and Buddhism have changed doctrinally over the centuries, Jainism has held fast to its original tradition.

In India, Jains constitute a tiny minority, numbering only half of 1 per cent of the population. There have been periods of cordial relations between Jains and Hindus. Marriages are sometimes arranged for men and women between the two traditions in some regions of India. Sometimes, at least on the American continent, there have been temples accommodating both faiths. Historically, however, there have also been times of conflict and tension.

Tension and intolerance have occurred in South India, where Hindu devotional poets frequently converted Jain kings to become followers of Visnu or Siva. Thus Pandyan kings from Madurai in South India were persuaded to become followers of Siva by Saivite saints in the eighth and ninth centuries. The Hoysala king Bittideva was converted to Vaisnavism by the teacher Ramanuja and was given the name Visnu Vardhana. Hindu texts in the Tamil language show considerable animosity towards the Jains, and inscriptions in the state of Tamil Nadu bear eloquent testimony to the persecution of Jains.

Although there was considerable interaction and mutual borrowing leading to a shared corpus of myth and ritual between the Hindu and Jain traditions, throughout the centuries the Jains have held fast to their own retelling and interpretations of the myth and to rituals and beliefs that have never compromised their unique identity.

The unique characteristics of the Jain tradition have safeguarded its identity from a fate that would have been almost inevitable: to become absorbed as one of the many sects of the amorphous Hindu tradition. The Jain and Buddhist traditions began at about the same time, but their historical roles differ. The Jains remained in India as an identifiable minority, while Buddhism eventually lost much of its identity in India but successfully spread elsewhere in Asia.

Although by the tenth century the Hindu *Bhagavata purana* included (albeit patronizingly) Siddhartha Gautama, the Buddha, as one of the many incarnations of Visnu, Mahavira was never considered to be

Vasudha Narayanan, "The Jain Tradition," in *World Religions: Eastern Traditions* (New York: Oxford University Press, 2002), 190–191.

one. However, this Hindu text did identify Rsabha, the first Jain *tirthankara,* as a partial incarnation of Visnu and Hinduized many of the Jain details. Rsabha and Parsva are portrayed with certain iconographic characteristics that are associated with the Hindu deity Visnu. The name Rsabha means "bull," and his emblem, like that of the Hindu god Siva, is the bull. Parsva, like Visnu, is seen with a serpent serving as his umbrella. On the other hand, the Jains have their own versions of the *Ramayana* and the *Mahabharata.* In recounting one of the myths, the Jain tradition associates the Hindu god Krsna (variously seen as the eighth or ninth incarnation of Visnu) as the cousin of the twenty-second *tirthankara,* Neminatha.

The relationship between the Jain and Hindu traditions has been somewhat ambiguous in post-independence India. While the religious identity of the Jains has not been compromised, their legal and social identities are somewhat blurred. Since India does not have a uniform civil code, Jains and Sikhs are included under the Hindu family law. Thus, marriage, divorce, and inheritance are all governed by the law applying to Hindus. Legal texts observe that the courts in India have always applied the Hindu law to Jain cases in the absence of a Jain custom that directly contradicts the Hindu law.

Socially, some Jains in India and especially in the diaspora, while proud of their heritage and identity, simply identify themselves as "Hindu" when asked about their religion. They do this, they say, because many Westerners are not familiar with the Jain tradition and the explanations seem tedious in a casual conversation. Interestingly, while these Jains seem comfortable identifying themselves as Hindu to social acquaintances, they are quite clear about their distinctive religious identity at home and among close friends.

STUDY QUESTIONS

1. What are the Five Great Vows of Jainism?
2. Who are the *tirthankaras*? How are they regarded in Jainism?
3. What *tirthankara* do Jains revere the most? What form did his asceticism take?
4. What are the main tenets of the *Digambara* sect? Of the *Shvetambara* sect?
5. How are these four things related: Mahavira, *kevala*, *samsara*, and *jina*?
6. What occupations do Jains generally shun? Why?
7. How are the following concepts related in Jainism: *jiva*, *kevala*, karma, and *samsara*?
8. True or false: Jainism holds that mere belief in God or gods is enough to secure the blessings of enlightenment. Explain.
9. Explain the Jain attitude toward God and gods.
10. Describe three forms of Jain devotional practice.

FURTHER READING

A. L. Basham, *The Wonder That Was India* (New York: Grove Press, 1954).

John Bowker, ed., *The Oxford Dictionary of World Religions* (Oxford: Oxford University Press, 1997).

Paul Dundas, *The Jains* (London: Routledge, 2002).

Ainslie T. Embree, ed., *Sources of Indian Tradition*, 2nd ed. (New York: Columbia University Press, 1988).

Jaini S. Padmanabh, *The Jaini Path of Purification* (Columbia, MO: South Asia Books, 2001).

Jyoti Prasad Jain, *Religion and Culture of the Jains* (New Delhi: Bharatiya Jnanpith, 1983).

N. Shanta, *The Unknown Pilgrims: The Voice of the Sadhvis: The History, Spirituality and Life of the Jaina Women Ascetics* (Delhi: Indian Books Centre, 1997).

Arvind Sharma, ed., *Today's Woman in World Religions* (Albany: State University of New York Press, 1994).

ONLINE

Jainism: Principles, Tradition and Practices, "Jainism: Introduction," http://www.cs.colostate.edu/~malaiya/jainhlinks.html (December 22, 2015).

Jain World, http://www.jainworld.com/index.htm (December 22, 2015).

5 Buddhism

Buddhism was virtually unheard of in Europe and North America until the mid-1800s, and it did not attract significant numbers of adherents in the West until the twentieth century. Now with 460 million adherents worldwide, it is the fourth-largest world religion and one of the fastest-growing religious traditions in America. It offers several metaphysical, epistemological, and moral theories and has become for many people a source of values relevant to debates about war, animal rights, the environment, capital punishment, and other issues.

BUDDHIST COMPLEXITIES

The term *Buddhism* disguises the religion's intricacies. Although Buddhists everywhere may hold in common some teachings of the Buddha, these core beliefs are few, allowing a great many meandering trails within a broad doctrinal highway. Buddhism therefore has no single set of authorized practices or a common compilation of doctrines or a universal statement of the articles of faith. Instead there are many schools of thought and practice in Buddhism (some would say *Buddhisms*), Zen Buddhism and Tibetan Buddhism being only the most familiar.

In some respects, Buddhism is the antithesis of what most people in the West think of as a religion. It posits no creator God, no all-powerful all-knowing deity that rules the universe, takes an interest in humans, or answers prayers. It teaches that the Buddha himself was neither God nor the child of a God. He was instead the ultimate teacher and an example for all Buddhists to follow. In accordance with the Buddha's wishes, Buddhism has no central religious authority. There is no Buddhist pope; there are only the Buddha's teachings. An individual achieves salvation not through faith in God, but primarily through his or her own efforts, by self-discipline and self-transformation. Buddhists must work out their own salvation.

According to Buddhist sources, the teachings of the Buddha astonished many of his day who were used to the doctrines and practices of Indian religions. In contrast to the orthodoxies of the time, the Buddha rejected the caste system, extreme asceticism, the practice of animal sacrifice, the authority of the *Vedas*, submission to the Brahmins as priests, and the existence of the soul (a permanent, unchanging identity). Contradicting the Hindu social conventions, he taught that women should not be barred from the spiritual life he proposed—they too could attain enlightenment. Contrary to doctrines of the major Western religious traditions, he was nontheistic in the sense that he had no use for the idea of a personal creator God. He believed that gods, goddesses, and demons exist, but that they are—like all other g things—finite, vulnerable, and mortal. They are trapped in the cycle of death and re-irth just as humans are. He therefore renounced religious devotion to any deity.

Buddhist scriptures point out that on some deep questions about the nature of reality—questions that most religions try to address—the Buddha was silent. He refused to conjecture about what happens after death, whether the universe was eternal, whether it was infinite, whether body and soul were the same thing, and what constitutes the divine. He taught that such speculations were pointless since they overlooked what was truly important in existence: the fact of suffering and the path of liberation from it. A person who spends his time trying to answer these imponderable questions, he said, is like a man struck by an arrow who will not pull it out until he has determined all the mundane facts about the arrow, bow, and archer—and dies needlessly while gathering the information.

THE BUDDHA'S LIFE

During a time of wrenching social change and clashing religious viewpoints, Buddhism arose in northern India (now southern Nepal) in the sixth century BCE. The spiritual landscape was dotted by religious and philosophical worldviews of all sorts, with each one competing for recognition and the allegiance of devotees. The practices advocated by various groups included meditation, celibacy, animal sacrifices, vegetarianism, nonviolence, worship of numerous gods, and **asceticism** (the denial of physical comfort or pleasures for religious ends). Some believed in rebirth and karma; some did not. Some accepted the notion of spiritual progress through one's own efforts; others denied it. Some thought that the actions of humans are never done freely but are fated to occur; some insisted that humans have free will.

Even though the sacred literature of Buddhism is ancient, revered, and voluminous, scholars must view it with a measure of judicious skepticism. Part of the reason is that for the first four hundred years of Buddhist history, the Buddha's teachings were passed along via an oral tradition, with monks reciting them from memory and risking errors in transmission.

FIGURE 5.1 An image of the Buddha, the earliest representation, appears on a gold coin minted by King Kanishka I around 120 CE.

And over the centuries, the written canon has been emended, expanded, and reinterpreted. Such scholarly caution is especially appropriate for the materials regarding the life of the Buddha, which are incomplete and intertwined with legend and symbolism.

Nevertheless, there is a traditional biographical account recognized by most Buddhists, and it goes something like this. In perhaps 563 BCE (the exact year is debated by specialists), the man destined to become the Buddha is born a prince in the tiny kingdom of Sakya in northern India and given the name Siddhartha Gautama. Siddhartha means "he whose aim is accomplished," and Gautama is a family name. Later many would call him Sakyamuni, "the sage of Sakya." At age sixteen, he marries a princess, and thirteen years later they have a son, Rahula.

The story goes that Siddhartha's father, a ruler named Suddhodana, wants his son to succeed him, so he surrounds him with luxury and shields him from all evidence of misery in the outside world. If the prince learns that the world is full of suffering, he might be tempted to renounce his comfortable life and become a monk. But all of Suddhodana's designs fail, for at age twenty-nine the prince sees what are called the Four Passing Sights, and they change his life forever. As legend has it, he ventures beyond the palace walls several times

BUDDHISM TIMELINE

BCE

563–483 Life of the Buddha

486 First Buddhist Council

386 Second Buddhist Council

265–232 Reign of King Asoka

250 Third Buddhist Council

c. 250 Buddhism established in Nepal and Sri Lanka

c. 25 Recording of the Pali Canon

CE

First century Buddhism spreads throughout Central Asia.

c. 100 *Lotus Sutra* composed in India

372 Buddhism established in Korea

538 Buddhism established in Japan

632 Buddhism becomes the official religion of Tibet.

Late Eighth century Mahayana spreads in Vietnam.

1887–1945 Buddhism in Japan officially supports militarism and the conquest of Korea, Taiwan, and part of China.

1950 World Council of Buddhists is established.

1989 The Dalai Lama is awarded the Nobel Peace Prize.[1]

and is shocked to see a decrepit old man, a diseased man, and a dead man. These three disturbing sights open his eyes to the unavoidable pain and impermanence of life and force him to question the meaning of it all. Then he encounters the fourth sight—a serene and detached **samana**, a wandering philosopher who had renounced all physical comforts to live as a beggar in search of the truth. Siddhartha decides that evening to lead such a life to pursue answers to the questions that haunt him. He leaves behind his wife, his son, his luxury, and his wealth to take up the alms bowl and begin his quest.

Seeking the wisdom that would help him transcend suffering and mortality, for six years he rambles about as a devoted *samana*, trying the spiritual regimens of renowned teachers. He masters the yogic meditation techniques of one teacher, then swiftly learns the meditation methods of another. But neither regimen gives Siddhartha the deep enlightenment for which he searches. He then tries severe asceticism, exposing himself to brutal heat and cold, holding his breath for extended periods, and fasting until his hair falls out and he is practically skin and bones. Eventually he concludes that such extreme self-denial is also a dead end. He thinks that if he continues his asceticism, he will not achieve enlightenment and will die trying.

So at age thirty-five Siddhartha begins to travel on what is known as the Middle Way to true wisdom—a path between self-gratification (which he practiced in his youth) and the self-mortification of asceticism. After finally deciding to give up the latter, he takes food to revive himself. At one point he sits under a large fig tree (called the *Bodhi*, or enlightenment, tree) to meditate. According to legend, he remains under the tree all night, meditating more and more deeply yet becoming increasingly conscious and aware. Early in the night he has a vision of all his past lives. Later he glimpses the actual workings of karma, watching how the rebirths of other people are reflected in their deeds committed in previous lives. Then he sees the true nature of suffering and death and how to end them forever. With this final insight, he reaches at dawn what he has been searching for—Enlightenment, or Awakening, the attainment of perfect understanding of the true nature of the universe, of life and death, and of suffering and liberation. After this momentous event, he is to be known by the title *the Buddha*, meaning "The Enlightened One" or "The Awakened One."

At first the Buddha wonders whether it is possible to teach his new wisdom to others, for the new insights are deep, perhaps too deep to be understood by the rest of humanity. He decides, however, that some people will indeed be able to grasp the truth, and—in his great compassion—he sets out to teach it to the world.

His first pupils are five ascetics he had befriended when they were all practicing severe asceticism together. Initially they shun him for abandoning the ways of self-denial, but eventually they see that he is different, transformed—he has achieved ultimate enlightenment—so they listen to him. To these five devoted followers, the Buddha preaches his first sermon in the Deer Park at present-day Sarnath. He preaches the **dharma**, Buddhism's core teachings systematized in the Four Noble Truths and the Noble Eightfold Path (discussed in the next section). The *dharma* embodies the ultimate truth about the nature of reality, the nature and cause of suffering, and the means for transcending suffering and its recurrence in continuous cycles of death and rebirth. Thus, in his first sermon, the Buddha is said to have started the turning of the Wheel of *Dharma*.

The five ascetics become the Buddha's devoted disciples, whom he ordains as the first members of his *sangha*, or monastic order. Eventually they also achieve enlightenment, becoming *arahats*—"worthy ones," or saints of Buddhism. The Buddha sends his disciples far and wide to teach the *dharma*, and soon Buddhism has a few more *arahats* and thousands of monks, disciples, and other followers. Eventually the Buddha is persuaded to allow

Buddhist nuns to be part of the *sangha*. People begin to respond to the Buddha's message in part because it is universal: he declares that all people are welcome to embrace the *dharma* and seek liberation from suffering—both men and women, rich and poor, priests and laymen, kings and members of the lowliest castes.

After his enlightenment, the Buddha spends the next forty-five years walking the roads and paths of northern India, spreading his message. Finally, at the age of eighty, in the village of Kusinara, the Buddha lies down on a couch between two trees and dies calmly, uttering at the last, "And now, O priests, I take my leave of you; all the constituents of being are transitory; work out your salvation with diligence."[2]

Before he dies, however, his disciples ask him who should lead them after he is gone. He replies that they should let the *dharma* lead them and rely on their own spiritual efforts:

> You must be your own lamps, be your own refuges. Take refuge in nothing outside yourselves. Hold firm to the truth as a lamp and a refuge, and do not look for refuge to anything besides yourselves.[3]

From the Buddha's death until about the first century CE, Buddhism fanned out from its territory of origin in all directions, becoming a world religion in the process. It became strongly established in Sri Lanka, where one of the oldest Buddhist canons of scripture (the Pali Canon) was preserved. In this first five hundred years, what became known as the two great branches of Buddhism arose in India before spreading elsewhere: *Theravada* (or the Way of the Elders) and *Mahayana* (or Great Vehicle). Theravada is now prevalent in Sri Lanka and the Southeast Asian countries of Myanmar (Burma), Laos, Thailand, and Cambodia. Mahayana exists in China, Tibet, and the East Asian nations of Mongolia, Japan, Vietnam, and Korea. Today most Buddhists follow the Mahayana tradition. Vajrayana (the "Thunderbolt Vehicle" or "Diamond Vehicle") is an important strain of Mahayana and the central pillar of Tibetan Buddhism. Some, however, think Vajrayana so distinctive that it should be considered a third branch of Buddhism (after Theravada and Mahayana). Thus Vajrayana adherents say the tradition is a "third turning of the wheel of the *dharma*." In any case, it arose out of India after Theravada and Mahayana and spread to Nepal, Tibet, Mongolia, and Bhutan.

THE BUDDHA'S TEACHINGS

The sacred writings say the Buddha meant his teachings to be useful—to be a realistic, accurate appraisal of our burdensome existence and how to rise above it. To a surprising degree, some aspects of his approach were rational and empirical. He tried to provide a reasonable explanation for the problem of existence and offer a plausible solution. Generally he thought people should not accept his views on faith but test them out through their own experience in everyday life. The Buddha declares,

> Do not believe in anything simply because you have heard it. Do not believe in traditions simply because they have been handed down for many generations. Do not believe in anything simply because it is spoken and rumored by many. Do not believe in anything simply because it is found written in your religious books. Do not believe in anything merely on the authority of your teachers and elders. But when, after observation and analysis, you find anything that agrees with reason, and is conducive to the good and benefit of one and all, then accept it and live up to it.[4]

Here the Buddha sounds like a philosophical skeptic and agnostic—not at all what we would expect from a religious leader.

The heart of the Buddha's system of teachings about the true nature of reality and how to live correctly to transcend it (the *dharma*) is the Four Noble Truths:

1. Life is suffering.
2. Suffering is caused by desires ("craving" or "thirst").
3. To banish suffering, banish desires.
4. Banish desires and end suffering by following the Noble Eightfold Path.

The First Noble Truth is that living brings suffering and dissatisfaction, or **dukkha**. In the traditional Buddhist way of putting it, "birth is painful, old age is painful, sickness is painful, death is painful, sorrow, lamentation, dejection, and despair are painful. Contact with unpleasant things is painful, not getting what one wishes is painful."[5] *Dukkha* comes in small and large doses—from mild stress and frustration to the agonies of devastating disease and the heartbreak of overwhelming loss and grief. But in any dose, suffering and dissatisfaction are inherent in living: an inescapable cost of existence.

A fundamental element of *dukkha* is impermanence (**anicca**)—the fact that things do not last, that whatever pleasures we enjoy soon fade, that whatever we possess we eventually lose, that whatever we do will be undone by time. The very transitory nature of life brings suffering, dissatisfaction, and pain.

Dukkha also arises because of another fact of life: **anatta**, the impermanence of the self, or not-self, or no-soul. A person—the "I" that we each refer to—is merely an ever-changing, fleeting assemblage of mental states or processes. It's the belief in a permanent self that spawns "craving," greed, selfishness, and egocentrism, and these lead to misery. But facing up to the fact of no-self makes room for selflessness and compassion for the rest of the world.

The thought of not-self frightens people, but to most Buddhists, *anatta* is a very soothing doctrine. As one Buddhist monk says,

> When you open the mind to the truth, then you realize there is nothing to fear. What arises passes away, what is born dies, and is not self—so that our sense of being caught in an identity with this human body fades out. We don't see ourselves as some isolated, alienated entity lost in a mysterious and frightening universe. We don't feel overwhelmed by it, trying to find a little piece of it that we can grasp and feel safe with, because we feel at peace with it. Then we have merged with the Truth.[6]

This focus on *dukkha* may seem like a dreary perspective on life, but it sets the stage for the Buddha's more optimistic views on the ultimate conquest of suffering. His message is not that we are doomed to unremitting suffering but that there is a way to escape our torment, to attain true and lasting happiness.

The Second Noble Truth is that the cause of *dukkha* is selfish desire ("craving" or "thirst")—desire for things that cannot sate our thirst, that arise from our grasping egos, that we can never truly obtain no matter how hard we try. We desire possessions, pleasures, power, money, life, beliefs, ideals, and more. We want things to be different from what they are or to remain the way they are forever. But we can never have any of these for long because everything is ephemeral, constantly changing. We have no distinct, permanent identity; the "self" is no more than a locus of shifting, flowing energy. Such an insubstantial, transient thing can never acquire anything permanent, even if permanent objects exist. We desire this or that, but our desires are continually frustrated. The result is discontent, unhappiness, and pain—*dukkha*.

The Third Noble Truth is that suffering can be extinguished if selfish desire is extinguished: *dukkha* will end if self-centered craving ends. As the Buddha says,

> Now this, O monks, is the noble truth concerning the destruction of suffering. Truly, it is the destruction of this very thirst. It is the laying aside of, the getting rid of, the being free from, the harboring no longer of this thirst. This, O monks, is the noble truth concerning the destruction of suffering.[7]

To quench selfish desires and therefore to end *dukkha* is to attain **nirvana**, the ultimate aim of all Buddhist practice and the liberation to which all the Buddha's teachings point. It is the extinguishing of the flames of desire (*nirvana* literally means *extinguish*) and all that accompanies it—greed, hatred, pride, delusion, and more. It is also the blossoming of contentment and inner peace, the "quietude of the heart." Buddhist scholar and monk Walpola Rahula describes it like this:

> He who has realized the Truth, Nirvana, is the happiest being in the world. He is free from all "complexes" and obsessions, the worries and troubles that torment others. His mental health is perfect. He does not repent the past, nor does he brood over the future. He lives fully in the present. Therefore he appreciates and enjoys things in the purest sense without self-projections. He is joyful, exultant, enjoying the pure life, his faculties pleased, free from anxiety, serene and peaceful. As he is free from selfish desire, hatred, ignorance, conceit, pride, and all such "defilements," he is pure and gentle, full of universal love, compassion, kindness, sympathy, understanding and tolerance. His service to others is of the purest, for he has no thought of self. He gains nothing, accumulates nothing, not even anything spiritual, because he is free from the illusion of Self, and the "thirst" for becoming.[8]

Nirvana is manifested both in life and at death. In life, it is—as Rahula suggests—a psychological and moral transformation and, ultimately, an enlightened way of living. At death, for an enlightened one, the continuing cycle, or wheel, of death and rebirth ends. *Dukkha*, the ever-recurring pain of existence, stops. And the controlling force behind the turning wheel—karma—ceases. So *nirvana*'s quenching of "defilements" not only quenches *dukkha* in life, but it also terminates the repeating pattern of death and rebirth. And by attaining *nirvana*, one acquires the title of *arhat*, a Buddhist saint.

Beyond this profound release, what *nirvana* entails at one's death is uncertain. The Buddha insisted that *nirvana* is beyond description and impossible to imagine, for it is neither annihilation nor survival of a soul. He said that people should devote themselves to attaining it rather than trying to plumb its depths. Buddhist sources, however, refer to *nirvana* with words such as *freedom*, *absolute truth*, *peace*, and *bliss*.

In Buddhism, one's cycle of repeated deaths and rebirths—**samsara**—is a painful process that can go on for millennia unless there is release from it through *nirvana*. The thing that wanders from one life to the next (what we refer to as "I") is not an eternally existing, permanent soul, self, or *atman*, but an ever-changing mix of personality fragments that recombine in each new life. The Buddha's classic illustration of this point is a flame (the "I") that is transferred from one candle to another. Only one flame is passed among multiple candles, so there is some continuity from one candle to the next—but the flame itself is also different from moment to moment.

Karma in Buddhism is just as it is in Hinduism: it's the universal principle that determines the characteristics and quality of each future life. But unlike Hinduism, Buddhism does not posit an *atman* that is subject to karma. In the Buddha's view of karma, through their own moral choices and acts people are free to try to change their karma and its associated results, and no one is trapped in a given level of existence forever. There is always the hope of rising to a higher point through spiritual effort or of halting the cycle of rebirths altogether through *nirvana.*

The notions of rebirth and karma lead naturally to the Buddhist attitude of compassion, tolerance, and kindness for all living things. After all, every being must follow the karmic current, being reborn as many different creatures from the lowest to the highest. Each human being has an implied empathetic connection with all other beings (humans, animals, and others) because he or she is likely to have *been* such beings at one time or another and to have endured the same kind of pain and grief they have.

The Fourth Noble Truth says the way to extinguish selfish desires and to attain *nirvana* is to follow the Noble Eightfold Path. The Path consists of eight factors or modes of practice

BACKGROUND

Zen

As Mahayana Buddhism spread throughout Asia and adapted to local cultures, it took on new forms that eventually became distinctive branches of the Mahayana tradition. A well-known one is called *Ch'an* in China and *Zen* in Japan. Generally it holds that *nirvana* is attained through personal effort with little or no help from Buddhas, **bodhisattvas** (those who are to become Buddhas), or teachers. It downplays scriptural study, rational thought, the deliverances of faith, Buddha worship, and incredibly long and laborious journeys toward enlightenment. Some in this school say enlightenment occurs gradually over time; others insist that it happens suddenly like a lightning strike. In either case, awakening comes after practicing meditation or performing some other highly focused action. Such exercises are meant to tap into the potential for Buddhahood (called *Buddha-nature*) that is inherent in everyone.

To many Zen Buddhists, abstractions and logical thinking are obstacles in the road to enlightenment. The Truth cannot be reasoned out; it must be accessed intuitively through direct experience. According to Zen, one way to quell the reasoning mind and open the door to insight is to meditate on a **koan**, an insoluble logic puzzle that's meant to confuse and dampen the intellect so enlightenment can occur. Initiates meditate on koans until rational thought is overcome and insight breaks through. Familiar koans include "What is the sound of one hand clapping?" and "What was your face before your parents were born?"

The primary type of meditation used in Zen is *zazen*, or sitting meditation. As one scholar says,

> *Zazen* . . . is used as the main basis for both awareness and *koan* meditations, though the meditator is also encouraged to develop awareness, and work with his *koan*, in any posture. Zen . . . attaches great importance to establishing correct posture in sitting meditation. The lower spine curves inwards, with the rest of the back straight and the abdomen completely relaxed. . . . The initial task of the meditator is to learn to dampen down wandering thoughts by counting and following the breath. . . .
>
> Once the meditator has learnt how to control his wandering thoughts to some extent, he may go on to develop high degrees of awareness while sitting . . . Here, the meditator cultivates *nothing but* sitting, in full awareness of the here-and-now of sitting . . . . The meditator sets out to be in a state in which he is not trying to think, nor trying not to think; he just sits with no deliberate thought.[9]

whose purpose is the development, or perfection, of the three fundamental aspects of Buddhist life: *wisdom*, *moral conduct*, and *mental discipline*, or focus. The eight factors have been described as "steps," as if they should be done in order, but they are actually intended to be implemented in concert. Each one complements and enhances the others, and a complete life cultivates them all. Together they constitute a way of purposeful living that the Buddha is said to have discovered through his own experience—the "Middle Way" or "Middle Path" between the extremes of brutal asceticism and sensual self-indulgence.

Inevitably different interpretations of the Buddha's teachings arose among his followers. Eventually these differences and the interactions of Buddhism with a variety of cultures in later centuries led to a panoply of schools of thought and adaptations in the Theravada and Mahayana traditions. Scholars attribute Buddhism's successful transplantation across cultures to several factors, including the religion's tolerance of competing religious beliefs, its lack of focus on doctrinal matters, and its emphasis on freedom of thought for its adherents.

MODERN CHALLENGES TO BUDDHISM

Like other religions, Buddhism has had to deal with the unstoppable juggernaut known as the modern world. This era in world history has unleashed social and ideological changes that the Buddha could not have imagined. For decades Buddhism in all its forms has been confronted with the diverging beliefs and practices of other faiths (pluralism and globalization), ideological pressures from nonreligious worldviews (secularism), an overwhelming economic ethic based on selfishness and material gain (capitalism and consumerism), the persuasive demands for fairness from long-ignored groups (women's rights, gay rights, and minority rights), political systems that persecute religious traditions (communism, fascism, and authoritarianism), critical investigations of religious doctrines and assumptions (science and modern scholarship), and some intractable problems that cannot be ignored (war, poverty, homelessness, environmental degradation, and more). In most cases, Buddhism has responded to these challenges by revising old ideas, generating new ones, or creating different traditions altogether. The changes have occurred not in Buddhism as a whole but in particular Buddhist sects or groups. The result is a Buddhism composed of a multitude of Buddhisms that are more diverse than in any other time in history.

Women and Buddhism

One issue that stands out among the many is the status of women. Most religions, East and West, have had to wrestle with this concern, and they continue to do so. Many observers would say that religions of all stripes are inherently patriarchal, that they have always been glaring examples of institutional inequality. The issue surfaces in Buddhism in part because, from its inception, the tradition has demonstrated an ambivalent attitude toward women. After the Buddha established a monastic order for males, he was asked to form a similar order for women—that is, for Buddhist nuns. At first he resisted the idea but eventually relented, noting that men and women were spiritual equals, both able to progress toward the highest wisdom and attain enlightenment. But he also insisted that the nuns be subordinate to the monks.

With rare exceptions, in many Buddhist traditions this unequal status has been the rule, even for women who have devoted their lives to Buddhist practice and ideals. Over the centuries, a few female monastic orders were established, but many of these withered away for lack of support from the government, the community, or the men's monastic orders. Some Buddhist traditions do ordain women (for example, Mahayana Buddhism in Korea and Vietnam), but in general Buddhism is still led by men who oppose full equality for women, ordained or not.

This form of discrimination continues despite the enormous contribution that women have made—and still make—to institutional Buddhism. Women help maintain the shrines, cook meals for the monks, perform rituals, make the pilgrimages, and (in some cases) sustain monasteries and temples through patronage. Despite their inferior status, thousands of women worldwide have chosen to live as unofficial nuns, walking the same austere path that monks do, taking vows of poverty, piety, and service.

A CLOSER LOOK

Buddhism and Science

Does Buddhism conflict with science? For several reasons, many Buddhists believe it does not. First, Buddhism is thought to be empirical, just as science is. The Buddha urged his followers to take nothing on faith but to test it out in their own experience. The current Dalai Lama has echoed this sentiment: "If there's good, strong evidence from science that such and such is the case and this is contrary to Buddhism, then we will change."[10] In addition, some elements of Buddhist cosmology seem to agree, at least superficially, with ideas in modern science: Every event has a cause, everything is connected or interdependent in some fundamental way, no eternally immutable objects exist (the whole cosmos is in flux). And of course the principles of Buddhist morality do not collide with science, because science is not in that line of work.

But philosophers of science would say something like this: science's job is to test theories, and it judges the worth of theories according to certain criteria (including how well the theory fits with existing theories or evidence, how many assumptions it makes, and whether it has successfully predicted any novel phenomena). If a theory is not needed to explain a phenomenon (because science explains it better), the theory is discredited. Scientists would reject the theory that Zeus causes lightning because they have much better theories to explain lightning. By this measure, scientists would say, many Buddhist theories would be rejected—for example, hungry ghosts, demons, gods, spiritual realms, karma, and reincarnation or rebirth. And the evidence for such theories provided by the Buddhist's direct experience (meditation or mystical practice) must also be rejected. We can accept truths acquired through meditation or mysticism, says the scientist, only if they can be corroborated by our usual tests based on reason and evidence—and these truths fail the test.

How can a Buddhist respond to such allegations? Here are three ways: (1) the Buddhist can, on various grounds, deny the scientific view altogether (or large parts of it); (2) the Buddhist can agree with the scientists and reject Buddhism entirely; or (3) the Buddhist can embrace his or her religion but only after stripping out the scientifically dubious content. Some who take this last path may end up with a Buddhism that fits better with our scientific age, and some may arrive at a purely secular Buddhism, accepting only ideas that are supported, or at least not refuted, by science. The secular Buddhist, for example, may accept meditation for its scientifically proven physiological and psychological benefits and can embrace the ethical content for its moral guidance.

Socially Engaged Buddhism

Every religious tradition must somehow come to terms with humanity's most pressing social problems. Some respond by opposing change—by maintaining or reviving a rigid adherence to a conservative past. Others preserve their core values while adapting practices and attitudes to a new world. Buddhism is in the latter category. Many Buddhists have found ways to apply Buddhist principles to some of the direst social ills of our time. Buddhist responses to social and political troubles have sometimes been disastrous (for instance, the violent conflict between the Buddhist majority and the Hindu and Muslim minority in Sri Lanka), but usually the Buddhist way has been benign or beneficial. For many, Buddhist values—compassion, equanimity, empathy, selflessness, nonviolence, generosity, and tolerance—are the relevant remedies for the afflictions of the contemporary world.

The tradition's altruistic approach to the planet's woes are part of what is referred to as "socially engaged Buddhism," the application of Buddhist principles to alleviate social, political, and economic suffering. Among the more prominent organizations and people involved in such work are the following:

The Buddhist Peace Fellowship. Some of its more recent projects include marches and letter-writing campaigns for peace in Afghanistan, the Middle East, Tibet, and Myanmar; support for efforts to end genocide in Darfur; efforts in the United States to end life sentences without parole for thirteen- and fourteen-year-old children; and campaigns against land mines in war-torn countries.

Daw Aung San Suu Kyi. This internationally known woman of courage uses Buddhist values to counter the forces of violence, injustice, ignorance, and fear. About her the *New York Times* says,

> Winner of the Nobel Peace Prize in 1991, Daw Aung San Suu Kyi is the leading pro-democracy opposition leader in Myanmar, formerly known as Burma, one of the world's most isolated and repressive nations. Ms. Aung San Suu Kyi spent most of the past two decades under detention after her party, the National League for Democracy, won an overwhelming victory in the 1990 elections but was denied power by the military junta, which has ruled since 1962. She was released from house arrest in November 2010.[11]

Buddhist Environmentalism ("Green Buddhism"). "Green Buddhism" refers to a wide range of individuals and organizations that address environmental issues through Buddhist principles such as interdependence, non-harm (*ahimsa*), and compassion. They are active around the globe. For example, in Cambodia activists have promoted seedling germination, tree planting, and water and wood management. In China they have conducted river and lake cleanups, the cataloging of local vegetation and animals, and the monitoring of the conditions of grasslands, wetlands, and ponds.

BUDDHIST SCRIPTURES

Buddhism does not have a single compilation of writings thought to be *the* authoritative Buddhist text. Instead, Buddhist scriptures consist of multiple sets of texts that are astonishingly extensive (much more voluminous than the Christian Bible), variously expressed in

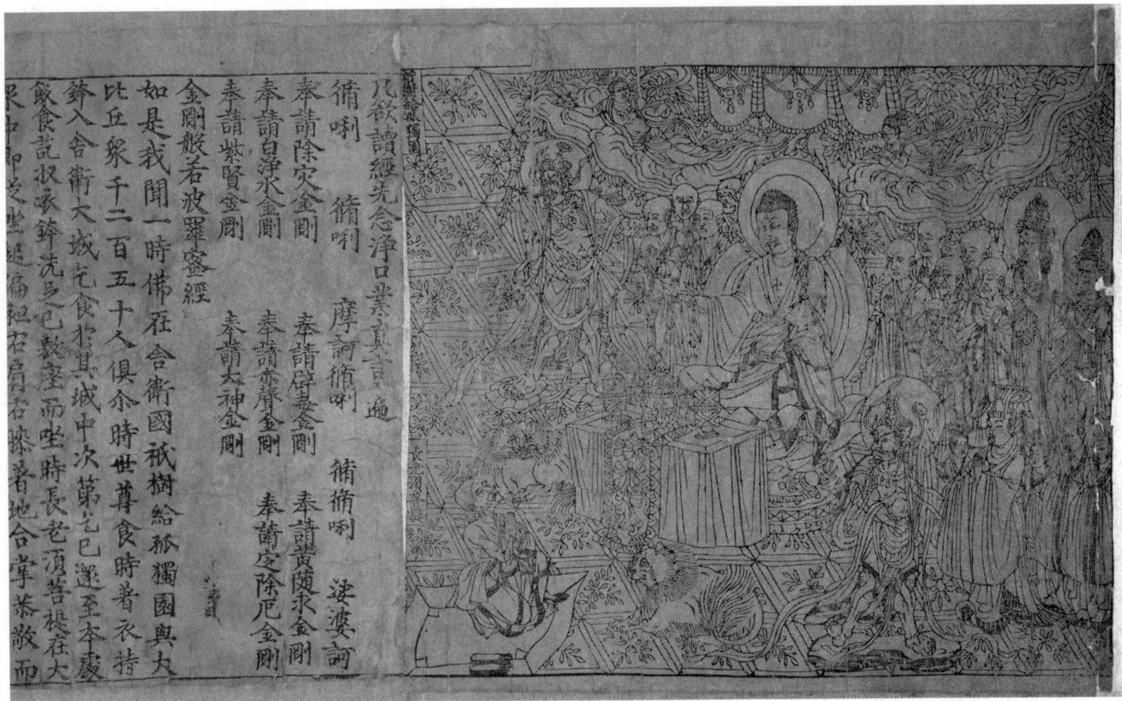

FIGURE 5.2 Frontispiece of the Diamond Sutra of Dunhuang, 868 CE. This manuscript is the oldest known printed book in the world; it appeared 587 years before the Gutenberg Bible.

different Buddhist traditions, and categorized in diverse ways. They are all based on oral transmission of the Buddha's teachings by the *sangha* and contain two kinds of writings: (1) the discourses or sermons of the Buddha and (2) various commentaries or elaborations on the Buddha's teachings by Buddhist scholars.

A complete authoritative collection of such writings is known as a *canon*. Several Buddhist canons exist, the most widely accepted being the Pali Canon, so named because it was written in Pali, an ancient language of India much like the one that the Buddha spoke. Preserved by the Theravada branch of Buddhism in Sri Lanka from at least the first century CE, this canon includes a core of teachings accepted by all Buddhist schools of thought. And much of its text is also included in the canons of other Buddhist camps.

The Pali Canon is called the *Tripitaka* ("three baskets"), a reference to its three principal parts: the *Sutra pitaka* (the Buddha's discourses, his major teachings), the *Vinaya pitaka* (the rules of discipline for the *sangha*), and the *Abhidharma pitaka* (commentary and systemization of the Buddha's teachings by scholars). The *Sutra pitaka* is further divided into five "collections": the Longer Discourses, the Shorter Discourses, the Connected Teachings, the Graduated Teachings, and the Small Book Collection. The last is a miscellany that includes aphoristic sayings of the Buddha, hymns of the elder monks and nuns, and story-poems recounting the Buddha's past lives.

NOTES

1. Adapted mostly from David Levinson, ed., *Religion: A Cross-Cultural Dictionary* (New York: Oxford University Press, 1996), ix–xiv.

2. Henry Clarke Warren, trans., *The Buddha in Translations: Passages from the Buddhist Sacred Books* (Whitefish, MT: Kessinger Publishing, 2005), from the *Maha-Parinibbana-Sutta* (v. and vi.) of the *Digha-Nikaya*.

3. As quoted in William T. deBary, ed., *Sources of Indian Tradition* (New York: Columbia University Press, 1958), vol. 1, 110.

4. *Anguttara Nikaya, Kalama Sutra*, in F. L. Woodward and E. M. Hare, trans., *The Book of Gradual Sayings*, 5 vols. (London: PTS, 1932–1936).

5. E. J. Thomas, trans., "Pali Sermons, the First Sermon," in *Samyutta*, V, 420 (London: Kegan Paul International, 1935), 29–31.

6. Ajahn Sumedho, cited in Satnacitto Bhikku, ed., *Buddha-Nature* (London: World Wide Fund for Nature, 1989).

7. Dhammacakapparattana Sutta, 1–8, in T. W. Rhys Davids, trans., *Buddhist Sutta: Sacred Books of the East* (Oxford: Oxford University Press, 1881), 146–155.

8. Walpola Rahula, *What the Buddha Taught* (New York: Grove Press, 1979), 43.

9. Peter Harvey, *An Introduction to Buddhism: Teachings, History and Practices* (Cambridge: Cambridge University Press, 1990), 270–271.

10. Dalai Lama, quoted in Pamela Weintraub, "Masters of the Universe," *Omni*, March 1990, 89.

11. "Daw Aung San Suu Kyi," New York Times, 26 July 2012, http://topics.nytimes.com/top/reference/timestopics/people/a/daw_aung_san_suu_kyi/index.html (July 26, 2012).

KEY TERMS

anatta The impermanence of the self; or not-self, or no-soul.

anicca Impermanence; the ephemeral nature of everything.

asceticism The denial of physical comfort or pleasures for religious ends.

bodhisattva A being who is eventually to be a Buddha.

dharma Buddhism's core teachings systematized in the Four Noble Truths and the Noble Eightfold Path.

dukkha The inevitable suffering and dissatisfaction of existence.

karma The universal principle that governs the characteristics and quality of each rebirth, or future life.

koan An insoluble logic puzzle that's meant to confuse and dampen the intellect so enlightenment can occur.

nirvana A state of bliss and well-being attained when one extinguishes the flames of desire and thus halts the repeating cycle of death and rebirth.

samana A wandering philosopher who has renounced all physical comforts to live as a beggar in search of the truth.

samsara One's cycle of repeated deaths and rebirths.

READINGS

TEACHINGS

The Awakened One

The *Dhammapada* is a canonical text that dates to ancient times, yet it has had broad appeal in the modern world. It exists in several versions, is rendered in verse, and is widely quoted. Its title suggests that it contains inspiring affirmations of the Buddha.

179. Whose victory is not turned into defeat,
Whose victory no one in this world reaches,
That Awakened One whose range is limitless,
Him, the trackless, by what track will you lead?

180. For whom craving there is not, the netlike, the clinging,
To lead him wheresoever,
That Awakened One whose range is limitless,
Him, the trackless, by what track will you lead?

181. Those who are intent on meditating, the wise ones,
Delighting in the calm of going out,
Even gods long for them,
The Fully Enlightened Ones, the mindful.

182. Difficult is the attainment of the human state.
Difficult the life of mortals.
Difficult is the hearing of dhamma true.
Difficult the appearance of Awakened Ones.

183. Refraining from all that is detrimental
The attainment of what is wholesome,
The purification of one's mind:
This is the instruction of Awakened Ones.

184. Forbearing patience is the highest austerity;
Nibbana [*Nirvana*] is supreme, the Awakened Ones say.
One who has gone forth is not one who hurts another,
No harasser of others is a recluse.

185. No faultfinding, no hurting, restraint in the *patimokkha*,
Knowing the measure regarding food, solitary bed and chair,
Application, too, of higher perception:
This is the instruction of the Awakened Ones.

186. Not even with a rain of golden coins
Is contentment found among sensual pleasures
"Sensual pleasures are of little delight, are a misery."
Knowing so, the wise one

187. Takes no delight
Even for heavenly sensual pleasures.
One who delights in the ending of craving
Is a disciple of the Fully Enlightened One.

The Dhammapada, John Ross Carter and Mahinda Palihawadana, trans. (New York: Oxford University Press, 1987), 34–36.

188. Many for refuge go
To mountains and to forests,
To shrines that are groves or trees—
Humans who are threatened by fear.
189. This is not a refuge secure,
This refuge is not the highest.
Having come to this refuge,
One is not released from all misery.
190. But who to the Buddha, Dhamma,
And Sangha as refuge has gone,
Sees with full insight
The Four Noble Truths;
191. Misery, the arising of misery,
And the transcending of misery,
The Noble Eightfold Path
Leading to the allaying of misery.
192. This, indeed, is a refuge secure.
This is the highest refuge.
Having come to this refuge,
One is released from all misery.

The Five Precepts

Every Buddhist is expected to adhere to minimum moral standards or virtues known as the Five Precepts. Much more is demanded of monks, who must conduct themselves not only according to the Precepts but also by a list of strict monastic rules. The first and foremost precept prohibits the killing of any living being.

"I UNDERTAKE to observe the rule
to abstain from taking life;
to abstain from taking what is not given;
to abstain from sensuous misconduct;
to abstain from false speech;
to abstain from intoxicants as tending to cloud the mind."

The first four precepts are explained by Buddhaghosa as follows:

(1) "Taking life" means to murder anything that lives. It refers to the striking and killing of living beings. "Anything that lives"—ordinary people speak here of a "living being," but more philosophically we speak of "anything that has the life-force." "Taking life" is then the will to kill anything that one perceives as having life, to act so as to terminate the life-force in it, in so far as the will finds expression in bodily action or in speech. With regard to animals it is worse to kill large ones than small. Because a more extensive effort is involved. Even where the effort is the same, the difference in substance must be considered. In the case of humans the killing is the more blameworthy the more virtuous they are. Apart from that, the extent of the offence is proportionate to the intensity of the wish to kill. Five factors are involved: a living being, the perception of a living being, a thought of murder, the action of carrying it out, and death as a result of it. And six are the ways in which the offence may be carried out: with one's own hand, by instigation, by missiles, by slow poisoning, by sorcery, by psychic power.

(2) "To take what is not given" means the appropriation of what is not given. It refers to the removing of someone else's property, to the stealing of

Buddhist Scriptures, Edward Conze, trans. (New York: Penguin Books, 1959), 70–73.

it, to theft. "What is not given" means that which belongs to someone else. "Taking what is not given" is then the will to steal anything that one perceives as belonging to someone else, and to act so as to appropriate it. Its blameworthiness depends partly on the value of the property stolen, partly on the worth of its owner. Five factors are involved: someone else's belongings, the awareness that they are someone else's, the thought of theft, the action of carrying it out, the taking away as a result of it. This sin, too, may be carried out in six ways. One may also distinguish unlawful acquisition by way of theft, robbery, underhand dealings, stratagems, and the casting of lots.

(3) "Sensuous misconduct"—here "sensuous" means "sexual," and "misconduct" is extremely blameworthy bad behaviour. "Sensuous misconduct" is the will to transgress against those whom one should not go into, and the carrying out of this intention by unlawful physical action. By "those one should not go into," first of all men are meant. And then also twenty kinds of women. Ten of them are under some form of protection, by their mother, father, parents, brother, sister, family, clan, co-religionists, by having been claimed from birth onwards, or by the king's law. The other ten kinds are: women bought with money, concubines for the fun of it, kept women, women bought by the gift of a garment, concubines who have been acquired by the ceremony which consists in dipping their hands into water, concubines who once carried burdens on their heads, slave girls who are also concubines, servants who are also concubines, girls captured in war, temporary wives. The offence is the more serious, the more moral and virtuous the person transgressed against. Four factors are involved: someone who should not be gone into, the thought of cohabiting with that one, the actions which lead to such cohabitation, and its actual performance. There is only one way of carrying it out: with one's own body.

(4) "False"—this refers to actions of the voice, or actions of the body, which aim at deceiving others by obscuring the actual facts. "False speech" is the will to deceive others by words or deeds. One can also explain: "False" means something which is not real, not true. "Speech" is the intimation that that is real or true. "False speech" is then the volition which leads to the deliberate intimation to someone else that something is so when it is not so. The seriousness of the offence depends on the circumstances. If a householder, unwilling to give something, says that he has not got it, that is a small offence; but to represent something one has seen with one's own eyes as other than one has seen it, that is a serious offence. If a mendicant has on his rounds got very little oil or ghee, and if he then exclaims, "What a magnificent river flows along here, my friends!," that is only a rather stale joke, and the offence is small; but to say that one has seen what one has not seen, that is a serious offence. Four factors are involved: something which is not so, the thought of deception, an effort to carry it out, the communication of the falsehood to someone else. There is only one way of doing it: with one's own body.

"To abstain from"—one crushes or forsakes sin. It means an abstention which is associated with wholesome thoughts. And it is threefold: (I) one feels obliged to abstain, (II) one formally undertakes to do so, (III) one has lost all temptation not to do so.

(I) Even those who have not formally undertaken to observe the precepts may have the conviction that it is not right to offend against them. So it was with Cakkana, a Ceylonese boy. His mother was ill, and the doctor prescribed fresh rabbit meat for her. His brother sent him into the field to catch a rabbit, and he went as he was bidden. Now a rabbit had run into a field to eat of the corn, but in its eagerness to get there had got entangled in a snare, and gave forth cries of distress. Cakkana followed the sound, and thought: "This rabbit has got caught there, and it will make a fine medicine for my mother!" But then he thought again: "It is not suitable for me that, in order to preserve my mother's life, I should deprive someone else of his life." And so he released the rabbit, and said to it: "Run off, play with the other rabbits in the wood, eat grass and drink water!" On his return he told the story to his brother, who scolded him. He then went to his mother, and said to her: "Even without having been told, I know quite clearly that I should not deliberately deprive any living being of life." He then fervently resolved that these truthful words of his might make his mother well again, and so it actually happened.

(II) The second kind of abstention refers to those who not only have formally undertaken not to offend against the precepts, but who in addition are willing to sacrifice their lives for that. This can be illustrated by a layman who lived near Uttaravarddhamana. He had received the precepts from Buddharakkhita, the Elder. He then went to plough his field, but found that his ox had got lost. In his search for the ox he climbed up the mountain, where a huge snake took hold of him. He thought of cutting off the snake's head with his sharp knife, but on further reflection he thought to himself: "It is not suitable that I, who have received the Precepts from the venerable Guru, should break them again." Three times he thought, "My life I will give up, but not the precepts!" and then he threw his knife away. Thereafter the huge viper let him go, and went somewhere else.

The last kind of abstention is associated with the holy Path. It does not even occur to the Holy Persons to kill any living being.

The Enlightenment

Perhaps the best telling of the life or legend of the Buddha is found in the Buddhacarita ("The Acts of the Buddha"). The following section of the text describes how one night the Buddha passed through several phases of trance finally to attain enlightenment. He (1) recollected all his past lives, (2) acquired "the supreme heavenly eye" by which he saw the cycle of death and rebirth experienced by all people, (3) entered into a profound meditation on the nature of the world and the source of all suffering, and (4) and finally "reached the state of all-knowledge"—Awakening.

Now that he had defeated Mara's violence by his firmness and calm, the Bodhisattva, possessed of great skill in Transic meditation, put himself into trance, intent on discerning both the ultimate reality of things and the final goal of existence. After he had gained complete mastery over all the degrees and kinds of trance:

1. In the *first watch* of the night he recollected the successive series of his former births. "There was I so and so; that was my name; deceased from there I came here"—in this way he remembered thousands of births, as though living them over again. When he had recalled his own births and deaths in all these various lives of his, the Sage, full of pity, turned his compassionate mind towards other living beings, and he thought to himself: "Again and again they must leave the people they regard as their own, and must go on elsewhere, and that without ever stopping. Surely this world is unprotected and helpless, and like a wheel it turns round and round." As he continued steadily to recollect the past thus, he came to the definite conviction that this world of Samsara is as unsubstantial as the pith of a plantain tree.

2. Second to none in valour, he then, in the *second watch* of the night, acquired the supreme heavenly *eye,* for he himself was the best of all those who have sight. Thereupon with the perfectly pure heavenly eye he looked upon the entire world, which appeared to him as though reflected in a spotless

Buddhacarita, Edward Conze, trans., in *Buddhist Scriptures* (New York: Penguin Books, 1959), 49–52.

mirror. He saw that the decease and rebirth of beings depend on whether they have done superior or inferior deeds. And his compassionateness grew still further. It became clear to him that no security can be found in this flood of Samsaric existence, and that the threat of death is ever-present. Beset on all sides, creatures can find no resting place. In this way he surveyed the five places of rebirth with his heavenly eye. And he found nothing substantial in the world of becoming, just as no core of heartwood is found in a plantain tree when its layers are peeled off one by one.

3. Then, as the *third watch* of that night drew on, the supreme master of trance turned his meditation to the real and essential nature of this world: "Alas, living beings wear themselves out in vain! Over and over again they are born, they age, die, pass on to a new life, and are reborn! What is more, greed and dark delusion obscure their sight, and they are blind from birth. Greatly apprehensive, they yet do not know how to get out of this great mass of ill." He then surveyed the twelve links of conditioned coproduction and saw that, beginning with ignorance, they lead to old age and death, and, beginning with the cessation of ignorance, they lead to the cessation of birth, old age, death, and all kinds of ill.

When the great seer had comprehended that where there is no ignorance whatever, there also the karma-formations are stopped—then he had achieved a correct knowledge of all there is to be known, and he stood out in the world as a Buddha. He passed through the eight stages of Transic insight, and quickly reached their highest point. From the summit of the world downwards he could detect no self anywhere. Like the fire, when its fuel is burnt up, he became tranquil. He had reached perfection, and he thought to himself: "This is the authentic Way on which in the past so many great seers, who also knew all higher and all lower things, have travelled on to ultimate and real truth. And now I have obtained it!"

4. At that moment, in the *fourth watch* of the night, when dawn broke and all the ghosts that move and those that move not went to rest, the great seer took up the position which knows no more alteration, and the leader of all reached the state of all-knowledge. When, through his Buddhahood, he had cognized this fact, the earth swayed like a woman drunken with wine, the sky shone bright with the Siddhas who appeared in crowds in all the directions, and the mighty drums of thunder resounded through the air. Pleasant breezes blew softly, rain fell from a cloudless sky, flowers and fruits dropped from the trees out of season—in an effort, as it were, to show reverence for him. Mandarava flowers and lotus blossoms, and also water lilies made of gold and beryl, fell from the sky on to the ground near the Shakya sage, so that it looked like a place in the world of the gods. At that moment no one anywhere was angry, ill, or sad; no one did evil, none was proud; the world became quite quiet, as though it had reached full perfection. Joy spread through the ranks of those gods who longed for salvation; joy also spread among those who lived in the regions below. Everywhere the virtuous were strengthened, the influence of Dharma increased, and the world rose from the dirt of the passions and the darkness of ignorance. Filled with joy and wonder at the Sage's work, the seers of the solar race who had been protectors of men, who had been royal seers, who had been great seers, stood in their mansions in the heavens and showed him their reverence. The great seers among the hosts of invisible beings could be heard widely proclaiming his fame. All living things rejoiced and sensed that things went well. Mara alone felt deep displeasure, as though subjected to a sudden fall.

For seven days He dwelt there—his body gave him no trouble, his eyes never closed, and he looked into his own mind. He thought: "Here I have found freedom," and he knew that the longings of his heart had at last come to fulfilment. Now that he had grasped the principle of causation, and finally convinced himself of the lack of self in all that is, he roused himself again from his deep trance, and in his great compassion he surveyed the world with his Buddha-eye, intent on giving it peace. When, however, he saw on the one side the world lost in low views and confused efforts, thickly covered with the dirt of the passions, and saw on the other side the exceeding subtlety of the Dharma of emancipation, he felt inclined to take no action. But when he weighed up the significance of the pledge to enlighten all beings he had taken in the past, he became again more favourable to the idea of proclaiming the path to Peace. Reflecting in his mind on this question, he also considered that, while some people have a great deal of passion, others have but little. As soon as Indra and Brahma, the two chiefs of those who dwell in the heavens, had grasped the Sugata's intention to proclaim the path to Peace, they shone brightly and came up to him, the weal of the world their concern. He remained there on his seat, free from all evil and successful in his aim. The most excellent Dharma which he had seen was his most excellent companion. His two visitors gently and reverently spoke to him these words, which were meant for the weal of the world: "Please do not condemn all those that live as unworthy of such treasure! Oh, please engender pity in your heart for beings in this world! So varied is their endowment, and while some have much passion, others have only very little. Now that you, O Sage, have yourself crossed the ocean of the world of becoming, please rescue also the other living beings who have sunk so deep into suffering! As a generous lord shares his wealth, so may also you bestow your own virtues on others! Most of those who know what for them is good in this world and the next, act only for their own advantage. In the world of men and in heaven it is hard to find anyone who is impelled by concern for the weal of the world." Having made this request to the great seer, the two gods returned to their celestial abode by the way they had come. And the sage pondered over their words. In consequence he was confirmed in his decision to set the world free.

The Recollection of Death

BUDDHAGHOSA

Buddhaghosa, a Theravadin Buddhist in the fourth century CE, taught that few things are as beneficial to a Buddhist as a profound meditation on the certainty of death. He says, "As a result of the recollection of death one reflects on the fact that one is sure to die, gives up the search for what is unworthy, and steadily increases one's agitation until one has lost all sluggishness." Here Buddhaghosa ponders death from eight different perspectives.

In "the recollection of death," the word "death" refers to the cutting off of the life-force which lasts for the length of one existence. Whoso wants to develop it, should in seclusion and solitude wisely set up attention with the words: "Death will take place, the life-force will be cut off," or (simply), "Death, death." But if somebody takes up an unwise attitude (to this problem of death), then sorrow will arise in him when he recalls the death of a loved person, like the grief of a mother when she thinks of the death of the dear child whom she has borne; and joy will arise when he recalls the death of an unloved person, like

Buddhaghosa's Commentary on Death, Edward Conza, trans., in *Thirty Years of Buddhist Studies* (New Delhi: Munshiram Manoharlal Publishers, 1968), 87–94.

the rejoicing of a foe who thinks of an enemy's death; and when he recalls the death of an indifferent person, no perturbation will arise in him, just as the man who all day long burns corpses looks on dead bodies without perturbation; when, finally, he recalls his own death, violent trembling arises in him, as in a frightened man who sees before him a murderer with his sword drawn. And all this is the result of a lack in mindfulness, (reasonable) perturbation, and cognition.

Therefore the Yogin should look upon beings killed or dead here and there, and advert to the death of beings who died after having first seen prosperity. To this (observation) he should apply mindfulness, perturbation and cognition, and set up attention with the words, "Death will take place." and so on. When he proceeds thus, he proceeds wisely, i.e. he proceeds expediently. For only if someone proceeds in this way will his hindrances be impeded, will mindfulness be established with death for its object, and will some degree of concentration be achieved.

If this is not enough (to produce access), he should recall death from the following eight points of view:

1. As a murderer, standing in front of him.
2. From the (inevitable) loss of (all) achievement.
3. By inference.
4. Because one's body is shared with many others.
5. From the weakness of the stuff of life.
6. From the absence of signs.
7. Because the life-span is limited.
8. From the shortness of the moment.

1. "AS A MURDERER STANDING IN FRONT OF HIM" means, "as if a murderer were standing in front of him." One should recall that death stands in front of us just like a murderer, who confronts us with his drawn sword raised to our neck, intending to cut off our head. And why? Because death comes together with birth, and deprives us of life.

a) As a budding mushroom shoots upwards carrying soil on its head, so beings from their birth onwards carry decay and death along with them. For death has come together with birth, because everyone who is born must certainly die. Therefore this living being, from the time of his birth onwards, moves in the direction of death, without turning back even for a moment;

b) just as the sun, once it has arisen, goes forward in the direction of its setting, and does not turn back for a moment on the path it traverses in that direction; *c*) or as a mountain stream rapidly tears down on its way, flows and rushes along, without turning back even for a moment. To one who goes along like that, death is always near; *d*) just as brooks get extinguished when dried up by the summer heat, *e*) as fruits are bound to fall from a tree early one day when their stalks have been rotted away by the early morning mists; *f*) as earthenware breaks when hit with a hammer; *g*) and as dewdrops are dispersed when touched by the rays of the sun. Thus death, like a murderer with a drawn sword, has come together with birth. Like the murderer who has raised his sword to our neck, so it deprives us of life. And there is no chance that it might desist.

2. "BY THE FAILURE OF ACHIEVEMENT," which means: Here in this world achievement prospers only so long as it is not overwhelmed by failure. And there is no single achievement that stands out as having transcended the (threat of) failure.

Moreover, all health ends in sickness, all youth in old age, all life in death; wherever one may dwell in the world, one is afflicted by birth, overtaken by old age, oppressed by sickness, struck down by death. Through realizing that the achievements of life thus end in the failure of death, he should recollect death from the failure of achievement.

3. "BY INFERENCE," means that one draws an inference for oneself from others. And it is with seven kinds of person that one should compare oneself: those great in fame, great in merit, great in might, great in magical power, great in wisdom, Pratyekabuddhas, and fully enlightened Buddhas.

In what manner? This death has assuredly befallen even those (kings) like Mahasammata, Mandhatu, Mahasudassana, Dalhanemin and Nimippabhuti, who possessed great fame, a great retinue, and who abounded in treasures and might. How then could it be that it will not befall also me?

"The greatly famous, noble kings,
Like Mahasammata and others,

They all fell down before the might of death.
What need is there to speak of men like us?"

(And so for the other kinds of distinction.)

In this way he draws from others, who have achieved great fame, and so on, an inference as to himself, i.e. that death is common to himself and to them. When he recalls that, "as for those distinguished beings so also for me death will take place," then the subject of meditation attains to access.

4. BECAUSE ONE'S BODY IS SHARED WITH MANY OTHERS": This body is the common property of many. It is shared by the eighty classes of parasitic animals, and it incurs death as a result of their turbulence. Likewise it belongs to the many hundreds of diseases which arise within it, as well as to the outside occasions of death, such as snakes, scorpions, and so on.

For just as, flying from all directions, arrows, spears, lances, stones, and so on, fall on a target placed at the cross roads, so on the body also all kinds of misfortune are bound to descend. And through the onslaught of these misfortunes it incurs death. Hence the Lord has said: "Here, monks, a monk, when the day is over and night comes round, thinks to himself: many are, to be sure, for me the occasions of death: a snake, or a scorpion, or a centipede may bite me; thereby I may lose my life, and that may act as an obstacle (to my spiritual progress). Or I may stumble and fall, or the food I have eaten may upset me, or the bile may trouble me, or the phlegm, or the winds which cut like knives; and thereby I may lose my life, and that may act as an obstacle" (*Anguttara III,* 306).

5. "FROM THE WEAKNESS OF THE STUFF OF LIFE": This life-force is without strength and feeble. For the life of beings is bound up with *a*) breathing in and out, *b*) the postures, *c*) heat and cold, *d*) the (four) great primaries, and *e*) with food.

a) It goes on only as long as it can obtain an even functioning of breathing in and out; as soon, however, as air issues from the nose without re-entering, or enters without going out again, one is considered dead. *b*) Again, it goes on only as long as it can obtain an even functioning of the four postures; but through the preponderance of one or the other of these the vital activities are cut off. *c*) Again, it goes on as long as it can obtain the even functioning of heat and cold; but it fails when oppressed by excessive heat or cold. *d*) Again, it goes on as long as it can obtain the even functioning of the (four) great primaries; but through the disturbance of one or the other of them (i.e.) of the solid, fluid, etc., element, the life of even a strong person is extinguished, be it by the stiffening of his body, or because his body has become wet and putrid from dysentery, and so on, or because it is overcome by a high temperature, or because his sinews are torn. *e*) Again, life goes on only as long as one obtains solid food, at suitable times; when one cannot get food, it gets extinguished.

6. "FROM THE ABSENCE OF SIGNS," because one cannot determine (the time of death, etc.). "From the absence of a definite limit," that is the meaning. For one says with regard to the death of beings:

a) Life's duration, *b*) sickness, *c*) time, *d*) the place where the body is cast off, *e*) the future destiny. These are five things about this animate world, which never can be known for certain, for no sign exists.

a) There is no sign (i.e. no clear indication) of the duration of life, because one cannot determine that so long will one live, and no longer. For beings may die in the first embryonic state, or in the second, third, or fourth, or after one month, or two, three, four, five or ten months, at the time when they issue from the womb, and further still at any time within or beyond one hundred years.

b) There is also no sign of the (fatal) sickness, insofar as one cannot determine that beings will die of this or that sickness, and no other; for beings may die from a disease of the eyes, or the ears, or any other.

c) There is also no sign of the time, insofar as one cannot determine that one will have to die just at this time of day and no other; for beings may die in the morning, or at midday, or at any other time.

d) There is also no sign as to the laying down of the body; for, when one is dying, one cannot determine that the body should be laid down just here and not anywhere else. For the body of those born within a village may fall away outside the village; and those born outside a village may perish inside one; those born on land may perish in water, those born in water may perish on land; and so this might be expanded in various ways.

e) There is also no sign of the future destiny, insofar as one cannot determine that one who has deceased there will be reborn here. For those who have deceased in the world of the gods may be reborn among men, and those deceased in the world of men may be reborn in the world of the gods, or anywhere else. In this way the world revolves round the five kinds of rebirth like an ox yoked to an oil-pressing mill.

7. "BECAUSE THE LIFE-SPAN IS LIMITED." Brief is the life of men at present; he lives long who lives for a hundred years, or a little more. Hence the Lord has said: "Short, oh monks, is the life-span of men, transient, having its sequel elsewhere; one should do what is wholesome, one should lead a holy life, no one who is born can escape death; he lives long who lives for a hundred years, or a little more.

"Short is the life of men, the good must scorn it,
And act as if their turban were ablaze.
For death is surely bound to come" (*Samyutta* I, 108).

Furthermore, the whole Araka-Sutta (*Anguttara* IV, 136–8) with its seven similes should be considered in detail: (i.e. Life is fleeting, and passes away quickly, *a*) like dewdrops on the tips of blades of grass, which soon dry up when the sun rises; *b*) or like the bubbles which rain causes in water, and which burst soon; *c*) or like the line made by a stick in water, which vanishes soon; *d*) or like a mountain brook, which does not stand still for a moment; *e*) or like a gob of spittle spat out with ease; *f*) or like a lump of meat thrown into a hot iron pot, which does not last long; *g*) or like a cow about to be slaughtered; each time she raises her foot she comes nearer to death).

Furthermore, He said: "If, oh monks, a monk develops the recollection of death in such a way that he thinks—'may I just live for one day and night—for one day—for as long as it takes to eat an alms-meal—for as long as it takes to chew and swallow four or five lumps of food—and I will then attend to the Lord's religion, and much surely will still be done by me'—then such monks are said to lead heedless lives, and they develop in a sluggish way the recollection of death which aims at the extinction of the outflows. But if, oh monks, a monk develops the recollection of death in such a way that he thinks— 'may I just live for so long as it takes to chew and swallow one lump of food—were I to live just long enough to breathe in after breathing out, or to breathe out after breathing in'—then such monks are said to lead watchful lives, and they develop keenly the recollection of death which aims at the extinction of the outflows" (*Anguttara* III, 305–6). And the span of life is brief like a mere swallowing of four or five lumps of food, and it cannot be trusted.

8. "FROM THE SHORTNESS OF THE MOMENT." In ultimate reality beings live only for an exceedingly brief moment, for it (life) lasts just as long as one single moment of thought. Just as a cart-wheel, whether it rolls along or stands still, always rests on one single spot of the rim; just so the life of beings lasts for one single moment of thought. As soon as that thought has ceased, the being also is said to have ceased. As it has been said: "In the past thought-moment one has lived, but one does not live and one will not live in it; in the future thought-moment one has not lived, but one does live, and one will live; in the present thought-moment one has not lived, but one does live, and one will not live in it.

"Our life and our whole personality,
All our joys and all our pains,
Are bound up with one single thought,
And rapidly that moment passes.
And those skandhas which are stopped,
For one who's dying, or one remaining here,
They all alike have gone away,
And are no longer reproduced.
Nothing is born from what is unproduced;
One lives by that which is at present there.
When thought breaks up, then all the world is dead.
So't is when final truth the concept guides " (*Niddesa* I, 42).

Result: When he recollects (death) from one or the other of these eight points of view, his mind by repeated attention becomes practised therein, mindfulness with death for its object is established, the hindrances are impeded, the Jhana-limbs become manifest. But, because of the intrinsic nature of the object and the agitation it produces, the Jhana only reaches access and not full ecstasy.

Benefits: And the monk who is devoted to this recollection of death is always watchful, he feels disgust for all forms of becoming, he forsakes the hankering after life, he disapproves of evil, he does not hoard up many things, and with regard to the necessities of life he is free from the taint of stinginess. He gains familiarity with the notion of impermanence, and, when he follows that up, also the notions of ill and not-self will stand out to him. At the hour of death, beings who have not developed the recollection of death, feel fear, fright and bewilderment, as if they were suddenly attacked by wild beasts, ghosts, snakes, robbers or murderers. He, on the contrary, dies without fear and bewilderment. If in this very life he does not win deathlessness, he is, on the dissolution of his body, bound for a happy destiny.

The Heart of Perfect Wisdom Sutra

This short Mahayana sutra (sermon), composed about 350 CE, has been regarded as conveying the essence of the doctrine of emptiness. In Buddhist history, the concept of emptiness was first connected to the notion of *anatta*—there is no permanent self or soul; the self is just an ever-changing, fleeting collection of mental processes. Later the doctrine was applied to the whole universe: ultimately everything is devoid of a permanent, enduring essence. In the Heart Sutra, to grasp the true nature of things—their emptiness—is finally to attain perfect wisdom.

I. THE INVOCATION

Homage to the Perfection of Wisdom, the lovely, the holy!

II. THE PROLOGUE

Avalokita, the holy Lord and Bodhisattva, was moving in the deep course of the wisdom which has gone beyond. He looked down from on high, he beheld but five heaps, and he saw that in their own-being they were empty.

III. THE DIALECTICS OF EMPTINESS: FIRST STAGE

Here, O Sariputra, form is emptiness, and the very emptiness is form; emptiness does not differ from form, form does not differ from emptiness; whatever is form, that is emptiness, whatever is emptiness, that is form. The same is true of feelings, perceptions, impulses, and consciousness.

The Heart of Perfect Wisdom Sutra, Edward Conze, trans., in *Buddhist Scriptures* (New York: Penguin Books, 1959), 162–164.

IV. THE DIALECTICS OF EMPTINESS: SECOND STAGE

Here, O Sariputra, all dharmas are marked with emptiness; they are not produced or stopped, not defiled or immaculate, not deficient or complete.

V. THE DIALECTICS OF EMPTINESS: THIRD STAGE

Therefore, O Sariputra, in emptiness there is no form, nor feeling, nor perception, nor impulse, nor consciousness; no eye, ear, nose, tongue, body, mind; no forms, sounds, smells, tastes, touchables or objects of mind; no sight-organ-element, and so forth, until we come to: no mind-consciousness-element; there is no ignorance, no extinction of ignorance, and so forth, until we come to: there is no decay and death, no extinction of decay and death; there is no suffering, no origination, no stopping, no path; there is no cognition, no attainment, and no non-attainment.

VI. THE CONCRETE EMBODIMENT AND PRACTICAL BASIS OF EMPTINESS

Therefore, O Sariputra, it is because of his indifference to any kind of personal attainment that a Bodhisattva, through having relied on the perfection of wisdom, dwells without thought-coverings. In the absence of thought-coverings he has not been made to tremble, he has overcome what can upset, and in the end he attains to Nirvana.

VII. FULL EMPTINESS IS THE BASIS ALSO OF BUDDHAHOOD

All those who appear as Buddhas in the three periods of time fully awake to the utmost, right and perfect enlightenment because they have relied on the perfection of wisdom.

VIII. THE TEACHING BROUGHT WITHIN REACH OF THE COMPARATIVELY UNENLIGHTENED

Therefore one should know the Prajnaparamita as the great spell, the spell of great knowledge, the utmost spell, the unequalled spell, allayer of all suffering, in truth—for what could go wrong? By the Prajnaparamita has this spell been delivered. It runs like this: Gone, Gone, Gone beyond, Gone altogether beyond, O what an awakening, All Hail!

This completes the Heart of Perfect Wisdom.

The Lotus Sutra: A Parable

This parable tells a tale, but it is also an argument for using "skillful means" in teaching Buddhist doctrines. *Skillful means* refers to various ways of tailoring the message of the dharma to individuals so it will appeal to them. This approach may seem dishonest to some, but this sutra argues that such tactics are sometimes necessary tools of persuasion that ultimately benefit people.

Let us suppose the following case, Sariputra. In a certain village, town, borough, province, kingdom, or capital, there was a certain housekeeper, old, aged, decrepit, very advanced in years, rich, wealthy, opulent; he had a great house, high, spacious, built a long time ago and old, inhabited by some two, three, four, or five hundred living beings. The house had but one door, and a thatch; its terraces were tottering, the bases of its pillars rotten, the coverings and plaster of the walls loose. On a sudden the whole house was from every side put in conflagration by a mass of fire. Let us suppose that the man had many little boys, say five, or ten, or even twenty, and that he himself had come out of the house.

Now, Sariputra, that man, on seeing the house from every side wrapt in a blaze by a great mass of fire, got afraid, frightened, anxious in his mind, and made the following reflection: I myself am able to come out from the burning house through the door, quickly and safely, without being touched or scorched by that great mass of fire; but my children, those young boys, are staying in the burning house, playing, amusing, and diverting themselves with all sorts of sports. They do not perceive, nor know, nor understand, nor mind that the house is on fire, and do not get afraid. Though scorched by that great mass of fire, and affected with such a mass of pain, they do not mind the pain, nor do they conceive the idea of escaping.

The man, Sariputra, is strong, has powerful arms, and (so) he makes this reflection: I am strong, and have powerful arms; why, let me gather all my little boys and take them to my breast to effect their escape from the house. A second reflection then presented itself to his mind: This house has but one opening; the door is shut; and those boys, fickle, unsteady, and childlike as they are, will, it is to be feared, run hither and thither, and come to grief and disaster in this mass of fire. Therefore I will warn them. So resolved, he calls to the boys: Come, my children; the house is burning with a mass of fire; come, lest ye be burnt in that mass of fire, and come to grief and disaster. But the ignorant boys do not heed the words of him who is their well-wisher; they are not afraid, not alarmed, and feel no misgiving; they do not care, nor fly, nor even know nor understand the purport of the word "burning"; on the contrary, they run hither and thither, walk about, and repeatedly look at their father; all, because they are so ignorant, Then the man is going to reflect thus: The house is burning, is blazing by a mass of fire. It is to be feared that myself as well as my children will come to grief and disaster. Let me therefore by some skillful means get the boys out of the house. The man knows the disposition of the boys, and has a clear perception of their inclinations. Now these boys happen to have many and manifold toys to play with, pretty, nice, pleasant, dear, amusing, and precious. The man, knowing the disposition of the boys, says to them: My children, your toys, which are so pretty, precious, and admirable, which you are so loth to miss, which are so various and multifarious, (such as) bullock-carts,

The Lotus Sutra, H. Kern, trans., in *Saddharma-Pundarika or The Lotus of the True Law* (New York: Dover Publications, 1963), 72–79.

goat-carts, deer-carts, which are so pretty, nice, dear, and precious to you, have all been put by me outside the house-door for you to play with. Come, run out, leave the house; to each of you I shall give what he wants. Come soon; come out for the sake of these toys. And the boys, on hearing the names mentioned of such playthings as they like and desire, so agreeable to their taste, so pretty, dear, and delightful, quickly rush out from the burning house, with eager effort and great alacrity, one having no time to wait for the other, and pushing each other on with the cry of "Who shall arrive first, the very first?"

The man, seeing that his children have safely and happily escaped, and knowing that they are free from danger, goes and sits down in the open air on the square of the village, his heart filled with joy and delight, released from trouble and hindrance, quite at ease. The boys go up to the place where their father is sitting, and say: "Father, give us those toys to play with, those bullock-carts, goat-carts, and deer-carts." Then, Sariputra, the man gives to his sons, who run swift as the wind, bullock-carts only, made of seven precious substances, provided with benches, hung with a multitude of small bells, lofty, adorned with rare and wonderful jewels, embellished with jewel wreaths, decorated with garlands of flowers, carpeted with cotton mattresses and woolen coverlets, covered with white cloth and silk, having on both sides rosy cushions, yoked with white, very fair and fleet bullocks, led by a multitude of men. To each of his children he gives several bullock-carts of one appearance and one kind, provided with flags, and swift as the wind. That man does so, Sariputra, because being rich, wealthy, and in possession of many treasures and granaries, he rightly thinks: Why should I give these boys inferior carts, all these boys being my own children, dear and precious? I have got such great vehicles, and ought to treat all the boys equally and without partiality. As I own many treasures and granaries, I could give such great vehicles to all beings, how much more then to my own children. Meanwhile the boys are mounting the vehicles with feelings of astonishment and wonder. Now, Sariputra, what is thy opinion? Has that man made himself guilty of a falsehood by first holding out to his children the prospect of three vehicles and afterwards giving to each of them the greatest vehicles only, the most magnificent vehicles?

Sariputra answered: By no means, Lord; by no means, Sugata. That is not sufficient, O Lord, to qualify the man as a speaker of falsehood, since it only was a skilful device to persuade his children to go out of the burning house and save their lives. Nay, besides recovering their very body, O Lord, they have received all those toys. If that man, O Lord, had given no single cart, even then he would not have been a speaker of falsehood, for he had previously been meditating on saving the little boys from a great mass of pain by some able device. Even in this case, O Lord, the man would not have been guilty of falsehood, and far less now that he, considering his having plenty of treasures and prompted by no other motive but the love of his children, gives to all, to coax them, vehicles of one kind, and those the greatest vehicles. That man, Lord, is not guilty of falsehood.

The venerable Sariputra having thus spoken, the Lord said to him: Very well, very well, Sariputra, quite so; it is even as thou sayest. So, too, Sariputra, the Tathagata, &c., is free from all dangers, wholly exempt from all misfortune, despondency, calamity, pain, grief, the thick enveloping dark mists of ignorance. He, the Tathagata, endowed with Buddha-knowledge, forces, absence of hesitation, uncommon properties, and mighty by magical power, is the father of the world, who has reached the highest perfection in the knowledge of skillful means, who is most merciful, long-suffering, benevolent, compassionate. He appears in this triple world, which is like a house the roof and shelter whereof are decayed, (a house) burning by a mass of misery, in order to deliver from affection, hatred, and delusion the beings subject to birth, old age, disease, death, grief, wailing, pain, melancholy, despondency, the dark enveloping mists of ignorance, in order to rouse them to supreme and perfect enlightenment. Once born, he sees how the creatures are burnt, tormented, vexed, distressed by birth, old age, disease, death, grief, wailing, pain, melancholy, despondency; how for the sake of enjoyments, and prompted by sensual desires, they severally suffer various pains. In consequence both of what in this world they are seeking and what they have acquired, they will in a future state suffer various pains, in hell, in the brute creation, in the realm of Yama; suffer such pains as poverty in the world of gods or men, union with hateful persons or things, and separation from the beloved ones. And whilst incessantly whirling in that mass of evils they are sporting, playing, diverting themselves; they do not fear, nor dread, nor are they seized with terror; they do not know, nor mind; they are not startled, do not try to escape, but are enjoying themselves in that triple world which is like unto a burning house, and run hither and thither. Though overwhelmed by that mass of evil, they do not conceive the idea that they must beware of it.

Under such circumstances, Sariputra, the Tathagata reflects thus: Verily, I am the father of these beings; I must save them from this mass of evil, and bestow on them the immense, inconceivable bliss of Buddha-knowledge, wherewith they shall sport, play, and divert themselves, wherein they shall find their rest.

Then, Sariputra, the Tathagata reflects thus: If, in the conviction of my possessing the power of knowledge and magical faculties, I manifest to these beings the knowledge, forces, and absence of hesitation of the Tathagata, without availing myself of some device, these beings will not escape. For they are attached to the pleasures of the five senses, to worldly pleasures; they will not be freed from birth, old age, disease, death, grief, wailing, pain, melancholy, despondency, by which they are burnt, tormented, vexed, distressed. Unless they are forced to leave the triple world which is like a house the shelter and roof whereof is in a blaze, how are they to get acquainted with Buddha-knowledge?

Now, Sariputra, even as that man with powerful arms, without using the strength of his arms, attracts his children out of the burning house by an able device, and afterwards gives them magnificent, great carts, so, Sariputra, the Tathagata, the Arhat, &c., possessed of knowledge and freedom from all hesitation, without using them, in order to attract the creatures out of the triple world which is like a burning house with decayed roof and shelter, shows, by his knowledge of able devices, three vehicles, viz. the vehicle of the disciples, the vehicle of the Pratyekabuddhas, and the vehicle of the Bodhisattvas. By means of these three vehicles he attracts the creatures and speaks to them thus: Do not delight in this triple world, which is like a burning house, in these miserable forms, sounds, odours, flavours, and contacts. For in delighting in this tripleworld ye are burnt, heated, inflamed with the thirst inseparable from the pleasures of the five senses. Fly from this triple world; betake yourselves to the three vehicles: the vehicle of the disciples, the vehicle of the Pratyekabuddhas, the vehicle of the Bodhisattvas. I give you my pledge for it, that I shall give you these three vehicles; make an effort to run out of this triple world. And to attract them I say: These vehicles are grand, praised by the Aryas, and provided with most pleasant things; with such you are to sport, play, and divert yourselves in a noble manner. Ye will feel the great delight of the faculties, powers, constituents of Bodhi, meditations, the (eight) degrees of emancipation, self-concentration, and the results of self-concentration, and ye will become greatly happy and cheerful.

Buddha Nature

PETER HARVEY

The Buddhist scholar Peter Harvey discusses ways that the Buddha has been portrayed in scripture and commentary. The Buddha is said to be no mere mortal, but neither is he a god nor the son of a god as Jesus was supposed to be. Some think he was thoroughly human but then transcended his humanness when he attained enlightenment. In early Buddhist texts, he is portrayed as an *arhat* (a Buddhist saint), but later he is described as exceeding *arhats* in knowledge and power.

While modern Theravadins sometimes say that the Buddha was "just a human," such remarks have to be taken in context. They are usually intended to contrast the Buddha with Jesus, seen as the "Son of God," and to counter the Mahayana view of the Buddha's nature, which sees it as far above the human. These remarks may also be due to a somewhat demythologized view of the Buddha. In the Pali Canon, Gotama was seen as *born* a human, though one with extraordinary abilities due to the perfections built up in his long *Bodhisatta* career. Once he had attained enlightenment, though, he could no longer be called a "human," as he had perfected and transcended his humanness. This idea is reflected in a *Sutta* passage where the Buddha was asked whether he was a god (*deva*) or a human. In reply, he said that he had gone beyond the deep-rooted unconscious traits that would make him a god or human, and was therefore to be seen as a *Buddha*, one who had grown up in the world but who had now gone beyond it, as a lotus grows from the water but blossoms above it unsoiled.

Peter Harvey, *An Introduction to Buddhism* (Cambridge: Cambridge University Press, 1990), 28.

Cutting Through Spiritual Materialism

CHOGYAM TRUNGPA

Chogyam Trungpa asserts that the biggest obstacle on the way to genuine spirituality is ego. We may think we are following the right path to enlightenment, but we may instead be strengthening our ego-centeredness through spiritual techniques. He calls this kind of

Chogyam Trungpa, *Cutting Through Spiritual Materialism* (Boston: Shambhala, 2008), 1–12.

delusion *spiritual materialism*. Following the true path means clearing away the confusion, the heart of which is our deluded notion that we have a continuous, permanent self.

Walking the spiritual path properly is a very subtle process; it is not something to jump into naively. There are numerous sidetracks which lead to distorted, ego-centered version of spirituality; we can deceive ourselves into thinking we are developing spiritually when instead we are strengthening our egocentricity through spiritual techniques. This fundamental distortion may be referred to as *spiritual materialism.*

These talks first discuss the various ways in which people involve themselves with spiritual materialism, the many forms of self-deception into which aspirants may fall. After this tour of the sidetracks along the way, we discuss the broad outlines of the true spiritual path.

The approach presented here is a classical Buddhist one—not in a formal sense, but in the sense of presenting the heart of the Buddhist approach to spirituality. Although the Buddhist way is not theistic, it does not contradict the theistic disciplines. Rather the differences between the ways are a matter of emphasis and method. The basic problems of spiritual materialism are common to all spiritual disciplines. The Buddhist approach begins with our confusion and suffering and works toward the unraveling of their origin. The theistic approach begins with the richness of God and works toward raising consciousness so as to experience God's presence. But since the obstacles to relating with God are our confusions and negativities, the theistic approach must also deal with them. Spiritual pride, for example, is as much a problem in theistic disciplines as in Buddhism.

According to the Buddhist tradition, the spiritual path is the process of cutting through our confusion, of uncovering the awakened state of mind. When the awakened state of mind is crowded in by ego and its attendant paranoia, it takes on the character of an underlying instinct. So it is not a matter of building up the awakened state of mind, but rather of burning out the confusions which obstruct it. In the process of burning out these confusions, we discover enlightenment. If the process were otherwise, the awakened state of mind would be a product, dependent upon cause and effect and therefore liable to dissolution. Anything which is created must, sooner or later, die. If enlightenment were created in such a way, there would always be the possibility of ego reasserting itself, causing a return to the confused state. Enlightenment is permanent because we have not produced it: we have merely discovered it. In the Buddhist tradition the analogy of the sun appearing from behind the clouds is often used to explain the discovery of enlightenment. In meditation practice we clear away the confusion of ego in order to glimpse the awakened state. The absence of ignorance, of being crowded in, of paranoia, opens up a tremendous view of life. One discovers a different way of being.

The heart of the confusion is that man has a sense of self which seems to him to be continuous and solid. When a thought or emotion or event occurs, there is a sense of someone being conscious of what is happening. You sense that *you* are reading these words. This sense of self is actually a transitory, discontinuous event, which in our confusion seems to be quite solid and continuous. Since we take our confused view as being real, we struggle to maintain and enhance this solid self. We try to feed it pleasures and shield it from pain. Experience continually threatens to reveal our transitoriness to us, so we continually struggle to cover up any possibility of discovering our real condition. "But," we might ask, "if our real condition is an awakened state, why are we so busy trying to avoid becoming aware of it?" It is because we have become so absorbed in our confused view of the world, that we consider it real, the only possible world. This struggle to maintain the sense of a solid, continuous self is the action of ego.

Ego, however, is only partially successful in shielding us from pain. It is the dissatisfaction which accompanies ego's struggle that inspires us to examine what we are doing. Since there are always gaps in our self-consciousness, some insight is possible.

An interesting metaphor used in Tibetan Buddhism to describe the functioning of ego is that of the "three lords of materialism": the "lord of form," the "lord of speech," and the "lord of mind." In the discussion of the three lords which follows, the words *materialism* and *neurotic* refer to the action of ego.

The lord of form refers to the neurotic pursuit of physical comfort, security, and pleasure. Our highly organized and technological society reflects our preoccupation with manipulating physical surroundings so as to shield ourselves from the irritations of the raw, rugged, unpredictable aspects of life. Push-button elevators, pre-packaged meat, air-conditioning, flush toilets, private funerals, retirement programs, mass production, weather satellites, bulldozers, fluorescent lighting, nine-to-five jobs, television—all are attempts to create a manageable, safe, predictable, pleasurable world.

The lord of form does not signify the physically rich and secure life situations we create per se. Rather it refers to the neurotic preoccupation that drives us to create them, to try to control nature. It is ego's ambition to secure and entertain itself, trying to avoid all irritation. So we cling to our pleasures and possessions; we fear change or force change; we try to create a nest or playground.

The lord of speech refers to the use of intellect in relating to our world. We adopt sets of categories which serve as handles, as ways of managing phenomena. The most fully developed products of this tendency are ideologies, the systems of ideas that rationalize, justify, and sanctify our lives. Nationalism, communism, existentialism, Christianity, Buddhism—all provide us with identities, rules of action, and interpretations of how and why things happen as they do.

Again, the use of intellect is not in itself the lord of speech. The lord of speech refers to the inclination on the part of ego to interpret anything that is threatening or irritating in such a way as to neutralize the threat or turn it into something "positive" from ego's point of view. The lord of speech refers to the use of concepts as filters to screen us from a direct, perception of what is. The concepts are taken too seriously; they are used as tools to solidify our world and ourselves. If a world of nameable things exists, then "I" as one of the nameable things exists as well. We wish not to leave any room for threatening doubt, uncertainty, or confusion.

The lord of mind refers to the effort of consciousness to maintain awareness of itself. The lord of mind rules when we use spiritual and psychological disciplines as the means of maintaining our self-consciousness, of holding on to our sense of self. Drugs, yoga, prayer, meditation, trances, various psychotherapies—all can be used in this way.

Ego is able to convert everything to its own use, even spirituality. For example, if you have learned of a particularly beneficial meditation technique of spiritual practice, then ego's attitude is, first, to regard it as an object of fascination and, second, to examine it. Finally, since ego is seemingly solid and cannot really absorb anything, it can only mimic. Thus ego tries to examine and imitate the practice of meditation and the meditative way of life. When we have learned all the tricks and answers of the spiritual game, we automatically try to imitate spirituality, since real involvement would require the complete elimination of ego, and actually the last thing we want to do is to give up the ego completely. However, we cannot experience that which we are trying to imitate; we can only find some area within the bounds of ego that seems to be the same thing. Ego translates everything in terms of its own state of health, its own inherent qualities. It feels a sense of great accomplishment and excitement at having been able to create such a pattern. At last it has created a tangible accomplishment, a confirmation of its own individuality.

If we become successful at maintaining our self-consciousness through spiritual techniques, then genuine spiritual development is highly unlikely. Our mental habits become so strong as to be hard to penetrate. We may even go so far as to achieve the totally demonic state of complete "egohood."

Even though the lord of mind is the most powerful in subverting spirituality, still the other two lords can also rule the spiritual practice. Retreat to nature, isolation, simplicity, quiet, high people—all can be ways of shielding oneself from irritation, all can be expressions of the lord of form. Or perhaps religion may provide us with a rationalization for creating a secure nest, a simple but comfortable home, for acquiring an amiable mate, and a stable, easy job.

The lord of speech is involved in spiritual practice as well. In following a spiritual path we may substitute a new religious ideology for our former beliefs, but continue to use it in the old neurotic way. Regardless of how sublime our ideas may be, if we take them too seriously and use them to maintain our ego, we are still being ruled by the lord of speech.

Most of us, if we examine our actions, would probably agree that we are ruled by one or more of the three lords. "But," we might ask, "so what? This is simply a description of the human condition. Yes, we know that our technology cannot shield us from war, crime, illness, economic insecurity, laborious work, old age, and death; nor can our ideologies shield us from doubt, uncertainty, confusion, and disorientation; nor can our therapies protect us from the dissolution of the high states of consciousness that we may temporarily achieve and the disillusionment and anguish that follow. But what else are we to do? The three lords seem too powerful to overthrow, and we don't know what to replace them with."

The Buddha, troubled by these questions, examined the process by which the three lords rule. He questioned why our minds follow them and whether there is another way. He discovered that the three lords seduce us by creating a fundamental myth: that we are solid beings. But ultimately the myth is false, a huge hoax, a gigantic fraud, and it is the root of our suffering. In order to make this discovery he had to break through very elaborate defenses erected by the three lords to prevent their subjects from discovering the fundamental deception which is the source of their power. We cannot in any way free ourselves from the domination of the three lords unless we too cut through, layer by layer, the elaborate defenses of these lords.

The lords' defenses are created out of the material of our minds. This material of mind is used by the lords in such a way as to maintain the basic myth of solidity. In order to see for ourselves how this process works we must examine our own experience. "But how," we might ask, "are we to conduct the examination? What method or tool are we to use?" The method that the Buddha discovered is meditation. He discovered that struggling to find answers did not work. It was only when there were gaps in his struggle that insights came to him. He began to realize that there was a sane, awake quality within him which manifested itself only in the absence of struggle. So the practice of meditation involves "letting be."

There have been a number of misconceptions regarding meditation. Some people regard it as a trancelike state of mind. Others think of it in terms of training, in the sense of mental gymnastics. But meditation is neither of these, although it does involve dealing with neurotic states of mind. The neurotic state of mind is not difficult or impossible to deal with. It has energy, speed, and a certain pattern. The practice of meditation involves *letting be*—trying to go with the pattern, trying to go with the energy and the speed. In this way we learn how to deal with these factors, how to relate with them, not in the sense of causing them to mature in the way we would like, but in the sense of knowing them for what they are and working with their pattern.

There is a story regarding the Buddha which recounts how he once gave teaching to a famous sitar player who wanted to study meditation. The musician asked, "Should I control my mind or should I completely let go?" The Buddha answered, "Since you are a great musician, tell me how you would tune the strings of your instrument." The musician said, "I would make them not too tight and not too loose." "Likewise," said the Buddha, "in your meditation practice you should not impose anything too forcefully on your mind, nor should you let it wander." That is the teaching of letting the mind *be* in a very open way, of feeling the flow of energy without trying to subdue it and without letting it get out of control, of going with the energy pattern of mind. This is meditation practice.

Such practice is necessary generally because our thinking pattern, our conceptualized way of conducting our life in the world, is either too manipulative, imposing itself upon the world, or else runs completely wild and uncontrolled. Therefore, our meditation practice must begin with ego's outermost layer, the discursive thoughts which continually run through our minds, our mental gossip. The lords use discursive thought as their first line of defense, as the pawns in their effort to deceive us. The more we generate thoughts, the busier we are mentally and the more convinced we are of our existence. So the lords are constantly trying to activate these thoughts, trying to create a constant overlapping of thoughts so that nothing can be seen beyond them. In true meditation there is no ambition to stir up thoughts, nor is there an ambition to suppress them. They are just allowed to occur spontaneously and become an expression of basic sanity. They become the expression of the precision and the clarity of the awakened state of mind.

If the strategy of continually creating overlapping thoughts is penetrated, then the lords stir up emotions to distract us. The exciting, colorful, dramatic quality of the emotions captures our attention as if we were watching an absorbing film show. In the practice of meditation we neither encourage emotions nor repress them. By seeing them clearly, by allowing them to be as they are, we no longer permit them to serve as a means of entertaining and distracting us. Thus they become the inexhaustible energy which fulfills egoless action.

In the absence of thoughts and emotions the lords bring up a still more powerful weapon, concepts. Labeling phenomena creates a feeling of a solid definite world of "things." Such a solid world reassures us that we are a solid, continuous thing as well. The world exists, therefore I, the perceiver of the world, exist. Meditation involves seeing the transparency of concepts, so that labeling no longer serves as a way of solidifying our world and our image of self. Labeling becomes simply the act of discrimination. The lords have still further defense mechanisms, but it would be too complicated to discuss them in this context.

By the examination of his own thoughts, emotions, concepts, and the other activities of mind, the Buddha discovered that there is no need to struggle to prove our existence, that we need not be subject to the rule of the three lords of materialism. There is no need to struggle to be free; the absence of struggle is in itself freedom. This egoless state is the attainment of buddhahood. The process of transforming the material of mind from expressions of ego's ambition into expressions of basic sanity and enlightenment through the practice of meditation—this might be said to be the true spiritual path.

Guidelines for Studying the Way

EIHEI DOGEN

Eihei Dogen (1200–1253 CE) was an influential Zen philosopher and the author of numerous texts. He is regarded as the most important master in Japanese Buddhism and the greatest advocate of Zen and its practice of "sitting meditation" known as zazen. For Dogen, zazen is the way to achieve "not thinking," a state in which all thoughts, concepts, and judgments are silenced, all attachments drop away, and mindfulness ensues. In this state comes awakening. In this passage Dogen explains what is and is not involved in true enlightenment.

Zen Master Dogen, in Kazuaki Tanahashi, ed., *Moon in a Dewdrop* (New York: North Point Press, 1985), 31–33.

You should arouse the thought of enlightenment.

The thought of enlightenment has many names but they all refer to one and the same mind.

Ancestor Nagarjuna said, "The mind that fully sees into the uncertain world of birth and death is called the thought of enlightenment."

Thus if we maintain this mind, this mind can become the thought of enlightenment.

Indeed, when you understand discontinuity the notion of self does not come into being, ideas of name and gain do not arise. Fearing the swift passage of the sunlight, practice the way as though saving your head from fire. Reflecting on this ephemeral life, make endeavor in the manner of Buddha raising his foot.

When you hear a song of praise sung by a kinnara god or a kalavinka bird, let it be as the evening breeze brushing against your ears. If you see the beautiful face of Maoqiang or Xishi, let it be like the morning dewdrops coming into your sight. Freedom from the ties of sound and form naturally accords with the essence of the way-seeking mind.

If in the past or present, you hear about students of small learning or meet people with limited views, often they have fallen into the pit of fame and profit and have forever missed the buddha way in their life. What a pity! How regrettable! You should not ignore this.

Even if you read the sutras of the expedient or complete teaching, or transmit the scriptures of the exoteric or esoteric schools, without throwing away name and gain it cannot be called arousing the thought of enlightenment.

Some of these people say, "The thought of enlightenment is the mind of supreme, perfect enlightenment. Do not be concerned with the cultivation of fame or profit."

Some of them say, "The thought of enlightenment is the insight that each thought contains three thousand realms."

Some of them say, "The thought of enlightenment is the dharma gate, 'Each thought is unborn.'"

Some of them say, "The thought of enlightenment is the mind of entering the buddha realm."

Such people do not yet know and mistakenly slander the thought of enlightenment. They are remote from the buddha way.

Try to reflect on the mind concerned only with your own gain. Does this one thought blend with the nature and attributes of the three thousand realms? Does this one thought realize the dharma gate of being unborn? There is only the deluded thought of greed for name and love of gain. There is nothing which could be taken as the thought of enlightenment.

From ancient times sages have attained the way and realized dharma. Although as an expedient teaching they lived ordinary lives, still they had no distorted thought of fame or profit. Not even attached to dharma, how could they have worldly attachment?

The thought of enlightenment, as was mentioned, is the mind which sees into impermanence. This is most fundamental, and not at all the same as the mind pointed to by confused people. The understanding that each thought is unborn or the insight that each thought contains three thousand realms is excellent practice after arousing the thought of enlightenment. This should not be mistaken.

Just forget yourself for now and practice inwardly—this is one with the thought of enlightenment. We see that the sixty-two views are based on self. So when a notion of self arises, sit quietly and contemplate it. Is there a real basis inside or outside your body now? Your body with hair and skin is just inherited from your father and mother. From beginning to end a drop of blood or lymph is empty. So none of these are the self. What about mind, thought, awareness, and knowledge? Or the breath going in and out, which ties a lifetime together: what is it after all? None of these are the self either. How could you be attached to any of them? Deluded people are attached to them. Enlightened people are free of them.

You figure there is self where there is no self. You attach to birth where there is no birth. You do not practice the buddha way, which should be practiced. You do not cut off the worldly mind, which should be cut off. Avoiding the true teaching and pursuing the groundless teaching, how could you not be mistaken?

PRACTICES

A Buddhist-American Monk

HENG SURE

Heng Sure from the Berkeley Buddhist Monastery explains what it's like to be an American Buddhist trying to incorporate cultural aspects of a Buddhist tradition from Asia.

I grew up in the 1950s and 1960s in Toledo, Ohio, of Scots-Irish ancestry and was president of my high school student council as well as my church's Methodist Youth Fellowship. The culture I grew up in was as mainstream Midwestern American as corn on the cob. My first encounter with Asian religious culture happened when I took a Chinese language class in high school and picked up a bilingual ancient Buddhist scripture in the local public library. I knew I had to find out why the book's Chinese characters felt strangely familiar and compelling. In college my roommate introduced me to Buddhist meditation. Later, he became a disciple and ordained monk under a Chinese Buddhist Ch'an Master. One day, I drove to Gold Mountain Monastery to visit my former roommate.

Inside the door of Gold Mountain, my first impressions were physical. I noticed the chill in the air, smelled the sandalwood incense, and marveled at the three large Buddhas seated in full lotus posture on a raised dais with gold-colored dragons curling around the roof. When I heard the tapping of a "wooden fish" drum and the rhythmic chanting of *mantras*, I looked at the Caucasian monks and nuns wearing robes and bowing in the Buddha hall and saw my former college roommate. He was sitting beside Master Hsuan Hua and translating his Mandarin Chinese Dharma talk into English. His head was shaven, and he wore a long robe and a dark brown sash clasped over his left shoulder. If it were not for the audio headphones over his ears, he might have stepped out of a T'ang Dynasty court painting. I had an epiphany: I knew I had returned to my spiritual home.

Three years after entering Gold Mountain, I knelt on a platform in a monastery in rural northern California called the City of Ten Thousand Buddhas and professed the many vows taken by Buddhist monastics since the time of the Buddha, twenty-five hundred years ago. Strange to say, promising to live with so many precepts felt not at all repressive. Instead, as I stepped into the lineage of monks and nuns of ages past, my heart felt liberated and joyful. By taking the *bhiksu* precepts, I set aside the cultural perspective in which I had been raised and entered a new, yet ancient, Buddhist culture. I became a celibate monk, a vegetarian, a mendicant. I vowed to replace my previous cultural lifestyle with the values of the Buddha's Sangha. Taking the vows is a ritual process; living in

Heng Sure, "Encountering Buddhist Culture," in Donald W. Mitchell, *Buddhism: Introducing the Buddhist Experience* (Oxford: Oxford University Press, 2008), 393–395.

the religious culture those vows express requires bone-deep changes. When I think back to what I went through in making these changes, certain peak experiences emerge from the mist of memory.

One of those moments was learning to bow. Bowing is a basic practice in Chinese monastic life and popular Chinese Buddhist culture. My initial experience with bowing was full of hesitation and questions. On Saturday mornings at Gold Mountain Monastery the Western monks and nuns lead the newcomers in bowing to an English translation of the repentance liturgy of Medicine Master Buddha. Men and women bowed on two sides of the hall while chanting passages of Buddhist texts and the names of Buddhas and bodhisattvas. When I bowed the first few times, pictures from Sunday school arose in mind. I recalled stories of God punishing the Israelites for worshiping graven idols. How was bowing to Buddha images any different? For a long time the gesture seemed forced and unnatural, but I stuck with it in large part because there was a vegetarian lunch immediately afterward and I was a graduate student cooking for myself in a studio apartment in Berkeley. After half an hour of bowing and chanting I realized my body felt unusually comfortable. My thoughts slowed down, my breathing was deep and regular, and tension left my shoulders. Bowing felt like yoga, only more spiritually focused.

Bowing also allowed my mind to contemplate the text of the liturgy. The bowing provided a space, and the following words of the Dharma-teaching went deep into my consciousness:

> Therefore the sicknesses of living beings are one single illusory sickness, and the medicines given by the Thus Come One are, likewise, one illusory medicine. . . . So we can know that all the Dharma spoken by the Thus Come One has a single quality and a single flavor. It is the quality of liberation, the quality of leaving [affliction], the quality of cessation, and ultimately, the quality of Nirvana. In the end, it returns to emptiness.

Bowing to this deep insight felt transformative and healing. Master Hua instructed that bowing was not for the purpose of getting anything from a Buddha, for example. Instead, we bowed to get rid of pride and arrogance and to create room for goodness in our minds once pride was gone. This made sense and answered my question as to how my bowing now is different from idolatry. As I adopted this Buddhist practice, it resonated with values that are part of American culture informed by Christianity: the overcoming of pride in the pursuit of goodness. Bowing with my head at shoe-top level, it was more difficult to feel arrogant. I felt humble and soft as I contemplated how many of my mistakes in life had come from loneliness, from a feeling of brokenness and alienation from others. On Saturday mornings at Gold Mountain, when the bowing was over, I felt relieved of a burden, lighter and more connected with the world around me and the people in it. The feeling of connection remained for hours. Bowing became a daily practice I willingly and literally threw myself into.

When I eventually moved over to the monastery from Berkeley, I asked my monk-roommate for an appropriate practice to deepen my cultivation. He suggested I bow to a *sutra* text, one character at a time. This immediately struck me as a ridiculous notion. I was studying for my master's degree at a prestigious public university, and I had learned to read a number of books, journals, and newspapers at once. Bowing down to one Chinese character at a time in one book simply seemed too slow. He anticipated my reluctance and said, "Don't think about it, don't talk about it, just do it, and tell me later how it felt."

I lit a stick of incense, opened the *Flower Adornment Sutra*, and, grumbling to myself that this was a waste of time, made the first bow to the first character: *da* for "great," or "large." One hour later, I had bowed my way onto just the second page. But in the process, my mind had downshifted into a slower gear, in tune with my bowing. I contemplated the characters one by one and had another epiphany: While reading great books slowly enhances comprehension and appreciation, bowing at each character in a book moves the mind toward an even deeper level of comprehension and appreciation. This deeper comprehension and appreciation is not only for each word, but it also gradually reduces the inner chatter that had been part of my everyday state. By letting the six senses concentrate on one thing, the *sutra* text as a sacred object while bowing, I experienced my mind interacting with writing in a whole new way.

The practice of bowing to a *sutra* became my first door into Buddhist spiritual culture.

Since then, I have dedicated years of my monastic formation to bowing, to making ritual prostrations. I made a pilgrimage at one point in my early monastic formation, bowing to the ground once every three steps. It took thirty-three months of steady walking and bowing to travel from South Pasadena, California, up the Pacific Coast Highway to the City of Ten Thousand Buddhas in Ukiah. The pace of bowing and the insights gained from putting my body prone to the ground for those months amended my views concerning such Buddhist practices as bowing and pilgrimage. Using the whole body in practice affects the mind and spirit in unexpected ways; putting the heart and the head on the same physical plane while one is wide awake seems to heal the mind and bring the world around one to life.

Meditation

DAMIEN KEOWN

Damien Keown, a professor of Buddhism at Goldsmiths College, University of London, and a Fellow of the Royal Asiatic Society, explains the nature and practice of Buddhist meditation.

But what exactly *is* meditation? Meditation may be defined as an altered state of consciousness which is induced in a controlled manner. There is nothing very mysterious about it, and people slip in and out of trance-like states akin to meditation spontaneously in the course of waking life. A good deal of waking life is punctuated by daydreams, reveries, and fantasies in which the mind withdraws to contemplate an interior landscape. Sometimes these reveries can be quite absorbing, as when driving a car one suddenly finds oneself at the destination with very little recollection of the trip. Taking drugs may also produce effects not unlike those experienced in meditation.

. . . The goal of meditation is not to be "elsewhere" but to be right here, fully conscious and aware. The aim is to "get one's head together," and become mentally concentrated rather than fragmented. A laser beam provides a good analogy: when light is diffuse it is relatively powerless, but when focused and concentrated it can cut through steel. Or, to use sound as a metaphor rather than light, the aim of meditation is to screen out mental "static" and reduce the mental "chatter" which dissipates psychic energy.

Meditational theory recognizes a close relationship between body and mind, so before the mind can become completely calm the body must be composed. The traditional posture for meditation is to sit cross-legged, using a cushion if necessary, with the back straight, head slightly inclined, and hands resting in the lap. This is known as the "lotus posture" . . . Although it may feel unnatural at first to a

Damien Keown, *Buddhism: A Very Short Introduction* (Oxford: Oxford University Press, 1996), 86–89.

beginner, with a little practice this position can be held for long periods of time. It allows the meditator to breathe in a deep and relaxed way and to remain comfortable but alert. Meditation can be performed in any position which is comfortable, but if the position is too comfortable there is a risk of falling asleep. Control of the mind when asleep is obviously very difficult, although there is a Tibetan practice known as "dream yoga" in which awareness is cultivated during lucid dreams.

Once a comfortable posture has been established a suitable object for meditation is chosen. When the Buddha left home he studied separately with two teachers of meditation, and it can reasonably be assumed that what they taught him—namely how to enter and abide in a deep state of trance—was typical of the meditation practised at the time. What instructions would the Buddha's two teachers have given to their student? We cannot know for sure, but they may have advised him to concentrate on his breathing, or to repeat a *mantra* silently to himself. Alternatively, they might have placed an object a few feet away—perhaps a small everyday item such as a pot or a flower—and instructed him to study it carefully, noting every detail until he could recreate a perfect mental image of the object with his eyes closed. The object of these exercises is for the mind to become completely engrossed in the object until the awareness of subject and object dissolves in a unified field of consciousness.

Meditation is by no means easy to master, since the mind continually throws up distractions. Buddhist sources compare the mind to a monkey which swings through the trees, taking hold of one branch after another. . . . Firm and steady concentration comes only with regular practice and it normally takes several months before results are achieved. Learning to meditate is a bit like learning to play a musical instrument: it requires determination, commitment, and daily practice.

No Need for Precepts

BANKEI

Bankei (1622–1693) was an iconoclastic teacher of Zen. His views on the subject were often in conflict with the mainstream Zen of his day. He insists that if Buddhists were to attain Buddha Mind, they would not need formal precepts to guide their actions—they would naturally and spontaneously do what's right.

PRECEPTS

A certain master of the Precepts School asked: "Doesn't your Reverence observe the precepts?"

The Master said: "Originally, what people call the precepts were all for wicked monks who broke the rules; for the man who abides in the Unborn Buddha Mind, there's no need for precepts. The precepts were taught to help sentient beings—they weren't

Bankei, *Bankei Zen*, Peter Haskel, trans. (New York: Grove Weidenfeld, 1984), 7–8.

taught to help buddhas! What everyone has from his parents innately is the Unborn Buddha Mind alone, so abide in the Unborn Buddha Mind. When you abide in the Unborn Buddha Mind, you're a living buddha here today, and that living buddha certainly isn't going to concoct anything like taking the precepts, so there aren't any precepts for him to take. To concoct anything like taking the precepts is not what's meant by the Unborn Buddha Mind. When you abide in the Unborn Buddha Mind, there's no way you can violate the precepts. From the standpoint of the Unborn, the precepts too are secondary, peripheral concerns; in the place of the Unborn, there's really no such thing as precepts. . . ."

THE SAME OLD THING

"A certain teacher of Buddhism told me: 'Instead of teaching the same old thing in your sermons day after day, you ought to throw in a few Buddhist miracle stories once in a while and give people a refreshing change of pace.' Of course, he could be right. I may be thickheaded, but provided something is really helpful to people, then, thickheaded or not, I'm not beyond memorizing one or two old stories if I put my mind to it. However, teaching this sort of thing is like feeding poison to sentient beings. And feeding people poison is something I certainly can't do!"

The Koan Exercise

D. T. SUZUKI

The aim of Zen practice is to short-circuit the reasoning mind so insight can rise to the surface. One way to accomplish this, say Zen masters, is to meditate on a koan, an insoluble logic puzzle, until rational thought is vanquished and true understanding comes unbidden. Here D. T. Suzuki, Zen's foremost proponent in English, explains how koans work.

WHAT IS A KOAN?

A koan, according to one authority, means "a public document setting up a standard of judgment," whereby one's Zen understanding is tested as to its correctness. A koan is generally some statement made by an old Zen master, or some answer of his given to a questioner. The following are some that are commonly given to the uninitiated:

1. A monk asked T'ung-shan, "Who is the Buddha?" "Three *chin* of flax."
2. Yun-men was once asked, "When not a thought is stirring in one's mind, is there any error here?" "As much as Mount Sumeru."
3. Chao-chou answered, "*Wu*!" (*mu* in Japanese) to a monk's question, "Is there Buddha-nature in a dog?" *Wu* literally means "not" or "none," but when this is ordinarily given as a koan, it has no reference to its literal signification; it is "*Wu*" pure and simple.

D. T. Suzuki, *Zen Buddhism* (New York: Doubleday, 1956), 134–137.

4. When Ming the monk overtook the fugitive Hui-neng, he wanted Hui-neng to give up the secret of Zen. Hui-neng replied, "What are your original features which you have even prior to your birth?"
5. A monk asked Chao-chou, "What is the meaning of the First Patriarch's visit to *China*?" "The cypress tree in the front courtyard."
6. When Chao-chou came to study Zen under Nan-chuan, he asked, "What is the Tao (or the Way)?" Nan-chuan replied, "Your everyday mind, that is the Tao."
7. A monk asked, "All things are said to be reducible to the One, but where is the One to be reduced?" Chao-chon answered, "When I was in the district of Ch'ing I had a robe made that weighed seven *chin.*"
8. When P'ang the old Zen adept first came to Ma-tsu in order to master Zen, he asked, "Who is he who has no companion among the ten thousand things of the world?" Matsu replied, "When you swallow up in one draught all the water in the Hsi Chiang, I will tell you."

When such problems are given to the uninitiated for solution, what is the object of the master? The idea is to unfold the Zen psychology in the mind of the uninitiated, and to reproduce the state of consciousness, of which these statements are the expression. That is to say, when the koans are understood the master's state of mind is understood, which is satori and without which Zen is a sealed book.

In the beginning of Zen history a question was brought up by the pupil to the notice of the master, who thereby gauged the mental state of the questioner and knew what necessary help to give him. The help thus given was sometimes enough to awaken him to realization, but more frequently than not puzzled and perplexed him beyond description, and the result was an ever-increasing mental strain or "searching and contriving" on the part of the pupil, of which we have already spoken in the foregoing pages. In actual cases, however, the master would have to wait for a long while for the pupil's first question, if it were coming at all. To ask the first question means more than half the way to its own solution, for it is the outcome of a most intense mental effort for the questioner to bring his mind to a crisis. The question indicates that the crisis is reached and the mind is ready to leave it behind. An experienced master often knows how to lead the pupil to a crisis and to make him successfully pass it. This was really the case before the koan exercise came in vogue, as was already illustrated by the examples of Lin-chi, Nan-yueh, and others.

As time went on there grew up many "questions and answers" (*mondo* in Japanese) which were exchanged between masters and pupils. And with the growth of Zen literature it was perfectly natural now for Zen followers to begin to attempt an intellectual solution or interpretation of it. The "questions and answers" ceased to be experiences and intuitions of Zen consciousness, and became subjects of logical inquiry. This was disastrous, yet inevitable. Therefore the Zen master who wished for the normal development of Zen consciousness and the vigorous growth of Zen tradition would not fail to recognize rightly the actual state of things, and to devise such a method as to achieve finally the attainment of the Zen truth.

The method that would suggest itself in the circumstances was to select some of the statements made by the old masters and to use them as pointers. A pointer would then function in two directions: (1) To check the working of the intellect, or rather to let the intellect see by itself how far it can go, and also that there is a realm into which it as such can never enter; (2) To effect the maturity of Zen consciousness which eventually breaks out into a state of satori.

When the koan works in the first direction there takes place what has been called "searching and contriving." Instead of the intellect, which taken by itself forms only a part of our being, the entire personality, mind and body, is thrown out into the solution of the koan. When this extraordinary state of spiritual tension, guided by an experienced master, is made to mature, the koan works itself out into what has been designated as the Zen experience. An intuition of the truth of Zen is now attained, for the wall against which the Yogin has been beating hitherto to no purpose breaks down, and an entirely new vista opens before him. Without the koan the Zen consciousness loses its pointer, and there will never be a state of satori. A psychological *impasse* is the necessary antecedent of satori. Formerly, that is, before the days of the koan exercise, the antecedent pointer was created in the consciousness of the Yogin by his own intense spirituality. But when Zen became systematized owing to the accumulation of Zen literature in the shape of "questions and answers" the indispensability of the koan had come to be universally recognized by the masters.

The worst enemy of Zen experience, at least in the beginning, is the intellect, which consists and insists in discriminating subject from object. The discriminating intellect, therefore, must be cut short if Zen consciousness is to unfold itself, and the koan is constructed eminently to serve this end.

On examination we at once notice that there is no room in the koan to insert an intellectual interpretation. The knife is not sharp enough to cut the koan open and see what are its contents. For a koan is not a logical proposition but the expression of a certain mental state resulting from the Zen discipline. For instance, what logical connection can there be between the Buddha and "three *chin* of flax"? or between the Buddha-nature and "*Wu*"? or between the secret message of Bodhidharma and "a cypress tree"? In a noted Zen textbook known as *Hekiganshu* (*Pi-yen-chi* in Chinese) Yuan-wu gives the following notes concerning the "three *chin* of flax," showing how the koan was interpreted by those pseudo-Zen followers who failed to grasp Zen:

> "There are some people these days who do not truly understand this koan; this is because there is no crack in it to insert their intellectual teeth. By this I mean that it is altogether too plain and tasteless. Various answers have been given by different masters to the question, 'What is the Buddha?' One said, 'He sits in the Buddha Hall.' Another said, 'The one endowed with the thirty-two marks of excellence.' Still another, 'A bamboo-root whip.' None, however, can excel T'ung-shan's 'three *chin* of flax' as regards its irrationality, which cuts off all passage of speculation. Some comment that T'ung-shan was weighing flax at the moment, hence the answer. Others say that it was a trick of equivocation on the part of T'ung-shan; and still others think that as the questioner was not conscious of the fact that he was himself the Buddha, T'ung answered him in this indirect way."

When Things Fall Apart

PEMA CHODRON

Pema Chodron uses traditional Buddhist wisdom to confront life's pain, disappointment, and loss. She says that often in the midst of our suffering, we are on the verge of discovering something about ourselves or seeing how the pain can be a gift. When things fall apart, we can experience a kind of testing and a kind of healing.

Gampo Abbey is a vast place where the sea and the sky melt into each other. The horizon extends infinitely, and in this vast space float seagulls and ravens. The setting is like a huge mirror that exaggerates the sense of there being nowhere to hide. Also, since it is a monastery, there are very few

Pema Chodron, *When Things Fall Apart* (Boston: Shambhala, 1997), 7–13.

means of escape—no lying, no stealing, no alcohol, no sex, no exit.

Gampo Abbey was a place to which I had been longing to go. Trungpa Rinpoche asked me to be the director of the abbey, so finally I found myself there. Being there was an invitation to test my love of a good challenge, because in the first years it was like being boiled alive.

What happened to me when I got to the abbey was that everything fell apart. All the ways I shield myself, all the ways I delude myself, all the ways I maintain my well-polished self-image—all of it fell apart. No matter how hard I tried, I couldn't manipulate the situation. My style was driving everyone else crazy, and I couldn't find anywhere to hide.

I had always thought of myself as a flexible, obliging person who was well liked by almost everyone. I'd been able to carry this illusion throughout most of my life. During my early years at the abbey, I discovered that I had been living in some kind of misunderstanding. It wasn't that I didn't have good qualities, it was just that I was not the ultimate golden girl. I had so much invested in that image of myself, and it just wasn't holding together anymore. All my unfinished business was exposed vividly and accurately in living Technicolor, not only to myself, but to everyone else as well.

Everything that I had not been able to see about myself before was suddenly dramatized. As if that weren't enough, others were free with their feedback about me and what I was doing. It was so painful that I wondered if I would ever be happy again. I felt that bombs were being dropped on me almost continuously, with self-deceptions exploding all around. In a place where there was so much practice and study going on, I could not get lost in trying to justify myself and blame others. That kind of exit was not available.

A teacher visited during this time, and I remember her saying to me, "When you have made good friends with yourself, your situation will be more friendly too."

I had learned this lesson before, and I knew that it was the only way to go. I used to have a sign pinned up on my wall that read: "Only to the extent that we expose ourselves over and over to annihilation can that which is indestructible be found in us." Somehow, even before I heard the Buddhist teachings, I knew that this was the spirit of true awakening. It was all about letting go of everything.

Nevertheless, when the bottom falls out and we can't find anything to grasp, it hurts a lot. It's like the Naropa Institute motto: "Love of the truth puts you on the spot." We might have some romantic view of what that means, but when we are nailed with the truth, we suffer. We look in the bathroom mirror, and there we are with our pimples, our aging face, our lack of kindness, our aggression and timidity—all that stuff.

This is where tenderness comes in. When things are shaky and nothing is working, we might realize that we are on the verge of something. We might realize that this is a very vulnerable and tender place, and that tenderness can go either way. We can shut down and feel resentful or we can touch in on that throbbing quality. There is definitely something tender and throbbing about groundlessness.

It's a kind of testing, the kind of testing that spiritual warriors need in order to awaken their hearts. Sometimes it's because of illness or death that we find ourselves in this place. We experience a sense of loss—loss of our loved ones, loss of our youth, loss of our life.

I have a friend dying of AIDS. Before I was leaving for a trip, we were talking. He said, "I didn't want this, and I hated this, and I was terrified of this. But it turns out that this illness has been my greatest gift." He said, "Now every moment is so precious to me. All the people in my life are so precious to me. My whole life means so much to me." Something had really changed, and he felt ready for his death. Something that was horrifying and scary had turned into a gift.

Things falling apart is a kind of testing and also a kind of healing. We think that the point is to pass the test or to overcome the problem, but the truth is that things don't really get solved. They come together and they fall apart. Then they come together again and fall apart again. It's just like that. The healing comes from letting there be room for all of this to happen: room for grief, for relief, for misery, for joy.

When we think that something is going to bring us pleasure, we don't know what's really going to happen. When we think something is going to give us misery, we don't know. Letting there be room for not knowing is the most important thing of all. We try to do what we think is going to help. But we don't know. We never know if we're going to fall flat or sit up tall. When there's a big disappointment, we don't know if that's the end of the story. It may be just the beginning of a great adventure.

I read somewhere about a family who had only one son. They were very poor. This son was extremely precious to them, and the only thing that mattered to his family was that he bring them some financial support and prestige. Then he was thrown from a horse and crippled. It seemed like the end of their lives. Two weeks after that, the army came into the village and took away all the healthy, strong men to fight in the war, and this young man was allowed to stay behind and take care of his family.

Life is like that. We don't know anything. We call something bad; we call it good. But really we just don't know.

When things fall apart and we're on the verge of we know not what, the test for each of us is to stay on that brink and not concretize. The spiritual journey is not about heaven and finally getting to a place that's really swell. In fact, that way of looking at things is what keeps us miserable. Thinking that we can find some lasting pleasure and avoid pain is what in Buddhism is called samsara, a hopeless cycle that goes round and round endlessly and causes us to suffer greatly. The very first noble truth of the Buddha points out that suffering is inevitable for human beings as long as we believe that things last—that they don't disintegrate, that they can be counted on to satisfy our hunger for security. From this point of view, the only time we ever know what's really going on is when the rug's been pulled out and we can't find anywhere to land. We use these situations either to wake ourselves up or to put ourselves to sleep. Right now—in the very instant of groundlessness—is the seed of taking care of those who need our care and of discovering our goodness.

I remember so vividly a day in early spring when my whole reality gave out on me. Although it was before I had heard any Buddhist teachings, it was what some would call a genuine spiritual experience. It happened when my husband told me he was having an affair. We lived in northern New Mexico. I was standing in front of our adobe house drinking a cup of tea. I heard the car drive up and the door bang shut. Then he walked around the corner, and without warning he told me that he was having an affair and he wanted a divorce.

I remember the sky and how huge it was. I remember the sound of the river and the steam rising up from my tea. There was no time, no thought, there was nothing—just the light and a profound, limitless stillness. Then I regrouped and picked up a stone and threw it at him.

When anyone asks me how I got involved in Buddhism, I always say it was because I was so angry with my husband. The truth is that he saved my life. When that marriage fell apart, I tried hard—very, very hard—to go back to some kind of comfort, some kind of security, some kind of familiar resting place. Fortunately for me, I could never pull it off. Instinctively I knew that annihilation of my old dependent, clinging self was the only way to go. That's when I pinned that sign up on my wall.

Life is a good teacher and a good friend. Things are always in transition, if we could only realize it. Nothing ever sums itself up in the way that we like to dream about. The off-center, in-between state is an ideal situation, a situation in which we don't get caught and we can open our hearts and minds beyond limit. It's a very tender, nonaggressive, open-ended state of affairs.

To stay with that shakiness—to stay with a broken heart, with a rumbling stomach, with the feeling of hopelessness and wanting to get revenge—that is the path of true awakening. Sticking with that uncertainty, getting the knack of relaxing in the midst of chaos, learning not to panic—this is the spiritual path. Getting the knack of catching ourselves, of gently and compassionately catching ourselves, is the path of the warrior. We catch ourselves one zillion times as once again, whether we like it or not, we harden into resentment, bitterness, righteous indignation—harden in any way, even into a sense of relief, a sense of inspiration.

Every day we could think about the aggression in the world, in New York, Los Angeles, Halifax,

Taiwan, Beirut, Kuwait, Somalia, Iraq, everywhere. All over the world, everybody always strikes out at the enemy, and the pain escalates forever. Every day we could reflect on this and ask ourselves, "Am I going to add to the aggression in the world?" Every day, at the moment when things get edgy, we can just ask ourselves, "Am I going to practice peace, or am I going to war?"

Rules for Zazen

MASTER DOGEN

How should one practice *zazen*, the sitting meditation at the heart of Zen? Master Dogen provides one of the more detailed sets of instructions.

1

Practicing Zen is zazen. For zazen a quiet place is suitable. Lay out a thick mat. Do not let in drafts or smoke, rain or dew. Protect and maintain the place where you settle your body. There are examples from the past of sitting on a diamond seat and sitting on a flat stone covered with a thick layer of grass.

Day or night the place of sitting should not be dark; it should be kept warm in winter and cool in summer.

2

Set aside all involvements and let the myriad things rest. Zazen is not thinking of good, not thinking of bad. It is not conscious endeavor. It is not introspection. Do not desire to become a buddha; let sitting or lying down drop away. Be moderate in eating and drinking. Be mindful of the passing of time, and engage yourself in zazen as though saving your head from fire. On Mt. Huangmei the Fifth Ancestor practiced zazen to the exclusion of all other activities.

3

When sitting zazen, wear the kashaya and use a round cushion. The cushion should not be placed all the way under the legs, but only under the buttocks. In this way the crossed legs rest on the mat and the backbone is supported with the round cushion. This is the method used by all buddha ancestors for zazen.

Sit either in the half-lotus position or in the full-lotus position. For the full-lotus put the right foot on the left thigh and the left foot on the right thigh. The toes should lie along the thighs, not extending beyond. For the half-lotus position, simply put the left foot on the right thigh.

Zen Master Dogen, *Moon in a Dewdrop*, Dan Welch and Kazuaki Tanahashi, trans. (New York: North Point Press, 1985), 29–30.

4

Loosen your robes and arrange them in an orderly way. Place the right hand on the left foot and the left hand on the right hand, lightly touching the ends of the thumbs together. With the hands in this position, place them next to the body so that the joined thumbtips are at the navel.

Straighten your body and sit erect. Do not lean to the left or right; do not bend forward or backward. Your ears should be in line with your shoulders, and your nose in line with your navel.

Rest your tongue against the roof of your mouth, and breathe through your nose. Lips and teeth should be closed. Eyes should be open, neither too wide, nor too narrow. Having adjusted body and mind in this manner, take a breath and exhale fully.

Sit solidly in samadhi and think not-thinking. How do you think not-thinking? Nonthinking. This is the art of zazen.

Zazen is not learning to do concentration. It is the dharma gate of great ease and joy. It is undefiled practice-enlightenment.

In the eleventh month, first year of Kangen [1243], this was taught to the assembly at Yoshimine Monastery, Yoshida County, Echizen Province.

CONTEMPORARY CHALLENGES

Freedom in Exile

THE DALAI LAMA

The Fourteenth Dalai Lama, Nobel laureate and spiritual leader of the Tibetans, gives a detailed account of his daily religious practice. "[A]s a Buddhist," he says, "I see no distinction between religious practice and daily life."

When I was not quite three years old, a search party that had been sent out by the Government to find the new incarnation of the Dalai Lama arrived at Kumbum monastery. It had been led there by a number of signs. One of these concerned the embalmed body of my predecessor, Thupten Gyatso, the Thirteenth Dalai Lama, who had died aged fifty-seven in 1933. During its period of sitting in state, the head was discovered to have turned from facing south to north-east. Shortly after that the Regent, himself a senior lama, had a vision. Looking into the waters of the sacred lake, Lhamoi Lhatso, in southern Tibet, he clearly saw the

Dalai Lama, *Freedom in Exile* (New York: Harper Collins, 1990), 10–11, 204–207.

Tibetan letters *Ah*, *Ka* and *Ma* float into view. These were followed by the image of a three-storeyed monastery with a turquoise and gold roof and a path running from it to a hill. Finally, he saw a small house with strangely shaped guttering. He was sure that the letter *Ah* referred to Amdo, the north-eastern province, so it was there that the search party was sent.

By the time they reached Kumbum, the members of the search party felt that they were on the right track. It seemed likely that if the letter *Ah* referred to Amdo, then *Ka* must indicate the monastery at Kumbum—which was indeed three storeyed and turquoise roofed. They now only needed to locate a hill and a house with peculiar guttering. So they began to search the neighbouring villages. When they saw the gnarled branches of juniper wood on the roof of my parents' house, they were certain that the new Dalai Lama would not be far away. Nevertheless, rather than reveal the purpose of their visit, the group asked only to stay the night. The leader of the party, Kewtsang Rinpoche, then pretended to be a servant and spent much of the evening observing and playing with the youngest child in the house.

The child recognised him and called out "Sera Lama, Sera Lama." Sera was Kewtsang Rinpoche's monastery. Next day they left—only to return a few days later as a formal deputation. This time they brought with them a number of things that had belonged to my predecessor, together with several similar items that did not. In every case, the infant correctly identified those belonging to the Thirteenth Dalai Lama saying, "It's mine. It's mine." This more or less convinced the search party that they had found the new incarnation. However, there was another candidate to be seen before a final decision could be reached. But it was not long before the boy from Taktser was acknowledged to be the new Dalai Lama. I was that child. . . .

As for my own religious practice, I try to live my life pursuing what I call the Bodhisattva ideal. According to Buddhist thought, a Bodhisattva is someone on the path to Buddhahood who dedicates themselves entirely to helping all other sentient beings towards release from suffering. The word Bodhisattva can best be understood by translating the *Bodhi* and *Sattva* separately: *Bodhi* means the understanding or wisdom of the ultimate nature of reality, and a *Sattva* is someone who is motivated by universal compassion. The Bodhisattva ideal is thus the aspiration to practise infinite compassion with infinite wisdom. As a means of helping myself in this quest, I choose to be a Buddhist monk. There are 253 rules of Tibetan monasticism (364 for nuns) and by observing them as closely as I can, I free myself from many of the distractions and worries of life. Some of these rules mainly deal with etiquette, such as the physical distance a monk should walk behind the abbot of his monastery; others are concerned with behaviour. The four root vows concern simple prohibitions: namely that a monk must not kill, steal or lie about his spiritual attainment. He must also be celibate. If he breaks any one of these, he is no longer a monk.

I am sometimes asked whether this vow of celibacy is really desirable and indeed whether it is really possible. Suffice to say that its practice is not simply a matter of suppressing sexual desires. On the contrary, it is necessary fully to accept the existence of these desires and to transcend them by the power of reasoning. When successful, the result on the mind can be very beneficial. The trouble with sexual desire is that it is a blind desire. To say "I want to have sex with this person" is to express a desire which is not intellectually directed in the way that "I want to eradicate poverty in the world" is an intellectually directed desire. Furthermore, the gratification of sexual desire can only ever give temporary satisfaction. Thus as Nagarjuna, the great Indian scholar, said:

> When you have an itch, you scratch.
> But not to itch at all
> Is better than any amount of scratching.

Regarding my actual daily practice, I spend, at the very least, five and a half hours per day in prayer, meditation and study. On top of this, I also pray whenever I can during odd moments of the day, for example over meals and whilst travelling. In this last case, I have three main reasons for doing so: firstly, it contributes towards fulfilment of my daily duty; secondly, it helps to pass the time productively; thirdly, it assuages fear! More seriously though, as a Buddhist, I see no distinction between religious practice and daily life. Religious practice is a twenty-four-hour occupation. In fact, there are prayers prescribed for every activity from waking to washing, eating and even sleeping. For Tantric practitioners, those exercises which are undertaken during deep sleep and in the dream state are the most important preparation for death.

However, for myself, early morning is the best time for practice. The mind is at its freshest and sharpest then. I therefore get up at around four o'clock. On waking, I begin the day with the recitation of *mantras*. I then drink hot water and take my medicine before making prostrations in salutation of the Buddhas for about half an hour. The purpose of this is twofold. Firstly, it increases one's own merit (assuming proper motivation) and secondly, it is good exercise. After my prostrations, I wash—saying prayers as I do so. Then I generally go outside for a walk, during which I make further recitations, until breakfast at around 5.15 A.M. I allow about half an hour for this meal (which is quite substantial) and whilst eating read scriptures.

From 5.45 A.M. until around 8.00 A.M., I meditate, pausing only to listen to the 6.30 news bulletin of the BBC World Service. Then, from 8.00 A.M. until noon, I study Buddhist philosophy. Between then and lunch at 12.30, I might read either official papers or newspapers, but during the meal itself I again read scripture. At 1.00 P.M., I go to my office, where I deal with government and other matters and give audiences until 5.00 P.M. This is followed by another short period of prayer and meditation as soon as I get back home. If there is anything worthwhile on television, I watch it now before having tea at 6.00 P.M. Finally, after tea, during which I read scripture once more, I say prayers until 8.30 or 9.00 P.M., when I go to bed. Then follows very sound sleep.

Of course, there are variations to this routine. Sometimes during the morning I will participate in a *puja* or, in the afternoon, I will deliver a teaching. But, all the same, I very rarely have to modify my daily practice—that is my morning and evening prayers and meditation.

The rationale behind this practice is quite simple. During the first part of it when I make prostrations, I am "taking refuge" in the Buddha, the *Dharma* and the *Sangha*. The next stage is to develop *Bodhichitta* or a Good Heart. This is done firstly by recognising the impermanence of all things and secondly by realising the true nature of being which is suffering. On the basis of these two considerations, it is possible to generate altruism.

To engender altruism, or compassion, in myself, I practise certain mental exercises which promote love towards all sentient beings, including especially my so-called enemies. For example, I remind myself that it is the actions of human beings rather than human beings themselves that make them my enemy. Given a change of behaviour, that same person could easily become a good friend.

The remainder of my meditation is concerned with *Sunya* or Emptiness, during which I concentrate on the most subtle meaning of Interdependence. Part of this practice involves what is termed "deity yoga," *lhai naljor*, during which I use different *mandalas* to visualise myself as a succession of different "deities." (This should not, however, be taken to imply belief in independent external beings.) In so doing, I focus my mind to the point where it is no longer preoccupied with the data produced by the senses. This is not a trance, as my mind remains fully alert; rather it is an exercise in pure consciousness. What exactly I mean by this is hard to explain: just as it is difficult for a scientist to explain in words what is meant by the term "space-time." Neither language nor everyday experience can really communicate the meaning experience of "pure mind." Suffice to say that it is not an easy practice. It takes many years to master.

One important aspect of my daily practice is its concern with the idea of death. To my mind, there are two things that, in life, you can do about death. Either you can choose to ignore it, in which case you may have some success in making the idea of it go away for a limited period of time, or you can confront the prospect of your own death and try to analyse it and, in so doing, try to minimise some of the evitable suffering that it causes. Neither way can you actually overcome it. However, as a Buddhist, I view death as a normal process of life, I accept it as a reality that will occur while I am in *Samsara*. Knowing that I cannot escape it, I see no point in worrying about it. I hold the view that death is rather like changing one's clothes when they are torn and old. It is not an end in itself. Yet death is unpredictable—you do not know when and how it will take place. So it is only sensible to take certain precautions before it actually happens.

Thich Nhat Hanh on Engaged Buddhist Ethics

SALLIE B. KING

In the aftermath of the war in Vietnam and the great suffering and pain it caused, many Vietnamese Buddhists looked for ways to apply Buddhist principles to the social and political conflicts that plagued the country. One approach came from Thich Nhat Hanh, a Vietnamese Zen master, poet, and the architect of a distinctive form of "engaged Buddhism." His answer to brutality and violence is to attain a compassionate Buddha nature and to develop a kind of deep empathy with both victim and victimizer.

When Diem fell, the activist Buddhists of Vietnam found themselves virtually overnight in a position of tremendous power and prominence. The eyes of the people of Vietnam, as well as of all the global parties to the conflict, were upon them. What should they do next? Completely unprepared, they needed to understand their role both in the light of their immediate situation and in the context of Buddhist values.

Events moved too fast, with crisis following crisis, and time was too short for anything like an adequate consideration of the issues. Yet the issues were there, were wrestled with, and continue to be wrestled with. Prominent among Buddhist activists publicly contemplating the principled foundation of Buddhist social activism was and is Thich Nhat Hanh. In his works written during the war and since, we see one creative attempt to come to Buddhist terms with the imperative posed by the "lotus in a sea fire": Vietnam.

What kind of ethical principles are embodied in the engaged Buddhism of Thich Nhat Hanh? We can open this by examining one of his poems.

Please Call Me By My True Names

Do not say that I'll depart tomorrow
because even today I still arrive.

Look deeply: I arrive in every second
to be a bud on a spring branch,
to be a tiny bird, with wings still fragile,
learning to sing in my new nest,
to be a caterpillar in the heart of a flower,
to be a jewel hiding itself in a stone.

I still arrive, in order to laugh and to cry,
in order to fear and to hope,
the rhythm of my heart is the birth and
death of all that are alive.

I am the mayfly metamorphosing on the
surface of the river,
and I am the bird which, when spring comes,
arrives in time to eat the mayfly.

I am the frog swimming happily in the
clear water of a pond,
and I am also the grass-snake who
approaching in silence,
feeds itself on the frog.

I am the child in Uganda, all skin and bones,
my legs as thin as bamboo sticks,

Sallie B. King, "Thich Nhat Hanh and the Unified Buddhist Church of Vietnam" in Christopher S. Queen and Sallie B. King, eds., *Engaged Buddhism* (Albany: State University of New York Press, 1996), 338–342.

and I am the arms merchant, selling deadly
weapons to Uganda.

I am the 12-year-old girl, refugee
on a small boat,
who throws herself into the ocean after
being raped by a sea pirate,
and I am the pirate, my heart not yet capable
of seeing and loving.

I am a member of the politburo, with
plenty of power in my hands,
and I am the man who has to pay his
"debt of blood" to my people,
dying slowly in a forced labor camp.

My joy is like spring, so warm it makes
flowers bloom in all walks of life.
My pain is like a river of tears, so full it
fills up the four oceans.

Please call me by my true names,
so I can hear all my cries and my laughs
at once,
so I can see that my joy and pain are one.

Please call me by my true names,
so I can wake up,
and so the door of my heart can be left open,
the door of compassion.

This poem locates ordinary human morality in the same realm as animal and even plant behavior. He says "I" am a bud, a tiny bird, a caterpillar. This reflects traditional Buddhist ideas about the nature of human being: we humans are not a special class, different in our essential nature from other forms of life. We are beings who live many lives, and in the endless round of birth after birth, we are born sometimes in the form of human beings, sometimes in animal forms, sometimes as gods, sometimes as hell beings, sometimes in other mythological forms. Given this idea, it is natural to locate human behavior and even human morality in the same realm as that of other life forms.

How, then, do animals behave? The mayfly metamorphoses; the bird eats the mayfly. The frog swims happily, the grass-snake eats the frog. Is there good and evil here? Is there right and wrong? We certainly do not ordinarily think so. As the Taoists say, "The Tao is not humane"; in other words, Mother Nature does not operate by our standards of right and wrong; morality does not apply in the nonhuman world of nature.

Nhat Hanh goes on to create a parallel between the snake eating the frog and the arms merchant selling deadly weapons to Uganda, to the detriment of the starving Ugandan child. Again, he parallels these with the sea pirate who rapes a 12-year-old Vietnamese boat-girl, who in her anguish throws herself into the sea. Is there not right and wrong here? Are these not great evils being committed against innocent children? Any moral system would surely recognize the unequivocal wrong of such acts. How can Nhat Hanh suggest that the sea pirate and the arms merchant are in any way like the blameless bird or the snake?

In Nhat Hanh's view, the sea pirate and the arms merchant are indeed like the bird and the snake. All are driven in their actions by the same forces: hunger seeks satiation, fear seeks to avoid what is feared, revulsion seeks to avoid the repulsive, desire seeks to attain the desired, power seeks to exercise dominance. Human ideas of good and bad are meaningless in this context, as Nhat Hanh reveals by his repeated use of the word "I." I am the frog and I am the snake: if I were born a frog I would enjoy swimming in the pond; if I were born a snake, I would seek a frog for dinner. Likewise, Nhat Hanh says, "if I had been born in the village of the pirate and raised in the same conditions as he was, I am now the pirate." It is important to recall that in the Buddhist view there is no soul or self that could be in its essence good or bad. While we live in samsara—the world of birth after birth after birth, the world of confusion and ignorant passions—we are conditioned beings. What I am is the product of my karma, my past actions in this life and previous lives. But if my karma causes me to be born in conditions of abject poverty, ignorance, and hopelessness, the person I become in this life will be the product of these conditions. So just as the snake behaves as it does on the basis of the conditions of its birth and its experiences in this life, so do human beings.

Two implications follow from this perspective. First, there is of course sorrow for the starving Ugandan child and the Vietnamese boat-girl; they also are the victims of the conditions of their birth. The first principle of Buddhism is suffering. The entire point of Buddhism from beginning to end is to eradicate suffering; this is the goal of each and every sincere Buddhist. So this is by no means a heartless view, despite the parallel drawn between the mayfly and frog on the one hand and the Ugandan and Vietnamese children on the other.

If the first principle of Buddhism is suffering, the second principle is the necessity of looking carefully at suffering, not turning one's face from it, seeing it clearly and understanding its roots. And part of seeing suffering clearly is feeling strongly that suffering; Nhat Hanh says I am the Ugandan child, I am the Vietnamese boat-girl. He not only feels sorry for them, he indicates that it is possible and necessary to feel complete empathy with the victims of hardship. Nhat Hanh says, "I feel the hunger, the misery, the despair that those children feel; the identical feelings that are in their hearts are in mine; there is no separation between us." This is surely the very opposite of heartlessness, and in fact suggests a degree of emotional commitment more intense than that usually expected in our Western ideas of pity.

Second, there is no judgment called for with respect to the sea pirate or the arms merchant, any more than there is for the snake and the bird. If you or I had been born under those conditions, you or I would be the sea pirate or arms merchant and as Nhat Hanh puts it, "I cannot condemn myself so easily." Furthermore, "If you take a gun and shoot the pirate," he says, "you shoot all of us," not only because that could and would be me if I were born under such circumstances but also "because all of us are to some extent responsible for this state of affairs." This reflects Nhat Hanh's emphasis upon the interconnections that constitute conditioned origination, *pratitya-samutpada.* Everything that exists comes into being as a result of certain causes and conditions. These causes and conditions, in turn, are all interlocking and interdependent in an endlessly complex way. Therefore, in this view, everything that happens is related, albeit distantly for the most part, to everything else that happens. In that sense, I am, and each one of you is, partially responsible for the arms merchant's and the sea pirate's actions. In that sense, there is clearly no place for one person to sit in judgment upon another here.

Does it follow that morality is to be ignored altogether? By no means; we have already seen the morality implicit in Nhat Hanh's identification with both victim and victimizer. The end of his poem suggests the hoped-for state of morality. "Please call me by my true names" says Nhat Hanh. I am the joy and the sorrow; I am the killer and the killed. We cannot simply identify with the boat-girl and affirm her suffering while negating the sea pirate as "bad." Through identifying with both, we can overcome such a dualistic attitude toward the complexities of suffering. Through this identification with both good and bad, through meditative discovery of the impulses behind one's own "goodness" and "badness" one can finally put aside these categories and "wake up," opening one's heart to compassion.

We may take the compassion of which Nhat Hanh speaks as a reference to Buddha nature. Buddha nature is our "true self," our true identity, whose nature is constituted by wisdom and compassion. In Mahayana thought, Buddha nature is absolutely differentiated from ego personality. The latter lives in and is conditioned by the samsaric world of ethical judgment. Buddha nature has no relation to that world, but is naturally and spontaneously compassionate, selfless, and altruistic. Thus there is a "goodness," called "compassion," beyond dualistic, judgmental "good and evil." This is the hoped-for moral condition.

In sum, this poem expresses an affirmation of a naturally compassionate Buddha nature as well as experiential identification with both victim and victimizer. In the context of an imperative to eliminate suffering, this produces Nhat Hanh's engaged Buddhism.

Regarding the means for making this vision a reality, all of Nhat Hanh's writings on socially engaged Buddhism emphasize the necessity of meditative and/or mindfulness practice. That this must be so follows directly from what was just stated. Both experiential identification with victim and victimizer and actualization of Buddha nature ordinarily are not attained without meditative practice. Both require self-knowledge beyond the level of ego personality as well as the ability to act in a way free of ego involvement. These are fruits of meditative practice. Consequently, an emphasis upon the necessity of meditative practice for the social activist is probably the most fundamental of Nhat Hanh's teachings. His work, *The Miracle of Mindfulness,* was written during the war years for the sake of students of the School of Youth for Social Service. Its message was the integration of meditation into their social work; its content was instruction in mindfulness practices that could be used in the context of wartime service to others. *Being Peace,* written for Western peace activists, has the same message: in order to make peace, one must "be peace"—that is, by practicing mindfulness in the midst of all one's activities.

Women in Buddhism

ROY C. AMORE AND JULIA CHING

Roy C. Amore and Julia Ching contend that the status of women in Buddhism is ambiguous. The Buddha warned monks that women could be a distraction, yet he instituted an order of nuns. Unlike other religious traditions, Buddhism did not regard women as the property of men, and in some Buddhist texts, women are considered just as capable of achieving enlightenment as men are. Yet male–female inequality is still the norm in some areas of Buddhism.

In most countries, Buddhism has historically been a monastic religion with celibate monks. The exception is Japan, where monastic celibacy has long been abolished. As a monastic tradition, Buddhism has emphasized otherworldly values while also encouraging almsgiving and the protection of life. In our own time, the Buddhist religion all over the world has been active in promoting global peace. While it is not possible to deal with the entire range of Buddhist attitudes towards a variety of social problems, we shall single out for discussion a special issue: the position of women.

There is a profound ambiguity about the status of women in Buddhism, as is the case in most traditional religions. This ambiguity may be found in the early texts themselves. Sakyamuni cautions the *bhiksus* [monks] against women as a distraction:

> "How are we to conduct ourselves, Lord, with regard to womankind?"
>
> "Don't see them, Ananda."
>
> "But if we should see them, what are we to do?"

Roy C. Amore and Julia Ching, "The Buddhist Tradition," in Willard G. Oxtoby, ed., *World Religions: Eastern Traditions* (Oxford: Oxford University Press, 2002), 291–292.

"Abstain from speech, Ananda."

"But if they should speak to us, Lord, what are we to do?"

"Keep wide awake, Ananda."

On the one hand, Sakyamuni is said to have resisted the formation of the *bhiksuni samgha* [the order of Buddhist nuns], and when he reluctantly agreed to institute it, he predicted that its existence would prove detrimental to the length of time that his teachings would endure. On the other hand, he did institute such a *samgha* and encouraged his stepmother and other close relatives to join it. The main reason for starting a *bhiksuni samgha* was that women were as capable as men of attaining levels of higher spiritual achievement, including the spiritual goal of becoming an *arhat*.

Early Buddhist history shows other evidence of women's ambiguous status. On the positive side, the texts describe approvingly the important role played by some rich women who were early benefactors of Buddhism. One book of the Pali Canon, the *Therigatha*, is devoted solely to the poems of early *bhiksunis* [nuns]. The ethic of non-violence discouraged the physical abuse of women and children. Buddhism did not define women as the "property" of men in the way that many traditional religions did:

And be it woman, be it man for whom
Such chariot doth wait, by that same car
Into Nirvana's presence shall they come.

On the negative side, female monks had a lower status than male monks. The *bhiksu samgha* officially outranked the *bhiksuni samgha*, an individual *bhiksu* outranked an individual *bhiksuni*, and *bhiksunis* were not allowed to reach *bhiksus*. The *bhiksuni samgha* has died out in many Buddhist countries for various reasons. In general, the *bhiksuni samgha* was more vulnerable because it was smaller and less connected to political power, so when times were hard, its survival precarious. . . .

Currently the biggest obstacle to re-establishing a *bhiksuni samgha* is that Buddhist rules require ordinations to be performed by at least five senior *samgha* members of the same sex as those being ordained. This rule has worked well as a way of discouraging schismatic ordination lineages, but whenever the main female ordination line has been lost, the only way to restore it has been to import senior *bhiksunis* from another country. Now, these are hard to find.

Despite this drawback, Theravada Buddhist laywomen are very active in their religion, both at home and in the temples. There are organizations of women Buddhists, in Thailand, for example, who live a pious life and devote themselves to the service of others. They are not ordained *bhiksunis*, but some have taken vows of poverty and service, somewhat along the lines of Roman Catholic nuns. Some of these women are not interested in becoming *bhiksunis* because they feel they have more freedom to serve others if they are not bound by the *vinaya* rules. This option is especially appealing to women whose children are grown or who are otherwise free of family responsibilities.

The status of women in some of the Mahayana texts is somewhat higher than it is in the earlier texts. The Mahayana movement was more sympathetic than earlier forms of Buddhism towards the laity and the rituals the laity practised, such as stupa worship. It raised the status of all lay Buddhists, but the higher status of the laity is especially noticeable in the case of female Buddhists, for the texts mention outstanding laywomen. Women were considered capable of making spiritual progress towards enlightenment.

One reason for this change may be that Mahayana tended to be less dominated by monasticism, which tends to be a stronghold of patriarchal attitudes. But the raising of the status of laywomen must have raised women's status in the *samgha* too, for Mahayana scriptures include references to wise *bhiksunis*. The reverse must have been true as well. We should not overstate the case, however. The status of women in the Mahayana tradition was not equal to that of the men, and the ancient role of laymen and laywomen in Hinayana was probably not all that lowly. Certainly contemporary Theravada lay Buddhists revere the *samgha*, but they do not feel that their own status in comparison is a lowly one.

STUDY QUESTIONS

1. What are the Four Passing Sights? How did they affect the young Buddha?
2. What is the Buddha's Middle Way?
3. What are the Four Noble Truths? What is the Noble Eightfold Path?
4. What is *nirvana*? *Samsara*? *Anatta*? *Dukkha*? The *Dharma*?
5. What is karma? How does karma affect one's future?
6. In what Asian countries does Theravada Buddhism predominate? And Mahayana Buddhism?
7. How does Theravada differ from Mahayana? Which tradition is more conservative?
8. What are the main characteristics of Zen Buddhism?
9. What is a koan? How is it used in Zen?
10. What are some of the obstacles that have prevented Buddhist women from attaining equal status with Buddhist men?

FURTHER READING

Satnacitto Bhikku, ed., *Buddha-Nature* (London: World Wide Fund for Nature, 1989).

Peter Harvey, *An Introduction to Buddhism: Teachings, History and Practices* (Cambridge: Cambridge University Press, 1990).

Steven Heine, *Buddhism in the Modern World* (New York: Oxford University Press, 2003).

Christmas Humphreys, *Zen Buddhism* (New York: MacMillan, 1971).

Damien Keown, *Buddhism: A Very Short Introduction* (Oxford: Oxford University Press, 1996).

David Levinson, ed., *Religion: A Cross-Cultural Dictionary* (New York: Oxford University Press, 1996).

Donald W. Mitchell, *Buddhism: Introducing the Buddhist Experience* (New York: Oxford University Press, 2008).

Willard G. Oxtoby, ed., *World Religions: Eastern Traditions* (Oxford: Oxford University Press, 2002).

Walpola Rahula, *What the Buddha Taught* (New York: Grove Press, 1979).

Arvind Sharma, ed., *Today's Woman in World Religions* (Albany: State University of New York Press, 1994).

Henry Clarke Warren, trans., *The Buddha in Translations: Passages from the Buddhist Sacred Books* (Whitefish, MT: Kessinger Publishing, 2005).

F. L. Woodward and E. M. Hare, trans., *The Book of Gradual Sayings*, 5 vols. (London: PTS, 1932–1936).

ONLINE

Buddhanet.net, "Basic Buddhism Guide," http://www.buddhanet.net/e-learning/basic-guide.htm (December 22, 2015).

Shambhala, http://shambhala.org/ (December 22, 2015).

Tricycle, http://www.tricycle.com/ (December 22, 2015).

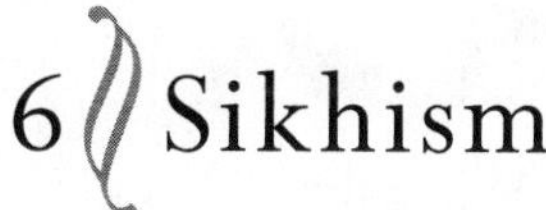

6 Sikhism

Sikhism is the world's fifth-largest religion, after Christianity, Islam, Hinduism, and Buddhism. Estimates of the number of Sikh adherents worldwide vary, but a safe approximation is around 24 million, 80 to 90 percent of whom live in the Punjab in northern India. In 2004, about 400,000 resided in North America, and 360,000 in the United Kingdom.[1] Like most religious traditions, Sikhism has a founder, scriptures, a sacred shrine, unique practices, and a history going back hundreds of years. It is no more mysterious or esoteric than other religions, yet it is often poorly understood, even in countries where many Sikhs live. Sikhism is sometimes thought to comprise an unoriginal mix of Islam and Hinduism, or to simply constitute Hinduism in new dress. Media reports give the impression that Sikhism is

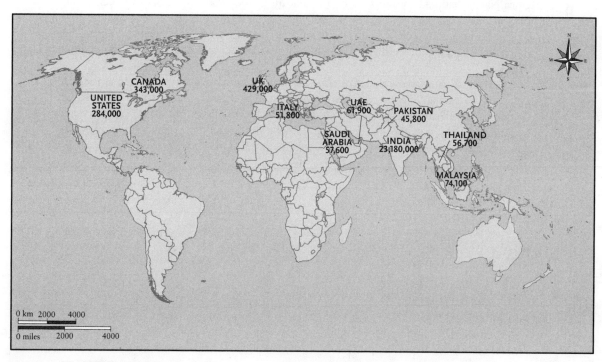

MAP 6.1 World Sikh population.

upied with violent conflict, and in the West, because Sikh men wear turbans, they been taken for Muslims. The facts about Sikhism, however, show a different side of the dition.

BEGINNINGS

Sikhism began with the spiritual teacher Guru Nanak (1469–1539), the first of ten successive Gurus revered (but not worshipped) by all Sikhs and credited with helping to develop the tradition over two-and-one-half centuries. Guru Nanak declared that the disagreements between Hindus and Muslims over doctrine were pointless, because doctrines are the result of deficient understanding of the real essence of God. God's true way, he said, is neither Muslim nor Hindu. Theology can never penetrate to God's divine nature, and neither can the performance of rituals, idol worship, ceremonies, pilgrimages, asceticism, priests, and superstitions. Only devotional praise of God—mainly through meditation on scripture, sacred words, and hymns—can lead to an inner union with God and therefore liberation from the cycle of death and rebirth.

Guru Nanak spent his years teaching the path he advocated, composing hymns (which were later incorporated into the Sikh canon), encouraging Hindus and Muslims to set aside their differences and join him on the true path, and founding the Sikh community, or **Panth**. Guru Nanak had gathered around him a handful of followers called *Sikhs*, which means "students" or "disciples." From his disciples he eventually chose a successor, Angad (1504–1552), who like all ten of Sikhism's great spiritual leaders wore the honorific of *Guru*. Tradition has it that by appointing Angad, Guru Nanak initiated the Panth, which has endured ever since.

The third Guru, Amar Das (1479–1574), is thought to have institutionalized a principle that Guru Nanak had introduced: caste has nothing to do with a Sikh's prospects for spiritual liberation or with status within the Panth. With this view in mind, Guru Amar Das promoted the practice of **langar**, the sharing of food among Sikhs and non-Sikhs alike in places of worship (**gurdwaras**) regardless of caste, wealth, or position.

A CLOSER LOOK

Sikhism's Ten Gurus

1. Guru Nanak (1469–1539)
2. Guru Angad (1504–1552)
3. Guru Amar Das (1479–1574)
4. Guru Ram Das (1534–1581)
5. Guru Arjan (1563–1606)
6. Guru Hargobind (1595–1644)
7. Guru Har Rai (1630–1661)
8. Guru Hari Krishan (1656–1664)
9. Guru Tegh Bahadur (1621–1675)
10. Guru Gobind Singh (1666–1708)

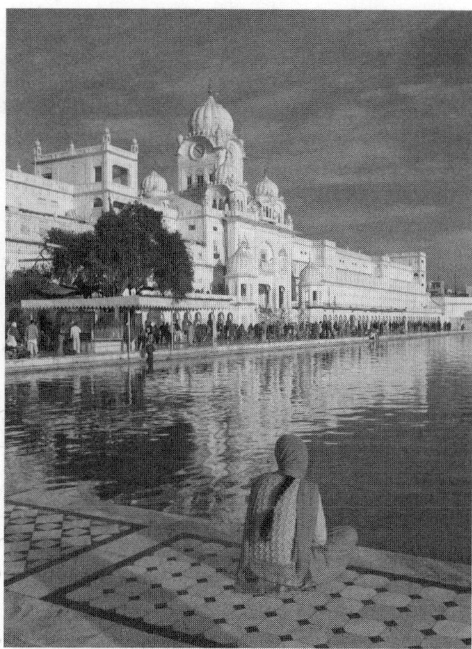

FIGURE 6.1 The Golden Temple (the Harmandir Sahib) in Amritsar, Punjab, India, is one of Sikhism's holiest places and a symbol of brotherhood and equality.

The fifth Guru, Arjan (1563–1606), is known for three far-reaching changes in the Sikh tradition. First, he completed construction of Sikhism's most sacred shrine, the gurdwara known as the Golden Temple at Amritsar, Sikhism's spiritual capital. Second, because of continued attacks on Sikhs by the Muslim Mughal empire, he held that Sikhs should be ready and able to defend themselves if the need arises. (As it turned out, Guru Arjan died at the hands of the Mughals, a martyr in the eyes of contemporary Sikhs.) From this time on, Sikhism was no longer a purely pacifist tradition preoccupied with interior devotion. Third, Guru Arjan compiled the **Adi Granth**, the most revered and authoritative scriptures of Sikhism.

According to tradition, the tenth Guru, Gobind Singh (1666–1708), proclaimed that he was the last of the human Gurus and that after his death Sikhs must look to the *Adi Granth* and the Panth for guidance. The holy scriptures and the Panth would constitute the supreme Sikh Guru. To mark this distinction the *Adi Granth* would be revered as Guru Granth Sahib, and the Sikh community would be known as Guru Panth. Today in every gurdwara, a large, adorned copy of the *Adi Granth* is prominently displayed and treated as an honored guest. When the scriptures are present, Sikhs maintain, the Guru is present.

Guru Gobind Singh also established a holy order within the Panth—the **Khalsa**, a special community of committed Sikh believers. The dominant view among Sikhs is that by setting up this body, he hoped to create a loyal and disciplined core of believers (men and women) who could defend Sikhs against their enemies. The first recruits were five men who were willing to

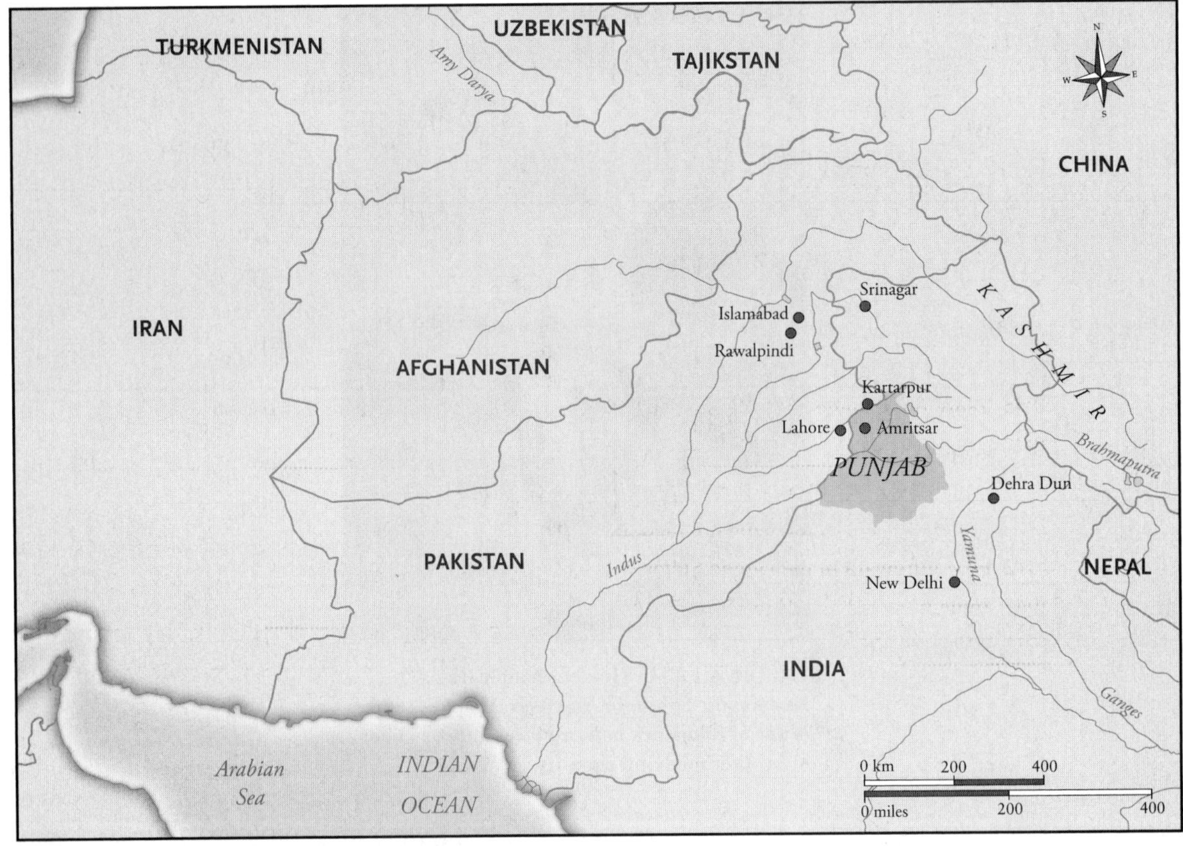

MAP 6.2 **Significant sites in the history of Sikhism.**

pledge allegiance to the Guru and to die for the cause. According to tradition, Guru Gobind Singh required all members of the Khalsa (known as the "Pure Ones") to symbolize their commitment by wearing the Five Ks (so called because the name of each item begins with a *k* in the language of the Punjab). The Five Ks are uncut hair, a comb, a short sword, an iron or steel bracelet, and a pair of white cotton shorts. Today members of the Khalsa don these same objects (or contemporary versions of them) and agree to a code of conduct (called the *Rahit*). Male members also wear turbans, which have become common among all Sikh men and now symbolize Sikhism generally. (In the United States, men who wear turbans are most likely Sikhs.) Khalsa Sikhs customarily add *Singh* to a male child's name and *Kaur* to a female child's.

BELIEFS

Sikhism teaches that there is only one God, whom Sikhs call *Vahiguru* (formerly *Akal Purakh*), one divinity in the universe—an eternal, timeless, genderless, self-existent Creator and Sustainer of everything that exists. God is invisible and formless; he does not express

SIKH TIMELINE

CE

1200–1757 Muslim rule of North India

1469–1539 Life of Nanak, founder of Sikhism

1563–1606 Life of Arjan, the fifth Guru

1666–1708 Life of Gobind Singh, tenth Guru

1699 Establishment of the Khalsa

1757 British rule established in India

1845–1846 First Anglo-Sikh War

1848–1849 Second Anglo-Sikh War

1873 Founding of the Singh Sabha reform movement

1911 First gurdwara in the United Kingdom

1912 First gurdwara in the United States

1947 India wins independence from Britain.

1950 The *Rahit Maryada* is published.

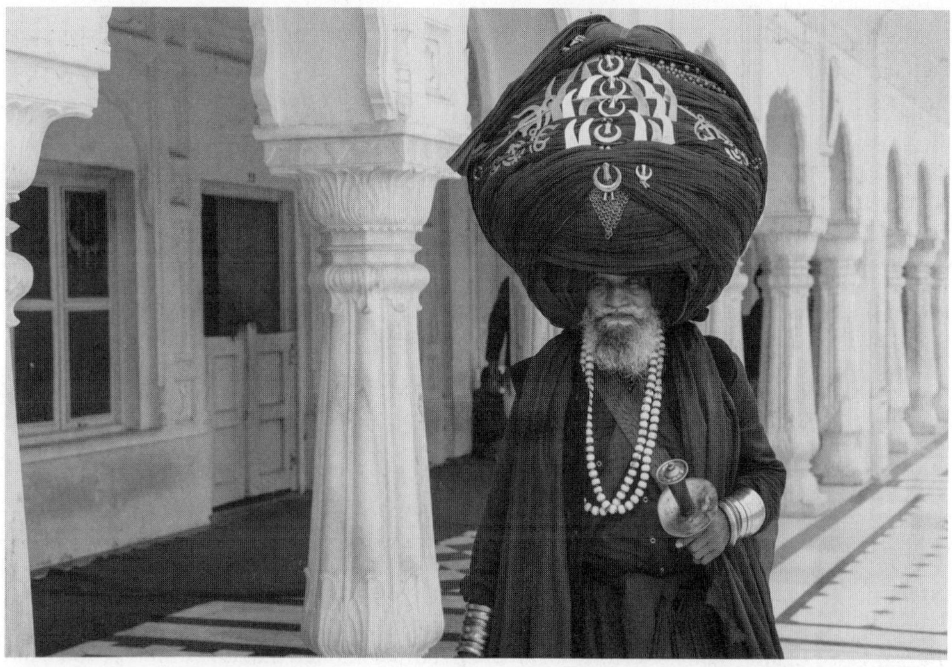

FIGURE 6.2 A Sikh man in Amritsar, India, wears an oversize turban at the Golden Temple.

his divinity through incarnations such as the avatars of Hinduism. God is said to be both transcendent (existing beyond the world) and immanent (existing and acting within the world). God cannot be equated with his creation, but he is present within it. Everything is an expression of his being. For humans, he is the ultimate Guru.

We can see God's immanence in the world (in physical reality and in ourselves) in **hukam**, the divine Order of things. In *hukam* there is a harmony that is proof of the divine harmony of God. To align our lives with this harmony is to align ourselves with *Akal Purakh*, which is the central aim of Sikhism.

But humans in their natural state are alienated from God and blinded by their egoistic focus on external things and by the illusion that they exist separately from God. As long as they remain spiritually aloof from *Akal Purakh*, they will be forever bound to the agonizing rounds of death and rebirth (*samsara*). God, however, through his grace has provided a way for men and women to come to know him, to harmonize themselves with the divine Order, and to unite with him and achieve liberation (*mukti*). (The *Adi Granth* asserts, "Past actions determine the nature of our birth, but grace alone reveals the door to liberation.") They can approach God through devotional meditation on the "divine name" (*nam*), which signifies the nature and glory of *Akal Purakh*. To grasp the meanings of the *nam* is to leap beyond ordinary understanding and to become one with God, finally attaining deliverance. As one scholar says,

> The term *nam* . . . is a summary expression for the whole nature of Akal Purakh and all that constitutes the divine being. . . . Anything that may be affirmed concerning Akal Purakh constitutes an aspect of the divine Name, and a sufficient understanding of the divine name provides the essential means to deliverance. . . . The *nam* is the ever-present and all-pervading presence of Akal Purakh, and whoever perceives this presence gains access to the means of mystical unity with Akal Purakh. In that condition of supreme peace lies liberation. . . .[2]

Deep meditation on the *nam* can be mastered through constant practice of *nam simaran*, "remembrance of the name":

> A simple version of this technique consists of repeating a word or expression that summarizes the meaning of the divine Name and thus Akal Purakh (terms such as *sat-nam* or *vahiguru*). *Kirtan* (the singing of appropriate hymns) is another form of *nam simaran*, for in this manner also devout believers can attune themselves to the divine. A third method (the most sophisticated version) is a technique of meditation that inwardly reflects upon the meaning of the divine Name, with the intention of bringing one's whole being into harmony with the divine harmony of Name.[3]

For Sikhs, external shows of piety—rituals, self-denial, pilgrimages, and the like—are of no help in overcoming *samsara*. But internal piety—the inward state of unity with divine Reality—breaks the circle of eternal birth and death.

SIKH SCRIPTURES

As we have seen, the *Adi Granth* constitutes the most significant and venerated scriptures of Sikhism. It is known not only as Guru Granth Sahib, but also as Granth Sahib, Guru Granth, and Sri Guru Granth Sahib. Guru Arjan is said to have compiled the *Adi Granth* in 1603 and

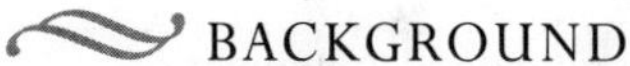 BACKGROUND

Women and Sikhism

Officially, Sikhism gives men and women equal standing in religious and social matters. As Guru Nanak says,

> Of woman are we born, of woman conceived . . .
>
> Woman we befriend, by woman do civilizations continue . . .
>
> It is through woman that order is maintained.
>
> Then why call her inferior from whom all great ones are born?[4]

But the ideal of gender equality in Sikhism has yet to be fully achieved. Consider the views of two Sikhism commentators:

> [W]hen non-Sikhs visit a gurdwara they are often favourably surprised to see a woman publicly reading from the scriptures and men distributing food in the *langar*, and they comment on the striking evidence of the equality of men and women. At the same time, in Sikh society, as in other societies, both men and women acquire and pass on a complex of spoken and unspoken norms about gender roles. Moreover, certain religious roles are almost always played by men. The *panj piare* [five beloved ones], whether marching in festival processions or administering *amrit* [the water of immortality] in the *khande di pahul* ceremony, are nearly always men. It is true that in North America, from the 1970s, there have been instances of females taking this part . . . but these are exceptions.[5]

> The answer is that the sociological patterns governing the beliefs and behaviour of most Sikhs do not permit equal treatment of men and women. . . . Women may be kindly and respectfully treated, and their lives may be rendered thoroughly satisfactory by the consideration which may be shown to them, but power rests with the males and patriarchy indisputably rules.[6]

1604 CE. It contains a large collection of hymns and poems by (1) the first five Gurus (Gurus Nanak, Angad, Amar Das, Ram Das, and Arjan) and the ninth Guru (Tegh Bahadur); (2) several Muslim and Hindu mystics, including the saint-poet Kabir; and (3) poets associated with the Gurus.

The basic language of the *Adi Granth* is similar to contemporary Punjabi and Hindi, but some regional variations are present as well as some words from other languages such as Arabic, Persian, and Sanskrit. The script is called Gurmukhi. Contemporary copies of the scriptures are standardized, all consisting of exactly 1,430 pages. This edition occupies a place of honor in gurdwaras, usually resting during the day on a cushion under a canopy and reposing in the evening in another room. It is treated as the physical embodiment of the Guru.

The *Dasam Granth* is another authoritative collection of writings, traditionally thought to have been written mostly by Guru Gobind Singh. Two hundred years ago the *Dasam Granth* was considered Sikh scripture on a par with the *Adi Granth*, but now it is generally regarded as secondary although still highly respected. Most adherents rarely read it, and few gurdwaras recite it, although some Sikhs (especially the Nihangs) revere it as highly as they do the *Adi Granth*.

The *Dasam Granth* is 1,428 pages long, is written in verse, and consists of a variety of texts: autobiographical compositions attributed to Guru Gobind Singh; hymns and prayers also by the Guru; miscellaneous texts (poems about the religions of India and a list of weapons and warriors); and mystical tales and anecdotes about gods, goddesses, and women. The latter make up over three quarters of the volume.

The *Rahit* (more precisely, the *Rahit Maryada*) is the code of conduct and statement of doctrine that specifies the acceptable behavior and beliefs of Sikhs who are members of the Khalsa. According to tradition, the *Rahit* is largely based on the lectures of Guru Gobind Singh, but this claim has been controversial. Although the *Rahit* is addressed to the Khalsa, it has become the official guide to the principles and practice of all Sikhs, and it has helped to clarify and solidify what it means to be a member of the Panth. Sikhs must reflect on God, read the scriptures, obey the Guru, respect the *Adi Granth*, pray daily, perform rites correctly, ignore the strictures of caste and class, tithe, and serve the needs of others, whether Sikh or not. They should not steal, gamble, use tobacco or other drugs, or commit infanticide or adultery. The final, approved version of the *Rahit Maryada* was approved in 1950.

NOTES

1. *Religious Tolerance* (based on data from adherents.com, realsikhism.com, and other sites), www.religioustolerance.com, accessed June 4, 2014.
2. Hew McLeod, *Sikhism* (New York: Penguin Books, 1997), 98–99.
3. *Ibid.*, 99–100.
4. Guru Nanak, *Asa* 19, *Adi Granth* 473, in *The Feminine Principle in the Sikh Vision of the Transcendent* (Cambridge: Cambridge University Press, 1993), 30.
5. Eleanor Nesbitt, *Sikhism: A Very Short Introduction* (Oxford: Oxford University Press, 2005), 112–113.
6. McLeod, 249.

KEY TERMS

Adi Granth (Guru Granth Sahib) Sikhism's most revered and authoritative scriptures.

gurdwara A Sikh place of worship.

hukam The divine Order of everything.

Khalsa The elite community of committed Sikh believers.

langar The sharing of food among all Sikhs regardless of caste, wealth, or position.

Panth The Sikh community.

READINGS

TEACHINGS

Hymns of Guru Gobind Singh

Guru Gobind Singh not only compiled the final version of the *Adi Granth*, he also composed his own writings. These are not part of Sikh scripture, but they are revered nonetheless. They are known as the *Dasam Granth*, a collection of over two thousand hymns. Here are two of them.

4

One man by shaving his head
Hopes to became a holy monk,
Another sets up as a Yogi
Or some other kind of ascetic.
Some call themselves Hindus:
Others call themselves Musulmans.
Among these there are the Shiahs,
There are the Sunis also,
And yet man is of one race in all the world;
God as Creator and God as Good,
God in His Bounty and God in His Mercy,
Is all one God. Even in our errors,
We should not separate God from God!
Worship the One God,
For all men the One Divine Teacher.
All men have the same form,
All men have the same soul.

5

He is in the temple as He is in the mosque:
He is in the Hindu worship as He is in the Muslim prayer;
Men are one though they appear different,
Gods and demons who guard the treasures
Of the god of riches, the musicians celestial
The Hindus and the Muslims are all one,
Have each the habits of a different environments,
But all men have the same eyes, the same body,
The same form compounded of the same four elements,
Earth, air, fire, and water.
Thus the Abhekh of the Hindus and the Allah of Muslims are one,
The Koran and the Purans praise the same Lord.
They are all of one form,
The One Lord made them all.

Guru Gobind Singh, "The Dasam Granth," in *Selections from the Sacred Writings of the Sikhs,* Trilochan Singh et al., trans. (London: George Allen and Unwin, 1960), 268–269.

Hymns of Guru Amar Das

The third guru, Guru Amar Das, was a reformer who reorganized Sikh congregations. Here are some of his 907 verses, which form part of the *Adi Granth.*

5

If the mind is unclean, all else is unclean;
And ceremonial washings cannot wash the mind.
This world is the realm of illusion:
There are few who grasp the Real.
O my mind, remember the Holy Name!
That is the precious gift of the Guru to men.
Were a man to learn all the postures of the most austere Yogis,
And mortify all his senses,
Not so would he cleanse the mind, or discard self-will.
There is no cure for the mind's sickness
But taking shelter at the Guru's feet.
To meet the Guru is to experience
A change of outlook that cannot be described.
Saith Nanak: From the mind of him who dies to self
Through meeting the Guru, and is reborn through the Guru's Word,
All uncleanness is removed.

6

Self-will is opposed to the Holy Name. The two cannot dwell in one house.
None can serve in a state of self-will, and the self-willed mind is worthless.
O my mind, fix thyself upon God's Name, and practise the Guru's Word.
By obeying God's Will, thou graspest Him, and sheddest thy self-will.
Self-will is the cause of all shapes and their coming into being:
It is the source of illusion, and veils the Reality from us.
The self-willed man cannot love God or understand His Will;
The soul is imprisoned in self-will and the Name cannot dwell in the heart.
But when a man meets the True Guru his self-will is destroyed,
And then the Truth alighteth in his heart to abide there
So, practising truth, a man lives in Truth
And, serving God who is Truth, is absorbed in Him.

7

All men have access to the Guru
But a mere glimpse of the Guru does not save them;
Without understanding of the Guru's Word
The self is not made clean nor the love of the Name implanted;
Some through God's Grace give up all self-will and sinfulness
And are made one with God:
Others, saith Nanak, at the sight of the Guru
Die to self, through the Guru's love,
And are at once made one with the Divine Spirit.

Guru Amar Das, "Adi Guru Granth," in *Selections from the Sacred Writings of the Sikhs*, Trilochan Singh et al., trans. (London: George Allen and Unwin, 1960), 133–134.

Hymns of Guru Ram Das

Guru Ram Das was the fourth Guru and the son-in-law of Guru Amar Das. *The Adi Granth* contains 679 of his hymns.

3

Deep in me there is a longing to see Thee, O my Beloved!
The Lord who hath given me the grace of love for Him
Knoweth how deep is my love. I would be a sacrifice to the Guru
Who has made me at one with the Lover Who dwelt afar!
Lord, I am a sinner seeking sanctuary at Thy Gates
In the hope that even I, utterly without merit,
May through Thy Grace be blessed with union with Thee.
Our sins are unnumbered: no count to our errors:
Thou, who art Justice, art also Mercy, O Lord.
Cleanse me, O Lord, of my stains, as it may please Thee.
I am a sinner saved by the Guru's society:
He has saved me by bearing witness to the Holy Name!
O True Guru, how can I speak of thy virtues?
When thou but speakest, I am transported with wonder.
Who, but the True Guru, could save a sinner like me?
Guru, thou art my father and my mother,
Thou art my friend, and hast wrought my salvation,
Thou art my most precious peace, and best knowest my soul!
Here below I was a wanderer and helpless,
None cared for me, but even I, wretch, have found honour
Through the society of the True Guru.
Glory, glory to the True Guru, saith Nanak,
Since, in his company,
Sorrow and pain have departed!

4

He who deems himself a Sikh of the true Guru
Should rise betimes and contemplate the Name.
In the early hours of the morning he should rise and bathe
And cleanse his soul in a tank of nectar,
As he repeats the Name the Guru taught him.
Thus he washes away the sins of his soul.
Then at dawn he should sing the hymns of the Guru.
And throughout all the busyness of the day
He should hold in his heart the Name.
He who repeats the Name with every breath
Such a Sikh is indeed dear to the Guru:
The Sikh that wins the favour of the Lord
Has received the gift of the Lord's Name from the Guru
Nanak seeks to kiss the dust under the feet of such a Sikh
Who utters the Name and inspires others to do so!

Guru Ram Das, "Adi Guru Granth," in *Selections from the Sacred Writings of the Sikhs*, Trilochan Singh et al., trans. (London: George Allen and Unwin, 1960), 143–144.

The Death of Guru Nanak

There have been many biographical studies of Sikhism's first great teacher, Guru Nanak. They are based on nonscriptural stories of questionable accuracy. Here is one such anecdote recounting Nanak's death.

Guru Baba Nanak then went and sat under a withered acacia which immediately produced leaves and flowers, becoming verdant again. Guru Angad prostrated himself. Baba Nanak's wife began to weep and the various members of his family joined her in her grief . . . The assembled congregation sang hymns of praise and Baba Nanak passed into an ecstatic trance. While thus transported, and in obedience to the divine will, he sang the hymn entitled *The Twelve Months*. It was early morning and the time had come for his final departure . . . His sons asked him, "What will happen to us?" The Guru reassured them. "Even the Guru's dogs lack nothing, my sons," he said. "You shall be abundantly supplied with food and clothing, and if you repeat the Guru's name you will be liberated from the bondage of human life."

Hindus and Muslims who had put their faith in the divine Name began to debate what should be done with the Guru's corpse. "We shall bury him," said the Muslims. "No, let us cremate his body," said the Hindus. "Place flowers on both sides of my body," said Baba Nanak, "flowers from the Hindus on the right side and flowers from the Muslims on the left. If tomorrow the Hindus' flowers are still fresh let my body be burned, and if the Muslims' flowers are still fresh let it be buried."

Baba Nanak then commanded the congregation to sing. They sang *Kirtan Sohila* and *Arati* . . . Baba Nanak then covered himself with a sheet and passed away. Those who had gathered around him prostrated themselves, and when the sheet was removed they found that there was nothing under it. The flowers on both sides remained fresh, and both Hindus and Muslims took their respective shares. All who were gathered there prostrated themselves again.

Puratan, "The Death of Baba Nanak," in *Textual Sources for the Study of Sikhism*, W. H. McLeod, trans. (Chicago: University of Chicago Press, 1984), 25.

The Rahit: Code of Conduct

Here is an excerpt from the *Sikh Rahit Maryada*, the Sikh code of conduct. It took centuries for Sikh scholars to compile this final version of the *Rahit*. It was published in 1950 and became a code of proper behavior and worship that Sikhs generally accepted as authoritative.

Sikh Rahit Maryada, from *Textual Sources for the Study of Sikhism*, W. H. McLeod, trans. (Chicago: University of Chicago Press, 1984), 79–81.

A Sikh should rise early (3 a.m. to 6 a.m.) and having bathed he should observe *nam japan* by meditating on God. Each day a Sikh should read or recite the order known as the "Daily Rule" (*nit-nem*). The Daily Rule comprises the following portions of scripture: Early morning (3 a.m.–6 a.m.): *Japji, Jap,* and the *Ten Savayyas* (5.1) . . . In the evening at sunset: *Sodar Rahiras* (5.2) . . . At night before retiring: *Sohila* (5.3). At the conclusion of the selections set down for early morning and evening (*Sodar Rahiras*) the prayer known as *Ardas* must be recited (5.4).

The influence of the Gurus' words is best experienced in a religious assembly (*sangat*). Each Sikh should therefore join in sangat worship, visiting gurdwaras and drawing inspiration from the sacred scripture in the sangat's presence. In each gurdwara the *Guru Granth Sahib* should be opened daily. . . . The *Guru Granth Sahib* must be treated with great reverence while it is being opened, read, or closed. When it is to be opened it should be laid under a canopy in a place which is clean and tidy. It should be set on a stool or lectern over which a clean cloth covering has been spread. Cushions should be used to support it while it is open and a mantle should be provided for covering it when it is not being read. A whisk should be provided for use when it is open. . . . Shoes must be removed before entering a gurdwara. Feet, if unclean, should be washed. . . . Whenever a Sikh enters a gurdwara his first duty must be to bow before the Guru Granth Sahib, touching the floor with his forehead. . . . No Sikh may sit bareheaded in the presence of the sangat or an opened Guru Granth Sahib. . . .

The only works which may be sung as kirtan in a sangat are those which are recorded in the sacred scriptures (1.2–3) or the commentaries on sacred scripture composed by Bhai Gurdas and Bhai Nand Lal (1.4).

A practice to be commended is for each Sikh regularly to read right through the entire contents of the *Guru Granth Sahib*, planning his daily instalments in such a way that he completes the task in four to eight weeks (or whatever period may be convenient for him). . . . An unbroken reading of the *Guru Granth Sahib* (*akhand path*) may be held in time of distress or to mark an occasion of particular joy. Such a reading takes approximately forty-eight hours, the actual reading continuing without interruption. . . .

Each Sikh should live and work in accordance with the principles of Gurmat. Gurmat may be defined as follows:

(a) To worship only the one supreme God (*Akal Purakh*) spurning all other gods and goddesses.
(b) To accept as the means of deliverance only the ten Gurus, the *Guru Granth Sahib*, and the works of the ten Gurus.
(c) To believe that the same spirit was successively incarnated in the ten individual Gurus.
(d) To reject caste distinctions and untouchability; magical amulets, mantras, and spells; auspicious omens, days, times, planets and astrological signs; the ritual feeding of Brahmans to sanctify or propitiate the dead; oblation for the dead; the superstitious waving of lights; [traditional] obsequies; fire sacrifices; ritual feasting or libations; sacred tufts of hair or ritual shaving; fasting for particular phases of the moon; frontal marks, sacred threads and sanctified rosaries; worshipping at tombs, temples or cenotaphs; idol worship; and all other such superstitions . . .
(g) A knowledge of Gurmukhi is essential for Sikhs (1.2[10]) . . .
(i) Do not cut a child's hair . . .
(r) When Sikhs meet they should greet each other by saying, "Vahiguru ji ka Khalsa, Vahiguru ji ki fateh" [Hail to the Guru's Khalsa! Hail to the victory of the Guru!]. This is the correct form for both men and women . . .
(t) A Sikh must wear a kachh (4.5[43]) and a turban. Apart from these garments he may wear whatever he chooses. The turban is optional for women.

Selections from the Japji

Japji is the portion of Sikh scripture that contains the core teachings of Sikhism. It is a long poem recited each day during morning prayers. The Japji speaks of God's greatness and grace, salvation by meditating on his name, and God as the source and sustainer of all creation.

2

Through His Will He creates all the forms of things,
But what the form of His Will is, who can express?
All life is shaped by His ordering,
By His ordering some are high, some of low estate,
Pleasure and pain are bestowed as His Writ ordaineth.

Some through His Will are graciously rewarded,
Others must grope through births and deaths;
Nothing at all, outside His Will, is abiding.
O Nanak, he who is aware of the Supreme Will
Never in his selfhood utters the boast: "It is I."

3

Those who believe in power,
Sing of His power;
Others chant of His gifts
As His messages and emblems;
Some sing of His greatness,
And His gracious acts;
Some sing of His wisdom
Hard to understand;
Some sing of Him as the fashioner of the body.
Destroying what He has fashioned;
Others praise Him for taking away life
And restoring it anew.

Some proclaim His Existence
To be far, desperately far, from us;
Others sing of Him
As here and there a Presence
Meeting us face to face.

To sing truly of the transcendent Lord
Would exhaust all vocabularies, all human powers of expression,
Myriads have sung of Him in innumerable strains.
His gifts to us flow in such plentitude
That man wearies of receiving what God bestows;
Age on unending age, man lives on His bounty;
Carefree, O Nanak, the Glorious Lord smiles.

4

The Lord is the Truth Absolute,
True is His Name.
His language is love infinite;
His creatures ever cry to Him;
"Give us more, O Lord, give more";
The Bounteous One gives unwearyingly.

Adi Granth 1.1–11, from *Selections from the Sacred Writings of the Sikhs*, Trilochan Singh, Bhai Jodh Singh, et al., trans. (London: George Allen and Unwin, 1960), 28–35.

What then should we offer
That we might see His Kingdom?
With what language
Might we His love attain?

In the ambrosial hours of fragrant dawn
Think upon and glorify
His Name and greatness.
Our own past actions
Have put this garment on us,
But salvation comes only through His Grace.

O Nanak, this alone need we know,
That God, being Truth, is the one Light of all.

5

He cannot be installed like an idol,
Nor can man shape His likeness.
He made Himself and maintains Himself
On His heights unstained for ever;
Honoured are they in His shrine
Who meditate upon Him.

Sing thou, O Nanak, the psalms
Of God as the treasury
Of sublime virtues.
If a man sings of God and hears of Him,
And lets love of God sprout within him,
All sorrow shall depart;
In the soul, God will create abiding peace.

The Word of the Guru is the inner Music;
The Word of the Guru is the highest Scripture;
The Word of the Guru is all pervading.
The Guru is Siva, the Guru is Vishnu and Brahma,
The Guru is the Mother goddess.

If I knew Him as He truly is
What words could utter my knowledge?
Enlightened by God, the Guru has unravelled one mystery
"There is but one Truth, one Bestower of life;
May I never forget Him."

6

I would bathe in the holy rivers
If so I could win His love and grace;
But of what use is the pilgrimage
If it pleaseth Him not that way?

What creature obtains anything here
Except through previous good acts?
Yet hearken to the Word of the Guru
And his counsel within thy spirit
Shall shine like precious stone.

The Guru's divine illumination
Has unravelled one mystery;
There is but one Bestower of life
May I forget Him never.

7

Were a man to live through the four ages,
Or even ten times longer,
Though his reputation were to spread over the nine shores,
Though the whole world were to follow in his train,
Though he were to be universally famous,
Yet lacking God's grace, in God's presence
Such a man would be disowned;
Such a man would be merely a worm among vermin
And his sins will be laid at his door.
On the imperfect who repent, O Nanak, God bestows virtue,

On the striving virtuous He bestows increasing blessedness.
But I cannot think there is any man so virtuous
Who can bestow any goodness on God.

8

By hearkening to the Name
The disciple becomes a Master,
A guide, a saint, a seraph;
By hearkening to the Name
The earth, the bull that bears it
And the heavens are unveiled.

By hearkening to the Name
Man's vision may explore
Planets, continents, nether regions.
Death vexes not in the least
Those that hearken to the Name;
They are beyond Death's reach.

Saith Nanak, the saints are always happy;
By hearkening to the Name
Sorrow and sin are destroyed.

9

By hearkening to the Name
Mortals obtain the godliness
Of Siva, Brahma and Indra;

By hearkening to the Name
The lips of the lowly
Are filled with His praise.
By hearkening to the Name
The art of Yoga and all the secrets
Of body and mind are unveiled.
By hearkening to the Name
The Vedic wisdom comes,
And also the knowledge of the shastras and smritis.

Saith Nanak, the saints are always happy;
By hearkening to the Name
Sorrow and sin are destroyed.

10

Hearkening to the Name bestows
Truth, divine wisdom, contentment.
To bathe in the joy of the Name
Is to bathe in the holy places.

By hearing the Name and reading it
A man attains to honour;
By hearkening, the mind may reach
The highest blissful poise
Of meditation on God.

Saith Nanak, the saints are always happy;
By hearkening to the Name
Sorrow and sin are destroyed.

11

By hearkening to the Name,
Man dives deep in an ocean of virtues;
By hearkening to the Name
The disciple becomes an apostle,
A prelate, a sovereign of souls.

By hearkening to the Name
The blind man sees the way;
By hearkening to the Name
Impassable streams are forded.

Saith Nanak, the saints are always happy;
By hearkening to the Name
Sorrow and sin are destroyed.

PRACTICES

The Rite of Khalsa Initiation

HEW MCLEOD

The Khalsa is a community of Sikh believers who have an especially strong allegiance to their religion and who promise to adhere strictly to the Sikh code of conduct (the Rahit) and to wear the Five Ks symbolizing that commitment. The Sikh scholar Hew McLeod describes the ceremony that initiates believers into the holy order.

Khalsa initiation is open to anyone who lives a worthy life and who affirms belief in the principles represented by the Khalsa. It is not limited to Punjabis. At the place of initiation an open copy of the Guru Granth Sahib is required, together with at least seven Amrit-dhari Sikhs, each wearing the Five Ks. One of the seven sits with the Guru Granth Sahib and another stands at the door, while the remaining five (the Panj Piare) administer the actual initiation. Men or women may serve in either capacity, though in fact the responsibility is almost always assumed by males. Prior to the ceremony they should bathe and wash their hair. The five who are to conduct the initiation should be physically sound, possessing both eyes, ears, legs and arms, and they should be free from chronic diseases. No one who has been convicted of transgressing the Rahit should be selected.

Those who are to receive initiation must be old enough to understand the meaning of the ceremony. They too should bathe, wash their hair and appear wearing the Five Ks. No symbols associated with any other religion may be worn, nor are ear-rings and nose ornaments acceptable. Prior to receiving initiation the initiants should stand reverently before the Guru Granth Sahib with palms joined.

One of the five officiants then addresses them on the faith they are to serve, and after an appropriate prayer which looks forward to the preparation of *amrit* a *hukam* is taken. The officiants place a large iron bowl on a pedestal and, pouring in fresh water, they add soluble sweets. They then adopt the "heroic posture" (*bir asan*), kneeling around the bowl with the right knee placed on the ground and the left knee kept upright.

Next the following compositions are recited: *Japji*, *Jap*, the *Ten Savayyas*, *Benati Chaupai*, and the six prescribed stanzas from *Anand Sahib*. The person reciting them should do so with his left hand placed on the rim of the bowl, using his right hand to stir the *amrit* with a two-edged sword (*khanda*). The other four keep both hands on the bowl, with their eyes fixed on the *amrit*. When the appointed passages have been completed, one of the officiants should recite *Ardas*. The candidates should then adopt the "heroic posture" and each should cup his/her hands, placing the right hand over the left. Five times a handful of *amrit* is given and is drunk by the candidate, the

Hew McLeod, *Sikhism* (New York: Penguin Books, 1997), 144–145.

officiant each time calling out, "*Vahiguruji ka Khalsa! Vahiguruji ki fateh!*" Each time the recipient, after drinking the *amrit*, will reply with the same words. His/her eyes are then touched with the *amrit* five times, and five times it is sprinkled on his/her hair. Each time the officiant repeats the same greeting and each time the candidate replies with the same words. Any *amrit* which is left is consumed by the candidates, all drinking in turn from the same vessel.

After this the five officiants impart the Name of Vahiguru to the initiates by saying in unison the Basic Credal Statement (the *Mul Mantra*), requiring the initiates to repeat it after them. One of them then expounds to the initiates the meaning of the Rahit, which they are undertaking to obey. Among its several injunctions are a promise always to keep the Five Ks and scrupulously to avoid the four cardinal prohibitions (*kurahit*). The four *kurahit* are:

1. Cutting one's hair or having it cut.
2. Consuming meat which has been slaughtered according to the Muslim rite (*halal* meat, or *kuttha*).
3. Extra-marital sexual intercourse.
4. Using tobacco.

The initiants are also urged to have no dealings with other initiated Sikhs who cut their hair, or with Sikhs who smoke. They should regard it as a duty always to support the Panth, setting aside one tenth of their earnings *(das-vandh)* for the Guru's service. A list of offences against the Rahit which warrant a penance is given. This includes associating with those who can be regarded as belonging to one of the Five Reprobate Groups believed to have been denounced by Guru Gobind Singh. It also specifies eating from the same dish as a person who has not received Khalsa initiation or is an apostate Sikh (*patit*); dyeing one's beard; giving or receiving a cash dowry; and consuming any drug or intoxicant.

At the conclusion of this homily, one of Panj Piare recites *Ardas* and a sixth member, sitting in attendance with the Guru Granth Sahib, takes a *hukam*. Any of the newly initiated who does not have a name chosen from the Guru Granth Sahib is renamed and the ceremony concludes with the distribution of *karah prasad*, all newly initiated Sikhs receiving it from the same dish.

Devotions: The Prakaash

SIRI KIRPAL KAUR KHALSA

Here is a first-person account of the Sikh worship service known as the Prakaash ("brightening"), the devotional practice that accompanies the opening of Sikh scripture in a gurdwara (Sikh temple).

We are about to begin *prakaash* (literally "brightening"), the process of opening the *Siri Guru Granth Sahib,* the Sikh Guru, for the day. In most Gurdwaras, prakaash occurs in the early morning, well before the service. People who live in homes with a formal set up for the Guru—like me—do prakaash early in the

Siri Kirpal Kaur Khalsa, "The Prakaash," in *Sikh Spiritual Practice* (Winchester, UK: O Books, 2010), 79–84.

morning in their homes too. But where the main sanctuary of the Gurdwara must serve several functions—as is true in Eugene—we do prakaash just before the service begins.

One of the things I love about Sikh services is their informality. It's not uncommon for a Sikh to show up for a service and be asked to participate in some special way. That happens today when someone hands me a long sword (called a *Siri Sahib*) as prakaash is about to start. The lady who does so then opens the doors to the upper cupboard where the *Siri Guru Granth Sahib* rests between appearances. And we begin.

We all proclaim *Waheguru ji ka Khalsa! Waheguru ji ki Fateh!* Translation: "The Pure Ones belong to God! Victory belongs to God!" We are acknowledging that everything that has happened or will happen is done by God . . . and only by God. We make this proclamation before and after nearly everything we do in Gurdwara. For simplicity's sake, I will indicate this proclamation with words like "We make our proclamation . . ." throughout this chapter.

We bow our foreheads to the ground, which is tricky for me because of the sword. Then we stand with our hands folded as best we can while the lady who opened the cupboard recites a short version of the *Ardas*, the supplication or prayer we'll look at in more detail later in this chapter. We recite the last two lines of the prayer together, then bow our heads to the ground again. As we all rise, we make our proclamation.

The lady who recited the Ardas then places a *ramala* (cloth of honor) on top of her head, lifts the ramala-covered Guru from the cupboard, and places it on her head. I walk in front of the Guru as a sort of honor guard carrying the unsheathed Siri Sahib. Walking behind the Guru is a young man waving a fancy flywhisk. As we walk, we chant *Sat Naam, Sat Naam, Sat Naam Jee, Waa Hay Guroo, Waa Hay Guroo, Waa Hay Guroo Jee.* There are many chants we could use while carrying the Guru. The one we chant today is essentially untranslatable, but praises Truth, praises God's ecstatic wisdom and grace, and praises God's Name.

Our little procession wends its way into the large room across the hall. Under a ceiling-hung, gold and white canopy (it could be any color) sits the *palki sahib*, the Guru's resting place—a cross between a throne, an altar, a bed and a palanquin. Indeed, in the Guru's room is a palki sahib resembling a miniature four-poster brass bed, complete with its own little canopy. The palki sahib we are heading for is more open—a low table with a miniature mattress, covered first with a clean white sheet that drapes down onto the floor. Completely covering this sheet are *ramalas* —a cross between altar cloths and robes of honor—always of the finest fabrics, of any color. Today's ramalas are brilliant green satin with gold fringes and Sikh symbols appliqued in gold. One of the large ramalas drapes gracefully down from the palki sahib onto the sheet-covered floor. There are other ramalas around the edges of the palki sahib. The entire ensemble rests on carpeted floors covered with clean white sheets.

To the side of the palki sahib are two small tables. The small wooden table to the left as we come bearing the Guru into the room will receive the *Gurprashaad*—literally "Gift of the Guru"—the sweet you could call Sikh communion food. The one to the right looks like part of a brass bed ensemble and contains a translation of the *Siri Guru Granth Sahib.* As a mark of respect, this is covered with a ramala also—the one today has a subtle pattern in gold.

Vases filled with greenery, pink roses and some white flowers I don't identify sit on coasters flanking the palki sahib. On the large floor-touching ramala are a large *Adi Shakti* symbol (often called a *Khanda* for the double-edged sword in the center of the symbol), three artistically arranged *chakras* (large steel rings that warriors used to wear on their heads for protection), and a couple of other Siri Sahibs. Pictures of several human Sikh Gurus adorn the walls. These decorations—and any others we might use—are all optional, but help create a rich and respectful atmosphere.

The lady carrying the Guru walks behind the palki sahib where no ramalas cascade to the floor. She lays the Guru on the palki and then sits cross-legged in front of the Guru. I lay the sword down with the other Siri Sahibs. The young man stands behind the Guru and waves the flywhisk as we proceed.

While the lady removes the gold ramala covering the Guru and unwraps the white cotton wrapping cloths one by one, we begin singing the *Shabad* (Sikh hymn) *Mayraa Man Lochai.* (This is the series of poetic letters that turned young Arjan into *Guru Arjan Dev*, the Fifth Guru, as we saw in the chapter on the Shabad Guru.) We could sing any Shabad or Sikh mantra. Placing a small ramala on top of the Guru, the lady lifts the Guru up on her own ramala-covered head again. The young man and I help her fold up the wrapping cloths. Then she sets out three small pillows in the center of the palki sahib in a C-shape, with the opening of the C facing her. These will prop up the Guru for reading. Laying the spine of the *Siri Guru Granth Sahib* carefully in the center of the central pillow, the lady opens first the front cover, inserting a small ramala between the cover and the pages with the help of the young man. She repeats the process with the back cover with my help.

It's now time to take our first *Hukam*. Hukam literally means "command." It's a random reading from the *Siri Guru Granth Sahib* and is the Guru's message for the occasion—in this case, the Gurdwara worship service about to begin. The Guru's word is law for any devout Sikh. So we listen carefully to the Hukam and do our best to follow what it says. Sometimes that's very clear. I recall the time our house was burglarized. Seeing the burglars as God testing us, I had no further problems with it (I thought), except for the hassle of police and wailing neighbors. So when the police held a meeting in our neighborhood, I decided not to go . . . until I got a Hukam the morning of the meeting that said something like, "I consort with thieves, but avoid the righteous." I went to the meeting!

Both of today's Hukams will be more subtle. The lady opens the *Siri Guru Granth Sahib* randomly, then reads a complete Shabad in Gurmukhi. When she finishes, she makes the proclamation and we all join in.

Then I read the English translation:

Gauree Reverend Kabir:
Why mourn when one dies?
Mourn if one remains forever alive.
I shall not die as the world dies.
For I have now met the Life-giving God. (Pause.)
One perfumes the body with sandalwood,
And in that pleasure forgets supreme bliss.
There is one well and five water carriers.
Even with a broken rope the foolish ones continue trying to draw water.
Says Kabir, through deliberation I have gained understanding:
For me there are no more wells and no more water carriers.

At the end, I make the proclamation and everyone present joins in.

Clearly, this Hukam is about releasing undue attachment to physical life and paying more attention to the life of the soul. But as the Guru's words ring through the corridors of my consciousness, I hear the Guru telling me to drop certain expectations I have for the day and enjoy what is given instead. That proves to be excellent advice.

We have now completed prakaash. A great many Sikhs, including me, have miniature Gurdwaras inside our homes. Inside those miniature Gurdwaras, we perform prakaash nearly every morning, and *Sukhasan*—which we'll look at later in this chapter—nearly every evening. Usually in our homes, the *Siri Guru Granth Sahib* stays on its palki sahib, so there is no procession in or out. But for prakaash, we always recite an Ardas, open the *Siri Guru Granth Sahib,* and take a Hukam for the day.

While we perform prakaash, a young man dressed in clean blue jeans and t-shirt enters the Gurdwara, bows to the Guru and gives an offering as soon as the *Siri Guru Granth Sahib* is unwrapped. He listens respectfully to the Hukam, then bows his forehead to the ground, puts his hands together and quietly leaves the Gurdwara. He's on his way to work at the local Indian restaurant. It's fairly common for Sikhs to stop by an open Gurdwara for a few minutes to receive the Guru's *Darshan*—the experience or vision one has when one is in the company of someone or something deeply holy.

Now it's my turn to bow at the Guru's Feet, my turn to receive the Guru's Darshan and align myself with the Guru's understanding. I do that by bringing my forehead to the ground in front of the Guru. As I bow, I place a monetary offering on top of the large, floor-touching ramala. Although money is the usual offering, other gifts are welcome. There was one occasion when I ran out of money while traveling and gave the Guru the only thing I had to give—an unopened box of graham crackers. Monetary offerings keep the lights on and pay other bills. The graham crackers were probably served to the *sangat* (congregation) during *langar* (the communal meal) after the next Gurdwara service. Giving paves the way to receive. Giving upfront turns the offering into an act of honest devotion without strings.

Bringing the forehead to the ground is a spiritual technology in its own right. I am bringing blood to my brain and activating my pituitary and pineal glands—thereby awakening my intuition and higher consciousness. I am not bowing to a book, a thing of paper, ink and binding. I am bowing to the embodied *Shabad Guru*—the Teacher through divine sound and song of Infinite wisdom, knowledge and ecstasy, whose story we looked at in an earlier chapter. Symbolically, I am giving my head to the Guru and stating that the Guru's wisdom rules me. In addition, I am picking up the dust of the feet of the Saints (their understanding), and joining the Company of the Holy by granting the dust of my feet to someone else. It's an act of humility and an act of utmost self-exaltation.

CONTEMPORARY CHALLENGES

Feminine Dimensions of Sikh Faith

WILLARD G. OXTOBY

The religion scholar Willard Oxtoby explains the apparent inconsistency in Sikhism between the more liberal attitudes toward women found in the writings of the gurus and the more conservative views exemplified in Sikh practice. For example, the gurus taught the social equality of men and women and had high regard for the unique roles that women assume in life. Social egalitarianism is demonstrated in the tradition of men and women sharing the duties involved in community meals (the *langar*). But some Sikhs regard menstruation and childbirth as spiritually polluting, and in many gurdwaras the sexes are segregated.

Sikh religious literature is almost completely the work of men, and the community's institutions have been almost completely staffed by men. In this the Sikh tradition differs little from other major religions. And where the Sikhs are most visibly distinguished from other groups, in hair and headgear, the

Willard T. Oxtoby, "The Sikh Tradition," in *World Religions: Eastern Traditions* (Oxford: Oxford University Press, 2002), 152–154.

masculine attire is prominent. Moreover, to think of the Khalsa as a military brotherhood is to confirm an impression of the Sikh tradition as male-centred.

Of course half the Sikhs through the centuries, including many members of the Khalsa, have been women, and feminine perspectives in the tradition are crucial for any picture of it to be adequate for today's needs. Encouraged by advances in scholarship on other religious traditions, some recent interpreters of the Sikh experience, especially Sikhs overseas, have begun to assemble a picture that allows scope for women's perspectives. Their insights have followed several lines.

First is the evaluation of women's historical roles. Discussing caste, we have already characterized the *gurus* as socially egalitarian. Today, interpreters are recruiting them as forerunners of women's liberation as well, seeing in the early Panth a community of equal spiritual access for male and female. Pivotal in such a reading is the hymn by Guru Nanak:

> Of woman are we born, of woman conceived,
> To woman engaged, to woman married.
> Woman we befriend, by woman do civilizations continue.
> When a woman dies, a woman is sought for.
> It is through woman that order is maintained.
> Then why call her inferior from whom all great ones are born?
> Woman is born of woman;
> None is born but of woman.
> The One, who is Eternal, alone is unborn.

To Sikh women today, these words signify an attitude that was revolutionary in Guru Nanak's time, when Muslim women were secluded and many Hindu widows were expected to join their deceased husbands on the funeral pyre. Sikh women are seen as partners, not property. Married family life—not asceticism or celibacy—is extolled as the ideal for human social fulfilment. And because women and men shared the practical and symbolic roles associated with the community meals of the *langar*, interpreters argue, women were equally valued in religious contexts.

While appreciating the positive side to these ideals, we urge caution in supposing that they were fully implemented. Women and men did gather together for worship in the early Panth, but gurdwara practice today still often segregates the sexes. And the hymn above says that a widower seeks to remarry, but is silent about what a woman is to do when her husband dies.

A second aspect to modern thinking about women's place in the tradition is the evaluation of women's roles as distinctive. Women, not men, give birth, as the hymn above states. Guru Nanak's word for woman here is *bhandu*, etymologically "vessel." Creation pours forth from woman. But—important in Indian tradition—so does pollution, particularly with the discharge of blood in childbirth and menstruation. On this point, a feminist reading of Nanak makes him a revolutionary who condemns the notion of pollution as false:

> If pollution attaches to birth, then pollution is everywhere (for birth is universal).
> Cow-dung [used as fuel] and firewood breed maggots. . . .
> How can we then believe in pollution, when pollution inheres within staples?
> Says Nanak, pollution is not washed away by purificatory rituals;
> Pollution is removed by true knowledge alone.

Still open to discussion is whether such a text denies the existence of pollution through bodily discharges or whether it assumes it in order to state that spiritual insight is of higher value.

A third line of interpretation is to value the metaphorical or symbolic role of femininity. Here again Guru Nanak's hymns offer a resource, for they are rich in bridal imagery. The created universe is the bride, and God is the groom. Modern Sikh fiction likewise finds religious analogies in the adornments of South Asian bridal costume and the anticipation that weddings provide. And again the question to ask of such imagery is whether the female role is one of true equivalency: is not the groom, or God as groom, the master in the relationship? On this point, Sikhs do see God as either male or female.

But birth imagery can be set against bridal imagery. On a descriptive level, many references in Sikh religious literature speak of humans as born of women and as first nurtured by women. Symbolically, however, they imply a deity who gives birth to creation and nurtures it.

> Who is our Mother? Who the Father?
> Where have we come from?
> The child's first attraction is to the mother's breast milk;
> Second, to the recognition of the mother and father.

The divine, which gives birth to the human, has a bond with its offspring that many today wish to read as uniquely feminine. It is the womb from which we come, the breast at which we suckle. The bond between divine and human is like that between mother and child. Interpreters see the primacy of the female explicit in the second of the passages above, where our initial experience is of the mother. They see it also implicit in the mention of mother before father in numerous references like both of the above.

For interpreting the divine as mother, or mother as divine, the Sikh heritage offers a treasury of material useful in today's discussions of women's role in religion. Indeed, since the Sikh sacred literature comprises mainly poetry, it has the advantage of multiple meanings and associations. It speaks of the tangible things of everyday life, at the same time evoking a sense of the intangible and transcendent. It is possible to find a perspective of God as feminine to be symbolically present in Sikh poetry partly because in poetry words often convey several meanings at the same time.

A question is still open. Is such a reading compatible with the rest of Sikh theology? If, as Sikh thought holds, divinity is truly formless—if it is beyond the categories and images that we humans use to describe it—then it is beyond femininity as well. It may be useful to speak of God as mother, and also as father, when operating poetically or metaphorically, but God is beyond both when we speak of ultimates. Feminist consciousness may bring out for Sikhs a new awareness of the female, but classical Sikh doctrine already provides the resources for devotion to an ultimate reality that relativizes gender.

STUDY QUESTIONS

1. What is the Khalsa? Adi Granth? The Panth?
2. What is Guru Nanak's opinion of caste, pilgrimages, and priests?
3. From what Sikh principle did the practice of *langar* arise?
4. What is the significance of the "Name"?
5. What changes in the Sikh tradition is Guru Arjan known for?
6. How is God characterized in Sikhism?
7. What are the five *k*s?
8. Who or what is *Akal Purakh*?
9. What is *nam simaran*? What is its purpose?
10. What is the *Dasam Granth*?

FURTHER READING

John Bowker, ed., *The Oxford Dictionary of World Religions* (Oxford: Oxford University Press, 1997).

Siri Kirpal Kaur Khalsa, *Sikh Spiritual Practice* (Winchester, UK: O Books, 2010).

W. H. McLeod, *Guru Nanak and the Sikh Religion* (Delhi: Oxford University Press, 1968).

W. H. McLeod, trans., *Textual Sources for the Study of Sikhism* (Chicago: University of Chicago Press, 1984).

Eleanor Nesbitt, *Sikhism: A Very Short Introduction* (Oxford: Oxford University Press, 2005).

Trilochan Singh, Bhai Jodh Singh, et al., trans., *Selections from the Sacred Writings of the Sikhs* (London: George Allen and Unwin, 1960).

ONLINE

Sikhs.org, "Introduction to Sikhism," http://www.sikhs.org/summary.htm (December 21, 2015).

BBC, "Sikhism," http://www.bbc.co.uk/religion/religions/sikhism/ (December 21, 2015).

7 Confucianism

Confucianism is a school of thought that arose out of ancient China and, along with Daoism, has been a dominant philosophical system there for hundreds of years. For many, it is also a religion or a secular outlook with strong religious elements. Its effect on Chinese and East Asian life, culture, and government has been enormous—comparable to the influence of Christianity, Judaism, and Islam in the West. Until the early twentieth century, Confucian virtues and training were required of anyone entering Chinese civil service, and even now under communist rule China holds to its Confucian roots in everyday life. Elsewhere in the East (especially in Korea, Japan, and Vietnam), Confucian ethics and ideals have remodeled society, providing moral underpinning and guidance to social relationships at all levels.

Part of the appeal of Confucianism is that in times of ideological confusion it has offered plausible answers to essential philosophical questions: What kind of person should I be? What kind of society is best? What are my moral obligations to my family, those who rule, and the rest of humanity? In the twenty-first century, millions of people are attracted to the answers supplied by this two-thousand-year-old tradition.

Many of the elements of Confucianism were part of Chinese culture long before Confucius arrived on the scene. In fact, he claimed merely to transmit the wisdom of the ancients to new generations, but what he transmitted plus what he added became the distinctive Confucian worldview. From early Chinese civilization came the Confucian emphasis on rituals and their correct performance, the veneration of ancestors, social and cosmic harmony, virtuous behavior and ideals, and the will of Heaven (or *Tian*), the ultimate power and organizing principle in the universe.

LIFE OF CONFUCIUS

Into this mix of characteristically Eastern ideas and practices there appeared in 551 BCE the renowned thinker we call Confucius (the Westernized spelling), otherwise known as K'ung Ch'iu or K'ung Fu-tzu (Master K'ung). According to legend and very sketchy information about his life, he was born to a poor family in the tiny Chinese state of Lu. He had no formal schooling, but he studied on his own and thereby achieved a high level of learning and drew a few students to him.

In his day China was being rocked by social upheaval as the Zhou Dynasty (1111–249 BCE) began to disintegrate into greedy and quarrelsome kingdoms. Confucius hoped to return

CONFUCIANISM TIMELINE

BCE

c. 1766–1123 Shang Dynasty

1122–256 Zhou Dynasty

c. 563 (or perhaps 566) Birth of the Buddha

551–479 Confucius

? Laozi Possibly a contemporary of Confucius'

c. 483 Death of the Buddha

c. 450 Organization of Daoist canon into three Caverns

c. 391–308 Mencius

c. 286 Zhuangzi dies.

Second century Confucianism becomes a state religion.

Second century Daoism as a religion begins.

200 Buddhism has spread to Nepal, Sri Lanka, and Central Asia.

CE

c. 61 Buddhism spreads to China.

594 Buddhism becomes the official religion of Japan .

1368–1644 Ming Dynasty

1868 Shinto is designated the official religion of Japan; Buddhism is repressed.

1921 Founding of Communist Party

1973–1974 Anti-Confucianism campaign

China to its golden age when emperors were sages and government fostered order and virtue. He served briefly at age fifty in the Lu government as police commissioner, and during the next thirteen years he visited other Chinese states trying to persuade the rulers to implement his philosophy of wise government. One leader after another turned him down. He spent the rest of his life teaching his philosophy and contributing to the Confucian works known as the *Five Classics*. He died in 479 without his ideas having achieved wide acceptance. Only later did his views become a major influence.

CONFUCIAN TEACHINGS

Confucianism, especially later forms of it, has always featured some religious or divine aspects. Confucius himself believed in the supreme deity Heaven, asserting that we should align ourselves with its will. But in general he veered away from the supernatural beliefs of

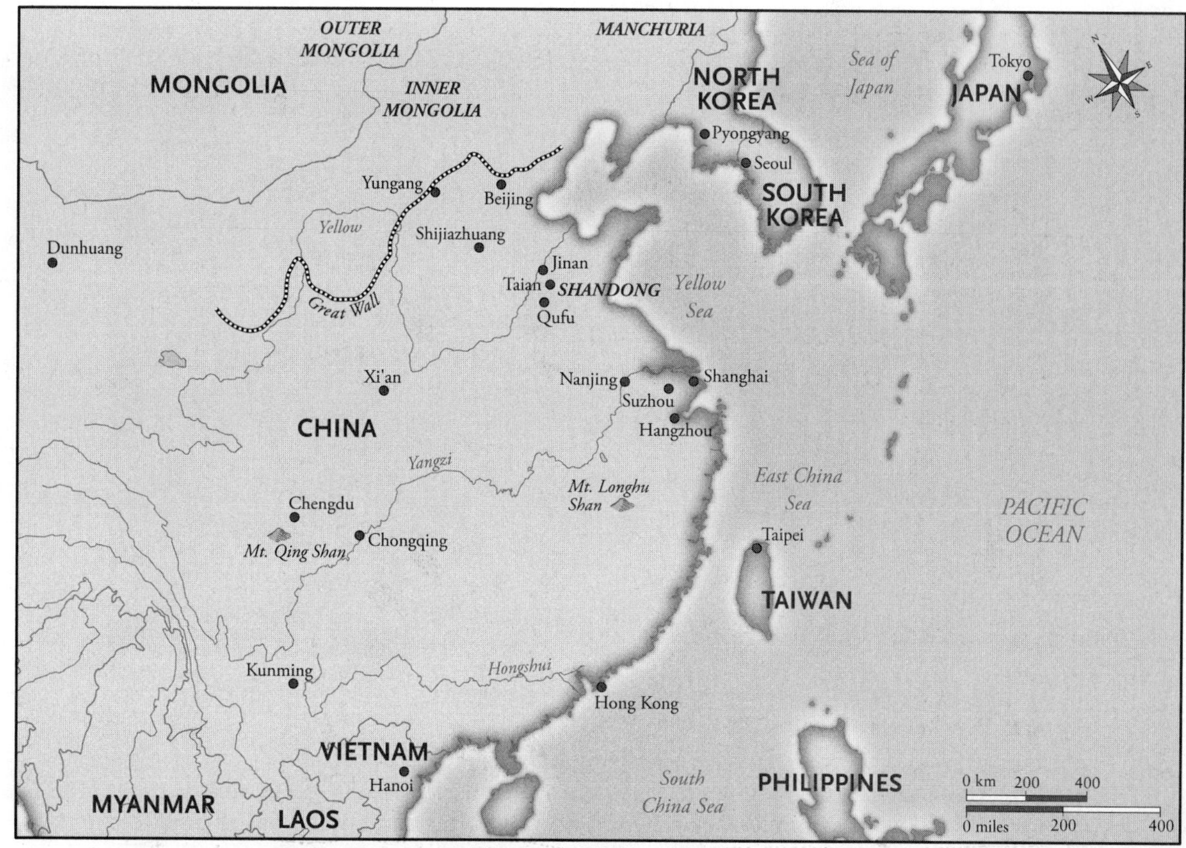

MAP 7.1 Important Confucian and Daoist sites in China.

the past, for his main interest was teaching a humanistic doctrine centered on social relationships. His aim was the creation of harmony and virtue in the world—specifically in individuals, in the way they interacted with one another, and in how they were treated by the state. He saw his teachings as a remedy for the social disorder, corruption, and inhumanity existing all around him, from the lowest levels of society to the highest.

Confucianism assumes a particular cosmology derived from ancient Chinese religion. The basic idea is that the universe is an ordered and interrelated system comprising the heavens, nature, humans, gods, and society. The system's ideal state is harmony among all its interlinked parts. Through Confucianism, human relationships are arranged so they harmonize with the workings of the cosmos, so the cosmos harmonizes society, so society returns harmony to the cosmos.

In this worldview, all such relationships and all things are made possible through **qi** (or *ch'i*), the vital energy that permeates and empowers everything. *Qi* consists of two opposing but complementary forces known as **yin** (denoting the dark, feminine, yielding, or cloudy aspects of the world) and **yang** (denoting the light, masculine, active, or sunny aspects). *Yin* and *yang* are apparent in such opposing pairs as shade and sun, night and day, soft and hard, and female and male. Through their continual back-and-forth struggles, they bring forth the innumerable forms and processes of the cosmos.

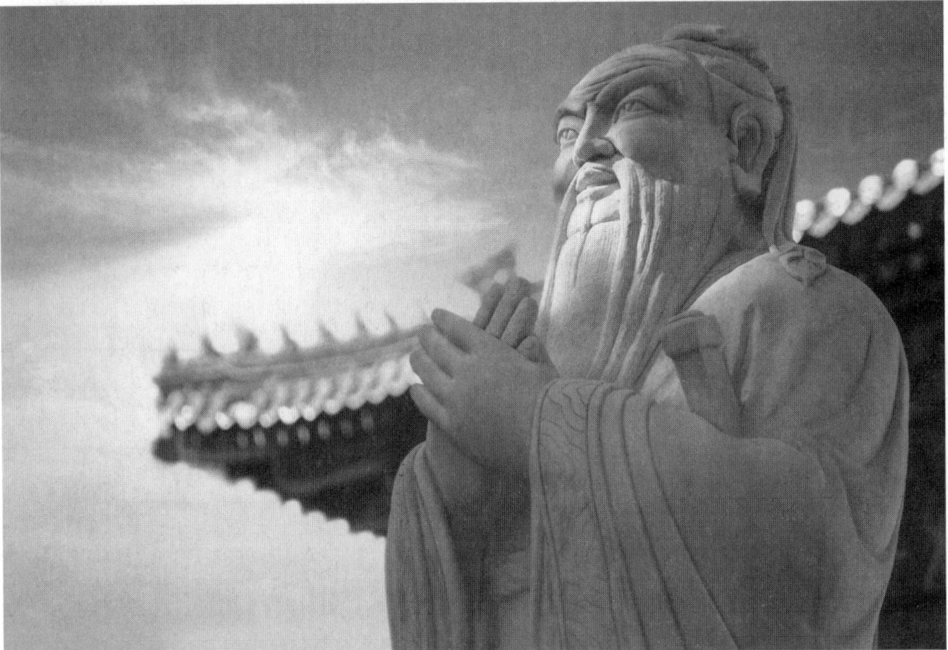

FIGURE 7.1 **A stone statue of Confucius stands outside Beijing's Temple of Confucius.**

In Confucianism, the ideal moral life is generated through the practice of *li* and *ren*. **Li** has several meanings, including ritual, etiquette, principle, and propriety, but its essence is conscientious behavior and right action. To follow *li* is to conduct yourself in your dealings with others according to moral and customary norms, and to act in this way is to contribute to social stability and harmony. **Ren** is about social virtues; it encompasses benevolence, sympathy, kindness, generosity, respect for others, and human-heartedness. At its core is the imperative to work for the common good and to recognize the essential worth of others regardless of their social status. The expression of these virtues is governed by the notion of reciprocity (*shu*), what has been called Confucius' (negative) golden rule: "Never do to others what you would not like them to do to you."[1] (The Christian golden rule is stated positively: "Do unto others as you would have them do unto you.")

Confucius urges people not merely to try to live according to *li* and *ren* but to excel at such a life, to become a "superior person" (a *junzi*), a noble. Contrary to history and custom, Confucius' idea of nobility has nothing to do with noble blood; true nobility, he says, comes from noble virtues and wisdom, and these anyone can acquire. He refers to a man who embodies this kind of nobility as a *gentleman*. We get a glimpse of the gentleman in the *Analects*, the main Confucian text:

> Tzu-kung asked about the true gentleman. The Master [Confucius] said, He does not preach what he practises till he has practised what he preaches. . . .
>
> The Master said, A gentleman can see a question from all sides without bias. The small man is biased and can see a question only from one side.

> The Master said, the Ways of the true gentleman are three. I myself have met with success in none of them. For he that is really Good is never unhappy, he that is really wise is never perplexed, he that is really brave is never afraid. Tzu-kung said, That, Master, is your own Way!
>
> Tzu-lu asked about the qualities of a true gentleman. The Master said, He cultivates in himself the capacity to be diligent in his tasks. . . . The Master said, He cultivates in himself the capacity to ease the lot of other people. . . . The Master said, He cultivates in himself the capacity to ease the lot of the whole populace.[2]

So living by *li* and *ren* requires self-cultivation and action—learning the moral norms, understanding the virtues, and acting to apply these to the real world. Being a superior person, then, demands knowledge and judgment as well as devotion to the noblest values and virtues.

In Confucianism, individuals are not like atoms: they are not discrete, isolated units of stuff defined only by what they're made of. Individuals are part of a complex lattice of social relationships that must be taken into account. So in Confucian ethics, *ren* tells us what virtues apply to social relationships generally, and the text called the "Five Relationships" details the most important connections and the specific duties and virtues associated with particular relationships. These relationships are between parent and child, elder brother and younger brother, husband and wife, elder and junior, and ruler and subject. Harmony will pervade society, says Confucius, when (1) parents provide for their children, and children respect and obey their parents and care for them in their old age; (2) elder brothers look after younger brothers, and the younger show deference to the elder; (3) husbands support and protect wives, and wives obey husbands and tend to children and the household; (4) elders show consideration for the younger, and the younger respect and heed elders; and (5) rulers care for and protect subjects, and subjects are loyal to rulers.

The relationship on which all others are based is that of parent and child or, as Confucius would have it, father and son. The son owes the father respect, obedience, and support—an obligation that Confucianism calls "filial piety." The central feature of this relationship is that it is hierarchical. Father and son are not equal partners; the son is subordinate. The other

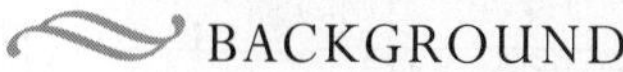
BACKGROUND

Confucianism and the Modern World

Is Confucianism relevant to contemporary life? A number of Confucianism scholars say yes. For example:

> Despite the disappearance of the Confucian state, Confucian ideals have continued to underpin East Asian civilizations. A new wave of Confucian scholars in the twentieth and twenty-first centuries—including Mou Tsung-san, Carson Chang, and Tu Weiming—has reinterpreted Confucianism in the light of the modern world. The city-state of Singapore under Lee Kuan Yew and the Republic of China on Taiwan have looked to the ideas of Confucianism as being central to morality and social harmony. Finally, Confucianism has been identified as a vital part of the mixture that has contributed to the booming economies of East Asia in recent decades. It is clear that the Confucian tradition remains fundamental to the assumptions and actions of East Asians and, although diffused through family, society, culture, and political structures, is unmistakably present and formative.[3]

four relationships are also hierarchical, with the wife subordinate to the husband, the younger brother to the older, the junior to the elder, and the subject to the ruler. And as in filial piety, the subordinates have a duty of obedience and respect, and the superiors are obligated to treat the subordinates with kindness and authority, as a father would. Confucius believes that if everyone conscientiously assumes his or her proper role, harmony, happiness, and goodness will reign in the land.

On filial piety, Confucius had this to say:

> Meng I Tzu asked about the treatment of parents. The Master said, Never disobey! When Ch'ih was driving his carriage for him, the Master said, Meng asked me about the treatment of parents and I said, Never disobey! Fan Ch'ih said, In what sense did you mean it? The Master said, While they are alive, serve them according to ritual. When they die, bury them according to ritual and sacrifice to them according to ritual. . . .
>
> Tzu-yu asked about the treatment of parents. The Master said, "Filial sons" nowadays are people who see to it that their parents get enough to eat. But even dogs and horses are cared for to that extent. If there is no feeling of respect, wherein lies the difference?[4]

The virtue of filial piety is still a strong force in China today, as this scholar explains:

> In China, loyalty to the family has been one's first loyalty. No lad in China ever comes of age, in the Western sense. It is still true that his whole service is expected to be devoted to the family until death, and he is expected to obey his father and, when his father dies, his eldest brother, with a perfect compliance. This has meant in the past that every father has a great and grave responsibility to fulfill toward his family. He must seek to produce virtue in his sons by being himself the best example of it. The fact that the present communist government speaks of making itself "father and

FIGURE 7.2 During three great dynasties—Yuan, Ming, and Qing (1271–1911)—people could pay homage to Confucius at the Temple of Confucius in Beijing.

elder brother" and claims for itself the first loyalty of every citizen has not totally invalidated the personal virtue of filial piety in the context of family life.[5]

Today the influence of the Confucian virtue of filial piety helps to explain why there is in much of Asia a greater emphasis on meeting obligations to family, community, and state than on ensuring individual rights and personal freedom.

THE CONFUCIAN CANON

The teachings of Confucianism are found in a vast assemblage of writings that date back centuries and have probably been as revered in the East as the Bible has been in the West (although the Confucian texts are considered the work of men, not God). The heart of the canon consists of two sets of texts—the *Five Classics* and the *Four Books.* They contain Confucian teachings and perhaps some of Confucius' words, but scholars now think that even though he may have borrowed from them or edited some of them, he probably did not write them. We possess many of Confucius' sayings because we have a putative record of his conversations with his students (in the *Analects*).

The basic contents and structure of the canon are as follows. The *Five Classics* are:

- *The Book of History* (or *Historical Documents*)—A history of ancient Chinese rulers and their kingdoms detailed in historical records and early dynasty speeches. Some of the documents date back seventeen centuries. It also includes commentary on moral issues and a discussion of the principles of good government.
- *The Book of Changes* (*Yi Jing*; also *I Ching*)—A how-to guide for the practice of divination, plus metaphysical conjecture. It articulates the doctrines of early Chinese

A CLOSER LOOK

Confucianism: Secular and Sacred

Confucianism may be a world religion, but it also has a secular side that has attracted millions of people past and present. Scholars agree that the humanistic, this-worldly aspect of the tradition is large and unmistakable. Consider:

> The Confucian faith is fundamentally humanistic, which lays the responsibility for a better world and for a secured future, not in the hands of a supremely detached God, but in the hands of ordinarily engaged humans. In this sense, Confucianism opens up a different approach to the meaning of life and the meaning of death. When Zengzi felt a resting peace at his impending death, he demonstrated the completion of his mission in the world. When Fan Zhongyan (989–1052) said that he was the first to be concerned with the problems of the world and the last to enjoy its pleasure . . . he was summarising the Confucian meaning of life in a paradigmatic statement. For a Confucian, the meaning of life can be realised only in learning and practice through self-cultivation and self-transformation, in committing oneself to the welfare of the family, community and society, and in effecting a lasting influence over the world by one's achievement in moral and cultural realms.[6]

religion, portraying an entirely interconnected universe striving for a balance of yin and yang forces. In this world there is no room for a creator God or a creation story like the one found in Genesis and other religious texts.

- *The Book of Poetry* (or *Book of Songs*)—An ancient anthology of 305 poems, or songs, some of which were allegedly chosen by Confucius. Most of them are written in rhymed quatrains, a style that eventually became the preferred form for all Chinese poetry.
- *The Book of Rites*—An ancient compendium of instructions and rules regarding ceremonies for the nobility.
- *Springs and Autumns*—A history of the Chinese state of Lu (722–481 BCE) where Confucius was born, highlighting moral and political decay.

The *Four Books* are:

- The *Analects*—A compilation of the dialogues of Confucius and his students, focusing on virtue and harmony in individuals and society. With its pithy sayings embodying the essential ideas of the philosophy of Confucius, it has rivaled the Bible in its influence on humankind through the ages. Its chief concern is the duties of human beings in this world, the spiritual perfection of humanity through virtue, propriety, and ritual in everyday life. Its emphasis on the here and now leaves no room for metaphysical speculation or musings about a personal God, original sin, or reward in heaven.
- The *Great Learning*—An account of the education and self-cultivation required to become a morally noble person.
- The *Doctrine of the Mean*—A philosophical discussion of how human nature is linked to the cosmos and how achieving balance in one's life aligns one with the cosmic order.
- The *Book of Mencius*—A compilation of the teachings of Mencius, a Confucian philosopher who arrived on the scene long after Confucius and who sought to produce a complete and coherent account of Confucianism.

NOTES

1. *Analects*, 15: 23, Arthur Waley, trans. *The Analects of Confucius* (New York: Macmillan, 1939).
2. *Analects*, 2: 13–14, 14: 30, 14: 45, Arthur Waley, trans.
3. Jennifer Oldstone-Moore, *Confucianism* (Oxford: Oxford University Press, 2002).
4. *Analects*, 2: 5, 7, Arthur Waley, trans.
5. John B. Noss, *A History of the World's Religions* (New York: Macmillan, 1994), 323.
6. Xinzhong Yao, *An Introduction to Confucianism* (Cambridge: Cambridge University Press, 2000), 285.

KEY TERMS

li Conscientious behavior and right action; also, ritual, etiquette, principle, or propriety.

qi (or ***ch'i***) The vital energy that permeates and empowers everything.

ren Social virtues such as benevolence, sympathy, kindness, and generosity; essentially, the imperative to work for the common good and to recognize the essential worth of others regardless of their social status.

yang The light, masculine, active, or sunny properties of *qi*.

yin The dark, feminine, yielding, or cloudy aspects of the *qi*.

READINGS

TEACHINGS

Selections from *The Analects*

In *The Analects* we learn about the views of Confucius through conversations with his students. His emphasis is on how to live virtuously and harmoniously in society, in the family, and in the state. He teaches that society is most harmonious when leaders are "noble men" (virtuous and wise), when they govern with humaneness and fatherly concern, when they observe the proprieties and rituals of society (*li*), and when they cultivate a strong sense of moral rightness in themselves and their subjects. An essential value that everyone should cultivate is filial piety, a respect for authority, rituals, and elders.

1.1 The Master said, "To learn and then have occasion to practice what you have learned—is this not satisfying? To have friends arrive from afar—is this not a joy? To be patient even when others do not understand—is this not the mark of the gentleman?"

1.4 Master Zeng said, "Every day I examine myself on three counts: in my dealings with others, have I in any way failed to be dutiful? In my interactions with friends and associates, have I in any way failed to be trustworthy? Finally, have I in any way failed to repeatedly put into practice what I teach?"

1.6 The Master said, "A young person should be filial when at home and respectful of his elders when in public. Conscientious and trustworthy, he should display a general care for the masses but feel a particular affection for those who are Good. If he has any strength left over after manifesting these virtues in practice, let him devote it to learning the cultural arts (*wen*. . .)."

1.8 The Master said, "If a gentleman is not serious, he will not inspire awe, and what he learns will be grasped only superficially. Let your actions be governed by dutifulness and trustworthiness, and do not accept as a friend one who is not your equal. If you have committed a transgression, do not be afraid to change your ways."

1.9 Master Zeng said, "Take great care in seeing off the deceased and sedulously maintain the sacrifices to your distant ancestors, and the common people will sincerely return to Virtue."

1.10 Ziqin asked Zigong, "When our Master arrives in a state, he invariably finds out about its government. Does he actively seek out this information? Surely it is not simply offered to him!"

Confucius Analects, Edward Slingerland, trans. (Indianapolis: Hackett, 2003).

Zigong answered, "Our Master obtains it through being courteous, refined, respectful, restrained and deferential. The Master's way of seeking it is entirely different from other people's way of seeking it, is it not?"

1.11 The Master said, "When someone's father is still alive, observe his intentions; after his father has passed away, observe his conduct. If for three years he does not alter the ways of his father, he may be called a filial son."

1.14 The Master said, "The gentleman is not motivated by the desire for a full belly or a comfortable abode. He is simply scrupulous in behavior and careful in speech, drawing near to those who possess the Way in order to be set straight by them. Surely this and nothing else is what it means to love learning."

2.1 The Master said, "One who rules through the power of Virtue is analogous to the Pole Star: it simply remains in its place and receives the homage of the myriad lesser stars."

2.3 The Master said, "If you try to guide the common people with coercive regulations (*zheng* . . .) and keep them in line with punishments, the common people will become evasive and will have no sense of shame. If, however, you guide them with Virtue, and keep them in line by means of ritual, the people will have a sense of shame and will rectify themselves."

2.4 The Master said, "At fifteen, I set my mind upon learning; at thirty, I took my place in society; at forty, I became free of doubts; at fifty, I understood Heaven's Mandate; at sixty, my ear was attuned; and at seventy, I could follow my heart's desires without overstepping the bounds of propriety."

2.9 The Master said, "I can talk all day long with Yan Hui without him once disagreeing with me. In this way, he seems a bit stupid. And yet when we retire and I observe his private behavior, I see that it is in fact worthy to serve as an illustration of what I have taught. Hui is not stupid at all."

2.13 Zigong asked about the gentleman. The Master said, "He first expresses his views, and then acts in accordance with them."

2.17 The Master said, "Zilu, remark well what I am about to teach you! This is wisdom: to recognize what you know as what you know, and recognize what you do not know as what you do not know."

2.20 Ji Kangzi asked, "How can I cause the common people to be respectful, dutiful, and industrious?"

The Master said, "Oversee them with dignity, and the people will be respectful; oversee them with filiality and kindness, and the people will be dutiful; oversee them by raising up the accomplished and instructing those who are unable, and the people will be industrious."

4.2 The Master said, "Without Goodness, one cannot remain constant in adversity and cannot enjoy enduring happiness. Those who are Good feel at home in Goodness, whereas those who are clever follow Goodness because they feel that they will profit (*li* . . .) from it."

4.7 The Master said, "People are true to type with regard to what sort of mistakes they make. Observe closely the sort of mistakes a person makes—then you will know his character."

4.10 The Master said, "With regard to the world, the gentleman has no predispositions for or against any person. He merely associates with those he considers right."

4.14 The Master said, "Do not be concerned that you lack an official position, but rather concern yourself with the means by which you might become established. Do not be concerned that no one has heard of you, but rather strive to become a person worthy of being known."

4.18 The Master said, "In serving your parents you may gently remonstrate with them. However, once it becomes apparent that they have not taken your criticism to heart you should be respectful and not oppose them, and follow their lead diligently without resentment."

4.25 The Master said, "Virtue is never solitary; it always has neighbors."

5.26 Yan Hui and Zilu were in attendance. The Master said to them, "Why do you not each speak to me of your aspirations?"

Zilu answered, "I would like to be able to share my carts and horses, clothing and fur with my fellow students and friends, without feeling regret."

Yan Hui answered, "I would like to avoid being boastful about my own abilities or exaggerating my accomplishments."

Zilu then said, "I would like to hear of the Master's aspirations."

The Master said, "To bring comfort to the aged, to inspire trust in my friends, and be cherished by the youth."

7.7 The Master said, "I have never denied instruction to anyone who, of their own accord, offered up as little as a bundle of silk or bit of cured meat."

7.16 The Master said, "Eating plain food and drinking water, having only your bent arm as a pillow—certainly there is joy to be found in this! Wealth and eminence attained improperly concern me no more than the floating clouds."

7.21 The Master did not discuss prodigies, feats of strength, disorderly conduct, or the supernatural.

7.37 The Master said, "The gentleman is self-possessed and relaxed, while the petty man is perpetually full of worry."

8.11 The Master said, "If a person has talents as fine as the Duke of Zhou, but is arrogant and mean-spirited, the rest of his qualities are not worth notice."

8.13 The Master said, "Be sincerely trustworthy and love learning, and hold fast to the good Way until death. Do not enter a state that is endangered, and do not reside in a state that is disordered. If the Way is being realized in the world then show yourself; if it is not, then go into reclusion. In a state that has the Way, to be poor and of low status is a cause for shame; in a state that is without the Way, to be wealthy and honored is equally a cause for shame."

9.10 Whenever the Master saw someone who was wearing mourning clothes, was garbed in full official dress, or was blind, he would always rise to his feet even if the person was his junior. When passing such a person, he would always hasten his step.

9.18 The Master said, "I have yet to meet a man who loves Virtue as much as he loves female beauty."

11.12 Zilu asked about serving ghosts and spirits. The Master said, "You are not yet able to serve people—how could you be able to serve ghosts and spirits?"

"May I inquire about death?"

"You do not yet understand life—how could you possibly understand death?"

12.1 Yan Hui asked about Goodness. The Master said, "Restraining yourself and returning to the rites . . . constitutes Goodness. If for one day you managed to restrain yourself and return to the rites, in this way you could lead the entire world back to Goodness. The key to achieving Goodness lies within yourself—how could it come from others?"

12.4 Sima Niu asked about the gentleman. The Master replied, "The gentleman is free of anxiety and fear."

"'Free of anxiety and fear'—is that all there is to being a gentleman?"

"If you can look inside yourself and find no faults, what cause is there for anxiety or fear?"

12.7 Zigong asked about governing. The Master said, "Simply make sure there is sufficient food, sufficient armaments, and that you have the confidence of the common people."

Zigong said, "If sacrificing one of these three things became unavoidable, which would you sacrifice first?"

The Master replied, "I would sacrifice the armaments."

Zigong said, "If sacrificing one of the two remaining things became unavoidable, which would you sacrifice next?"

The Master replied, "I would sacrifice the food. Death has always been with us, but a state cannot stand once it has lost the confidence of the people."

12.16 The Master said, "A gentleman helps others to realize their good qualities, rather than their bad. A petty person does the opposite."

12.18 Ji Kangzi was concerned about the prevalence of robbers in Lu and asked Confucius about how to deal with this problem. Confucius said, "If you could just get rid of your own excessive desires, the people would not steal even if you rewarded them for it."

13.1 Zilu asked about governing. The Master replied, "Precede the common people in accepting the burden of labor." When asked to elaborate, he added, "Do not slacken in your efforts."

13.4 Fan Chi asked to learn about plowing and growing grain [from Confucius]. The Master said, "When it comes to that, any old farmer would be a better teacher than I."

He asked to learn about growing fruits and vegetables. The Master said, "When it comes to that, any old gardener would be a better teacher than I."

Fan Chi then left. The Master remarked, "What a common fellow . . . that Fan Chi is! When a ruler loves ritual propriety, then none among his people will dare to be disrespectful. When a ruler loves rightness, then none among his people will dare not to obey. When a ruler loves trustworthiness, then none of his people will dare to not be honest. The mere existence of such a ruler would cause the common people throughout the world to bundle their children on their backs and seek him out. Of what use, then, is the study of agriculture?"

13.13 The Master said, "If you simply correct yourself, what difficulties could you encounter in government service? If you cannot correct yourself, how can you expect to correct others?"

13.18 The Duke of She said to Confucius, "Among my people there is one we call 'Upright Gong.' When his father stole a sheep, he reported him to the authorities."

Confucius replied, "Among my people, those who we consider 'upright' are different from this: fathers cover up for their sons, and sons cover up for their fathers. 'Uprightness' is to be found in this."

13.24 Zigong asked, "What would you make of a person whom everyone in the village likes?"

The Master said, "I would not know what to make of him."

"What about someone whom everyone in the village hates?"

"I would still not know. Better this way: those in the village who are good like him, and those who are not good hate him."

14.22 Zilu asked about serving one's lord. The Master replied, "Do not deceive him. Oppose him openly."

15.30 The Master said, "To make a mistake and yet to not change your ways—this is what is called truly making a mistake."

16.8 The Master said, "The gentleman stands in awe of three things: the Mandate of Heaven, great men, and the teachings of the sages. The petty person does not understand the Mandate of Heaven, and thus does not regard it with awe; he shows disrespect to great men, and ridicules the teachings of the sages."

16.10 Confucius said, "There are nine things upon which a gentleman focuses his attention: when looking, he focuses on seeing clearly; when listening, he focuses on being discerning; in his expression, he focuses on being amiable; in his demeanor, he focuses on being reverent; in his speech, he focuses on being dutiful; in his actions, he focuses on being respectful; when in doubt, he focuses on asking questions; when angry, he focuses on thinking about the potential negative consequences of his anger; and when seeing gain, he focuses upon what is right."

17.3 The Master said, "Only the very wise and the very stupid do not change."

Selections from *The Book of Mencius*

Mencius (c. 391–308 BCE) was a Confucian thinker who echoed and elaborated many of Confucius' ideas. He taught that good leaders should care for the people while striving for personal virtue and moral goodness, that humans are inherently good, and that the people have a right to rebel against a leader who becomes corrupt or cruel. This latter idea, a very modern notion, was considered extremely radical in Mencius's day, and in some places it still is. Mencius expended much energy opposing two doctrines that he regarded as pernicious: (1) the view that morality is based on calculations of benefit or harm to people and (2) the notion that people should look out for their own well-being while ignoring the welfare of society.

1 Mencius went to see King Hui of Liang. The king said, "Sir. You've come here with little concern for the thousand *li* (approximately one-sixth of a mile). Surely you've brought something that will be of profit to my state?" Mencius responded, "Why must Your Majesty use the word 'profit'? Surely, it is true goodness and righteousness alone that matter. If the king were to say, 'What will be of profit to my state?' and the high officials were to say, 'What will be of profit to my family?' and gentlemen and commoners were to say, 'What will be of profit to myself?' everyone above and below would turn to attacking one another for profit and the state thereby would be put in grave danger. If the ruler of a state of ten thousand chariots were killed, it would be sure to be by someone from a thousand chariot state; and, if the ruler of a state of a thousand chariots were killed, it would be sure to be by someone from a family of one hundred chariots. To take a thousand from ten thousand or one hundred from one thousand can hardly be considered a little, yet those who put profit before righteousness are not satisfied until they seize it all. Never has a person given to true goodness abandoned those close to him; never has a person given to righteousness treated his lord as an afterthought. Let Your Majesty say, 'It is true goodness and righteousness alone that matter.' Why must Your Majesty use the word 'profit'?" (1A.1)

2 [In reply to a question from King Hui of Liang about government, Mencius responds:]

"Do not interfere with the farming seasons and the crops will be more than can be consumed; do not let finely meshed nets be cast in ponds and lakes and the fish and turtles will be more than can be consumed; let axes enter the mountain groves only at the appropriate time and the timber will be more than can be used. When crops and fish and turtles are more than can be consumed, and timber is more than can be used, the people will nurture the living and mourn the dead in contentment. Their nurturing of the living and the mourning of the dead in contentment: such is the beginning of the kingly way. Let mulberry trees be planted in households of five *mu* (approximately one-sixth of an acre) and fifty-year-olds can wear silk; do not let the times for breeding chickens, pigs, dogs, and hogs be neglected, and the seventy-year-olds can eat meat. In fields of one hundred *mu*, do not deprive them of the seasons, and families of several mouths will never go hungry. Be attentive to instruction in the village schools and set forth the principles of filial piety, and fraternal respect and those with graying hair will not be on the roads carrying heavy loads on their backs and heads. It is impossible in a state where seventy-year-olds wear silk and eat meat, and the black-haired people suffer from neither hunger nor cold, for the ruler not

Mencius, Daniel K. Gardner, trans., in *The Four Books* (Indianapolis: Hackett, 2007), 53–55, 61–62, 65, 77–79, 88–89, 95–96, 103.

to be regarded as a true king. If pigs and hogs eat the food meant for the people and you know not how to restrain them, and if there are famished dying on the roads and you know not how to distribute aid from the granaries and then say, 'It is not me; it is just a bad year,' how is this any different from mutilating and killing a person and then saying, 'It is not me; it is the weaponry.' Let the king not put blame on a bad year and all under heaven will come to him." (1A.3)

5 Mencius said to King Xuan of Qi: "Suppose one of Your Majesty's ministers entrusts his wife and children to a friend and then takes leave to journey to Chu, only to find, upon his return, that his wife and children suffer from cold and famine: What should be done?" He said, "Break off the friendship." He said, "Suppose the chief judge proved incapable of managing the junior judges: What should be done?" The king said, "Remove him." Suppose that all within the four borders is not well governed: What should be done?" The king looked around to his left and to his right and then spoke of other matters. (1B.6)

6 King Xuan of Qi asked, "Is it the case that Tang banished Jie and King Wu cut down Zhou?" Mencius responded, "So it says in the records." King Xuan said, "Is it permissible for a minister to murder his sovereign?" Mencius said, "A thief of true goodness is called 'thief'; a thief of righteousness is called 'criminal.' Thieves and criminals are called good-for-nothings. I have heard of the punishment of the good-for-nothing Zhou; I have not heard of the murder of a sovereign." (1B.8)

8 All people have a mind-and-heart that cannot bear to see the suffering of others. Former kings had a mind-and-heart that could not bear to see the suffering of others and thus had governments that could not bear to see the suffering of others. Ruling all under heaven was as simple for them as rolling it in the palm of the hand. Here is why I say that all men have a mind-and-heart that cannot bear to see the suffering of others: Today, no matter the person, if he suddenly comes upon a young child about to fall into a well, his mind-and-heart fills with alarm and is moved to compassion. It is not because he wishes to ingratiate himself with the parents of the young child; nor is it because he seeks renown among villagers and friends; nor is it because he would hate the bad reputation. From this we can see that to be without a mind-and-heart of compassion is not to be human; to be without a mind-and-heart that is ashamed of evil in oneself and hates it in others is not [to] be human; to be without a mind-and-heart of humility and deference is not to be human; to be without a mind-and-heart of right and wrong is not to be human. The mind-and-heart of compassion is the seed of benevolence; the mind-and-heart that is ashamed of evil in oneself and hates it in others is the seed of righteousness; the mind-and-heart of humility and deference is the seed of propriety; the mind-and-heart of right and wrong is the seed of wisdom. People have these four seeds just as they have the four limbs. To have these four seeds but to deny their potential in oneself is to rob from oneself. To deny their potential in the ruler is to rob from the ruler. All of us have these four seeds within us; if we know to develop and bring each to completion, it will be like a blaze catching fire or a spring finding a path. He who is able to bring them to completion is capable of preserving all within the four seas; he who doesn't complete them is incapable of caring for his parents. (2A.6)

17 Mencius said, "The actualization of true goodness is serving our parents; the actualization of righteousness is obeying our elder brothers; the actualization of wisdom is understanding these two [true goodness and righteousness] and never departing from them; the actualization of rites is the regulation and adornment of these two. The actualization of music is taking delight in these two. Where there is delight they come to life, and once they come to life how can they be stopped? And when they cannot be stopped, our feet and hands will begin to dance without our realizing it." (4A.27)

18 Mencius said, "When the sovereign is truly good, everybody will be truly good; when the sovereign is righteous, everybody will be righteous." (4B.5)

22 Mencius said, "The superior man advances persistently along the proper path, hoping to get it for himself. Getting it for himself he rests in it at ease; resting in it at ease he trusts in it deeply; trusting in it deeply he penetrates its source in

whatever is around him. It is for this reason that the superior man hopes to get it for himself." (4B.14)

32 Gongduzi said, "Gaozi says, 'In human nature there is neither good nor bad.' Others say, 'Human nature can be made to be good or made to be bad, which is why in the time of Wen and Wu the people were fond of goodness and in the time of Yu and Li people were fond of malice.' Still others say, 'There is human nature that is good and human nature that is not good, which is why when Shun was ruler there still was Xiang, why with Gusou as his father there still was Shun, and why with Zhou as son of their older brother and their ruler to boot there still were Viscount Qi of Wei and Prince Bigan.' Now you say, 'Human nature is good.' Does this mean that these others are wrong?"

Mencius responded, "Our natural tendency is to do good. This is what I mean by its [i.e., the nature's] being good. Doing what is not good is not the fault of our natural disposition. Each and every one of us possesses the mind-and-heart of compassion; the mind-and-heart that is ashamed of evil in oneself and detests it in others; the mind-and-heart of respectfulness and reverence; and the mind-and-heart of right and wrong. The mind-and-heart of compassion is true goodness; the mind-and-heart that is ashamed of evil in oneself and hates it in others is righteousness; the mind-and-heart of respectfulness and reverence is propriety; and the mind-and-heart of right and wrong is wisdom. True goodness, righteousness, propriety, and wisdom are not welded on to us from without. We possess them from the very beginning, but we just do not think about it. Thus it is said, 'Seek and you will find it; let go of it and you will lose it.' That some are at twice, five times, or an infinite remove from others in this respect is owing to their inability to give full realization to their natural disposition.

"The *Book of Odes* says,

Heaven gives birth to the multitude of people
Once there is a thing there is a norm for it.
Holding fast to what makes us human
People take delight in this excellent virtue of theirs. [#260]

"Confucius said, 'Whoever wrote this ode knew the Way. Thus, once there is a thing, there is sure to be a norm for it. And because people hold fast to what makes us human, they take delight in this outstanding virtue of theirs.'" (6A.6)

39 Mencius said, "A person, in giving full realization to his mind-and-heart, knows his nature; and knowing his nature, he knows heaven. By preserving his mind-and-heart and nurturing his nature, he serves heaven. Whether his life is to be short or long does not weigh on him; he cultivates himself and waits for death. This is how he stands firm in his fate." (7A.1)

42 Mencius said, "The ten thousand things are all complete within me. Nothing brings greater joy than to look within and find that I am true to myself. Try your hardest to treat others empathetically—this is the shortest way to true goodness." (7A.4)

60 Mencius said, "There is no better way to nurture the mind-and-heart than to have few desires. Here is a person with few desires: there may be occasions when he fails to preserve it [the original mind-and-heart], but they will be few. Here is a person with many desires: there may be occasions when he preserves it, but they will be few." (7B.35)

Human Nature Is Evil

XUNZI

Xunzi (c. 310–211 BCE) was an astute and influential commentator on Confucius, although he parted from the master in several ways. Unlike Confucius, Xunzi believed that people are essentially bad and that to keep them in line rulers must govern with a heavy hand and tight reins. People can be trained to be good, but a ruler should never relax his grip.

The inborn nature of man is certainly that of the petty man. If he is without a teacher and lacks the model, he will see things solely in terms of benefit to himself. As the nature of man is assuredly that of the petty man, if the age in which he lives is chaotic, he will acquire its chaotic customs. For this reason, he will use the small to redouble what is small and use the chaotic to begat more chaos. If the gentleman does not use the power inherent in his circumstances to control them, then he will have no means to develop their inherent possibilities. Now the mouth and stomach of a man can only lead to smacking and chewing away, feasting and gorging himself to satisfaction. How can they be aware of ritual principles and his moral duty? Or know when to offer polite refusals or to yield precedence? Or know shame more keenly or sharpen what he accumulates? If a man lacks a teacher and the model, then his mind will be just like his mouth and stomach.

Now if a man were caused to live without ever having tasted the meat of pastured and grain-fed animals or rice and millet, but knew only beans, coarse greens, dregs and husks, then he would be satisfied with such food. Were there suddenly to arrive a platter filled with the finest and most delicate of meats, he would look at them with astonishment and exclaim: "What strange things!" But since when savored, they are not unpleasing to the nose; when tasted, they are sweet to the mouth; and when eaten, they are satisfying to the body, everyone who tries them will reject their old foods and choose these new ones instead.

Consider the way of the Ancient Kings and the guiding principles of humanity and justice. Are they not the means by which we live together in societies, by which we protect and nurture each other, by which we hedge in our faults and refine each other, and by which together we become tranquil and secure? Consider then the way of Jie and Robber Zhi. Does it not contrast with that of the Ancient Kings just as the meat of pastured and grain-fed animals contrasts with dregs and husks! Though this is so, many men still become like them and few like the Ancient Kings. Why is this? I say: They are uncultivated rustics. A lack of cultivation is a misfortune common to the whole world; it is the greatest calamity for man and does him the greatest harm. Anciently it was said:

> The humane man delights in proclaiming and manifesting it to others.

If it is proclaimed and manifested, smoothed and polished, imitated and repeated, then the myopic will suddenly become comprehensive, the uncultivated suddenly refined, and the stupid suddenly wise. If this could not be done, though a Tang or Wu held supreme power, what advantage would result,

Xunzi, 4.10, *Xunzi: A Translation and Study of the Complete Works*, vol. I, John Knoblock, trans. (Stanford, CA: Stanford University Press, 1988), 192–193.

and though a Jie or Zhou Xin held supreme power, what damage could they cause? But when Tang and Wu lived, the world followed them and order prevailed, and when Jie and Zhou Xin lived, the world followed them and was chaotic. How could this be if such were contrary to the essential nature of man because certainly it is as possible for a man to be like the one as like the other?

Confucianism as Religious Humanism

JULIA CHING

Julia Ching addresses the question of how to categorize Confucius and Confucianism. Many have wondered whether he is a philosopher or a religious leader, and whether Confucianism is a secular or religious worldview. For her part, Ching contends that Confucius is an original thinker and that Confucianism is "a humanism that is open to religious values."

In the West, people are accustomed to an image of Confucius as a wise man or a sage, propounding a teaching about how to live a virtuous life, much as did Socrates in ancient Greece. Socrates is regarded as a humanist; in fact, he was condemned by the state for misleading youth, for turning them away from the gods of their fathers. Confucius had his own struggles with the state, but died a natural death. As a teacher, he too instructed the young in ideals different from those of the world around them. And extant records indicate that he seldom touched on religious matters. He is known as a humanist, and today's secular society tends to understand all humanists as secularists or at least religious agnostics.

Many Western philosophers are not sure that Confucius was even a philosopher, if by that word one is referring to a "professional" philosopher, who analyses language and concepts or offers a systematic teaching about the world or human existence. Many would see him simply as propounding a practical wisdom without much speculative content. But then, many of these people have hardly ever read Confucius. They might even say that they have attempted some reading, and found it unattractive, since works like the *Analects* of Confucius, which gives the conversations between the master and the disciple, have at first sight too much of an *ad hoc* character without any challenging profundity.

But there are also exceptions. The American philosopher Herbert Fingarette is known for his work, *Confucius: The Secular as Sacred* (1972). He singles out Confucius' love of ritual and discovers in this a sacred or religious dimension. Fingarette acknowledges philosophical value in Confucius, although he refrains from delving into the more metaphysical side of Confucius' teachings.

The German philosopher Karl Jaspers counts Confucius among the Great Philosophers, the "paradigmatic individuals," together with Socrates, Jesus of Nazareth and the Buddha Gautama. In each case,

Julia Ching, *Chinese Religions* (Maryknoll, NY: Orbis Books, 1993), 51–52.

we have a man who lived in a time of a social crisis, and sought to respond to this through special teachings aimed at all people. In each case as well, disciples were gathered, without regard to social backgrounds. In all cases, the teachings were not of abstract metaphysics but concern with the higher order of things (the "Rites" or *li*, the Law or Torah, or the Dharma). These individuals offered their own critical interpretation of this higher order in opposition to external conformism and hypocrisy and in favour of an interior disposition. All lived what they preached, and represented a very high personal *ethic,* which expressed itself in clear moral demands.

Within China itself, debates have also taken place in our own times about how to evaluate or categorise Confucius and his teachings. We are not speaking here of the diatribes that raged during the Anti-Confucius Campaign (1973–74) that have been discredited as politically motivated. We are referring to differences of opinion regarding how to view Confucius, and whether Confucianism should be considered a philosophy or a religion. The presupposition in Communist China is that Karl Marx was the greatest philosopher the world ever produced and that philosophy is superior to religion. To call a tradition a religion is therefore to put it in a place that is lower than that of philosophy, but higher than that of "superstition." Thus those scholars (including Fung Yu-lan and Kuang Yaming) who have more respect for Confucianism prefer to see it as a philosophy, while others who have less respect for it (especially Ren Jiyu) prefer to call it a religion.

In our own case, removed from ideological considerations, and also from any presumed superiority of philosophy over religion or vice versa, we shall regard Confucius mainly as a seminal thinker, and describe Confucianism as a humanism that is open to religious values. Here we are using the term Confucianism broadly, to include not merely the Master's original teachings, but also those teachings of later disciples that became integrated into the school of Confucius or the doctrinal and ritual system called Confucianism.

The Confucian Way of Being Religious

TU WEI-MING

Tu Wei-Ming sees Confucianism as a "way of being religious" and as a fundamental concern for "the secular as sacred." We can define this way, he says, as "ultimate self-transformation as a communal act and as a faithful dialogical response to the transcendent."

Being religious, in the Confucian perspective, informed by sacred texts such as *Chung-yung*, means being engaged in the process of learning to be fully human. We can define the Confucian way of being religious as *ultimate self-transformation as a communal act and as a faithful dialogical response to the transcendent.* This is also the Confucian prescription for learning to be fully human. Using the

Tu Wei-Ming, *Centrality and Commonality* (Albany: State University of New York Press, 1989), 93–98.

categories of thought enunciated in the preceding chapters, we can say that Confucian religiosity is expressed through the infinite potential and the inexhaustible strength of each human being for self-transcendence. Three interrelated dimensions are involved here: the person, the community, and the transcendent.

The Confucian conviction that a person's self-cultivation is the root of social order and that universal peace depends on social order has far-reaching implications for our perception of the linkage between the person and the community on the one hand and the community and the transcendent on the other. For example, the private, psychological management of one's emotive state is not separate from the well-being of the public; social responsibility and religious faith are not conflicting demands. The movement from the self via the community to Heaven is predicated on a holistic vision of human self-transcendence that the compartmentalized methods of psychology, sociology, or theology which are characteristic of academic "disciplines" in modern universities, are grossly inadequate to grasp.

The conviction that what we do as ordinary citizens within the confines of our private homes is socially and politically important and what we do as public servants performing our roles and functions in the mundane world is religiously significant reflects a deep Confucian concern for "the secular as sacred." In the post-Machiavellian, Hobbesian, Mandan and Freudian age, it is extremely difficult to imagine that there is or can ever be an organismic unity that underlies the person, the community and the transcendent. Indeed, any insinuation that these connections are still whole may give the impression of a prelapsarian worldview, a worldview that can still be imagined but is no longer viable as a spiritual and intellectual option for the sophisticated modern mind.

The Confucians do not glorify a utopia that historically has never existed but describe what we naturally and inevitably are as human beings. As the Confucians argue, it is more difficult to imagine ourselves as isolable individuals than as centers of relationships constantly interacting with one another in a dynamic network of human-relatedness. Similarly, it is more difficult to believe in an omnipotent God who violates rules of nature for mysterious reasons than in enduring cosmic patterns discoverable by human rationality. I do not mean to challenge the doctrine of individualism which has inspired generation after generation to search for autonomy, independence and dignity, or the concept of an all-mighty God which continues to be informed by sophisticated theological argumentation. I simply want to note that, despite its apparent naivete, the concept of organismic unity is predicated on an inclusive humanist vision. The Confucian way of being religious is a means of understanding of that vision.

"Ultimate self-transformation" implies that the process of learning to be human never ends (even though the Confucians do not subscribe to the "existentialist" belief that since our existence precedes our essence we can shape our nature according to our own independent action through conscious living). Our inescapable humanity specifies the minimum condition, the lowest common denominator; "ultimate" refers to the greatest possible realization of that humanity. "Self-transformation" suggests that although we are not what we ought to be, we can reach the highest state of humanity through personal cultivation. Learning to be fully human is to learn to become a sage (an authentic manifestation of our nature, indeed our essence as ordained by Heaven). Since the sage is genuinely human, the aim of self-transformation is not to go beyond humanity but to realize it as completely as possible. We can never embody our humanity in its all-embracing fullness.

The statement that we are naturally and inescapably human and that we must endeavor to learn to be fully human may appear paradoxical. If we are already human, why must we try to learn to be human? It seems easier to comprehend the thesis that to transcend the state of being human is to become superior to what is still human, to become superhuman or divine. However, the Confucian insistence that ultimate self-transformation does not go beyond humanity but realizes it is a substantive ethicoreligious claim. The minimum requirement—that one is human—serves as the basis for the maximum realization of humanity, just as a tiny stream serves as the beginning of the mighty Yangtze. We cannot deny that there is water in the tiny stream, but we must admit that the greatness of the water in the Yangtze has given it a qualitatively different significance.

The metaphor that humanity, like water, must reach a high enough level for it to flow suggests that the Confucians conceive of humanity as dynamic. Self-transformation, symbolized by an ever-broadening and ever-deepening stream of humanity, is a process of "establishing" (*li*) and "enlarging" (*ta*). It is radically different from one's quest for inner spirituality as an isolable individual. In this context, "ultimate" connotes the full realization of humanity: its maximum fulfillment as well as its highest point of attainment.

If we envision the ultimate self-transformation of a fellow human being as a stream gushing forth from its springs, then as that stream establishes and enlarges itself, it will meet other streams. The confluence of two or more streams is what we refer to as *the communal act.* To the Confucians, one cannot establish and enlarge oneself through spiritual transformation without encountering like-minded people. Even if we imagine a subterranean stream making its way alone to the ocean, we must assume that it benefits from other sources. A defining characteristic of Confucian religiousness is its emphasis on the fiduciary community as an irreducible reality in ultimate self-transformation.

One becomes fully human within a community. The Confucians believe that normally it is desirable to establish fruitful communication with the transcendent through communal participation. Only in extraordinary circumstances, such as the case of Ch'u Yuan, who was the only sober person in a drunken multitude, can we appeal to Heaven directly. Such an action—facing Heaven alone as an isolated individual without reference to one's community—has grave consequences for the community as a whole as well as for the individual. It must be undertaken with extreme care and even a sense of tragedy. The preferred course of action is to integrate all levels of the community (family, neighborhood, clan, race, nation, world, universe, cosmos) into the process of self-transformation. The Confucians believe that this gradual process of inclusion is inherent in the project of learning to be fully human.

The Confucians advocate a humanism that neither denies nor slights the transcendent. I use the term "inclusive humanism" to underscore the comprehensiveness of the concept of humanity in the Confucian perspective and to differentiate it from the familiar forms of exclusive secular humanism. In light of Confucian inclusive humanism, the process of learning to be fully human entails not only communal participation but also *a faithful dialogical response to the transcendent.* The willingness—which implies one's ability—to open up to the dimension of reality that can never be completely apprehended by human rationality, is not only an imagination but also an action. This opening up is a fulfillment of humanity as well as an answer to the Mandate of Heaven. The mutuality of Heaven and man (in the gender neutral sense of humanity) makes it possible to perceive the transcendent as immanent. To suggest that the full meaning of Heaven can be embodied in our humanity would be blasphemous. Rather, our inborn ability to respond to the bidding of Heaven impels us to extend our human horizon continuously so that the immanent in our nature assumes a transcendent dimension.

To become fully human, in this sense, one must establish a constant dialogical relationship with Heaven. The Confucian faith in the perfectibility of human nature through self-effort is, strictly speaking, a faith in self-transcendence. The godlike sage is the co-creator of the universe not because the transcendent is totally humanized but because the human is ultimately transformed by means of a faithful dialogical response to the transcendent. The fiduciary community, as a defining characteristic of Confucian religiosity, is not governed by social ethics devoid of reference to the transcendent. On the contrary, the community based on trust rather than on contract is itself a sacred confirmation that human nature is ordained by Heaven. It may not be far-fetched to suggest that in the Confucian sense our "covenant" with Heaven is the full realization of humanity as Heaven's own ultimate transformation.

Sacred Space

JENNIFER OLDSTONE-MOORE

This selection explains the nature and meaning of "sacred space" as adherents experience it in Confucianism. In Confucianism the distinction between the sacred and the profane is blurred; still, there is space that is unambiguously recognized as sacred space. This is "primarily ritual space, and ranges from simple sites where small offerings are made, to grand imperial spaces where complex rites are conducted."

In Confucianism there is frequently no clear distinction between the sacred and the profane—the sacred may be encountered in nature and in the world at large, as well as in temples, shrines, and the home. Space that is specifically designated as sacred is primarily ritual space, and ranges from simple sites where small offerings are made, to grand imperial spaces where complex rites are conducted.

Since the end of the traditional Confucian state, many temples have decayed or declined in use. However, some have been restored and maintained and, in 1988, amid lavish celebrations, a new Confucian temple was opened in Andong county in Korea—ceremonies were performed to install the ritual tablets of eighteen Chinese disciples and eighteen Korean scholars of Confucianism.

Confucian temples are monuments to human beings rather than to gods and serve to honor Confucius and his disciples, as well as worthy scholars through the ages. The human orientation of the temples is further emphasized by the general lack of images and statues—instead, Confucius' name, as well as the names of his disciples and illustrious followers, are inscribed on tablets which act as the focus of veneration.

Members of the state bureaucracy traditionally honored Confucius in twice-yearly sacrifices on the equinoxes. The most important offering was on Confucius' birthday, which is still celebrated at Confucian temples. The event generally falls on September 28 and is celebrated as "Teacher's Day" in Taiwan. Participants dress in the garb of ancient China, perform dance and music, and offer sacrifices to the great sage.

Confucian temple architecture echoes the architecture of the emperor's palace—notably, the north–south axis on which the important halls are located. The temples are built on a square base, and internally they are symmetrical, with each wall a mirror-image of the one opposite, conveying the order associated with Confucian thought. Temples were public spaces—results of civil service examinations were posted in them and they were also used for training in music and ritual.

Jennifer Oldstone-Moore, *Confucianism* (Oxford: Oxford University Press, 2002), 63–69.

The first Confucian temple was built in Qufu in Shandong province in 478 BCE, the year after Confucius' death. Official sacrifices to Confucius began in 195 BCE, when the Han emperor offered a Grand Sacrifice at Qufu; the Han later adopted Confucianism as the basis of the state cult. Adjacent to the temple is the Kong family mansion, the home of the direct descendants of Confucius from the first century BCE, when the Han government granted the family a fiefdom and title. Later dynasties also supported the temple and the family with grants of land and imperial funds. The Confucian temple and the family mansion have defined and, through the extent of their landholdings, dominated Qufu. Beginning in the Ming dynasty, the district magistrate's office was located within the mansion compound; the only other residence also to serve as a government office was the imperial palace.

Other places of import for the Confucian tradition are schools and academies. These were centers for moral formation, places that provided the means and context to experience the ultimate as prescribed by Zhu Xi's "investigation of things," constituted communities for Confucian scholars, and were the locus for many rituals honoring the Great Sage. Schools supported by the state were established in Korea, China, and Vietnam. In China, although the wealthiest had the easiest access to education, most dynasties sought to make education available to exceptional students regardless of background or ability to pay. Schools were staffed by men who had received a classical Confucian education or had passed but not taken up a government appointment. In premodern East Asia, numerous academies in China and Korea were places of advanced learning where scholars and their disciples gathered to discuss Confucian thought, and to compile, preserve, and, in the last several centuries, publish texts. Scholars attached to an academy might be assigned a room and a stipend. Some academies still exist today: Korea's Seongkyunkwan University, which was the center of Confucian studies in Seoul, continues to perform rites for Confucians twice yearly, and still, theoretically, controls the local Confucian schools, of which there are more than 200.

South of the emperor's palace in Beijing is a large sacred complex that was one of the holiest sites of imperial China: the Temple of Heaven. Here, the emperor would perform rituals such as the annual sacrifices on the winter solstice when *yin* energy was at its peak and *yang*, bringing growth, warmth, and light, was just beginning to reemerge. As the Son of Heaven, the sole intermediary between Heaven (Tian) and the empire (Tian Xia, "All under Heaven"), he alone could perform such sacrifices. Through his sacrifices, the emperor of China played his part to guarantee cosmic order.

The Temple of Heaven was sacred ground—commoners were not allowed even to watch the silent procession of the emperor and his entourage from the imperial palace to the temple. On the winter solstice, the emperor offered incense, jade, silk, and wine. He sacrificed a red bullock, symbolizing *yang*, and prostrated himself nine times (nine is considered the most *yang* of numbers) before the altar to Heaven.

For most people, however, the family altar and the ancestral shrine are the most significant places of sacred activity. The home itself is the basic unit of Confucian practice—it is here that important relationships are played out, and where individuals receive the training that will shape them into virtuous members of the family and society. The altar—where gods and spirits as well as family ancestors may reside—is usually in the main living space of the house. Manuals outlining procedures for ritual carefully delineate correct placement of spirit tablets, which house ancestors. The tablets include the names of individual ancestors and birth and death dates, and often the number of sons. When three to five generations have passed, tablets are taken to the ancestral shrine where they receive regular sacrifices which are conducted by the extended family.

Confucianism affirms the sacrality of the universe. Human destiny, which is realized through fulfilment of one's social roles, is as much a part of cosmic order as any aspect of nature. Human virtues are evident in the patterns of creation, such as the regularity of the nodes on bamboo, which is associated with human constancy. Certain features of the landscape—for example, rivers, caves, and mountains—are believed to possess spiritual power. In China, Taishan (Mount Tai), the most important of five sacred mountains, was seen as a provider of fertility, a preventer of natural disasters, and a symbol of stability. It was worshiped as part of the folk tradition in spring and fall to ensure a successful planting and an abundant harvest. It was also the site of the rare *feng* and *than* sacrifices. These rituals, addressed to Heaven and Earth, were performed by emperors to mark the founding of a new dynasty or the achievements of the emperor who requested favor for the dynasty from Heaven and Earth.

According to Confucian thought, the links between Heaven and humankind, and the responsiveness of Heaven to human affairs, were manifest in nature. The emperor's mandate to govern and his fulfilment of ritual duties and continued virtuous rule were evident in the regular and predictable motion of heavenly bodies, the successful growth of crops, and the continuation of order in the empire. If Heaven was not satisfied with the emperor, the harmony and regular rhythms of the natural and human worlds would be disrupted. Portents of chaos, such as floods, earthquakes, famine, drought, and uprisings, indicated Heaven's displeasure—and if they continued, they could ultimately legitimate the replacement of the dynasty.

Confucian Holy Rite

HERBERT FINGARETTE

The Confucius scholar Herbert Fingarette acknowledges that in Confucianism there are unmistakable elements of the secular, the humanistic, and the this-worldly. But he sees something else that he thinks has been overlooked: "belief in magical powers of profound importance."

The remarks which follow are aimed at revealing the magic power which Confucius saw, quite correctly, as the very essence of human virtue. It is finally by way of the magical that we can also arrive at the best vantage point for seeing the holiness in human existence which Confucius saw as central. In the twentieth century this central role of the holy in Confucius's teaching has been largely ignored because we have failed to grasp the existential point of that teaching.

Specifically, what is needed (and is here proposed) is a reinterpretation which makes use of contemporary philosophical understanding. In fact such a reinterpretation casts, by reflection as it were, illumination into dimensions of our own philosophical thought, which have remained in shadow.

The distinctive philosophical insight in the *Analects*, or at least in its more authentic "core," was quickly obscured as the ideas of rival schools infected Confucius's teaching. It is not surprising that this insight, requiring as it does a certain emphasis on the magical and religious dimensions of the *Analects,* is absent from the usual Western-influenced interpretations of modern times. Today the *Analects* is read, in its main drift, either as an empirical,

Herbert Fingarette, *Confucius: The Secular as Sacred* (Prospect Heights, IL: Waveland Press, 1972), 1–9.

humanist, this-worldly teaching or as a parallel to Platonist-rationalist doctrines. Indeed, the teaching of the *Analects* is often viewed as a major step toward the explicit rejection of superstition or heavy reliance on "supernatural forces."

There is no doubt that the world of the *Analects* is profoundly different in its quality from that of Moses, Aeschylus, Jesus, Gautama Buddha, Lao-tzu [Laozi] or the Upanishadic teachers. In certain obvious respects the *Analects* does indeed represent the world of a humanist and a traditionalist, one who is, however, sufficiently traditional to render a kind of pragmatic homage, when necessary, to the spirits.

"Devote yourself to man's duties," says the Master; "respect spiritual beings but keep distance." (6:20) He suited the deed to the precept and himself "never talked of prodigies, feats of strength, disorders, or spirits." (7:20) In response to direct questions about the transcendental and supernatural he said: "Until you are able to serve men, how can you serve spiritual beings? Until you know about life, how can you know about death?" (11:11)

If we examine the substance of the *Analects* text, it is quickly evident that the topics and the chief concepts pertain primarily to our human nature, comportment and relationships. Merely to list some of the constantly recurring themes suffices for our present purposes: Rite (*li*), Humaneness (*jen*), Reciprocity (*shu*), Loyalty (*chung*), Learning (*bsueh*), Music (*yueh*), and the concepts by which are defined the familial-social relationships and obligations (prince, father, etc.).

The this-worldly, practical humanism of the *Analects* is further deepened by the teaching that the moral and spiritual achievements of man do not depend on tricks or luck or on esoteric spells or on any purely external agency. One's spiritual condition depends on the "stuff' one has to begin with, on the amount and quality of study and good hard work one puts into "shaping" it. Spiritual nobility calls for persistence and effort. "First the difficult. . . ." (6:20) "His burden is heavy and his course is long. He has taken *jen* as his burden—is that not heavy?" (8:7) What disquieted Confucius was "leaving virtue untended and learning unperfected, hearing about what is right but not managing either to turn toward it or to reform what is evil." (7:3) The disciple of Confucius was surely all too aware that his task was one calling not for amazement and miracle but for constant "cutting, filing, carving, polishing" (1:15) in order to become a fully and truly human being, a worthy participant in society. All this seems the very essence of the antimagical in outlook. Nor does it have the aura of the Divine.

Yet, in spite of this dedicated and apparently secular prosaic moralism, we also find occasional comments in the *Analects* which seem to reveal a belief in magical powers of profound importance. By "magic" I mean the power of a specific person to accomplish his will directly and effortlessly through ritual, gesture and incantation. The user of magic does not work by strategies and devices as a means toward an end; he does not use coercion or physical forces. There are no pragmatically developed and tested strategies or tactics. He simply wills the end in the proper ritual setting and with the proper ritual gesture and word; without further effort on his part, the deed is accomplished. Confucius's words at times strongly suggest some fundamental magical power as central to this way. (In the following citations, the Chinese terms all are central to Confucius's thought, and they designate powers, states and forms of action of fundamental value.) . . .

"Is *jen* far away? As soon as I want it, it is here." (7:29)

"Self-disciplined and ever turning to *li*—everyone in the world will respond to his *jen*." (12:1)

Shun, the great sage-ruler, "merely placed himself gravely and reverently with his face due South (the ruler's ritual posture); that was all" (i.e., and the affairs of his reign proceeded without flaw). (15:4)

The magical element always involves great effects produced effortlessly, marvelously, with an irresistible power that is itself intangible, invisible, unmanifest. "With correct comportment, no commands are necessary, yet affairs proceed." (13:6) "The character of a noble man is like wind, that of ordinary men like grass; when the wind blows the grass must bend." (12:19) "To govern by *te* is to be like the North Polar Star; it remains in place while all the other stars revolve in homage about it." (2:1)

Such comments can be taken in various ways. One may simply note that, as Duyvendak remarks, the "original magical meaning" of 2:1 is "unmistakable," or that the ritual posture of Shun in 15:4 is "a state of the highest magical potency." In short, one may admit that these are genuine residues of "superstition" in the *Analects*.

However, many modern interpreters of the *Analects* have wished to read Confucius more "sympathetically," that is, as one whose philosophic claims would have maximum validity for us in our own familiar and accepted terms. To do this these commentators have generally tried to minimize to the irreducible the magical claims in the *Analects*. For it is accepted as an axiom in our times that the goal of direct action by incantation and ritual gesture cannot be taken as a serious possibility. (The important exception to this general acceptance of the axiom, to be discussed later, is contemporary "linguistic analysis." But the import of this work has as yet hardly extended beyond the world of professional philosophy.)

The suggestion of magic and marvel so uncongenial to the contemporary taste may be dissipated in various ways: only one of the sayings I have quoted comes from the portion of the *Analects*—Books 3 to 8—that has been most widely of all accepted as "authentic" in the main. The other sayings might be among the many interpolations, often alien in spirit to Confucius, which are known to be in the received text. Or one might hold that the magical element is quite restricted in scope, applying only to the ruler or even the perfect ruler alone. Still another possible method of "interpreting away" the "magical" statements is to suppose that Confucius was merely emphasizing and dramatizing the otherwise familiar power of setting a good example. In short, on this view we must take the "magical" sayings as being poetic statements of a prosaic truth. Finally, one might simply argue that Confucius was not consistent on the issue—perhaps that he was mainly and characteristically antimagic, but, as might well be expected, he had not entirely freed himself of deep-rooted traditional beliefs.

All of these interpretations take the teaching of a magical dimension to human virtue as an obstacle to acceptance by the sophisticated citizen of the twentieth century. The magic must be interpreted away or else treated as a historically understandable failure on Confucius's part. I prefer to think we can still learn from Confucius on this issue if we do not begin by supposing the obvious meaning of his words as unacceptable.

Rather than engage in polemics regarding these other interpretations, I shall devote the remainder of my remarks to a positive exposition of what I take to be the genuine and sound magical view of man in Confucius's teaching. I do not hold that my interpretation is correct to the exclusion of all others. There is no reason to suppose that an innovator such as Confucius distinguishes all possible meanings of what he says and consciously intends only one of these meanings to the exclusion of all others. One should assume the contrary. Of the various meanings of the Confucian magical teaching, I believe the one to be elaborated in the following remarks is authentic, central and still unappreciated.

Confucius saw, and tried to call to our attention, that the truly, distinctively human powers have, characteristically, a magical quality. His task, therefore, required, in effect, that he reveal what is already so familiar and universal as to be unnoticed. What is necessary in such cases is that one come upon this "obvious" dimension of our existence in a new way, in the right way. Where can one find such a new path to this familiar area, one which provides a new and revealing perspective? Confucius found the path: we go by way of the notion of *li*.

One has to labor long and hard to learn *li*. The word in its root meaning is close to "holy ritual," "sacred ceremony." Characteristic of Confucius's teaching is the use of the language and imagery of *li* as a medium within which to talk about the entire body of the *mores,* or more precisely, of the authentic tradition and reasonable conventions of society. Confucius taught that the ability to act according to *li* and the will to submit to *li* are essential to that perfect and peculiarly human virtue or power which can be man's. Confucius thus does two things here: he calls our attention to the entire body of tradition and convention, and he calls upon us to see all this by means of a metaphor, through the imagery of sacred ceremony, holy rite.

The (spiritually) noble man is one who has labored at the alchemy of fusing social forms (*li*) and raw personal existence in such a way that they transmuted into a way of being which realizes *te,* the distinctively human virtue or power.

Te is realized in concrete acts of human intercourse, the acts being of a pattern. These patterns have certain general features, features common to all such patterns of *li*: they are all expressive of "man-to-man-ness," of reciprocal loyalty and respect. But the patterns are also specific: they differentiate and they define in detail the ritual performance-repertoires which constitute civilized, i.e., truly human patterns of mourning, marrying and fighting, of being a prince, a father, a son and so on. However, men are by no means conceived as being mere standardized units mechanically carrying out prescribed routines in the service of some cosmic or social law. Nor are they self-sufficient, individual souls who happen to consent to a social contract. Men become truly human as their raw impulse is shaped by *li.* And *li* is the fulfillment of human impulse, the civilized expression of it—not a formalistic dehumanization. *Li* is the specifically humanizing form of the dynamic relation of man-to-man.

The novel and creative insight of Confucius was to see this aspect of human existence, its form as learned tradition and convention, in terms of a particular revelatory image: *li,* i.e., "holy rite," "sacred ceremony," in the usual meaning of the term prior to Confucius.

In well-learned ceremony, each person does what he is supposed to do according to a pattern. My gestures are coordinated harmoniously with yours—though neither of us has to force, push, demand, compel or otherwise "make" this happen. Our gestures are in turn smoothly followed by those of the other participants, all effortlessly. If all are "self-disciplined, ever turning to *li,*" then all that is needed—quite literally—is an initial ritual gesture in the proper ceremonial context; from there onward everything "happens." What action did Shun (the Sage-ruler) take? "He merely placed himself gravely and reverently with his face due south; that was all." (15:4) Let us consider in at least a little detail the distinctive features of action emphasized by this revelatory image of Holy Rite.

It is important that we do not think of this effortlessness as "mechanical" or "automatic." If it is so, then, as Confucius repeatedly indicates, the ceremony is dead, sterile, empty: there is no *spirit* in it. The truly ceremonial "takes place"; there is a kind of spontaneity. It happens "of itself." There is life in it because the individuals involved do it with seriousness and sincerity. For ceremony to be authentic one must "participate in the sacrifice"; otherwise it is as if one "did not sacrifice at all." (3:12) To put it another way, there are two contrasting kinds of failure in carrying out *li*: the ceremony may be awkwardly performed for lack of learning and skill; or the ceremony may have a surface slickness but yet be dull, mechanical for lack of serious purpose and commitment. Beautiful and effective ceremony requires the personal "presence" to be fused with learned ceremonial skill. This ideal fusion is true *li* as sacred rite.

Confucius characteristically and sharply contrasts the ruler who uses *li* with the ruler who seeks to attain his ends by means of commands, threats, regulations, punishments and force. (2:3) The force of coercion is manifest and tangible, whereas the vast (and sacred) forces at work in *li* are invisible and intangible. *Li* works through spontaneous coordination rooted in reverent dignity. The perfection in Holy Rite is esthetic as well as spiritual.

CONTEMPORARY CHALLENGES

The Revival of Confucian Values

XINZHONG YAO

Xinzhong Yao notes that although Confucianism has been regarded in Mainland China as irrelevant and outdated, it is still very much alive and in fact is now enjoying a revival. "Elements of Confucian heritage," Xinzhong says, "have been transmitted to the present, either hidden in Nationalist and Communist doctrines, principles, ethics, public opinions and the system of a bureaucratic elite, etc., or implicitly underlying the whole structure of Chinese community . . . in whatever forms it may take, either capitalist or socialist, Nationalist or Communist."

With the Confucian retreat from political, social and economic stages in East Asia since the end of the nineteenth century, the Confucian influence has been limited to a small area of learning, seemingly viable only among the traditionally minded people and merely as a social and psychological background of their activities. The political and religious role of Confucianism in Mainland China has long been deemed the "doctrinal furnishing" of feudalism and aristocracy, and its values and ideals have been severely undermined both by radical revolutionaries and by radical liberals. For most academics and lay people, Confucianism represented the shadow of the past, the symbol and the reason for a backward, disadvantaged and powerless China. As a result, three irreversible changes have taken place in relation to Confucianism: Confucian organisations and institutions have disappeared, Confucian scholars have lost their social identity, and Confucian rituals no longer have spiritual values. Confucianism seems to have been reduced to being merely a theory or a doctrine without practical meaning, an old paradigm lacking influence on and relevance to modern life, and Mainland China, the homeland of Confucianism, appears to have become the least Confucian in East Asia.

This is, of course, only one side of the story. The umbilical cord between the Confucian tradition and modern China cannot easily be severed. Elements of Confucian heritage have been transmitted to the present, either hidden in Nationalist and Communist doctrines, principles, ethics, public opinions and the system of a bureaucratic elite, etc., or implicitly underlying the whole structure of Chinese community (family, community, society and the state), in whatever forms it may take, either capitalist or socialist, Nationalist or Communist. The link between the Three Principles of the People (Nationalism, Democracy and the Livelihood of the People) initiated by Sun Zhongshan (1866–1925) and the Confucian vision of the Grand Unity Society (*datong shehui*) is so strong that very few people would deny that there exists a succession from the latter to the former. And

Xinzhong Yao, *An Introduction to Confucianism* (Cambridge: Cambridge University Press, 2000), 274–279.

Communism inherited a great deal from the Confucian moral code, so much so that David Nivison argued a long time ago that Communist ethics and Confucianism were not very different in practice. This hidden heritage makes it possible for a revival of Confucianism after many years in which its development was impeded.

Since the beginning of the 1980s Confucianism has been on the rise again in many states and areas of East Asia, although the reasons and motives behind its popularity are quite different from one state to another. In any case, the revival of Confucianism is not simply a return to tradition, nor is it intended as a wholesale restoration of the old practice and learning. The awakening consciousness of Confucianism is related to the renewal of culture and the transformation of traditions in order to redefine cultural identity and to guide social and economic development. In the search for a new form of Confucianism, traditional Confucianism is consciously divided into two parts, "Confucianism as the source of moral values" and "Confucianism as the structure of a traditional society," which correspond, to some extent, to Ninian Smart's separation between "doctrinal Confucianism" and "religious Confucianism," or to Modern New Confucians' division between "the Confucian tradition" or "idealistic and cultural Confucianism" and "the Confucian China" or "dynastic and social Confucianism." It is agreed among scholars in Confucian Studies that while the social structure of old Confucianism has long been demolished, its doctrinal and idealistic values remain inherent in Chinese psychology and underlie East Asian peoples' attitudes and behaviour: "Recent anthropological, sociological, and political surveys all point to the pervasive presence of Confucian ethics in belief, attitude, and behaviour across all strata throughout China"; and that "Confucian culture is still at work in the everyday lives of the Korean people, and it is now being renovated or reproduced."

Despite criticism and caution about the relevance of Confucianism to modernisation, Confucianism is nevertheless gradually regaining some of the space it traditionally held in people's lives and in the mind of intellectuals. As a traditional organisation, Confucianism may not yet have obtained any new identity, and the old systems and social structures may never be appreciated again. But Confucian values are no longer disliked, and some of them have become appealing, albeit with certain political motives. For example, self-cultivation (*xiu shen*) as the basis for governing the state and bringing peace to the world has been accepted as politically correct and therefore has deliberately been adopted as a means of re-establishing moral standards among students, as shown when the Graduates' Society of Beijing University published its manifesto on self-cultivation in 1994, calling for all students to start with cultivating good habits and moral virtues. The combination of Confucian values and modern qualities creates a new title for business leaders, "Confucian entrepreneurs" (*ru shang*), praising their Confucian virtues demonstrated in industrial and commercial activities, such as humaneness (*ren*), trustfulness (*xin*), sincerity (*cheng*) and altruism (the *People's Daily*, 15 January 1998). Some people enthusiastically talk about "Marxist Confucianism" or "Confucian Marxism," while others see an opportunity in the economic experience of East Asia to merge Confucianism and free-market economy to formulate a new doctrine, Capitalist Confucianism or Confucian Capitalism (*rujiao ziben zhuyi*). Along with these new understandings of the nature and functions of Confucianism, efforts have also been made to rejuvenate and rehabilitate Confucian institutions, and interests in the Confucian education system, including its examinations and academies, are on the increase. For example, after the interval of more than half a century, the traditional civil service examination, which bears the hallmark of Confucianism and which was "adopted by Western nations in the 19th and 20th centuries," has partly been adopted as a modern means to recruit civil servants in Mainland China. Confucian academies (*shu yuan*) are no longer regarded as "feudal institutes" but praised as centres of learning and education, as indicated clearly in the celebration of the 1,000th anniversary of Hunan University in 1996, during which a modern university seems to have been deemed a legitimate successor of the famous Neo-Confucian Academy, Yuelu Shuyuan. In some Chinese communities in Hong Kong, Taiwan and South East Asia, a variety of Confucian organisations have been established aiming at restoring the religious functions of Confucianism. For example, the Confucian Academy of Hong Kong (*Kongjiao Xueyuan*) and its three affiliated schools list the following four objectives in their constitution: (1) to strive for the Government's recognition of Confucianism as a religion; (2) to strive for designating Confucius' birthday as a national holiday; (3) to incorporate Confucian doctrines into the curricula of primary, secondary and tertiary education institutions; and (4) to encourage the establishment of Confucius Temples or Confucian Youth Centres in cities and towns far and wide across the country.

These may not be enough for Confucianism to reclaim the glorious image of its past. However, nobody would deny that it has become gradually relevant again to today's social/personal and religious life. There are obvious signs indicating that aspects of the Confucian ethics are still useful and valuable, that the uniqueness of Confucian religiosity is being recognised as an important dimension of human spirituality, and that the Confucian speculation on metaphysical views is considered conducive to the healthy growth of the global village. If in the past it was true that an understanding of the Chinese and East Asian peoples and their societies was impossible without an appreciation of Confucianism, then it has now become true that a picture of China and East Asia which takes no account of Confucianism is partial and superficial. It is against this background that Bak argues that "Confucianism still continues to exert a die-hard influence and it is concluded that without sufficient knowledge of Korean Confucianism it is difficult to predict what the future of Korean thought might be."

Confucianism thus revived does not exist as an isolated tradition behind the process of East Asian modernisation. It is essentially a moderation of the disagreement between Confucian traditionalism and moralism on the one side, and western democracy, capitalism and individualism on the other. New Confucianism is not a wholesale revival of the tradition, but as a transformed doctrine provides useful elements for modern society. New Confucian values are really "post-Confucian" values, as they have been transformed into modern values. The deep concern with human nature and destiny is what new Confucianism accounts for. It is in this sense that Japanese Confucian scholar Okada Takehiko even said that "We don't really need to have Confucianism as Confucianism in the future. All we need is the respect for human life and human dignity . . . thus one's focus must remain upon the issue of respect for human life and human dignity, not the name of the tradition."

To the question of what key element makes Confucianism relevant to modern life and modern society, some people single out Confucian clanism (*jiazu zhuyi*) as the sole reason for its modern relevance. It is indeed that Confucian clanism is culturally and psychologically very important for an East Asian society. Family values are indeed important for the stability and continuity of a modern society, and it has been observed that "In the post-Confucian states, family continues to serve as a vital institution for social cohesiveness, moral education, spiritual growth and, not infrequently, capital formation." However, there are also arguments opposing any identification of the Confucian modern value with traditional clanism. At least three reasons have been put forward with regard to why clanism cannot be the key for the Confucian relevance to the twenty-first century. Firstly, clan structure in East Asia is going through rapid changes, and traditional family relations as defined by Confucian legal and moral codes have fallen short of the requirements of mobility, flexibility, equality, and democracy that characterise a modern society. Confucianism in conjunction with clanism contributes to a social fabric in which personal connections rather than codes of public conduct are of importance, and that is against the fundamental principles of modernity. Secondly, traditional clanism has brought about too many negative by-products. It is argued that the core of traditional family ethics hinders the implementation of market economy and economic reform, because it would generate a modern version of the old customs including the precedence of seniority, favouritism, hierarchy, patriarchal attitudes, and sheer moralism, which slow down, if not stop, the process of modernisation. Thirdly, while family values are the driving force behind the emerging East Asian economies, "family businesses" are facing serious challenges from international market economies and competition. What Kim has examined in Korea where business is run in kinship networks and what Yamamoto has observed in Japan where the familistic link is seen as part of the "Spirit of Japanese Capitalism" have been refuted by recent evidence that traditional family businesses are becoming more a problem than an advantage for East Asian economies. East Asia is being forced to give up its economic pattern based on traditional clan structure.

What makes Confucianism a living tradition for the twenty-first century cannot be any fixed pattern of family, social and political life but rather its moral and spiritual values. Among these values, three are especially of significance for the Confucian future: its concern about moral responsibilities, its emphasis on the importance of transmission of values, and its humanistic understanding of life. It is believed that these three values are the most important elements for Confucian relevance to the future, because they will make a significant contribution to an ethic of responsibility, give a new momentum to the establishment of a comprehensive education system, and help people in their search for ultimate meaning in a temporary life.

STUDY QUESTIONS

1. Who is Master K'ung?
2. What is *qi*?
3. What is yin? What is yang?
4. What is *li*? What is *ren*?
5. What was Confucius' main aim in teaching his views?
6. What cosmology does Confucianism assume?
7. What is Confucius' idea of true nobility?
8. How is Confucianism relevant to contemporary life?
9. What is filial piety?
10. What are the two main parts of the Confucian canon?

FURTHER READING

Julia Ching, *Chinese Religions* (Maryknoll, NY: Orbis Books, 1993).

H. G. Creel, *Confucius and the Chinese Way* (New York: Harper Torchbooks, 1960).

W. T. De Bary, *Sources of Chinese Tradition*, 2 vols. (New York: Columbia University Press, 2001, 2002).

Herbert Fingarette, *Confucianism: The Secular as Sacred* (Prospect Heights, IL: Waveland Press, 1972).

Daniel K. Gardner, trans., *The Four Books* (Indianapolis: Hackett, 2007).

John B. Noss, *A History of the World's Religions* (New York: Macmillan, 1994).

Jennifer Oldstone-Moore, *Confucianism: Origins, Beliefs, Practices, Holy Texts, and Sacred Places* (New York: Oxford University Press, 2002).

Edward Slingerland, trans., *Confucius Analects* (New York: Hackett, 2003).

Anna Sun, *Confucianism as a World Religion* (Princeton, NJ: Princeton University Press, 2013).

Xinzhong Yao, *An Introduction to Confucianism* (Cambridge: Cambridge University Press, 2000).

ONLINE

The New Yorker, "Confucius Comes Home," http://www.newyorker.com/magazine/2014/01/13/confucius-comes-home (December 23, 2015).

Internet Encyclopedia of Philosophy, "Confucianism," https://en.wikipedia.org/wiki/Confucianism (December 23, 2015).

8 Daoism

For two thousand years *Daoism* (or *Taoism*) has been molding Chinese culture and changing the character of religions in the East. It has both philosophical and religious sides, and each of these has many permutations. It gets its name from the impossible-to-define notion of **Dao**, which has been translated as "the Way" or "the Way of Nature."

Laozi (Lao-tzu) is the supposed author of the classical Daoist text that bears his name (also called the *Daodejing, Classic of the Way and Its Power*), destined to become, along with Confucius' *Analects*, one of the two most respected books in Chinese writings. Scholars are unsure whether Laozi (which means "Old Master") is an historical figure or a product of legend, but most agree that if Laozi was real, he probably lived in the sixth century BCE and may have been a contemporary of Confucius. The second most important text in philosophical Daoism is the *Zhuangzi* (*Chuang Tzu*), also named after its presumed author. Regardless of their authorship, these two books laid the groundwork for a Daoist religious and philosophical tradition that influenced Chinese thinkers and nobles and shaped the worldviews of the Chinese right up to the present.

TEACHINGS

The Dao is the mysterious first principle of the universe: it is the eternal source of all that is real and the invisible process and underpinning of the world. It is the Way—the impersonal power that gives order and stability to the cosmos. Like the force of gravity, the Dao holds everything together, gives shape and structure to what is, and determines the way that everything must go. The *Zhuangzi* characterizes the Dao as literally everything—it is the whole of all that exists, and we are of this whole. The *Zhuangzi* asserts,

> In the universe, all things are one. For him who can but realize his indissoluble unity with the whole, the parts of his body mean no more than so much dust and dirt, and death and life, end and beginning, are no more to him than the succession of day and night. They are powerless to disturb his tranquility.[1]

When it comes to the concept of the Dao, the West seems to parallel the East. The pre-Socratic Greek philosopher Heraclitus declared that there is a source of all that exists, the fount of rationality, a first principle of the cosmos that he called *logos*. And there are

FIGURE 8.1 Laozi (Lao-tzu) is the supposed author of the classical Daoist text that bears his name. Here Laozi is depicted riding on the back of a water buffalo as he retires into the realm of the immortals.

hints of a similar cosmic force elsewhere in Western thought—in Aristotle's Unmoved Mover, for example, and in Christianity's omnipotent God.

If the descriptions of the Dao seem obscure or perplexing, it cannot be otherwise, the Daoist would say. For the Dao is beyond words; it is "nameless" (unnameable) and thus can only be hinted at. As the *Daodejing* says,

> The way that cannot be spoken of
> Is not the constant way;
> The name that can be named
> Is not the constant name.
> The nameless was the beginning of heaven and earth;
> The named was the mother of the myriad creatures. . . .
> There is a thing confusedly formed,
> Born before heaven and earth.
> Silent and void

DAOISM TIMELINE

BCE

c. 563 (or perhaps 566) Birth of the Buddha

551–479 Confucius

Sixth century (?) Laozi; possibly a contemporary of Confucius'

c. 483 Death of the Buddha

c. 391–308 Mencius

c. 286 Zhuangzi dies.

CE

Second century Confucianism becomes a state religion.

Second century Daoism as a religion begins.

200 Buddhism has spread to Nepal, Sri Lanka, and Central Asia.

It stands alone and does not change,
Goes round and does not weary.
It is capable of being the mother of the world.
I know not its name
So I style it "the way."
I give it the makeshift name of "the great."[2]

A fundamental notion in Daoism is that since everything and everyone is subject to the power of the Dao, since nothing can withstand its inexorable flow, the best human life is one lived in harmony with it. To live well is to go with the current of the Dao; to struggle against the stream is to invite discord, strife, and woe. The good Daoist, then, discerns the way of nature, the "grain of the universe," and lets the cosmic order guide his or her life.

Living in harmony with the Dao means realizing the virtue of **wu-wei**—inactive action, or effortless action. This paradoxical attitude does not amount to passivity or apathy. According to some scholars it suggests acting effortlessly without straining or struggling and without feverish obsession with the objects of desire. To others it implies acting naturally, spontaneously, without predetermined ideas of how things should go. Thus the Daoist does not try to take charge of a problem, for that often just makes matters worse. She instead acts instinctively and efficiently, letting the solution unfold naturally, waiting for the right moment, harnessing the flow of the Dao by using the natural momentum in the situation, letting change happen by doing nothing. The Daoist is wise like the fighter who rolls with a punch, using its force to come round and return the blow, expending almost no energy of her own. In either interpretation, the point is not to interfere with nature but to let nature follow its own path.

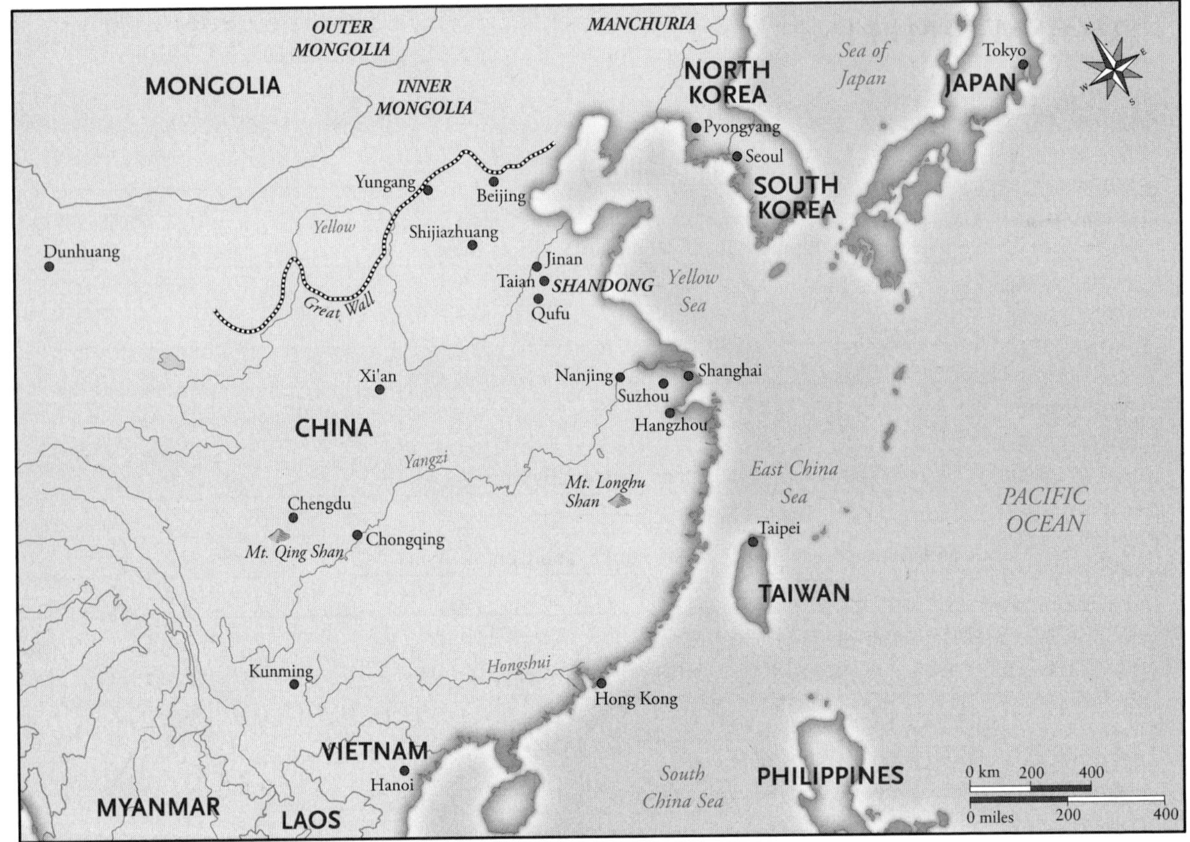

MAP 8.1 Important Confucian and Daoist sites in China.

Daoists differ on exactly what attitudes *wu-wei* implies. To many it suggests a rejection of worldly pleasures or a disregard for society and its conventions and values (like those stressed in Confucianism). The *Daodejing* makes explicit this abhorrence of regimented life:

Exterminate the sage, discard the wise,
And the people will benefit a hundredfold;
Exterminate benevolence, discard rectitude,
And the people will again be filial;
Exterminate ingenuity, discard profit,
And there will be no more thieves and bandits.
These three, being false adornments, are not enough
And the people must have something to which they can attach themselves:
Exhibit the unadorned and embrace the uncarved block,
Have little thought of self and as few desires as possible.[3]

To some Daoists, *wu-wei* implies the opposite: a Daoism consistent with the demands of everyday life and Confucian values.

Laozi says that even in matters of governance, struggle and strain are useless, but *wu-wei* accomplishes much:

Govern the state by being straightforward;
Wage war by being crafty;
But win the empire by not being meddlesome.
How do I know that it is like that?
By means of this.
The more taboos there are in the empire
The poorer the people;
The more sharpened tools the people have
The more benighted the state;
The more skills the people have
The further novelties multiply;
The better known the laws and edicts
The more thieves and robbers there are.
Hence the sage says,
I take no action and the people are transformed of themselves;
I prefer stillness and the people are rectified of themselves;
I am not meddlesome and the people prosper of themselves;
I am free from desire and the people of themselves become simple like the uncarved block.[4]

In the *Daodejing*, *wu-wei* seems to imply a nearly invisible, hands-off, small-scale government. The job of the wise ruler is to shield the people from excessive regulation, overbearing laws and decrees, and unsettling ideas. Such policies may bring people closer to the natural order, but they have also been criticized as a recipe for despotism.

A CLOSER LOOK

Is Humankind One with the Universe?

Some commentators have pointed out that Daoism and Western religions are worlds apart in their views on the relationship between humans and nature. This is how one scholar makes this point:

> In the Western intellectual tradition it has commonly been taken for granted that man's mind, or his essential nature, enjoys a special and rather intimate relationship with the essential nature of the universe. For Judaism and Christianity the basis for this is laid in the first chapter of Genesis, which says both that God created man in his own image and that God created the heaven and the earth. In Greek thought, at least as it is represented by Plato, while the basis may be different the conviction that man stands in a special position with regard to the universe is no less strong.
>
> In philosophic Taoism [Daoism], on the other hand, as we see it especially in the *Chuang-tzu* [*Zhuangzi*], there is no special relationship between man, or man's mind, and the nature of the universe.[5]

In the *Zhuangzi* there is a strong emphasis on mystically uniting with the Dao. The process involves seeing that there is no gap between yourself and nature and transcending all conceptual distinctions and contrasts of the mind. Such divisions are impediments to becoming one with the Dao. Thus the Dao cannot be known through rational thought; it must be grasped by nonrational means, through a mystical experience.

PRACTICES

Religious Daoism developed alongside philosophical Daoism, and the two have often been intertwined while fostering their own distinct schools and teachings. (Daoism now boasts of over eighty prominent movements.) The main interest of religious Daoism has been to align the practitioner ever closer to the Dao and to achieve immortality, either spiritual or physical. To this end, a host of diverse practices have been adopted, including diet and exercises, offerings to deities, the drinking of chemical elixirs to restore energy, breathing techniques to focus cosmic *qi* energy, "sexual hygiene" (sex plus yoga) to capture and use the body's power, rituals and liturgical acts for renewal and salvation, exorcism rituals, yoga and meditation for balancing the body's yin and yang ("inner alchemy"), the burning of incense and sacred writings, examination of the morality of behavior, and celebrations and rituals throughout the lunar year.

FIGURE 8.2 **In Bodgahya, India, a monk meditates under a *bodhi* tree, the same kind of tree under which the Buddha is said to have meditated and found enlightenment.**

BACKGROUND

Daoist Meditation

Daoists use three different kinds of meditation, usually together. Livia Kohn explains:

> The three forms [of meditation] are concentrative meditation, insight meditation, and ecstatic excursions. . . . Concentration comes first. It is a basic exercise in fixation of mind, the focusing of attention on one single spot, the cultivation of one-pointedness. The classical expression is "guarding the One." Besides simply "to concentrate," this also means to secure the presence of the gods within the body. Just as concentration in meditation practice in general is the foundation for contemplation or higher spiritual exercises, so the rooting of the gods in Taoism [Daoism] leads to insight and ecstatic journeys to the otherworld.
>
> Insight is a concept borrowed from Buddhism and coupled closely with the notion of mindfulness. Here the attention is not fixed in one single spot but kept moving, either within the body or in the outside world. Practitioners notice, literally "observe," self and others and evaluate them in a particular new way, applying the worldview of the Tao [Dao] to their lives and being. They gain new insights by adapting their conscious understanding of all to the point of view of the Tao [Dao].
>
> Ecstatic excursions are travels to the realms of the otherworld that go back originally to the journeys of shamans. Leaving the physical body behind, the soul of the meditator surges up and beyond, meeting divine powers and spirits of the stars.[6]

Among the latter is the communal ceremony known as the **jiao**. It is a community-wide, multiday liturgy conducted by Daoist priests to implore the gods to bless everyone with health and good fortune. The intent is serious, but the atmosphere is festive and raucous, much like a carnival in the West.

Religious Daoism also includes the worship or petition of deities and super-beings. As one scholar notes,

> Daoism evolved a pantheon of innumerable spiritual beings, gods, or celestials and immortals, as well as deified heroes and forces of nature. Together, they make up a divine hierarchy, resembling a state bureaucracy. The hierarchy includes mythical figures, as well as many who were divinized human beings, under the supremacy of the highest deity. During the second century BCE, this was the Taiyi ("Great One").[7]

THE DAOIST CANON

The Daoist body of scriptures, known as the *Daozang*, is immense, consisting of 1,120 volumes added over fifteen hundred years and revered by multiple Daoist traditions. For the most part, its authority rests on its putative source—sacred knowledge revealed to adepts in trance or mystical states. It may be the largest—certainly one of the largest—compilations of scripture in existence.

The *Daozang*'s books have been sorted into three main divisions known as the *Three Caverns*: (1) the *Cavern of Perfection*, (2) the *Cavern of Mystery*, and (3) the *Cavern of Spirit*. To these three, four supplements are attached. One consists of scripture grounded in the *Daodejing*; another is the notable text the *Classic of the Great Peace*; a third is a discourse on alchemy; and the fourth comprises the scriptures of the Heavenly Masters tradition.

Each Cavern covers a host of diverse topics expressed through many genres: commentaries, moral codes, hymns, histories, genealogies, revelations, instructions for conducting rituals, discussions of sacred talismans, biographies of Daoist "saints," and treatises on alchemy, astrology, numerology, and other esoteric lore.

The *Daodejing* is the most respected and influential book in the Daoist canon, regarded as the founding scripture of Daoism and thought to be the handiwork of several authors and compilers. In Confucian metaphysics, *Tian* is the foremost power and organizing principle in the universe, but in the *Daodejing* the Dao is the primal, unproduced substance from which everything—even *Tian*—comes.

The *Daodejing* is short and epigrammatic (some would say *cryptic*) and divided into two books, together containing eighty-one chapters or sections. It is the most commonly translated text in Chinese and the most famous Chinese work in the West. The *Daodejing* is the reason a few dozen books in English begin their titles with "The Dao (or Tao) of . . ." (as in *The Tao of Physics*).

The other supremely important book, second only to the *Daodejing*, is the *Zhuangzi*. It comprises thirty-three chapters, the first seven of which are alleged to be the work of Zhuangzi himself. Whereas the *Daodejing* is aphoristic, the *Zhuangzi* is anecdotal and allegorical. Unlike the *Daodejing*, it eschews politics, focusing instead on inactive action (*wu-wei*) and meditation. It says that the Dao cannot be grasped through rational processes; only practices that bypass the intellect and grasp the truth intuitively will suffice.

NOTES

1. *Chuang Tzu*, 7. 18b; Welhelm, Dschuang Dsi, 158.
2. *Tao Te Ching*, 1, 25, D. C. Lau, trans. (New York: Penguin Classics, 1963).
3. *Ibid.*, 19.
4. *Ibid.*, 57.
5. Herrlee G. Creel, *What Is Taoism?* (Chicago: University of Chicago Press, 1970), 25.
6. Livia Kohn, trans., *The Taoism Experience: An Anthology* (Albany: State University of New York Press, Albany, 1993), 191.
7. Julia Ching, "East Asian Religions" in *World Religions: Eastern Traditions*, Willard G. Oxtoby, ed. (Oxford: Oxford University Press, 2002).

KEY TERMS

Dao The "Way" in Daoism, the mysterious first principle of the universe, the eternal source of all that is real and the underpinning of the world.

jiao A community-wide liturgy conducted by Daoist priests to implore the gods to bless everyone with health and good fortune.

wu-wei Inactive action, or effortless action.

READINGS

TEACHINGS

Selections from the *Daodejing*

The *Daodejing* is the most revered book of all the Daoist scriptures. Many presume that its author is Laozi, but others say the book actually has several authors. Its central concern is of course the Dao and how to align one's life with it. "Be like heaven and merge with the Dao," it says. "One with the Dao, you will last long."

The Tao [Dao] is empty.
Use it,
It will never overflow;
Abysmal it is—
The ancestor of all beings.

Blunting blades,
Opening knots,
Joining light,
Merging with dust.
Profound it is—
Like something eternal.

I do not know.
Whose child is it?
Its appearance precedes the gods.

Heaven and earth are not benevolent,
They take the myriad beings as mere straw dogs.
The sage is not benevolent,
He takes the hundred families as mere straw
dogs.

The space between heaven and earth,
Isn't it like a bellows?
Empty, yet never bent;
Active, yet reaching ever farther.

Speak much, repeat again—
No, much better to guard it in your midst!

The valley spirit does not die,
It is called the mysterious female.
The gate of the mysterious female
Is called the root of heaven and earth.

Forever and ever, it exists continuously,
Use it. yet you'll never wear it out.
Highest goodness is like water.
It benefits the myriad beings
And never contends.
By never contending
It is without fault.

It rests in what the multitude disdain,
Thus it is close to the Tao.

Daodejing, ch. 4–6, 8, 14, 16, 21, 25, 32, 34, Livia Kohn, trans., *The Taoist Experience: An Anthology* (Albany: State University of New York, Albany, 1993).

Rest in goodness like you stand on the earth,
Make your mind as good as the abyss is deep.
Join goodness to become fully benevolent,
Speak pure goodness for mutual trust.

Be straight in goodness when you govern,
Serve goodness as much as you can,
Then you will move with goodness at all times.

Look at it and do not see it:
We call it invisible.
Listen to it and do not hear it:
We call it inaudible.
Touch it and do not feel it:
We call it subtle.

These three cannot be better understood,
They merge and become one.

Infinite and boundless, it cannot be named.
It belongs to where there are no beings.
It may be called the shape of no-shape,
It may be called the form of no-form.

Call it vague and obscure.
Meet it, yet you cannot see its head,
Fo1low it, yet you cannot see its back.
Grasp the Tao of old and control existence now.
Know the beginnings of old—
And have a thread to the Tao.

Attain utmost emptiness,
Maintain steadfast tranquility.

The myriad beings are alive,
And I see thereby their return.
All these beings flourish,
But each one returns to its root.

Return to the root means tranquility,
It is called recovering life.

To recover life is called the eternal.
To know the eternal is called enlightenment.

If you don't know the eternal,
You will fall into error and end in disaster.

Know the eternal and forgive;
Forgive and be altruistic.
Be altruistic and embrace all;
Embrace all and be like heaven.

Be like heaven and merge with the Tao,
One with the Tao, you will last long.
You may die but will never perish.

Forgiveness of great virtue
Flows from the Tao alone.
The Tao may appear as a being,
Yet is just vague, only obscure.

Obscure it is! It is vague!
In its midst, some appearance.
Vague it is! It is obscure!
In its midst, some being.

Serene it is! It is profound!
In its midst, some essence.
True this essence, nothing but so true!
In its midst, some trust.

From the old to today
Its name never vanished,
To open the beginnings of all.

How do I know what those beginnings
are?
From this alone.

There is a being, in chaos yet complete;
It preceded even heaven and earth.
Silent it is, and solitary;
Standing alone, it never changes;
It moves around, yet never ends.
Consider it the mother of all-under-heaven.

I do not know its name.
To call it something, I speak of Tao.
Naming its strength, I call it great.

Great—that means it departs.
Depart—that means it is far away.
Far away—that means it will return.

Therefore the Tao is great,
Heaven is great,
Earth is great,
The king, too, is great.

In this enclosure, there are these four greats,
And the king rests as one of them.
The king follows earth,
Earth follows heaven,
Heaven follows the Tao.
The Tao follows only itself.

The Tao—eternal, nameless, simple.
Although small,
It is subject to neither heaven nor earth.

Kings and lords maintain it,
And the myriad beings come to them.
Heaven and earth are in harmony,
And sweet dew falls.

People do not order it,
It is everywhere equally.

First you control it, then names appear.
Yet once there are names,
Knowledge must arise of when to stop.
Know when to stop
And you will never perish.

Compare how the Tao is in all-under-heaven
To the converging of rivers and valleys
Toward the great streams and endless oceans.

Great Tao—overflowing!
Can be left and right!

The myriad beings rely on it to be born.
It never turns them away.
Its merit, so perfect—
Yet claims no fame for its existence.

It clothes and nurtures the myriad beings—
Yet claims no position as their chief.
Always free from desires—
Call it small!

The myriad beings return to it—
And yet never make it their chief.
Call it great!

To its very end
It does not think itself great.
Thus
It can perfect its greatness.

Selections from the *Zhuangzi*

This excerpt insists that by grasping the Dao, we can understand events and circumstances and thus know how to deal with them to avoid harm. We can, in other words, correctly apply *wu-wei.*

"The Way is without beginning or end, but things have their life and death—you cannot rely upon their fulfillment. One moment empty, the next moment full—you cannot depend upon their form. The years cannot be held off; time cannot be stopped. Decay, growth, fullness, and emptiness end and then begin again. It is thus that we must describe the plan of the Great Meaning and discuss the principles of the ten thousand things. The life of things is a gallop, a headlong dash—with every movement they alter, with every moment they shift. What should you do and what should you not do? Everything will change of itself, that is certain!"

"If that is so," said the Lord of the River, "then what is there valuable about the Way?"

Jo of the North Sea said, "He who understands the Way is certain to have command of basic principles. He who has command of basic principles is certain to know how to deal with circumstances. And he who knows how to deal with circumstances will not allow things to do him harm. When a man

Zhuangzi, sec. 17, Burton Watson, trans., *Chuang Tzu: Basic Writings* (New York: Columbia University Press, 1964, 1996), 103–104.

has perfect virtue, fire cannot burn him, water cannot drown him, cold and heat cannot afflict him, birds and beasts cannot injure him. I do not say that he makes light of these things. I mean that he distinguishes between safety and danger, contents himself with fortune or misfortune, and is cautious in his comings and goings. Therefore nothing can harm him."

The Dao of Ecology

HUSTON SMITH

Huston Smith calls for a new attitude toward nature that avoids our current view of the world as something separate from us that should be plundered or coldly examined. Daoism provides this new perspective, he says. Through Daoism we necessarily see ourselves and the world as interdependent, complementary, sympathetic, numinous, holistic, and unified.

The Tao cannot be objectively described, then, in the sense of being depicted in a way that is logically consistent and intuitively plausible to all. To assume the contrary would be to continue in the Western objectivist mistake. The only approaches to it are the way of letters and the way of life. The way of letters is the poet's way: by verbal wizardry to trigger an astral projection of our moods and imaginings to another plane. The way of life is different. It requires long years of cultivation, for it requires altering not one's imagination but one's self; transforming one's sentiments, attitudes, and outlook until, a new perceptual instrument having been forged, a new world swings into view.

This world of the accomplished Taoist, of the man whose psychic integration has progressed to the point where not only are his inner forces harmonized but the sum of these are attuned to his enveloping surround—what is this world of the perfected Taoist like?

It is the Realm of the Great Infinite. Here too let us acknowledge that even the accomplished Taoist can have only the slightest sense of what this realm is really like. We approach it as men, with minds and senses that suffice for our needs but fall as far short in their capacity to discern reality's ultimate nature as an amoeba's intelligence founders before Einstein; if physicists like David Bohm and Phillip Morrison can suspect that the levels of size in the universe—transstellar, mega, macro, micro, subquantum—are infinite, a sage may be pardoned his hunch that its value-reaches are comparably beyond our ken. To be in any way manageable our question must be modified to read: What is the profoundest view of the Realm of the Great Infinite available to man?

1. It is a realm of relativity. Perhaps, as Kierkegaard put the matter, existence *is* a system—for God; for man, who is within it, system it can never be. Within it, all is perspectival. The flower, in front of the candle to me, is behind it to my wife. One stone is light compared to a second, heavy compared to a third. The pitch of a locomotive's whistle is constant for the engineer; to a

Huston Smith, "Tao Now" in *Earth Might Be Fair*, Ian G. Barbour, ed. (Englewood Cliffs, NJ: Prentice-Hall, 1972), 74–81.

bystander it falls. Nothing can be absolutely positioned, for we lack the absolute framework such positioning would require. If this is true of perception and thought, it must also hold of course for language. It being impossible to say everything at once, every statement is perforce partial; it is one-sided. But the world itself, being in us and around us, is never one-sided. All this holds, of course, for the present statement. Naturally I shall try to make my account of the Tao as cogent as possible, for if I begin to fail glaringly, I shall myself lose interest as quickly as will you. Still, somewhere in my words there will be a flaw—that's a priori; somewhere in my depiction is a value counterpart of the surd Goedel spotted in mathematics: a point that contradicts something I say elsewhere or collides with a piece of your considered experience. We should not bemoan this buckle in our logic, for it keeps us moving, keeps us from settling down, insists on an extension in our horizons if it is to be smoothed out. If it doesn't show itself today, it will tomorrow.

2. It is a realm of interpenetration and interdependence. It is not one in a simple sense that excludes distinctions and could be visualized as the clear light of the void, a sky unflecked with clouds, or the sea without a wave. Distinctions abound, but the domains they establish cohere. "Heaven and Earth and I live together, and therein all things and I are one" (Chuang Tzu).

> Thirty spokes joined at the hub.
> From their non-being [i.e., the point at which their distinctnesses disappear in the hub itself]
> Comes the function of the wheel (Lao Tzu).

Multiplicity is itself a unity. As nothing exists by itself, all things being in fact interdependent, no phenomenon can be understood by divorcing it from its surround. Indeed, it is the underlying unity that provides the possibility *for* distinctions. Thus even parts that appear discordant unite at some level to form a whole: "Tweedledum and Tweedledee / *Agreed* to have a battle." Or like elderly chess players who, having done their utmost to vanquish each other, at game's end push back the board, light up cigarettes, and review the moves as friends. Being is organic. Peculiarities dissolve, parts fuse into other parts. Each individual melds into other individuals and through this melding makes its contribution, leaves its mark.

This complementary interpenetration is symbolized in many ways in China. One of the best-known ways is the *yin-yang*, a circle divided into black and white halves, not by a straight line but by one that meanders, leading white into black domain and allowing black to lap back into the white. Moreover, a white dot stakes its claim in the deepest recesses of black, while a black dot does likewise in the central citadel of the white. All things do indeed carry within themselves the seeds of their own antitheses. And the opposites are bonded; banded together by the encompassing circle that locks both black and white in inseparable embrace.

On a two-dimensional surface, no symbol can rival the yang-yin in depicting the Great Infinite's complementing interpenetration, but because it remains to the end two-dimensional, it needs supplementing. Our two cats when they sleep lapped over one another are a three-dimensional yin-yang, and indeed when they fight they form a four-dimensional one. But man needs to feel the play of these forces in himself kinesthetically, not just observe them in others. So the Chinese created *Tai Chi*, the Great Polarity, a discipline that cuts right across our disparate categories of calisthenics, dance, martial arts, and meditation. In lieu of a film strip I insert here some notes I once jotted down at a Tai Chi class:

> Everything a little curved; nothing extended or pushed to the limit. Expansive gestures (out and up) are yang, ingathering gestures (down and in) are yin. No side of the body exclusively one or the other. Yang dissolves at once into yin, yin gathers strength to become yang. Down becomes up, up down. All is lightness and freedom. As soon as it's done, stop; no sooner heavy than grows light. Strong, then immediately release. Energy reserved, highly volatile, capable of being deployed in any direction, at any point. So finely balanced that a fly cannot alight nor feather be added.

Apocryphal like all such stories, yet making its point, is the account of the great master, Yang Chien Ho. Birds were unable to take off from his palm because as their feet pushed down to spring, his hand dropped concomitantly. Drawing a cocoon thread is another image; if there is no pressure the thread isn't drawn, but the instant there is too much the thread snaps.

3. Viewed extrovertively, under the aspect of yang, the interrelatedness of existence shows forth as the Great Creativity. From a single primordial atom the entire universe derives: galaxies, nebulae, island universes, pushing forward faster and faster. Potentiality explodes into actuality, infinitely. Every possibility must be exploited, each nook and cranny filled. Thereby diversity is accomplished. When attention shifts from this multiplicity to its relatedness, the Great Sympathy comes into view. As sympathy, Tao synthesizes; as creativity it proliferates. The two movements complement; creativity flows from one to all, sympathy from all to one. Without sympathy multiplicity would be chaos, whereas without creativity sympathy would lack province. They proceed together, hand in hand, partners in the Tao's sublime ecology. Chuang Tzu's illustration, characteristically homey, is the centipede. At the points at which they touch the earth its legs are a hundred or so, but on a higher level such orchestration! It is through the many that the one enacts its versatility.

Perceived thus in the context of the Tao, nature to the Chinese was no disenchanted causal mechanism floating on the foundation of nothingness. It was undergirded by an eternal numinous reality from which life proceeds and which inclines it towards harmony. Underlying the visible—our phenomenal world, the "realm of the ten thousand things"—is something of immense importance that is invisible. The essential relation between the two is nonduality. Life's dependability, mingling with nature's, betokens a hidden oneness in the bosom of the multiple, a total interdependence at the heart of the spheres. A rhythm falls upon the visible, breaking it into day and night, summer and winter, male and female, but these divisions are caught up and ordered in a superior integration that resolves the tensions and reconciles the irreconcilable. Heaven and earth agree. They are united in a hymn for a double choir, an antiphony on a cosmic scale. It is a concentric vision, the vision of society set like a stone in nature, and nature set similarly in the deep repose of eternity.

V. THE LADDER OF ASCENT

To experience reality as just described results in sensing a friendly continuity between one's own life and the Tao, and a willingness to blend with its ways. There comes also a shift toward *yes* and away from *no* where the claims of the nonego are concerned and a consequent freedom and elation as the boundaries of confining selfhood melt down. A generalized sense of life's enlargement and well-being commences. How to get into this state—the question of method—lies outside the scope of this paper, but I will note five stages through which the aspirant is said to pass.

1. He begins with the world as it appears to men generally, composed of discrete and apparently self-subsisting entities that are related only in such ways as empirical observation discloses.

2. The second stage involves a dramatic awakening in which the world's undifferentiated aspect is realized. This is the world known to mystics and a good many artists. Individual selfhood vanishes; one becomes merged with the Great Self, Emptiness, or the Void.

3. But we live in the everyday world, the world of relativity and separate things. So the next step is to realize that noumena and phenomena, the relative and absolute worlds of stages one and two respectively, are but two aspects of one reality. With feet planted in the absolute the aspirant is directed to look anew at the relative world that he previously took to be the only world. He must come to see that the phenomenal is in truth but the aspect under which the noumenon is perceived. Absolute and relative completely interpenetrate without obstruction or hindrance. They are one and the same thing. With this realization the aspirant discovers that everything in the world about him, every tree and rock, every hill and star, every bit of dust and dirt, as well as every insect, plant, and animal, himself included, are manifestations of the Tao and their movements are functionings of the Tao. Everything, just as it is, is in essence holy.

4. But more lies ahead. One must come to see that the things that have already come to be recognized as manifestations of the Tao together form one

complete and total whole by means of harmonious and unobstructed penetration, interconvertibility, and identification with each other. Everything in the universe is realized to be constantly and continuously, freely and harmoniously interpenetrating, interconverting itself with every other thing. A favorite symbol here is Indra's net, each intersection of which lodges a jewel that reflects all the other jewels in the net together with the reflections each of them contained. The problem with this symbol is the same as that which we encountered in connection with the yin-yang, a net, too, is static, whereas the point is to grasp dynamically the Tao whose nature is always to move on. This requires that the grasper himself be forever in the mood of moving, this being the character of life itself. Taoist terms are, for the most part, dynamic rather than static, terms like "entering-into" and "being-taken-in," or "taking-in," "embracing-and-pervading," and "simultaneous-unimpeded-diffusion."

5. Finally, and characteristically Chinese, there is "the return to the natural." Having come to recognize every element in the world and every act as holy and indispensable to the total universe, as this realization deepens and grows increasingly profound, it is no longer necessary to think explicitly about such things. It is enough for things to be affirmed in their own right; each moment can be responded to naturally and spontaneously as sufficient in itself. It is in this culminating state that one realizes with Master Nansen that "the everyday mind is Tao." Trudging through the snow a master and disciple were surprised by a rabbit that sprang out of nowhere and bounded across their path. "What would you say of that?" the master asked. "It was like a god!" the disciple answered. As the master seemed unimpressed with the answer, the disciple returned the question: "Well, what would you say it was?" "It was a rabbit!"

VI. QUIETISM: THE TEST OF THE THEORY

Every position has its problematic, a shoal that, navigated or foundered upon, determines whether the system stands or falls. For Taoism the danger is quietism, the reading of its pivotal *wu wei* (no action) doctrine as admonishing us to do as little as possible or in any case nothing contrary to natural impulse. If everything is an aspect of Tao and thereby holy exactly as it is, why change it? Or to put the question another way: Since, although the Tao's parts are always in flux, its balance of forces is constant, why try to shift its parts from one place to another?

The path that winds past this precipice is a narrow one, and time and again China fell off it. Indeed, one can read the entire history of philosophical Taoism, as well as Buddhism in its Taoist variant (Ch'an), as one long struggle to keep from reading Chuang Tzu's "Do nothing, and everything will be done" as counselling sloth and rationalizing privilege. What other reading is possible? If the answer is "none," the jig's up. If Taoism ends up admonishing us to lounge around while tsetse flies bite us, to sink back in our professional settees, handsomely upholstered by endowments amassed from exorbitant rents in ghetto slums; if Taoism suggests that we rest on our oars while our nation mashes peasant countrysides in Southeast Asia, the sooner it is forgotten the better.

The doctrine cannot be stated to preclude such misreading, but the misreading itself can, with care, be avoided. Helpful to doing so is the realization that Taoist assertions are made from the far side of the self/other divide, being in this respect the Orient's equivalent of "Love God and do what you please." *Wu wei* can be read unequivocally only after one has attained Tao-identification. At that point one will continue to act—the Tao, we recall, is never static; to be in it is to be always in the mood of moving—but the far shore attained, one need do nothing save what comes naturally, for what needs doing will claim one's will directly. Unobscured by attachment to one's own perquisites, the suffering of the dispossessed will draw one spontaneously to their side. Until that point is reached there must be labors that are not wholly spontaneous as we try to act our way into right thinking while concomitantly thinking our way into right action.

The Tao is not unilateral yin. Sensing that even in China when the Tao hits man's mind it tends to enter a yang phase, Taoism sought to redress the balance, but the balance itself was its true concern. "Now yin, now yang: that is the Tao" (*The Great Commentary*).

The formulation is exact; countering man's disposition to put yang first, Taoism throws its ounces on the side of yin, but to recover the original wholeness. That emphasis is what we need as well. "Heroic materialism" is the phrase Kenneth Clark used on the concluding program of his *Civilization* series to characterize our Western achievement; pointing to the Manhattan skyline he noted that it had been thrown up in a century, about a third of the time it took the Middle Ages to build a cathedral. With an impunity Asia would not have believed possible, we have indulged ourselves in a yang trip the likes of which was never before essayed. And we are still here; we haven't capsized. But if we have arrived at a point where taste as well as prudence counsels a redressing, the Tao stands waiting in the wings with "now yin" as its first suggestion. It doesn't ask us to dismantle our machines; civilization needn't be deyanged. Its call is simply to open the sluice gates of our Great Sympathy to let it catch up with our Great Creativity. The virtues of mastery and control we have developed to near perfection, but life can't proceed on their terms alone.

To enter a friendship, to say nothing of marriage, with an eye to control is to sully the relationship from the start. Complementing the capacity to control is the capacity to surrender—to others in love and friendship, to duty in conscience, to life itself in some sustaining way. The same holds for possessions and complexity; we know well the rewards that they can bestow, while knowing less well the complementing rewards that derive from simplicity. When a Western musicologist was seeking help in deciphering the score of certain Tibetan chants, he was informed by the Karmapa that they "could only be understood by a perfect being, there being so much to hear in a single note." And fronting Eiheiji is Half-Dipper bridge, so-called because whenever Dogen dipped water from the river he used only half a dipperful, returning the rest to the river. Such sayings and behavior are difficult for us to understand; they tend to be beyond our comprehension. But if we were to feel the beauty of the river and a oneness with the water, might we not feel its claims on us and do as Dogen did? It is our own true nature, our natural "uncarved block" as the Taoist would say, to do so.

Simplicity and surrender can appear as high-ranking values only in a world one trusts and to which one feels at deepest level attuned. If the Taoist approach to nature was not based on reasoned strategy and well-planned attack, it was because such stratagems appeared unneeded. Western civilization has tended to regard the world either as mystery to be entered through religious initiation or as antagonist to be opposed with technological adroitness or stoical courage. Greek tragedy and philosophy set the tone for this; modern science and technology have amplified it a hundredfold. Western man has been at heart Promethean; therein lie both his greatness and his absurdity. Taoism does not try to beat or cajole the universe or the gods; it tries to join them. The Western stoic tries this tack too, but from the premise of antagonistic wills to be reconciled by obedience or overcome by dogged refusal. To Asia the problem is a matter of ignorance and enlightenment. If seventeenth-to-nineteenth-century science saw the world as mechanism and twentieth-century science is seeing it (with its holism, reciprocity, and growth) as resembling more an organism, is it possible that the twenty-first century will see it as—what? Is the savingly indefinite word "spirit" appropriate? "If I could say impersonal person, it would be that" (Sokei-an).

> There is a being, wonderful, perfect;
> It existed before heaven and earth.
> How quiet it is!
> How spiritual it is!
> It stands alone and it does not change.
> It moves around and around, but does not on this account suffer.
> All life comes from it.
> It wraps everything with its love as in a garment, and yet it claims no honor, it does not demand to be Lord.
> I do not know its name, and so I call it Tao, the Way, and I rejoice in its power.

PRACTICES

T'ai Chi

AL CHUNG-LIANG HUANG

T'ai chi is an ancient discipline that reflects Daoist beliefs in cosmic order and energy. Daoists and non-Daoists say they practice it for physical health, stress reduction, longevity, mental discipline, and spiritual well-being. The slow, fluid movements are meant to increase and balance the flow of ch'i energy throughout the body. Here is a t'ai chi master explaining t'ai chi theory and practice.

In this culture, we rely so much on the mind that we become separated from other aspects of our living. An exercise, a discipline like t'ai chi immediately points out where you lack, where you go astray. Why do you find something that is so easy to understand intellectually, so difficult to do? This division between thinking and doing is so clear; it takes so long to really find that yin/yang balance.

The yin/yang symbol is the interlocking, melting together of the flow of movement within a circle. The similar—and at the same time obviously contrasting—energies are moving *together.* Within the black area there is a white dot and within the white fish shape, there is a black dot. The whole idea of a circle divided in this way is to show that within a unity there is duality and polarity and contrast. The only way to find real balance without losing the centering feeling of the circle is to think of the contrasting energies moving together and in union, in harmony, interlocking. In a sense this is really like a white fish and a black fish mating. It's a union and flowing interaction. It's a kind of consummation between two forces, male and female, mind and body, good and bad. It's a very important way of living. People identify with this kind of concept in the Orient much more than in our Western culture, where the tendency is to identify with one force and to reject the contrasting element. If you identify with only one side of the duality, then you become unbalanced. T'ai chi can help you to realize how you are unbalanced and help you to become centered again as you reestablish a flow between the two sides. So don't get stuck in a corner, because a circle has no corners. If you think in this way, you open up more, and you don't feel like you have to catch up with anything.

Someone said that the difference between an Oriental man and a Western man is this: The Oriental man is very empty and light up here in the head and very heavy down here in the belly and he feels very secure. The Western man is light in the belly and very heavy up here in the head, so he topples over. In our Western society so much is in the head, so much is in talking and thinking about things, that we can analyze everything to pieces and it's still distant from us, still not really understood. We have so many mechanical gadgets to do our work for us that our

Al Chung-liang Huang, *Embrace Tiger, Return to Mountain* (Moab, UT: Real People Press, 1973), 12–13, 19, 183–185.

bodies are underemphasized. In order to regain balance we have to emphasize the body and we must work with the mind-body together.

Some people realize that their bodies need more work, so they run, jog, ride bicycles, swim, and then say "O.K. I have done my share of exercise." But this is still a separation of "body time" and "mind time," like the separation of work and play that most people experience. You work very hard so that you can take a vacation and come to a beautiful place to enjoy yourself. This brings a separation in your life. Working shouldn't be such a chore. Playing shouldn't be such a straining for fun, fun, fun. Work and play can combine. Nonverbal activities are a very important way to regain balance and find unity in your life. When you stop talking you have a chance to open up and become receptive to what is happening in your body and to what is going on around you.

T'ai chi is one of the many ways to help you to discipline your body and find a way to release that tension within you. T'ai chi can be a way of letting your body really teach you and be with you and help you to get through the conflicts you encounter every day. . . .

This is why in t'ai chi practice we do not count: We work on a continuous flow. This is another aspect of t'ai chi, which ties in exactly with the *I Ching* [*Yi Jing*], the *Book of Changes*. Change is yin and constant is yang, or vice versa. So the constant thing is that we all can fit into the changing rise and fall. The change is constant; the constant is change. In movement, we learn to really understand this intellectual concept. Part of our everyday conflict is how to cope with the changes and how to be happy with the constant. We are usually bored with the constant, and we get frantic with the change. We have all kinds of gimmicks: "Meditate!" "Pull yourself together!" "Relax!" "Do therapy!" But these all boil down to one thing: Accept *both* the constant and the change. Learn how to be resilient and responsive to your surroundings, to time, and to yourself.

In t'ai chi practice, you move very slowly. By moving very slowly you have time to be aware of all the subtle details of your movement and your relationship to your surroundings. It's so slow that you really have no way of saying this is slower than that or faster than that. You reach a level of speed that is like slow motion, in which everything is just happening. You slow it to the point that you are fully involved in the process of each moment as it happens. You transcend the form and any concern you might have to achieve some particular motif. . . .

Pay attention to the circular movement of your breathing. Allow the breathing pattern to really circulate inside of you, inside of your torso. Let it flow into your arms, up to your neck, to the top of your head, and down the backbone into your legs. Then energy can begin to expand to all directions at once. Feel all the energy from outside coming towards you, and your energy reaching out as your arms begin to lift. The rising of your arms is balanced by a sinking into your base, as the energy of the circle expands. Think of an expansion instead of a cut-and-dried hand-lift and knee-bend. Try this first movement several times. Think of that expansion into all directions from the center of your body and then the coming together, the collecting back to straight upright center support. Let that feeling of energy open you out into a curving yin/yang intertwining up/down flow as you expand in your arms and settle into your base. Then the outward energy curves and turns inward as your arms sink and your pelvis rises and you return to center. This energy must be a part of you; you must never move as an objective outsider observing. You must always be inside of it, with it. This is the only way you can do t'ai chi.

When you prepare for the beginning of your t'ai chi, you first allow your stance to become uneven until it begins to settle into evenness. Then you begin to sense the space all around you, including the space that's beyond the floor. This way you will feel that you are suspended in the middle of a sphere of energy. As you move, you play with this energy that comes from all sides. You play with the horizontal curve, the vertical curve, the slanting curve, the curve beneath you and above you—all over, all around.

In China you would have to practice this beginning movement for many months before the master would allow you to do anything else. There is a good reason for this. In the beginning you are fragmented. You think about your wrist, or maybe your elbow; you think of the knee and then you think of the spine. You do serial things, because your experience is still in bits and pieces. When you really get a sense of doing this movement, it all happens simultaneously. You sense all events, all the directions, all the energies going, without having to consciously direct your attention to your wrist or elbow or shoulder. It all happens together: a sense of time, personal connection—one on-going, flowing, immediate sequential flash.

So when you practice t'ai chi in the morning, just do this first movement for a while. It's *plenty* to work on. You only get bored if you focus on the outside, the peripheral, instead of the inside, the essential. If I put it very simply t'ai chi is this one movement—that's all.

Now, let t'ai chi happen and let the essence take over. Embrace Tiger, Return to Mountain: The first and the last and all major variations of this one movement will develop slowly like waves moving in and rolling out. Recall the different ways you have been practicing breathing with this circular motif. Reach outward to embrace all the energy around you. Your arms gather in, cross, and lift up to about chest level, and then you relax your elbows and let your hands revolve. Then gently push all this energy down into your tant'ien—Return to Mountain. Let your arms return to rest at your sides as all this energy settles and simmers down. Keep flowing through. Remember the sensation of the stone falling into water, with your elbows drooping and pulling down. Your chest feels hollow, the tongue is loose, touching the palate gently; the breathing passages are open. Just keep feeling the energy moving within your stillness.

The change of energy curves, the level curves. There is no stopping and beginning; it's ongoing. You are very steady. You feel very constant and very still as you move, and you feel the motion within your stillness. Movement and stillness become one. One is not a static point. One is a moving one, one is a changing one, one is everything. One is all the movement you can possibly do with the human body. One is also that stillness suspended, flowing, settling, in motion. You do not stand still now in contrast to your moving around. All the energy that you can possibly use in the whole spectrum of your expression is settling, contained within this form of t'ai chi. It is not a confinement or elimination of the rest of your energy levels and your energy varieties, but they must be connected to become this one feeling.

Wherever you are, whatever you do, you can always come back to this marvelous sense of stillness, the feeling of yourself, very, very much *here*. This is your reference point; this is your stability. This is your life force that gives you balance. This is your home you carry around with you wherever you are. This is your powerhouse, your reservoir, your endless inexhaustible resource, that center you that is teaching and sharing and working with all of us these past few days. And the movement goes on and on and on.

Quiet Sitting with Master Yinshi

JIANG WEIQIAO

Breathing exercises have been used in China for hundreds of years, and they are still common practice in contemporary Daoism. Practitioners do them to try to achieve health, longevity, and spiritual awareness. Here is a set of breathing instructions compiled from ancient sources and updated in the early twentieth century by Jiang Weiqiao (Master Yinshi).

Livia Kohn, trans., "Quiet Sitting with Master Yinshi," in *The Taoist Experience* (Albany: State University of New York Press, 1993), 136–141.

Breathing is one of the most essential necessities of human life, even more so than food and drink. Ordinary people are quite familiar with the idea that food and drink are important to maintain life, that they will starve if left without it for a while. But they hardly ever turn around to think about the importance of breathing and that air is even more essential to life than anything else.

This has to do with the fact that in order to obtain food and drink people have to go to work and earn money, so they come to value these things as important commodities. Breathing, on the other hand, is done by taking in the air of the atmosphere of which there is no limit and which cannot be exhausted. There is no need to labor and pay for the air we breathe; thus people tend to overlook the importance of this function.

Yet if you stop eating and drinking, you may still survive for a couple of days, even as long as a whole week. However, if you stop up your nostrils and mouth you will be dead within minutes. This fact alone shows that breathing is far more important than food.

In discussing methods of breathing, two main types can be distinguished: natural breathing and regulated breathing.

NATURAL BREATHING

One exhalation and one inhalation are called one breath. The respiratory organs in the body are the nose on the outside and the lungs on the inside. The two wings of the lungs are positioned within the upper torso so that through the motion of the respiration the entire area expands and contracts. Such is the law of nature. However, in ordinary people, the respiration never expands or contracts the lungs to their full capacity. They only use the upper section of the lungs while their lower section hardly ever is employed at all. Because of this they cannot gain the full advantage of deep breathing, their blood and body fluids are not refreshed, and the various diseases gain easy entry. Any of this has as yet nothing to do with natural breathing.

Natural breathing is also called abdominal breathing. Every single inhalation, every single exhalation must always go deep down into the stomach area. During inhalation, when the air enters the lungs, they are filled to capacity and as a result their lower section expands. This in turn presses against the diaphragm and pushes it downward. Therefore, during inhalation, the chest area is completely relaxed while the stomach area is curved toward the outside.

Again, during exhalation the stomach area contracts, the diaphragm is pushed upward against the lungs and thereby causes the old and turbid breath to be expelled from their depth. Once it is all dispersed outside, no used air remains within. Therefore in this kind of breathing, although it makes use mostly of the lungs, it is the area of the stomach and the diaphragm which expands and contracts. This is the great method of breathing naturally by which the blood and the body fluids are kept fresh and active.

Not only during and prior to meditation should this method be employed, but always: whether walking, staying, sitting, or lying down, one can breathe deeply and naturally in any given circumstance.

Breathing Instructions

1. Contract the lower abdomen when breathing out. Thereby the diaphragm is pushed upward, the chest area is tensed, and all used breath, even from the lower part of the lungs, is expelled entirely.
2. Breathe in fresh air through the nostrils. Let it fill the lungs to capacity so that the diaphragm is pushed down and the stomach area expands.
3. Gradually lengthen and deepen your inhalations and exhalations. The stomach will get stronger and more stable. Some people say that one should hold the breath for a short moment at the end of an inhalation. This is called stopping respiration. According to my own experience, this is not good for beginners.
4. As you go along, let the respiration gradually grow subtler and finer until the entering and leaving of the breath is very soft. With prolonged practice you will cease to be consciously aware of the respiration and feel as if you weren't breathing at all.

5. Once the state of non-respiration is reached, you can truly be without inhalations and exhalations. Even though you have special organs for breathing, you won't feel any longer that you are using them. At the same time the breath will by and by come to enter and leave through all the body. This is the perfection of harmonious breathing. However, as a beginner you should never try to attain this intentionally. Always obey nature and go along with what you can do.

REGULATED BREATHING

Regulated breathing is also known as "reversed breathing." It resembles natural breathing in that it is very deep and soft and should always reach as far as the stomach area. On the other hand, it reverses the movements of the stomach. The upward and downward movement of the diaphragm is accordingly different from its activity during natural breathing. It is called "reversed" precisely because it reverses the pattern proper to natural breathing.

Practical Instructions

1. Exhale slow and far; let the stomach area expand freely, and make sure that the stomach is strong and full.
2. Let the lower abdomen be full of breath, the chest area slack, and the diaphragm completely relaxed.
3. Inhale slowly and deeply into the diaphragm. Let the fresh air fill the lungs so that they expand naturally. At the same time contract the abdomen.
4. As the lungs are filled with breath they will press down, while the stomach, contracted, will push up. The diaphragm is therefore pressed in from above and below; its movement is thereby getting subtler and subtler.
5. When the chest area is fully expanded, the stomach region may be contracted, yet it should not be entirely empty. Independent of whether you inhale or exhale, the center of gravity must always be solidly established beneath the navel. Thus the stomach area remains strong and full.
6. All respiration should be subtle and quiet. Especially during the practice of quiet sitting it should be so fine that you don't hear the sound of your own breathing. In the old days some people claimed that inhalations should be slightly longer than exhalations. Nowadays some say that exhalations should be slightly longer than inhalations. As far as I can tell, it is best to keep their length equal.

To summarize: Independent of whether you practice natural breathing or regulated breathing, the aim is always to activate the diaphragm. In the case of regulated breathing, the diaphragm is worked by means of human power. It reverses natural breathing and thus causes the diaphragm to stretch even farther, to move even more smoothly. For this reason I never enter my meditation practice without first practicing regulated breathing for a little while.

This is also the reason why I have recommended its use in my book. Since its publication many students have begun the practice. Some found the prescribed breathing exercises useful, others didn't. For this reason, always remain aware that even though regulated breathing is controlled by the human mind, it cannot be learned by human means alone. It is not a mere distortion of natural breathing, but its development, and should be learned in accordance with nature.

BREATHING EXERCISES

Both natural and regulated breathing have the following eight instructions in common:

1. Sit cross-legged and erect; take the same posture as in quiet sitting.
2. First breathe short breaths, then gradually lengthen them.
3. All breaths should be slow and subtle, quiet and long. Gradually they enter deeper into the abdomen.
4. Always inhale through the nose. Do not inhale through the mouth. The nose is the specific organ of respiration. There are tiny hairs on the inside of the nostrils which are easily blocked and obstructed.

The mouth, on the other hand, is not made primarily for respiration, and if you use it for breathing it will usurp the proper function of the nose. This in turn will lead to the gradual obstruction of the nose. More than that, by breathing through the mouth any number of bacteria and dirt particles will enter the body, and diseases are easily conceived. Therefore always keep the mouth closed, not only during breathing and meditation practice.

5. Once your breathing gets purer and warmer with prolonged practice, lengthen the individual breaths. The limit of lengthening is reached when it takes you a whole minute to breathe in and out one single breath. However, never forget that this cannot be forced.
6. The practice of slow and subtle breathing can be continued any time, any place.
7. During quiet sitting there should be no thoughts and no worries. If you have to pay constant attention to your respiration, the mind cannot be truly calm. Therefore it is best to practice breathing before and after every sitting.
8. Before and after quiet sitting, practice respiration. Pick a place that has good fresh air. Take about five to ten minutes for the exercise.

BREATHING AND THE LOWERING OF THE PIT OF THE STOMACH

In my discussion of posture above [in a separate section], I already spoke about the reason why the pit of the stomach should be lowered. Nevertheless, since this lowering is also of central importance in breathing, I come back to it now. Generally, if the pit of the stomach is not lowered, the respiration cannot be harmonized. Then the effectiveness of quiet sitting will not come to bear.

Repeating thus what I said before, students should pay attention to the following points:

1. During the breathing exercise, beginners should be aware of the pit of the stomach being firm and solid. It thus interferes with the breath, which cannot be harmonized properly. This is because the diaphragm is not yet able to move up and down freely. A beginner should overcome this difficulty with determination and not falter before it.
2. Should you become aware that your breathing is obstructed it this way, never try to force it open. Rather, let it take it natural course by gently focusing your attention on the lower abdomen.
3. Relax your chest so that the blood circulation does not press upon the heart. The pit of the stomach will then be lowered naturally.
4. Practice this over a long period. Gradually the chest and the diaphragm will feel open and relaxed. The breathing will be calm and subtle, deep and continuous. Every inhalation and exhalation will reach all the way to the center of gravity below the navel. This, then, is proof that the pit of the stomach has been effectively lowered.

Qingjing Jing

The *Qingjing Jing* is an ancient text still used in Daoism to inspire and exhort adherents to follow the Way. It is a devotional book, written in rhythmic verse to make it easier to memorize and recite. Here is the *Qingjing Jing* in its entirety.

Livia Kohn, trans., *The Qingjing Jing* in *The Taoist Experience* (Albany: State University of New York Press, 1993), 24–29.

The Great Tao has no form;
It brings forth and raises heaven and earth.
The Great Tao has no feelings;
It regulates the course of the sun and the moon.

The Great Tao has no name;
It raises and nourishes the myriad beings.
I do not know its name—
So I call it Tao.

The Tao can be pure or turbid, moving or tranquil.
Heaven is pure, earth is turbid;
Heaven is moving, earth is tranquil.
The male is moving, the female is tranquil.

Descending from the origin,
Flowing toward the end,
The myriad beings are being born.

Purity—the source of turbidity,
Movement—the root of tranquility.

Always be pure and tranquil;
Heaven and earth
Return to the primordial.

The human spirit is fond of purity,
But the mind disturbs it.
The human mind is fond of tranquility,
But desires meddle with it.

Get rid of desires for good,
And the mind will be calm.
Cleanse your mind,
And the spirit will be pure.

Naturally the six desires won't arise,
The three poisons are destroyed.
Whoever cannot do this
Has not yet cleansed his mind,
His desires are not yet driven out.

Those who have abandoned their desires:
Observe your mind by introspection—
And see there is no mind.

Then observe the body,
Look at yourself from without—
And see there is no body.

Then observe others by glancing out afar—
And see there are no beings.

Once you have realized these three,
You observe emptiness!

Use emptiness to observe emptiness,
And see there is no emptiness.
When even emptiness is no more,
There is no more nonbeing either.

Without even the existence of nonbeing
There is only serenity,
Profound and everlasting.

When serenity dissolves in nothingness—
How could there be desires?
When no desires arise
You have found true tranquility.

In true tranquility, go along with beings;
In true permanence, realize inner nature.
Forever going along, forever tranquil—
This is permanent purity, lasting tranquility.

In purity and tranquility,
Gradually enter the true Tao.
When the true Tao is entered,
It is realized.

Though we speak of "realized,"
Actually there is nothing to attain.
Rather, we speak of realization
When someone begins to transform the myriad beings.

Only who has properly understood this
Is worthy to transmit the sages' Tao.

The highest gentleman does not fight;
The lesser gentleman loves to fight.
Highest Virtue is free from Virtue;
Lesser Virtue clings to Virtue.

All clinging and attachments
Have nothing to do with the Tao or the Virtue.

People fail to realize the Tao
Because they have deviant minds.

Deviance in the mind
Means the spirit is alarmed.

Spirit alarmed,
There is clinging to things.
Clinging to things,
There is searching and coveting.

Searching and coveting,
There are passions and afflictions.
Passions, afflictions, deviance, and imaginings
Trouble and pester body and mind.

Then one falls into turbidity and shame,
Ups and downs, life and death.
Forever immersed in the sea of misery,
One is in eternity lost to the true Tao.

The Tao of true permanence
Will naturally come to those who understand.
Those who understand the realization
of the Tao
Will rest forever in the pure and tranquil.

The Lady of Great Mystery

Even though male–female inequality was the norm in China in classical times, some exceptional women became sages and what we might call saints. From the Daoist canon comes this story of one such woman, a reputed immortal who could perform miracles.

The Lady of Great Mystery had the family name Zhuan and was personally called He. When she was a little girl she lost first her father and after a little while also her mother.

Understanding that living beings often did not fulfill their destined lifespans, she felt sympathy and sadness. She used to say: "Once people have lost their existence in this world, they cannot recover it. Whatever has died cannot come back to life. Life is so limited! It is over so fast! Without cultivating the Tao, how can one extend one's life?"

She duly left to find enlightened teachers, wishing to purify her mind and pursue the Tao. She obtained the arts of the Jade Master and practiced them diligently for several years.

As a result she was able to enter the water and not get wet. Even in the severest cold of winter she would walk over frozen rivers wearing only a single garment. All the time her expression would not change, and her body would remain comfortably warm for a succession of days.

The Lady of Great Mystery could also move government offices, temples, cities, and lodges. They would appear in other places quite without moving from their original location. Whatever she pointed at would vanish into thin air. Doors, windows, boxes, or caskets that were securely locked needed only a short flexing of her finger to break wide open. Mountains would tumble, trees would fall at the pointing of her hand. Another short gesture would resurrect them to their former state.

One day she went into the mountains with her disciples. At sunset she took a staff and struck a stone. The stone at once opened wide, leading into a grotto-world fully equipped with beds and benches, screens and curtains. It also had a kitchen and larder, full with wine and food. All was just like it would be in the world of everyday life.

The Lady of Great Mystery could travel ten thousand miles, yet at the same time continue to stay nearby. She could transform small things to be suddenly big, and big things to be small. She could spit

Livia Kohn, trans., *The Taoist Experience* (Albany: State University of New York Press, 1993), 291–292.

fire so big it would rise up wildly into heaven, and yet in one breath she could extinguish it again.

She was also able to sit in the middle of a blazing fire, while her clothes would never be even touched by the flames. She could change her appearance at will: one moment she was an old man, the next a small child. She could also conjure up a cart and horse to ride back and forth in if she did not want to walk.

The Lady of Great Mystery perfectly mastered all thirty-six arts of the immortals. She could resurrect the dead and bring them back to life. She saved innumerable people, but nobody knew what she used for her dresses or her food, nor did anybody ever learn her arts from her. Her complexion was always that of a young girl; her hair stayed always black as a raven. Later she ascended into heaven in broad daylight. She was never seen again.

CONTEMPORARY CHALLENGES

Daoism in the Twenty-First Century

WILLIAM A. YOUNG

Like all other major religions, Daoism has been forced to adapt to the modern world, advancing in some ways and retreating in others. Here is one assessment of Daoism's status in the current century.

Religious Daoism today is found principally in Taiwan and Hong Kong, as well as Chinese communities in Malaysia, Thailand, Singapore, and wherever sizeable Chinese groups have settled (for example, San Francisco). In these communities Daoist priests are visible and very active. They perform rituals of healing for individuals and lead communal worship.

Daoist monasteries were closed in the People's Republic of China, and have not been as readily reopened in recent years as other religious institutions. According to the official policy of the Communist government, Daoism is a superstition rather than a religion and therefore does not have the same protections as Christianity, Buddhism, and Islam. However, the government has moderated its position, and allowed (and in some cases supported) the rebuilding of Daoist temples. Daoism is also being reintroduced into other public places. For example, restaurants are being allowed to display small altars to Daoist deities of wealth and protection. Individuals in China are also less reserved about their observance of Daoist traditions. For example, paper "hell bank notes" are openly burned by relatives of those who have died, in order to improve the ancestors' status in the afterlife.

The growing popularity of *tai-ch'i*, the exercise regimen and approach to the martial arts based on the Daoist teachings, is evidence of the vitality of Daoism in the twenty-first century. The principles of yielding,

William A. Young, *The World's Religions* (Upper Saddle River, NJ: Pearson, 2005), 120–121.

softness, centeredness, slowness, balance, suppleness, and rootedness found in *tai-ch'i* are all drawn from Daoism. The influence of Daoist philosophy is seen in the names of movements in the *tai-ch'i* form, such as Push the Boat with the Current, and Wind Sweeps the Plum Blossoms. The influence of "religious" Daoism, especially its astrological elements, is seen in other *tai-ch'i* movements, such as Step Up to Seven Stars, and Embrace the Moon.

The influence of Daoism is also seen in the growing popularity of the practice of *feng shui* (the art of reading the *yin* and *yang* forces present in particular settings, in order to insure the harmony of buildings and activities), and acupuncture.

The rapidly growing new religious movement known as *Falun Gong* . . . also draws on Daoism in its teachings.

In East Asia the teachings of philosophical Daoism were largely absorbed into the meditation school of Buddhism. The tradition is still preserved, however, by individuals (including many in the West) who find in the *Daodejing* and other classical texts an appealing philosophy of life. Its teachings of the return to a natural way of life are particularly attractive amidst the conflicts and turmoil of an increasingly frenetic world.

STUDY QUESTIONS

1. What is the ultimate goal in life according to Daoism?
2. How does Daoism differ from Confucianism?
3. What is the Dao?
4. Who is Laozi? Who is Zhuangzi?
5. What is the *Daodejing*?
6. What is *wu-wei*?
7. In the *Daodejing*, what kind of government does *wu-wei* seem to imply?
8. What has been the main interest of religious Daoism?
9. What is the *Daozang*? What importance does it have in the Daoist tradition?
10. How do Daoists and Confucianists differ in their conceptions of the ultimate force in the universe?

FURTHER READING

Ian G. Barbour, ed., *Earth Might Be Fair* (Englewood Cliffs, NJ: Prentice-Hall, 1972).

Herrlee G. Creel, *What Is Taoism?* (Chicago: University of Chicago Press, 1970).

Livia Kohn, trans., *The Taoism Experience: An Anthology* (Albany: State University of New York Press, Albany, 1993).

D. C. Lau, trans., *Tao Te Ching* (New York: Penguin Classics, 1963).

John B. Noss, *A History of the World's Religions* (New York: Macmillan, 1994).

Huston Smith, *The World's Religions* (San Francisco: HarperSanFrancisco, 1991).

Burton Watson, trans., *Chuang Tzu* (New York: Columbia University Press, 1964, 1996).

ONLINE

Internet Encyclopedia of Philosophy, "Daoist Philosophy," http://www.iep.utm.edu/daoism/ (December 21, 2015).

Daoist Studies, "Daoism and Daoist Studies," http://www.daoiststudies.org/ (December 23, 2015).

9 Shinto

From Japan's early history to the modern, democratic, technologically savvy Japan of today, Shinto has been a defining force in the lives of the Japanese. It is hundreds of years old, has endured the rise and fall of empires, and has weathered competition from other religions. Yet it remains a significant influence on society's attitudes, behavior, religious practice, and sense of identity. Shinto's heartiness seems all the more remarkable when we consider that it offers no founder, no clearly articulated set of doctrines, no system of ethics, and no counterpart to what other religions call holy scripture.

BELIEFS AND PRACTICES

Shinto does not derive its name from a founder or an ancient text. It got its name from Chinese—and it did so out of necessity. According to Umeda Yoshimi, of the International Shinto Foundation,

> The ancient beliefs were given the name "Shinto" only when faced with competition from the newly-imported Buddhist religion, which reached Japan in 538. That is, in order to distinguish traditional Japanese forms of belief from Buddhism, a word having connections with Chinese Taoism was sought and employed to convey the meaning "the way of *kami*" ("Shinto" is written with two Chinese characters: the first, *shin*, is used to write the native Japanese word *kami*, meaning "divinity" or "numinous entity," and the second character, *tō*, is used to write the native word *michi*, meaning "way").
>
> The term "Shinto" first appears in the historical chronicle *Nihon Shoki* compiled in 720 CE, where it refers to religious observances, *kami* and shrines, but not until the 12th century was it used as it is today, to denote a body of religious doctrines.[1]

The central concept in Shinto is the **kami**, divine powers of the cosmos in the form of deities, features of nature, and exceptional humans (emperors and ancestors, for example). (Shinto means "the way of the *kami*.") As Motoori Norinaga, an eighteenth-century Shinto scholar, says,

> [I]t may be said that *kami* signifies, in the first place, the deities of heaven and earth that appear in the ancient records and also the spirits of the shrines where they are worshipped. It is hardly necessary to say that it includes human beings. It also includes such objects as birds, beasts, trees, plants, seas, mountains, and so forth. In ancient usage, anything whatsoever which was outside the ordinary, which possessed power, or which was awe-inspiring was called *kami*.[2]

The *kami* are thought to be divine life forces—the powers through which life is created and expressed. They bring to humanity the blessings of harmony, happiness, success, bounty, and fertility (although a few of them are destructive). Through worship at public and household shrines—that is, through prayers, offerings, and rituals of purification—adherents try to appease the *kami*, hoping to win their favor in small and large endeavors. In Japan, there are thousands of shrines in public places, and many others in households. More than any adherence to doctrines or creeds, actions performed in recognition of the *kami* reflect the core of Shinto and the underlying ethos of the Japanese.

Kami is everywhere, and so everywhere exists the divine. The cosmos is a sacred place, and humans are themselves divine children of the *kami*. Contrary to the prevailing Western view, in Shinto humans are intrinsically good. They may become spiritually contaminated, but the contaminants can be removed to restore their inherent goodness.

The dichotomies that permeate Western religions—good and evil, right and wrong, sin and forgiveness, heaven and hell—are absent in Shinto. This is how one commentator expresses the point:

> Shinto in those early times had no clear philosophy or ethics, and it still does not today. It expressed an attitude of joyful acceptance of life and a feeling of closeness to nature. Life and death were seen as part of the normal processes of nature. There was no struggle between good and evil. The only concern was with ritual purity, perhaps originating in part from sanitary measures and certainly contributing to the Japanese love of bathing and their record of being undoubtedly the world's cleanest people throughout history. *Kami* were felt to be everywhere and were worshipped and prayed to as beneficent forces. These were the simple beliefs of Shinto in earliest times, and they remain the heart of Shinto today.[3]

SHINTO TIMELINE

BCE

c. 483 Death of the Buddha

200 Buddhism has spread to Nepal, Sri Lanka, and Central Asia.

CE

c. 61 Buddhism spreads to China.

Second century Confucianism becomes a state religion.

Second century Daoism as a religion begins.

538 Buddhism and Confucianism are introduced to Japan.

594 Buddhism becomes the official religion of Japan.

712 *Kojiki* completed

720 *Nihongi* completed

1730–1801 Life of Shinto scholar Motoori Norinaga

1868 Creation of State Shinto in Japan; repression of Buddhism

1945 End of World War II; Japan surrenders; Shinto is no longer the state religion

FIGURE 9.1 The Yasaka Jinja Shrine, one of the great Shinto shrines of Gion District, Kyoto, Japan. The shrine includes several buildings, a main hall, and a stage.

Shinto's lack of a system of ethics has not been a serious problem for the tradition, because it has freely adapted moral norms and metaphysical ideas from Confucianism and Buddhism. Today most Japanese seem to be comfortable with this fusion and regard the three worldviews as complementary.

In modern Japan, there are three classifications of Shinto. Shrine Shinto is the variety practiced by most devotees at the thousands of Shinto shrines. At a shrine (called a **jinja**, "dwelling place of the *kami*") a worshipper appeals to the *kami* (in the form of gods or other manifestations) by performing rituals, saying prayers, or making offerings. Such pleas are supposed to influence the *kami* to improve a person's well-being or circumstances or to aid dead ancestors or the nation. The greatest and purest shrine is said to be the Grand Shrine at Ise, dedicated to the Sun Goddess Amaterasu. Sect Shinto comprises several Shinto movements that began in the nineteenth century and continue to this day. The founders, many of them women, were compelling figures who claimed shamanistic powers and promised down-to-earth rewards such as health and worldly success. Folk Shinto (which can overlap with the other kinds) refers to the Shinto of many ordinary people who accept a diverse assortment of superstitious and magical beliefs and practices.

In the late nineteenth century, State Shinto arose. The Japanese government declared Shinto to be the official religion of the state, mandated enrollment of all households at Shinto shrines, claimed that Japan was favored and protected by *kami* deities (and was thus superior to other nations), and inaugurated the emperor cult by insisting that the emperor was "living *kami*," a god. State Shinto and the emperor cult have been indicted as major causes of Japan's extreme jingoism and its imperialist aggression against its Asian neighbors in the early twentieth century and against the United States and its allies in World War II. In 1945 the war ended State Shinto and forced the emperor to renounce his claim to divinity.

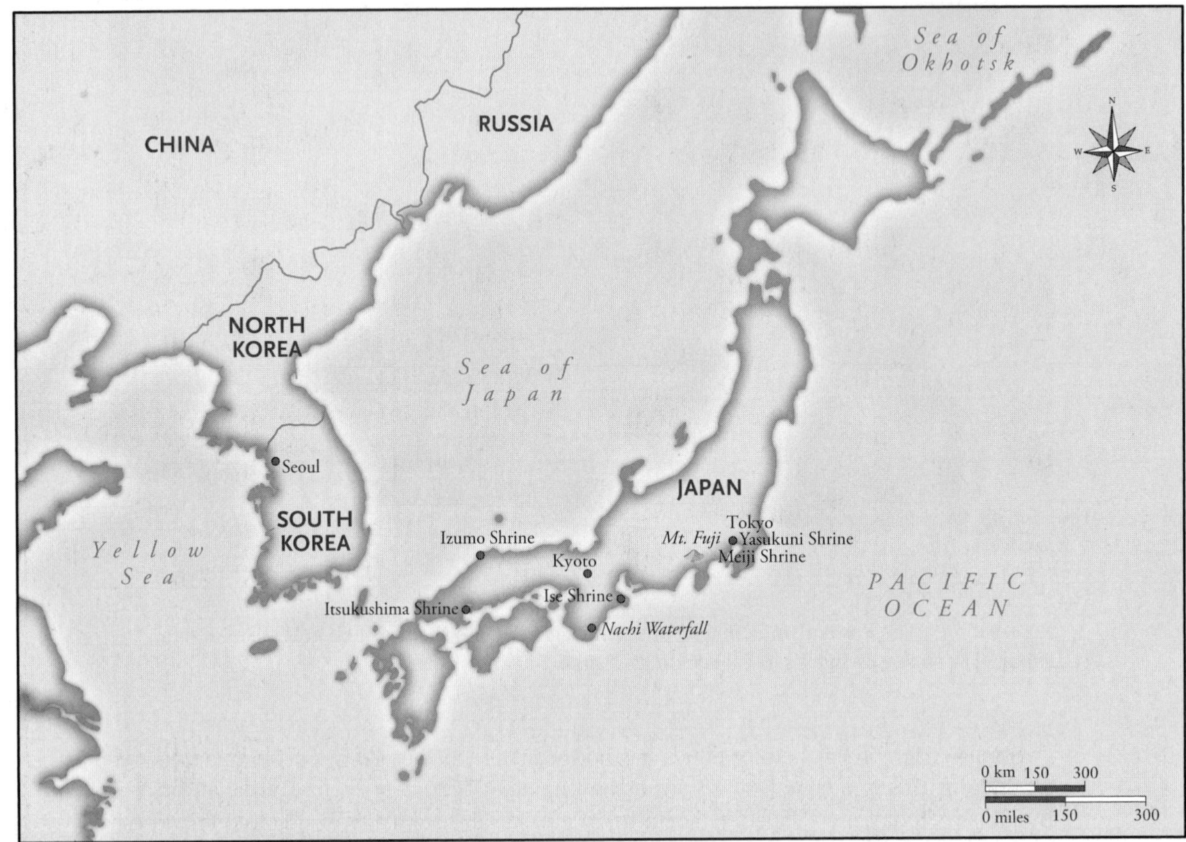

MAP 9.1 Significant sites in the history of Shinto.

SACRED WRITINGS

Shinto has no holy scriptures comparable to the Bible or the Quran, but it does have literature deeply revered by adherents and regarded as authoritative. The two central texts are the *Kojiki* (*Records of Ancient Matters*, 712 CE) and the *Nihongi*, or *Nihonshoki* (*Chronicles of Japan*, 720 CE). These relate the early history and mythologies of Japan while articulating Shinto's main ideas and practices. Until the end of World War II, these two classics were regarded by many Japanese as historical fact.

Together the *Kojiki* and the *Nihongi* detail unique creation myths, stories of primeval *kami*, a rudimentary cosmology, and an account of the relationship between the *kami* and human beings. The *Nihongi* creation story explains that in the beginning two *kami* called Izanami (female) and Izanagi (male) gave order to the elementary, chaotic universe. From their perch on the "floating bridge of heaven," they dipped a jeweled spear into the primal sea below and stirred the waters. When they raised the spear, drops fell from its tip and

A CLOSER LOOK

Are the Japanese Religious?

Despite the historically close connection between Shinto (and other religions) and the Japanese people, in opinion surveys most Japanese say they have no religious beliefs. How can this be? Ian Reader, a noted Shinto scholar, explains:

> In just about all surveys that have been carried out in recent decades the numbers of [Japanese] affirming religious belief have hovered somewhere around the 30 percent mark and those saying that they have no religious belief somewhere around the 65 percent mark. When, however, further questions are asked, it becomes clear that lack of belief does not mean lack of action, lack of concern or lack of relationship with religious issues. For example, when asked whether they consider religious feelings to be important, the Japanese are likely to respond positively, with an average around 70 percent or more stating that they are important and somewhere between 10 and 15 percent on average denying that they are. . . .
>
> Levels of belonging [to a religion] also have traditionally been high in Japan and continue to be so. It is common for people, even while denying that they are religious, to state that they are affiliated to Shinto and Buddhism, the two major institutional religious structures in Japan.[4]

FIGURE 9.2 The Meoto-iwa (Husband and Wife) rocks in Mie Prefecture is an iconic landmark in Japan that symbolizes the union between Izanagi and Izanami.

BACKGROUND

Shinto's This-Worldliness

To a greater extent than most other world religions, Shinto is markedly "this-worldly"—that is, it emphasizes happiness and well-being in this life rather than rewards or punishments in life hereafter. This is true of both early and contemporary Shinto. As Joseph M. Kitagawa says,

[The early Japanese] took it for granted that the natural world was the original world; that is, they did not look for another order of meaning behind the phenomenal, natural world—at least until they came under the influence of Sino-Korean civilization and Buddhism. The one-dimensional meaning structure of the early Japanese is implicit in the term *kami*. . . .[5]

formed the islands of Japan. They decided to live there, and together they produced other *kami*—Amaterasu (the sun goddess), Tsukiyomi (the moon god), Susa-no-o (the storm god), and other deities.

From the myths of the *Kojiki* and the *Nihongi*, several fundamental Shinto ideas emerge: the power and pervasiveness of the *kami*; the preeminence and uniqueness of the nation of Japan; the divinity of human beings as the children of the *kami*; the power of life and fertility; the descent of Japanese emperors from the *kami*; the preeminence of Amaterasu the sun goddess; and the absence of an all-powerful creator God.

NOTES

1. Umeda Yoshimi, "The Role of Shinto in Japanese Culture," address to the International Shinto Foundation, October 23, 2009.
2. Quoted in D. C. Holton, *The National Faith of Japan* (New York: E. P. Dutton, 1938), 23.
3. Edwin O. Reischauer (Introduction), in Stuart D. B. Picken, *Shinto: Japan's Spiritual Roots* (Tokyo: Kodansha International, 1980).
4. Ian Reader, *Religion in Contemporary Japan* (Honolulu: University of Hawaii Press, 1991), 6.
5. Joseph M. Kitagawa, *On Understanding Japanese Religion* (Princeton, NJ: Princeton University Press, 1987).

KEY TERMS

kami Divine powers of the cosmos in the form of deities, features of nature, and exceptional humans (emperors and ancestors, for example).

jinja A Shinto shrine, the "dwelling place of the *kami*."

READINGS

TEACHINGS

The Nihongi: The Kami Create Japan

The Japanese creation story begins with two deities, or kami: Izanagi and Izanami. From the "floating bridge of heaven" these two see that there is no land below. So they decide to create it. They dip the jeweled spear of heaven in the ocean, and the brine that drips from the spear point becomes the islands of Japan. Then they produce children to live on the created land.

Izanagi no Mikoto and Izanami no Mikoto stood on the floating bridge of Heaven, and held counsel together, saying: "Is there not a country beneath?"

Thereupon they thrust down the jewel-spear of Heaven, and groping about therewith found the ocean. The brine which dripped from the point of the spear coagulated and became an island which received the name of Ono-goro-jima.

The two Deities thereupon descended and dwelt in this island. Accordingly they wished to become husband and wife together, and to produce countries.

So they made Ono-goro-jima the pillar of the centre of the land.

Now the male deity turning by the left, and the female deity by the right, they went round the pillar of the land separately. When they met together on one side, the female deity spoke first and said:—"How delightful! I have met with a lovely youth." The male deity was displeased, and said:—"I am a man, and by right should have spoken first. How is it that on the contrary thou, a woman, shouldst have been the first to speak? This was unlucky. Let us go round again." Upon this the two deities went back, and having met anew, this time the male deity spoke first, and said:—"How delightful! I have met a lovely maiden."

Then he inquired of the female deity, saying:—"In thy body is there aught formed?" She answered, and said:—"In my body there is a place which is the source of femininity." The male deity said:—"In my body again there is a place which is the source of masculinity. I wish to unite this source-place of my body to the source-place of thy body." Hereupon the male and female first became united as husband and wife.

Now when the time of birth arrived, first of all the island of Ahaji was reckoned as the placenta, and their minds took no pleasure in it. Therefore it received the name of Ahaji no Shima.

Next there was produced the island of Oho-yamato no Toyo-aki-tsu-shima.

W. G. Aston, trans., *Nihongi*, Book 1 (Rutland, VT: Charles E. Tuttle, 1972), 10–17.

Next they produced the island of Iyo no futa-na, and next the island of Tsukushi. Next the islands of Oki and Sado were born as twins. This is the prototype of the twin-births which sometimes take place among mankind.

Next was born the island of Koshi, then the island of Ohoshima, then the island of Kibi no Ko.

Hence first arose the designation of the Oho-ya-shima country.

Nihongi: The Kami of the Sun and Moon

Izanagi and Izanami soon produce the Sun goddess and then the Moon god—brother and sister. They make other *kami*, not all of whom are well behaved.

After this Izanagi no Mikoto and Izanami no Mikoto consulted together, saying:—"We have now produced the Great-eight-island country, with the mountains, rivers, herbs, and trees. Why should we not produce someone who shall be lord of the universe?" They then together produced the Sun-Goddess, who was called Oho-hiru-me no muchi. . . .

The resplendent lustre of this child shone throughout all the six quarters. Therefore the two Deities rejoiced, saying:—"We have had many children, but none of them have been equal to this wondrous infant. She ought not to be kept long in this land, but we ought of our own accord to send her at once to Heaven, and entrust to her the affairs of Heaven."

At this time Heaven and Earth were still not far separated, and therefore they sent her up to Heaven by the ladder of Heaven.

They next produced the Moon-god. . . .

His radiance was next to that of the Sun in splendour. This God was to be the consort of the Sun-Goddess, and to share in her government. They therefore sent him also to Heaven.

Next they produced the leech-child, which even at the age of three years could not stand upright. They therefore placed it in the rock-camphor-wood boat of Heaven, and abandoned it to the winds.

Their next child was Sosa no wo no Mikoto. . . .

This God had a fierce temper and was given to cruel acts. Moreover he made a practice of continually weeping and wailing. So he brought many of the people of the land to an untimely end. Again he caused green mountains to become withered. Therefore the two Gods, his parents, addressed Sosa no wo no Mikoto, saying:—"Thou art exceedingly wicked, and it is not meet that thou shouldst reign over the world. Certainly thou must depart far away to the Nether-Land." So they at length expelled him.

W. G. Aston, trans., *Nihongi*, Book 1 (Rutland, VT: Charles E. Tuttle, 1972), 18–20.

Kojiki: Kami, the Netherworld, and the Eclipse of the Sun

In the world, three great *kami* come into existence, each with different attributes and powers. Then two more *kami* come into being. These five are the "heavenly *kami* of special standing," and together they produce a diverse set of *kami* offspring, including Izanagi and Izanami.

Later, Izanami dies giving birth to yet another *kami* (the fire god); she descends into hades from which Izanagi tries unsuccessfully to retrieve her. In the effort, he becomes contaminated. When he washes himself in a river on earth, three other *kami* come into existence—the Sun goddess (Amaterasu) to rule the Plain of High Heaven, the Moon god (Tsukiyomi) to rule the night, and the Valiant Male Kami (Susanoo) to rule the ocean.

The Sun goddess is so shocked by the bad behavior of her brother, Susanoo, that she hides in a heavenly cave, and the world goes dark. Then a host of *kami* try to entice her out of the cave. When she finally comes out, the world is illuminated once again.

BIRTH OF KAMI

At the beginning of heaven and earth, there came into existence in the Plain of High Heaven the Heavenly Center Lord Kami, next, the Kami of High Generative Force, and then the Kami of Divine Generative Force.

Next, when the earth was young, not yet solid, there developed something like reed-shoots from which the Male Kami of Excellent Reed Shoots and then Heavenly Eternal Standing Kami emerged.

The above five kami are the heavenly kami of special standing.

Then, there came into existence Earth Eternal Standing Kami, Kami of Abundant Clouds Field, male and female Kami of Clay, male and female Kami of Post, male and female Kami of Great Door, Kami of Complete Surface and his spouse, Kami of Awesomeness, Izanagi (kami-who-invites) and his spouse, Izanami (kami-who-is-invited).

BIRTH OF OTHER KAMI

After giving birth to the land, they proceeded to bear kami [such as the kami of the wind, of the tree, of the mountain, and of the plains]. But Izanami died after giving birth to the kami of fire.

Izanagi, hoping to meet again with his spouse, went after her to the land of Hades. When Izanami came out to greet him, Izanagi said, "Oh my beloved, the land which you and I have been making has not yet been completed. Therefore, you must return with me." To which Izanami replied, "I greatly regret that you did not come here sooner, for I have already partaken of the hearth of the land of hades. But let me discuss with the kami of hades about my desire to return. You must, however, not look at me." As she was gone so long, Izanagi, being impatient, entered the hall to look for her and found maggots squirming around the body of Izanami.

Izanagi, seeing this, was afraid and ran away, saying, "Since I have been to an extremely horrible and unclean land, I must purify myself." Thus, arriving at [a river], he purified and exorcised himself. When he washed his left eye, there came into existence the Sun Goddess, or Heavenly Illuminating Great Kami (Amaterasu), and when he washed his right eye, there emerged the Moon Kami (Tsukiyomi). Finally, as he washed his nose there came into existence Valiant Male Kami (Susanoo).

Greatly rejoiced over this, Izanagi removed his necklace, and giving it to the Sun Goddess, he gave her the mission to rule the Plain of High Heaven.

Kojiki, ch. 2, 12, 17, *Kojiki, Records of Ancient Matters*, in *The Great Asian Religions: An Anthology* (New York: Macmillan, 1969), 231–233.

Next he entrusted to the Moon Kami the rule of the realms of the night. Finally, he gave Valiant Male Kami the mission to rule the ocean.

WITHDRAWAL OF THE SUN GODDESS

[At one time] the Sun Goddess [shocked by the misdeeds of her brother, Valiant Male Kami] opened the heavenly rock-cave door and concealed herself inside. Then the Plain of High Heaven became completely dark, and all manner of calamities arose.

Then the 800 myriads of kami gathered in a divine assembly, and summoned Kami of the Little Roof in Heaven and Kami of Grand Bead to perform a divination. They hung long strings of myriad curved beads on the upper branches of a sacred tree, and hung a large-dimensioned mirror on its middle branches. They also suspended in the lower branches white and blue cloth. These objects were held by Kami of Grand Bead as solemn offerings, while Kami of the Little Roof in Heaven intoned liturgical prayers (*norito*). Meanwhile, Kami of Heavenly Strength hid himself behind the entrance of the rock-cave, and Kami of Heavenly Headgear bound her sleeves with a cord of vine, and stamped on an over-turned bucket which was placed before the rock-cave. Then she became kami-possessed, exposed her breasts and genitals. Thereupon, the 800 myriads of kami laughed so hard that the Plain of High Heaven shook with their laughter.

The Sun Goddess, intrigued by all this, opened the rock-cave door slightly, wondering why it was that the 800 myriads of kami were laughing. Then Kami of Heavenly Headgear said, "There is a kami nobler than you, and that is why we are happy and dancing." While she was speaking thus, Kami of the Little Roof and Kami of Grand Bead showed the mirror to the Sun Goddess. Thereupon, the Sun Goddess, thinking this ever more strange, gradually came out of the cave, and the hidden Kami of Grand Bead took her hand and pulled her out. Then as the Sun Goddess reappeared, the Plain of High Heaven was naturally illuminated.

Life Is Transitory

An idea that runs through Japanese texts is that life is fleeting. This poem elaborates on the motif, describing the ephemeral beauty of nature as a reminder of the shortness of human life.

It has been told from the beginning of the world
that life on earth is transitory. . . .
Indeed we see even in the sky
the moon waxes and wanes. . . .
In the spring
flowers decorate mountain-trees,
But in the autumn with dew and frost
leaves turn colors and fall on the ground. . . .
So it is with human life:
Rosy cheek and black hair turn their color;
The morning smile disappears in the evening
like the wind which blows away.
Changes continue in life like the water passing away,
And my tears do not stop over the uncertainty of life.

Manyoshu, 4: 226–227, in *The Great Asian Religions: An Anthology* (New York: Macmillan, 1969), 239.

Mount Fuji

Mount Fuji in Japan is regarded as a sacred place and the home c
poem extols the splendor of the mountain and the mysterious *ka*

Between the provinces of Kai and Suruga
  Stands the lofty peak of Fuji.
Heavenly clouds would not dare cross it;
  Even birds dare not fly above it.
The fire of volcano is extinguished by snow,
  and yet snow is consumed by fire.
It is hard to describe;
  It is impossible to name it.
One only senses
  the presence of a mysterious kami.
In the land of Yamato,
  the land of the rising sun,
The lofty Mount Fuji is its treasure
  and its tutelary kami. . . .
One is never tired of
  gazing at its peak in the province Suruga.

Manyoshu, 3: 319–321, in *The Great Asian Religions: An Anthology* (New York: Macmillan, 1969), 239.

PRACTICES

Rituals, Shrines, and Festivals

IAN READER

Shinto is a religion of ritual and devotion, not a system of doctrines and creeds. This reading explains the nature of some of these practices, how they are performed, and what their performance means to Japanese devotees.

There is a great emphasis in Shinto on beginnings, growth, fertility and celebration, and the events that occur in the lives of individuals, households and communities that bring them into a relationship with the *kami* and the shrine generally revolve around these themes. The ritual of *miyamairi*, in which the

Ian Reader, *Religion in Contemporary Japan* (Honolulu: University of Hawaii Press, 1991), 13–16.

hortly after birth to the local shrine to lessing and be placed under the protec- *kami* who is the guardian of the local ty and area, integrates the child into the mmunity and also, because of Shinto's ethnic s, into the wider community of Japan. Tradi- lly the household to which the child belonged s affiliated to the shrine: both individual and ousehold were its *ujiko*, parishioners, under the protection of the *kami* and with various obligations to help in its upkeep and to participate in and contribute to the annual (or seasonal) festivals which helped to draw the community together and provide a sense of social bonding. The shrine often served (and still does in some places) as a community centre, the setting for meetings and recreational activities as well as various religious events. In such terms the local shrine stood as a regional and territorial entity, a focus of the community of identity and belonging. It also formed, especially in earlier times when communications were not so highly developed, a link between the village and the wider Japanese world. Local shrines were often branch shrines of nationally known ones, enshrining *kami* of nationwide repute such as Hachiman, Tenjin, Inari or the *kami* venerated at the shrines of Ise: in fact two-thirds of Shinto shrines today enshrine one of these *kami*. The shrine thus, besides symbolising regional community, acted as a conduit uniting the village and its people with the wider social world of the Japanese nation.

In many respects Shinto has been, especially at local levels, more of an amorphous tradition of shrines related to local communities, identities and life cycles, and concerned with the maintenance of a continuing and productive relationship with the *kami* than anything else, and it is these themes that will concern us most here.

Although demographic changes have altered the religious landscape in recent years one can still find shrines that perform a centralising role in their local communities: contemporary change does not always sweep away all vestiges of earlier times. In order to illustrate the workings of Shinto in social terms and shed light on the major events that take place at shrines throughout the country I shall here describe one such shrine. Whether one could call it "typical" is a difficult question: with approximately 80,000 registered shrines in Japan there is probably no such place. However, the events celebrated and the times when people visit it are standard enough to make it as reasonable a microcosm of the overall as is possible. It is a shrine I came to know well not through academic research but because my wife and I lived near it for two years during which time we came to regard it as "our" local shrine (in a way that we never had with shrines in other places we had lived in Japan), announcing it as such to those who came to stay with us and making it our first port of call during the New Year's celebrations.

The area in which Katano shrine stands is situated halfway between the cities of Kyoto and Osaka, in an old rice-farming area that has, due to its proximity to both cities, become commuter territory, its fields built over as the population has increased dramatically in recent years. The whole area is a juxtaposition of new housing, old farmhouses, rice fields, apartment blocks, bars, *pachinko* [pinball gambling game] parlours, electrical stores and rice merchants, of frantic businessmen and office girls rushing for trains to the city in the morning, of housewives visiting the local market to buy food, and schoolgirls clustering in the music shop for posters and cassettes of the current idols—in short, the rather typical mixture of old and new, and the crowded jumble of buildings, telegraph wires, narrow streets and level-crossings that may be found virtually anywhere in contemporary urban Japan.

The shrine clearly benefited from the remaining local community of farmers and from the influx of new faces, for it managed to support a full-time priest who could call on the services of a number of assistants, especially *miko* or shrine maidens, at festivals. Although part of the shrine dated to the sixteenth century and was deemed a prefectural cultural asset it was hardly known outside the local region. Nor was it especially large, the whole area of the shrine, surrounded by an old mud and brick wall, being approximately 60 metres long and 50 wide.

While not attracting people from further afield the shrine was certainly an active centre for the local community. I used to go by it every day on my way to and from work and frequently saw people passing through the shrine and paying their respects to the *kami*. On Sundays there were often several babies being taken on the *miyamairi*, clad in a bright baby *kimono* with several lucky amulets attached to it: the priest would chant Shinto prayers while one of the shrine maidens performed a sacred dance and gave a symbolic purificatory blessing to the baby. The reason that Sundays are the most common day for such activities (and indeed for most shrine and temple visiting) is a pragmatic rather than a religious one: it is the only day most people in Japan have off work and hence the most convenient for such things.

Besides the general flow of passers-by, regular worshippers, babies receiving the *kami*'s blessing, people coming to pray for safety because it was their unlucky year (*yakudoshi*), and the occasional wedding that might be celebrated there, the shrine had a number of regular yearly events (*nenju gyoji*) that punctuated the year. In November the shrine, along with most others in Japan, came alive with the *shichigosan* (7-5-3) festival, in which girls of three and seven and boys of five are taken to the shrine to be further placed under the protective blessings of the *kami*. The chief day for this is 15 November (or, more commonly, the Sunday nearest that date) but the blessings are, as at most shrines, dispensed throughout the month. As with *miyamairi* and New Year it is an occasion for dressing up and for overt display: the children are dressed formally, usually in a bright kimono but sometimes in formal Western-style dress. Their parents also dress up for the occasion, usually in Western style. . . .

Probably the two most active times at the shrine were the *hatsumode* period in January and the annual shrine festival in mid-October, and at these two periods the shrine and the surrounding area became alive and active. The former is a nationwide and the latter a local festival specific to the shrine, although it has wider connotations for its roots are in the harvest celebrations that are still celebrated at countless other festivals throughout Japan at this time. There are festivals all the year round in Japan, and it is possible to find one occurring somewhere on virtually every day of the year, but certain periods, such as the beginning of the year, the traditional planting season of spring, the hot months of the summer which are eminently suited to relaxed evening festivals, and the period in mid-October are definitely peak times for festivals across the country.

The New Year's festival is both a national holiday, a time for celebration and relaxation, and a religious event with themes of regeneration, purification and renewal as the old year and whatever bad luck it contained are swept aside in a tide of noisy enjoyment. It is traditional to clean one's house thoroughly and to pay off all debts before the end of the year (indeed I have seen, in the national newspapers, reminders during the last days of the old year that this is the time to clean one's house), thus clearing away physically and metaphorically the residue of the past year so as to allow one to start again new. Throughout January there are numerous "first" festivals, such as the *hatsu Ebisu* ("first Ebisu") widely celebrated especially in the Kyoto-Osaka region from 9–11 January, which is the first festive day of the year of the popular deity Ebisu. All such festivals reiterate the theme of transition from old to new, of the sweeping away of the hindrances of the past and of fresh beginnings, expressing optimistic hopes for good fortune.

The New Year's festival is the largest of all these, and at this time it is customary to visit shrines (and some of the better-known temples as well) to pay one's respects to the *kami*, to ask for good luck and help in the coming year and to make resolutions fortified by the general mood of optimistic renewal. This is accompanied by a great changeover in religious amulets and talismans as new ones representing the power and benevolence of the *kami* and Buddhas are acquired and old ones are dispensed with. The most commonly procured of these at New Year is the *hamaya* (literally "evil-destroying arrow"), a symbolic arrow that is placed in the home as a protective talisman to drive away or absorb bad luck. Other lucky charms, talismans and amulets are also on sale at the shrines and temples, the income this produces often making an important contribution to the upkeep of the institutions. Often the talismans that are purchased are placed in the household *kamidana* [small shrine or altar in the home], thereby creating a further link between shrine and household, with the *kamidana* itself operating as a localised shrine in its own right sacralising the house itself.

At the same time the old amulets and talismans from the previous year are jettisoned, and most shrines and temples at this time designate a special place where these can be left. Some time later, usually in mid-January, these will be formally burnt in a purificatory rite, generally to the accompaniment of priests chanting prayers whose powers, along with the exorcistic nature of the fire, transform the impurities and eradicate the bad luck that have been absorbed by the amulets and talismans. The pollutions and hindrances of the past are thus dispensed with and the way is opened up, symbolised by the acquisition of new charms, for regeneration. Naturally, too, in the process of cyclical transition, those same, new talismans, will be brought back the next year to be burnt, in a continuing round of change and renewal.

CONTEMPORARY CHALLENGES

Japanese Religion in Modern Times

HOWARD W. FRENCH

Modern Japan is increasingly secular, with an overall lack of interest in religion, and several indicators suggest that Shinto is in decline. But Shinto is a very old religion, having adapted again and again to changes in culture and politics. It has survived. But will it adapt once more to the twenty-first century world?

Dressed smartly in a black skirt and a turquoise silk shirt with wide lapels, Yuka Sugimoto receives visitors in a sleek suite of offices these days, handing them a business card taken from a fancy zebra-skin wallet.

In both style and setting, this might be the greeting of a top business executive. It is hard to say, in fact, which would be the rarer position for a woman in today's Japan, corporate director or the job she holds: chief priest of a Shinto shrine.

Ms. Sugimoto has taken a creative approach to ensuring the survival of her 800-year-old shrine, which is nestled in a forest of office buildings between two of Tokyo's hippest and most bustling centers of youth culture, Shibuya and Harajuku.

Ms. Sugimoto offers purification rites and other religious services to the big media companies that surround her. She has also built a state-of-the-art shrine, complete with high-tech lighting and motorized

Howard W. French, "Japan Has Little Time for Old-Time Religion." *New York Times*, September 13, 2001.

shutters, renting fashionable office space to nearby businesses on the grounds.

Her innovative marketing of an old religion reflects the difficulty of all religions in an increasingly secular Japan. Shinto in particular seems to be losing support. Many urban shrines are finding that renting their land, always a premium in Japan's cities, is the best way to survive.

Walking up the steep stairway that leads to the shrine and through the concrete-paved courtyard of the complex, one could hardly guess that this was a place of worship were it not for the telltale thick rope hanging from a bell used to call the spirits.

That is just as well, said Ms. Sugimoto, because it had almost no visitors when it was a rustic copper-roofed structure built on a cedar and bamboo frame, before the renovation she directed three years ago.

Ms. Sugimoto, who became head priest eight years ago, after the death of her father, says the path she has taken is probably preferable to an advertising campaign to attract more visitors. "People say we should do public relations work, or make a Web page, but I'm not sure it would do any good," she said. "And if more people came, I'm not sure what I would do with them. I don't have the time to receive them, and can't afford to hire more staff."

The situation of Ms. Sugimoto's shrine encapsulates the plight of Shinto. The religion figures prominently in the news each August, when there is a debate about whether the prime minister should visit one of its most famous shrines, in Tokyo, which honors Japan's war dead.

People visit other famous shrines, and shrine visits are popular on select holidays, like the New Year. On the whole though, fewer and fewer Japanese are showing an interest.

Before World War II, it was virtually unheard of for a Shinto priest to be a woman, and the priesthood was usually passed from father to son. But with the lack of interest in religion and with families growing smaller, shrine priesthoods have had to open up to daughters, to keep them in the family. Priests go through a training period. Ms. Sugimoto is one of 25 women among the 404 head priests in Tokyo, according to the Association of Shinto Shrines.

Shinto is a faith that worships spirits that are found in all objects, living and inanimate.

The Japanese have traditionally managed to retain affiliations with several religions at once, apparently without conflict.

"The religious practice of an ordinary man is highly complicated: he is likely to be Shintoist as a Japanese, Buddhist in face of death and suffering, Confucian as a social being in general, personally often a Christian and, as a man of science, a materialist," wrote Kurt Singer, in a classic postwar book about Japanese society, "Mirror, Sword and Jewel."

The problem today, though, is the low level of overall interest in religion. A commonly cited indicator is wedding practices. A generation ago, 70 percent or more Japanese were married with Shinto rites, says Kenji Ishii, sociologist of religion at Kokugakuin University in Tokyo. Today, Christian-style weddings are in fashion, even though few Japanese identify themselves as Christians. Shinto marriages constitute fewer than 20 percent of the total.

Some experts in Shinto dispute the significance of wedding customs, though. "In the past the Japanese didn't really have wedding ceremonies," said Masato Uno, a professor of Japanese folklore at Edogawa Gakuen Women's Junior College. "The important event was the reception. This is really just a question of esthetics."

But there are other indicators of Shinto's decline, from statistics showing fewer shrine visits nationally to a decline in observance of the so-called 7-5-3 rites of passage for children on those birthdays, when their families go to a shrine for prayers.

With few people living in her shrine's vicinity, and an awareness that young people have little interest in shrine ceremonies generally, Ms. Sugimoto has pushed the business angle as far as she can. Her days are now spent performing purification ceremonies for television studios that hope for success with new plays or sitcoms, or blessing new construction sites to ward off accidents or earthquake damage.

"Japan is in recession and business may be down, especially for the construction companies," she said with a knowing grin. "But the flip side of this is that I receive requests from real estate companies to pray for an increase in tenants. We have a saying in Japan that people only pray when they are in trouble."

STUDY QUESTIONS

1. What is the *kami*?
2. In Shinto mythology, how did Japan come into existence?
3. What is a *jinja*?
4. In what way is Shinto "this-worldly"?
5. What is the relationship between humans and the *kami*?
6. How did State Shinto contribute to Japanese jingoism in World War II?
7. What is the *Kojiki*? What is the *Nihongi*?
8. What is shrine Shinto? What is folk Shinto?
9. What are some of the fundamental ideas that emerge from the myths of the *Kojiki* and the *Nihongi*?
10. Where did the term *Shinto* come from?

FURTHER READING

W. G. Aston, trans., *Nihongi: Chronicles of Japan from the Earliest Time to A.D. 697* (Rutland, VT: Charles E. Tuttle, 1972).

John Bowker, ed., *The Oxford Dictionary of World Religions* (Oxford: Oxford University Press, 1997).

Joseph M. Kitagawa, *On Understanding Japanese Religion* (Princeton, NJ: Princeton University Press, 1987).

John K. Nelson, *A Year in the Life of a Shinto Shrine* (Seattle: University of Washington Press, 1996).

Ian Reader, *Religion in Contemporary Japan* (Honolulu: University of Hawaii Press, 1991).

Motohisa Yamakage, *The Essence of Shinto: Japan's Spiritual Heart* (New York: Kodansha, 2012).

Wing-Tsit Chan et al., *The Great Asian Religions: An Anthology* (New York: Macmillan, 1969).

ONLINE

Encyclopedia of Shinto, http://eos.kokugakuin.ac.jp (December 25, 2015).

Jinja Honcho: Association of Shinto Shrines, http://www.jinjahoncho.or.jp/en/shinto/ (December 25, 2015).

10 Zoroastrianism

Zoroastrianism is probably the oldest of the prophetic world religions, dating back over three thousand years. It is also the smallest of the world religions, with perhaps no more than 190,000 adherents worldwide, most of them living in India (where Zoroastrians are known as *Parsis*) and the rest mostly in Iran, the United States, Canada, England, Australia, Singapore, and Persian Gulf countries. Today its presence is barely noticed on the world stage, even though it was once the official religion of three powerful Iranian empires that dominated much of the known world for twelve centuries. Zoroastrianism's influence on some of the main ideas of Judaism, Christianity, and Islam has been far greater than many contemporary believers realize.

ZARATHUSTRA AND HIS TEACHINGS

The founder of the tradition is Zarathustra (or Zoroaster, the Greek name), who flourished around northeast Iran (Persia). Some date his life at around 1200 BCE, but there is much debate about when he lived. He arose out of an Indo-Iranian culture that practiced a polytheistic religion led by priests who focused on rituals of fire, water, and animal sacrifice. According to tradition, he was a priest in that religion when, at age thirty, he received a revelation from the one true God, **Ahura Mazda**, the "Lord Wisdom," the world's one supreme deity. Zarathustra began to preach about Ahura Mazda's total goodness and incomparable power, the weakness and malevolence of the ancient Persian gods (the *daevas*), and the evil of **Angra Mainyu** ("Hostile Spirit"), the adversary of God and all that is good. God, Zarathustra asserted, is uncreated, eternal, wholly just, and all-knowing. He is the maker of every good thing in the cosmos, but Angra Mainyu is the author of all things evil, the one who brought death and destruction into Ahura Mazda's perfect universe. As the scholar Mary Boyce says,

> An essential element in this revelation is that the two primal Beings each made a deliberate choice . . . between good and evil, an act which prefigures the identical choice which every man must make for himself in this life. The exercise of choice changed the inherent antagonism between the two Spirits into an active one, which expressed itself, at a decision taken by Ahura Mazda, in creation and counter-creation, or, as the prophet put it, in the making of "life" and "not-life" (that is,

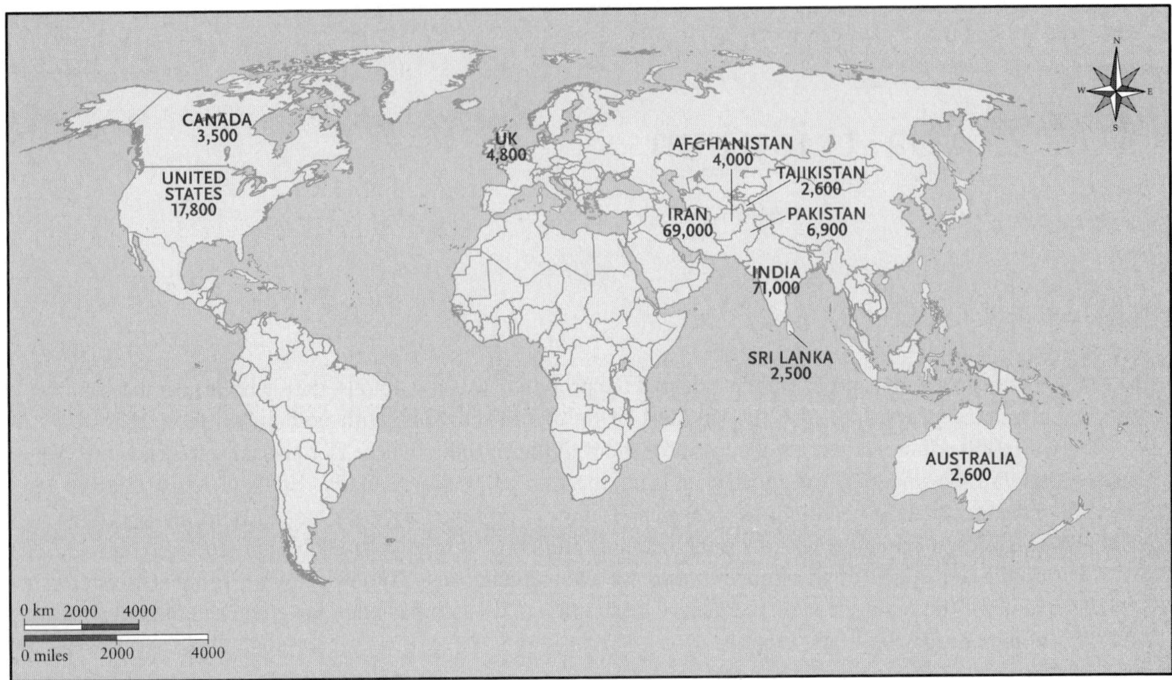

MAP 10.1 World Zoroastrian population.

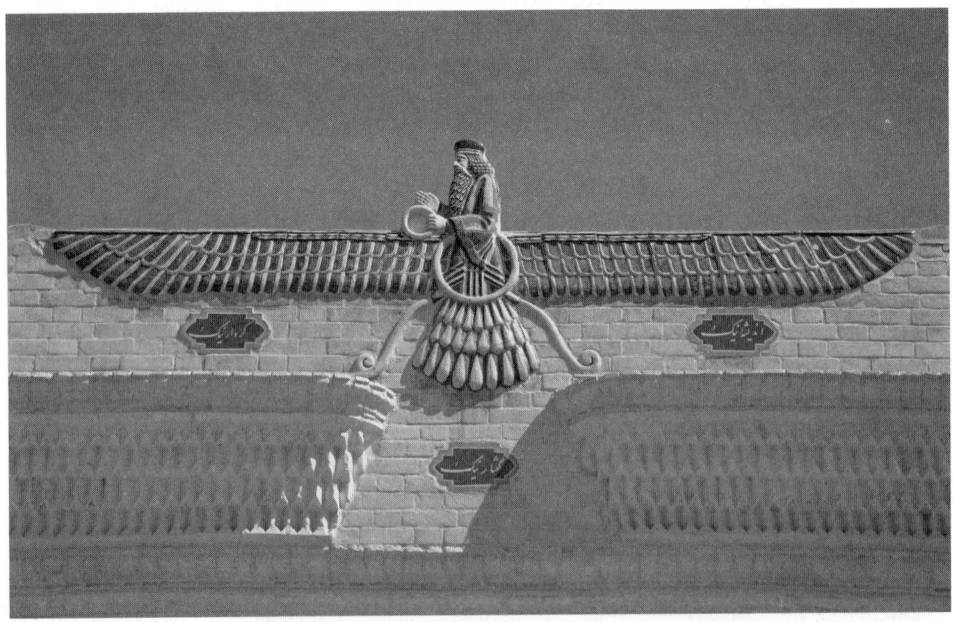

FIGURE 10.1 A statue of Ahura Mazda, "the one true God" in Zoroastrianism, is on display in Yazd, Iran.

ZOROASTRIANISM TIMELINE

BCE

c. 1200 Zarathustra flourishes in Iran.

550–530 Zoroastrianism is established as the Iranian religion by Cyrus the Great.

334–326 Conquest of Iran by Alexander the Great

CE

Seventh century Muslim conquest of Iran; slaughter and forced conversions

Eighth century Zoroastrians leave Iran due to Muslim oppression to live in India; the immigrants are known as Parsis.

Tenth century The Parsis settle in India.

1295–1304 Mongol rule of Iran; more oppression of non-Muslims

1719 Afghan army invades Iran; Zoroastrians of Kerman are slaughtered.

1796–1925 The Muslim Qajar dynasty in Iran, under which Zoroastrians were persecuted

1960 First World Zoroastrian Congress held in Tehran

1979 Ayatollah Khumayni assumes power in Iran; many Zoroastrians leave the country.

> death); for Ahura Mazda knew in his wisdom that if he became Creator and fashioned this world, the Hostile Spirit would attack it, because it was good, and it would become a battleground for their two forces, and in the end he, God, would win the great struggle there and be able to destroy evil, and so achieve a universe which would be wholly good forever.[1]

Ahura Mazda created other divine and beneficent beings, most notably the "Holy Immortals," who in his name promote good and fight evil. Humans are enlisted in this struggle, and their primary duty is the same—to strive for the good. It is the cardinal duty of Zoroastrians, then, to foster "good thoughts, good words, and good deeds." Humans have free will and must choose for themselves which side they will take in this cosmic morality play. (Zoroastrianism therefore avoids proselytizing, for that would be a form of compulsion, a constraint on free will.) In the Zoroastrian view, evil in the world (wickedness, suffering, injustice, and chaos) is not the philosophical and theological problem that it is in the three major Western religions. Evil exists in the world because the forces of evil bring it about.

Zarathustra taught that there is a hereafter in which individuals (rich and poor, high and low) are judged according to the amount of good and evil they produced in their time on earth. If the good outweighs the evil, they are deemed fit for paradise. If the evil outweighs the good, they are thrown into hell, the "House of the Lie," where they will experience a "long age of misery, of darkness, ill food and the crying of woe."

Finally, at the end of time, there will be a last judgment in which the righteous and the wicked will be judged according to their deeds and words in life. This is a judgment both of all who have been previously judged and of those who are alive at the time of this ultimate

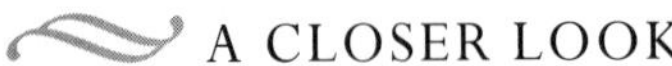 A CLOSER LOOK

Is Zoroastrianism Disappearing?

Some contemporary Zoroastrians fear that their three-thousand-year-old religion may soon die for lack of adherents. Consider this assessment:

> There is a palpable panic among Zoroastrians today—not only in the United States, but also around the world—that they are fighting the extinction of their faith. . . .
>
> While Zoroastrians once dominated an area stretching from what is now Rome and Greece to India and Russia, their global population has dwindled to 190,000 at most, and perhaps as few as 124,000. . . .
>
> "Survival has become a community obsession," said Dina McIntyre, an Indian-American lawyer in Chesapeake, Va., who has written and lectured widely on her religion.
>
> The Zoroastrians' mobility and adaptability has contributed to their demographic crisis. They assimilate and intermarry, virtually disappearing into their adopted cultures. And since the faith encourages opportunities for women, many Zoroastrian women are working professionals who, like many other professional women, have few children or none. . . .
>
> Although the collective picture is bleak, most individual Zoroastrians appear to be thriving. They are well-educated and well-traveled professionals, earning incomes that place them in the middle and upper classes of the countries where they or their families settled after leaving their homelands in Iran and India.[3]

verdict. It is a trial by fire; all humans must pass through a river of molten metal. The righteous will walk through it unharmed; the wicked will be consumed by it, dying a second and permanent death. The burning river will pour into hell, killing Angra Mainyu. It will purify the cosmos, eradicating all evil everywhere. The earth will release the bones of the righteous, who will then receive an immortal resurrected body. The world will return to the perfection it once enjoyed, and the righteous will dwell in it forever in happiness and blessedness.

So we can detect major doctrines of Zoroastrianism in contemporary Western religions. Some scholars even contend that Zoroastrianism was the first to adopt some beliefs that other religions eventually embraced. For example, Mary Boyce notes,

> Zoroaster was thus the first to teach the doctrines of an individual judgment, Heaven and Hell, the future resurrection of the body, the general Last Judgment, and life everlasting for the reunited soul and body. These doctrines were to become familiar articles of faith to much of mankind, through borrowings by Judaism, Christianity and Islam. . . .[2]

ZOROASTRIAN SCRIPTURES

The most revered collection of Zoroastrian scripture is the voluminous **Avesta** (which most likely means "The Injunction [of Zarathustra]"). It contains liturgical writings (hymns, poems, and prayers), laws of purity, histories and legends about Zarathustra, explanations of

BACKGROUND

Zoroastrian Burial

The traditional Zoroastrian burial ritual (called the "rite of exposure") is like none other. Here is a description:

> The Zoroastrian burial ritual is quite distinctive. In both scripture and tradition, decaying corpses would pollute the earth, the good creation. In India, where it is not illegal, Parsis [Zoroastrians who immigrated from Persia] have traditionally exposed bodies in "Towers of Silence," to be eaten by vultures. This tradition has been fading, however, both because the population of vultures has been rapidly declining as a result of toxic chemicals fed to cattle and, to some degree, because of hostility from Hindus. In most places disposal of bodies is now carried out by cremation.[4]

doctrine, exegesis of particular *Avestan* writings, speculations about the origins of the universe, and works of rudimentary science. Three-quarters of the early *Avesta* has been lost, with the oldest existing manuscript dating back to 1323 CE. What remains was written in a rare eastern Iranian language, and the *Avesta* itself is the only existing example of a work in this linguistic form. For centuries the *Avesta* lived only in recitation and was finally written down in the fifth century CE. Over the centuries, it was expanded to include many other texts

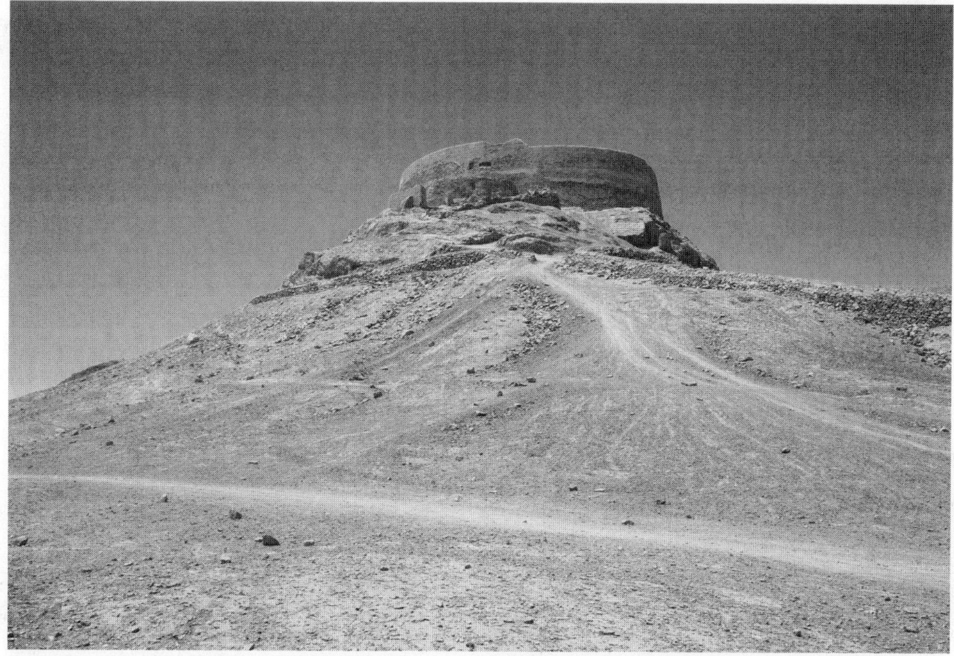

FIGURE 10.2 The dakhma, or "Tower of Silence," provides a space for exposure of the dead body to vultures and to the sun. This dakhma is located in Yazd, Iran.

by several authors in different eras. By tradition, however, the entire *Avesta* is ascribed to Zarathustra.

A large part of the *Avesta* consists of the *Yasna* (*Yasna* refers to Zoroastrian acts of worship), an ancient collection of liturgical writings in seventy-two sections. Part of the *Yasna* contains the *Gathas*, seventeen hymns that appear to have been written by Zarathustra himself. They are in the form of brief but passionate verses addressed to Ahura Mazda. In these, Zarathustra calls himself a *manthran*, someone who can write mantras, or inspired words of power.

The *Avesta* also includes the *Vendidad* ("Against the Daevas"), an assortment of writings concerned principally with laws of purity as a way to fend off evil beings; the *Visperad* ("Worship [of] All the Masters"), an addendum of invocations; the *Khorda Avesta*, the Zoroastrian book of common prayer for daily use by lay people; and *Zand* ("Interpretation"), exegeses and glosses of the *Avesta* (thus referred to as the *Zend Avesta*).

NOTES

1. Mary Boyce, *Zoroastrians: Their Religious Beliefs and Practices* (London: Routledge and Kegan Paul, 1979, 2001), 20–21.
2. *Ibid.*, 29.
3. Laurie Goodstein, "Zoroastrians Keep the Faith, and Keep Dwindling," *New York Times*, September 6, 2006, A1.
4. John C. Peterson, "Zoroastrianism," March 2012, *World Religions and Spirituality Project*, www.has.vcu.edu/wrs/profiles/Zoroastrianism (June 2, 2014).

KEY TERMS

Ahura Mazda The supreme God of Zoroastrianism; the "Lord Wisdom."

Angra Mainyu "Hostile Spirit," the adversary of God and all that is good.

Avesta The sacred text of Zoroastrianism.

READINGS

TEACHINGS

The Zoroastrian Creed

This excerpt from the *Avesta* is one of Zoroastrianism's oldest and most important statements of beliefs. It calls for believers to eschew the evil of the *daevas* and the Demon-of-the-Lie, and to embrace the good of Lord Ahura Mazda, the supreme deity of the universe. The last sentence sums up the creed: "Yea, to Ahura Mazda do I ascribe all good, and such shall be the worship of the Mazdayasnian belief!"

1. I drive the Daêvas hence; I confess as a Mazda-worshipper of the order of Zarathustra, estranged from the Daêvas, devoted to the lore of the Lord, a praiser of the Bountiful Immortals; and to Ahura Mazda, the good and endowed with good possessions, I attribute all things good, to the holy One, the resplendent, to the glorious, whose are all things whatsoever which are good; whose is the Kine, whose is Asha (the righteous order pervading all things pure), whose are the stars, in whose lights the glorious beings and objects are clothed.

2. And I choose Piety, the bounteous and the good, mine may she be. And therefore I loudly (deprecate all robbery and violence against the sacred) Kine, and all drought to the wasting of the Mazdayasnian villages.

3. Away from (?) their thoughts do I wish to lead (the thought of) wandering at will, (away the thought of) free nomadic pitching of the tent, for I wish to remove (?) all wandering from (their) Kine which abide in steadfastness upon this land; and bowing down in worship to Righteousness I dedicate my offerings with praise so far as that. Never may I stand as a source of wasting, never as a source of withering to the Mazdayasnian villages, not for the love of body or of life.

4. Away do I abjure the shelter and headship of the Daêvas, evil as they are; aye, utterly bereft of good, and void of virtue, deceitful in their wickedness, of (all) beings those most like the Demon-of-the-Lie, the most loathsome of existing things, and the ones the most of all bereft of good.

5. Off, off, do I abjure the Daêvas and all possessed by them, the sorcerers and all that hold to their devices, and every existing being of the sort; their thoughts do I abjure, their words and actions, and their seed (that propagate their sin); away do I abjure their shelter and their headship, and the iniquitous of every kind who act as Rakhshas act!

Thus and so in very deed might Ahura Mazda have indicated to Zarathustra in every question which Zarathustra asked, and in all the consultations in the which they two conversed together.

L. H. Mills, trans., *The Zend Avesta, Sacred Books of the East, Yasna 12* (Oxford: Oxford University Press, 1886).

6. Thus and so might Zarathustra have abjured the shelter and the headship of the Daêvas in all the questions, and in all the consultations with which they two conversed together, Zarathustra and the Lord.

And so I myself, in whatsoever circumstances I may be placed, as a worshipper of Mazda, and of Zarathustra's order, would so abjure the Daêvas and their shelter, as he who was the holy Zarathustra abjured them (once of old).

7. To that religious sanctity to which the waters appertain, do I belong, to that sanctity to which the plants, to that sanctity to which the Kine of blessed gift, to that religious sanctity to which Ahura Mazda, who made both Kine and holy men, belongs, to that sanctity do I. Of that creed which Zarathustra held, which Kavi Vîstâspa, and those two, Frashaostra and Gâmâspa; yea, of that religious faith which every Saoshyant who shall (yet come to) save (us), the holy ones who do the deeds of real significance, of that creed, and of that lore, am I.

8. A Mazda-worshipper I am, of Zarathustra's order; (so) do I confess, as a praiser and confessor, and I therefore praise aloud the well-thought thought, the word well spoken, and the deed well done;

9. Yea, I praise at once the Faith of Mazda, the Faith which has no faltering utterance, the Faith that wields the felling halbert, the Faith of kindred marriage, the holy (Creed), which is the most imposing, best, and most beautiful of all religions which exist, and of all that shall in future come to knowledge, Ahura's Faith, the Zarathustrian creed. Yea, to Ahura Mazda do I ascribe all good, and such shall be the worship of the Mazdayasnian belief!

To Ahura and the Fire

This prayer-hymn praises both Ahura Mazda and the spirit of fire while stressing the importance of morally upright living. In Zoroastrian temples, fire is a symbol of divine presence and moral purity.

1. We would approach You two, O (Ye) primeval ones in the house of this Thy holy Fire, O Ahura Mazda, Thou most bounteous Spirit! Who brings pollutions to this (Thy flame) him wilt Thou cover with pollutions (in his turn).

2. But as the most friendly do Thou give us zeal, O Fire of the Lord! and approach us, and with the loving blessing of the most friendly, with the praise of the most adored. Yea, may'st thou approach to aid us in this our greatest (undertaking) among the efforts of our zeal.

3. The Fire of Ahura Mazda art thou verily; yea, the most bounteous one of His Spirit, wherefore Thine is the most potent of all names (for grace), O Fire of the Lord!

4. And therefore we would approach Thee, (O Ahura!) with the help of Thy Good Mind (which Thou dost implant within us), with Thy (good) Righteousness, and with the actions and the words inculcated by Thy good wisdom!

5. We therefore bow before Thee, and we direct our prayers to Thee with confessions of our

L. H. Mills, trans., *The Zend Avesta, Sacred Books of the East, Yasna 36* (Oxford: Oxford University Press, 1886).

guilt, O Ahura Mazda! with all the good thoughts (which Thou dost inspire), with all the words well said, and the deeds well done, with these would we approach Thee.

6. And to Thy most beauteous body do we make our deep acknowledgments, O Ahura Mazda! to those stars (which are Thy body); and to that one, the highest of the high, [such as the sun was called]!

Hymn to Ahura

This hymn is another kind of affirmation of faith as well as a declaration of fervent commitment to Ahura Mazda.

1. Thus therefore do we worship Ahura Mazda, who made the Kine (the living creation), and the (embodied) Righteousness (which is incarnate in the clean), and the waters, and the wholesome plants, the stars, and the earth, and all (existing) objects that are good.

2. Yea, we worship Him for His Sovereign Power and His greatness, beneficent (as they are), and with priority among the Yazads who abide beside the Kine (and care for her protection and support).

3. And we worship Him under His name as Lord, to Mazda dear, the most beneficent (of names). We worship him with our bones, and with our flesh, (with our bodies and our life). And we worship the Fravashis of the saints, of holy men, and holy women;

4. And Righteousness the Best do we worship, the most beauteous, the Bountiful Immortal and that which is endowed with light in all things good.

5. And we worship the Good Mind (of the Lord), and His Sovereign Power, and the Good Faith, the good law of our thrift, and Piety the ready mind (within Thy folk)!

L. H. Mills, trans., *The Zend Avesta, Sacred Books of the East, Yasna 37* (Oxford: Oxford University Press, 1886).

Resurrection and Final Judgment

At the end of time, Ahura Mazda will raise the dead, both the evil and the good, beginning with the first human (Gayomard). Then all will be judged according to the good and evil they did in their mortal lives. All will have to walk through a river of molten metal: the good people will pass through unharmed, but the evil ones will be consumed. The molten metal will flow into hell and cleanse it, and the Evil Spirit (God's evil counterpart) will be destroyed. Then Ahura Mazda's kingdom will appear on earth, and the world will be made perfect (Frashegird) just as it was in the beginning.

Mary Boyce, trans. *Textual Sources for the Study of Zoroastrianism, Yasna 30* (Chicago: University of Chicago Press, 1984), 52–53.

Zardusht asked Ohrmazd: "From where shall the body be reassembled which the wind has blown away, and the water carried off? And how shall the resurrection take place?" Ohrmazd answered: "When I created the sky without pillars . . . ; and when I created the earth which bears all physical life . . . ; and when I set in motion the sun and moon and stars . . . ; and when I created corn, that it might be scattered in the earth and grow again, giving back increase . . . ; and when I created and protected the child in the mother's womb . . . ; and when I created the cloud, which bears water for the world and rains it down where it chooses; and when I created the wind . . . which blows as it pleases then the creation of each one of these was more difficult for me than the raising of the dead. For . . . consider, if I made that which was not, why cannot I make again that which was?"

First, the bones of Gayomard will be raised up, and then those of Mashya and Mashyanag, and then those of other people. In fifty-seven years the Soshyant will raise up all the dead. And all mankind will arise, whether just or wicked. Then the assembly of Isadvastar will take place. In that assembly, everyone will behold his own good or bad deeds, and the just will stand out among the wicked like white sheep among black. Fire and the yazad Airyaman will melt the metal in the hills and mountains, and it will be upon the earth like a river. Then all men will be caused to pass through that molten metal. . . . And for those who are just it will seem as if they are walking through warm milk; and for the wicked it will seem as if they are walking in the flesh through molten metal. And thereafter men will come together with the greatest affection, father and son and brother and friend. The Soshyant with his helpers will perform the yasna for restoring the dead. For that yasna they will slay the Hadayans bull; from the fat of that bull and the white haoma they will prepare ambrosia and give it to all mankind; and all men will become immortal, for ever and ever. Then Vahman will seize Akoman, Ardvahisht Indar, Shahrevar Savol, Spendarmad . . . Nanhaith, Hordad and Amurdad Turiz and Zairiz, Truthful Utterance Lying Utterance, and the just Srosh Eshm of the bloody club. Then there will remain the two Druj, Ahriman and the Demon of Greed. Ohrmazd will Himself come to the world as celebrating priest, and the just Srosh as serving priest; and He will hold the sacred girdle in His hands. And at that Gathic liturgy the Evil Spirit, helpless and with his power destroyed, will rush back to shadowy darkness through the way by which he had entered. And the molten metal will flow into hell; and the stench and filth in the earth, where hell was, will be burnt by that metal, and it will become clean. The gap through which the Evil Spirit had entered will be closed by that metal. The hell within the earth will be brought up again to the world's surface, and there will be Frashegird in the world.

Good and Evil

This selection draws a clear distinction between good and evil—between Ahura Mazda (Lord of Good Purpose) and the Wicked One (the Deceiver, Evil Spirit). These two "primal Spirits" are in continual conflict. In the beginning the former chose good; the latter chose evil. In the end those who follow the Wicked One will end up in hell (the Worst Existence); those who follow Ahura Mazda will reside in heaven (the House of Best Purpose).

Mary Boyce, trans., *Textual Sources for the Study of Zoroastrianism, Yasna 30* (Chicago: University of Chicago Press, 1984), 35.

(1) Truly for seekers I shall speak of those things to be pondered, even by one who already knows, with praise and worship for the Lord of Good Purpose, the excellently Wise One, and for Truth . . . . (2) Hear with your ears the best things. Reflect with clear purpose, each man for himself, on the two choices for decision, being alert indeed to declare yourselves for Him before the great requital. (3) Truly there are two primal Spirits, twins renowned to be in conflict. In thought and word, in act they are two: the better and the bad. And those who act well have chosen rightly between these two, not so the evildoers. (4) And when these two Spirits first came together they created life and not-life, and how at the end Worst Existence shall be for the wicked, but (the House of) Best Purpose for the just man. (5) Of these two Spirits the Wicked One chose achieving the worst things. The Most Holy Spirit, who is clad in hardest stone, chose right, and (so do those) who shall satisfy Lord Mazda continually with rightful acts. (6) The Daevas indeed did not choose rightly between these two, for the Deceiver approached them as they conferred. Because they chose worst purpose, they then rushed to Fury, with whom they have afflicted the world and mankind. (7) With Power He came to this world, by Good Purpose and by Truth. Then enduring Devotion gave body and breath . . . . (8) Then when retribution comes for these sinners, then, Mazda, Power shall be present for Thee with Good Purpose, to declare himself for those, Lord, who shall deliver the Lie into the hands of Truth. (9) And then may we be those who shall transfigure this world. O Mazda (and you other) Lords (Ahuras), be present to me with support and truth, so that thoughts may be concentrated where understanding falters. . . . (11) O men! when you learn the commands which Mazda has given, and both thriving and not-thriving, and what long torment (is) for the wicked and salvation for the just—then will it be as is wished with these things.

Fate of the Soul at Death

After death, people's souls must pass over the Chinvat Bridge, which crosses over hell far below. If they have chosen the good in their lifetimes, the bridge will be wide and easy to cross into heaven. If they have chosen evil, the bridge will narrow so that crossing is impossible, and they will fall into hell.

Zarathushtra said to Ahura Mazda . . . : "O Creator! where shall the rewards be, where shall the rewards be adjudged, where shall the rewards be concluded, where shall the rewards be reckoned up, which a man earns for his soul in the material world?" Then said Ahura Mazda: "After a man is dead, after his time is over, after the wicked demons, evil of thought, rend him completely, at dawn of the third night, the Radiant One (the Dawn) grows bright and shines, and Mithra, having good weapons, shining like the sun, arises and ascends the mountains which possess the bliss of Asha. The demon named Vizaresha ('He who drags away'), O Spitama Zarathushtra, leads the bound soul of the wicked man, the worshipper of demons. . . . It (the soul) goes along the paths created by time for both the wicked and the just, to the Mazda-created Chinvat Bridge. . . . There comes that beautiful one, strong, fair of form, accompanied by the two dogs. . . . She comes over high Hara, she takes the souls of the just over the Chinvat Bridge, to the rampart of the invisible yazatas. Vohu Manah rises from his golden throne. Vohu Manah exclaims: 'How have you come here, O just one, from the perilous world to the world without peril?' Contented, the souls of the just proceed to the golden thrones of Ahura Mazda and the Amesha Spentas, to the House of Song, the dwelling-place of Ahura Mazda, the dwelling-place of the Amesha Spentas, the dwelling-place of the just."

Mary Boyce, trans., *Textual Sources for the Study of Zoroastrianism, Vendidad 19* (Chicago: University of Chicago Press, 1984), 80.

PRACTICES

The Four Main Prayers

These prayers are essential to Zoroastrianism; adherents recite them repeatedly. The names of the prayers come from their opening words.

Ahuna vairyo

As the Master, so is the Judge to be chosen in accord with truth. Establish the power of acts arising from a life lived with good purpose, for Mazda and for the lord whom they made pastor for the poor.

Airyema ishyo

May longed-for Airyaman come to the support of the men and women of Zarathushtra, to the support of good purpose. The Inner Self which earns the reward to be chosen, for it I ask the longed-for recompense of truth, which Lord Mazda will have in mind.

Ashem vohu

Asha is good, it is best. According to wish it is, according to wish it shall be for us. Asha belongs to Asha Vahishta.

Yenhe hatam

Those Beings, male and female, whom Lord Mazda knows the best for worship according to truth, we worship them all.

Mary Boyce, trans., *Textual Sources for the Study of Zoroastrianism, Yasna 27, 54* (Chicago: Chicago University Press, 1984), 56–57.

Burial of the Dead

This excerpt lays out the requirements for a proper Zoroastrian burial. Since Zoroastrians regard a dead body as polluting, they avoid in-ground burials. Instead they prefer to place the dead in "towers of silence," high places where the body can be eaten by birds of prey or other scavengers. Where towers of silence are not available, alternative methods of burial are used.

[Zarathustra asked:] "O Maker of the material world, thou Holy One! Whither shall we bring, where shall we lay the bodies of the dead, O Ahura Mazda?"

Ahura Mazda answered: "On the highest summits, where they know there are always corpse-eating dogs and corpse-eating birds, O holy Zarathustra!

James Darmesteter, trans., *Vendidad 6: 44–51, Sacred Books of the East* (Oxford: Oxford University Press, 1880).

"There shall the worshippers of Mazda fasten the corpse, by the feet and by the hair, with brass, stones, or lead, lest the corpse-eating dogs and the corpse-eating birds shall go and carry the bones to the water and to the trees."

"If they shall not fasten the corpse, so that the corpse-eating dogs and the corpse-eating birds may go and carry the bones to the water and to the trees, what is the penalty that they shall pay?"

Ahura Mazda answered: "They shall be Peshôtanus: two hundred stripes with the Aspahê-astra, two hundred stripes with the Sraoshô-karana."

"Maker of the material world, thou Holy-one! Whither shall we bring, where shall we lay the bones of the dead, O Ahura Mazda?"

Ahura Mazda answered: "The worshippers of Mazda shall erect a building out of the reach of the dog, of the fox, and of the wolf, and wherein rain-water cannot stay.

"Such a building shall they erect, if they can afford it, with stones, mortar, and earth; if they cannot afford it, they shall lay down the dead man on the ground, on his carpet and his pillow, clothed with the light of heaven, and beholding the sun."

Zoroastrian Ceremonies

RUSTOM MASANI

The following is a modern commentary by the Zoroastrian scholar Rustom Masani on Zoroastrian rites of birth and death.

BIRTH CEREMONIES

"I prefer," says Ahura Mazda in the *Vendidad*, "a person with children to one without children." Even the soil feels happy where a man with children lives. This conviction makes the advent of a child doubly welcome in a Zoroastrian home. We do not find in the Avesta any reference to pregnancy rites. In the later Pahlavi and Persian books, however, we find references to certain rites. For instance, the *Sayast la Sayast* directs that during the days of pregnancy a fire may be maintained most carefully in the house. According to the *Vendidad*, the place for delivery must be very clean, dry, and least frequented by others. After delivery, the mother should avoid contact with fire, water, and the *baresman* (i.e. the sacred ceremonial apparatus) of the house. It enjoins a period of twelve days for such isolation in the case of a still-born child.

MARRIAGE CEREMONIES

After prolonged contact with the Hindus in India, the present-day followers of Zarathushtra have adopted

Rustom Masani, "Socio-Religions Ceremonies," in *Zoroastrianism: The Religion of the Good Life* (New Delhi: Cosmo, 2003), 143–158.

several Hindu marriage customs and ceremonies, but the strictly religious part of the ceremony, as performed by the officiating priests, is more or less orthodox Iranian and is conducted mainly in the later Pazand language. It consists of:

1. Preliminary benedictions.
2. Questions to the marrying couple and the witness on either side.
3. Joint address by the two officiating priests.

The senior priest blesses the couple in these words:

"May the Creator, the Omniscient Lord, grant you a progeny of sons and grandsons, plenty of means to provide yourselves, abiding love, bodily strength, long life for a hundred and fifty years."

Thrice during the course of the benediction a declaration of the witnesses and of the bride and bridegroom is taken by the priest. The witness on behalf of the bridegroom's family is first asked:

"In the presence of this assembly that has met together in the city of __ on __ day of __ month of the year __ of the era of Emperor Yazdagard of the Eassanian dynasty of auspicious Iran, say, whether you have agreed to take this maiden __ by name, in marriage for this bridegroom, in accordance with the rites and rules of the Mazdayasnans, promising to pay her 2,000 *dirams* of pure white silver and two *dinars* of real gold of the Nishapur coinage."

"I have agreed," replies the witness.

Then the following question is put to the other witness: "Have you and your family with righteous mind, and truthful thoughts, words, and actions, and for the increase of righteousness, agreed to give for ever this bride in marriage to ___?"

He replies: "We have agreed."

The priest then asks the couple: "Have you agreed to enter into this contract of marriage (and abide by it) till the last day of your life, with a righteous mind?"

Both reply: "We have agreed."

Then follows the recital of the *Paevandanama*, or *Ashirwad*, an address replete with benedictions, admonitions, and prayers, by the two officiating priests who keep on showering on the couple grains of rice as an emblem of happiness and plenty.

The *Ashirwad* is not merely a benedictory address; it is also a little sermon which closes with a short prayer. Likewise, the admonitory part of it is not merely a homily exhorting the bride and the bridegroom to cultivate good qualities, to do good and to shun evil; it is also a discourse for the entire assembly on worldly wisdom and a key to success in life. As an illustration, the following extracts may be noted:

"Do not quarrel with the revengeful. Never be a partner with an avaricious man. Do not be a comrade of a back-biter. Do not join the company of persons of ill-fame. Do not co-operate with the ill-informed. Do not enter into any discussion with persons of bad report. Speak in an assembly after mature consideration. Speak with moderation in the presence of kings."

"Oh, ye good men," says the officiating priest, "may good accrue to you as the result of perfect good thoughts, perfect good words, and perfect good deeds! May that piety come to you which is the best of all good. May not sinful life, which is the worst of all evil, come to you. . . . Righteousness is the best gift and happiness. Happiness to him who is righteous for the sake of the best righteousness!"

In the concluding paragraph of the *Ashirwad* the married couple is blest in these terms:

"May they have light and glory, physical strength, physical health, and physical success; wealth that may bring with it much happiness, children blest with innate wisdom, a very long life and the blissful paradise, which is due to the pious! May it be so as I wish it!"

FUNERAL CEREMONIES

It will be convenient to treat the funeral ceremonies and observances under the following two heads:

1. Ceremonies relating to the disposal of the dead.
2. Ceremonies relating to the soul.

DISPOSAL OF THE DEAD

To maintain fire, air, water, and earth pure and undefiled is a cardinal principle of the Zoroastrian creed. It is enjoined that the body of a person, after the soul has left it, should with due respect to the deceased be disposed of in such a manner as not to defile these elements or to injure the living. Accordingly, the followers of the creed do not burn or bury their dead, or consign them to the water. They merely expose the dead, on the top of a high hill, to the heat of the Sun, there to be devoured by carnivorous birds. Their funeral ceremonies are likewise based on the ancient Zoroastrian ideas of sanitation, segregation, and purification. All the ceremonies of this order appear to have anticipated the prophylactic measures taken in modern times for the prevention of epidemics, namely, (1) breaking the contact of the living with the real or supposed centre of infection, and (2) destroying such a centre itself. As a matter of precaution, all cases of death are treated as infectious, and the followers of the faith are warned that they should bring themselves, as little as possible, into contact with dead bodies.

Soon after death, the corpse is washed and a clean suit of clothes is put over it. The Kusti, or the sacred thread, is then put round the body with a prayer. The corpse is placed on the ground in a corner of the front room on large slabs of stone, or impermeable, hard, dry clods of earth. The hands art, folded upon the chest crosswise. After the corpse is placed on slabs of stone, one of the two professional corpse-bearers, to whom the body is entrusted, draws round it three *Kashas*, or circles, with a metallic bar or nail, thus reserving temporarily the marked plot of ground for the corpse so as to prevent the living from going near it and catching infection.

The dead body is then shown to a dog with two eye-like spots just above the eyes. It is believed that this particular kind of spotted (*Chathru Chasma*, literally, "the four-eyed") dog has the faculty to detect whether life in the body is extinct or not. It is expected to stare steadily at the body, if life is extinct; but not even to look at it if otherwise.

Fire is then brought into the room in a vase and is kept burning with fragrant sandalwood and frankincense. Before the fire sits a priest who recites the Avestan texts till the time of the removal of the corpse to the Tower, and keeps the fire burning. The corpse may be removed to the Tower at any time during the day, but not at night, as the body must be exposed to the Sun.

About an hour before the time fixed for the removal of the body to the Tower, two or, if the body is heavier, four *Nassasalars*, i.e. corpse-bearers, clothed completely in white, enter the house. In the case of a death due to an infectious disease, all the exposed parts of the body, except the face, are covered up, so as to prevent infection through any uncovered part. They carry a bier, called *gehan*, invariably made of iron, to remove the body. Wood being porous and, therefore, likely to carry and spread germs of disease and infection, its use is strictly prohibited in the funeral ceremonies.

The corpse-bearers place the bier by the side of the corpse. They then recite in a suppressed tone the following formula of grace, and remain silent up to the time of the final disposal of the corpse in the Tower of Silence.

"(We do this) according to the dictates of Ahura Mazda, according to the dictates of the Amesha-Spenta, according to the dictates of the Holy Sraosha, according to the dictates of Adarbad Maraspend, and according to the dictates of the Dastur of the age!"

They sit silent by the side of the corpse. If there is any occasion on which they must break silence, they do so in a subdued tone, without opening the lips.

Then follows the "Geh-Sarna" ceremony, i.e. the recital of the *Getha,* which is intended to be an admonition to the survivors to bear with fortitude the loss of the deceased. After this, the corpse is again shown, to the dog; the relatives and friends, who have by this time assembled at the house, then have a last look of the deceased. After the *geh-sarna* ceremony, the mourners pass, one by one, before the corpse, to have a last look and to bow before it as a mark of respect.

The corpse-bearers then cover the face with a piece of cloth and secure the body to the bier with a few straps of cloth. They carry the bier, out of the house and entrust it to the *Khandias*, another set of corpse-bearers, whose business it is to carry the bier on their shoulders to the Tower.

When the bier reaches the Tower, it is put on the ground outside; the corpse-bearers uncover the face, and those who have accompanied the funeral procession pay their respects and have a last look from a distance of at least three paces. After the dead body is once more exposed to the sight of the "four-eyed" dog, for the last time, the gate of the Tower is opened. The *Nassasalars*, who took the corpse out of the house and have accompanied the corpse to the last resting-place, now take over the bier from the carriers and take it into the Tower, and place the dead body on the space set apart for it. They then tear off the clothes from the body of the deceased and leave it on the floor of the Tower. Naked one comes into this world; naked one leaves it.

The body is exposed and left uncovered, so that the eye of the flesh-devouring birds may be drawn to it. The sooner it is eaten up, the fewer the chances of further decomposition, and the greater the safety of the living. The clothes removed from the corpse are thrown in a pit outside the Tower, where they are destroyed by the combined action of heat, air, and rain. In Bombay they are destroyed with sulphuric acid.

On completing their work the corpse-bearers lock the Tower. Thereupon an attendant claps his hands as a signal to all those who have accompanied the funeral procession and who have by this time taken their seats at some distance from the Tower. They all get up from their seats and recite the rest of the *Sraosh baj* prayer, of which, before joining the procession, they had recited only a part. This is followed by a short prayer, in which they say: "We repent of all our sins. Our respects to you (the souls of the departed). We remember here the souls of the dead who are the spirits of the holy."

THE TOWER OF SILENCE

"O Holy Creator of the Material World! Where are we to carry the bodies of the dead? O Ahura Mazda! Where are we to place them?" asks Zarathushtra in the *Vendidad*.

Ahura Mazda replies: "O Spitama Zarathushtra, on the most elevated place."

In the earliest times corpses were exposed on the summits of high mountains without any inclosures. When the bones were denuded of flesh by dogs, vultures and other carnivorous birds, and rendered absolutely dry, and desiccated in the course of a year, they were removed and preserved in *Astodans*, that is, receptacles for the preservation of bones, the stone-urns referred to by classical authors. The *Astodans* were made of stone, mortar, or any other durable substance capable of withstanding infection, as the means of the relatives of the deceased permitted. The existing Towers of Silence are so constructed as to secure the ready disposal of the flesh and the preservation of the bones; and it is recognized that the modern method is superior to the ancient, inasmuch as it does not involve defilement of a large area of ground and recognizes no distinction between the rich and the poor. All bones are disposed of in the same well, establishing equality of all in death.

THE BOMBAY TOWERS OF SILENCE

The best example of the modern method is to be seen in the Bombay Towers of Silence. It is a round, massive structure, built entirely of solid stone. A few steps from the ground lead to an iron gate which opens on a circular platform of solid stone with a circular well in the centre. The circular platform inside the Tower, about three hundred feet in circumference, is paved with large stone slabs, well-cemented, and divided into three rows of shallow, open receptacles, corresponding to the triad, good thought, good word, good deed. The first row is used for corpses of men, the second for corpses of women, and the third for corpses of children.

There are footpaths for corpse-bearers to move about. A deep central well (*bhandar*) in the Tower, about one hundred and fifty feet in circumference (the sides and bottom of which are also paved with stone slabs), is used for depositing the dry bones. The corpse is completely stripped of its flesh by vultures within an hour or two, and the bones of the denuded skeleton, when perfectly dried up by atmospheric influences and the powerful heat of the tropical sun, are thrown into this well, where they gradually crumble to dust, chiefly consisting of lime and phosphorus.

In the compound of the Tower, at a short distance from it, there is a small building called *sagri*, where a sacred fire is kept burning day and night. In *mofussil* towns, where it is not possible to do so, at least a light is kept burning.

CEREMONIES RELATING TO THE SOUL OF THE DECEASED

"O Ahura Mazda, Beneficent Spirit, Holy Creator of the material world! when a pious man dies, where dwells his soul for that night? . . . Where for the second night? . . . Where for the third night?" asks Zarathushtra in the *Hadokht Nask*.

Ahura Mazda replies: "It remains at the place of his body, singing the *Ustavaiti Gatha*, asking for blessedness: 'Blessedness to him whom Ahura Mazda of His own will grants blessedness!'"

If it is the soul of a wicked man, it remains within the precincts of this world for three nights. Remembering all the sinfulness of its past life and feeling at a loss where to go, it clamours: "Oh, Ahura Mazda! To what land shall I turn? Where shall I go?"

The soul of a dead person that thus remains within the precincts of this world is under the special protection of Sraosha, whom Ahura Mazda has appointed to guard the souls of men during life and after death. The religious ceremonies for the soul of the dead during the first three days are, therefore, performed in the name of, or with the propitiatory formulae of invocation (*Khshnuman*) of, Sraosha. The *Shayast-las-Shayast* enjoins: "During all the three days, it is necessary to perform the ceremony (*Yazisn of Sraosha*) because Sraosha will be able to save his soul from the hands of the *daevas* during the three days; and when one constantly performs a ceremony at every period (*gah*) in the three days, it is as good as though he should celebrate the whole religious ritual at one time.

At the commencement of every *gah*, two or more priests and the relatives of the deceased recite the *Sraosh baj* and the formula of the particular *gah*, and the *patit*, or the penitence prayer, with the *Khshnuman* of Sraosha. At night two priests perform the *Afringan* ceremony in honour of Sraosha. They sit on a carpet face to face, with an altar of fire and a metallic tray between them. The senior priest, who has the tray before him, is called the *Zaotar*, or invoking priest. The other, who has the altar of fire before him, is called the *Atarevaks*, or the nourisher of fire. The metallic tray contains a pot of pure water and a few flowers.

The Zaotar begins the Afringan, invoking in the course of the introductory portion, which is composed in the Pazand language, the protection of Sraosha upon the soul of the deceased, who is specifically mentioned by name in the prayer. Both the priests then recite together the seventh section of the *Sraosha Yacht*, which sings the praises of the *Yazata* for the protection it affords.

Besides these prayers and ceremonies, which are performed for three days and nights at the house of the deceased, the *Yasna* litany, and, sometimes, the *Vendidad* with the *Khshnuman* of Sraosha, are recited at an adjoining fire-temple for three successive mornings and nights. . . .

PASSAGE OF THE SOUL TO THE OTHER WORLD

On the dawn after the third night the soul is believed to pass on to the other world, crossing the bridge called *Chinvat*. This bridge is guarded by the Yazata *Mithra*. "When the third night ends and the day breaks, with the first appearance of light in the morning, the well-armed Mithra appears on the Elysian heights. This Yazata, who is known in the later books as *Meher Davar*, i.e. Meher the Judge, is assisted by *Rashnu*, the *Yazata* of Justice, and *Astad*, the *Yazata* of Truth. They judge the man's actions during his life time. If his good deeds outweigh the bad ones even by a small particle, his soul is allowed to pass over the bridge to Paradise; if his good deeds just balance his misdeeds, the soul goes to a place called *Hamestagan;* but if his misdeeds outweigh his good deeds, even by a particle, he is flung deep down into the abyss of hell."

The dawn after the third night after death is, therefore, regarded as a very important and solemn occasion for the performance of religious ceremonies for the benefit of the soul of the deceased. The ceremonies performed in the afternoon on the previous day are repeated; the *Afringan* and *Baj* prayers are recited, and other ceremonies are performed. This being the day of judgment, the relatives and friends of the dead join in prayer for God's mercy on his soul.

Baj ceremonies are recited, firstly in honour of the *Yazata Rashnu* and *Astad* together, who help the Yazata *Meher*; secondly, in honour of *Rama Khvastra*, who is the Yazata presiding on the rarefied atmosphere, or ether; thirdly, in honour of *Ardafravash*, i.e. the holy spirits of all the departed souls, whom the deceased has joined; and fourthly, in honour of *Sraosha*, who guided the soul of the deceased in its journey to the other world. When the *Baj* of *Ardafravash* is recited, a suit of white clothes, together with the sacred bread and other votive offerings, is consecrated by the priest. This suit of clothes is called *syav*. It is the *vastra* mentioned in the *Fravardin Yast*: "Who will praise us . . . with clothes in hand?" This suit of clothes is generally given as a gift to the priest or to the poor. The other principal occasion, on which the *Afringan-Baj* ceremonies should, according to the scriptural injunctions, be performed in honour of the dead, are the *Cheharum*, *Dahum*, *Siroz*, and *Salroz*, i.e. the fourth day, the tenth day, the thirtieth day, and the anniversary day.

Death does not put an end to the relation between the deceased and the surviving members of his family. According to the Zoroastrian belief, the holy spirit of the dead continues to take an interest in the living. If the surviving relations cherish his memory, remember him with gratitude and try to please him with pious thoughts, pious words, and pious deeds, the departed spirit takes an interest in their welfare, and assists them with invisible helping hands. Therefore, the most essential tribute with which a surviving relative can please the holy spirits of his departed dear ones consists of pious thoughts, words, and deeds. Thus the performance of meritorious and charitable deeds constitutes a connecting link between the living and the dead. The scriptures praise "the brilliant deeds of piety in which the souls of the deceased delight"; and on the days dedicated to the memory of the deceased, their relatives not only remember them and pray that their souls may rest in peace, but also distribute food and clothing among the poor of their community, and, if they can afford it, set aside various sums in charity.

CONTEMPORARY CHALLENGES

Zoroastrianism's Biggest Worry: Membership

ARIANE SHERINE

Compared to other religions, Zoroastrianism has only a small number of devotees, and this situation is not likely to change. Conversion to Zoroastrianism is generally disallowed; it is at least controversial. In this reading, Ariane Sherine ponders the implications for the survival of Zoroastrianism of the religion's rules limiting membership.

The exhibition on Zoroastrianism "The Everlasting Flame," currently showing at London's School of Oriental and African Studies, should perhaps be renamed "The Ever-Dwindling Flame." There are approximately 137,000 Parsi Zoroastrians left in the world, only 4,100 in the UK (they're outnumbered by heavy metal adherents on the latest census), and for every birth there are five deaths. Possibly the least inclusive community in existence—you can't convert to Zoroastrianism, and it is patrilineal—Zoroastrians need to widen their admission criteria fast, or go the way of the lesser Antillean macaw and the koala lemur.

I say this not because I'm after membership—the Zoroastrian beliefs of my mother's side of the family do not appeal—but because, as the wide-ranging SOAS exhibition amply demonstrates, it is a fascinating ancient community that predates even Judaism. Originating in Iran in approximately 1,500 BC, founded by the badass apocalyptic prophet Zoroaster, it is the first monotheistic religion, and is based on a simple equation of good (Ahura Mazda) versus evil (Ahriman). Good symbolises creativity, and evil is tantamount to destruction—in the event that there is more evil in the world than good, the planet will be destroyed, so all Zoroastrians must vow to live by the motto "good thoughts, good words, good deeds."

One of the leading world religions for a millennium, Zoroastrianism is best known for its fire temples. Followers believe fire symbolises God's purity and wisdom, so worship in front of a flame. It is also famous for its towers of silence, enclosed spaces where the dead bodies of Zoroastrians are placed to be devoured by vultures. The holy book is called the Avesta, split into two sections (much like the Old and New Testaments, full of stories and myths), and the initiation ritual is named the Navjote ceremony.

As the child of a female Zoroastrian, I was not permitted to follow in my mother's footsteps and undertake the Navjote; whether I am even allowed to call myself Parsi is debatable, although as it is an ethnicity, it is hard to know what else to term myself. And, as a non-Zoroastrian, I am not allowed into the fire temples.

Ariane Sherine, "Zoroastrianism Needs to Adapt Its Archaic Laws—or Die," *The Guardian*, http://www.theguardian.com (December 8, 2013).

The faith is inextricably linked to the Parsi and Irani communities—you don't find Zoroastrians of any other ethnicity. Although historical evidence suggests that many left ancient Persia for economic reasons, my late maternal grandfather gave me the traditional Parsi version of events. He stated that the Zoroastrians' exclusivity dates back to the seventh century, when Arab Muslims invaded ancient Persia and gave them the choice of converting to Islam or fleeing the country. Many chose the latter, and sailed to India in a fleet of ships. On arrival, the king of the Gujarat sent out a (possibly apocryphal) cup of milk filled to the brim, to signify that the country was overflowing with residents and couldn't accept any more.

The king of the Zoroastrians, however, returned the cup of milk with a spoonful of sugar sprinkled over the top, to indicate that the Zoroastrians wouldn't cause the country to overflow—they would merely sweeten the mixture. The Gujarati king admitted the seafaring refugees on three conditions: that they would promise not to eat beef; not to marry into the existing population; and not to convert any Hindus. The Zoroastrians have stuck rigidly to the latter two tenets ever since, leading to quips like: "We Zoroastrians aren't allowed to convert anyone. So we can go up to people's houses and knock on their doors—but then we have to run away."

Why, as an atheist, should I feel sadness at the decline of a faith that was never mine to begin with? Perhaps for the same reason that many people who don't believe in God have a soft spot for the religion of their ethnicity: nostalgia for my childhood, family ties, the memory of my beloved grandfather praying quietly in his *sedreh* and *kushti*. But I think it is more than that: Zoroastrianism and being a Parsi are intertwined, so much so that the terms are often used interchangeably. If the religion dies, all the traditions of the ethnicity will go with it.

I suspect that it will be too late by the time my fellow Parsis wake up to the fact that survival urgently depends on overruling archaic laws. Instead of basing their faith on rules established 1,300 years ago, the Zoroastrians need to adhere instead to the rules of evolution, and adapt or die. For the sake of history and humanity, I hope they choose the former.

STUDY QUESTIONS

1. What is *Avesta*? *Ahura Mazda*? *Angra Mainyu*?
2. Who is the founder of Zoroastrianism?
3. Where did Zoroastrianism arise?
4. In Zoroastrianism, what is the relationship between good and evil?
5. Is Zoroastrianism a monotheism or a polytheism?
6. What is the supreme duty of Zoroastrians?
7. According to Zoroastrianism, do humans have free will?
8. How does Zoroastrianism explain the presence of evil in the world?
9. What are three doctrines that can be traced to Zoroastrianism?
10. How are humans to be judged when they die? What happens in the last judgment?

FURTHER READING

John Bowker, ed., "Zoroaster," "Zoroastrianism," in *The Oxford Dictionary of World Religions* (Oxford: Oxford University Press, 1997).

Mary Boyce, *Textual Sources for the Study of Zoroastrianism* (Chicago: University of Chicago Press, 1984).

Mary Boyce, *Zoroastrians: Their Religious Beliefs and Practices* (London: Routledge and Kegan Paul, 1979, 2003).

Rustom Masani, *Zoroastrianism: The Religion of the Good Life* (New Delhi: Cosmo, 2003).

John B. Noss, *A History of the World's Religions* (New York: Macmillan, 1994).
Shaul Shaked, *Wisdom of the Sasanian Sages* (Boulder, CO: Mazda, 1979).
Michael Stausberg, *Zarathustra and Zoroastrianism: A Short Introduction* (London: Equinox Publishing, 2008).

ONLINE

Avesta, "Frequently Asked Questions on Zoroastrianism and the Avesta," Avesta.org (December 25, 2015).
The Zarathushtrian Assembly, http://www.zoroastrian.org/ (December 25, 2015).

11 Judaism

Few religious traditions are more intimately interwoven with history than Judaism. Jews will tell you that Judaism's sense of itself as a monotheistic faith with a continuing relationship with the one true God began over three thousand years ago when God revealed his law and established his covenant with Moses and the children of Israel. To Jews, the story of their trials and triumphs through the millennia confirms and illustrates the central elements of their faith. And that faith became the forefather of two other traditions, Christianity and Islam, whose own histories in turn became intertwined with Judaism.

HISTORY

The narrative of the ancient Israelites (or Hebrews) begins in what scholars call the Biblical period, which dawned in about the eighteenth century BCE and stretched for twelve hundred years into the sixth century BCE. The first few hundred years of this time span were the age of the patriarchs: Abraham, Isaac, and Jacob, the forebears of the ancient Hebrews. There is hardly any historical evidence that they existed; we have only the stories and legends found in the **Tanakh**, the Hebrew Bible (which includes what Christians call the *Old Testament*). The Bible records how God established a *covenant* (a contractual arrangement) with Abraham, agreeing to make him the father of a great nation if he and his descendants live righteously—that is, "keep [God's] statutes and observe his laws." Later God also made covenants with Abraham's son Isaac, Isaac's son Jacob (Israel), and Moses. The understanding in all these pacts was that God (called **Yahweh**, and written as YHWH in Hebrew) had chosen the Jewish people to be an example of righteousness to other nations. If they obey him, they will prosper; if they disobey him, he will punish them but never completely abandon them. As God declared in the Bible's Book of Leviticus (26.12), "I . . . will be your God and you shall be my people."

In the time of the patriarchs, the Israelites migrated to an area known as Canaan (later Palestine), the land that God had promised to Abraham and his progeny. Decades later a famine forced the Israelites out of Canaan and into Egypt, where the pharaoh enslaved them. But God had other plans for the descendants of Abraham, so he chose Moses to lead them out of bondage and into the wilderness, where they wandered for forty years but eventually reached the Promised Land. This is the Exodus story, which has become to all Jews a reminder of God's protection and his special relationship to them. It is commemorated each year in the Passover festival.

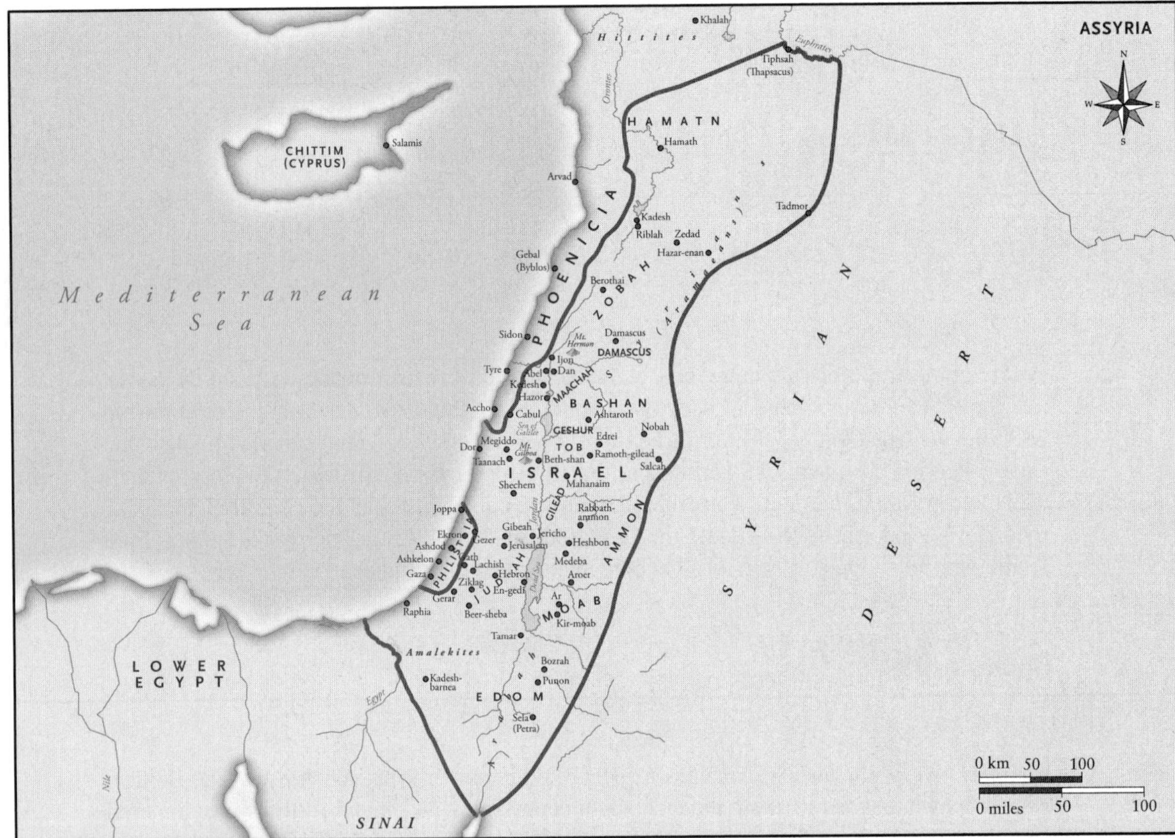

MAP 11.1 Ancient Israel.

As told in the Bible, the forty-year passage through the wilderness was of supreme importance because it was during the journey that the Israelites received the laws that would define them as a people. On Mount Sinai, Yahweh gave Moses the precepts of the Jewish religion, including the Ten Commandments, and Moses delivered them to the Israelites. For many Jews, it is in this imparting of the laws that Judaism began, and it is the Israelites' acceptance of them that made the people a distinctive religious tradition.

In the Biblical account, when the Israelites reached Canaan, they found they had to fight the current inhabitants (notably the Canaanites and the Philistines) to take the land that God had promised them. At this time Abraham's descendants consisted of twelve tribes linked only by a common heritage and religion, with each tribe led by a chief, or "judge," selected by consensus. But around 1000 BCE, this political system changed dramatically when the tribes were united into a kingdom ruled by David, the legendary slayer of the Philistine champion, Goliath the giant. (Tradition has it that David was also the author of many of the Psalms.) The monarchy was formed of necessity—to counter the military threat posed by the Philistines and other warring groups. To further consolidate his power, David captured Jerusalem—known later as "the City of David"—and declared it his capital. The people came to believe that David and his descendants were selected by Yahweh to reign over Israel through all time.

FIGURE 11.1 A drawing entitled "David Slays Goliath" by Paul Gustave Doré, printed in *The Holy Scriptures* (Stuttgart, Germany, 1885).

After David's death, the crown passed to his son, Solomon, renowned for his wisdom and wealth. It was during Solomon's reign that the kingdom of Israel reached the zenith of its glory, power, and territorial limits. For Jews, Solomon's greatest accomplishment was the building of Israel's First Temple, an opulent structure built on a hill in Jerusalem. But Solomon's policies alienated the ten tribes in the north, and when he died in 921 BCE, they broke away and formed their own kingdom, keeping the name *Israel* and designating Samaria as its capital. In response, the two southern tribes also established a kingdom, taking *Judah* (*Judea* in Greek) as its name and including Jerusalem in its territory.

In 722 BCE the Assyrians defeated the northern kingdom and dispersed the people, many of whom escaped to Judah. In 586 BCE Judah suffered a similar fate when the Babylonians conquered it, exiled its leaders to Babylon, and razed the Temple in Jerusalem. For Jews today, the Babylonian Exile and First Temple destruction are events that changed Jews and Judaism forever. These two catastrophes became a symbol of the Jews' suffering down through the ages.

The Exile brought home the reality of the Jewish **Diaspora**—Jewish communities existing outside the traditional land of Israel, a state of affairs still common throughout the world. The diaspora forced the Israelites to think of themselves not as a people tied to a physical kingdom (as *Judeans*, for example) but as adherents of a religious tradition known as *Judaism* carried on in many countries by *Jews*.

After the rebuilding of the Temple, many Jews latched onto a theme that has appeared occasionally in one form or another in Jewish history: the coming of the *messiah*. The original idea was that the messiah would be a human descendent of king David who would

JUDAISM TIMELINE

BCE

1700–600 The Biblical Period

1500–600 The *Vedas* composed

c. 1280 The Exodus from Egypt

c. 1210 Earliest historical evidence of the existence of Israel or Israelites

c. 1000 King David unites kingdom.

922 Death of Solomon and the breakup of the kingdom

722 Assyrians conquer northern kingdom.

586 Babylonians conquer Jerusalem; First Temple is destroyed; Hebrew leaders are exiled.

538 Persians conquer Babylon.

c. 515 Rebuilding of the Temple

331–323 Alexander the Great defeats Egypt, Persia, and Palestine.

166–164 Revolt of the Maccabees

CE

70 Jerusalem falls to the Romans; Second Temple is destroyed.

73 Masada falls to the Romans.

70–100 The Four Gospels are written.

354–430 Augustine

c. 570–632 Muhammad

1135–1204 Maimonides

1492 Jews are pushed out of Spain.

1648 Cossacks massacre 100,000 Jews in Ukraine and Poland.

1789 Jews are granted legal equality in the United States.

1792 France grants citizenship to Jews.

1889 Conservative Judaism breaks away from Reform.

1939–1945 World War II and *Shoah*

1948 State of Israel established

1967 The Six-Day War

reestablish the Jewish monarchy. During and after the Exile, the hope was that the messiah—an extraordinary king, priest, or prophet—would arrive in the future and achieve victory over evil, destroy the earthly powers, and reward the righteous. From those days to the present, there have always been diverse opinions about what would happen when the messiah appears. Many believers have expected that the messiah would bring an end to wicked regimes and to time itself, that there would be a resurrection of the dead, and that the righteous would inhabit God's new world. Theories about the messiah were rife in Jesus' time, and several self-proclaimed messiahs stepped forward. Jesus' followers declared him the messiah after his death. Many Jews are skeptical of these scenarios; Orthodox Jews, however, believe in some version of a messianic future.

Persian rule lasted from 538 to 331 BCE, when Persia was conquered by Alexander the Great. After Alexander a series of empires took control of Palestine: the Ptolemaic (established by Ptolemy, one of Alexander's generals); the Seleucid, from Syria; and the Roman. In this age of empires and the Second Temple, the Jews grew in number in both Palestine and the Diaspora, and Jewish priests and scribes completed the editing and compilation of the **Torah**, the first five books of the Hebrew scriptures, the books of Moses. (Here *Torah* refers to the

FIGURE 11.2 A drawing entitled "Moses Coming Down from Mount Sinai" by Paul Gustave Doré, 1866.

five books, but the word is also used to indicate the *Tanakh* with all the commentaries, or all the laws on a given subject.) The *Torah* thus became an essential part of Jewish life and has remained so to this day. And in a move that brought the scriptures to the attention of a much larger audience, the **Septuagint** was produced, a translation of the Hebrew texts into Greek.

From the time of the Seleucid domination of Palestine to about 100 CE, the story of the Jews was one of revolution against their foreign masters and of dissension among themselves. The internal conflicts usually arose over perceived threats to true Judaism, as it was defined by Jewish factions. A central issue was how Hellenized the Jewish religion should be—that is, how far Judaism should go toward adopting Greek ideas that were prevalent then throughout the known world. In 166 BCE a Jewish rebel group known as the Maccabees took Jerusalem back from the Seleucids and purged the Temple of the pagan adornments and rites. The revolt won for the Jews the freedom to practice their faith as they saw fit. Their term of independence lasted until 63 BCE, when a Roman army, led by a general named Pompey, seized Jerusalem and occupied Palestine. A hundred years later another revolt erupted (66–73 CE). This time the Jewish revolutionaries belonged to a political-religious faction known as the *Zealots*, who fought to rid Palestine of the Romans once and for all. But the Romans defeated them, killing and torturing many and destroying the Second Temple (70 CE). Toward the end of the war, the last undefeated Zealots and their families holed up in the mountain fortress called Masada, determined never to be taken alive. When the Romans finally stormed the fortress, they discovered that the entire population had committed suicide.

After the destruction of the Second Temple in 70 CE, Jewish leaders and scholars set about the task of preserving and defining Judaism, which seemed to some to be in danger of disappearing altogether. When the Temple was still standing, the religious practice of the Jews was centered there. The Temple was the place for prayer, services, and animal sacrifices, and priests were the spiritual guardians of both the Temple and the rituals. Now new modes of worship needed to be established. *Synagogues*, which had first appeared generations earlier, became the new focus of worship, study, and communal life. Synagogues had no priests and conducted no animal sacrifices, but they could be set up almost anywhere, and anyone could take part in the proceedings.

The priests vanished when the Temple was demolished, but another class of devotees arose to take their place: **rabbis**. These were clerical leaders who could explain the scriptures to the people and guide them in devotional practices. With the rabbis came a new emphasis on the piety of adherents. They taught that individuals needed no priest to perform acts of devotion and live morally upright lives. Judaism was not only communal but personal. Rabbis serve the same functions today.

In the following centuries, Judaism wrestled with Christian enmity but enjoyed Islamic tolerance and respect. From the beginning, Christians and Jews found reasons for mutual animosity and mistrust. Christians blamed Jews for Christ's death, and Jews repudiated the Christian view that Jesus was the Messiah. Both traditions competed for Rome's favor—and blamed each other for their troubles with Roman officials. The rift between them grew even larger when in the fourth century the Roman emperor Constantine converted to Christianity. A whole series of emperors then sought to repress and punish the Jews and encourage violence against them.

In the Middle Ages, the Jews of the Diaspora were frequently the victims of Christian hostility. Here is a scholar's description of the anti-Jewish fervor that arose around the time of the Christian Crusades:

> The launching of the Crusades at the end of the eleventh century produced such excitement against "infidels" that an open butchery of the Jews began, starting in Germany, where wholesale massacres took place, and spreading to the rest of Europe. After the butchery ran its course, orders of expulsion followed. In Germany, one town after another drove the Jews out, at least in law. They were expelled from England in 1290, and after two centuries of periodic expulsion and restoration, in 1394 they were denied residence in France. In Spain, persecution of the Jews accompanied the expulsion of the Moors, and in 1492 all unconverted Jews were ordered driven out.[1]

In this period, Jews often got better treatment from Muslims than they did from Christians. Although ultimately ambivalent about the Jews, Muhammad respected their monotheism, recognizing that Jews were "people of the book" with a religious and genealogical ancestor in common with Muslims: Abraham. In Muslim societies, Jews were often second-class citizens, but they still preferred to be ruled by Muslims rather than Christians. As David Noss says,

A CLOSER LOOK

Maimonides

Maimonides (1135–1204) was born in Cordova, Spain, a Muslim-ruled city whose intellectual life was among the liveliest and most permissive of the medieval world. That atmosphere changed in 1148 when the Muslim Almohads conquered Cordova and demanded that non-Muslims immediately convert or submit to exile or death. Having little choice, Maimonides and his family fled the city, traveling about for years, seeking refuge in Morocco, Palestine, and finally Egypt.

In Cairo, he served as court physician and Egypt's foremost rabbinic leader, all the while writing the works that would influence generations to come. His preeminent authority as a rabbinic jurist was forever established by his *Book of the Commandments*; the *Commentary on the Mishnah*; and the fourteen-volume *Code of Jewish Law*, the *Mishneh Torah*. His credentials as a philosopher were secured by his masterpiece, *The Guide for the Perplexed*.

Like ancient Greek thinkers and some philosophers of his day (including a few Arab scholars), Maimonides sought truth through reason and tried to apply rational methods of inquiry not just to philosophy and science but also to religious and biblical beliefs. This approach led him to argue in his *Guide for the Perplexed* that biblical and rabbinic writings embody, in figurative language, truths that can be discovered and demonstrated by philosophy. There can be no contradiction between religious texts and the deliverances of reason, although the former must be interpreted figuratively to agree with the latter. To interpret scripture literally is to fall into error. For example, scriptural language seems to suggest that God is corporeal and that he possesses essential attributes. But, Maimonides says, philosophy shows that these literal understandings are false, so the passages must be given a figurative meaning. God has no body and cannot be conceived of or described at all. We can only characterize God negatively (for instance, "God does not lack power" instead of "God is powerful"), which is simply a way of acknowledging that God is beyond our comprehension.

> In Palestine, Syria, and Babylonia, [Muslims] displayed toward the Jews not only tolerance but kindness, partly because the Jews looked upon them as deliverers from the Christians and the Zoroastrians and therefore lent them their service as spies and scouts, and partly for the reason that culturally, racially, and religiously there was a marked resemblance between them. . . .
>
> [But the] Turks came; the Jews again began to be oppressed. So, in the tenth and eleventh centuries, many Babylonian scholars set forth with their folk for Spain, at the other end of the world, where, since the eighth century, Jewish learning had been enjoying a heyday under the tolerant rule of the [Muslim] Moors. Here they joined forces with their Spanish brethren in creating the "golden age" of Jewish science, religious philosophy, and mysticism in the West.[2]

Several remarkable Jewish philosophers emerged from the climate of Muslim tolerance in Spain. The most able and learned among them was Maimonides, a twelfth-century thinker who became Judaism's most famous philosopher, known for his attempts to reconcile religious faith with reason.

BELIEFS

In the modern period (the seventeenth century to the present), Judaism has been interpreted in diverse ways, with various perspectives constituting different branches of the tradition. These branches have arisen against a background of traditional beliefs that have persisted through Judaism's history and that would likely be accepted by most (but certainly not all) Jews today. These core beliefs include the following: (1) God exists and is the Creator of the world, the one and only god, an incorporeal, eternal being; (2) God is worthy of worship; (3) God's law in the scriptures should be obeyed; (4) God has a unique relationship with the chosen; and (5) the Messiah (however described) will doubtless come to rescue his chosen from tyranny and injustice.

The principal branches of Judaism have arisen in the modern period as reform movements. Reformers wanted to modernize Jewish thinking, to take into account the far-reaching changes wrought in secular society since the Enlightenment. Or they wished to take small steps toward adapting Judaism to the new era but not to take the kinds of leaps toward the modern world that other Jews thought were needed.

Of all the major movements, *Reform Judaism* advocates the greatest changes in Judaism. It calls for discarding claims about a returning messiah, bodily resurrection of the dead, direct revelation from God, heaven and paradise, and the establishment of a Jewish nation (reformers declared that we are "no longer a nation, but a religious community"). Reform Judaism recommends dispensing with, or deemphasizing, many traditional customs or practices, such as Sabbath services in Hebrew (the vernacular was favored instead), rigid adherence to dietary and purity laws (circumcision, for example), and the ban on ordaining women as rabbis.

Orthodox Judaism is in sharp contrast to the Reform platform. It acknowledges the need to accommodate some aspects of modern life, but it rejects Reform's disavowal of divine revelation and traditional religious practice. Orthodox Judaism insists on rigorous observance of the laws and customs, such as the rules about obeying all the commandments regarding Sabbath obligations, eating only kosher meals, honoring all the ancient festivals, and maintaining the distinction between the religious roles of men and women.

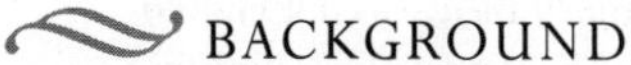 BACKGROUND

Who Is a Jew?

Contrary to what many non-Jews (including Adolf Hitler) have believed, there is no such thing as the "Jewish race." That is, there is no group of people who can be identified *genetically* as the Jews. Alan F. Segal explains:

> Is the Jewish Heritage by definition religious? The answer is yes and no. Yes, because it is possible to join the Jewish community through conversion, and many people have done so. On the other hand, the tradition is far more commonly inherited than chosen, and for that reason Judaism is frequently considered an "ethnic" religion.
>
> Some Jews have said yes to their ethnic identity while saying no to the religion. A substantial number of North Americans, Europeans, and Israelis identify themselves as Jews but do not take part in the religious tradition. Rather, they see themselves as members of a cultural community with distinctive literary and artistic traditions, foods and folkways, and roles in their various social and historical milieus. Religion, to them, is part of their culture, but not necessarily the defining part.[3]

Conservative Judaism is considered an intellectual midpoint between Reform and Orthodox. This stance allows the local language in worship and maintains equal roles for men and women in religious observance. But unlike Reform, it does not dispense with most customs; and unlike Orthodox, it does not refuse to drop any of them. Conservatives examine customs to see if there are historical reasons for altering or getting rid of them. If a custom is recent in Jewish history, it might be a candidate for elimination. If it is ancient, it may be regarded as well founded and thus legitimate.

SCRIPTURES

Like the sacred texts of many other religions, the Jewish canon is vast, a kind of anthology of revered volumes written by several authors and accumulated over many generations. The Hebrew Bible—the *Tanakh*—consists of thirty-nine books divided into three sections: (1) the *Torah* (the Five Books of Moses, "The Law"); (2) "The Prophets" (twenty-one books, some of them very short); and (3) "The Writings" (thirteen books, including Psalms and Proverbs). *Tanakh* is an acronym that comes from the first letters of the Hebrew names for each section.

The Hebrew Bible contains books that Christians call the "Old Testament," a term they use in opposition to their own scriptures, the "New Testament." But this label can be disconcerting to some Jews because it implies that the Hebrew scriptures have been rendered obsolete by the Christian canon.

The *Torah* (also the *Pentateuch*) is the most highly revered of all the sacred writings of Judaism. A first-century CE scholar named Hillel offered this famous summary of it: "What is hateful to you, do not to your fellow." According to tradition, Moses wrote all five books, receiving them directly from God on Mount Sinai. But Biblical scholarship indicates that they were written not by Moses but by four or five different authors writing from distinct perspectives.

The books in the *Tanakh*'s three sections are organized like this:

The Torah: Genesis, Exodus, Leviticus, Numbers, Deuteronomy
The Prophets:
"Former Prophets": Joshua, Judges, I Samuel, II Samuel, I Kings, II Kings
"Latter Prophets": Isaiah, Jeremiah, Ezekiel, The Twelve (Hosea, Joel, Amos, Obadiah, Jonah, Micah, Nahum, Habakkuk, Zephaniah, Haggai, Zechariah, Malachi)
The Writings: Psalms, Job, Proverbs, Ruth, Song of Songs, Ecclesiastes, Lamentations, Esther, Daniel, Ezra, Nehemiah, I Chronicles, II Chronicles

The *Torah* gives "the Laws," the rules of Jewish religious and ethical behavior. But the Laws, like any moral or legal code, are problematic if there are no interpretations or guidelines for applying the Laws to puzzling cases that inevitably arise in changing times and unusual circumstances. From this need for clarification came a tradition among Jewish scholars of commenting extensively on the *Torah*, a process that began in the sixth century BCE and continued for hundreds of years. The result was a body of commentary that became known as the "oral *Torah*" or "Oral Law," because its original mode of transmission was speech. But between the second and sixth century CE, it was committed to text. The final product is the **Talmud**, 2.5 million words of guidance and discussion of the Law. To many Jews, the *Talmud* is almost as sacred as the *Torah*.

The *Talmud* has two voluminous divisions: (1) the **Mishnah**, interpretations and applications of laws, compiled and edited in the second century CE; and (2) the **Gemara**, clarifications and commentaries on the *Mishnah* (c. 450–550 CE). There are two versions of the *Talmud*: the Jerusalem (or Palestinian) *Talmud* and the longer Babylonian *Talmud*. The Jerusalem *Talmud* (c. 400 CE) consists of the *Mishnah* and a *Gemara* from the Jewish scholars in Palestine; the Babylonian *Talmud* (c. 427–650 CE) consists of the same *Mishnah* and a different *Gemara* from the Jewish scholars in Babylon. Generally Jews regard the Babylonian *Talmud* as the more authoritative version.

NOTES

1. David S. Noss, "Judaism in Its Early Phases," in *A History of the World's Religions* (Upper Saddle River, NJ: Prentice Hall, 2003), 435.
2. David S. Noss, "The Religious Development of Judaism," in *A History of the World's Religions* (Upper Saddle River, NJ: Prentice Hall, 2003), 431–432.
3. Alan F. Segal, "Jewish Traditions," in *World Religions: Western Traditions*, Willard G. Oxtoby, ed. (Oxford: Oxford University Press, 2011), 71.

KEY TERMS

Diaspora Jewish communities existing outside the traditional land of Israel.

Gemara A body of commentary combined with the *Mishnah*, which together make up the *Talmud*.

Mishnah A collection of commentaries and elucidations on the *Torah*; the written version of the Oral Law.

rabbis Clerical leaders.

Septuagint Hebrew scriptures translated into Greek.

Talmud Authoritative writings consisting of the *Mishnah* and the *Gemara.*

Tanakh The Hebrew Bible; what Christians call the *Old Testament.*

Torah (1) The books of Moses, the first five books of the Hebrew Bible. (2) The *Tanakh* with all the commentaries. (3) All the laws on a given subject.

Yahweh The name of God in Judaism; written as YHWH in Hebrew.

READINGS

TEACHINGS

The Creation Story

Within the first three chapters of Genesis (book one of the Torah), two different stories of creation are told. In the first one (Genesis 1:1–2:4), God creates in the first five days the world and the earth with all its vegetation and living creatures. Then on the sixth day, God creates man and woman in his own image and commands them to populate and master the earth. On the seventh day, God ceases his work and declares the day holy.

In the second creation story (Genesis 2:4–3:24), God first creates man (Adam), then vegetation and living creatures in the Garden of Eden. He fashions woman (Eve) from the man's rib. Eve is tempted by the serpent and breaks God's commandment about not eating fruit from the tree of knowledge of good and bad, and she shares the fruit with Adam. God then punishes them for their transgression: Eve must endure the pain of childbirth; Adam must work by the sweat of his brow for food; and they are both made mortal and banished from the garden.

Genesis 1:1–3:24, *Tanakh: A New Translation of the Holy Scriptures* (Philadelphia: Jewish Publication Society, 1985).

1 1When God began to create heaven and earth—2the earth being unformed and void, with darkness over the surface of the deep and a wind from God sweeping over the water—3God said, "Let there be light"; and there was light. 4God saw that the light was good, and God separated the light from the darkness. 5God called the light Day, and the darkness He called Night. And there was evening and there was morning, a first day.

6God said, "Let there be an expanse in the midst of the water, that it may separate water from water." 7God made the expanse, and it separated the water which was below the expanse from the water which was above the expanse. And it was so. 8God called the expanse Sky. And there was evening and there was morning, a second day.

9God said, "Let the water below the sky be gathered into one area, that the dry land may appear." And it was so. 10God called the dry land Earth, and the gathering of waters He called Seas. And God saw that this was good. 11And God said, "Let the earth sprout vegetation: seed-bearing plants, fruit trees of every kind on earth that bear fruit with the seed in it." And it was so. 12The earth brought forth vegetation: seed-bearing plants of every kind, and trees of every kind bearing fruit with the seed in it. And God saw that this was good. 13And there was evening and there was morning, a third day.

14God said, "Let there be lights in the expanse of the sky to separate day from night; they shall serve as signs for the set times—the days and the years; 15and they shall serve as lights in the expanse of the sky to shine upon the earth." And it was so. 16God made the two great lights, the greater light to dominate the day and the lesser light to dominate the night, and the stars. 17And God set them in the expanse of the sky to shine upon the earth, 18to dominate the day and the night, and to separate light from darkness. And God saw that this was good. 19And there was evening and there was morning, a fourth day.

20God said, "Let the waters bring forth swarms of living creatures, and birds that fly above the earth across the expanse of the sky." 21God created the great sea monsters, and all the living creatures of every kind that creep, which the waters brought forth in swarms, and all the winged birds of every kind. And God saw that this was good. 22God blessed them, saying, "Be fertile and increase, fill the waters in the seas, and let the birds increase on the earth." 23And there was evening and there was morning, a fifth day.

24God said, "Let the earth bring forth every kind of living creature: cattle, creeping things, and wild beasts of every kind." And it was so. 25God made wild beasts of every kind and cattle of every kind, and all kinds of creeping things of the earth. And God saw that this was good. 26And God said, "Let us make man in our image, after our likeness. They shall rule the fish of the sea, the birds of the sky, the cattle, the whole earth, and all the creeping things that creep on earth." 27And God created man in His image, in the image of God He created him; male and female He created them. 28God blessed them and God said to them, "Be fertile and increase, fill the earth and master it; and rule the fish of the sea, the birds of the sky, and all the living things that creep on earth."

29God said, "See, I give you every seed-bearing plant that is upon all the earth, and every tree that has seed-bearing fruit; they shall be yours for food. 30And to all the animals on land, to all the birds of the sky, and to everything that creeps on earth, in which there is the breath of life, [I give] all the green plants for food," And it was so. 31And God saw all that He had made, and found it very good. And there was evening and there was morning, the sixth day.

2 1The heaven and the earth were finished, and all their array. 2On the seventh day God finished the work that He had been doing, and He ceased on the seventh day from all the work that He had done. 3And God blessed the seventh day and declared it holy, because on it God ceased from all the work of creation that He had done. 4Such is the story of heaven and earth when they were created:

When the LORD God made earth and heaven—5when no shrub of the field was yet on earth and no grasses of the field had yet sprouted, because the LORD God had not sent rain upon the earth and there was no man to till the soil, 6but a flow would well up from the ground and water the whole surface of the earth—7the LORD God formed man from the dust of the earth. He blew into his nostrils the breath of life, and man became a living being.

[8]The LORD God planted a garden in Eden, in the east, and placed there the man whom He had formed. [9]And from the ground the LORD God caused to grow every tree that was pleasing to the sight and good for food, with the tree of life in the middle of the garden, and the tree of knowledge of good and bad.

[10]A river issues from Eden to water the garden, and it then divides and becomes four branches. [11]The name of the first is Pishon, the one that winds through the whole land of Havilah, where the gold is. ([12]The gold of that land is good; bdellium is there, and lapis lazuli.) [13]The name of the second river is Gihon, the one that winds through the whole land of Cush. [14]The name of the third river is Tigris, the one that flows east of Asshur. And the fourth river is the Euphrates.

[15]The LORD God took the man and placed him in the garden of Eden, to till it and tend it. [16]And the LORD God commanded the man, saying, "Of every tree of the garden you are free to eat; [17]but as for the tree of knowledge of good and bad, you must not eat of it; for as soon as you eat of it, you shall die."

[18]The LORD God said, "It is not good for man to be alone; I will make a fitting helper for him." [19]And the LORD God formed out of the earth all the wild beasts and all the birds of the sky, and brought them to the man to see what he would call them; and whatever the man called each living creature, that would be its name. [20]And the man gave names to all the cattle and to the birds of the sky and to all the wild beasts; but for Adam no fitting helper was found. [21]So the LORD God cast a deep sleep upon the man; and, while he slept, He took one of his ribs and closed up the flesh at that spot. [22]And the LORD God fashioned the rib that He had taken from the man into a woman; and He brought her to the man. [23]Then the man said,

"This one at last
Is bone of my bones
And flesh of my flesh.
This one shall be called Woman,
For from man was she taken."

[24]Hence a man leaves his father and mother and clings to his wife, so that they become one flesh.

[25]The two of them were naked, the man and his wife, yet they felt no shame.

3 [1]Now the serpent was the shrewdest of all the wild beasts that the LORD God had made. He said to the woman, "Did God really say: You shall not eat of any tree of the garden?" [2]The woman replied to the serpent, "We may eat of the fruit of the other trees of the garden. [3]It is only about fruit of the tree in the middle of the garden that God said: 'You shall not eat of it or touch it, lest you die.'" [4]And the serpent said to the woman, "You are not going to die, [5]but God knows that as soon as you eat of it your eyes will be opened and you will be like divine beings who know good and bad." [6]When the woman saw that the tree was good for eating and a delight to the eyes, and that the tree was desirable as a source of wisdom, she took of its fruit and ate. She also gave some to her husband, and he ate. [7]Then the eyes of both of them were opened and they perceived that they were naked; and they sewed together fig leaves and made themselves loincloths.

[8]They heard the sound of the LORD God moving about in the garden at the breezy time of day; and the man and his wife hid from the LORD God among the trees of the garden. [9]The LORD God called out to the man and said to him, "Where are you?" [10]He replied, "I heard the sound of You in the garden, and I was afraid because I was naked, so I hid." [11]Then He asked, "Who told you that you were naked? Did you eat of the tree from which I had forbidden you to eat?" [12]The man said, "The woman You put at my side—she gave me of the tree, and I ate." [13]And the LORD God said to the woman, "What is this you have done!" The woman replied, "The serpent duped me, and I ate." [14]Then the LORD God said to the serpent,

"Because you did this,
More cursed shall you be
Than all cattle
And all the wild beasts:
On your belly shall you crawl
And dirt shall you eat
All the days of your life.
[15]I will put enmity
Between you and the woman,
And between your offspring and hers;
They shall strike at your head,
And you shall strike at their heel."

16And to the woman He said,
"I will make most severe
Your pangs in childbearing;
In pain shall you bear children.
Yet your urge shall be for your husband,
And he shall rule over you."
17To Adam He said, "Because you did as your wife
said and ate of the tree about which I commanded
you, 'You shall not eat of it,'
Cursed be the ground because of you;
By toil shall you eat of it
All the days of your life:
18Thorns and thistles shall it sprout for you.
But your food shall be the grasses of the field;
19By the sweat of your brow
Shall you get bread to eat,
Until you return to the ground—
For from it you were taken.
For dust you are,
And to dust you shall return."
20The man named his wife Eve, because she was
the mother of all the living. 21And the LORD God
made garments of skins for Adam and his wife, and
clothed them.
22And the LORD God said, "Now that the man
has become like one of us, knowing good and bad,
what if he should stretch out his hand and take also
from the tree of life and eat, and live forever!" 23So
the LORD God banished him from the garden of
Eden, to till the soil from which he was taken. 24He
drove the man out, and stationed east of the garden
of Eden the cherubim and the fiery ever-turning
sword, to guard the way to the tree of life.

The Covenant with Noah

God determines that all the people of the earth—except Noah—are wicked and should be destroyed, so he sends a great flood that covers the whole earth and drowns everyone. Only Noah and his family are spared. After the flood, God makes a covenant with Noah, pledging never again to destroy the earth and its inhabitants by water. This is the first such covenant in the *Tanakh*; others will follow in later eras.

9 1God blessed Noah and his sons, and said to
them, "Be fertile and increase, and fill the earth.
2The fear and the dread of you shall be upon all the
beasts of the earth and upon all the birds of the
sky—everything with which the earth is astir—and
upon all the fish of the sea; they are given into your
hand. 3Every creature that lives shall be yours to eat;
as with the green grasses, I give you all these. 4You
must not, however, eat flesh with its life-blood in it.
5But for your own life-blood I will require a reckoning: I will require it of every beast; of man, too, will
I require a reckoning for human life, of every man
for that of his fellow man!
6Whoever sheds the blood of man,
By man shall his blood be shed;
For in His image
Did God make man.
7Be fertile, then, and increase; abound on the earth
and increase on it."
8And God said to Noah and to his sons with him,
9"I now establish My covenant with you and your
offspring to come, 10and with every living thing that

Genesis 9:1–17, *Tanakh: A New Translation of the Holy Scriptures* (Philadelphia: Jewish Publication Society, 1985).

is with you—birds, cattle, and every wild beast as well—all that have come out of the ark, every living thing on earth. [11]I will maintain My covenant with you: never again shall all flesh be cut off by the waters of a flood, and never again shall there be a flood to destroy the earth."

[12]God further said, "This is the sign that I set for the covenant between Me and you, and every living creature with you, for all ages to come. [13]I have set My bow in the clouds, and it shall serve as a sign of the covenant between Me and the earth. [14]When I bring clouds over the earth, and the bow appears in the clouds, [15]1 will remember My covenant between Me and you and every living creature among all flesh, so that the waters shall never again become a flood to destroy all flesh. [16]When the bow is in the clouds, I will see it and remember the everlasting covenant between God and all living creatures, all flesh that is on earth. [17]That," God said to Noah, "shall be the sign of the covenant that I have established between Me and all flesh that is on earth."

The Covenant with Abraham

The next divine covenant is between God and Abraham (called Abram at first), an "everlasting covenant throughout the ages." God vows to make Abraham the father of many nations and to give to him and his offspring the land of Canaan. He declares that the sign of this covenant will be circumcision of all Hebrew males.

17 [1]When Abram was ninety-nine years old, the LORD appeared to Abram and said to him, "I am El Shaddai. Walk in My ways and be blameless. [2]I will establish My covenant between Me and you, and I will make you exceedingly numerous."

[3]Abram threw himself on his face; and God spoke to him further, [4]"As for Me, this is My covenant with you: You shall be the father of a multitude of nations. [5]And you shall no longer be called Abram, but your name shall be Abraham, for I make you the father of a multitude of nations. [6]I will make you exceedingly fertile, and make nations of you; and kings shall come forth from you. [7]I will maintain My covenant between Me and you, and your offspring to come, as an everlasting covenant throughout the ages, to be God to you and to your offspring to come. [8]I assign the land you sojourn in to you and your offspring to come, all the land of Canaan, as an everlasting holding. I will be their God."

[9]God further said to Abraham, "As for you, you and your offspring to come throughout the ages shall keep My covenant. [10]Such shall be the covenant between Me and you and your offspring to follow which you shall keep: every male among you shall be circumcised. [11]You shall circumcise the flesh of your foreskin, and that shall be the sign of the covenant between Me and you. [12]And throughout the generations, every male among you shall be circumcised at the age of eight days. As for the homeborn slave and the one bought from an outsider who is not of your offspring, [13]they must be circumcised, homeborn, and purchased alike. Thus shall My covenant be marked in your flesh as an everlasting pact. [14]And if any male who is uncircumcised fails to circumcise

Genesis 17:1–27, *Tanakh: A New Translation of the Holy Scriptures* (Philadelphia: Jewish Publication Society, 1985).

the flesh of his foreskin, that person shall be cut off from his kin; he has broken My covenant."

15And God said to Abraham, "As for your wife Sarai, you shall not call her Sarai, but her name shall be Sarah. 16I will bless her; indeed, I will give you a son by her. I will bless her so that she shall give rise to nations; rulers of peoples shall issue from her." 17Abraham threw himself on his face and laughed, as he said to himself, "Can a child be born to a man a hundred years old, or can Sarah bear a child at ninety?" 18And Abraham said to God, "O that Ishmael might live by Your favor!" 19God said, "Nevertheless, Sarah your wife shall bear you a son, and you shall name him Isaac; and I will maintain My covenant with him as an everlasting covenant for his offspring to come. 20As for Ishmael, I have heeded you. I hereby bless him. I will make him fertile and exceedingly numerous. He shall be the father of twelve chieftains, and I will make of him a great nation. 21But My covenant I will maintain with Isaac, whom Sarah shall bear to you at this season next year." 22And when He was done speaking with him, God was gone from Abraham.

23Then Abraham took his son Ishmael, and all his homeborn slaves and all those he had bought, every male in Abraham's household, and he circumcised the flesh of their foreskins on that very day, as God had spoken to him. 24Abraham was ninety-nine years old when he circumcised the flesh of his foreskin, 25and his son Ishmael was thirteen years old when he was circumcised in the flesh of his foreskin. 26Thus Abraham and his son Ishmael were circumcised on that very day; 27and all his household, his homeborn slaves and those that had been bought from outsiders, were circumcised with him.

The Exodus

In the book of Exodus we read the central story of the Jewish tradition: the escape of the Israelites from bondage in Egypt. The pharaoh had enslaved them, but one of them—Moses—was spared enslavement because he was adopted into the pharaoh's house. When Moses became an adult, God chose him to lead the Israelites out of slavery and into the land that God had promised Abraham and his descendants. After God struck down all the first-born Egyptians, the pharaoh allowed Moses and his people to leave. To this day, the annual Passover feast commemorates the events surrounding the liberation of the people.

12 29In the middle of the night the LORD struck down all the first-born in the land of Egypt, from the first-born of Pharaoh who sat on the throne to the first-born of the captive who was in the dungeon, and all the firstborn of the cattle. 30And Pharaoh arose in the night, with all his courtiers and all the Egyptians—because there was a loud cry in Egypt, for there was no house where there was not someone dead. 31He summoned Moses and Aaron in the night and said, "Up, depart from among my people, you and the Israelites with you! Go, worship the LORD as you said! 32Take also your flocks and your herds, as you said, and begone! And may you bring a blessing upon me also!"

33The Egyptians urged the people on, impatient to have them leave the country, for they said, "We shall all be dead." 34So the people took their dough before it was leavened, their kneading bowls wrapped in

Exodus 12:1–51; 14:1–31, *Tanakh: A New Translation of the Holy Scriptures* (Philadelphia: Jewish Publication Society, 1985).

their cloaks upon their shoulders. [35]The Israelites had done Moses' bidding and borrowed from the Egyptians objects of silver and gold, and clothing. [36]And the LORD had disposed the Egyptians favorably toward the people, and they let them have their request; thus they stripped the Egyptians.

[37]The Israelites journeyed from Raamses to Succoth, about six hundred thousand men on foot, aside from children. [38]Moreover, a mixed multitude went up with them, and very much livestock, both flocks and herds. [39]And they baked unleavened cakes of the dough that they had taken out of Egypt, for it was not leavened, since they had been driven out of Egypt and could not delay; nor had they prepared any provisions for themselves.

[40]The length of time that the Israelites lived in Egypt was four hundred and thirty years; [41]at the end of the four hundred and thirtieth year, to the very day, all the ranks of the LORD departed from the land of Egypt. [42]That was for the LORD a night of vigil to bring them out of the land of Egypt; that same night is the LORD'S, one of vigil for all the children of Israel throughout the ages.

[43]The LORD said to Moses and Aaron: This is the law of the passover offering: No foreigner shall eat of it. [44]But any slave a man has bought may eat of it once he has been circumcised. “No bound or hired laborer shall eat of it. [46]It shall be eaten in one house: you shall not take any of the flesh outside the house; nor shall you break a bone of it. [47]The whole community of Israel shall offer it. [48]"If a stranger who dwells with you would offer the passover to the LORD, all his males must be circumcised; then he shall be admitted to offer it; he shall then be as a citizen of the country. But no uncircumcised person may eat of it. [49]There shall be one law for the citizen and for the stranger who dwells among you.

[50]And all the Israelites did so; as the LORD had commanded Moses and Aaron, so they did.

[51]That very day the LORD freed the Israelites from the land of Egypt, troop by troop.

14 [1]The LORD said to Moses: [2]Tell the Israelites to turn back and encamp before Pi-hahiroth, between Migdol and the sea, before Baal-zephon; you shall encamp facing it, by the sea. [3]Pharaoh will say of the Israelites, “They are astray in the land; the wilderness has closed in on them.” [4]Then I will stiffen Pharaoh's heart and he will pursue them, that I may gain glory through Pharaoh and all his host; and the Egyptians shall know that I am the LORD.

And they did so.

[5]When the king of Egypt was told that the people had fled, Pharaoh and his courtiers had a change of heart about the people and said, “What is this we have done, releasing Israel from our service?” [6]He ordered his chariot and took his men with him; [7]he took six hundred of his picked chariots, and the rest of the chariots of Egypt, with officers in all of them. [8]The LORD stiffened the heart of Pharaoh king of Egypt, and he gave chase to the Israelites. As the Israelites were departing defiantly, boldly, [9]the Egyptians gave chase to them, and all the chariot horses of Pharaoh, his horsemen, and his warriors overtook them encamped by the sea, near Pi-hahiroth, before Baal-zephon.

[10]As Pharaoh drew near, the Israelites caught sight of the Egyptians advancing upon them. Greatly frightened, the Israelites cried out to the LORD. [11]And they said to Moses, “Was it for want of graves in Egypt that you brought us to die in the wilderness? What have you done to us, taking us out of Egypt? [12]Is this not the very thing we told you in Egypt, saying, ‘Let us be, and we will serve the Egyptians, for it is better for us to serve the Egyptians than to die in the wilderness’?” [13]But Moses said to the people, “Have no fear! Stand by, and witness the deliverance which the LORD will work for you today; for the Egyptians whom you see today you will never see again. [14]The LORD will battle for you; you hold your peace!”

[15]Then the LORD said to Moses, “Why do you cry out to Me? Tell the Israelites to go forward. [16]And you lift up your rod and hold out your arm over the sea and split it, so that the Israelites may march into the sea on dry ground. [17]And I will stiffen the hearts of the Egyptians so that they go in after them; and I will gain glory through Pharaoh and all his warriors, his chariots and his horsemen. [18]Let the Egyptians know that I am LORD, when I gain glory through Pharaoh, his chariots, and his horsemen.”

[19]The angel of God, who had been going ahead of the Israelite army, now moved and followed behind them; and the pillar of cloud shifted from in front of

them and took up a place behind them, [20]and it came between the army of the Egyptians and the army of Israel. Thus there was the cloud with the darkness, and it cast a spell upon the night, so that the one could not come near the other all through the night.

[21]Then Moses held out his arm over the sea and the LORD drove back the sea with a strong east wind all that night, and turned the sea into dry ground. The waters were split, [22]and the Israelites went into the sea on dry ground, the waters forming a wall for them on their right and on their left. [23]The Egyptians came in pursuit after them into the sea, all of Pharaoh's horses, chariots, and horsemen. [24]At the morning watch, the LORD looked down upon the Egyptian army from a pillar of fire and cloud, and threw the Egyptian army into panic. [25]He locked the wheels of their chariots so that they Moved forward with difficulty. And the Egyptians said, "Let us flee from the Israelites, for the LORD is fighting for them against Egypt."

[26]Then the LORD said to Moses, "Hold out your arm over the sea, that the waters may come back upon the Egyptians and upon their chariots and upon their horsemen." [27]Moses held out his arm over the sea, and at daybreak the sea returned to its normal state, and the Egyptians fled at its approach. But the LORD hurled the Egyptians into the sea. [28]The waters turned back and covered the chariots and the horsemen—Pharaoh's entire army that followed them into the sea; not one of them remained. [29]But the Israelites had marched through the sea on dry ground, the waters forming a wall for them on their right and on their left.

[30]Thus the LORD delivered Israel that day from the Egyptians. Israel saw the Egyptians dead on the shore of the sea. [31]And when Israel saw the wondrous power which the LORD had wielded against the Egyptians, the people feared the LORD; they had faith in the LORD and His servant Moses.

The Mosaic Covenant

After escaping from Egypt, the Israelites journeyed to the wilderness of Sinai, and there God made another covenant with them: obey my laws, and "you shall be my treasured possession among all the peoples." Then on Mount Sinai God delivered to Moses the Ten Commandments.

19 [1]On the third new moon after the Israelites had gone forth from the land of Egypt, on that very day, they entered the wilderness of Sinai. [2]Having journeyed from Rephidim, they entered the wilderness of Sinai and encamped in the wilderness. Israel encamped there in front of the mountain, [3]and Moses went up to God. The LORD called to him from the mountain, saying, "Thus shall you say to the house of Jacob and declare to the children of Israel: [4]'You have seen what I did to the Egyptians, how I bore you on eagles' wings and brought you to Me. [5]Now then, if you will obey Me faithfully and keep My covenant, you shall be My treasured possession among all the peoples. Indeed, all the earth is Mine, [6]but you shall be to Me a kingdom of priests and a holy nation.' These are the words that you shall speak to the children of Israel."

[7]Moses came and summoned the elders of the people and put before them all that the LORD had

Exodus 19:1–25; 20:1–18, *Tanakh: A New Translation of the Holy Scriptures* (Philadelphia: Jewish Publication Society, 1985).

commanded him. [8]All the people answered as one, saying, "All that the LORD has spoken we will do!" And Moses brought back the people's words to the LORD. [9]And the LORD said to Moses, "I will come to you in a thick cloud, in order that the people may hear when I speak with you and so trust you ever after." Then Moses reported the people's words to the LORD, [10]and the LORD said to Moses, "Go to the people and warn them to stay pure today and tomorrow. Let them wash their clothes. [11]Let them be ready for the third day; for on the third day the LORD will come down, in the sight of all the people, on Mount Sinai. [12]You shall set bounds for the people round about, saying, 'Beware of going up the mountain or touching the border of it. Whoever touches the mountain shall be put to death: [13]no hand shall touch him, but he shall be either stoned or shot; beast or man, he shall not live.' When the ram's horn sounds a long blast, they may go up on the mountain."

[14]Moses came down from the mountain to the people and warned the people to stay pure, and they washed their clothes. [15]And he said to the people, "Be ready for the third day: do not go near a woman."

[16]On the third day, as morning dawned, there was thunder, and lightning, and a dense cloud upon the mountain, and a very loud blast of the horn; and all the people who were in the camp trembled. [17]Moses led the people out of the camp toward God, and they took their places at the foot of the mountain.

[18]Now Mount Sinai was all in smoke, for the LORD had come down upon it in fire; the smoke rose like the smoke of a kiln, and the whole mountain trembled violently. [19]The blare of the horn grew louder and louder. As Moses spoke, God answered him in thunder. [21]The LORD came down upon Mount Sinai, on the top of the mountain, and the LORD called Moses to the top of the mountain and Moses went up. [21]The LORD said to Moses, "Go down, warn the people not to break through to the LORD to gaze, lest many of them perish. [22]The priests also, who come near the LORD, must stay pure, lest the LORD break out against them." [23]But Moses said to the LORD, "The people cannot come up to Mount Sinai, for You warned us saying, 'Set bounds about the mountain and sanctify it.'" [24]So the LORD said to him, "Go down, and come back together with Aaron; but let not the priests or the people break through to come up to the LORD, lest He break out against them." [25]And Moses went down to the people and spoke to them.

20 [1]God spoke all these words, saying:

[2]I the LORD am your God who brought you out of the land of Egypt, the house of bondage: [3]You shall have no other gods besides Me.

[4]You shall not make for yourself a sculptured image, or any likeness of what is in the heavens above, or on the earth below, or in the waters under the earth. [5]You shall not bow down to them or serve them. For I the LORD your God am an impassioned God, visiting the guilt of the parents upon the children, upon the third and upon the fourth generations of those who reject Me, [6]but showing kindness to the thousandth generation of those who love Me and keep My commandments.

[7]You shall not swear falsely by the name of the LORD your God; for the LORD will not clear one who swears falsely by His name.

[8]Remember the sabbath day and keep it holy. [9]Six days you shall labor and do all your work, [10]but the seventh day is a sabbath of the LORD your God: you shall not do any work—you, your son or daughter, your male or female slave, or your cattle, or the stranger who is within your settlements. [11] For in six days the LORD made heaven and earth and sea, and all that is in them, and He rested on the seventh day; therefore the LORD blessed the sabbath day and hallowed it.

[12]Honor your father and your mother, that you may long endure on the land that the LORD your God is assigning to you.

[13]You shall not murder.

You shall not commit adultery.

You shall not steal.

You shall not bear false witness against your neighbor.

[14]You shall not covet your neighbor's house: you shall not covet your neighbor's wife, or his male or female slave, or his ox or his ass, or anything that is your neighbor's.

[15]All the people witnessed the thunder and lightning, the blare of the horn and the mountain smoking; and when the people saw it, they fell back and

stood at a distance. 16"You speak to us," they said to
Moses, "and we will obey; but let not God speak to
us, lest we die." 17Moses answered the people, "Be
not afraid; for God has come only in order to test
you, and in order that the fear of Him may be ever
with you, so that you do not go astray." 18So the
people remained at a distance, while Moses approached the thick cloud where God was.

The Holiness Code

In the books of Exodus, Leviticus, and Deuteronomy, several sets of moral and religious laws, or codes, are set forth for the Israelites to follow. In Leviticus 17 through 26, the laws known as the Holiness Code are stated in detail. Here is the nineteenth chapter.

19 1The LORD spoke to Moses, saying: 2Speak to
the whole Israelite community and say to them:
You shall be holy, for I, the LORD your God, am
holy.
3You shall each revere his mother and his father,
and keep My sabbaths: I the LORD am your God.
4Do not turn to idols or make molten gods for
yourselves: I the LORD am your God.
5When you sacrifice an offering of well-being to
the LORD, sacrifice it so that it may be accepted on
your behalf. 6It shall be eaten on the day you sacrifice it, or on the day following; but what is left by the
third day must be consumed in fire. 7If it should be
eaten on the third day, it is an offensive thing, it will
not be acceptable. 8And he who eats of it shall bear
his guilt, for he has profaned what is sacred to the
LORD; that person shall be cut off from his kin.
9When you reap the harvest of your land, you
shall not reap all the way to the edges of your field,
or gather the gleanings of your harvest. 10You shall
not pick your vineyard bare, or gather the fallen fruit
of your vineyard; you shall leave them for the poor
and the stranger: I the LORD am your God.
11You shall not steal; you shall not deal deceitfully
or falsely with one another. 12You shall not swear
falsely by My name, profaning the name of your
God: I am the LORD.
13You shall not defraud your fellow. You shall not
commit robbery. The wages of a laborer shall not
remain with you until morning.
14You shall not insult the deaf, or place a stum-
bling block before the blind. You shall fear your
God: I am the LORD.
15You shall not render an unfair decision: do not
favor the poor or show deference to the rich; judge
your kinsman fairly. 16Do not deal basely with your
countrymen. Do not profit by the blood of your
fellow: I am the LORD.
17You shall not hate your kinsfolk in your heart.
Reprove your kinsman but incur no guilt because of
him. 18You shall not take vengeance or bear a grudge
against your countrymen. Love your fellow as yourself: I am the LORD.
19You shall observe My laws.
You shall not let your cattle mate with a different
kind; you shall not sow your field with two kinds of
seed; you shall not put on cloth from a mixture of
two kinds of material.
20If a man has carnal relations with a woman who is
a slave and has been designated for another man, but

Leviticus 19:1–37, *Tanakh: A New Translation of the Holy Scriptures* (Philadelphia: Jewish Publication Society, 1985).

has not been redeemed or given her freedom, there shall be an indemnity; they shall not, however, be put to death, since she has not been freed. 21But he must bring to the entrance of the Tent of Meeting, as his guilt offering to the LORD, a ram of guilt offering. 22With the ram of guilt offering the priest shall make expiation for him before the LORD for the sin that he committed; and the sin that he committed will be forgiven him.

23When you enter the land and plant any tree for food, you shall regard its fruit as forbidden. Three years it shall be forbidden for you, not to be eaten. 24In the fourth year all its fruit shall be set aside for jubilation before the LORD; 25and only in the fifth year may you use its fruit—that its yield to you may be increased: I the LORD am your God.

26You shall not eat anything with its blood. You shall not practice divination or soothsaying. 27You shall not round off the side-growth on your head, or destroy the side-growth of your beard. 28You shall not make gashes in your flesh for the dead, or incise any marks on yourselves: I am the LORD.

29Do not degrade your daughter and make her a harlot, lest the land fall into harlotry and the land be filled with depravity. 30You shall keep My sabbaths and venerate My sanctuary: I am the LORD.

31Do not turn to ghosts and do not inquire of familiar spirits, to be defiled by them: I the LORD am your God.

32You shall rise before the aged and show deference to the old; you shall fear your God: I am the LORD.

33When a stranger resides with you in your land, you shall not wrong him. 34The stranger who resides with you shall be to you as one of your citizens; you shall love him as yourself, for you were strangers in the land of Egypt: I the LORD am your God.

35You shall not falsify measures of length, weight, or capacity. 36You shall have an honest balance, honest weights, an honest *ephah*, and an honest *hin*.

I the LORD am your God who freed you from the land of Egypt. 37You shall faithfully observe all My laws and all My rules: I am the LORD.

The Entry into Canaan

The book of Joshua tells the story of how the Israelites enter Canaan. Again they are directed to obey God's laws. They carry the Ark of the Covenant across the Jordan river into Canaan, and the Israelite army begins the campaign to destroy and dispossess the peoples living there, as God has commanded.

1 1After the death of Moses the servant of the LORD, the LORD said to Joshua son of Nun, Moses' attendant:

2"My servant Moses is dead. Prepare to cross the Jordan, together with all this people, into the land that I am giving to the Israelites. 3Every spot on which your foot treads I give to you, as I promised Moses. 4Your territory shall extend from the wilderness and the Lebanon to the Great River, the River Euphrates [on the east]—the whole Hittite country—and up to the Mediterranean Sea on the west. 5No one shall be able to resist you as long as you live. As I was with Moses, so I will be with you; I will not fail you or forsake you.

6"Be strong and resolute, for you shall apportion to this people the land that I swore to their fathers to

Joshua 1:1–18; 3:1–17, *Tanakh: A New Translation of the Holy Scriptures* (Philadelphia: Jewish Publication Society, 1985).

assign to them. 7But you must be very strong and resolute to observe faithfully all the Teaching that My servant Moses enjoined upon you. Do not deviate from it to the right or to the left, that you may be successful wherever you go. 8Let not this Book of the Teaching cease from your lips, but recite it day and night, so that you may observe faithfully all that is written in it. Only then will you prosper in your undertakings and only then will you be successful.

9"I charge you: Be strong and resolute; do not be terrified or dismayed, for the LORD your God is with you wherever you go."

10Joshua thereupon gave orders to the officials of the people: 11"Go through the camp and charge the people thus: Get provisions ready, for in three days' time you are to cross the Jordan, in order to enter and possess the land that the LORD your God is giving you as a possession."

12Then Joshua said to the Reubenites, the Gadites, and the half-tribe of Manasseh, 13"Remember what Moses the servant of the LORD enjoined upon you, when he said: 'The LORD your God is granting you a haven; He has assigned this territory to you.' 14Let your wives, children, and livestock remain in the land that Moses assigned to you on this side of the Jordan; but every one of your fighting men shall go across armed in the van of your kinsmen. And you shall assist them 15until the LORD has given your kinsmen a haven, such as you have, and they too have gained possession of the land that the LORD your God has assigned to them. Then you may return to the land on the east side of the Jordan, which Moses the servant of the LORD assigned to you as your possession, and you may possess it."

16They answered Joshua, "We will do everything you have commanded us and we will go wherever you send us. 17We will obey you just as we obeyed Moses; let but the LORD your God be with you as He was with Moses! 18Any man who flouts your commands and does not obey every order you give him shall be put to death. Only be strong and resolute!". . .

3 1Early next morning, Joshua and all the Israelites set out from Shittim and marched to the Jordan. They did not cross immediately, but spent the night there. 2Three days later, the officials went through the camp 3and charged the people as follows: "When you see the Ark of the Covenant of the LORD your God being borne by the levitical priests, you shall move forward. Follow it—4but keep a distance of some two thousand cubits from it, never coming any closer to it—so that you may know by what route to march, since it is a road you have not traveled before." 5And Joshua said to the people, "Purify yourselves, for tomorrow the LORD will perform wonders in your midst."

6Then Joshua ordered the priests, "Take up the Ark of the Covenant and advance to the head of the people." And they took up the Ark of the Covenant and marched at the head of the people.

7The LORD said to Joshua, "This day, for the first time, I will exalt you in the sight of all Israel, so that they shall know that I will be with you as I was with Moses. 8For your part, command the priests who carry the Ark of the Covenant as follows: When you reach the edge of the waters of the Jordan, make a halt in the Jordan."

9And Joshua said to the Israelites, "Come closer and listen to the words of the LORD your God. 10By this," Joshua continued, "you shall know that a living God is among you, and that He will dispossess for you the Canaanites, Hittites, Hivites, Perizzites, Girgashites, Amorites, and Jebusites: 11the Ark of the Covenant of the Sovereign of all the earth is advancing before you into the Jordan. 12Now select twelve men from the tribes of Israel, one man from each tribe. 13When the feet of the priests bearing the Ark of the LORD, the Sovereign of all the earth, come to rest in the waters of the Jordan, the waters of the Jordan—the water coming from upstream—will be cut off and will stand in a single heap."

14When the people set out from their encampment to cross the Jordan, the priests bearing the Ark of the Covenant were at the head of the people. 15Now the Jordan keeps flowing over its entire bed throughout the harvest season. But as soon as the bearers of the Ark reached the Jordan, and the feet of the priests bearing the Ark dipped into the water at its edge, 16the waters coming down from upstream piled up in

a single heap a great way off, at Adam, the town next
to Zarethan; and those flowing away downstream to
the Sea of the Arabah (the Dead Sea) ran out completely. So the people crossed near Jericho.
17The priests who bore the Ark of the LORD'S Covenant stood on dry land exactly in the middle of the Jordan, while all Israel crossed over on dry land, until the entire nation had finished crossing the Jordan.

Psalms of David

The Book of Psalms is a compilation of 150 hymns and prayers, 73 of which are attributed to David (although scholars have questioned his authorship). Some Psalms praise God; some implore him for help in bad times; some may have been recited or sung in Temple worship. Jews—individually and collectively—recite them in times of grief or crisis. Psalm 23 is well known by both Jews and non-Jews.

8

2O LORD, our Lord,
How majestic is Your name throughout the earth,
You who have covered the heavens with Your splendor!
3From the mouths of infants and sucklings
You have founded strength on account of Your foes,
to put an end to enemy and avenger.
4When I behold Your heavens, the work of Your fingers,
the moon and stars that You set in place,
5what is man that You have been mindful of him,
mortal man that You have taken note of him,
6that You have made him little less than divine,
and adorned him with glory and majesty;
7You have made him master over Your handiwork,
laying the world at his feet,
8sheep and oxen, all of them,
and wild beasts, too;
9the birds of the heavens, the fish of the sea,
whatever travels the paths of the seas.
10O LORD, our Lord, how majestic is Your name throughout
the earth!

23

1The LORD is my shepherd;
I lack nothing.
2He makes me lie down in green pastures;
He leads me to water in places of repose;
3He renews my life;
He guides me in right paths
as befits His name.
4Though I walk through a valley of deepest darkness,
I fear no harm, for You are with me;

Psalms 8, 23, 27, 51, *Tanakh: A New Translation of the Holy Scriptures* (Philadelphia: Jewish Publication Society, 1985).

Your rod and Your staff—they comfort me.
5You spread a table for me in full view of my enemies;
You anoint my head with oil;
my drink is abundant.
6Only goodness and steadfast love shall pursue me
all the days of my life,
and I shall dwell in the house of the LORD
for many long years.

27

1The LORD is my light and my help;
whom should I fear?
The LORD is the stronghold of my life,
whom should I dread?
2When evil men assail me
to devour my flesh—
it is they, my foes and my enemies,
who stumble and fall.
3Should an army besiege me,
my heart would have no fear;
should war beset me,
still would I be confident.
4One thing I ask of the LORD,
only that do I seek:
to live in the house of the LORD
all the days of my life,
to gaze upon the beauty of the LORD,
to frequent His temple.
5He will shelter me in His pavilion
on an evil day,
grant me the protection of His tent,
raise me high upon a rock.
6Now is my head high
over my enemies roundabout;
I sacrifice in His tent with shouts of joy,
singing and chanting a hymn to the LORD.
7Hear, O LORD, when I cry aloud;
have mercy on me, answer me.
8 In Your behalf my heart says:
"Seek My face!"
O LORD, I seek Your face.
9Do not hide Your face from me;
do not thrust aside Your servant in anger;
You have ever been my help.
Do not forsake me, do not abandon me,
O God, my deliverer.
10Though my father and mother abandon me,
the LORD will take me in.
11Show me Your way, O LORD,
and lead me on a level path
because of my watchful foes.
12Do not subject me to the will of my foes,
for false witnesses and unjust accusers
have appeared against me.
13Had I not the assurance
that I would enjoy the goodness of the LORD
in the land of the living . . .
14Look to the LORD;
be strong and of good courage!
O look to the LORD!

51

3Have mercy upon me, O God,
as befits Your faithfulness;
in keeping with Your abundant compassion,
blot out my transgressions.
4Wash me thoroughly of my iniquity,
and purify me of my sin;
5for I recognize my transgressions,
and am ever conscious of my sin.
6Against You alone have I sinned,
and done what is evil in Your sight;
so You are just in Your sentence,
and right in Your judgment.
7Indeed I was born with iniquity;
with sin my mother conceived me.
8Indeed You desire truth about that which is hidden;
teach me wisdom about secret things.
9Purge me with hyssop till I am pure;

wash me till I am whiter than snow.
10 Let me hear tidings of joy and gladness;
let the bones You have crushed exult.
11 Hide Your face from my sins;
blot out all my iniquities.
12 Fashion a pure heart for me, O God;
create in me a steadfast spirit.
13 Do not cast me out of Your presence,
or take Your holy spirit away from me.
14 Let me again rejoice in Your help;
let a vigorous spirit sustain me.
15 I will teach transgressors Your ways,
that sinners may return to You.
16 Save me from bloodguilt,
O God, God, my deliverer,
that I may sing forth Your beneficence.
17 O LORD, open my lips,
and let my mouth declare Your praise.
18 You do not want me to bring sacrifices;
You do not desire burnt offerings;
19 True sacrifice to God is a contrite spirit; God, You will not despise
a contrite and crushed heart.

The Babylonian Conquest and Exile

In 586 BCE the Babylonians conquered the Israelites, exiled their leaders and skilled workers to Babylon, and destroyed the (First) Temple in Jerusalem. The Babylonian Exile and First Temple destruction had an incalculable effect on Jews and Judaism. This is how the book of 2 Kings relates the story.

24 1 In his days, King Nebuchadnezzar of Babylon came up, and Jehoiakim became his vassal for three years. Then he turned and rebelled against him. 2 The LORD let loose against him the raiding bands of the Chaldeans, Arameans, Moabites, and Ammonites; He let them loose against Judah to destroy it, in accordance with the word that the LORD had spoken through His servants the prophets. 3 All this befell Judah at the command of the LORD, who banished [them] from His presence because of all the sins that Manasseh had committed, 4 and also because of the blood of the innocent that he shed. For he filled Jerusalem with the blood of the innocent, and the LORD would not forgive.

5 The other events of Jehoiakim's reign, and all of his actions, are recorded in the Annals of the Kings of Judah. 6 Jehoiakim slept with his fathers, and his son Jehoiachin succeeded him as king. 7 The king of Egypt did not venture out of his country again, for the king of Babylon had seized all the land that had belonged to the king of Egypt, from the Wadi of Egypt to the River Euphrates.

8 Jehoiachin was eighteen years old when he became king, and he reigned three months in Jerusalem; his mother's name was Nehushta daughter of Elnathan of Jerusalem. 9 He did what was displeasing to the LORD, just as his father had done. 10 At that time, the troops of King Nebuchadnezzar of Babylon marched against Jerusalem, and the city came under siege. 11 King Nebuchadnezzar of Babylon advanced against the city while his troops were besieging it. 12 Thereupon King Jehoiachin of Judah, along with his mother,

2 Kings 24:8–20; 25:1–17, *Tanakh: A New Translation of the Holy Scriptures* (Philadelphia: Jewish Publication Society, 1985).

and his courtiers, commanders, and officers, surrendered to the king of Babylon. The king of Babylon took him captive in the eighth year of his reign. [13]He carried off from Jerusalem all the treasures of the House of the LORD and the treasures of the royal palace; he stripped off all the golden decorations in the Temple of the LORD—which King Solomon of Israel had made—as the LORD had warned. [14]He exiled all of Jerusalem: all the commanders and all the warriors—ten thousand exiles—as well as all the craftsmen and smiths; only the poorest people in the land were left. [15]He deported Jehoiachin to Babylon; and the king's wives and officers and the notables of the land were brought as exiles from Jerusalem to Babylon. [16]All the able men, to the number of seven thousand—all of them warriors, trained for battle—and a thousand craftsmen and smiths were brought to Babylon as exiles by the king of Babylon. [17]And the king of Babylon appointed Mattaniah, Jehoiachin's uncle, king in his place, changing his name to Zedekiah.

[18]Zedekiah was twenty-one years old when he became king, and he reigned eleven years in Jerusalem; his mother's name was Hamutal daughter of Jeremiah of Libnah. [19]He did what was displeasing to the LORD, just as Jehoiakim had done. [20]Indeed, Jerusalem and Judah were a cause of anger for the LORD, so that He cast them out of His presence.

25 Zedekiah rebelled against the king of Babylon. [1]And in the ninth year of his reign, on the tenth day of the tenth month, Nebuchadnezzar moved against Jerusalem with his whole army. He besieged it; and they built towers against it all around. [2]The city continued in a state of siege until the eleventh year of King Zedekiah. [3]By the ninth day [of the fourth month] the famine had become acute in the city; there was no food left for the common people.

[4]Then [the wall of] the city was breached. All the soldiers [left the city] by night through the gate between the double walls, which is near the king's garden—the Chaldeans were all around the city; and [the king] set out for the Arabah. [5]But the Chaldean troops pursued the king, and they overtook him in the steppes of Jericho as his entire force left him and scattered. [6]They captured the king and brought him before the king of Babylon at Riblah; and they put him on trial. [7]They slaughtered Zedekiah's sons before his eyes; then Zedekiah's eyes were put out. He was chained in bronze fetters and he was brought to Babylon.

[8]On the seventh day of the fifth month—that was the nineteenth year of King Nebuchadnezzar of Babylon—Nebuzaradan, the chief of the guards, an officer of the king of Babylon, came to Jerusalem. [9]He burned the House of the LORD, the king's palace, and all the houses of Jerusalem; he burned down the house of every notable person. [10]The entire Chaldean force that was with the chief of the guard tore down the walls of Jerusalem on every side. [11]The remnant of the people that was left in the city, the defectors who had gone over to the king of Babylon—and the remnant of the population—were taken into exile by Nebuzaradan, the chief of the guards. [12]But some of the poorest in the land were left by the chief of the guards, to be vinedressers and field hands.

[13]The Chaldeans broke up the bronze columns of the House of the LORD, the stands, and the bronze tank that was in the House of the LORD; and they carried the bronze away to Babylon. [14]They also took all the pails, scrapers, snuffers, ladles, and all the other bronze vessels used in the service. [15]The chief of the guards took whatever was of gold and whatever was of silver: firepans and sprinkling bowls. [16]The two columns, the one tank, and the stands that Solomon provided for the House of the LORD—all these objects contained bronze beyond weighing. [17]The one column was eighteen cubits high. It had a bronze capital above it; the height of the capital was three cubits, and there was a meshwork [decorated] with pomegranates about the capital, all made of bronze. And the like was true of the other column with its meshwork.

Mishnah: The Ethics of the Fathers

The Ethics of the Fathers (Tractate Avot) is the best-known part of the *Mishnah*, which is a huge collection of oral law in the *Talmud*. It is mostly an assemblage of comments or proverbs. This first part of the *Avot* follows the transmission of the oral law from Moses to the rabbis who committed it to writing.

1 Moses received the Torah at Sinai. He conveyed it to Joshua; Joshua to the elders; the elders to the prophets; and the prophets transmitted it to the men of the Great Assembly. The latter emphasized three principles: Be deliberate in judgment; raise up many disciples; and make a fence to safeguard the Torah.

2 Simeon the Just was of the last survivors of the Great Assembly. He used to say: The world rests on three foundations: the Torah; the divine service; and the practices of lovingkindness between man and man.

3 Antigonus of Soho received the tradition from him. He was accustomed to say: Be not like servants who serve their master because of the expected reward, but be like those who serve a master without expecting a reward; and let the fear of God be upon you.

4 Yose ben Yoezer of Zeredah and Yose ben Yohanan of Jerusalem received the tradition from them. Yose ben Yoezer of Zeredah said: Let your house be a gathering place for wise men; sit attentively at their feet, and drink of their words of wisdom with eagerness.

5 Yose ben Yohanan of Jerusalem said: Let your home be a place of hospitality to strangers; and make the poor welcome in your household; and do not indulge in gossip with women. This applies even with one's own wife, and surely so with another man's wife. The sages generalized from this: He who engages in profuse gossiping with women causes evil for himself and neglects the study of the Torah, and he will bring upon himself retributions in the hereafter.

6 Joshua ben Perahya and Nittai the Arbelite received the tradition from them. Joshua ben Perahya said: Get yourself a teacher; and acquire for yourself a companion; and judge all people favorably.

7 Nittai the Arbelite said: Avoid an evil neighbor; do not associate with the wicked; and do not surrender your faith in divine retribution.

8 Judah ben Tabbai and Simeon ben Shatah received the traditions from them. Judah ben Tabbai said: Let not the judge play the part of the counselor; when two litigants stand before you, suspect both of being in the wrong; and when they leave after submitting to the court's decree, regard them both as guiltless.

9 Simeon ben Shatah said: Search the witnesses thoroughly and be cautious with your own words lest you give them an opening to false testimony.

10 Shemaya and Abtalyon received the traditions from them. Shemaya said: Love work; hate domineering over others; and do not seek the intimacy of public officials.

11 Abtalyon said: Sages, be precise in your teachings. You may suffer exile to a place where heresy is rampant, and your inexact language may lead your disciples astray, and they will lose their faith, thus leading to a desecration of the divine name.

12 Hillel and Shammai received the tradition from them. Hillel said: Be of the disciples of Aaron. Love peace and pursue peace; love your fellow creatures and bring them near to the Torah.

13 He also said: He who strives to exalt his name will in the end destroy his name; he who does not increase his knowledge decreases it; he who

Misnah, The Talmud: Selected Writings, Ben Zion Bokser, trans. (New York: Paulist Press, 1989), 219–221.

does not study has undermined his right to life; and he who makes unworthy use of the crown of the Torah will perish.

14 He also said: If I am not for myself who will be? But if I am for myself only, what am I? And if not now, when?

15 Shammai said: Set a fixed time for the study of the Torah; say little and do much; and greet every person with a cheerful countenance.

16 Rabban Gamaliel said: Provide yourself with a teacher, and extricate yourself from doubt; and do not habitually contribute your tithes by rough estimates.

17 Simeon his son said: All my life I was raised among scholars and I found that no virtue becomes a man more than silence; what is more essential is not study but practice; and in the wake of many words is sin.

18 Rabban Simeon ben Gamaliel said: The world rests on three foundations: truth, justice, and peace. As it is written (Zech 8:16): "You shall administer truth, justice and peace within your gates."

Maimonides: Thirteen Principles of the Jewish Faith

The great Jewish philosopher Maimonides (1135–1204) drafted a set of thirteen principles that he thought constituted the heart of the Jewish faith. Jews accepted them, and they are still respected. In 1885, however, Reform Judaism issued its own statement of principles (called the Pittsburgh Platform) that rejects Maimonides's view of Judaism.

1. I believe with perfect faith that God is the Creator and Ruler of all things. He alone has made, does make, and will make all things.
2. I believe with perfect faith that God is One. There is no unity that is in any way like His. He alone is our God—He was, He is, and He will be.
3. I believe with perfect faith that God does not have a body. Physical concepts do not apply to Him. There is nothing whatsoever that resembles Him at all.
4. I believe with perfect faith that God is first and last.
5. I believe with perfect faith that it is only proper to pray to God. One may not pray to anyone or anything else.
6. I believe with perfect faith that all the words of the prophets are true.
7. I believe with perfect faith that the prophecy of Moses is absolutely true. He was the chief of all prophets, both before and after him.
8. I believe with perfect faith that the entire Torah that we now have is that which was given to Moses.
9. I believe with perfect faith that this Torah will not be changed, and that there will never be another given by God.
10. I believe with perfect faith that God knows all of man's deeds and thoughts. It is thus written (Psalm 33:15), "He has molded every heart together, He understands what each one does."
11. I believe with perfect faith that God rewards those who keep His commandments, and punishes those who transgress Him.
12. I believe with perfect faith in the coming of the Messiah. No matter how long it takes, I will await his coming every day.
13. I believe with perfect faith that the dead will be brought back to life when God wills it to happen.

Moses Maimonides, *Thirteen Principles of the Jewish Faith*, in *Essential Judaism*, George Robinson, ed. (New York: Pocket Books, 2000), 416–417.

Reform Judaism: The Pittsburgh Platform, 1885

Reform Judaism advocated dramatic changes in Judaism. For example, it dispensed with claims about a returning messiah, bodily resurrection of the dead, and the establishment of a Jewish nation (reformers declared that we are "no longer a nation, but a religious community"). Further, it sought to downplay many traditional practices, such as Sabbath services in Hebrew and rigid adherence to dietary and purity laws. The following is a formal Declaration of Principles, adopted in 1885 and still accepted by Reform Judaism.

1. We recognize in every religion an attempt to grasp the Infinite, and in every mode, source or book of revelation held sacred in any religious system the consciousness of the indwelling of God in man. We hold that Judaism presents the highest conception of the God-idea as taught in our Holy Scriptures and developed and spiritualized by the Jewish teachers, in accordance with the moral and philosophical progress of their respective ages. We maintain that Judaism preserved and defended amid continual struggles and trials and under enforced isolation, this God-idea as the central religious truth for the human race.

2. We recognize in the Bible the record of the consecration of the Jewish people to its mission as the priest of the one God, and value it as the most potent instrument of religious and moral instruction. We hold that the modern discoveries of scientific researches in the domain of nature and history are not antagonistic to the doctrines of Judaism, the Bible reflecting the primitive ideas of its own age, and at times clothing its conception of divine Providence and Justice dealing with men in miraculous narratives.

3. We recognize in the Mosaic legislation a system of training the Jewish people for its mission during its national life in Palestine, and today we accept as binding only its moral laws, and maintain only such ceremonies as elevate and sanctify our lives, but reject all such as are not adapted to the views and habits of modern civilization.

4. We hold that all such Mosaic and rabbinical laws as regulate diet, priestly purity, and dress originated in ages and under the influence of ideas entirely foreign to our present mental and spiritual state. They fail to impress the modern Jew with a spirit of priestly holiness; their observance in our days is apt rather to obstruct than to further modern spiritual elevation.

5. We recognize, in the modern era of universal culture of heart and intellect, the approaching of the realization of Israel's great Messianic hope for the establishment of the kingdom of truth, justice, and peace among all men. We consider ourselves no longer a nation, but a religious community, and therefore expect neither a return to Palestine, nor a sacrificial worship under the sons of Aaron, nor the restoration of any of the laws concerning the Jewish state.

6. We recognize in Judaism a progressive religion, ever striving to be in accord with the postulates of reason. We are convinced of the utmost necessity of preserving the historical identity with our great past. Christianity and Islam, being daughter religions of Judaism, we appreciate their providential mission, to aid in the spreading of monotheistic and moral truth. We acknowledge that the spirit of broad humanity of our age is our ally in the fulfillment of our mission, and therefore we extend the hand of fellowship to all who cooperate with us in the establishment of the reign of truth and righteousness among men.

7. We reassert the doctrine of Judaism that the soul is immortal, grounding the belief on the divine nature of human spirit, which forever finds bliss in righteousness and misery in wickedness. We reject as

The Pittsburgh Platform, 1885, Meeting of Reform Rabbis, Mayer Wise presiding, Nov. 16–19, 1885.

ideas not rooted in Judaism, the beliefs both in bodily resurrection and in Gehenna and Eden (Hell and Paradise) as abodes for everlasting punishment and reward.

8. In full accordance with the spirit of the Mosaic legislation, which strives to regulate the relations between rich and poor, we deem it our duty to participate in the great task of modern times, to solve, on the basis of justice and righteousness, the problems presented by the contrasts and evils of the present organization of society.

To Be a Jew

ELIE WIESEL

Elie Wiesel (1928–2016) was born in what is now part of Romania. At age fifteen he and his family were uprooted from their home and shipped by the Nazis to the Auschwitz concentration camp. In the brutal camp system of Nazi Germany, his mother, his younger sister, and his father died. Wiesel was imprisoned at the camp at Buchenwald when it was finally liberated in 1945. Later he became a journalist, wrote over sixty books, and became a university professor. In 1986 he won the Nobel Prize for peace. In this excerpt he tries to answer the question: After all the suffering that Jews have endured in history, including the nightmare of the Holocaust, what does it mean to be a Jew?

Once upon a time, in a distant town surrounded by mountains, there lived a small Jewish boy who believed himself capable of seeing good in evil, of discovering dawn within dusk and, in general, of deciphering the symbols, both visible and invisible, lavished upon him by destiny.

To him, all things seemed simple and miraculous: life and death, love and hatred. On one side were the righteous, on the other the wicked. The just were always handsome and generous, the miscreants always ugly and cruel. And God in His heaven kept the accounts in a book only He could consult. In that book each people had its own page, and the Jewish people had the most beautiful page of all.

Naturally, this little boy felt at ease only among his own people, in his own setting. Everything alien frightened me. And alien meant not Moslem or Hindu, but Christian. The priest dressed in black, the woodcutter and his ax, the teacher and his ruler, old peasant women crossing themselves as their husbands uttered oath upon oath, constables looking gruff or merely preoccupied—all of them exuded a hostility I understood and considered normal, and, therefore without remedy.

I *understood* that all these people, young and old, rich and poor, powerful and oppressed, exploiters and exploited, should want my undoing, even my death. True, we inhabited the same landscape, but that was yet another reason for them to hate me. Such is man's nature: he hates what disturbs him, what eludes him. We depended on the more or less unselfish tolerance of the "others," yet our life followed its

Elie Wiesel, *A Jew Today* (New York: Vintage, 1978), 3–16.

own course independently of theirs, a fact they clearly resented. Our determination to maintain and enrich our separate history, our separate society, confused them as much as did that history itself. A living Jew, a believing Jew, proud of his faith, was for them a contradiction, a denial, an aberration. According to their calculations, this chosen and accursed people should long ago have ceased to haunt a mankind whose salvation was linked to the blood-stained symbol of the cross. They could not accept the idea of a Jew celebrating his Holy Days with song, just as they celebrated their own. That was inadmissible, illogical, even unjust. And the less they understood us, the more I understood them.

I felt no animosity. I did not even hate them at Christmas or Easter time when they imposed a climate of terror upon our frightened community. I told myself: They envy us, they persecute us because they envy us, and rightly so; surely *they* were the ones to be pitied. Their tormenting us was but an admission of weakness, of inner insecurity. If God's truth subsists on earth in the hearts of mortals, it is our doing. It is through us that God has chosen to manifest His will and outline His designs, and it is through us that He has chosen to sanctify His name. Were I in their place I, too, would feel rejected. How could they not be envious? In an odd way, the more they hunted me, the more I rationalized their behavior. Today I recognize my feelings for what they were: a mixture of pride, distrust and pity.

Yet I felt no curiosity. Not of any kind, or at any moment. We seemed to intrigue them, but they left me indifferent. I knew nothing of their catechism, and cared less. I made no attempt to comprehend the rites and canons of their faith. Their rituals held no interest for me; quite the contrary, I turned away from them. Whenever I met a priest I would avert my gaze and think of something else. Rather than walk in front of a church with its pointed and threatening belfry, I would cross the street. To see was as frightening as to be seen; I worried that a visual, physical link might somehow be created between us. So ignorant was I of their world that I had no idea that Judaism and Christianity claimed the same roots. Nor did I know that Christians who believe in the eternity and in the divinity of Christ also believe in those of God, *our* God. Though our universes existed side by side, I avoided penetrating theirs, whereas they sought to dominate ours by force. I had heard enough tales about the Crusades and the pogroms, and I had repeated enough litanies dedicated to their victims, to know where I stood. I had read and reread descriptions of what inquisitors, grand and small, had inflicted on Jews in Catholic kingdoms; how they had preached God's love to them even as they were leading them to the stake. All I knew of Christianity was its hate for my people. Christians were more present in my imagination than in my life. What did a Christian do when he was alone? What were his dreams made of? How did he use his time when he was not engaged in plotting against us? But none of this really troubled me. Beyond our immediate contact, our public and hereditary confrontations, he simply did not exist.

My knowledge of the Jew, on the other hand, sprang from an inexhaustible source: the more I learned, the more I wanted to know. There was inside me a thirst for knowledge that was all-enveloping, all-pervasive, a veritable obsession.

I knew what it meant to be a Jew in day-to-day life as well as in the absolute. What we required was to obey the Law; thus one needed first to learn it, then to remember it. What was required was to love God and that which in His creation bears His seal. And His will would be done.

Abraham's covenant, Isaac's suspended sacrifice, Jacob's fiery dreams, the revelation at Sinai, the long march through the desert, Moses' blessings, the conquest of Canaan, the pilgrimages to the Temple in Jerusalem, Isaiah's and Habakkuk's beautiful but harsh words, Jeremiah's lamentations, the Talmudic legends: my head was abuzz with ancient memories and debates, with tales teeming with kings and prophets, tragedies and miracles. Every story contained victims, always victims, and survivors, always survivors. To be a Jew meant to live with memory.

Nothing could have been easier. One needed only to follow tradition, to reproduce the gestures and sounds transmitted through generations whose end product I was. On the morning of Shavuoth there I was with Moses receiving the Law. On the eve of Tishah b'Av, seated on the floor, my head covered with ashes, I wept, together with Rabbi Yohanan Ben-Zakkai, over the destruction of the city that had been thought indestructible. During the week of Hanukkah, I rushed to the aid of the Maccabees; and on Purim, I laughed, how I laughed, with Mordecai, celebrating his victory over Haman. And week after week, as we blessed the wine during Shabbat meals, I accompanied the Jews out of Egypt—yes, I was forever leaving Egypt, freeing myself from bondage. To be a Jew meant creating links, a network of continuity.

With the years I learned a more "sophisticated," more modern vocabulary. I was told that to be a Jew means to place the accent simultaneously and equally on verb and noun, on the secular and the eternal, to prevent the one from excluding the other or succeeding at the expense of the other. That it means to serve God by espousing man's cause, to plead for man while recognizing his need of God. And to opt for the Creator *and* His creation, refusing to pit one against the other.

Of course, man must interrogate God, as did Abraham; articulate his anger, as did Moses; and shout his sorrow, as did Job. But only the Jew opts for Abraham—who questions—and for God—who is questioned. He claims every role and assumes every destiny: he is both sum and synthesis.

I shall long, perhaps forever, remember my Master, the one with the yellowish beard, telling me, "Only the Jew knows that he may oppose God as long as he does so in defense of His creation." Another time he told me, "God gave the Law, but it is up to man to interpret it—and his interpretation is binding on God and commits Him."

Surely this is an idealized concept of the Jew. And of man. And yet it is one that is tested every day, at every moment, in every circumstance.

At school I read in the Talmud: Why did God create only one man? The answer: All men have the same ancestor. So that no man, later, could claim superiority over another.

And also: A criminal who sets fire to the Temple, the most sacred, the most revered edifice in the world, is punishable with only thirty-nine lashes of the whip; let a fanatic kill him and *his* punishment would be death. For all the temples and all the sanctuaries are not worth the life of a single human being, be he arsonist, profanator, enemy of God and shame of God.

Painful irony: We were chased from country to country, our Houses of Study were burned, our sages assassinated, our school-children massacred, and still we went on tirelessly, fiercely, praising the inviolate sanctity of life and proclaiming faith in man, any man.

An extraordinary contradiction? Perhaps. But to be a Jew is precisely to reveal oneself within one's contradictions by accepting them. It means safeguarding one's past at a time when mankind aspires only to conquer the future; it means observing Shabbat when the official day of rest is Sunday or Friday; it means fervently exploring the Talmud, with its seemingly antiquated laws and discussions, while outside, not two steps away from the heder or the yeshiva, one's friends and parents are rounded up or beaten in a pogrom; it means asserting the right of spirituality in a world that denies spirituality; it means singing and singing again, louder and louder, when all around everything heralds the end of the world, the end of man.

All this was really so. The small Jewish boy is telling only what he heard and saw, what he lived himself, long ago. He vouches for its truth.

Yes, long ago in distant places it all seemed so simple to me, so real, so throbbing with truth. Like God, I looked at the world and found it good, fertile, full of meaning. Even in exile, every creature was in its place and every encounter was charged with promise. And with the advent of Shabbat, the town changed into a kingdom whose madmen and beggars became the princes of Shabbat.

I shall never forget Shabbat in my town. When I shall have forgotten everything else, my memory will still retain the atmosphere of holiday, of serenity pervading even the poorest houses: the white tablecloth, the candles, the meticulously combed little girls, the men on their way to synagogue. When my town shall fade into the abyss of time, I will continue to remember the light and the warmth it radiated on Shabbat. The exalting prayers, the wordless songs of the Hasidim, the fire and radiance of their Masters.

On that day of days, past and future suffering and anguish faded into the distance. Appeased man called on the divine presence to express his gratitude.

The jealousies and grudges, the petty rancors between neighbors could wait. As could the debts and worries, the dangers. Everything could wait. As it enveloped the universe, the Shabbat conferred on it a dimension of peace, an aura of love.

Those who were hungry came and ate; and those who felt abandoned seized the outstretched hand; and those who were alone, and those who were sad, the strangers, the refugees, the wanderers, as they left the synagogue were invited to share the meal in any home; and the grieving were urged to contain their tears and come draw on the collective joy of Shabbat.

The difference between us and the others? The others, how I pitied them. They did not even know what they were missing; they were unmoved by the beauty, the eternal splendor of Shabbat.

And then came the Holocaust, which shook history and by its dimensions and goals marked the end of a civilization. Concentration-camp man discovered the anti-savior.

We became witnesses to a huge simplification. On the one side there were the executioners and on the other the victims. What about the onlookers, those who remained neutral, those who served the executioner simply by not interfering? To be a Jew then meant to fight both the complacency of the neutral and the hate of the killers. And to resist—in any way, with any means. And not only with weapons. The Jew who refused death, who refused to believe in death, who chose to marry in the ghetto, to circumcise his son, to teach him the sacred language, to bind him to the threatened and weakened lineage of Israel—that Jew was resisting. The professor or shopkeeper who disregarded facts and warnings and clung to illusion, refusing to admit that people could so succumb to degradation—he, too, was resisting. There was no essential difference between the Warsaw ghetto fighters and the old men getting off the train in Treblinka: because they were Jewish, they were all doomed to hate, and death.

In those days, more than ever, to be Jewish signified *refusal.* Above all, it was a refusal to see reality and life through the enemy's eyes—a refusal to resemble him, to grant him that victory, too.

Yet his victory seemed solid and, in the beginning, definitive. All those uprooted communities, ravaged and dissolved in smoke; all those trains that crisscrossed the nocturnal Polish landscapes; all those men, all those women, stripped of their language, their names, their faces, compelled to live and die according to the laws of the enemy, in anonymity and darkness. All those kingdoms of barbed wire where everyone looked alike and all words carried the same weight. Day followed day and hour followed hour, while thoughts, numb and bleak, groped their way among the corpses, through the mire and the blood.

And the adolescent in me, yearning for faith, questioned: Where was God in all this? Was this another test, one more? Or a punishment? And if so, for what sins? What crimes were being punished? Was there a misdeed that deserved so many mass graves? Would it ever again be possible to speak of justice, of truth, of divine charity, after the murder of one million Jewish children?

I did not understand, I was afraid to understand. Was this the end of the Jewish people, or the end perhaps of the human adventure? Surely it was the end of an era, the end of a world. That I knew, that was all I knew.

As for the rest, I accumulated uncertainties. The faith of some, the lack of faith of others added to my perplexity. How could one believe, how could one not believe, in God as one faced those mountains of ashes? Who would symbolize the concentration-camp experience—the killer or the victim? Their confrontation was so striking, so gigantic that it had to include a metaphysical, ontological aspect: would we ever penetrate its mystery?

Questions, doubts. I moved through the fog like a sleepwalker. Why did the God of Israel manifest such hostility toward the descendants of Israel? I did not know. Why did free men, liberals and humanists, remain untouched by Jewish suffering? I did not know.

I remember the midnight arrival at Birkenau. Shouts. Dogs barking. Families together for the last time, families about to be torn asunder. A young Jewish boy walks at his father's side in the convoy of men; they walk and they walk and night walks with them toward a place spewing monstrous flames, flames devouring the sky. Suddenly an inmate crosses the ranks and explains to the men what they are seeing, the truth of the night: the future, the absence of future; the key to the secret, the power of evil. As he speaks, the young boy touches his father's arm as though to reassure him, and whispers, "This is impossible, isn't it? Don't listen to what he is telling us, he only wants to frighten us. What he says is impossible, unthinkable, it is all part of another age, the Middle Ages, not the twentieth century, not modern history. The world, Father, the civilized world would not allow such things to happen."

And yet the civilized world did know, and remained silent. Where was man in all this? And culture, how did it reach this nadir? All those spiritual leaders, those thinkers, those philosophers enamored of truth, those moralists drunk with justice—how was one to reconcile their teachings with Josef Mengele, the great master of selections in Auschwitz? I told myself that a grave, a horrible error had been committed somewhere—only, I knew neither its nature nor its author. When and where had history taken so bad a turn? . . .

Which brings us back to where we started: to the relations between Jews and Christians, which, of course, we had been forced to revise. For we had been struck by a harsh truth: in Auschwitz all the Jews were victims, all the killers were Christian.

I mention this here neither to score points nor to embarrass anyone. I believe that no religion, people or nation is inferior or superior to another; I dislike facile triumphalism, for us and for others. I dislike self-righteousness. And I feel closer to certain Christians—as long as they do not try to convert me to their faith—than to certain Jews. I felt closer to John XXIII and to François Mauriac than to self-hating Jews. I have more in common with an authentic and tolerant Christian than with a Jew who is neither authentic nor tolerant. I stress this because what I am about to say will surely hurt my Christian friends. Yet I have no right to hold back.

How is one to explain that neither Hitler nor Himmler was ever excommunicated by the church? That Pius XII never thought it necessary, not to say indispensable, to condemn Auschwitz and Treblinka? That among the S.S. a large proportion were believers who remained faithful to their Christian ties to the end? That there were killers who went to confession between massacres? And that they all came from Christian families and had received a Christian education?

In Poland, a stronghold of Christianity, it often happened that Jews who had escaped from the ghettos returned inside their walls, so hostile did they find the outside world; they feared the Poles as much as the Germans. This was also true in Lithuania, in the Ukraine, in White Russia and in Hungary. How is one to explain the passivity of the population as it watched the persecution of its Jews? How explain the cruelty of the killers? How explain that the Christian in them did not make their arms tremble as they shot at children or their conscience bridle as they shoved their naked, beaten victims into the factories of death? Of course, here and there, brave Christians came to the aid of Jews, but they were few: several dozen bishops and priests, a few hundred men and women in all of Europe.

It is a painful statement to make, but we cannot ignore it: as surely as the victims are a problem for the Jews, the killers are a problem for the Christians.

Yes, the victims remain a serious and troubling problem for us. No use covering it up. What was there about the Jew that he could be reduced so quickly, so easily to the status of victim? I have read all the answers, all the explanations. They are all inadequate. It is difficult to imagine the silent processions marching toward the pits. And the crowds that let themselves be duped. And the condemned who, inside the sealed wagons and sometimes on the very ramp at Birkenau, continued not to see. I do not understand. I understand neither the killers nor the victims.

To be a Jew during the Holocaust may have meant not to understand. Having rejected murder as a means of survival and death as a solution, men and women agreed to live and die without understanding.

For the survivor, the question presented itself differently: to remain or not to remain a Jew. I remember our tumultuous, anguished debates in France after the liberation. Should one leave for Palestine and fight in the name of Jewish nationalism, or should one, on the contrary, join the Communist movement and promulgate the ideal of internationalism? Should one delve deeper into tradition, or turn one's back on it? The options were extreme: total commitment or total alienation, unconditional loyalty or repudiation.

There was no returning to the earlier ways and principles. The Jew could say: I have suffered, I have been made to suffer, all I can do is draw closer to my own people. And that was understandable. Or else: I have suffered too much, I have no strength left, I withdraw, I do not wish my children to inherit this suffering. And that, too, was understandable.

And yet, as in the past, the ordeal brought not a decline but a renascence of Jewish consciousness and a flourishing of Jewish history. Rather than break his ties, the Jew strengthened them. Auschwitz made him stronger. Even he among us who espouses so-called universal causes outside his community is motivated by the Jew in him trying to reform man even as he despairs of mankind. Though he may be in a position to become something else, the Jew remains a Jew.

Throughout a world in flux, young Jews, speaking every tongue, products of every social class, join in the adventure that Judaism represents for them, a phenomenon that reached its apex in Israel and Soviet Russia. Following different roads, these pilgrims take part in the same project and express the same defiance: "They want us to founder, but we will let our joy explode; they want to make us hard, closed to solidarity and love, well, we will be obstinate but filled with compassion." This is the challenge that justifies the hopes the Jew places in Judaism and explains the singular marks he leaves on his destiny.

Thus there would seem to be more than one way for the Jew to assume his condition. There is a time to question oneself and a time to act; there is a time to tell stories and a time to pray; there is a time to build and a time to rebuild. Whatever he chooses to do, the Jew becomes a spokesman for all Jews, dead and yet to be born, for all the beings who live through him and inside him.

His mission was never to make the world Jewish but, rather, to make it more human.

God in Search of Man

ABRAHAM JOSHUA HESCHEL

Abraham Joshua Heschel (1907–1972), was a leading Jewish theologian and philosopher. In this reading, he tries to explain God's relationship with humankind. He declares that the crucial link is not man's search for God, but God's search for man.

Most theories of religion start out with defining the religious situation as man's search for God and maintain the axiom that God is silent, hidden and unconcerned with man's search for Him. Now, in adopting that axiom, the answer is given before the question is asked. To Biblical thinking, the definition is incomplete and the axiom false. The Bible speaks not only of man's search for God but also of *God's search for man.* "Thou dost hunt me like a lion," exclaimed Job (10:16).

"From the very first Thou didst single out man and consider him worthy to stand in Thy presence." This is the mysterious paradox of Biblical faith: *God*

Abraham Joshua Heschel, *God in Search of Man: A Philosophy of Judaism* (New York: Farrar, Straus and Giroux, 1955), 136–143.

is pursuing man. It is as if God were unwilling to be alone, and He had chosen man to serve Him. Our seeking Him is not only man's but also His concern, and must not be considered an exclusively human affair. His will is involved in our yearnings. All of human history as described in the Bible may be summarized in one phrase: *God is in search of man.* Faith in God is a response to God's question.

Lord, where shall I find Thee?
High and hidden in Thy place;
And where shall I not find Thee?
The world is full of Thy glory.
I have sought Thy nearness;
With all my heart have I called Thee,
And going out to meet Thee
I found Thee coming toward me.
Even as, in the wonder of Thy might,
In holiness I have beheld Thee,
Who shall say he bath not seen Thee?
Lo, the heavens and their hosts
Declare the awe of Thee,
Though their voice be not heard.

When Adam and Eve hid from His presence, the Lord called: *Where art thou* (Genesis 3:9). It is a call that goes out again and again. It is a still small echo of a still small voice, not uttered in words, not conveyed in categories of the mind, but ineffable and mysterious, as ineffable and mysterious as the glory that fills the whole world. It is wrapped in silence; concealed and subdued, yet it is as if all things were the frozen echo of the question: *Where art thou?*

Faith comes out of awe, out of an awareness that we are exposed to His presence, out of anxiety to answer the challenge of God, out of an awareness of our being called upon. Religion consists of *God's question and man's answer.* The way *to* faith is the way *of* faith. The way to God is a way of God. Unless God asks the question, all our inquiries are in vain.

The answer lasts a moment, the commitment continues. Unless the awareness of the ineffable mystery of existence becomes a permanent state of mind, all that remains is a commitment without faith. To strengthen our alertness, to refine our appreciation of the mystery is the meaning of worship and observance. For faith does not remain stationary. We must continue to pray, continue to obey to be able to believe and to remain attached to His presence.

Recondite is the dimension where God and man meet, and yet not entirely impenetrable. He placed within man something of His spirit (see Isaiah 63:10), and "it is the spirit in a man, the breath of the Almighty, that makes him understand" (Job 32:8).

FAITH IS AN EVENT

Men have often tried to give itemized accounts of why they must believe that God exists. Such accounts are like ripe fruit we gather from the trees. Yet it is beyond all reasons, beneath the ground, where a seed starts to become a tree, that the act of faith takes place.

The soul rarely knows how to raise its deeper secrets to discursive levels of the mind. We must not, therefore, equate the act of faith with its expression. The expression of faith is an affirmation of truth, a definite judgment, a conviction, while faith itself is *an event,* something that happens rather than something that is stored away; it is *a moment* in which the soul of man communes with the glory of God.

Man's walled mind has no access to a ladder upon which he can, on his own strength, rise to knowledge of God. Yet his soul is endowed with translucent windows that open to the beyond. And if he rises to reach out to Him, it is a reflection of the divine light in him that gives him the power for such yearning. We are at times ablaze against and beyond our own power, and unless man's soul is dismissed as an insane asylum, the spectrum analysis of that ray is evidence for the truth of his insight.

For God is not always silent, and man is not always blind. His glory fills the world; His spirit hovers above the waters. There are moments in which, to use a Talmudic phrase, heaven and earth kiss each other; in which there is a lifting of the veil at the horizon of the known, opening a vision of what is eternal in time. Some of us have at least once experienced the momentous realness of God. Some of us have at least caught a glimpse of the beauty, peace, and power that flow through the souls of those who are devoted to Him. There may come a moment like a thunder in the soul, when man is not only aided, not only guided by God's mysterious hand, but also taught how to aid, how to guide other beings. The voice of Sinai goes on for ever: "These words the Lord spoke unto all your assembly in the mount out of the midst of the fire, of the cloud, and of the thick darkness, with *a great voice that goes on for ever.*"

A FLASH IN THE DARKNESS

The fact that ultimately the living certainty of faith is a conclusion derived from acts rather than from logical premises is stated by Maimonides:

"Do not imagine that these great mysteries are completely and thoroughly known to any of us. By no means: sometimes truth flashes up before us with daylight brightness, but soon it is obscured by the limitations of our material nature and social habits, and we fall back into a darkness almost as black as that in which we were before. We are thus like a person whose surroundings are from time to time lit up by lightning, while in the intervals he is plunged into pitch-dark night. Some of us experience such flashes of illumination frequently, until they are in almost perpetual brightness, so that the night turns for them into daylight. That was the prerogative of the greatest of all prophets (Moses), to whom God said: *But as for thee, stand thou here by Me* (Deuteronomy 5:28), and concerning whom Scripture said: *the skin of his face sent forth beams* (Exodus 32:39). Some see a single flash of light in the entire night of their lives. That was the state of those concerning whom it is said: *they prophesied that time and never again* (Numbers 11:25). With others again there are long or short intermissions between the flashes of illumination, and lastly there are those who are not granted that their darkness be illuminated by a flash of lightning, but only, as it were, by the gleam of some polished object or the like of it, such as the stones and [phosphorescent] substances which shine in the dark night; and even that sparse light which illuminates us is not continuous but flashes and disappears as if it were the *gleam of the ever-turning sword* (Genesis 3:24). The degrees of perfection in men vary according to these distinctions. Those who have never for a moment seen the light but grope about in their night are those concerning whom it is said: *They know not, neither will they understand; they walk on in darkness* (Psalms 82:5). The Truth is completely hidden from them in spite of its powerful brightness, as it is also said of them: *And now men see not the light which is bright in the skies* (Job 37:21). These are the great mass of mankind. . . ."

Only those who have gone through days on which words were of no avail, on which the most brilliant theories jarred the ear like mere slang; only those who have experienced ultimate not-knowing, the voicelessness of a soul struck by wonder, total muteness, are able to enter the meaning of God, a meaning greater than the mind.

There is a loneliness in us that hears. When the soul parts from the company of the ego and its retinue of petty conceits; when we cease to exploit all things but instead pray the world's cry, the world's sigh, our loneliness may hear the living grace beyond all power.

We must first peer into the darkness, feel strangled and entombed in the hopelessness of living without God, before we are ready to feel the presence of His living light.

"And it shall come to pass, when I bring a cloud over the earth, that the bow shall be seen in the cloud" (Genesis 9:14). When ignorance and confusion blot out all thoughts, the light of God may suddenly burst forth in the mind like a rainbow in the sky. Our understanding of the greatness of God comes about as an act of illumination. As the Baal Shem said, "like a lightning that all of a sudden illumines the whole world, God illumines the mind of man, enabling him to understand the greatness of our Creator." This is what is meant by the words of the Psalmist: "He sent out His arrows and scattered [the clouds]; He shot forth lightnings and discomfited them." The darkness retreats, "The channels of water appeared, the foundations of the world were laid bare" (Psalms 18:15–16).

The essence of Jewish religious thinking does not lie in entertaining a concept of God but in the ability to articulate a memory of moments of illumination by His presence. Israel is not a people of definers but a people of witnesses: "Ye are My witnesses" (Isaiah 43:10). Reminders of what has been disclosed to us are hanging over our souls like stars, remote and of mind-surpassing grandeur. They shine through dark and dangerous ages, and their reflection can be seen in the lives of those who guard the path of conscience and memory in the wilderness of careless living.

Since those perennial reminders have moved into our minds, wonder has never left us. Heedfully we stare through the telescope of ancient rites lest we lose the perpetual brightness beckoning to our souls. Our mind has not kindled the flame, has not produced these principles. Still our thoughts glow with their light. What is the nature of this glow, of our faith, and how is it perceived?

RETURN TO GOD IS AN ANSWER TO HIM

We do not have to discover the world of faith; we only have to recover it. It is not a *terra incognita,* an unknown land; it is a forgotten land, and our relation to God is a palimpsest rather than *a tabula rasa.* There is no one who has no faith. Every one of us stood at the foot of Sinai and beheld the voice that proclaimed, *I am the Lord thy God.* Every one of us participated in saying, *We shall do and we shall hear.* However, it is the evil in man and the evil in society silencing the depth of the soul that block and hamper our faith. "It is apparent and known before Thee that it is our will to do Thy will. But what stands in the way? The leaven that is in the dough (the evil impulse) and the servitude of the kingdoms."

In the spirit of Judaism, our quest for God is a return to God; our thinking of Him is a recall, an attempt to draw out the depth of our suppressed attachment. The Hebrew word for repentance, *teshuvah,* means *return.* Yet it also means *answer.* Return to God is an answer to Him. For God is not silent. "Return O faithless children, says the Lord" (Jeremiah 3:14). According to the understanding of the Rabbis, daily, at all times, "A Voice cries: in the wilderness prepare the way of the Lord, make straight in the desert a highway for our God" (Isaiah 40:3). "The voice of the Lord cries to the city" (Micah 6:9).

"Morning by morning He wakens my ear to hear as those who are taught" (Isaiah 50:4). The stirring in man to turn to God is actually a "reminder by God to man." It is a call that man's physical sense does not capture, yet the "spiritual soul" in him perceives the call. The most precious gifts come to us unawares and remain unnoted. God's grace resounds in our lives like a staccato. Only by retaining the seemingly disconnected notes do we acquire the ability to grasp the theme.

Is it possible to define the content of such experiences? It is not a perception of a thing, of anything physical; nor is it always a disclosure of ideas hitherto unknown. It is primarily, it seems, an enhancement of the soul, a sharpening of one's spiritual sense, an endowment with a new sensibility. It is a discovery of what is in time, rather than anything in space.

Just as clairvoyants may see the future, the religious man comes to sense the present moment. And this is an extreme achievement. For the present is the presence of God. Things have a past and a future, but only God is pure presence.

A SPIRITUAL EVENT

But if insights are not physical events, in what sense are they real?

The underlying assumption of modern man's outlook is that objective reality is physical: all nonmaterial phenomena can be reduced to material phenomena and explained in physical terms. Thus, only those types of human experiences which acquaint us with the quantitative aspects of material phenomena refer to the real world. None of the other types of our experience, such as prayer or the awareness of the presence of God, has any objective counterpart. They are illusory in the sense that they do not acquaint us with the nature of the objective world.

In modern society, he who refuses to accept the equation of the real and the physical is considered a mystic. However, since God is not an object of a physical experience, the equation implies the impossibility of His existence. Either God is but a word not designating anything real or He is at least as real as the man I see in front of me.

This is the premise of faith: Spiritual events are real. Ultimately all creative events are caused by spiritual acts. The God who creates heaven and earth is the God who communicates His will to the mind of man.

"In Thy light we shall see light" (Psalms 36:10). There is a divine light in every soul, it is dormant and eclipsed by the follies of this world. We must first awaken this light, then the upper light will come upon us. In Thy light which is within us will we see light (Rabbi Aaron of Karlin).

We must not wait passively for insights. In the darkest moments we must try to let our inner light go forth. "And she rises while it is yet night" (Proverbs 31:15).

Observing the Sabbath

GEORGE ROBINSON

In this reading, George Robinson, author of *Essential Judaism: A Complete Guide to Beliefs and Rituals*, delves into what he considers the deeper meaning of the Sabbath.

In the Torah it is written, "On the seventh day God finished the work . . . and ceased from all the work . . . and God blessed the seventh day and declared it holy, because on it God ceased from all the work of creation . . ." (Genesis 2:2–3).

Most people reading that passage find it a bit of a shock. "On the seventh day God finished the work. . . ." But what did God create on the seventh day? Didn't God "cease . . . from all the work of creation" on the seventh day? What God created on the seventh day, the ancient rabbis tell us, was . . . rest.

The Hebrew word used here is *menuhah*, and "rest" is an inadequate translation. To say that *Shabbat Menuhah* means a "Sabbath of rest" only tells half the story. In the Shabbat liturgy we are given a more complete, many layered understanding of the word. It is, the *Minkhah / afternoon* service tells us, "a rest of love freely given, a rest of truth and

George Robinson, "Shabbat," *Essential Judaism* (New York: Pocket Books 2000), 81–86.

sincerity, a rest in peace and tranquility, in quietude and safety." Yet, at the same time, it is a rest yoked in the same breath to "holiness." And inextricably linked to that concept is the fact that this rest comes from the Almighty and exists so that we might glorify God's name, to bring holiness to God.

Shabbat is the only Jewish holiday whose timing does not depend on the calendar at all—seven days are seven days, regardless of the phases of the moon. Like the Creation itself, it is beyond human influence. And its observance, in turn, informs the way most of the other holidays are celebrated.

The Sabbath is the only day of observance mentioned in the Ten Commandments. In the first version of the Decalogue we are enjoined to "Remember the Sabbath day and keep it holy" (Exodus 20:8); in the second version, we are told to "observe" the Sabbath (Deuteronomy 5:12). What more compelling evidence can one find for the paramount importance of this day?

But not to work? An enforced rest? The rabbis who began to codify Jewish law (*halakhah*) during the time of the Second Temple specified thirty-nine categories of prohibited activities—and objects associated with those activities are *muktzeh* / literally, *set aside*—based on the activities that were involved in the building of the Tabernacle as described in the Tanakh, the Hebrew Bible. One should not handle a hammer or money. One should not rearrange the books on a shelf. What sort of holiday is this?

We are commanded in the Torah "Six days shall you labor and do all your work." To abstain from labor on the seventh day is, as Abraham Joshua Heschel says in his magnificent little book *The Sabbath: Its Meaning for Modern Man*, "not a depreciation but an affirmation of labor, a divine exaltation of its dignity." We are suddenly lifted out of the process of time, removed from the world of natural and social change. Instead of creating the world anew, we are at one with the world created.

We are not beasts of burden. We should not live to work. We should not be chained to routine. Shabbat unchains us. As Heschel states,

> To set one day a week for freedom, a day on which we do not use the instruments which have been so easily turned into weapons of destruction, a day for being with ourselves, a day of detachment from the vulgar, of independence of external obligations, a day on which we stop worshipping the idols of technical civilization, a day on which we use no money, a day of armistice in the economic struggle with our fellow men and the forces of nature—is there any institution that holds out a greater hope for [humanity's] progress than the Sabbath? (p. 28)

Shabbat is meant to be a day of peace, *Shabbat shalom*, the peace of the Sabbath. It offers us a chance for peace with nature, with society, and with ourselves. The prohibitions on work are designed to make us stop—if only for one day of the week—our relentless efforts to tame, to conquer, to subdue the earth and everything on it. The prohibition against making fire is also said by the rabbis to mean that one should not kindle the fires of controversy against one's fellow humans. And, finally, the Sabbath offers us a moment of quiet, of serenity, of self-transcendence, a moment that allows us to seek and perhaps achieve some kind of internal peace.

Shabbat is also a time of joy, of good food and wine (even if the food preparation must be done beforehand). Judaism is most decidedly not an ascetic religion. It is no accident that it is considered a *mitzvah* [a commandment] . . . to have sexual relations with your spouse on the Sabbath.

The concept of *oneg shabbat / joy in the Sabbath* is so crucial that any sadness is banished. Fast days are postponed a day if they should fall on Shabbat (except for Yom Kippur). Active mourning is expressly forbidden on the Sabbath. Funerals are put off until Sunday and mourners do not sit *shivah* on Shabbat. Indeed, the only time they can leave their homes during the week of mourning is to come to synagogue for the Sabbath observance. On Friday night, they sit outside the sanctuary during *Kabbalat Shabbat / Welcoming the Sabbath,* entering after *L'kha Dodi* has been sung; worshippers greet them with the words, "May God console you among the other mourners of Zion and Jerusalem."

In the post-biblical literature the Sabbath is depicted in two related guises, as a bride (*kallah*) and as a queen (*malkah*). These two personifications of the day can tell us a bit more about how we are to understand this unusual—indeed, unique—religious holiday.

There is a Midrash (a rabbinic commentary in parable form) about *Shabbat ha-Kallah / the Sabbath Bride.* When God created the days of the week, each of them was given a mate—Sunday had Monday, Tuesday had Wednesday, and Thursday had Friday. Only the Sabbath was alone. The Sabbath pointed this out to God, whose answer was to give it to the people Israel as their mate, a bride. (Interestingly, in Hebrew the days are numbered rather than named, with one exception, Shabbat, providing more evidence of how this "bride" stands out from the rest of the week.)

Why a bride? As Samuel Dresner, a contemporary Conservative rabbi, points out, "The symbol of a bride is love, devotion, and joy—an inward feeling." One prepares for the Sabbath with all the fervor and yearning with which one prepares for a bride.

Shabbat ha-Malkah / the Sabbath Queen evokes different feelings. If the Sabbath Bride may be said to represent the "remember" part of the Decalogue's commandments regarding the Sabbath, the Sabbath Queen represents "observe." She is the stern avatar of the laws governing the day. The Sabbath, Dresner writes, "cannot be observed haphazardly." One does not achieve the peace of the Sabbath without observing the rules that lead to that rest. A Jew "makes" Shabbat; it doesn't just come at the end of the week.

Both of these facets of Shabbat are essential to a full realization of the day. A Sabbath without the Bride would be a cold, lifeless recitation of rules and prayers with nothing motivating them but rote and subjugation to a higher will. A Sabbath without the Queen would be without substance or focus, short-lived good feelings with nothing to show for them. The Jewish observance of the Sabbath is an attempt to find an appropriate balance between these two aspects of the day.

An example of that balance: The rabbis of the Gaonic period (sixth to twelfth centuries) cautioned: "There is nothing more important, according to the Torah, than to preserve human life. . . . Even when there is the slightest possibility that a life may be at stake one may disregard every prohibition of the law." This doctrine, called *pikuakh nefesh / saving a soul* applies to the laws governing Shabbat and the festivals; a doctor must act to save another person, even though it means she is "working" on the Sabbath. A sick person may not fast if it threatens his life.

But the Sabbath was designed to be "a delight," as our liturgy tells us. It is a time when families and friends gather together for meals, songs, and stories. The Friday night rituals of candle lighting, making *kiddush* (blessing the wine for the holiday), and *ha-Motzi / blessing the bread* are followed the next day by the tradition of the *se'udah sh'lishit / third meal*, on Shabbat afternoon, another festive gathering, often accompanied by Torah study and lively discussion, and finished off with more singing of *z'mirot / songs.* Even as the Sabbath ends, there is a tradition that allows us to extend the pleasure, the *melaveh malkah / farewell to the Queen,* when Jews gather to reluctantly bid goodbye to the Sabbath after *Havdalah*, with more songs, food, and wine.

As Heschel observes, the Sabbath is the one day on the Jewish calendar for which there are no appurtenances necessary to partake of its holiness—no *shofar* to blow as on Rosh Hashanah, no "four species" to wave as on Sukkot, no *matzah,* no *tefillin,* not even the Tabernacle. Just a group of Jews and the Sabbath, all holiness in itself.

Yom Kippur

HERMAN WOUK

Here is a brief commentary on the Jewish holiday Yom Kippur, an authoritative explanation of the meaning, history, and observance of this important day on the Jewish calendar. Observance of Yom Kippur, the author says, "still binds Jews to their identity when all other links have rusted through or snapped."

Jews who never enter a synagogue or temple at any other time, Jews of all shades of thought—Conservative, Reform, orthodox, unaffiliated, atheistic—somehow manage to crowd their way into a congregation for at least an hour or two on Yom Kippur. They will pay high, even the membership fee for the whole year, in order to do so.

This mass behavior has affected synagogue and temple architecture. Designers keep inventing different shapes and compartmentations to allow for a flood of people one day of the year, while trying to avoid the glum spectacle at other times of a handful of worshippers confronting a forlorn rabbi in an almost empty hall. No wholly satisfying solution has yet been found to this puzzle. It has the fascination of an enduring mathematical riddle, like squaring the circle.

So certain is the American Jew of this one fact about Judaism—the importance of Yom Kippur—that he has won recognition of the day from civic authorities. In cities with a large Jewish population Yom Kippur is virtually a legal holiday. Ordinary business calendars note the day. Everywhere schools and employers accept as a matter of course the absence of Jewish pupils and workers. To a certain extent Yom Kippur has carried along with it in popular esteem the Jewish New Year, Rosh Hashana. Together the two observances comprise a major religious event, the High Holy Days, or Days of Awe. The Talmud calls the period from Rosh Hashana to Yom Kippur *The Ten Days of Repentance.*

What is this hypnotic observance which still binds Jews to their identity when all other links have rusted through or snapped?

LEGAL DESCRIPTION OF DAYS OF AWE

The statute governing the days is bare and brief. It is in Leviticus, Chapter 23, verses 24–29:

> In the seventh month, on the first day of the month, you shall have a rest-day, a day of remembrance, horn-blowing, and holy assembly. You shall not do any servile work, and you shall bring an offering to the Lord.
>
> The tenth day of this seventh month is the Day of Atonement. It shall be a holy assembly for you. You shall afflict your souls, and bring an offering to the Lord. You shall do no work on this same day, for it is a day of atonement, to atone for you before the Lord your God. Every soul that is not afflicted on this day shall be cut off from its people. Every soul that does any kind of work on this day, I shall cause to be lost from among its people.
>
> You shall do no work. It is an everlasting law, for all your generations wherever you shall live. It is a

Herman Wouk, *This Is My God: The Jewish Way of Life* (Doubleday and Company, Inc. 1959), 85–88.

> sabbath, a rest-day for you, and you shall afflict your souls. Beginning on the ninth of the month in the evening, from evening to evening, you shall keep your sabbath.

The seventh Hebrew month, *Tishri*, is in harvest time, usually in September and October. The Days of Awe precede the Sukos feast, which starts at the full moon. There is no explanation in the Torah for the rite of horn-blowing on the first of Tishri, and the day is called the start of the seventh month, not of the New Year. We must look to other sources to understand the ceremonial as it now exists.

Yom Kippur, on the other hand, is today exactly what it is called in the Torah: a day of atonement and of ascetic discipline, a day of "afflicting the soul."

An account of the Atonement ceremony takes up the whole of Chapter 16 of the Book of Leviticus. This was the one day of the year when Aaron entered the dread silent space, sealed off by a curtain, in the western end of the sanctuary in the desert: the holy of holies, the place of the Presence, the place where the stone tables of the law, and the broken fragments of the first tables, lay in the golden Holy Ark, under a massive gold lid ornamented with two cherubim. The Talmud describes how the high priest went about this same awesome rite in the last days of the Second Temple.

What the high priest did on this day, in the desert sanctuary and in the two temples, was to seek forgiveness for himself, the priesthood, and all Israel, for transgressions of God's law. When the ceremonies, lasting nearly all day, came to an end without mishap, the news sped from the Temple throughout Jerusalem, touching off jubilation everywhere. Yom Kippur in Temple times was therefore a two-sided day, filled with solemnity and dread, but marked also by exciting pageantry and, in its closing hours, by an outburst of public gaiety.

What has come down to us today is only the solemnity, the asceticism, the sense of confronting one's Maker face to face in judgment, the awareness of time passing and of life's sands running out. The law codes tell us that Atonement Day should have gladness in it. They suggest white vestments for the worshippers, to symbolize confidence in a renewal of purity through the mercy of God. But since the fall of Jerusalem any gaiety that was in Yom Kippur has faded. Our Atonement Day is a time of mordant grieving melodies, of bowed heads and wrung hearts. No one who has heard the *Kol Nidre* chanted at sunset when the holy day begins can doubt that the worshippers are carrying out literally a law many thousands of years old, and afflicting their souls.

"Afflicting one's soul" traditionally means five abstentions: from eating and drinking, from sex, from bathing, from anointing the body with oil (the Oriental hygienic practice), and from the wearing of leather shoes. The last four are the abstinences of a newly bereaved mourner, and the rabbis enacted them on Yom Kippur to add to the awe of the day. Fasting is a law of the Torah. Today almost every Jew who has any religious impulse abstains from eating and drinking for the twenty-four hours of Yom Kippur.

The community spends the whole day in the synagogue. The Yom Kippur liturgy is by far the longest in the Hebrew religion. All the prayers turn on the theme of repentance before judgment, of release from sin and error, as do the Rosh Hashana prayers; for the day of horn-blowing is part of the Judgment and Atonement drama. Together the two prayer books picture the Days of Awe in one grand metaphor, which runs through dozens of prose-poems, dithyrambs, litanies, confessional tables, and soliloquies.

The Seder

GEORGE ROBINSON

This excerpt provides an account of the complex structure and spiritual significance of the Passover Seder ceremony.

The entire *seder* is similarly heavy with meaning. The word *seder* literally means "order" and the *seder* is nothing if not orderly. At the center of the table is the *seder* plate, which holds a hard-boiled egg, a roasted bone, *maror / bitter herbs* (usually horseradish), *kharoset* (a mixture of chopped apples, nuts, cinnamon, wine, and in some recipes honey), *karpas / greens* (usually parsley or watercress), and a small cup or saucer of salt water. In addition, there is a plate holding three *matzahs,* covered with a cloth. Everyone at the table will have *a Haggadah / the Telling*, the book containing the special liturgy for the evening meal.

Essentially, the evening has fourteen elements, which occur in a prescribed order:

1. *Kadesh:* The *seder* opens with the recitation of the festival *kiddush* over a glass of wine. Everyone drinks their first of four glasses of wine.
2. *Urkhatz:* The ritual washing of the hands, as in the hand-washing before eating bread, but with the blessing omitted.
3. *Karpas:* The leafy greens are dipped in the salt water and, after the blessing for *karpas* is recited, they are eaten.
4. *Yakhatz:* The middle *matzah* from the center of the table is broken in half. One portion will be hidden for the *afikoman,* to be eaten at the very end of the meal. The tradition is for the host to hide it and for the children to search for it, ransoming it back to the leader at the end of the meal. (In some families, the tradition is reversed, with the children hiding the *afikoman,* and the parents searching.)
5. *Maggid:* The first part of the *Haggadah* is now read. This section of the *seder* includes the Four Questions, the list of the ten plagues, the story of the Exodus, an explanation of the significance of the Paschal lamb, *matzah*, *maror*, the first part of *Hallel*, and second and third glasses of wine.
6. *Rakhtsah:* Again the hands are washed, this with the blessing recited.
7. *Motzi Matzah:* The *matzah* is eaten, with a blessing for eating unleavened bread. The blessing serves the same purpose as the blessing for eating bread in a non-Passover meal; it signals the beginning of the meal proper.
8. *Maror:* The bitter herb is dipped in the *kharoset* and eaten, with an appropriate blessing.
9. *Korekh:* A sandwich of bitter herb and *kharoset* on *matzah is* eaten, as was the custom in the time of Hillel (first century B.C.E.) to eat the Paschal sacrifice together with the *matzah* and *maror.*
10. *Shukhan Orekh:* Dinner is served and eaten, a full and festive meal.
11. *Tsafun:* The *afikoman,* representing the Paschal sacrifice, is ransomed and eaten, officially ending the meal. After this no more food should be eaten.
12. *Barekh: Birkat ha-Mazon / Grace after meals* is recited.
13. *Hallel:* The remainder of the *Hallel* psalms are recited.

George Robinson, "The Seder," *Essential Judaism* (New York: Pocket Books, 2000), 121–125.

14. *Nirtzah:* The celebration is "accepted," and those assembled declare, "Next year in Jerusalem." In Jerusalem, they say, *"L'shana ha-ba'ah bi-Yerushalayim ha-benuyah / Next year in a Jerusalem rebuilt."* This is followed by spirited singing of Pesakh songs like *Adir Hu, Khad Gadya / An Only Kid*, and *Ekhad Mi Yode'a / Who Knows One?*

A *seder* is a joyous occasion, a gathering of family and friends that should include not only the recitation of the *Haggadah,* but a spirited discussion with many questions and debate of the meaning of the holiday. With a large meal, the entire evening can last into the early hours of the morning and, in an Orthodox household, the meal itself may not be served until well past midnight.

But what does it all mean? Of course, the *Haggadah* itself is largely occupied with explaining the significance of the elements of the *seder,* and their relevance to the agricultural aspects of a major spring festival are self-evident (the greens for the arrival of spring, the egg a symbol of fertility and renewal, the roasted bone a reference to the Paschal sacrifice at the Temple). After all, Pesakh is also known as *Khag ha-Aviv / Festival of Spring.* But the historical/religious aspects are worth some further exploration, bringing us back to the themes of slavery and freedom, exile and home, once more.

Certainly the symbolic nature of the *maror* and the salt water are obvious—the bitterness of slavery and the tears of the Israelites. The *kharoset* relates to the mortar from which the Jewish slaves made bricks for the Pharaoh's storehouse cities, and the shankbone echoes the Paschal lambs' blood with which Israelites marked the lintels of their doorways, signaling their presence to the Angel of Death so that he would not take their first-born (but would *pass over*). But it is equally significant that we are asked in a small way to experience them again at Pesakh and at every Pesakh. The *Haggadah* is very explicit about this: one is to retell the story of the Exodus as if he, too, had been liberated from slavery in Egypt. Indeed, this idea is conveyed emphatically at several points in the text, echoing the words of the *Sh'ma,* "I am Adonai your God, who brought you out of Egypt to be your God," words that we repeat each day.

In the same prayer, we are instructed to teach the word "to your children," or as the phrase goes that recurs throughout Jewish liturgy, *"Idor va-dor" / "from generation to generation."* Hence the enormous importance of children in Pesakh observance.

The Four Questions are asked by the youngest child at the table. Colloquially known as *Ma nishtana* from their opening words "how different," the questions deal with the eating of *matzah, maror,* and *karpas,* and the practice of eating the Pesakh meal while reclining. By asking these questions, the youngest child allows an adult at the table to explain each of these practices and thereby to fulfill the obligation to tell the story to one's children.

Likewise, the *Haggadah* tells the parable of the Four Sons, each representing one of the types of personality to whom we must impart the story of the Exodus, the wise child, the simple child, the wicked child, and the child who is unable to ask. And the entire ritual of the *afikoman* is clearly designed to keep the kids interested until after dinner has been finished.

The number four recurs throughout the *seder.* In addition to the Four Questions and the Four Sons, we drink four glasses of wine. The four glasses of wine are said to represent the four nations that drove the Jews into exile, the Chaldeans, the Medes, the Greeks, and the Romans, or the four national characteristics that the Jews retained in slavery that allowed them to survive captivity in Egypt—they kept their Hebrew names; did not lose touch with their own language; maintained their ethical standards; and did not inform on one another. Perhaps the most compelling explanation, however, is that the four glasses of wine represent the four promises God made to the Israelites in Exodus 6: "I will liberate you. . . . I will deliver you. . . . I will redeem you. . . . I will take you to me as a people."

The strongest evidence for this interpretation is the custom of reserving a glass of wine at the table for the prophet Elijah, whose return to earth will herald the coming of the Messianic Age, a time of peace and prosperity for all. We sing of his greatness, *Eliahu ha-Navi / Elijah the Prophet,* while holding the door to our homes open for him to partake of our Pesakh hospitality. As such, the hope of his coming is nothing less than an expression of our belief in the Creator's promise of a final redemption and of *dam ha-bah / the World to Come*. This fifth cup of wine corresponds to the fifth promise of Exodus, "*v'heveiti. . . . / and I will bring you to the land which I promised your fathers.*"

Pesakh is one of the most home-oriented of Jewish holidays. In the synagogue, there are few changes in the actual text of the liturgy. Generally, it follows the standard practice of festival services, adding *Hallel*, *Ya'aleh v'Yavo*, and a *Yizkor* service in Ashkenazi congregations on the last day. One additional prayer that is unique to the holiday is the *Tefillat Tal / Prayer for Dew,* which is recited before *Musaf* on the first day. Like the Prayer for Rain, it calls on God to remember the needs of a people who live on the land and need water to survive. The special *megillah* read on the Shabbat which falls during the holiday is the Song of Songs, no doubt chosen for its spirited invocation of spring. The intermediate days of the festival, *Khol ha-Moed*, are subject to the same rules as the intermediate days of Sukkot. The final day of the festival is treated as a full holiday.

The great sixteenth-century rabbi, Yehudah Loewe of Prague, known as the Maharal, wrote that the Exodus marked a fundamental change in the nature of the Jewish people, that through the liberation from Egypt they acquired the nature of free men and women, a nature that has not changed over centuries, despite all the suffering and captivity subsequently inflicted on them. Thus it may be truly said that God takes us out of Egypt each day, just as our liturgy tells us.

CONTEMPORARY CHALLENGES

Meaning from Suffering

VIKTOR FRANKL

During World War II, Viktor Frankl was a prisoner in a Nazi concentration camp where he lost nearly everything but his life. His father, mother, brother, and wife perished in such camps or died in the gas chambers. The question that his experience provoked was: Under such circumstances, how can anyone find a reason to live? What could give an inconceivably tragic life meaning? His answer is: "To live is to suffer; to survive is to find meaning in suffering."

Let us first ask ourselves what should be understood by "a tragic optimism." In brief it means that one is, and remains, optimistic in spite of the "tragic triad," as it is called in logotherapy, a triad which consists of those aspects of human existence which may be circumscribed by (1) pain; (2) guilt; and (3) death.

Viktor E. Frankl, *Man's Search for Meaning* (New York: Pocket Books, 1959), 161–179.

This chapter, in fact, raises the question, How is it possible to say yes to life in spite of all that? How, to pose the question differently, can life retain its potential meaning in spite of its tragic aspects? After all, "saying yes to life in spite of everything," to use the phrase in which the title of a German book of mine is couched, presupposes that life is potentially meaningful under any conditions, even those which are most miserable. And this in turn presupposes the human capacity to creatively turn life's negative aspects into something positive or constructive. In other Words, what matters is to make the best of any given situation. "The best," however, is that which in Latin is called *optimum*—hence the reason I speak of a tragic optimism, that is, an optimism in the face of tragedy and in view of the human potential which at its best always allows for: (1) turning suffering into a human achievement and accomplishment; (2) deriving from guilt the opportunity to change oneself for the better; and (3) deriving from life's transitoriness an incentive to take responsible action.

It must be kept in mind, however, that optimism is not anything to be commanded or ordered. One cannot even force oneself to be optimistic indiscriminately, against all odds, against all hope. And what is true for hope is also true for the other two components of the triad inasmuch as faith and love cannot be commanded or ordered either.

To the European, it is a characteristic of the American culture that, again and again, one is commanded and ordered to "be happy." But happiness cannot be pursued; it must ensue. One must have a reason to "be happy." Once the reason is found, however, one becomes happy automatically. As we see, a human being is not one in pursuit of happiness but rather in search of a reason to become happy, last but not least through actualizing the potential meaning inherent and dormant in a given situation.

This need for a reason is similar in another specifically human phenomenon—laughter. If you want anyone to laugh you have to provide him with a reason, e.g., you have to tell him a joke. In no way is it possible to evoke real laughter by urging him, or having him urge himself, to laugh. Doing so would be the same as urging people posed in front of a camera to say "cheese," only to find that in the finished photographs their faces are frozen in artificial smiles.

In logotherapy, such a behavior pattern, is called "hyper-intention." It plays an important role in the causation of sexual neurosis, be it frigidity or impotence. The more a patient, instead of forgetting himself through giving himself, directly strives for orgasm, i.e., sexual pleasure, the more this pursuit of sexual pleasure becomes self-defeating. Indeed, what is called "the pleasure principle" is, rather, a fun-spoiler.

Once an individual's search for a meaning is successful, it not only renders him happy but also gives him the capability to cope with suffering. And what happens if one's groping for a meaning has been in vain? This may well result in a fatal condition. Let us recall, for instance, what sometimes happened in extreme situations such as prisoner-of-war camps or concentration camps. In the first, as I was told by American soldiers, a behavior pattern crystallized to which they referred as "give-up-itis." In the concentration camps, this behavior was paralleled by those who one morning, at five, refused to get up and go to work and instead stayed in the hut, on the straw wet with urine and feces. Nothing—neither warnings nor threats—could induce them to change their minds. And then something typical occurred: they took out a cigarette from deep down in a pocket where they had hidden it and started smoking. At that moment we knew that for the next forty-eight hours or so we would watch them dying. Meaning orientation had subsided, and consequently the seeking of immediate pleasure had taken over.

Is this not reminiscent of another parallel, a parallel that confronts us day by day? I think of those youngsters who, on a worldwide scale, refer to themselves as the "no future" generation. To be sure, it is not just a cigarette to which they resort; it is drugs.

In fact, the drug scene is one aspect of a more general mass phenomenon, namely the feeling of meaninglessness resulting from a frustration of our existential needs which in turn has become a universal phenomenon in our industrial societies. Today it is not only logotherapists who claim that the feeling of meaninglessness plays an ever increasing role in the etiology of neurosis. As Irvin D. Yalom of Stanford University states in *Existential Psychotherapy*: "Of forty consecutive patients applying for therapy at a psychiatric outpatient clinic . . . twelve (30 percent) had some major problem involving meaning (as adjudged from self-ratings, therapists, or independent judges)." Thousands of miles east of Palo Alto, the situation differs only by 1 percent; the most recent pertinent statistics indicate that in Vienna, 29 percent of the population complain that meaning is missing from their lives.

As to the causation of the feeling of meaninglessness, one may say, albeit in an oversimplifying vein, that people have enough to live by but nothing to live for; they have the means but no meaning. To be sure, some do not even have the means. In particular, I think of the mass of people who are today unemployed. Fifty years ago, I published a study devoted to a specific type of depression I had diagnosed in cases of young patients suffering from what I called "unemployment neurosis." And I could show that this neurosis really originated in a twofold erroneous identification: being jobless was equated with being useless, and being useless was equated with having a meaningless life. Consequently, whenever I succeeded in persuading the patients to volunteer in youth organizations, adult education, public libraries and the like—in other words, as soon as they could fill their abundant free time with some sort of unpaid but meaningful activity—their depression disappeared although their economic situation had not changed and their hunger was the same. The truth is that man does not live by welfare alone.

Along with unemployment neurosis, which is triggered by an individual's socioeconomic situation, there are other types of depression which are traceable back to psychodynamic or biochemical conditions, whichever the case may be. Accordingly, psychotherapy and pharmacotherapy are indicated respectively. Insofar as the feeling of meaninglessness is concerned, however, we should not overlook and forget that, per se, it is not a matter of pathology; rather than being the sign and symptom of a neurosis, it is, I would say, the proof of one's humanness. But although it is not caused by anything pathological, it may well cause a pathological reaction; in other words, it is potentially pathogenic. Just consider the mass neurotic syndrome so pervasive in the young generation: there is ample empirical evidence that the three facets of this syndrome—depression, aggression, addiction—are due to what is called in logotherapy "the existential vacuum," a feeling of emptiness and meaninglessness.

It goes without saying that not each and every case of depression is to be traced back to a feeling of meaninglessness, nor does suicide—in which depression sometimes eventuates—always result from an existential vacuum. But even if each and every case of suicide had not been *undertaken* out of a feeling of meaninglessness, it may well be that an individual's impulse to take his life would have been *overcome* had he been aware of some meaning and purpose worth living for.

If, thus, a strong meaning orientation plays a decisive role in the prevention of suicide, what about intervention in cases in which there is a suicide risk? As a young doctor I spent four years in Austria's largest state hospital where I was in charge of the pavilion in which severely depressed patients were accommodated—most of them having been admitted after a suicide attempt. I once calculated that I must have explored twelve thousand patients during those four years. What accumulated was quite a store of experience from which I still draw whenever I am confronted with someone who is prone to suicide. I explain to such a person that patients have repeatedly told me how happy they were that the suicide attempt had not been successful; weeks, months, years later, they told me, it turned out that there *was* a solution to their problem, an answer to their question, a meaning to their life. "Even if things only take such a good turn in one of a thousand cases," my explanation continues, "who can guarantee that in your case it will not happen one day, sooner or later? But in the first place, you have to live to see the day on which it may happen, so you have to survive in order to see that day dawn, and from now on the responsibility for survival does not leave you."

Regarding the second facet of the mass neurotic syndrome—aggression—let me cite an experiment once conducted by Carolyn Wood Sherif. She had succeeded in artificially building up mutual aggressions between groups of boy scouts, and observed that the aggressions only subsided when the youngsters dedicated themselves to a collective purpose—that is, the joint task of dragging out of the mud a carriage in which food had to be brought to their camp. Immediately, they were not only challenged but also united by a meaning they had to fulfill.

As for the third issue, addiction, I am reminded of the findings presented by Annemarie von Forstmeyer who noted that, as evidenced by tests and statistics, 90 percent of the alcoholics she studied had suffered from an abysmal feeling of meaninglessness. Of the drug addicts studied by Stanley Krippner, 100 percent believed that "things seemed meaningless."

Now let us turn to the question of meaning itself. To begin with, I would like to clarify that, in the first place, the logotherapist is concerned with the potential meaning inherent and dormant in all the single situations one has to face throughout his or her life. Therefore, I will not be elaborating here on the meaning of one's life as a whole, although I do not deny that such a long-range meaning does exist. To invoke an analogy, consider a movie: it consists of thousands upon thousands of individual pictures, and each of them makes sense and carries a meaning, yet the meaning of the whole film cannot be seen before its last sequence is shown. However, we cannot understand the whole film without having first understood each of its components, each of the individual pictures. Isn't it the same with life? Doesn't the final meaning of life, too, reveal itself, if at all, only at its end, on the verge of death? And doesn't this final meaning, too, depend on whether or not the potential meaning of each single situation has been actualized to the best of respective individuals' knowledge and belief?

The fact remains that meaning, and its perception, as seen from the logotherapeutic angle, is completely down to earth rather than afloat in the air or resident in an ivory tower. Sweepingly, I would locate the cognition of meaning—of the personal meaning of a concrete situation—midway between an "aha" experience along the lines of Karl Buhler's concept and a Gestalt perception, say, along the lines of Max Wertheimer's theory. The perception of meaning differs from the classical concept of Gestalt perception insofar as the latter implies the sudden awareness of a "figure" on a "ground," whereas the perception of meaning, as I see it, more specifically boils down to becoming aware of a possibility against the background of reality or, to express it in plain words, to becoming aware of what can be done about a given situation.

And how does a human being go about finding meaning? As Charlotte Buhler has stated: "All we can do is study the lives of people who seem to have found their answers to the questions of what ultimately human life is about as against those who have not." In addition to such a biographical approach, however, we may as well embark on a biological approach. Logotherapy conceives of conscience as a prompter which, if need be, indicates the direction in which we have to move in a given life situation. In order to carry out such a task, conscience must apply a measuring stick to the situation one is confronted with, and this situation has to be evaluated in the light of a set of criteria, in the light of a hierarchy of values. These values, however, cannot be espoused and adopted by us on a conscious level—they are something that we *are*. They have crystallized in the course of the evolution of our species; they are founded on our biological past and are rooted in our biological depth. Konrad Lorenz might have had something similar in mind when he developed the concept of a biological *a priori*, and when both of us recently discussed my own view on the biological foundation of the valuing process, he enthusiastically expressed his accord. In any case, if a pre-reflective axiological self-understanding exists, we may assume that it is ultimately anchored in our biological heritage.

As logotherapy teaches, there are three main avenues on which one arrives at meaning in life. The first is by creating a work or by doing a deed. The second is by experiencing something or encountering someone; in other words, meaning can be found not only in work but also in love. Edith Weisskopf-Joelson observed in this context that the logotherapeutic "notion that experiencing can be as valuable as achieving is therapeutic because it compensates for our one-sided emphasis on the external world of achievement at the expense of the internal world of experience."

Most important, however, is the third avenue to meaning in life: even the helpless victim of a hopeless situation, facing a fate he cannot change, may rise above himself, may grow beyond himself, and by so doing change himself. He may turn a personal tragedy into a triumph. Again it was Edith Weisskopf-Joelson who . . . once expressed the hope that logotherapy "may help counteract certain unhealthy trends in the present-day culture of the United States, where the incurable sufferer is given very little opportunity to be proud of his suffering and to consider it ennobling rather than degrading" so that "he is not only unhappy, but also ashamed of being unhappy."

For a quarter of a century I ran the neurological department of a general hospital and bore witness to my patients' capacity to turn their predicaments into human achievements. In addition to such practical experience, empirical evidence is also available which supports the possibility that one may find meaning in suffering. Researchers at the Yale University School of Medicine "have been impressed by the number of prisoners of war of the Vietnam war who explicitly claimed that although their captivity was extraordinarily stressful—filled with torture, disease, malnutrition, and solitary confinement—they nevertheless . . . benefited from the captivity experience, seeing it as a growth experience."

But the most powerful arguments in favor of "a tragic optimism" are those which in Latin are called *argumenta ad hominem*. Jerry Long, to cite an example, is a living testimony to "the defiant power of the human spirit," as it is called in logotherapy. To quote the *Texarkana Gazette*, "Jerry Long has been paralyzed from his neck down since a diving accident which rendered him a quadriplegic three years ago. He was 17 when the accident occurred. Today Long can use his mouth stick to type. He 'attends' two courses at Community College via a special telephone. The intercom allows Long to both hear and participate in class discussions. He also occupies his time by reading, watching television and writing." And in a letter I received from him, he writes: "I view my life as being abundant with meaning and purpose. The attitude that I adopted on that fateful day has become my personal credo for life: I broke my neck, it didn't break me. I am currently enrolled in my first psychology course in college. I believe that my handicap will only enhance my ability to help others. I know that without the suffering, the growth that I have achieved would have been impossible."

Is this to say that suffering is indispensable to the discovery of meaning? In no way. I only insist that meaning is available in spite of—nay, even through—suffering, provided . . . that the suffering is unavoidable. If it is avoidable, the meaningful thing to do is to remove its cause, for unnecessary suffering is masochistic rather than heroic. If, on the other hand, one cannot change a situation that causes his suffering, he can still choose his attitude. Long had not been chosen to break his neck, but he did decide not to let himself be broken by what had happened to him.

As we see, the priority stays with creatively changing the situation that causes us to suffer. But the superiority goes to the "know-how to suffer," if need be. And there is empirical evidence that—literally—the "man in the street" is of the same opinion. Austrian public-opinion pollsters recently reported that those held in highest esteem by most of the people interviewed are neither the great artists nor the great scientists, neither the great statesmen nor the great sports figures, but those who master a hard lot with their heads held high.

In turning to the second aspect of the tragic triad, namely guilt, I would like to depart from a theological concept that has always been fascinating to me. I refer to what is called *mysterium iniquitatis*, meaning, as I see it, that a crime in the final analysis remains inexplicable inasmuch as it cannot be fully traced back to biological, psychological and/or sociological factors. Totally explaining one's crime would be tantamount to explaining away his or her guilt and to seeing in him or her not a free and responsible human being but a machine to be repaired. Even criminals themselves abhor this treatment and prefer to be held responsible for their deeds. From a convict serving his sentence in an Illinois penitentiary I received a letter in which he deplored that "the criminal never has a chance to explain himself. He is offered a variety of excuses to choose from. Society is blamed and in many instances the blame is put on the victim." Furthermore, when I addressed the prisoners in San Quentin, I told them that "you are human beings like me, and as such you were free to commit a crime, to become guilty. Now, however, you are responsible for overcoming guilt by rising above it, by growing beyond yourselves, by changing for the better." They felt understood. And from Frank E. W., an ex-prisoner, I received a note which stated that he had "started a logotherapy group for ex-felons. We are 27 strong and the newer ones are staying out of prison through the peer strength of those of us from the original group. Only one returned—and he is now free."

As for the concept of collective guilt, I personally think that it is totally unjustified to hold one person responsible for the behavior of another person or a collective of persons. Since the end of World War II, I have not become weary of publicly arguing against the collective guilt concept. Sometimes, however, it takes a lot of didactic tricks to detach people from their superstitions. An American woman once confronted me with the reproach, "How can you still write some of your books in German, Adolf Hitler's language?" In response, I asked her if she had knives in her kitchen, and when she answered that she did, I acted dismayed and shocked, exclaiming, "How can you still use knives after so many killers have used them to stab and murder their victims?" She stopped objecting to my writing books in German.

The third aspect of the tragic triad concerns death. But it concerns life as well, for at any time each of the moments of which life consists is dying, and that moment will never recur. And yet is not this transitoriness a reminder that challenges us to make the best possible use of each moment of our lives? It certainly is, and hence my imperative: *Live as if you were living for the second time and had acted as wrongly the first time as you are about to act now.*

In fact, the opportunities to act properly, the potentialities to fulfill a meaning, are affected by the irreversibility of our lives. But also the potentialities alone are so affected. For as soon as we have used an opportunity and have actualized a potential meaning, we have done so once and for all. We have rescued it into the past wherein it has been safely delivered and deposited. In the past, nothing is irretrievably lost, but rather, on the contrary, everything is irrevocably stored and treasured. To be sure, people tend to see only the stubble fields of transitoriness but overlook and forget the full granaries of the past into which they have brought the harvest of their lives: the deeds done, the loves loved, and last but not least, the sufferings they have gone through with courage and dignity.

From this one may see that there is no reason to pity old people. Instead, young people should envy them. It is true that the old have no opportunities, no possibilities in the future. But they have more than that. Instead of possibilities in the future, they have realities in the past—the potentialities they have actualized, the meanings they have fulfilled, the values they have realized—and nothing and nobody can ever remove these assets from the past.

In view of the possibility of finding meaning in suffering, life's meaning is an unconditional one, at least potentially. That unconditional meaning, however, is paralleled by the unconditional value of each and every person. It is that which warrants the indelible quality of the dignity of man. Just as life remains potentially meaningful under any conditions, even those which are most miserable, so too does the value of each and every person stay with him or her, and it does so because it is based on the values that he or she has realized in the past, and is not contingent on the usefulness that he or she may or may not retain in the present.

More specifically, this usefulness is usually defined in terms of functioning for the benefit of society. But today's society is characterized by achievement orientation, and consequently it adores people who are successful and happy and, in particular, it adores the young. It virtually ignores the value of all those who are otherwise, and in so doing blurs the decisive difference between being valuable in the sense of dignity and being valuable in the sense of usefulness. If one is not cognizant of this difference and holds that an individual's value stems only from his present usefulness, then, believe me, one owes it only to personal inconsistency not to plead for euthanasia along the lines of Hitler's program, that is to say, "mercy" killing of all those who have lost their social usefulness, be it because of old age, incurable illness, mental deterioration, or whatever handicap they may suffer.

Confounding the dignity of man with mere usefulness arises from a conceptual confusion that in turn may be traced back to the contemporary nihilism transmitted on many an academic campus and many an analytical couch. Even in the setting of training analyses such an indoctrination may take place. Nihilism does not contend that there is nothing, but it states that everything is meaningless. And George A. Sargent was right when he promulgated the concept of "learned meaninglessness." He himself remembered a therapist who said, "George, you must realize that the world is a joke. There is no justice, everything is random. Only when you realize this will you understand how silly it is to take yourself seriously. There is no grand purpose in the universe. It just *is*. There's no particular meaning in what decision you make today about how to act."

One must not generalize such a criticism. In principle, training is indispensable, but if so, therapists should see their task in immunizing the trainee against nihilism rather than inoculating him with the cynicism that is a defense mechanism against their own nihilism.

Logotherapists may even conform to some of the training and licensing requirements stipulated by the other schools of psychotherapy. In other words, one may howl with the wolves, if need be, but when doing so, one should be, I would urge, a sheep in wolf's clothing. There is no need to become untrue to the basic concept of man and the principles of the philosophy of life inherent in logotherapy. Such a loyalty is not hard to maintain in view of the fact that as Elisabeth S. Lukas once pointed out, "throughout the history of psychotherapy, there has never been a school as undogmatic as logotherapy." And at the First World Congress of Logotherapy (San Diego, California, November 6–8, 1980) I argued not only for the rehumanization of psychotherapy but also for what I called "the degurufication of logotherapy." My interest does not lie in raising parrots that just rehash "their master's voice," but rather in passing the torch to "independent and inventive, innovative and creative spirits."

Sigmund Freud once asserted, "Let one attempt to expose a number of the most diverse people uniformly to hunger. With the increase of the imperative urge of hunger all individual differences will blur, and in their stead will appear the uniform expression of the one unstilled urge." Thank heaven, Sigmund Freud was spared knowing the concentration camps from the inside. His subjects lay on a couch designed in the plush style of Victorian culture, not in the filth of Auschwitz. *There*, the "individual differences" did *not* "blur" but, on the contrary, people became more different; people unmasked themselves, both the swine and the saints. And today you need no longer hesitate to use the word "saints": think of Father Maximilian Kolbe who was starved and finally murdered by an injection of carbolic acid at Auschwitz and who in 1983 was canonized.

You may be prone to blame me for invoking examples that are the exceptions to the rule. "*Sed omnia praeclara tam difficilia quam rara sunt*" (but everything great is just as difficult to realize as it is rare to find) reads the last sentence of the *Ethics of Spinoza*. You may of course ask whether we really need to refer to "saints." Wouldn't it suffice just to refer to *decent* people? It is true that they form a minority. More than that, they always will remain a minority. And yet I see therein the very challenge to join the minority. For the world is in a bad state, but everything will become still worse unless each of us does his best.

So, let us be alert—alert in a twofold sense:
Since Auschwitz we know what man is capable of.
And since Hiroshima we know what is at stake.

Jewish Feminism

JUDITH PLASKOW

Judith Plaskow believes, as other Jewish feminists do, that Judaism excludes women. The heart of her critique is that throughout Jewish theology, there is a widespread and consistent conception of women as "Other."

In an article on the situation of Jewish women, Cynthia Ozick offers fourteen "meditations" pointing to the sociological status of the woman question in Judaism. The subordination of women, she argues, is not deeply rooted in Torah but is the result of historical custom and practice, which can be halakhically repaired. Only in her last meditation does she raise the great "what if?": what if the Otherness of women is not simply a matter of Jewish incorporation of surrounding social attitudes but is in part created and sustained by Torah itself? What if the subordination of women in Judaism is rooted in theology, in the very foundations of the Jewish tradition?

The fact that Ozick postpones this question to the end of her paper, that she is reluctant to explore the theological underpinnings of women's status, places her in the mainstream of Jewish feminism. The Jewish women's movement of the past decade has been and remains a civil-rights movement rather than a movement for "women's liberation." It has been a movement concerned with the images and status of women in Jewish religious and communal life, and with halakhic and institutional change. It has been less concerned with analysis of the origins and bases of women's oppression that render change necessary. It has focused on getting women a piece of the Jewish pie; it has not wanted to bake a new one!

There are undoubtedly many reasons for Jewish feminism's practical bent; absence of a strong Jewish theological tradition; the minority status of Jews in American culture; the existence of laws (e.g., divorce) that have the power to destroy women's lives and thus require immediate remedy. But such emphasis is no less dangerous for being comprehensible. If the Jewish women's movement addresses itself only to the fruits but not the bases of discrimination, it is apt to settle for too little in the way of change. It may find that the full participation of women in Jewish life—should it come—will only bring to light deeper contradictions in Jewish imagery and symbolism. And most likely, far-reaching change will not come until these contradictions are examined and exorcised. It is time, therefore, to confront the full extent of our disablement as Jewish women in order that we may understand the full implications of our struggle.

Of the issues that present themselves for our attention, *halakhah* [the Jewish system of laws] has been at the center of feminist agitation for religious change, and it is to *halakhah* that Ozick turns in the hope of altering women's situation. But while this issue has been considered and debated frequently in the last ten years, it is specific *halakhot* that have been questioned and not the fundamental presuppositions of the legal system. The fact that women are not counted in a *minyan*, that we are not called to the Torah, that we are silent in the marriage ceremony and shackled when it comes to divorce—these disabilities have been recognized, deplored, and in non-Orthodox

Judith Plaskow, "The Right Question Is Theological," in Susannah Heschel, ed., *On Being a Jewish Feminist* (New York: Schocken Books, 1985), 223–232.

Judaism, somewhat alleviated. The *implications* of such laws, their essentially nonarbitrary character, has received less attention, however. Underlying specific *halakhot*, and *outlasting their amelioration or rejection*, is an assumption of women's Otherness far more basic than the laws in which it finds expression. If women are not part of the congregation, if we stand passively under the *huppah*, if, even in the Reform movement, we have become rabbis only in the last ten years, this is because men—and not women with them—define Jewish humanity. Men are the actors in religious and communal life because they are the normative Jews. Women are "other than" the norm; we are less than fully human.

This Otherness of women is a presupposition of Jewish law in its most central formulations. In the last section of her article on Jewish women, finally turning to the sacral nature of women's status, Ozick points out that the biblical passion for justice does not extend to women. Women's position in biblical law as "part of the web of ownership" is taken as simply the way things are; it is not perceived as or named "injustice." One great "Thou shalt not"—"Thou shalt not lessen the humanity of women"—is absent from the Torah. The Otherness of women basic to the written law also underlies the Mishnaic treatment of women. Jacob Neusner points out that the Mishnah's Division of Women deals with women in states of transition, whose uncertain status threatens the stasis of the community. The woman who is about to enter into a marriage or who has just left one requires close attention. The law must regularize her irregularity, facilitate her transition to the normal state of wife and motherhood, at which point she no longer poses a problem. The concerns of the Division, and even the fact of its existence, assume a view of women as "abnormal" or "irregular" and therefore requiring special sanctification. While the mechanisms of sanctification are elaborated extensively, the need for it is never questioned. It is simply presupposed by the text.

That women have a "special" status, one that is taken for granted by the tradition, is underlined by another factor: all reasons given for women's legal disabilities—e.g., they are exempt from positive time-bound commandments because of household responsibilities; they are closer to God and therefore do not need as many commands—presuppose the sex-role division they seek to explain. But while the origins of this division are thus hidden from us—they remain part of the broader historical question of the roots of female subordination—the division itself is imaged and elaborated in clear and specific terms. As in the Christian tradition, in which the Otherness of women is expressed in the language of mind/body dualism, Judaism tenders a similar distinction between *ruhniut* [spirituality] and *gashmiut* [physicality], men and women. The need to regulate women is articulated not as a general problem but as the need to control their unruly female sexuality because of its threat to the spirituality of men.

This fear of women as sexual beings finds expression in both halakhic and aggadic sources. Neusner suggests that it lies just under the surface of the Mishnah's whole treatment of women. Even where a text's explicit topic is the economics of property transfer, it is the anomaly of female sexuality, with its "dreadful threat of uncontrolled shifts in personal status and material possession," that is the motive of legislation. But rabbinic concern with female sexuality need not always be deduced from discussion of other matters. The rabbinic laws concerning modesty, with their one-sided emphasis on the modesty of women, make clear that it is women who endanger public morality through their ability to tempt men. These careful regulations of dress and exposure lack any sense of reciprocity, any sense that men tempt women and may therefore also be defined as tempters. Woman may be a bag of filth; "it [may be] better to walk behind a lion than behind a woman," but apparently men are different since there is no danger in a woman's walking behind a man!

The concepts of woman as Other and as temptress are certainly not new to Jewish feminism. They were articulated by Rachel Adler in her classic essay on women and *halakhah*, elaborated by others, and recently reiterated by Ozick. These writers seem not to have fully understood the implications of their own categories, however, for they tend to assume that the Otherness of women will disappear if only the community is flexible enough to rectify halakhic injustices. Would this were true! But the issue is far deeper than is suggested by this assumption.

Indeed, the situation of the Jewish woman might well be compared to the situation of the Jew in non-Jewish culture. The Gentile projection of the Jew as Other—the stranger, the demon, the human not-quite-human—is repeated in—or should one say partly *modelled on?*—the Jewish understanding of the Jewish woman. She too is the stranger whose life is lived parallel to man's, the demoness who stirs him, the partner whose humanity is different from his own. And just as legal changes have ameliorated the situation of the Jews without ever lifting the suspicion of our humanity, so legal change will not restore the full humanity of the Jewish woman. Our legal disabilities are a *symptom* of a pattern of projection that lies deep in Jewish thinking. They express and reflect a fundamental stance toward women that must be confronted, addressed and rooted out at its core. While it is Jewish to hope that changes in *halakhah* might bring about changes in underlying attitudes, it is folly to think that justice for women can be achieved simply through halakhic mechanisms when women's plight is not primarily a product of *halakhah.*

But this is just one issue. The Otherness of women is also given dramatic expression in our language about God. Here, we confront a great scandal: the God who supposedly transcends sexuality, who is presumably one and whole, is known to us through language that is highly selective and partial. The images we use to describe God, the qualities we attribute to God, draw on male pronouns and male experience and convey a sense of power and authority that is clearly male in character. The God at the surface of Jewish consciousness is a God with a voice of thunder, a God who as Lord and King rules his people and leads them into battle, a God who forgives like a father when we turn to him. The female images that exist in the Bible and (particularly the mystical) tradition form an underground stream that reminds us of the inadequacy of our imagery without, however, transforming its overwhelmingly male nature. The hand that takes us out of Egypt is a male hand—both in the Bible and in our contemporary imaginations.

Perceiving the predominance of male language is not the same as understanding its importance, however. Ozick, for instance, begins her article with the question of God and dismisses it quickly. She does not deny the dominance of male imagery, but argues that reflection on the absence of female anthropomorphisms "can only take us to quibbles about the incompetence of pronouns." If the Jewish-woman question is unrelated to theology, theological questions can only lead to dead ends. But as with Ozick's treatment of *halakhah,* this position seriously underestimates the depth of the issue. Religious symbols are significant and powerful communications. Since through them, a community expresses its sense and experience of the world, it cannot allow missing pronouns to determine its sense of reality! The maleness of God is not arbitrary—nor is it simply a matter of pronouns. It leads us to the central question, the question of the Otherness of women, just as the Otherness of women leads to the maleness of God.

Anthropologist Clifford Geertz offers us important insights into the function of religious language. In an essay on "Religion as a Cultural System," Geertz argues that religious symbols express both the sensibility and moral character of a people and the way in which it understands and structures the world. Symbols are simultaneously *models of* a community's sense of ultimate reality and *models for human* behavior and the social order. The Sabbath, for example, as a model of God's action in creating the world, is also a model for the Jewish community which, like God, rests on the seventh day. The double reference of symbols, up and down, enforces a community's sense of its symbols' factuality and appropriateness. If God rested on the seventh day, can we fail to do so, and how can our doing so not bring us closer to God?

If we apply Geertz's analysis to the issue of male God-language, it is clear that such language also functions as a model-of and model-for. This language both tells us about God's nature (it is, after all, the only way we know God) and justifies a human community which reserves power and authority to men. When Mortimer Ostow used the maleness of God as an argument against the ordination of women rabbis, he made the connection between language and authority painfully clear. But we do not need Ostow's honesty to grasp the implications of our language; language speaks for itself. If God is male, and we are in God's image, how can maleness *not* be the norm of Jewish humanity? If maleness is normative, how can women not be Other? And if women are Other, how can we not speak of God in language drawn from the male norm?

One consequence of the nature of male God-imagery as a model for community is that the prayer book becomes testimony against the participation of women in Jewish religious life. Women's greater access to Jewish learning, our increased leadership in synagogue ritual only bring to the surface deep contradictions between equality for women and the tradition's fundamental symbols and images for God. While the active presence of women in congregations should bespeak our full membership in the Jewish community, the language of the service conveys a different message. It impugns the humanity of women and ignores our experience, rendering that experience invisible, even in the face of our presence. But since language is not a halakhic issue, we cannot change this situation through halakhic repair. It is not "simply" that *halakhah* presupposes the Otherness of women but that this Otherness reflects and is reflected in our speech about God. The equality of women in the Jewish community requires the radical transformation of our religious language in the form of recognition of the feminine aspects of God.

Here we encounter a problem; for it is impossible to mention the subject of female language without the specter of paganism being raised. For critics of (this aspect of) Jewish feminism, introducing female God-language means reintroducing polytheism into the tradition and abdicating all that made Judaism distinctive in the ancient world. While, on the one hand, cries of "paganism" couch the question of language in dishonest and hysterical terms, they also make clear that the issue evokes deep emotional resonances. Rationally, it seems contradictory to argue that the Jewish God transcends sexuality, that anthropomorphism—while necessitated by the limits of our thought—is not to be taken literally; and at the same time to insist that a broadening of anthropomorphic language will destroy the tradition. As Rita Gross asks in her article on Jewish God-language: "If we do not mean that God is male when we use masculine pronouns and imagery, then why should there be any objections to using female imagery and pronouns as well?" Use of sexually dimorphic images may be the best way to acknowledge the limits of language and God's fullness, so that the inclusion of women becomes, at the same time, an enrichment of our concept of God.

But the issue of female God-language touches chords that are not reached or responded to by rational discussion, and so such arguments do not do. The exclusive worship of Jahweh was the result of a long, drawn-out struggle, not simply with the people of the land, but with the many within Israel who wanted to maintain Goddess-worship alongside the worship of God. The victory of Jahwehism entailed suppression of the female side of divinity (and of women as members of the cult), almost as if any recognition the feminine was accorded might overwhelm the precarious ascendency of God. The gods could seemingly be superseded, their qualities included in the many-named God and recognized as aspects of himself. But the goddesses were apparently too real and too vital for their attributes to be incorporated in this way.

It might seem we are now distant enough from paganism to understand the historical context of suppression of the Goddess without feeling the need to refight this struggle. But if Ba'al is impotent and voiceless, an object of purely theoretical condemnation, the Goddess still evokes resistance which is vehement and deeply felt. Albeit through the lens of our monotheistic tradition, she seems to speak to us as powerfully as ever. Yet this is itself a strong argument for the incorporation of female language into the tradition. It is precisely because she is not distant that the Goddess must be recognized as a part of God. For the God who does not include her is an idol made in man's image, a God over against a female Other—not the Creator, source of maleness and femaleness, not the relativizer of all gods and goddesses who nonetheless includes them as part of God's self. Acknowledging the many aspects of the Goddess among the names of God becomes a measure of our ability to incorporate the feminine and women into a monotheistic religious framework. At the same time, naming women's experience as part of the nature of the deity brings the suppressed experience of women into the Jewish fold.

This brings us to our last issue, one that is closely related to the other two. As Ozick points out in a particularly eloquent meditation, the Jewish tradition is not the product of the entire Jewish people, but of Jewish men alone! Of course women have lived Jewish history and carried its burdens, shaped our experience to history and history to ourselves. But ours is not the history passed down and recorded; the texts committed to memory or the documents studied; the arguments fought, refought, and finely honed. Women have not contributed to the formation of the written tradition, and thus tradition does not reflect the specific realities of women's lives.

This fact, which marks so great a loss to tradition and to women, is cause and reflection both of the Otherness of women and the maleness of God. Women are not educated as creators of tradition because we are Other, but of course we remain Other when we are seen through the filter of male experience without ever speaking for ourselves. The maleness of God calls for the silence of women as shapers of the holy, but our silence in turn enforces our Otherness and a communal sense of the "rightness" of the male image of God. There is a "fit" in other words, a tragic coherence between the role of women in the community, and its symbolism, law, and teaching. The Otherness of women is part of the fabric of Jewish life.

Once again, and now most clearly, we are brought up against the impotence of halakhic change. For *halakhah* is part of the system that women have not had a hand in creating, neither in its foundations, nor as it was developed and refined. Not only is this absence reflected in the content of *halakhah,* it may also be reflected in its very form. How can we presume that if women add their voices to the tradition, *halakhah* will be our medium of expression and repair? How can we determine in advance the channels through which the tradition will become wholly Jewish, i.e., a product of the whole Jewish people, when women are only beginning consciously to explore the particularities of our own Jewishness? To settle on *halakhah* as the source of justice for women is to foreclose the question of women's experience when it has scarcely begun to be raised.

Clearly, the implications of Jewish feminism, while they include halakhic restructuring, reach beyond *halakhah* to transform the bases of Jewish life. Feminism demands a new understanding of Torah, God, and Israel: an understanding of Torah that begins with acknowledgment of the profound injustice of Torah itself. The assumption of the lesser humanity of women has poisoned the content and structure of the law, undergirding women's legal disabilities and our subordination in the broader tradition. This assumption is not amenable to piecemeal change. It must be utterly eradicated by the withdrawal of projection from women—the discovery that the negative traits attributed to women are also in the men who attribute them, while the positive qualities reserved for men are also in women. Feminism demands a new understanding of God that reflects and supports the redefinition of Jewish humanity. The long-suppressed femaleness of God, acknowledged in the mystical tradition, but even here shaped and articulated by men, must be recovered and reexplored and reintegrated into the Godhead. Last, feminism assumes that these changes will be possible only when we come to a new understanding of the community of Israel which includes the whole of Israel and which therefore allows women to speak and name our experience for ourselves. The outcome of these new understandings is difficult to see in advance of our turning. It is clear, however, that the courage, concern, and creativity necessary for a feminist transformation of Judaism will not be mustered by evading the magnitude of the required change.

STUDY QUESTIONS

1. What is the Diaspora? *Talmud*? *Tanakh*? *Torah*? Yahweh?
2. What was God's covenant with the Jewish patriarch?
3. What important event in Biblical history occurred on Mount Sinai?
4. What part did David play in Jewish history?

5. To Jews, what was Solomon's most important action during his reign?
6. What is the Exile? What happened during this event? How did it affect the Jews?
7. What is the significance of the Romans' destruction of the Second Temple in 70 CE?
8. What is Reform Judaism? What is Orthodox Judaism?
9. How does Maimonides' *Thirteen Principles* conflict with the principles of Reform Judaism expressed in the Pittsburgh Platform?
10. What is the Babylonian *Talmud*?

FURTHER READING

David Ariel, *What Do Jews Believe?* (New York: Schocken Books, 1995).

John Bowker, ed., *The Oxford Dictionary of World Religions* (Oxford: Oxford University Press, 1997).

Ronald Eisenberg, *The JPS Guide to Jewish Traditions* (Philadelphia: The Jewish Publication Society, 2004).

Abraham Joshua Heschel, *God in Search of Man: A Philosophy of Judaism* (New York: Farrar, Straus and Giroux, 1955).

Susannah Heschel, *On Being a Jewish Feminist* (New York: Schocken Books, 1983, 1995).

Nicholas de Lange and Miri Freud-Kandel, *Modern Judaism: An Oxford Guide* (Oxford: Oxford University Press, 2008).

John B. Noss, *A History of the World's Religions* (New York: Macmillan, 1994).

George Robinson, *Judaism: A Complete Guide to Beliefs, Customs, and Rituals* (New York: Pocket Books, 2000).

Norman Solomon, *Judaism: A Very Short Introduction* (Oxford: Oxford University Press, 1996).

Herman Wouk, *This Is My God* (New York: Pocket Books, 1959, 1970).

ONLINE

Chabad.org, http://www.chabad.org/library/article_cdo/aid/109866/jewish/Jewish-Beliefs.htm (December 25, 2015).

BBC, "Jewish Faith and God," http://www.bbc.co.uk/religion/religions/judaism (December 25, 2015).

Jewish Virtual Library, https://www.jewishvirtuallibrary.org/jsource/Judaism/jewnation.html (December 25, 2015).

Pew Research Center, "Jews and Judaism," http://www.pewforum.org/topics/jews-and-judaism/ (December 25, 2015).

12 Christianity

Christianity is both like and unlike most other major world religions. Like others, it can claim a vast number of adherents (about 2 billion worldwide); it comprises many subgroups that differ in belief and practice (actually, there are thousands of distinct denominations); it recognizes an authoritative scriptural canon; and its distinctive features have evolved from the words and deeds of a single revered founder (Jesus Christ). Not surprisingly, the main differences between Christianity and other traditions also lie in the life and message of its founder. From the very beginning, Christians have derived diverse interpretations from the Jesus narrative, and these conflicting views have not hampered the tradition but expanded it.

HISTORY

For a hundred years, historians have been trying to piece together a historically accurate picture of the life of Jesus. The job has not been easy. Our best and earliest sources of historical information about Jesus (virtually our *only* sources) are the Gospels, the first four books of the New Testament: Matthew, Mark, Luke, and John. (The many non-Biblical sources from ancient times are hardly any help at all.) But as historical records, these scriptural texts are less than satisfactory. A leading New Testament historian explains why:

> The problem is that these books were not written to provide objective biographical information about Jesus. They were *Gospels*, that is, proclamations of the good news that Jesus brings salvation to the world. The books were written decades after the events they narrate, by people who were not eyewitnesses, who are telling the tales in a different language from Jesus', based on oral traditions that the authors themselves had heard and that had circulated by word of mouth decade after decade before being written down. These traditions were modified when they were told and retold, and modified further when written down.[1]

Story of Jesus

Nevertheless, from a critical reading of the Gospels, historians have been able to surmise this much: Jesus was born in 4 BCE to two Jews, Joseph and Mary, in a town in Galilee called Nazareth. As an adult he spent time in the company of an apocalyptic prophet known as John the Baptist, who baptized him. Afterwards Jesus began two or three years of preaching, mingling with outcasts and those deemed sinners, and gathering twelve devoted disciples around him. He caused a commotion in the Temple in Jerusalem where he offended the

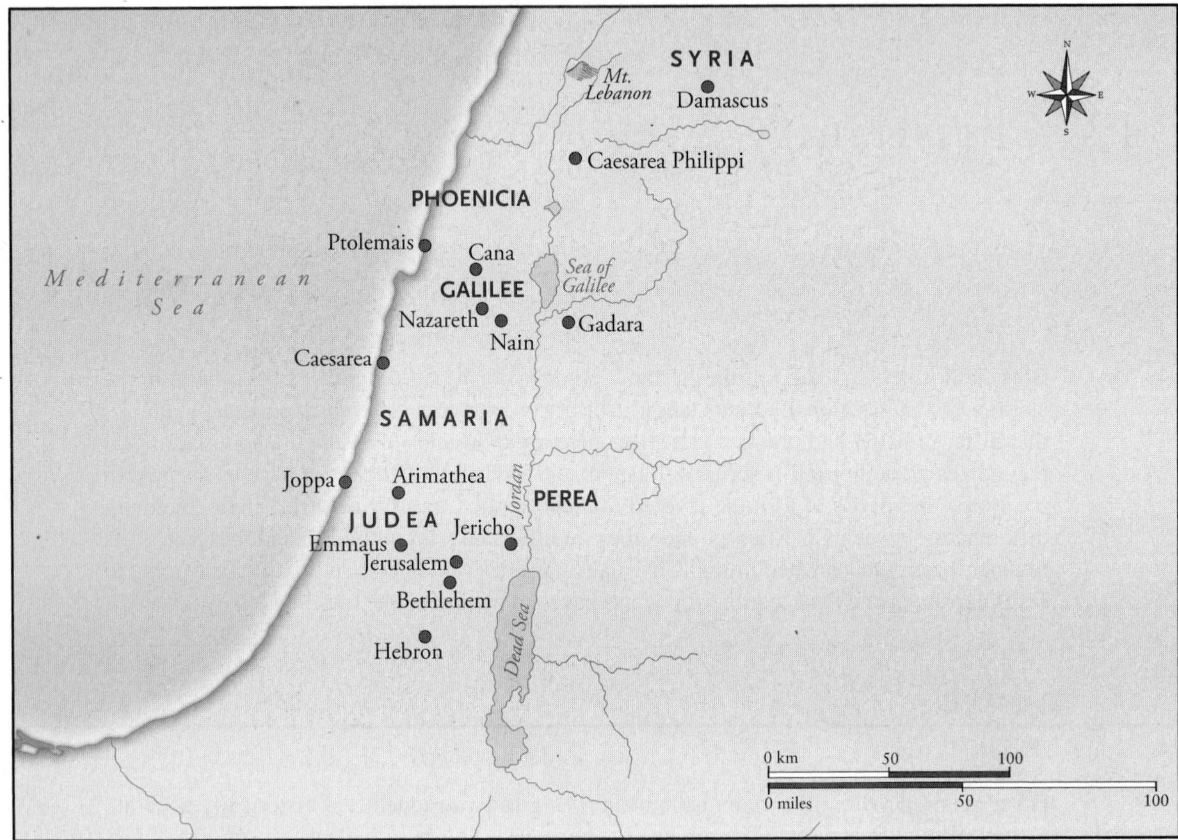

MAP 12.1 Palestine during the time of Jesus.

Temple priests, and this led to his arrest, apparently arranged by the priests. After a perfunctory trial, the Roman prefect Pontius Pilate sentenced him to be crucified. Some time after his execution, his followers began to spread the good news about a divine Jesus who was sacrificed for the sins of humankind, rose from the dead, ascended into heaven, and promised to return to earth very soon.

Palestine was under harsh Roman rule at the time, and apocalyptic ideas—beliefs that God would soon destroy all evil forces and usher in a new earthly kingdom of justice and righteousness—were common among Jews (and later among Christians). From various self-proclaimed prophets came sermons about the coming of a messiah—either a great human king, a leader like Moses, or a powerful liberator from heaven. Many figures in Jesus' time claimed to be the messiah and acquired a reputation for performing miracles, healing the sick, casting out demons, and raising the dead. Historians say that into this environment Jesus came, also preaching an apocalyptic message. According to the second Gospel, Jesus' teachings amounted to "The time has been fulfilled, the kingdom of God is near; repent and believe in this good news!" (Mark 1:15). Jesus too was said to perform miraculous and supernatural feats, which were thought to be proof that his words and works

FIGURE 12.1 A stained glass window depicting the Bible story of St. John the Baptist baptizing Jesus in the Jordan River.

emanated from God. He was hesitant to claim the title of messiah, but his followers eagerly applied the word to him. He called God *father*, and himself the *Son of Man*.

Divisions

Most religions feature a diversity of beliefs; Christianity is no different. From the death of Jesus to the present day, Christianity has never been a unified, fully coherent tradition. From the beginning it has been amazingly disparate in doctrine, practice, organization, and accepted canon. In fact, in describing the tradition, modern scholars have suggested that it might be more precise to refer not to Christianity but to *Christianities*. This characterization is especially apt when applied to the first four centuries CE. In that era before the Christian canon was solidified, Christians called *Gnostics* believed that the material world was evil and that salvation was to be found in freeing the soul not from sin but from the human body. Only secret knowledge (*gnosis* in Greek) provided by Christ could lead to liberation. Other Christians were monotheists, while some were polytheistic. In the latter group were the *Marcionites*, who taught that there were two Gods—the wicked Old Testament God, and the loving New Testament God. Some Christians believed that Jesus was both divine and human; others that he was divine through and through; and some that he was 100 percent human. Another group of Christians insisted that Christianity was not distinct from Judaism but part of it, being the fulfillment of Jewish prophecy. A number of Christians accepted that Jesus

CHRISTIANITY TIMELINE

BCE

753 Founding of Rome

332–323 Conquests of Alexander the Great

166–164 Revolt of the Maccabees

40–4 Rome makes Herod king of the Jews.

CE

4 BCE–30 CE Life of Jesus

46–62 Paul's missionary work

65–70 Gospel of Mark

70 Jerusalem falls to the Romans; Second Temple is destroyed.

73 Masada falls to the Romans.

80–85 Gospels of Matthew and Luke

90–95 Gospel of John

100–130 Rise of Gnosticism

354–430 Augustine

367 Contents of New Testament determined

410 Rome is sacked by Visigoths.

1054 The Great Schism between Western and Eastern Christianity

1095 The first military crusade to liberate Jerusalem

1225–1274 Thomas Aquinas

1480 Spanish Inquisition founded

1517 Martin Luther posts his theses.

1545 Council of Trent

1611 Publication of King James Version of the Bible

1616 Galileo condemned by the Church for accepting heliocentric solar system

1859 Charles Darwin's *On the Origin of Species*

1948 Inaugural meeting of World Council of Churches

1962–1965 Second Vatican Council

died to bring salvation to humanity; others said that Jesus did nothing of the kind. Today some scholars characterize Jesus as an apocalyptic figure, while others say he was mostly a teacher of ethics.

Early Christians also argued over what to include in the Christian scriptures. Before the final compilation of the New Testament in the fourth century, there were many textual candidates for possible inclusion in the canon. There were other gospels (like the Gospel of Philip and the Gospel of Peter), other epistles (such as 3 Corinthians), and other Acts (like the Acts of John and the Acts of Paul)—all of which were putatively written by Jesus' apostles.

In the first few centuries, variant "Christian" doctrines competed with each other to be recognized as *the* genuine Christian beliefs. Eventually only one kind of Christianity won out over the others, and it was this winning tradition that defined "true" Christianity and proclaimed that the losing traditions were heretical. Likewise the winning tradition decided what books would be included in the "official" Christian canon. When the content of the New Testament was finalized, only twenty-seven books had made the cut. These twenty-seven now constitute the Christian canon of scripture. The books that did not make the cut have been denounced, ignored, or relegated to a lower status.

From Empire to Schism

Despite resistance from non-Christians and persecutions by the authorities, Christianity spread swiftly throughout the Roman Empire. From the outset, Christian monotheism clashed with the prevailing polytheism of the Greco-Roman world. Rome expected Christians to show respect for the officially sanctioned gods, and when they did not, the Roman authorities reacted with brutality—imprisoning, torturing, and killing Christians at will. Persecutions, however, failed to stop the growth of Christianity: the making of martyrs seemed only to create more Christians.

The plight of Christians, however, began to change after Emperor Constantine came to power (reign, 306–337). In 313 he enacted a policy of tolerance for Christians, giving them complete freedom to practice their religion. Later, under Emperor Theodosius I (reign, 379–395), Christianity's prospects improved again when it became the official religion of the empire.

Throughout this era, leaders of the Church (that is, the main Christian body) tried to achieve a consensus about various doctrines. They held several councils to resolve differences, eventually producing Church creeds that defined **orthodoxy** regarding the incarnation, the resurrection, the Holy Spirit, the hierarchy of the Church, the humanity and divinity of Christ, and the **Trinity** (now the doctrine that there is one God who exists in three persons—Father, Son, and Holy Spirit). Two statements of faith in particular had a strong impact on early Christians: the Nicene Creed (produced in 325 and expanded in 381) and the Apostles' Creed (evolved from the second century). The orthodox conception of the Trinity—the view accepted by most Christians today—was not fully worked out until the late fourth century.

Around that time, the Roman Empire divided the administration of its immense territories into western and eastern domains. Rome ruled the western sphere, Constantinople the eastern. Eventually the Church also split along these lines, with Western Christianity (the Latin or *Catholic Church*) being led by a pope in Rome, and Eastern Christianity (the *Orthodox Church*) being led by a patriarch in Constantinople. The theological gulf between these two was large and, apparently, unbridgeable. The **Great Schism**, as the east–west split is called, exposed huge doctrinal differences between the two versions of Christianity. The Eastern Church rejected the authority of the pope and resented the West's unilateral changes in the Nicene Creed concerning the nature of the Trinity. The Western Church disliked the East's veneration of icons, its endorsement of married priests, the use of vernacular languages in worship, and its refusal to submit to papal power. By the eleventh century, the great divide between East and West was complete and irreversible.

Augustine

Into these tumultuous times came Augustine (354–430), a Christian philosopher and theologian who had an enormous influence on Christian thought and on the West's appreciation of Plato and Aristotle. He affected Christian theology more than any other early Christian author, introduced Plato to generations of thinkers, and forced philosophers in every epoch to reckon with his ideas and authority. Pascal, Luther, Wittgenstein, and others had to take Augustine into account. He was the pivot point between Greco-pagan and Christian thinking, a transition that would change both the Church and future philosophy.

Augustine was born to a Christian mother (St. Monica) and pagan father (Patricius) in Roman North Africa (now Algeria). In his autobiography *Confessions*, he describes an idle youth spent in an uninhibited romp through sensuality. Before becoming a Christian, he became intrigued by a doctrine that seemed to shine new light on Christianity: **Neoplatonism**. This view is a blend of Plato's metaphysics (primarily concerning the theory of Forms) and other nonmaterialist or religious ideas. In the "Platonic books," Augustine found musings about an immaterial transcendent realm, about high and low levels of reality, about a supreme entity (the One in Plato), and about the possibility of knowledge of all these things. Moreover, Augustine thought he saw analogs of these concepts in the Christian worldview. After a very long, anguished struggle with these ideas, he finally converted to Christianity in 386 at age thirty-one and was baptized by St. Ambrose on Easter Day.

From both classical and Christian threads, Augustine wove a distinctive set of doctrines about God, the world, knowledge, ethics, and existence. In epistemology, metaphysics, and moral philosophy, he shaped new doctrines from old ideas and original analyses.

The Middle Ages

After a long, slow decline, the western part of the Roman Empire fell in the fifth century to a Germanic king, thus ending over a thousand years of Roman rule in the Western world. But Roman Christianity continued for centuries. By the beginning of the Middle Ages (lasting from about 500 to 1500 CE), the Latin Church had grown in power and number of adherents. The popes acquired complete authority in all religious matters, mostly in northern Europe and the western Mediterranean, and their influence in political affairs increased until they exerted unprecedented control over secular governments. Eventually the Church became the primary source of learning, culture, theology, and philosophy in the West. (Around the same time in the Arab world, the original Greek philosophical texts of Plato, Aristotle, and others were being rescued from oblivion and studied by Islamic scholars from India to Spain.) Among the educated, **scholasticism**—the study of philosophy as it relates to religion—became the dominant method for the pursuit of knowledge.

The supreme scholastic of the medieval period was Thomas Aquinas (1225–1274). He was born into a noble family in southern Italy and was eventually to become the greatest philosopher of the period and, to this day, the official theologian of the Roman Catholic Church. Because his family had decided that he should be a great church leader, they packed him off before the age of six to the Benedictine monastery of Monte Cassino for training. At fourteen, he was sent to the University of Naples for further study, and there his life took what his family considered a radical turn. At age twenty, he joined the scholarly Dominican order and pursued not a leadership position in the church, but the rarefied life of the intellect.

Becoming alarmed at Aquinas's change of plans, his family had him kidnapped and locked in the family castle for several months. When it became clear that he was not going to relinquish his scholarly ambitions, they released him, and he continued his studies and his writing at the University of Paris and in Cologne, Rome, Naples, Viterbo, and Orvieto.

Aquinas's great contribution to both philosophy and Christianity was his fusion of Aristotle's philosophy with Christian doctrines. In theology he distinguished between reason and faith, giving each its own domain of inquiry. Reason can be used to prove the existence of God, he says, but only through faith can we know such mysteries as the incarnation and the Trinity.

Aquinas produced significant works in many areas of philosophy, including logic, epistemology, ethics, and philosophy of religion. Nowadays he is most famous for his arguments for the existence of God and for his system of ethics known as *natural law theory*.

The Reformation

In the sixteenth century, the Latin Church was besieged by dissenters who called for reform in Church doctrine and practice. This chorus grew until it became a movement throughout Europe, a widespread protest against Church corruption and dogma known as the **Protestant Reformation**. Dramatic social changes aided and encouraged the reformers. These revolutionary forces included the Renaissance, a movement in literature and the arts emphasizing humanist concerns and classical (secular) learning; the invention of the printing press by Johann Gutenberg; the translation of the Bible from Latin into vernacular languages; and the rising power of cities and towns. Many voices throughout Europe insisted on reform, but the sharpest objections came from a German monk and scholar named Martin Luther (1483–1546). He detested the Church's extravagance, its corruption, and its selling of *indulgences* (ecclesiastical "vouchers" that authorized early release from purgatory). But his main protests concerned doctrinal issues. Contrary to traditional Church positions, he asserted that salvation had nothing to do with religious practice and good works; salvation was made possible only by Jesus' divine grace through faith. A person could be saved regardless of merit, for the sinner attains salvation through faith alone. Moreover, Luther declared, the ultimate authority on Christian doctrine is neither the pope nor the Church, but the holy scriptures, which believers could examine for themselves. To connect with God, the believer needed no priestly intermediary.

Originally the Protestant Reformation was meant only to reform the Church, but it soon caused a complete break with it. Luther acquired his own group of followers, and other reformers—such as John Calvin, John Knox, and Ulrich Zwingli—also preached distinct doctrines and garnered their own devotees. These doctrinal differences splintered the

 A CLOSER LOOK

Major Christian Traditions

	Population
Catholic	1,094,610,000
Protestant	800,640,000
Orthodox	260,380,000
Other (Mormons, Jehovah's Witnesses, Christian Science Church, et al.)	28,430,000
Total	2,184,060,000 (31.7% of world pop.)

Pew Research Center, "Religion and Public Life Project," www.pewforum.org (Pew Research Center, 2010).

Reformation. The result was not one breakaway Protestant faith group but many, large and small. Today there are thousands of Protestant denominations throughout the world, comprising some 800 million members, about one-third of all Christians. Some of the larger Protestant traditions (consisting of many separate denominations) include Lutherans, Anglicans, Baptists, Pentecostals, Presbyterians, United Church, Episcopalians, Adventists, and Methodists.[2]

SCRIPTURES

The Christian Scriptures consist of the Hebrew, or Jewish, bible (what Christians call the "Old Testament") and the New Testament (which reflects the teachings of Christianity). (The references to old and new testaments are inapt, because they imply erroneously that the Hebrew bible has been completely superseded by the new Christian writings. But to avoid confusion we will have to stick with the standard terms.) Together these two sets of writings form the Christian canon, the texts that most Christians recognize as having full authority on matters relating to their religion. As Christians see it, the Old Testament belongs in their canon because it describes an ancient covenant, or testament, between God and humans, a covenant that foreshadows a new one as recounted in the New Testament.

The New Testament consists of twenty-seven books, written in Greek at different times from 50 to 120 CE. In early Christianity, many books purporting to be genuine works of the apostles appeared, and Christians debated which books should be included in the canon. It was not until the fourth century that the canon was finalized. Some of the books were written under the name of their actual authors, but many texts that claimed to be written by Jesus' disciples were in fact penned by anonymous writers.

The New Testament books are categorized like this:

The Gospels: Matthew, Mark, Luke, John (stories and sayings of Jesus, the "good news" of Christianity)

Acts: The Acts of the Apostles (early Christian narratives of events from the death of Jesus to the end of Paul's ministry)

Epistles:

I. **Paul's letters:** Romans, 1 and 2 Corinthians, Galatians, Ephesians, Philippians, Colossians, 1 and 2 Thessalonians, 1 and 2 Timothy, Titus, Philemon (thirteen letters purportedly written by Paul)

II. **General letters:** Hebrews, James, 1 and 2 Peter, 1, 2, and 3 John, Jude (eight letters with anonymous or doubtful authorship)

Apocalypse: The Revelation of John (book by a prophet describing the end of the world and the beginning of God's new kingdom)

Written 30 to 65 years after Jesus' death, the four Gospels give varying accounts of Jesus' birth, message, interactions with others, crucifixion, and resurrection. Despite their claim to have been written by four of Jesus' disciples, the actual authors are unknown. Matthew, Mark, and Luke are called the **Synoptic Gospels** because they are so similar in content, having been derived from the same set of writings.

Mark was written first, between 65 and 70. It portrays Jesus as the son of God, an extraordinary but misunderstood figure who came to earth to suffer, die, and be resurrected. Matthew was composed between 80 and 85, drawing its account from Mark and two other sources. In Matthew, Jesus is the Jewish messiah come to explain and fulfill Jewish law. Luke was written around the same time as Matthew, using some of the same sources. In Luke, Jesus is a prophet rejected by the Jews but now come to offer salvation to the Gentiles. John was the last gospel written, produced about ten years after the Gospel of Matthew. John drew from several sources that were apparently not used in the other gospels, and most of the book's stories about Jesus are not found in them. John speaks of Jesus as a divine being, the very "Word of God" who was with God in eternity—the one God sent to earth to impart God's truth to the world. He tells of the many "signs" of Jesus' divinity (miracles such as healing the blind man and resurrecting Lazarus), Jesus' discourse at the last supper, Jesus' betrayal by Judas, his trial before a Roman governor, his crucifixion and resurrection, and his postmortem appearances to his followers.

The Acts of the Apostles was composed by the same author who wrote the Gospel of Luke and at about the same time (80–85). It recounts the apostles' dissemination of the gospel to the Gentiles after Jesus' after-death appearances. We are told of the Holy Spirit's encounter with the apostles on the day of Pentecost, the spreading of the gospel to Palestine and all parts of the Empire, the conversion and preaching of Paul (a former persecutor of Christians), his establishment of churches in Asia Minor and Greece, and his arrest in Jerusalem and trial in Rome.

The epistles are letters (actually two are sermons) sent to churches and individuals, exhorting them in the faith and instructing them in doctrine. Thirteen of the twenty-one letters have traditionally been ascribed to Paul. Of these, scholars are sure that Paul wrote seven—Romans, 1 Corinthians, 2 Corinthians, Galatians, Philippians, 1 Thessalonians, and Philemon.

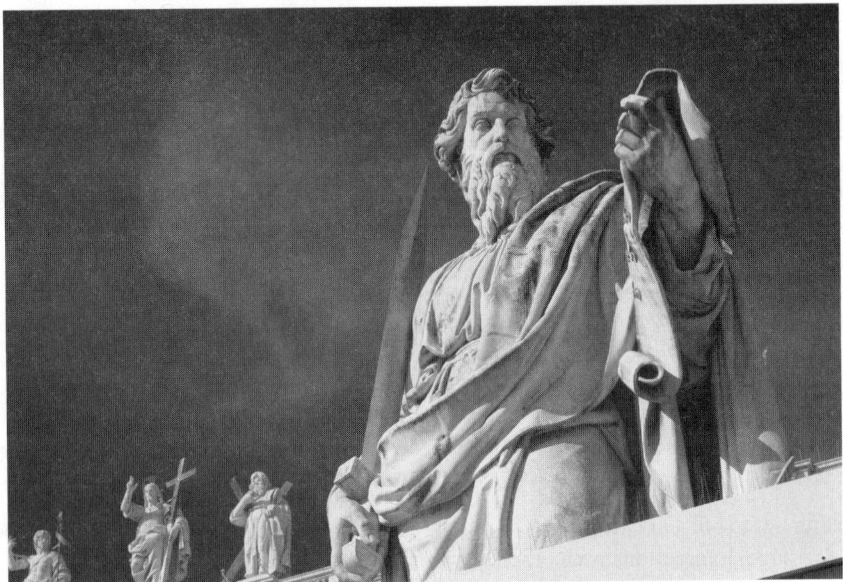

FIGURE 12.2 The Statue of the Apostle Paul in front of the Basilica of St. Peter, Vatican, Rome, Italy.

 BACKGROUND

The Problem with Scribes

Historians note an unsettling difficulty in precisely identifying the Christian canon: many different versions of the same New Testament books exist. This problem has arisen because of the way books of any kind were copied and distributed in ancient times. Bart Ehrman, an expert in Biblical studies, explains:

> Books in the ancient world . . . were copied by hand, one page, one sentence, one word, one letter at a time. There was no other way to do it. Since books were copied by hand, there was always the possibility that scribes would make mistakes and intentional changes in a book—any and every time it was copied. Moreover, when a new copy was itself copied, the mistakes and changes that the earlier scribe (copyist) made would have been reproduced, while the new scribe would introduce some mistakes and changes of his own. When that copy was then copied, more changes would be introduced. And so it went.
>
> Unfortunately, we do not have the originals of any of the books of the New Testament, or the first copies, or the copies of the first copies. What we have are copies made much later—in most cases hundreds of years later.
>
> How do we know that these copies were changed in the process of reproduction? Because we can compare the thousands of copies that we now have, which range in date from the second to the sixteenth centuries, to see if and how they differ from one another. What is striking is that they differ a lot. . . . Most of these differences are altogether minor and unimportant (misspelled words, changes of word order, the accidental omission of a line, etc.). But some of them are of immense importance.[3]

But three are most likely *not* written by Paul—1 Timothy, 2 Timothy, and Titus. And three are *possibly* not composed by Paul—Ephesians, Colossians, and 2 Thessalonians. Paul's missionary journeys and his writing of the letters took place between 46 and 62, a few years *before* the writing of the Gospels.

The Revelation of John is an example of a literary genre popular among Jews and early Christians—**apocalypse**, a work describing revelations of a cataclysmic future or world. Through a weird, symbolic narrative, the author (a prophet called John) evokes a vision of the end of the world when God destroys the old age and creates a new one for the righteous.

NOTES

1. Bart D. Ehrman, *A Brief Introduction to the New Testament*, 2nd ed. (New York: Oxford University Press, 2009), 128–129.
2. David B. Barrett et al., *World Christian Encyclopedia* (Oxford: Oxford University Press, 2001); Pew Research, "Religion and Public Life Project," http://www.pewresearch.org/ (Pew Research Center, 2011).
3. Ehrman, 7–8.

KEY TERMS

apocalypse A literary genre that describes revelations of a cataclysmic future or world.

Great Schism The final break between Western and Eastern Christianity, completed in the eleventh century.

Neoplatonism A view that blends Plato's metaphysics (primarily concerning the theory of Forms) and other nonmaterialist or religious ideas.

orthodoxy The generally accepted or authorized views on religious doctrine and practice.

Protestant Reformation A widespread, sixteenth-century call for reform in the Latin Church that resulted in the founding of Protestant denominations.

scholasticism In the Middle Ages, the study of philosophy as it relates to religion.

Synoptic Gospels The Gospels of Matthew, Mark, and Luke, which have similar content derived from the same set of writings.

the Trinity The doctrine that one God exists in three persons: Father, Son, and the Holy Spirit.

READINGS

TEACHINGS

The Sermon on the Mount

This passage—the well-known "Sermon on the Mount"—is the first of five of Jesus' sermons recounted in Matthew. In it Jesus proclaims a new way to understand Jewish law, lays out the duties of someone who follows him, and sets forth the requirements for entering the kingdom of heaven.

5 [1]When Jesus saw the crowds, he went up the mountain; and after he sat down, his disciples came to him. [2]Then he began to speak, and taught them, saying:

[3]"Blessed are the poor in spirit, for theirs is the kingdom of heaven.

[4]"Blessed are those who mourn, for they will be comforted.

"Blessed are the meek, for they will inherit the earth.

[6]"Blessed are those who hunger and thirst for righteousness, for they will be filled.

[7]"Blessed are the merciful, for they will receive mercy.

[8]"Blessed are the pure in heart, for they will see God.

[9]"Blessed are the peacemakers, for they will be called children of God.

[10]"Blessed are those who are persecuted for righteousness' sake, for theirs is the kingdom of heaven.

[11]"Blessed are you when people revile you and persecute you and utter all kinds of evil against you falsely on my account.

[12]"Rejoice and be glad, for your reward is great in heaven, for in the same way they persecuted the prophets who were before you.

[13]"You are the salt of the earth; but if salt has lost its taste, how can its saltiness be restored? It is no longer good for anything, but is thrown out and trampled under foot.

[14]"You are the light of the world. A city built on a hill cannot be hid. [15]No one after lighting a lamp puts it under the bushel basket, but on the lampstand, and it gives light to all in the house. [16]In the same way, let your light shine before others, so that they may see your good works and give glory to your Father in heaven.

[17]"Do not think that I have come to abolish the law or the prophets; I have come not to abolish but to fulfill. [18]For truly I tell you, until heaven and earth pass away, not one letter, not one stroke of a letter, will pass from the law until all is accomplished.

[19]Therefore, whoever breaks one of the least of these commandments, and teaches others to do the

Matthew 5:1–5: 48, 6:19–29, *New Revised Standard Version*, 1989, in *The New Oxford Annotated Bible* (Oxford: Oxford University Press, 2010).

same, will be called least in the kingdom of heaven; but whoever does them and teaches them will be called great in the kingdom of heaven. [20]For I tell you, unless your righteousness exceeds that of the scribes and Pharisees, you will never enter the kingdom of heaven.

[21]“You have heard that it was said to those of ancient times, ‘You shall not murder’; and ‘whoever murders shall be liable to judgment.’ [22]But I say to you that if you are angry with a brother or sister, you will be liable to judgment; and if you insult a brother or sister, you will be liable to the council; and if you say, ‘You fool,’ you will be liable to the hell of fire. [23]So when you are offering your gift at the altar, if you remember that your brother or sister has something against you, [24]leave your gift there before the altar and go; first be reconciled to your brother or sister, and then come and offer your gift. [25]Come to terms quickly with your accuser while you are on the way to court with him, or your accuser may hand you over to the judge, and the judge to the guard, and you will be thrown into prison. [26]Truly I tell you, you will never get out until you have paid the last penny.

[27]“You have heard that it was said, ‘You shall not commit adultery.’ [28]But I say to you that everyone who looks at a woman with lust has already committed adultery with her in his heart. [29]If your right eye causes you to sin, tear it out and throw it away; it is better for you to lose one of your members than for your whole body to be thrown into hell. [30]And if your right hand causes you to sin, cut it off and throw it away; it is better for you to lose one of your members than for your whole body to go into hell.

[31]“It was also said, ‘Whoever divorces his wife, let him give her a certificate of divorce.’ [32]But I say to you that anyone who divorces his wife, except on the ground of unchastity, causes her to commit adultery; and whoever marries a divorced woman commits adultery.

[33]“Again, you have heard that it was said to those of ancient times, ‘You shall not swear falsely, but carry out the vows you have made to the Lord.’ [34]But I say to you, Do not swear at all, either by heaven, for it is the throne of God, [35]or by the earth, for it is his footstool, or by Jerusalem, for it is the city of the great King. [36]And do not swear by your head, for you cannot make one hair white or black. [37]Let your word be ‘Yes, Yes’ or ‘No, No’; anything more than this comes from the evil one.

[38]“You have heard that it was said, ‘An eye for an eye and a tooth for a tooth.’ [39]But I say to you, Do not resist an evildoer. But if anyone strikes you on the right cheek, turn the other also; [40]and if anyone wants to sue you and take your coat, give your cloak as well; [41]and if anyone forces you to go one mile, go also the second mile. [42]Give to everyone who begs from you, and do not refuse anyone who wants to borrow from you.

[43]“You have heard that it was said, ‘You shall love your neighbor and hate your enemy.’ [44]But I say to you, Love your enemies and pray for those who persecute you, [45]so that you may be children of your Father in heaven; for he makes his sun rise on the evil and on the good, and sends rain on the righteous and on the unrighteous. [46]For if you love those who love you, what reward do you have? Do not even the tax collectors do the same? [47]And if you greet only your brothers and sisters, what more are you doing than others? Do not even the Gentiles do the same? [48]Be perfect, therefore, as your heavenly Father is perfect. . . .

6 [19]“Do not store up for yourselves treasures on earth, where moth and rust consume and where thieves break in and steal; [20]but store up for yourselves treasures in heaven, where neither moth nor rust consumes and where thieves do not break in and steal. [21]For where your treasure is, there your heart will be also.

[22]“The eye is the lamp of the body. So, if your eye is healthy, your whole body will be full of light; [23]but if your eye is unhealthy, your whole body will be full of darkness. If then the light in you is darkness, how great is the darkness!

[24]“No one can serve two masters; for a slave will either hate the one and love the other, or be devoted to the one and despise the other. You cannot serve God and wealth.

[25]“Therefore I tell you, do not worry about your life, what you will eat or what you will drink, or about your body, what you will wear. Is not life more than food, and the body more than clothing? [26]Look at the birds of the air; they neither sow nor reap nor

gather into barns, and yet your heavenly Father feeds them. Are you not of more value than they? [27]And can any of you by worrying add a single hour to your span of life? [28]And why do you worry about clothing? Consider the lilies of the field, how they grow; they neither toil nor spin, [29]yet I tell you, even Solomon in all his glory was not clothed like one of these. [30]But if God so clothes the grass of the field, which is alive today and tomorrow is thrown into the oven, will he not much more clothe you—you of little faith? [31]Therefore do not worry, saying, ‘What will we eat?’ or ‘What will we drink?’ or ‘What will we wear?’ [32]For it is the Gentiles who strive for all these things; and indeed your heavenly Father knows that you need all these things. [33]But strive first for the kingdom of God and his righteousness, and all these things will be given to you as well.

[34]“So do not worry about tomorrow, for tomorrow will bring worries of its own. Today's trouble is enough for today.

7 [1]“Do not judge, so that you may not be judged. [2]For with the judgment you make you will be judged, and the measure you give will be the measure you get. [3]Why do you see the speck in your neighbor's eye, but do not notice the log in your own eye? [4]Or how can you say to your neighbor, ‘Let me take the speck out of your eye,’ while the log is in your own eye? [5]You hypocrite, first take the log out of your own eye, and then you will see clearly to take the speck out of your neighbor's eye.

[6]“Do not give what is holy to dogs; and do not throw your pearls before swine, or they will trample them under foot and turn and maul you.

[7]“Ask, and it will be given you; search, and you will find; knock, and the door will be opened for you. [8]For everyone who asks receives, and everyone who searches finds, and for everyone who knocks, the door will be opened. [9]Is there anyone among you who, if your child asks for bread, will give a stone? [10]Or if the child asks for a fish, will give a snake? [11]If you then, who are evil, know how to give good gifts to your children, how much more will your Father in heaven give good things to those who ask him!

[12]“In everything do to others as you would have them do to you; for this is the law and the prophets.

[13]“Enter through the narrow gate; for the gate is wide and the road is easy that leads to destruction, and there are many who take it.

[14]For the gate is narrow and the road is hard that leads to life, and there are few who find it.

[15]“Beware of false prophets, who come to you in sheep's clothing but inwardly are ravenous wolves. [16]You will know them by their fruits. Are grapes gathered from thorns, or figs from thistles? [17]In the same way, every good tree bears good fruit, but the bad tree bears bad fruit. [18]A good tree cannot bear bad fruit, nor can a bad tree bear good fruit. [19]Every tree that does not bear good fruit is cut down and thrown into the fire. [20]Thus you will know them by their fruits.

[21]“Not everyone who says to me, ‘Lord, Lord,’ will enter the kingdom of heaven, but only the one who does the will of my Father in heaven. [22]On that day many will say to me, ‘Lord, Lord, did we not prophesy in your name, and cast out demons in your name, and do many deeds of power in your name?’ [23]Then I will declare to them, ‘I never knew you; go away from me, you evildoers.’

[24]“Everyone then who hears these words of mine and acts on them will be like a wise man who built his house on rock. [25]The rain fell, the floods came, and the winds blew and beat on that house, but it did not fall, because it had been founded on rock. [26]And everyone who hears these words of mine and does not act on them will be like a foolish man who built his house on sand. [27]The rain fell, and the floods came, and the winds blew and beat against that house, and it fell—and great was its fall!”

[28]Now when Jesus had finished saying these things, the crowds were astounded at his teaching, [29]for he taught them as one having authority, and not as their scribes.

Healing the Blind and Casting out Demons

Here Matthew describes two of the miracles that Jesus is said to have performed: healing two blind men, and curing a mute by casting out a demon.

9 27As Jesus went on from there, two blind men followed him, crying loudly, "Have mercy on us,
Son of David!" 28When he entered the house, the
blind men came to him; and Jesus said to them, "Do
you believe that I am able to do this?" They said to
him, "Yes, Lord." 29Then he touched their eyes and
said, "According to your faith let it be done to you."
30And their eyes were opened. Then Jesus sternly ordered them, "See that no one knows of this." 31But
they went away and spread the news about him
throughout that district.
32After they had gone away, a demoniac who was
mute was brought to him. 33And when the demon had
been cast out, the one who had been mute spoke; and
the crowds were amazed and said, "Never has anything like this been seen in Israel." 34But the Pharisees said, "By the ruler of the demons he casts out
the demons."

Matthew 9:27–34, *New Revised Standard Version*, 1989, in *The New Oxford Annotated Bible* (Oxford: Oxford University Press, 2010).

The Good Samaritan

Many of Jesus' teachings were presented as parables; "The Good Samaritan" is one of the most famous. In it, Jesus explains to a lawyer that the true meaning of "neighbor" is much broader than many think. We have moral obligations not just to our own ethnic group but also to those outside our group. Jesus illustrates the point with a story about a Samaritan who helps a Jew who has been beaten—even though the two groups are adversaries.

10 25Just then a lawyer stood up to test Jesus.
"Teacher," he said, "what must I do to inherit
eternal life?" 26He said to him, "What is written in
the law? What do you read there?" 27He answered,
"You shall love the Lord your God with all your
heart, and with all your soul, and with all your
strength, and with all your mind; and your neighbor
as yourself." 28And he said to him, "You have given
the right answer; do this, and you will live."
29But wanting to justify himself, he asked Jesus,
"And who is my neighbor?" 30Jesus replied, "A man
was going down from Jerusalem to Jericho, and fell
into the hands of robbers, who stripped him, beat
him, and went away, leaving him half dead. 31Now by

Luke 10:25–37, *New Revised Standard Version*, 1989, in *The New Oxford Annotated Bible* (Oxford: Oxford University Press, 2010).

chance a priest was going down that road; and when he saw him, he passed by on the other side. 32So likewise a Levite, when he came to the place and saw him, passed by on the other side. 33But a Samaritan while traveling came near him; and when he saw him, he was moved with pity. 34He went to him and bandaged his wounds, having poured oil and wine on them. Then he put him on his own animal, brought him to an inn, and took care of him. 35The next day he took out two denarii, gave them to the innkeeper, and said, 'Take care of him; and when I come back, I will repay you whatever more you spend.' 36Which of these three, do you think, was a neighbor to the man who fell into the hands of the robbers?" 37He said, "The one who showed him mercy." Jesus said to him, "Go and do likewise."

Arrest, Trial, Crucifixion, and Resurrection

Mark recounts Jesus' final hours, detailing his betrayal by Judas and the other disciples, his hearing before the Jewish counsel, his trial before the Roman governor Pilate, his denial by Peter as prophesied, Pilate satisfying the crowd by ordering Jesus' crucifixion, the crucifixion and burial, the women finding the tomb empty, and the young man declaring that Jesus had arisen and would meet them in Galilee.

14 43Immediately, while he was still speaking, Judas, one of the twelve, arrived; and with him there was a crowd with swords and clubs, from the chief priests, the scribes, and the elders. 44Now the betrayer had given them a sign, saying, "The one I will kiss is the man; arrest him and lead him away under guard." 45So when he came, he went up to him at once and said, "Rabbi!" and kissed him. 46Then they laid hands on him and arrested him. 47But one of those who stood near drew his sword and struck the slave of the high priest, cutting off his ear. 48Then Jesus said to them, "Have you come out with swords and clubs to arrest me as though I were a bandit? 49Day after day I was with you in the temple teaching, and you did not arrest me. But let the scriptures be fulfilled." 50All of them deserted him and fled.

51A certain young man was following him, wearing nothing but a linen cloth. They caught hold of him, 52but he left the linen cloth and ran off naked.

53They took Jesus to the high priest; and all the chief priests, the elders, and the scribes were assembled. 54Peter had followed him at a distance, right into the courtyard of the high priest; and he was sitting with the guards, warming himself at the fire. 55Now the chief priests and the whole council were looking for testimony against Jesus to put him to death; but they found none. 56For many gave false testimony against him, and their testimony did not agree. 57Some stood up and gave false testimony against him, saying, 58"We heard him say, 'I will destroy this temple that is made with hands, and in three days I will build another, not made with hands.'" 59But even on this point their testimony did not agree. 60Then the high priest stood up before them and asked Jesus, "Have you no answer? What is it that they testify against you?" 61But he was silent and did not answer. Again the high priest asked him, "Are you the Messiah, the Son of the Blessed One?"

Mark 14:43–16:8, *New Revised Standard Version*, 1989, in *The New Oxford Annotated Bible* (Oxford: Oxford University Press, 2010).

[62]Jesus said, "I am; and 'you will see the Son of Man seated at the right hand of the Power,' and 'coming with the clouds of heaven.'"

[63]Then the high priest tore his clothes and said, "Why do we still need witnesses? [64]You have heard his blasphemy! What is your decision?" All of them condemned him as deserving death. [65]Some began to spit on him, to blindfold him, and to strike him, saying to him, "Prophesy!" The guards also took him over and beat him.

[66]While Peter was below in the courtyard, one of the servant-girls of the high priest came by. [67]When she saw Peter warming himself, she stared at him and said, "You also were with Jesus, the man from Nazareth." [68]But he denied it, saying, "I do not know or understand what you are talking about." And he went out into the forecourt. Then the cock crowed. [69]And the servant-girl, on seeing him, began again to say to the bystanders, "This man is one of them." [70]But again he denied it. Then after a little while the bystanders again said to Peter, "Certainly you are one of them; for you are a Galilean." [71]But he began to curse, and he swore an oath, "I do not know this man you are talking about." [72]At that moment the cock crowed for the second time. Then Peter remembered that Jesus had said to him, "Before the cock crows twice, you will deny me three times." And he broke down and wept.

15 [1]As soon as it was morning, the chief priests held a consultation with the elders and scribes and the whole council. They bound Jesus, led him away, and handed him over to Pilate. [2]Pilate asked him, "Are you the King of the Jews?" He answered him, "You say so." [3]Then the chief priests accused him of many things. [4]Pilate asked him again, "Have you no answer? See how many charges they bring against you." [5]But Jesus made no further reply, so that Pilate was amazed.

[6]Now at the festival he used to release a prisoner for them, anyone for whom they asked. [7]Now a man called Barabbas was in prison with the rebels who had committed murder during the insurrection. [8]So the crowd came and began to ask Pilate to do for them according to his custom. [9]Then he answered them, "Do you want me to release for you the King of the Jews?" [10]For he realized that it was out of jealousy that the chief priests had handed him over. [11]But the chief priests stirred up the crowd to have him release Barabbas for them instead. [12]Pilate spoke to them again, "Then what do you wish me to do with the man you call the King of the Jews?" [13]They shouted back, "Crucify him!" [14]Pilate asked them, "Why, what evil has he done?" But they shouted all the more, "Crucify him!" [15]So Pilate, wishing to satisfy the crowd, released Barabbas for them; and after flogging Jesus, he handed him over to be crucified.

[16]Then the soldiers led him into the courtyard of the palace (that is, the governor's headquarters); and they called together the whole cohort. [17]And they clothed him in a purple cloak; and after twisting some thorns into a crown, they put it on him. [18]And they began saluting him, "Hail, King of the Jews!" [19]They struck his head with a reed, spat upon him, and knelt down in homage to him. [20]After mocking him, they stripped him of the purple cloak and put his own clothes on him. Then they led him out to crucify him.

[21]They compelled a passer-by, who was coming in from the country, to carry his cross; it was Simon of Cyrene, the father of Alexander and Rufus. [22]Then they brought Jesus to the place called Golgotha (which means the place of a skull). [23]And they offered him wine mixed with myrrh; but he did not take it. [24]And they crucified him, and divided his clothes among them, casting lots to decide what each should take.

[25]It was nine o'clock in the morning when they crucified him. [26]The inscription of the charge against him read, "The King of the Jews." [27]And with him they crucified two bandits, one on his right and one on his left. [29]Those who passed by derided him, shaking their heads and saying, "Aha! You who would destroy the temple and build it in three days, [30]save yourself, and come down from the cross!" [31]In the same way the chief priests, along with the scribes, were also mocking him among themselves and saying, "He saved others; he cannot save himself. [32]Let the Messiah, the King of Israel, come down from the cross now, so that we may see and believe." Those who were crucified with him also taunted him.

[33]When it was noon, darkness came over the whole land until three in the afternoon. [34]At three

o'clock Jesus cried out with a loud voice, "Eloi, Eloi, lema sabachthani?" which means, "My God, my God, why have you forsaken me?" 35When some of the bystanders heard it, they said, "Listen, he is calling for Elijah." 36And someone ran, filled a sponge with sour wine, put it on a stick, and gave it to him to drink, saying, "Wait, let us see whether Elijah will come to take him down." 37Then Jesus gave a loud cry and breathed his last. 38And the curtain of the temple was torn in two, from top to bottom. 39Now when the centurion, who stood facing him, saw that in this way he breathed his last, he said, "Truly this man was God's Son!"

40There were also women looking on from a distance; among them were Mary Magdalene, and Mary the mother of James the younger and of Joses, and Salome. 41These used to follow him and provided for him when he was in Galilee; and there were many other women who had come up with him to Jerusalem.

42When evening had come, and since it was the day of Preparation, that is, the day before the sabbath, 43Joseph of Arimathea, a respected member of the council, who was also himself waiting expectantly for the kingdom of God, went boldly to Pilate and asked for the body of Jesus. 44Then Pilate wondered if he were already dead; and summoning the centurion, he asked him whether he had been dead for some time. 45When he learned from the centurion that he was dead, he granted the body to Joseph. 46Then Joseph bought a linen cloth, and taking down the body, wrapped it in the linen cloth, and laid it in a tomb that had been hewn out of the rock. He then rolled a stone against the door of the tomb. 47Mary Magdalene and Mary the mother of Joses saw where the body was laid.

16 1When the sabbath was over, Mary Magdalene, and Mary the mother of James, and Salome bought spices, so that they might go and anoint him. 2And very early on the first day of the week, when the sun had risen, they went to the tomb. 3They had been saying to one another, "Who will roll away the stone for us from the entrance to the tomb?" 4When they looked up, they saw that the stone, which was very large, had already been rolled back. 5As they entered the tomb, they saw a young man, dressed in a white robe, sitting on the right side; and they were alarmed. 6But he said to them, "Do not be alarmed; you are looking for Jesus of Nazareth, who was crucified. He has been raised; he is not here. Look, there is the place they laid him. 7But go, tell his disciples and Peter that he is going ahead of you to Galilee; there you will see him, just as he told you." 8So they went out and fled from the tomb, for terror and amazement had seized them; and they said nothing to anyone, for they were afraid.

The Women at the Tomb

This is Matthew's account of the visit of the women to the tomb. It differs slightly from Mark's telling. For example, Mark says that the women "went out and fled from the tomb, for terror and amazement had seized them; and they said nothing to anyone, for they were afraid." But Matthew says that the women "left the tomb quickly with fear and great joy, and ran to tell his disciples."

Matthew 28:1–15, *New Revised Standard Version*, 1989, in *The New Oxford Annotated Bible* (Oxford: Oxford University Press, 2010).

28 1After the sabbath, as the first day of the week
was dawning, Mary Magdalene and the other
Mary went to see the tomb. 2And suddenly there was
a great earthquake; for an angel of the Lord, descending from heaven, came and rolled back the stone and
sat on it. 3His appearance was like lightning, and his
clothing white as snow. 4For fear of him the guards
shook and became like dead men. 5But the angel said
to the women, "Do not be afraid; I know that you are
looking for Jesus who was crucified. 6He is not here;
for he has been raised, as he said. Come, see the place
where he lay. 7Then go quickly and tell his disciples,
'He has been raised from the dead, and indeed he is
going ahead of you to Galilee; there you will see
him.' This is my message for you." 8So they left the
tomb quickly with fear and great joy, and ran to tell
his disciples. 9Suddenly Jesus met them and said,
"Greetings!" And they came to him, took hold of his
feet, and worshiped him. 10Then Jesus said to them,
"Do not be afraid; go and tell my brothers to go to
Galilee; there they will see me."

11While they were going, some of the guard went
into the city and told the chief priests everything that
had happened. 12After the priests had assembled with
the elders, they devised a plan to give a large sum of
money to the soldiers, 13telling them, "You must say,
'His disciples came by night and stole him away
while we were asleep.' 14If this comes to the governor's ears, we will satisfy him and keep you out of
trouble." 15So they took the money and did as they
were directed. And this story is still told among the
Jews to this day.

The Word Made Flesh

This passage, a poem, in the book of John is unlike the prefaces to the other gospels. It offers a meditation on the "divine word"—which was present from eternity with God and was God, a divine being who created the universe and provided life and the "light of humanity." It was and is none other than Jesus Christ, who became human, "brimming with generosity and truth."

1 1In the beginning there was the divine word and wisdom.
The divine word and wisdom was there with God,
and it was what God was.
2It was there with God from the beginning.
3Everything came to be by means of it;
and without it not one thing that exists came to be.
4In it was life,
and this life was the light of humanity.
5Light was shining in darkness,
and darkness did not master it.
6There appeared a man sent from God named John.
7He came to testify—to testify about the light—so everyone would believe through him. 8He was not the light; he came only to testify about the light.
9Genuine light—the kind that enlightens everyone—was coming into the world.
10Although it was in the world,
and the world came to be through it,
the world did not recognize it.
11It came to its own place,
but its own people were not receptive to it.

The Gospel of John, 1:1–18, in *The Complete Gospels*, Robert Miller, ed. (Salem, OR: Polebridge, 2010) 209–210.

[12]But to all who did embrace it,
to those who believed in it,
it gave the right to become children of God.
[13]They were born not from blood,
not from physical desire,
nor from male desire;
they were born out of God.
[14]The divine word and wisdom became human
and resided among us.
We have seen its glory,
glory appropriate
to a Father's only son,
brimming with generosity and truth.
[15]John testifies about him and has called out, "This is the one I was talking about when I said, 'The one who's coming after me ranks ahead of me, because he was before I was.'"
[16]From his richness
all of us benefited—
one gift after another.
[17]The Law was given through Moses;
mercy and truth came through Jesus the Anointed One.
[18]No one has ever seen God;
the only son, close to the Father's heart—he has disclosed ⟨him⟩.

The Ascension and Pentecost

The book of Acts recounts the events surrounding the early church after Jesus' death and resurrection. The themes include the spread of the gospel from the Jews to the Gentiles, persecutions by non-Christians, the arrival of the Holy Spirit, amazing feats of the apostles, and the conversion and ministry of the apostle Paul. The following selection from Acts relates the appearances of the resurrected Christ, his ascension into heaven, and the filling of the apostles with the Holy Spirit on the Jewish festival day known as Pentecost.

1 [1]In the first book, Theophilus, I wrote about all
that Jesus did and taught from the beginning
[2]until the day when he was taken up to heaven, after
giving instructions through the Holy Spirit to the
apostles whom he had chosen. [3]After his suffering he
presented himself alive to them by many convincing
proofs, appearing to them during forty days and
speaking about the kingdom of God. [4]While staying
with them, he ordered them not to leave Jerusalem,
but to wait there for the promise of the Father. "This,"
he said, "is what you have heard from me; [5]for John
baptized with water, but you will be baptized with
the Holy Spirit not many days from now."
[6]So when they had come together, they asked him,
"Lord, is this the time when you will restore the
kingdom to Israel?" [7]He replied, "It is not for you to
know the times or periods that the Father has set by
his own authority. [8]But you will receive power when
the Holy Spirit has come upon you; and you will be
my witnesses in Jerusalem, in all Judea and Samaria,
and to the ends of the earth." [9]When he had said this,
as they were watching, he was lifted up, and a cloud

Acts 1:1–14, 2:1–24, 2:40–47, *New Revised Standard Version*, 1989, in *The New Oxford Annotated Bible* (Oxford: Oxford University Press, 2010).

took him out of their sight. 10While he was going and they were gazing up toward heaven, suddenly two men in white robes stood by them. 11They said, "Men of Galilee, why do you stand looking up toward heaven? This Jesus, who has been taken up from you into heaven, will come in the same way as you saw him go into heaven."

12Then they returned to Jerusalem from the mount called Olivet, which is near Jerusalem, a sabbath day's journey away. 13When they had entered the city, they went to the room upstairs where they were staying, Peter, and John, and James, and Andrew, Philip and Thomas, Bartholomew and Matthew, James son of Alphaeus, and Simon the Zealot, and Judas son of James. 14All these were constantly devoting themselves to prayer, together with certain women, including Mary the mother of Jesus, as well as his brothers . . .

2 1When the day of Pentecost had come, they were all together in one place. 2And suddenly from heaven there came a sound like the rush of a violent wind, and it filled the entire house where they were sitting. 3Divided tongues, as of fire, appeared among them, and a tongue rested on each of them. 4All of them were filled with the Holy Spirit and began to speak in other languages, as the Spirit gave them ability.

5Now there were devout Jews from every nation under heaven living in Jerusalem. 6And at this sound the crowd gathered and was bewildered, because each one heard them speaking in the native language of each. 7Amazed and astonished, they asked, "Are not all these who are speaking Galileans? 8And how is it that we hear, each of us, in our own native language? 9Parthians, Medes, Elamites, and residents of Mesopotamia, Judea and Cappadocia, Pontus and Asia, 10Phrygia and Pamphylia, Egypt and the parts of Libya belonging to Cyrene, and visitors from Rome, both Jews and proselytes, 11Cretans and Arabs—in our own languages we hear them speaking about God's deeds of power." 12All were amazed and perplexed, saying to one another, "What does this mean?" 13But others sneered and said, "They are filled with new wine."

14But Peter, standing with the eleven, raised his voice and addressed them, "Men of Judea and all who live in Jerusalem, let this be known to you, and listen to what I say. 15Indeed, these are not drunk, as you suppose, for it is only nine o'clock in the morning. 16No, this is what was spoken through the prophet Joel:

17'In the last days it will be, God declares, that I will pour out my Spirit upon all flesh,
and your sons and your daughters shall prophesy,
and your young men shall see visions, and your old men shall dream dreams.
18Even upon my slaves, both men and women,
in those days I will pour out my Spirit; and they shall prophesy.
19And I will show portents in the heaven above
and signs on the earth below, blood, and fire, and smoky mist.
20The sun shall be turned to darkness and the moon to blood,
before the coming of the Lord's great and glorious day.
21Then everyone who calls on the name of the Lord shall be saved.'

22"You that are Israelites, listen to what I have to say: Jesus of Nazareth, a man attested to you by God with deeds of power, wonders, and signs that God did through him among you, as you yourselves know— 23this man, handed over to you according to the definite plan and foreknowledge of God, you crucified and killed by the hands of those outside the law. 24But God raised him up, having freed him from death, because it was impossible for him to be held in its power. . . . 40And he testified with many other arguments and exhorted them, saying, "Save yourselves from this corrupt generation." 41So those who welcomed his message were baptized, and that day about three thousand persons were added. 42They devoted themselves to the apostles' teaching and fellowship, to the breaking of bread and the prayers.

43Awe came upon everyone, because many wonders and signs were being done by the apostles. 44All who believed were together and had all things in common; 45they would sell their possessions and goods and distribute the proceeds to all, as any had need. 46Day by day, as they spent much time together in the temple, they broke bread at home and ate their food with glad and generous hearts, 47praising God and having the goodwill of all the people. And day by day the Lord added to their number those who were being saved.

Paul: Life After Death

This excerpt contains Paul's attempt to correct some mistaken ideas held by Christians in Corinth. Contrary to some Corinthians at the time, Paul teaches that there is indeed a resurrection of the body. Jesus' resurrection was a resurrection of the body, a glorified spiritual body. Likewise when Christ returns, Christians will experience a bodily resurrection, and the new bodies will be imperishable and glorified—bodies that will live forever in an afterlife.

15 12Now if Christ is proclaimed as raised from the dead, how can some of you say there is no resurrection of the dead? 13If there is no resurrection of the dead, then Christ has not been raised; 14and if Christ has not been raised, then our proclamation has been in vain and your faith has been in vain. 15We are even found to be misrepresenting God, because we testified of God that he raised Christ—whom he did not raise if it is true that the dead are not raised. 16For if the dead are not raised, then Christ has not been raised. 17If Christ has not been raised, your faith is futile and you are still in your sins. 18Then those also who have died in Christ have perished. 19If for this life only we have hoped in Christ, we are of all people most to be pitied.

20But in fact Christ has been raised from the dead, the first fruits of those who have died. 21For since death came through a human being, the resurrection of the dead has also come through a human being; 22for as all die in Adam, so all will be made alive in Christ. 23But each in his own order: Christ the first fruits, then at his coming those who belong to Christ. 24Then comes the end, when he hands over the kingdom to God the Father, after he has destroyed every ruler and every authority and power. 25For he must reign until he has put all his enemies under his feet. 26The last enemy to be destroyed is death. 27For "God has put all things in subjection under his feet." But when it says, "All things are put in subjection," it is plain that this does not include the one who put all things in subjection under him. 28When all things are subjected to him, then the Son himself will also be subjected to the one who put all things in subjection under him, so that God may be all in all. . . . 35But someone will ask, "How are the dead raised? With what kind of body do they come?" 36Fool! What you sow does not come to life unless it dies. 37And as for what you sow, you do not sow the body that is to be, but a bare seed, perhaps of wheat or of some other grain. 38But God gives it a body as he has chosen, and to each kind of seed its own body. 39Not all flesh is alike, but there is one flesh for human beings, another for fish. 40There are both heavenly bodies and earthly bodies but the glory of the heavenly is one thing and that of the earthly is another. 41There is one glory of the sun, and another glory of the moon and another glory of the stars; indeed, star differs from star in glory.

42So it is with the resurrection of the dead. What is sown is perishable, what is raised is imperishable. 43It is sown in dishonor, it is raised in glory. It is sown in weakness, it is raised in power. 44It is sown a physical body, it is raised a spiritual body. If there is a physical body, there is also a spiritual body. 45Thus it is written, "The first man, Adam, became a living being"; the last Adam became a life-giving spirit. 46But it is not the spiritual that is first, but the physical, and then the spiritual. 47The first man was from the earth, a man of dust; the second man is from heaven. 48As was the man of dust, so are those who

1 Corinthians 15:12–28, 35–57, *New Revised Standard Version*, 1989, in *The New Oxford Annotated Bible* (Oxford: Oxford University Press, 2010).

are of the dust; and as is the man of heaven, so are those who are of heaven. [49]Just as we have borne the image of the man of dust, we will also bear the image of the man of heaven.

[50]What I am saying, brothers and sisters, is this: flesh and blood cannot inherit the kingdom of God, nor does the perishable inherit the imperishables. [51]Listen, I will tell you a mystery! We will not all die, but we will all be changed, [52]in a moment, in the twinkling of an eye, at the last trumpet. For the trumpet will sound, and the dead will be raised imperishable, and we will be changed. [53]For this perishable body must put on imperishability, and this mortal body must put on immortality. [54]When this perishable body puts on imperishability, and this mortal body puts on immortality, then the saying that is written will be fulfilled:

"Death has been swallowed up in victory."
[55]Where, O death, is your victory?
Where, O death, is your sting?"

[56]The sting of death is sin, and the power of sin is the law. [57]But thanks be to God, who gives us the victory through our Lord Jesus Christ.

The Gnostic Gospel of Mary

In the early Christian centuries, many Christian movements competed with the prevailing orthodoxy. One of these was known as Gnosticism, or Gnostic Christianity. This version of Christianity differed significantly from orthodox views in several ways. The points of difference include (1) the conspicuous presence of feminine imagery or female personalities, as in the Gospel of Mary (Magdalene) excerpted here, (2) the view that salvation comes not from Christ's atonement but from secret knowledge (gnosis in Greek) grasped by some Gnostic believers, (3) the conception of salvation not as deliverance from sin but the emancipation of the soul from the evil body, and (4) the view that women can possess and share divine wisdom.

1 *(Six manuscript pages are missing.)*

2 [1]". . . Will m[a]tter then be utterly [destr]oyed or not?"

[2]The Savior replied, "Every nature, every modeled form, every creature, exists in and with each other. [3]They will dissolve again into their own proper root. [4]For the nature of matter is dissolved into what belongs to its nature.

[5]"Anyone with two ears able to hear should listen!"

3 [1]Then Peter said to him, "You have been explaining every topic to us; tell us one other thing. [2]What is the sin of the world?"

[3]The Savior replied, "There is no such thing as sin; [4]rather you yourselves are what produces sin when you act in accordance with the nature of adultery, which is called 'sin.' [5]For this reason, the Good came among you, pursuing ⟨the good⟩ which belongs to every nature. [6]It will set it within its root."

[7]Then he continued. He said, "This is why you get si[c]k and die: [8]because [you love] what de[c]ei[ve]s [you. [9]Anyone who] thinks should consider ⟨these matters⟩!

[10]"[Ma]tter gav[e bi]rth to a passion that has no Image because it derives from what is contrary to nature. [11]A disturbing confusion then occurred in the

Gospel of Mary, chs. 1–10 in *The Complete Gospels*, Robert Miller, ed. (Salem, OR: Polebridge, 2010), 337–342.

whole body. [12]That is why I told you, 'Become content at heart, [13]while also remaining discontent; indeed, become contented ⟨only⟩ in the presence of every ⟨true⟩ Image of nature.'

[14]"Anyone with two ears able to hear should listen!"

4 When the Blessed One had said these things, he greeted them all. "Peace be with you!" he said. [2]"Acquire my peace within yourselves!

[3]"Be on your guard [4]so that no one deceives you by saying, 'Look over here' or 'Look over there.' [5]For the Human One exists within you. [6]Follow it. [7]Those who search for it will find it.

[8]"Go then, preac[h] the good news about the kingdom. [9][Do] not lay down any rule beyond what I determined for you, [10]nor promulgate law like the lawgiver, or else you might be dominated by it."

[11]After he said these things, he left them.

5 But they were distressed and wept greatly. [2]"How are we going to go out to the rest of the world to announce the good news about the kingdom of the Human One?" they said. [3]"If they didn't spare him, how will they spare us?"

[4]Then Mary stood up. She greeted them all, addressing her brothers and sisters, [5]"Do not weep and be distressed nor let your hearts be irresolute. [6]For his grace will be with you all and will shelter you. [7]Rather we should praise his greatness, [8]for he has united us and made us ⟨true⟩ human beings."

[9]When Mary said these things, she turned their mind [to]ward the Good, [10]and they began to deba[t]e the wor[d]s of [the Savior].

6 [1]Peter said to Mary, "Sister, we know that the Savior loved you more than all other women. [2]Tell us the words of the Savior that you remember, the things which you know that we don't because we haven't heard them."

[3]Mary responded, "I will report to you [as much as] I remember that you don't know." And she began to speak these words to them.

7 [1]She said, "I saw the Master in a vision [2]and I said to him, 'Master, I saw you today in a vision.'

[3]"He answered me, 'Congratulations to you for not wavering at seeing me! [4]For where the mind is, there is the treasure.'

[5]I said to him, 'So now, Master, does a person who sees a vision see it ⟨with⟩ the soul ⟨or⟩ with the spirit?'

[6]"The Savior answered, 'A person does not see with the soul or with the spirit. [7]Rather the mind, which exists between these two, sees the vision an[d] that is w[hat . . .]

8 *(Four manuscript pages are missing.)*

9 "' . . . it.'

[2]"And Desire said, 'I did not see you go down, yet now I see you go up. [3]So why do you lie since you belong to me?'

[4]"The soul answered, 'I saw you. You did not see me nor did you know me. [5]You ⟨mis⟩took the garment ⟨I wore⟩ for my ⟨true⟩ self. [6]And you did not recognize me.'

[7]"After it had said these things, it left rejoicing greatly.

[8]"Again, it came to the third Power, which is called 'Ignorance.' [9][It] examined the soul closely, saying, 'Where are you going? [10]You are bound by wickedness. [11]Indeed you are bound! [12]Do not judge!'

[13]"And the soul said, 'Why do you judge me, since I have not passed judgment? [14]I have been bound, but I have not bound ⟨anything⟩. [15]They did not recognize me, but I have recognized that the universe is to be dissolved, both the things of earth and those of heaven.'

[16]"When the soul had overcome the third Power, it went upward and saw the fourth Power. [17]It had seven forms. [18]The first form is darkness; [19]the second is desire; [20]the third is ignorance; [21]the fourth is zeal for death; [22]the fifth is the realm of the flesh; [23]the sixth is the foolish wisdom of the flesh; [24]the seventh is the wisdom of the wrathful person. [25]These are the seven Powers of Wrath.

[26]"They interrogated the soul, 'Where are you coming from, human-killer, and where are you going, space-conqueror?'

[27]"The soul replied, saying, 'What binds me has been slain, and what surrounds me has been destroyed, and my desire has been brought to an end, and ignorance has died. [28]In a [wor]ld, I was set loose from a world [an]d in a type, from a type which is above, and ⟨from⟩ the chain of forgetfulness which exists in time.

[29]From this hour on, for the time of the due season of the age, I will receive rest i[n] silence.'"

[30]After Mary said these things, she was silent, [31]since it was up to this point that the Savior had spoken to her.

10 [1]Andrew sai[d, "B]rothers and sisters, what is your opinion of what was just said? [2]I for one do not believe that the S[a]vior said these things, for what she said appears to give views that are [dif] ferent from h[is th]ought."

[3]After examining these ma[tt]ers, ⟨Peter said⟩, "Has the Sa[vior] spoken secretly to a wo[m]an and ⟨not⟩ openly so that [we] would all hear? [4][Surely] he did[n't want to show] that [she] is more worthy than we are?"

Then [M]ary wept and said to Peter, "My brother Peter, what are you imagining? [6]Do you think that I have made all this up by myself or that I am telling lies about the Savior?"

[7]Levi said to Peter, "Peter, you are al[ways] rea[dy] to give in to you[r] perpetual inclination to anger. [8]And even now you're doing exactly that by questioning the woman as if you're her adversary. [9]For if the Savior made her worthy, just who do you think you are to reject her? [10]For he knew her completely (and) loved her stea[df]ast[ly].

[11]"Rath[e]r [we] should be ashamed and, once we have clothed [ou]rselves with the p[erfec]t Human, we should do what [w]e were commanded [12]and announce the good news, [13]and not be la[y]ing down any rules or maki[n]g laws."

[14]After he said [the]se things, Le[vi] le[ft] (and) began to anno[unce the good ne]ws.

[15][The Gos]pel according to Mary.

The Infancy Gospel of Thomas

Many would-be scriptures in Judaism and Christianity are labeled Apocrypha (Greek, "hidden things") because they are associated with the official canon but are not included in it. The Infancy Gospel of Thomas is one such book, as is the Gospel of Mary. The Infancy Gospel recounts legends about Jesus as a child from ages five to twelve. As a young boy he is portrayed as a brilliant, headstrong youngster who sometimes uses his divine powers for harmful and vicious purposes.

1 I, Thomas the Israelite, am reporting to you, all my non-Jewish brothers and sisters, to tell you about the extraordinary childhood of our Lord Jesus Christ—what he did after his birth in my part of the world. This is how it all started.

2 When this boy, Jesus, was five years old, he was playing at the ford of a rushing stream. [2]He was collecting the flowing water into ponds and with a single command he made the water instantly pure. [3]He then made soft clay and shaped it into twelve sparrows. He did this on the Sabbath, and a lot of other boys were playing with him.

[4]But when a Jew saw what Jesus was doing while playing on the Sabbath, he immediately went off and told Joseph, Jesus' father: "See here, your boy is at the ford and has violated the Sabbath by taking mud and making twelve birds with it."

[5]So Joseph went there, and as soon as he spotted him he shouted, "Why are you doing what's not permitted on the Sabbath?"

Infancy Gospel of Thomas, chs. 1–18, in *The Complete Gospels*, Robert Miller, ed. (Salem, OR: Polebridge, 2010), 381–383.

[6]But Jesus simply clapped his hands and shouted to the sparrows, "Go on, fly away, and remember me, you who are now alive!" And the sparrows took off and flew away noisily.

[7]The Jews watched with amazement, then left the scene to report to their leaders what they had seen Jesus doing.

3 The son of Annas the scholar was standing there with Jesus. He took a willow branch and drained the water Jesus had collected. [2]Jesus saw what had happened and got angry and said to him, "Damn you, you ungodly ignoramus! What harm were the ponds of water doing you? From now on you, too, will dry up like a tree, and you'll never produce leaves or roots or bear fruit."

[3]In an instant the boy had completely withered away. Then Jesus departed and left for the house of Joseph. [4]The parents of the boy who had withered away picked him up and were carrying him out, in grief because he was so young. And they came to Joseph and accused him: "It's your fault—your boy did all this."

4 Later on he was going through the village when a boy ran by and bumped him on the shoulder. Jesus got angry and said to him, "Your trip is over!" [2]And all of a sudden he fell down and died.

[3]Some people saw what had happened and said, "Where has this boy come from? Everything he says happens instantly!"

[4]The parents of the dead boy came to Joseph and blamed him, saying, "Teach your boy to bless and not curse, or else you can't live with us in the village. He's killing our children!"

5 So Joseph summoned his child and scolded him in private, "Why are you doing all this? These people hate and harass us because they are suffering."

[2]Jesus said, "I know that the words I spoke are not my own. Still, I'll keep quiet for your sake. But those people must take their punishment." At that very moment his accusers were struck blind.

[3]Those who saw this were very frightened and didn't know what to do. All they could say was, "Every word he says, whether good or bad, turns into a fact—a miracle, even!"

[4]When Joseph saw that Jesus had done such a thing, he got angry and grabbed his ear and pulled very hard. [5]The boy became infuriated with him and replied, "It's one thing for you to seek but not find; it's quite another for you to act this unwisely. [6]Don't you know that I don't really belong to you? Don't get me angry."

6 A teacher by the name of Zacchaeus was listening to everything Jesus was saying to Joseph, and was astonished. He said to himself, "He is just a child, and he's saying this!" [2]And so he summoned Joseph and said to him, "You have a bright child, and he has a good mind. Hand him over to me so he can learn his letters. I'll teach him everything he needs to know so he won't be out of control."

[3]Joseph replied, "No one can control this child except God alone. Don't consider him to be a small cross, brother."

[4]When Jesus heard Joseph saying this he laughed and said to Zacchaeus, "Believe me, teacher, what my father told you is true. [5]I am the Lord of these people and I'm present with you and have been born among you and am with you. [6]I know where you've come from and how long you'll live. Let me tell you, teacher, I existed when you were born. If you wish to be a perfect teacher, listen to me and I'll teach you a wisdom that no one else knows except for me and the One who sent me to you. [7]It's you who happen to be my student. I know how old you are and how long you have to live. [8]When you see the cross that my father mentioned, then you'll believe that everything I've told you is true."

[9]The Jews who were standing by and heard Jesus marveled and said, "How strange and paradoxical! This child is barely five years old and yet he says such things. In fact, we've never heard anyone say the kinds of things this child does."

[10]Jesus said to them in reply, "Are you really so amazed? Think about what I've said to you. The truth is that I also know when you were born, and your parents, and I announce this paradox to you: when the world was created, I existed along with the One who sent me to you."

[11]The Jews, once they heard the child speaking like this, got angry but were unable to say anything back. [12]But the child skipped forward and said to them, "I've made fun of you because I know that your tiny minds marvel at trifles."

[13]When, therefore, they thought that they were being comforted by the child's exhortation, the teacher said to Joseph, "Bring him to the classroom and I'll teach him the alphabet."

[14]Joseph took him by the hand and led him to the classroom. [15]The teacher wrote the alphabet for him and began the instruction by repeating the letter Alpha over and over again. But the child clammed up and did not answer him for a long time. [16]No wonder, then, that the teacher got angry and struck him on the head. The child took the blow calmly and replied to him, "I'm teaching you instead of being taught by you: I already know the letters you're teaching me, and your condemnation is great. To you these letters are like a bronze pitcher or a clashing cymbal, which can't produce glory or wisdom because it's all just noise. [17]No one can understand the extent of my wisdom." [18]When he got over being angry he rapidly recited the letters from Alpha to Omega.

Augustine's Confessions

Augustine's *Confessions* is a much-lauded spiritual autobiography, tracing his thoughts and deeds from his youthful debauchery to the moment of his conversion and beyond. He also wrote *City of God* (a synthesis of Christian and classical philosophy), *On the Trinity* (a commentary on the mysterious doctrine of the unity of three persons in one Godhead), and *On Free Will* (a dialogue about human choice).

Augustine found that in his search for wisdom there was a place for both faith and reason, both belief and understanding. He thought that to attain wisdom, belief had to come first, then understanding. On this point, a verse from the Bible spoke volumes to him: "Unless you believe, you shall not understand." So he came to believe in the Christian God, but he wanted more: he wanted to understand God and how He relates to the world and to him. (Centuries later, Thomas Aquinas and countless other philosopher-theologians would also see faith and reason as partners, not enemies.)

Book II: I will now call to mind my past foulness, and the carnal corruptions of my soul; not because I love them, but that I may love Thee, O my God. For love of Thy love I do it; reviewing my most wicked ways in the very bitterness of my remembrance, that Thou mayest grow sweet unto me (Thou sweetness never failing, Thou blissful and assured sweetness); and gathering me again out of that my dissipation, wherein I was torn piecemeal, while turned from Thee, the One Good, I lost myself among a multiplicity of things. For I even burnt in my youth heretofore, to be satiated in things below; and I dared to grow wild again, with these various and shadowy loves: my beauty consumed away, and I stank in Thine eyes; pleasing myself, and desirous to please in the eyes of men.

And what was it that I delighted in, but to love, and be loved? but I kept not the measure of love, of mind to mind, friendship's bright boundary: but out of the muddy concupiscence of the flesh, and the bubblings of youth, mists fumed up which beclouded and overcast my heart, that I could not discern the

Augustine, *Confessions*, Edward Bouverie Pusey, trans., 1909–1914, sacred-texts.com.

clear brightness of love from the fog of lustfulness. Both did confusedly boil in me, and hurried my unstayed youth over the precipice of unholy desires, and sunk me in a gulf of flagitiousnesses. Thy wrath had gathered over me, and I knew it not. I was grown deaf by the clanking of the chain of my mortality, the punishment of the pride of my soul, and I strayed further from Thee, and Thou lettest me alone, and I was tossed about, and wasted, and dissipated, and I boiled over in my fornications, and Thou heldest Thy peace, O Thou my tardy joy! Thou then heldest Thy peace, and I wandered further and further from Thee, into more and more fruitless seed-plots of sorrows, with a proud dejectedness, and a restless weariness. . . .

Book III: To Carthage I came, where there sang all around me in my ears a cauldron of unholy loves. I loved not yet, yet I loved to love, and out of a deep-seated want, I hated myself for wanting not. I sought what I might love, in love with loving, and safety I hated, and a way without snares. For within me was a famine of that inward food, Thyself, my God; yet, through that famine I was not hungered; but was without all longing for incorruptible sustenance, not because filled therewith, but the more empty, the more I loathed it. For this cause my soul was sickly and full of sores, it miserably cast itself forth, desiring to be scraped by the touch of objects of sense. Yet if these had not a soul, they would not be objects of love. To love then, and to be beloved, was sweet to me; but more, when I obtained to enjoy the person I loved, I defiled, therefore, the spring of friendship with the filth of concupiscence, and I beclouded its brightness with the hell of lustfulness; and thus foul and unseemly, I would fain, through exceeding vanity, be fine and courtly. I fell headlong then into the love wherein I longed to be ensnared. My God, my Mercy, with how much gall didst Thou out of Thy great goodness besprinkle for me that sweetness? For I was both beloved, and secretly arrived at the bond of enjoying; and was with joy fettered with sorrow-bringing bonds, that I might be scourged with the iron burning rods of jealousy, and suspicions, and fears, and angers, and quarrels. . . .

I resolved then to bend my mind to the holy Scriptures, that I might see what they were. But behold, I see a thing not understood by the proud, nor laid open to children, lowly in access, in its recesses lofty, and veiled with mysteries; and I was not such as could enter into it, or stoop my neck to follow its steps. For not as I now speak, did I feel when I turned to those Scriptures; but they seemed to me unworthy to be compared to the stateliness of Tully: for my swelling pride shrunk from their lowliness, nor could my sharp wit pierce the interior thereof. Yet were they such as would grow up in a little one. But I disdained to be a little one; and, swollen with pride, took myself to be a great one.

Therefore I fell among men proudly doting, exceeding carnal and prating, in whose mouths were the snares of the Devil, limed with the mixture of the syllables of Thy name, and of our Lord Jesus Christ, and of the Holy Ghost, the Paraclete, our Comforter. . . .

Book V: And for almost all those nine years, wherein with unsettled mind I had been their disciple, I had longed but too intensely for the coming of this Faustus. For the rest of the sect, whom by chance I had lighted upon, when unable to solve my objections about these things, still held out to me the coming of this Faustus, by conference with whom these and greater difficulties, if I had them, were to be most readily and abundantly cleared. When then he came, I found him a man of pleasing discourse, and who could speak fluently and in better terms, yet still but the self-same things which they were wont to say. But what availed the utmost neatness of the cup-bearer to my thirst for a more precious draught? Mine ears were already cloyed with the like, nor did they seem to me therefore better, because better said; nor therefore true, because eloquent; nor the soul therefore wise, because the face was comely, and the language graceful. But they who held him out to me were no good judges of things; and therefore to them he appeared understanding and wise, because in words pleasing. . . .

For after it was clear that he was ignorant of those arts in which I thought he excelled, I began to despair of his opening and solving the difficulties which perplexed me (of which indeed however ignorant, he might have held the truths of piety, had he not been a Manichee). . . .

To Milan I came, to Ambrose the Bishop, known to the whole world as among the best of men, Thy devout servant; whose eloquent discourse did then plentifully dispense unto Thy people the flour of Thy wheat, the gladness of Thy oil, and the sober inebriation of Thy wine. To him was I unknowing led by Thee, that by him I might knowingly be led to Thee. That man of God received me as a father, and showed me an Episcopal kindness on my coming. Thenceforth I began to love him, at first indeed not as a teacher of the truth (which I utterly despaired of in Thy Church), but as a person kind towards myself. And I listened diligently to him preaching to the people, not with that intent I ought, but, as it were, trying his eloquence, whether it answered the fame thereof, or flowed fuller or lower than was reported; and I hung on his words attentively; but of the matter I was as a careless and scornful looker-on; and I was delighted with the sweetness of his discourse, more recondite, yet in manner less winning and harmonious, than that of Faustus. Of the matter, however, there was no comparison; for the one was wandering amid Manichaean delusions, the other teaching salvation most soundly. But salvation is far from sinners, such as I then stood before him; and yet was I drawing nearer by little and little, and unconsciously. . . .

And while I opened my heart to admit "how eloquently he spake," there also entered "how truly he spake"; but this by degrees. For first, these things also had now begun to appear to me capable of defence; and the Catholic faith, for which I had thought nothing could be said against the Manichees' objections, I now thought might be maintained without shamelessness; especially after I had heard one or two places of the Old Testament resolved, and ofttimes "in a figure," which when I understood literally, I was slain spiritually. Very many places then of those books having been explained, I now blamed my despair, in believing that no answer could be given to such as hated and scoffed at the Law and the Prophets. Yet did I not therefore then see that the Catholic way was to be held, because it also could find learned maintainers, who could at large and with some show of reason answer objections; nor that what I held was therefore to be condemned, because both sides could be maintained. For the Catholic cause seemed to me in such sort not vanquished, as still not as yet to be victorious. . . .

Book VIII: But now, the more ardently I loved those whose healthful affections I heard of, that they had resigned themselves wholly to Thee to be cured, the more did I abhor myself, when compared with them. For many of my years (some twelve) had now run out with me since my nineteenth, when, upon the reading of Cicero's Hortensius, I was stirred to an earnest love of wisdom; and still I was deferring to reject mere earthly felicity, and give myself to search out that, whereof not the finding only, but the very search, was to be preferred to the treasures and kingdoms of the world, though already found, and to the pleasures of the body, though spread around me at my will. But I wretched, most wretched, in the very commencement of my early youth, had begged chastity of Thee, and said, "Give me chastity and continency, only not yet." For I feared lest Thou shouldest hear me soon, and soon cure me of the disease of concupiscence, which I wished to have satisfied, rather than extinguished. And I had wandered through crooked ways in a sacrilegious superstition, not indeed assured thereof, but as preferring it to the others which I did not seek religiously, but opposed maliciously. . . .

The very toys of toys, and vanities of vanities, my ancient mistresses, still held me; they plucked my fleshy garment, and whispered softly, "Dost thou cast us off? and from that moment shall we no more be with thee for ever? and from that moment shall not this or that be lawful for thee for ever?" And what was it which they suggested in that I said, "this or that," what did they suggest, O my God? Let Thy mercy turn it away from the soul of Thy servant. What defilements did they suggest! what shame! And now I much less than half heard them, and not openly showing themselves and contradicting me, but muttering as it were behind my back, and privily plucking me, as I was departing, but to look back on them. Yet they did retard me, so that I hesitated to burst and shake myself free from them, and to spring over whither I was called; a violent habit saying to me, "Thinkest thou, thou canst live without them?". . .

But when a deep consideration had from the secret bottom of my soul drawn together and heaped up all my misery in the sight of my heart; there arose a mighty storm, bringing a mighty shower of tears.

Which that I might pour forth wholly, in its natural expressions, I rose from Alypius: solitude was suggested to me as fitter for the business of weeping; so I retired so far that even his presence could not be a burden to me. Thus was it then with me, and he perceived something of it; for something I suppose I had spoken, wherein the tones of my voice appeared choked with weeping, and so had risen up. He then remained where we were sitting, most extremely astonished. I cast myself down I know not how, under a certain fig-tree, giving full vent to my tears; and the floods of mine eyes gushed out an acceptable sacrifice to Thee. And, not indeed in these words, yet to this purpose, spake I much unto Thee: and Thou, O Lord, how long? how long, Lord, wilt Thou be angry for ever? Remember not our former iniquities, for I felt that I was held by them. I sent up these sorrowful words: How long, how long, "to-morrow, and tomorrow?" Why not now? why not is there this hour an end to my uncleanness?

So was I speaking and weeping in the most bitter contrition of my heart, when, lo! I heard from a neighbouring house a voice, as of boy or girl, I know not, chanting, and oft repeating, "Take up and read; Take up and read." Instantly, my countenance altered, I began to think most intently whether children were wont in any kind of play to sing such words: nor could I remember ever to have heard the like. So checking the torrent of my tears, I arose; interpreting it to be no other than a command from God to open the book, and read the first chapter I should find. For I had heard of Antony, that coming in during the reading of the Gospel, he received the admonition, as if what was being read was spoken to him: Go, sell all that thou hast, and give to the poor, and thou shalt have treasure in heaven, and come and follow me: and by such oracle he was forthwith converted unto Thee. Eagerly then I returned to the place where Alypius was sitting; for there had I laid the volume of the Apostle when I arose thence. I seized, opened, and in silence read that section on which my eyes first fell: Not in rioting and drunkenness, not in chambering and wantonness, not in strife and envying; but put ye on the Lord Jesus Christ, and make not provision for the flesh, in concupiscence. No further would I read; nor needed I: for instantly at the end of this sentence, by a light as it were of serenity infused into my heart, all the darkness of doubt vanished away.

The Five Ways

THOMAS AQUINAS

Aquinas's five arguments have been tremendously influential right up to the present day—if for no other reason than that they have provoked an enormous amount of debate and criticism. For example, many philosophers and theologians have responded to Aquinas's first-cause argument (the second way). Aquinas maintains that everything we can observe has a cause, and it is clear that nothing can cause itself. For something to cause itself, it would have to exist prior to itself, which is impossible. Neither can something be caused by an infinite regress of causes—that is, a series of causes stretching to infinity. In any series of

Thomas Aquinas, *Summa Theologica*, Laurence Shapcote, trans. (London: O. P. Benziger Brothers, 1911).

causes, Aquinas says, there must be a first cause, which causes the second, which causes the third, and so on. But in an infinite series of causes, there would be no first cause and thus no subsequent causes, including causes existing now. So infinite regresses make no sense. Therefore, there must be a first cause of everything, and this first cause we call God.

Critics reply that just because an infinite chain of causes has no first cause, that doesn't mean that the chain of causes has no cause at all: in an infinite chain of causes, every link has a cause. Many philosophers see no logical contradiction in the idea of an infinite regress. They hold that the universe need not have had a beginning; it may be eternal, without beginning, and without a first cause or a first mover. The universe may have simply *always been.*

[Aquinas first identifies two objections to the thesis that God exists.]

OBJECTION 1. It seems that God does not exist, because if one of two contraries be infinite, the other would be altogether destroyed. But the name *God* means that He is infinite goodness. If, therefore, God existed, there would be no evil discoverable; but there is evil in the world. Therefore God does not exist.

OBJECTION 2. Further, it is superfluous to suppose that what can be accounted for by a few principles has been produced by many. But it seems that everything we see in the world can be accounted for by other principles, supposing God did not exist. For all natural things can be reduced to one principle, which is nature; and all voluntary things can be reduced to one principle, which is human reason, or will. Therefore there is no need to suppose God's existence.

On the Contrary, It is said in the person of God: *I am Who I am* (Ex. iii.14).

I answer that, The existence of God can be proved in five ways.

THE FIRST WAY: THE ARGUMENT FROM CHANGE

The first and clearest [way] is taken from the idea of motion. (1) Now it is certain, and our senses corroborate it, that some things in this world are in motion. (2) But everything which is in motion is moved by something else. (3) For nothing is in motion except insofar as it is potentiality in relation to that towards which it is in motion. (4) Now a thing causes movement in so far as it is in actuality. For to cause movement is nothing else than to bring something from potentiality to actuality; but a thing cannot be brought from potentiality to actuality except by something which exists in actuality, as, for example, that which is hot in actuality, like fire, makes wood, which is only hot in potentiality, to be hot in actuality, and thereby causes movement in it and alters it. (5) But it is not possible that the same thing should be at the same time in actuality and potentiality in relation to the same thing, but only in relation to different things; for what is hot in actuality cannot at the same time be hot in potentiality, though it is at the same time cold in potentiality. (6) It is impossible, therefore, that in relation to the same thing and in the same way anything should both cause movement and be caused, or that it should cause itself to move. (7) Everything therefore that is in motion must be moved by something else. If therefore the thing which causes it to move be in motion, this too must be moved by something else, and so on. (8) But we cannot proceed to infinity in this way, because in that cause there would be no first mover, and in consequence, neither would there be any other mover, for secondary movers do not cause movement except they be moved by a first mover, as, for example, a stick cannot cause movement unless it is moved by the hand. Therefore it is necessary to stop at some first mover which is moved by nothing else. And this is what we all understand God to be.

THE SECOND WAY: THE ARGUMENT FROM CAUSATION

The Second Way is taken from the idea of the Efficient Cause. (1) For we find that there is among material things a regular order of efficient causes. (2) But we do not find, nor indeed is it possible, that anything is the efficient cause of itself, for in that case it would be prior to itself, which is impossible. (3) Now it is not possible to proceed to infinity in efficient causes. (4) For if we arrange in order all efficient causes, the first is the cause of the intermediate, and the intermediate the cause of the last, whether the intermediate be many or only one. (5) But if we remove a cause the effect is removed; therefore, if there is no first among efficient causes, neither will there be a last or an intermediate. (6) But if we proceed to infinity in efficient causes there will be no first efficient cause, and thus there will be no ultimate effect, nor any intermediate efficient causes, which is clearly false. Therefore it is necessary to suppose the existence of some first efficient cause, and this men call God.

THE THIRD WAY: THE ARGUMENT FROM CONTINGENCY

The Third Way rests on the idea of the "contingent" and the "necessary" and is as follows: (1) Now we find that there are certain things in the Universe which are capable of existing and of not existing, for we find that some things are brought into existence and then destroyed, and consequently are capable of being or not being. (2) But it is impossible for all things which exist to be of this kind, because anything which is capable of not existing, at some time or other does not exist. (3) If therefore *all* things are capable of not existing, there was a time when nothing existed in the Universe. (4) But if this is true there would also be nothing in existence now; because anything that does not exist cannot begin to exist except by the agency of something which has existence. If therefore there was once nothing which existed, it would have been impossible for anything to begin to exist, and so nothing would exist now. (5) This is clearly false. Therefore all things are not contingent, and there must be something which is necessary in the Universe. (6) But everything which is necessary either has or has not the cause of its necessity from an outside source. Now it is not possible to proceed to infinity in necessary things which have a cause of their necessity, as has been proved in the case of efficient causes. Therefore it is necessary to suppose the existence of something which is necessary in itself, not having the cause of its necessity from any outside source, but which is the cause of necessity in others. And this "something" we call God.

THE FOURTH WAY: THE ARGUMENT FROM DEGREES OF EXCELLENCE

The Fourth Way is taken from the degrees which are found in things. (1) For among different things we find that one is more or less good or true or noble; and likewise in the case of other things of this kind. (2) But the words "more" or "less" are used of different things in proportion as they approximate in their different ways to something which has the particular quality in the highest degree—e.g., we call a thing hotter when it approximates more nearly to that which is hot in the highest degree. There is therefore something which is true in the highest degree, good in the highest degree and noble in the highest degree; (3) and consequently there must be also something which has being in the highest degree. For things which are true in the highest degree also have being in the highest degree (see Aristotle, *Metaphysics*, 2). (4) But anything which has a certain quality of any kind in the highest degree is also the cause of all the things of that kind, as, for example, fire which is hot in the highest degree is the cause of all hot things (as is said in the same book). (5) Therefore there exists something which is the cause of being, and goodness, and of every perfection in all existing things; and this we call God.

THE FIFTH WAY: THE ARGUMENT FROM HARMONY

The Fifth Way is taken from the way in which nature is governed. (1) For we observe that certain things which lack knowledge, such as natural bodies, work for an End. This is obvious, because they always, or at any rate very frequently, operate in the same way so as to attain the best possible result. (2) Hence it is clear that they do not arrive at their goal by chance, but by purpose. (3) But those things which have no knowledge do not move towards a goal unless they are guided by someone or something which does possess knowledge and intelligence—e.g., an arrow by an archer. Therefore, there does exist something which possesses intelligence by which all natural things are directed to their goal; and this we call God.

Reply Obj. 1. As Augustine says: *Since God is the highest good, He would not allow any evil to exist in His works, unless His omnipotence and goodness were such as to bring good even out of evil.* This is part of the infinite goodness of God, that He should allow evil to exist, and out of it produce good.

Reply Obj. 2. Since nature works for a determinate end under the direction of a higher agent, whatever is done by nature must be traced back to God as to its first cause. So likewise whatever is done voluntarily must be traced back to some higher cause other than human reason and will, since these can change and fail; for all things that are changeable and capable of defect must be traced back to an immovable and self-necessary first principle, as has been shown.

Orthodox Christianity

ERNST BENZ

Ernst Benz (1907–1978) was a German theologian and perhaps the most respected Western writer on the Eastern Orthodox Church. Here he examines the Eastern Church's most distinctive features and contrasts them with those of Western traditions.

[a] BASIC MYSTICISM. The theology of the Eastern Church has quite another complexion. The differences may not be too precisely defined, since to do so would involve us in a series of generalities to which there will be numerous exceptions. We may, however, say that the striking feature of Eastern Christianity is its lack of those very features that depend on a conception of religion as a legal relationship. Instead, the mystical aspect of the New Testament message comes far more strongly to the fore. Both Pauline and Johannine mysticism are given equal weight. There is little emphasis upon justification. Instead, the major

Ernst Benz, *The Eastern Orthodox Church* (New Brunswick, NJ: Aldine Transaction, 2009), 48–53.

themes of the Orthodox faith are the apotheosis, sanctification, rebirth, re-creation, resurrection and transfiguration of man; and not only man, but also the whole universe—for the Eastern Church has a characteristically cosmic approach. The central theme is not God's justice but his love. For this reason the total development of religious life both within the Church and within the consciousness of each individual believer has taken a course radically different from that of the Western Church.

This matter is particularly striking when we consider the sacrament of penance. In the Eastern Church, penance is not associated with the idea of justification but with the idea of the Christian's education to a life of sanctity. Penance was never conceived of in legal terms, with the result that the sacrament never became corrupted. No doctrine or practice of indulgences ever arose. Since penance was always viewed as a road to sanctity rather than as an act of compensation, there could be no thought of substituting money payments for performance of acts of atonement.

Similarly, in the absence of a judicial conception, the Western doctrine of purgatory and of posthumous salvation by acts of the Church could not spread through the Eastern Orthodox Church. The Eastern Church never pretended that its powers to bind and loosen extended to the realm of the dead. The Eastern Church considered that its only power to affect the dead lay in intercessory prayer. Underlying this was the premise that the union between believers and the Body of Christ of which they are a part is not destroyed by death. This union continues to exist within the Church. This mystical communion in the Body of Christ makes possible a continuation of intercession and of vicarious suffering. Under these circumstances the institution of the Mass for the Dead also retained its purity and escaped the degeneration that took place in the West.

[*b*] THE MYSTICAL INTERPRETATION OF THE CHURCH. The Orthodox view of the nature of the Church is likewise not based upon any legalistic system. To be sure, a legal element does enter into its conception of ecclesiastical office, above all of the office of the bishop and of apostolic succession. But the legalistic idea is nowhere dominant; it is simply embedded in the view of the Church as the Mystical Body of Christ, and of the Holy Spirit as the continuous stream of life within the Church. There was no room in the Eastern faith for the idea of a Church-state, or for a bishop's exceeding his spiritual prerogatives and intervening in secular affairs. Consequently, the Eastern Church remained unaffected by the rise of the feudalistic state. Conditions that were characteristic of the Christian Middle Ages in the West, where bishops turned into the feudal lords of their dioceses, the dioceses themselves becoming territories and the bishops neglecting the spiritual side of their offices in favor of their political duties and their recreations as members of the feudal aristocracy, were totally unknown in the East. The bishops of the Eastern Orthodox Church have always remained first and foremost ecclesiastical officials. Many Orthodox bishops, it is true, felt it necessary to oppose godless princes, to admonish them in the name of Christ, and to call upon them to do penance. But these bishops never felt that their spiritual powers entitled them to claim secular dominion, or to treat secular rulers as feudal vassals of the Church.

The legalistic principle is likewise absent from the way the ordinary Orthodox priest regards the nature of his priesthood. Nowhere in the Orthodox liturgy does the priest allude to his rightful title. Instead he repeatedly expresses his own sinfulness and unworthiness, emphasizing that he is no less a sinner than his parishioners. It is significant that in the Orthodox sacrament of penance the formula of absolution is not framed in declaratory terms. Instead of the Roman priest's "*Ego te absolvo*," the Orthodox priest says after confession: "My spiritual child, you have now confessed to my lowliness. I, miserable sinner, do not have the power to absolve a sin upon earth; only God can do that. But for the sake of those divine words which were spoken to the apostles after His resurrection, and which were: 'If you forgive the sins of any, they are forgiven; if you retain the sins of any, they are retained,' for the sake of those words and trusting in them, we say this: 'What you have confessed to my extreme lowliness, and also those things which you did not say, either from ignorance or from forgetfulness, whatever they are: may God forgive you for them in this world and the next.'"

In the matter of sanctity, the Eastern Church venerates the saints as spiritually gifted persons who have succeeded in living on earth the "angelic" life of the celestial Church. But their achievements are nowhere booked to the accounts of the Church as "supererogatory works," nor has the Church ever claimed a legal right from God to invest this "capital."

[*c*] APOTHEOSIS. The great theme of Orthodox theology has remained the incarnation of God and the apotheosis of man. Always the emphasis has been upon rebirth, the re-creation of man, his reshaping into a new creature, his being resurrected along with Christ and rising with Christ to God. Fulfillment of man's being and his transfiguration by grace are all-important to the Orthodox theologian. It is no wonder that the doctrine of justification has been given short shrift in Orthodox dogmatics. The most famous exposition of Orthodox dogma, that of John of Damascus (c. 700–50), does not even mention the idea of justification. So the Orthodox Church was never prompted to assert that the necessity for God's incarnation arose logically out of the doctrine of satisfaction: the very groundwork for such a doctrine was lacking. Not until Protestant ideas penetrated the East during the sixteenth and seventeenth centuries were the Orthodox theologians compelled to take a position on the doctrine of justification. The result was a "pseudomorphosis" of the whole of Orthodox theology. That is to say, a violent wrench was given to the entire theology.

The basic Orthodox attitude is again reflected in the conception of sin. Whereas the Western mind defines sin as a violation of the divinely established legal relationship between God and man, the Eastern mind—influenced by Greek philosophy—defines it as a diminution of essence, a loss of substance, a wound or infection of the original image of God, the which man is and ought to be. Redemption, therefore, is not primarily the restitution of a legal relationship that has been upset by sin. Rather, it is fulfillment, renewal, transfiguration, perfection, deification of man's being.

[d] THE PRIMACY OF LOVE. We have already said that the idea of love rather than of justice dominates Eastern religiosity. A characteristic instance of this is St. John Chrysostom's catechetic sermon on the parable of the toilers in the vineyard (Matt. 20:1–16). In the Eastern Church this sermon is to this day read from all pulpits. It is a triumphal hymn of the victory of love. Awareness of the overflowing fullness of divine love drives away all thought of any schemes of reckoning and satisfaction. Divine grace is bestowed as generously upon those who are called in the eleventh hour as upon those who were called in the eighth and ninth hours. "Ye who are first and ye who are last, receive your reward. Rich and poor, rejoice together. Ye who are dutiful and ye who are neglectful, honor the day. Ye who have fasted and ye who have not fasted, today is the day of your rejoicing. The table is laden; let all partake! The calf is fattened; let none depart hungry. All may partake in the feast of faith. All may partake of the wealth of goodness. Let none complain of poverty, for the kingdom for all is come. Let none mourn transgressions, for forgiveness has risen radiant from the grave. Let none fear death, for the Savior's death has freed us from death."

Such a pattern clearly excludes the doctrine of predestination. From the beginning, the Eastern Church secretly inclined toward the theory of universal salvation. Origen (c. 254) had developed this idea in his theory of eons. The Judgment at the end of our eon will not be the ultimate judgment, will not forever set apart the saved and the damned. It will only assign men their place in a new age of the universe (eon) in which everyone will have a fresh chance to ascend to glory. At the end of all eons everything evil will have been winnowed out; the fallen angels and even Satan himself will turn back to the divine Logos. The Church officially disavowed this doctrine; nevertheless a hankering for it persisted within Eastern Orthodox religious thought, and Eastern theologians have repeatedly revived it.

The legalistic temper of Western Christianity has, characteristically, enlarged upon the idea of eternal damnation to a point quite alien to the Orthodox Church. Both Thomas Aquinas and Calvin in describing the bliss of the saved, suggest that one of the pleasures of heaven will consist in looking down upon the torments of the eternally damned, for do not these torments glorify divine justice? Such attitudes, following as they do from the legalistic thinking of the West, are not to be found in the work of Eastern religious thinkers. Similarly the Eastern Church has never thought of Judgment Day in the strictly juristic terms customary in the West. It does not haggle over anyone's right to salvation or insist upon an individual's achievements or the achievements of the Church's saints and martyrs. There is only confidence in grace and in the "love of man—*philanthropia*," which is an attribute of the divine Logos. Confidence and, in addition, prayer for divine mercy.

For all these reasons the Orthodox Church could scarcely comprehend the theological principles of the Occidental Reformation, springing as these did from the need felt in the West for a religious approach based on a new interpretation of the doctrine of justification. The Reformers, of course, were attacking specific Roman Catholic doctrines and customs that Orthodoxy too had always rejected and fought—for example, papal primacy and the celibacy of the clergy. Here the Eastern Church was in full sympathy. But the central issue of justification interested only a few Orthodox theologians who had been educated in the West, such as Cyril Lukaris. These tried to insert the problem into Orthodox theology, but the grafted shoot soon withered.

In spite of this it would be wrong to view Eastern Orthodox and Western Christianity as absolutely antithetical to each other. A study of the liturgy and dogma of the East will reveal tendencies toward a legalistic view of the Church. The West, especially Roman Catholicism, can certainly claim its share of mystics. In fact, the history of the Western churches has been characterized by repeated renascences of mysticism. Recently, Roman Catholic theologians have given a great spur to the study of Orthodox liturgy and mysticism through exemplary editions and translations. Differences are more in the nature of nuances whereby the common tradition is given this or that alternate emphasis.

The Apostles' Creed

The Apostles' Creed, like many other declarations of faith developed over the centuries, tries to distinguish acceptable doctrines from unacceptable. In this case the unacceptable views were Gnosticism's contention that salvation comes only by way of secret knowledge, that God did not create the world, and that Jesus did not actually suffer and die for the sins of humankind.

I BELIEVE in God the Father Almighty, Maker of heaven and earth:

And in Jesus Christ his only Son our Lord: Who was conceived by the Holy Ghost, Born of the Virgin Mary: Suffered under Pontius Pilate, Was crucified, dead, and buried: He descended into hell, The third day he rose again from the dead: He ascended into heaven, And sitteth on the right hand of God the Father Almighty: From thence he shall come to judge the quick and the dead.

I believe in the Holy Ghost: The holy Catholic Church; The Communion of Saints: The Forgiveness of sins: The Resurrection of the body: And the Life everlasting. Amen.

The Apostles' Creed, in *The Book of Common Prayer* (London: Bagster, 1885).

The Nicene Creed

The Nicene Creed was the first church statement of faith to clearly state the doctrine of the Trinity. (The date of its origin is in dispute, but it was certainly in circulation by the fifth century.) Both Eastern and Western churches now use it.

I believe in one God, the Father Almighty, Maker of heaven and earth, and of all things visible and invisible.

And in one Lord Jesus Christ, the only-begotten Son of God, begotten of the Father before all worlds; God of God, Light of Light, very God of very God; begotten, not made, being of one substance with the Father, by whom all things were made.

Who, for us men for our salvation, came down from heaven, and was incarnate by the Holy Spirit of the virgin Mary, and was made man; and was crucified also for us under Pontius Pilate; He suffered and was buried; and the third day He rose again, according to the Scriptures; and ascended into heaven, and sits on the right hand of the Father; and He shall come again, with glory, to judge the quick and the dead; whose kingdom shall have no end.

And I believe in the Holy Ghost, the Lord and Giver of Life; who proceeds from the Father *and the Son*; who with the Father *and the Son* together is worshipped and glorified; who spoke by the prophets.

And I believe in one holy catholic and apostolic Church. I acknowledge one baptism for the remission of sins; and I look for the resurrection of the dead, and the life of the world to come. Amen.

The Nicene Creed, sacred-texts.com

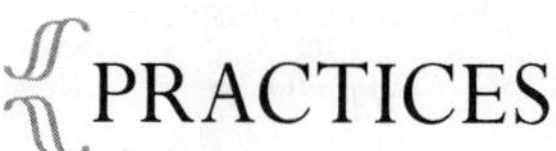

PRACTICES

Prayer and Fasting

Here are Jesus' instructions on prayer and fasting, including his famous example of a sincere and humble petition to God, "The Lord's Prayer." Several times he admonishes against verbose prayer, flamboyant fasting, and devotions designed merely to get attention.

Matthew 6:1–8, *New Revised Standard Version*, 1989, in *The New Oxford Annotated Bible* (Oxford: Oxford University Press, 2010).

6 1“Beware of practicing your piety before others in order to be seen by them; for then you have no reward from your Father in heaven.

2“So whenever you give alms, do not sound a trumpet before you, as the hypocrites do in the synagogues and in the streets, so that they may be praised by others. Truly I tell you, they have received their reward. 3But when you give alms, do not let your left hand know what your right hand is doing, 4so that your alms may be done in secret; and your Father who sees in secret will reward you.

5“And whenever you pray, do not be like the hypocrites; for they love to stand and pray in the synagogues and at the street corners, so that they may be seen by others. Truly I tell you, they have received their reward. 6But whenever you pray, go into your room and shut the door and pray to your Father who is in secret; and your Father who sees in secret will reward you.

7“When you are praying, do not heap up empty phrases as the Gentiles do; for they think that they will be heard because of their many words. 8Do not be like them, for your Father knows what you need before you ask him. . . .

9“Pray then in this way:
Our Father in heaven,
hallowed be your name.
10Your kingdom come.
Your will be done,
on earth as it is in heaven.
11Give us this day our daily bread.
12And forgive us our debts,
as we also have forgiven our debtors.
13And do not bring us to the time of trial,
but rescue us from the evil one.

14For if you forgive others their trespasses, your heavenly Father will also forgive you; 15but if you do not forgive others, neither will your Father forgive your trespasses.

16“And whenever you fast, do not look dismal, like the hypocrites, for they disfigure their faces so as to show others that they are fasting. Truly I tell you, they have received their reward. 17But when you fast, put oil on your head and wash your face, 18so that your fasting may be seen not by others but by your Father who is in secret; and your Father who sees in secret will reward you.

The Eucharist

This passage recounts the last meal (called the “Last Supper”) that Jesus shared with his disciples during the Jewish feast of Passover before his arrest and crucifixion. The Gospels of Matthew, Mark, and Luke (the Synoptic Gospels) say he used the bread and wine of the meals to symbolize his body and blood, which he offered up to atone for the sins of humanity. This symbolic gesture is commemorated in the Christian sacrament (rite) known as the Eucharist.

14 1It was two days before the Passover and the festival of Unleavened Bread. The chief priests and the scribes were looking for a way to arrest Jesus by stealth and kill him; 2for they said, “Not during the festival, or there may be a riot among the people.”

Mark 14:1–25, *New Revised Standard Version*, 1989, in *The New Oxford Annotated Bible* (Oxford: Oxford University Press, 2010).

[3]While he was at Bethany in the house of Simon the leper, as he sat at the table, a woman came with an alabaster jar of very costly ointment of nard, and she broke open the jar and poured the ointment on his head. [4]But some were there who said to one another in anger, "Why was the ointment wasted in this way? [5]For this ointment could have been sold for more than three hundred denarii, and the money given to the poor." And they scolded her. [6]But Jesus said, "Let her alone; why do you trouble her? She has performed a good service for me. [7]For you always have the poor with you, and you can show kindness to them whenever you wish; but you will not always have me. [8]She has done what she could; she has anointed my body beforehand for its burial. [9]Truly I tell you, wherever the good news is proclaimed in the whole world, what she has done will be told in remembrance of her."

[10]Then Judas Iscariot, who was one of the twelve, went to the chief priests in order to betray him to them. [11]When they heard it, they were greatly pleased, and promised to give him money. So he began to look for an opportunity to betray him.

[12]On the first day of Unleavened Bread, when the Passover lamb is sacrificed, his disciples said to him, "Where do you want us to go and make the preparations for you to eat the Passover?" [13]So he sent two of his disciples, saying to them, "Go into the city, and a man carrying a jar of water will meet you; follow him, [14]and wherever he enters, say to the owner of the house, 'The Teacher asks, Where is my guest room where I may eat the Passover with my disciples?' [15]He will show you a large room upstairs, furnished and ready. Make preparations for us there." [16]So the disciples set out and went to the city, and found everything as he had told them; and they prepared the Passover meal.

[17]When it was evening, he came with the twelve. [18]And when they had taken their places and were eating, Jesus said, "Truly I tell you, one of you will betray me, one who is eating with me." [19]They began to be distressed and to say to him one after another, "Surely, not I?" [20]He said to them, "It is one of the twelve, one who is dipping bread into the bowl with me. [21]For the Son of Man goes as it is written of him, but woe to that one by whom the Son of Man is betrayed! It would have been better for that one not to have been born."

[22]While they were eating, he took a loaf of bread, and after blessing it he broke it, gave it to them, and said, "Take; this is my body." [23]Then he took a cup, and after giving thanks he gave it to them, and all of them drank from it. [24]He said to them, "This is my blood of the covenant, which is poured out for many. [25]Truly I tell you, I will never again drink of the fruit of the vine until that day when I drink it new in the kingdom of God."

Baptism

In Matthew Jesus commands his disciples to win disciples throughout the world and baptize them in the name of the Trinity (Father, Son, and Holy Spirit). Thus he institutes the rite of baptism, which all Christians observe. Baptism has been interpreted by different denominations as "affusion" (pouring water over the head), "immersion" (submerging the whole body in water), or "aspersion" (sprinkling water over the head). What function baptism performs is also variable. It has been interpreted as washing away sins, symbolizing dying to sin and beginning a new devout life, and being admitted to the Christian community.

Matthew 28:16–20, *New Revised Standard Version*, 1989, in *The New Oxford Annotated Bible* (Oxford: Oxford University Press, 2010).

28 16 Now the eleven disciples went to Galilee, to the mountain to which Jesus had directed them. 17 When they saw him, they worshiped him; but some doubted. 18 And Jesus came and said to them, "All authority in heaven and on earth has been given to me. 19 Go therefore and make disciples of all nations, baptizing them in the name of the Father and of the Son and of the Holy Spirit, 20 and teaching them to obey everything that I have commanded you. And remember, I am with you always, to the end of the age."

Anointing the Sick

Pouring oil on persons represents the raising of their spiritual standing in God's eyes. The practice in Christianity of "anointing the sick" goes back to this passage in James. It is believed to be a method of healing, but it has also been added to the rites of baptism and ordination.

5 13 Are any among you suffering? They should pray. Are any cheerful? They should sing songs of praise. 14 Are any among you sick? They should call for the elders of the church and have them pray over them, anointing them with oil in the name of the Lord. 15 The prayer of faith will save the sick, and the Lord will raise them up; and anyone who has committed sins will be forgiven. 16 Therefore confess your sins to one another, and pray for one another, so that you may be healed. The prayer of the righteous is powerful and effective. 17 Elijah was a human being like us, and he prayed fervently that it might not rain, and for three years and six months it did not rain on the earth. 18 Then he prayed again, and the heavens gave rain and the earth yielded its harvest.

James 5:13–18, *New Revised Standard Version*, 1989, in *The New Oxford Annotated Bible* (Oxford: Oxford University Press, 2010).

The Didache: Teaching of the Apostles

The *Didache* (Greek, "teaching") is an early Christian handbook of instruction in various practices and beliefs: charity, prayer, baptism, fasting, the Eucharist, morality, the coming of Christ, and the proper way to welcome itinerant apostles, prophets, and other Christians.

The Didache: The Teaching of the Apostles, Charles H. Hoole, trans., 1894, sacred-texts.com.

I. There are two paths, one of life and one of death, and the difference is great between the two paths.

Now the path of life is this—first, thou shalt love the God who made thee, thy neighbour as thyself, and all things that thou wouldest not should be done unto thee, do not thou unto another. And the doctrine of these maxims is as follows. Bless them that curse you, and pray for your enemies. Fast on behalf of those that persecute you; for what thanks is there if ye love them that love you? do not even the Gentiles do the same. But do ye love them that hate you, and ye will not have an enemy. Abstain from fleshly and worldly lusts. If any one give thee a blow on thy right cheek, turn unto him the other also, and thou shalt be perfect; if any one compel thee to go a mile, go with him two; if a man take away thy cloak, give him thy coat also; if a man take from thee what is thine, ask not for it again, for neither art thou able to do so. Give to every one that asketh of thee, and ask not again, for the Father wishes that from his own gifts there should be given to all. Blessed is he who giveth according to the commandment, for he is free from guilt; but woe unto him that receiveth. For if a man receive being in need, he shall be free from guilt; but he who receiveth when not in need, shall pay a penalty as to why he received and for what purpose; and when he is in tribulation he shall be examined concerning the things that he has done, and shall not depart thence until he has paid the last farthing. For of a truth it has been said on these matters, Let thy almsgiving abide in thy hands until thou knowest to whom thou hast given. . . . .

III. My child, fly from everything that is evil, and from everything that is like to it. Be not wrathful, for wrath leadeth unto slaughter; be not jealous, or contentious, or quarrelsome, for from all these things slaughter ensues. My child, be not lustful, for lust leadeth unto fornication; be not a filthy talker; be not a lifter up of the eye, for from all these things come adulteries. My child, be not an observer of omens, since it leadeth to idolatry, nor a user of spells, nor an astrologer, nor a travelling purifier, nor wish to see these things, for from all these things idolatry ariseth. My child, be not a liar, for lying leadeth unto theft; be not covetous or conceited, for from all these things thefts arise. My child, be not a murmurer, since it leadeth unto blasphemy; be not self-willed or evil-minded, for from all these things blasphemies are produced; but be thou meek, for the meek shall inherit the earth; be thou long-suffering, and compassionate, and harmless, and peaceable, and good, and fearing alway the words that thou hast heard. Thou shalt not exalt thyself, neither shalt thou put boldness into thy soul. Thy soul shall not be joined unto the lofty, but thou shalt walk with the just and humble. Accept the things that happen to thee as good, knowing that without God nothing happens.

IV. My child, thou shalt remember both night and day him that speaketh unto thee the Word of God; thou shalt honour him as thou dost the Lord, for where the teaching of the Lord is given, there is the Lord; thou shalt seek out day by day the favour of the saints, that thou mayest rest in their words; thou shalt not desire schism, but shalt set at peace them that contend; thou shalt judge righteously; thou shalt not accept the person of any one to convict him of transgression; thou shalt not doubt whether a thing shall be or not. Be not a stretcher out of thy hand to receive, and a drawer of it back in giving. If thou hast, give by means of thy hands a redemption for thy sins. Thou shalt not doubt to give, neither shalt thou murmur when giving; for thou shouldest know who is the fair recompenser of the reward. Thou shalt not turn away from him that is in need, but shalt share with thy brother in all things, and shalt not say that things are thine own; for if ye are partners in what is immortal, how much more in what is mortal? Thou shalt not remove thine heart from thy son or from thy daughter, but from their youth shalt teach them the fear of God. Thou shalt not command with bitterness thy servant or thy handmaid, who hope in the same God as thyself, lest they fear not in consequence the God who is over both; for he cometh not to call with respect of persons, but those whom the Spirit hath prepared. And do ye servants submit yourselves to your masters with reverence and fear, as being the type of God. Thou shalt hate all hypocrisy and everything that is not pleasing to God; thou shalt not abandon the commandments of the Lord, but shalt guard that which thou hast received, neither adding thereto nor taking therefrom; thou shalt confess thy transgressions in the church, and shalt not come unto prayer with an evil conscience. This is the path of life. . . .

VII. But concerning baptism, thus baptize ye: having first recited all these precepts, baptize in the name of the Father, and of the Son, and of the Holy Spirit, in running water; but if thou hast not running water, baptize in some other water, and if thou canst not baptize in cold, in warm water; but if thou hast neither, pour water three times on the head, in the name of the Father, and of the Son, and of the Holy Spirit. But before the baptism, let him who baptizeth and he who is baptized fast previously, and any others who may be able. And thou shalt command him who is baptized to fast one or two days before.

VIII. But as for your fasts, let them not be with the hypocrites, for they fast on the second and fifth days of the week, but do ye fast on the fourth and sixth days. Neither pray ye as the hypocrites, but as the Lord hath commanded in his Gospel so pray ye: Our Father in heaven, hallowed be thy name. Thy kingdom come. Thy will be done as in heaven so on earth. Give us this day our daily bread. And forgive us our debt, as we also forgive our debtors. And lead us not into temptation, but deliver us from the evil: for thine is the power, and the glory, for ever. Thrice a day pray ye in this fashion.

IX. But concerning the Eucharist, after this fashion give ye thanks. First, concerning the cup. We thank thee, our Father, for the holy vine, David thy Son, which thou hast made known unto us through Jesus Christ thy Son; to thee be the glory for ever. And concerning the broken bread. We thank thee, our Father, for the life and knowledge which thou hast made known unto us through Jesus thy Son; to thee be the glory for ever. As this broken bread was once scattered on the mountains, and after it had been brought together became one, so may thy Church be gathered together from the ends of the earth unto thy kingdom; for thine is the glory, and the power, through Jesus Christ, for ever. And let none eat or drink of your Eucharist but such as have been baptized into the name of the Lord, for of a truth the Lord hath said concerning this, Give not that which is holy unto dogs.

X. But after it has been completed, so pray ye. We thank thee, holy Father, for thy holy name, which thou hast caused to dwell in our hearts, and for the knowledge and faith and immortality which thou hast made known unto us through Jesus thy Son; to thee be the glory for ever. Thou, Almighty Master, didst create all things for the sake of thy name, and hast given both meat and drink for men to enjoy, that we might give thanks unto thee, but to us thou hast given spiritual meat and drink, and life everlasting, through thy Son. Above all, we thank thee that thou art able to save; to thee be the glory for ever. Remember, Lord, thy Church, to redeem it from every evil, and to perfect it in thy love, and gather it together from the four winds, even that which has been sanctified for thy kingdom which thou hast prepared for it; for thine is the kingdom and the glory for ever. Let grace come, and let this world pass away. Hosanna to the Son of David. If any one is holy, let him come (to the Eucharist); if any one is not, let him repent. Maranatha. Amen. But charge the prophets to give thanks, so far as they are willing to do so. . . .

XIV. But on the Lord's day, after that ye have assembled together, break bread and give thanks, having in addition confessed your sins, that your sacrifice may be pure. But let not any one who hath a quarrel with his companion join with you, until they be reconciled, that your sacrifice may not be polluted, for it is that which is spoken of by the Lord. In every place and time offer unto me a pure sacrifice, for I am a great King, saith the Lord, and my name is wonderful among the Gentiles.

XV. Elect, therefore, for yourselves bishops and deacons worthy of the Lord, men who are meek and not covetous, and true and approved, for they perform for you the service of prophets and teachers. Do not, therefore, despise them, for they are those who are honoured among you, together with the prophets and teachers. Rebuke one another, not in wrath, but peaceably, as ye have commandment in the Gospel; and, but let no one speak to any one who walketh disorderly with regard to his neighbour, neither let him be heard by you until he repent. But your prayers and your almsgivings and all your deeds so do, as ye have commandment in the Gospel of our Lord.

Watch concerning your life; let not your lamps be quenched or your loins be loosed, but be ye ready, for ye know not the hour at which our Lord cometh. But be ye gathered together frequently, seeking what is suitable for your souls; for the whole time of your faith shall profit you not, unless ye be found perfect in the last time. For in the last days false prophets and seducers shall be multiplied, and the sheep shall be turned into wolves, and love shall be turned into hate; and because iniquity aboundeth they shall hate each other, and persecute each other, and deliver each other up; and then shall the Deceiver of the world appear as the Son of God, and shall do signs and wonders, and the earth shall be delivered into his hands; and he shall do unlawful things, such as have never happened since the beginning of the world. Then shall the creation of man come to the fiery trial of proof, and many shall be offended and shall perish; but they who remain in their faith shall be saved by the rock of offence itself. And then shall appear the signs of the truth; first the sign of the appearance in heaven, then the sign of the sound of the trumpet; and thirdly, the resurrection of the dead—not of all, but as it has been said, The Lord shall come and all his saints with him; then shall the world behold the Lord coming on the clouds of heaven.

The Prayer of Union

ST. TERESA OF AVILA

Teresa of Avila (1515–1582) was a Spanish Carmelite nun and mystic, one of the most beloved religious figures in Christianity. She founded the convent of St. Joseph at Avila and wrote several books, including *Way of Perfection*, an autobiography, and *The Interior Castle*, an excerpt from which follows. She reported having many visions and rapturous experiences, and she wrote *The Interior Castle* to explain her vision of a crystal castle made of seven rooms, or "mansions." For her, the castle symbolized the soul, and the mansions represented levels of the soul's spiritual development.

You will suppose that all there is to be seen in this Mansion has been described already, but there is much more to come yet, for, as I said, some receive more and some less. With regard to the nature of union, I do not think I can say anything further; but when the soul to which God grants these favours prepares itself for them, there are many things to be said concerning what the Lord works in it. Some of these I shall say now, and I shall describe that soul's state. In order the better to explain this, I will make use of a comparison which is suitable for the purpose; and which will also show us how, although this work is performed by the Lord, and we can do nothing to make His Majesty grant us this favour, we can do a great deal to prepare ourselves for it.

You will have heard of the wonderful way in which silk is made—a way which no one could invent but God—and how it comes from a kind of

St. Teresa of Avila, "5th Mansions," ch. II in *The Interior Castle* (Mineola, NY: Dover, 1946, 2007), 70–72.

seed which looks like tiny peppercorns (I have never seen this, but only heard of it, so if it is incorrect in any way the fault is not mine). When the warm weather comes, and the mulberry-trees begin to show leaf, this seed starts to take life; until it has this sustenance, on which it feeds, it is as dead. The silk-worms feed on the mulberry-leaves until they are full-grown, when people put down twigs, upon which, with their tiny mouths, they start spinning silk, making themselves very tight little cocoons, in which they bury themselves. Then, finally, the worm, which was large and ugly, comes right out of the cocoon a beautiful white butterfly.

Now if no one had ever seen this, and we were only told about it as a story of past ages, who would believe it? And what arguments could we find to support the belief that a thing as devoid of reason as a worm or a bee could be diligent enough to work so industriously for our advantage, and that in such an enterprise the poor little worm would lose its life? This alone, sisters, even if I tell you no more, is sufficient for a brief meditation, for it will enable you to reflect upon the wonders and the wisdom of our God. What, then, would it be if we knew the properties of everything? It will be a great help to us if we occupy ourselves in thinking of these wonderful things and rejoice in being the brides of so wise and powerful a King.

But to return to what I was saying. The silkworm is like the soul which takes life when, through the heat which comes from the Holy Spirit, it begins to utilize the general help which God gives to us all, and to make use of the remedies which He left in His Church—such as frequent confessions, good books and sermons, for these are the remedies for a soul dead in negligences and sins and frequently plunged into temptation. The soul begins to live and nourishes itself on this food, and on good meditations, until it is full grown—and this is what concerns me now: the rest is of little importance.

When it is full-grown, then, as I wrote at the beginning, it starts to spin its silk and to build the house in which it is to die. This house may be understood here to mean Christ. I think I read or heard somewhere that our life is hid in Christ, or in God (for that is the same thing), or that our life is Christ. (The exact form of this is little to my purpose.)

Here, then, daughters, you see what we can do, with God's favour. May His Majesty Himself be our Mansion as He is in this Prayer of Union which, as it were, we ourselves spin. When I say He will be our Mansion, and we can construct it for ourselves and hide ourselves in it, I seem to be suggesting that we can subtract from God, or add to Him. But of course we cannot possibly do that! We can neither subtract from, nor add to, God, but we can subtract from, and add to, ourselves, just as these little silkworms do. And, before we have finished doing all that we can in that respect, God will take this tiny achievement of ours, which is nothing at all, unite it with His greatness and give it such worth that its reward will be the Lord Himself. And as it is He Whom it has cost the most, so His Majesty will unite our small trials with the great trials which He suffered, and make both of them into one.

On, then, my daughters! Let us hasten to perform this task and spin this cocoon. Let us renounce our self-love and self-will, and our attachment to earthly things. Let us practise penance, prayer, mortification, obedience, and all the other good works that you know of. Let us do what we have been taught: and we have been instructed about what our duty is. Let the silkworm die—let it die, as in fact it does when it has completed the work which it was created to do. Then we shall see God and shall ourselves be as completely hidden in His greatness as is this little worm in its cocoon. Note that, when I speak of seeing God, I am referring to the way in which, as I have said, He allows Himself to be apprehended in this kind of union.

And now let us see what becomes of this silkworm, for all that I have been saying about it is leading up to this. When it is in this state of prayer, and quite dead to the world, it comes out a little white butterfly. Oh, greatness of God, that a soul should come out like this after being hidden in the greatness of God, and closely united with Him, for so short a time—never, I think, for as long as half an hour! I tell you truly, the very soul does not know itself. For think of the difference between an ugly worm and a white butterfly; it is just the same here. The soul cannot think how it can have merited such a blessing—whence such a blessing could have come to it, I meant to say, for it knows quite well that it has not merited it at all. It finds itself so anxious to praise the Lord that it would gladly be consumed and die a thousand deaths for His sake. Then it finds itself longing to suffer great trials and unable to do otherwise. It has the most vehement desires for penance, for solitude, and for all to know God. And hence, when it sees God being offended, it becomes greatly distressed. In the following Mansion we shall treat of these things further and in detail, for, although the experiences of this Mansion and of the next are almost identical, their effects come to have much greater power; for, as I have said, if after God comes to a soul here on earth it strives to progress still more, it will experience great things.

CONTEMPORARY CHALLENGES

Women in the New Testament

The traditional Christian perspective on women is ambivalent, favoring both respect for women and subordination to men. These attitudes derive from New Testament teachings. The following passage from Corinthians reminds the church that man was not created for woman, but woman was created for man. The verses from Timothy make a similar point: "I permit no woman to teach or to have authority over a man; she is to keep silent."

1 CORINTHIANS

11 [2]I commend you because you remember me in
everything and maintain the traditions just as I
handed them on to you. [3]But I want you to understand
that Christ is the head of every man, and the husband
is the head of his wife, and God is the head of Christ.
[4]Any man who prays or prophesies with something
on his head disgraces his head, [5]but any woman who
prays or prophesies with her head unveiled disgraces
her head—it is one and the same thing as having her
head shaved. [6]For if a woman will not veil herself,
then she should cut off her hair; but if it is disgraceful
for a woman to have her hair cut off or to be shaved,
she should wear a veil. [7]For a man ought not to have
his head veiled, since he is the image and reflection
of God; but woman is the reflection of man. [8]Indeed,
man was not made from woman, but woman from
man. [9]Neither was man created for the sake of
woman, but woman for the sake of man. [10]For this
reason a woman ought to have a symbol of authority
on her head, because of the angels. [11]Nevertheless, in
the Lord woman is not independent of man or man
independent of woman. [12]For just as woman came
from man, so man comes through woman; but all
things come from God. [13]Judge for yourselves: is it
proper for a woman to pray to God with her head

1 Corinthians 11:2–16, 1 Timothy 2:8–15, *New Revised Standard Version*, 1989, in *The New Oxford Annotated Bible* (Oxford: Oxford University Press, 2010).

unveiled? [14]Does not nature itself teach you that if a
man wears long hair, it is degrading to him, [15]but if a
woman has long hair, it is her glory? For her hair is
given to her for a covering. [16]But if anyone is disposed to be contentious—we have no such custom,
nor do the churches of God. . . .

1 TIMOTHY

2 [8]I desire, then, that in every place the men should
pray, lifting up holy hands without anger or
argument; [9]also that the women should dress themselves modestly and decently in suitable clothing, not
with their hair braided, or with gold, pearls, or expensive clothes, [10]but with good works, as is proper
for women who profess reverence for God. [11]Let a
woman learn in silence with full submission. [12]I
permit no woman to teach or to have authority over a
man; she is to keep silent. [13]For Adam was formed
first, then Eve; [14]and Adam was not deceived, but the
woman was deceived and became a transgressor.
[15]Yet she will be saved through childbearing, provided they continue in faith and love and holiness,
with modesty.

Women and Christianity

LINDA WOODHEAD

Linda Woodhead, a respected scholar of Christian studies, addresses the thorny problem of gender equality in the Christian world. She concludes that "the shift towards gender equality in modern Western societies poses a serious threat to traditional Christian imagery, teaching, and organization."

Christianity can no longer take male domination for granted, for the societies in which it is situated have been changing—particularly in the West. Of the several unprecedented changes that took place in advanced industrial societies in the last quarter of the 20th century, the move towards gender equality has been one of the most significant. Whilst genuine equality remains an elusive ideal, as an ideal at least it is now widely accepted. A recent survey of cultural values worldwide indicates that such acceptance is now the single most important cultural item separating affluent Western societies from less economically developed countries in the rest of the world. The difference can be traced back not only to cultural and educational differences, but to the much greater scarcity of resources outside the West. Where money and jobs are in short supply, men have always been more likely to try to preserve a monopoly than when they have nothing to lose by allowing women (relatively) free access to the labour market.

Of the many threats that Christianity has to face in modern times, gender equality is one of the most

Linda Woodhead, *Christianity: A Very Short Introduction* (Oxford: Oxford University Press, 2004), 140–141, 143–145.

serious, though perhaps the most underestimated by the churches. The more radical feminists had Christianity in their sights from the start. When Elizabeth Cady Stanton (1815–1902) set out to liberate women from their traditional shackles, for example, one of her first projects was a *Woman's Bible* in which the passages used by men to keep women in subjection were highlighted and critiqued. Although some early campaigners for female emancipation belonged to the churches, and though some church-related movements helped nurture women's entrance onto the public stage, the campaigners who embraced the feminist cause most wholeheartedly nearly always made a break from Church and Biblical Christianity (Mystical Christianity sometimes proved more compatible with feminism).

The rift between Christianity and feminism was exacerbated not so much by the churches' opposition to the cause, but by their general indifference. Even churches that supported the emancipation of slaves, the amelioration of the condition of the industrial working class, and the civil rights movement of the 1960s often failed to give similar support to the cause of women's liberation. So far as their own institutional life was concerned, a few of the more liberal Biblical and Mystical churches supported women's ministry as early as the late 19th century, but Church Christianity and conservative Biblical Christianity opposed the ordination of women with vigour. The Roman Catholic and Orthodox churches still refuse even to discuss the possibility of women's ordination.

An obvious consequence of the churches' continuing failure to support gender equality—in practice if not in theory—is the alienation of women and men sympathetic to the ideal. This is not to say that huge numbers of women leave the churches in a conscious act of protest, but that one of the reasons that each successive generation since the 1960s has been less likely to attend than the one before may be that many women and men are no longer in sympathy with the churches' implicit or explicit messages about gender roles. Women who refuse to submit to male authority may struggle with a religion that has male clergy, a male God, and a male saviour; and women who want a career on equal terms with men may be alienated by churches that privilege women's domestic roles. They may abandon Christianity altogether, try to reform it, or find themselves attracted to the new holistic forms of spirituality that tend to be run by women for women and which offer direct benefit in terms of personal empowerment.

But this cannot be the whole story, for despite women's defection from the churches (the single most important direct cause of congregational decline), they continue to attend in larger numbers than men. For some, it would seem, the traditional attractions of Christianity remain, not least its ability to affirm women's domestic roles and offer support to family life. Large numbers of women continue to enjoy the satisfactions of an intense relationship with Jesus Christ. Others, particularly in some of the more liberal and mystical forms of Christianity, are experimenting with new forms of spirituality that require less by way of female submission. Some women have been admitted to positions of authority in the church, and a handful have even become bishops.

In the southern hemisphere the story is different again, for here the number of women in the churches is growing rather than declining, and women play a significant rule in Christianity's recent growth. Although a traditional message about male headship is more common than in the West, masculine authority is tempered in Charismatic Christianity by the presence of the Holy Spirit. Not only can the Spirit be represented in feminine terms as gentle, flowing, loving, and nurturing, it also offers direct empowerment to all who admit it into their lives, irrespective of their sex. Far from remaining external, commanding, and forbidding, God as Spirit enters into the most intimate relationship with the believer, empowering from within. Rather than imposing its will from above, the Spirit works through individual lives, bodies, and personalities, conferring authority as it does so. Lest the empowered overreach themselves, however, the Spirit is checked by the Word. That which is contrary to scripture—and thus to male headship—may be condemned as the work of evil spirits rather than the Spirit of God. Given lack of support for gender equality in many of the poorer countries of the world, this message supports a wider social consensus.

The success of Christianity across the centuries may lie, in part, in the delicate balance it has managed to maintain between male and female interests. While supporting the former, it has also made significant concessions to the latter. While affirming masculine domination, it has tempered and qualified it by emphasizing the importance of the gentler, more loving, more feminine virtues. While presenting a rhetoric of egalitarianism, it has ensured that male privilege has been firmly embedded in its own life. In this way it has been able to uphold patriarchal arrangements, whilst subjecting them to critique and control. Equally, it has managed to affirm women and appeal to them, without encouraging them to rebel against their masters. By appealing to greater numbers of women than to men, but in retaining and supporting male control, it may have achieved the best possible outcome in the male-dominated societies of which it has been an integral part.

The shift towards gender equality in modern Western societies poses a serious threat to traditional Christian imagery, teaching, and organization. For men, Christianity's role in reinforcing masculine domination becomes less relevant, whilst for women its usefulness as a way of gaining access to male power and subverting it from within becomes less important. As women as well as men come to place greater authority on the value of their own unique subjective-lives, they become more resistant to the ready-made roles into which the church would have them fit—however highly exalted. Outside the West, however, where full gender equality wins far less support, Christianity's delicate balancing act continues to prove effective. One might say that Christianity is most successful as a 'woman's religion' when it finds itself in a 'man's world'—a world it helps to reinforce, whilst ameliorating its excesses.

STUDY QUESTIONS

1. Recount the story of Jesus that historians have been able to piece together.
2. What are some of the issues that divided the early Christians?
3. What is the *Great Schism*?
4. What is *scholasticism*? The *Trinity*?
5. What is the Protestant Reformation and what are some of the major changes in Christianity that followed from it? What were some of the charges that reformers made against the Catholic Church?
6. What are the *Synoptic Gospels*?
7. How is the *New Testament* organized?
8. What is an epistle? What is an *apocalypse*?
9. How does the Gospel of John portray Jesus?
10. Who wrote the Synoptic Gospels?

SUGGESTED READING

John Bowker, ed., *The Oxford Dictionary of World Religions* (Oxford: Oxford University Press, 1997).

Tim Dowley and David Wright, *Introduction to the History of Christianity* (Minneapolis: Fortress Press, 1995).

Bart D. Ehrman, *A Brief Introduction to the New Testament* (New York: Oxford University Press, 2009).

Bart D. Ehrman, *Lost Christianities: The Battle for Scripture and the Faiths We Never Knew* (New York: Oxford University Press, 2003).

Clyde L. Manschreck, ed., *A History of Christianity*, vol. 2 (Upper Saddle River, NJ: Prentice Hall, 1964).

George Marsden, *Understanding Fundamentalism and Evangelicalism* (Grand Rapids, MI: William B. Eerdmans, 1991).

John McManners, ed., *The Oxford Illustrated History of Christianity* (Oxford: Oxford University Press, 1990).

The New Oxford Annotated Bible: New Revised Standard Version, With the Apocrypha, Michael D. Coogan, ed. (Oxford: Oxford University Press, 2010).

Ray C. Petry, ed., *A History of Christianity*, vol. 1 (Upper Saddle River, NJ: Prentice Hall, 1962).

St. Teresa of Avila, *The Interior Castle*, E. Allison Peers, trans. and ed. (New York: Dover, 1946).

Linda Woodhead, *Christianity: A Very Short Introduction* (Oxford: Oxford University Press, 2004).

ONLINE

BBC, "Christianity," http://www.bbc.co.uk/religion/religions/christianity/ (December 25, 2015).

Catholic Online, http://www.catholic.org/ (December 25, 2015).

Frontline: PBS, "The Diversity of Early Christianity," http://www.pbs.org/wgbh/pages/frontline/shows/religion/first/diversity.html (December 25, 2015).

Orthodox Church in America, https://oca.org/orthodoxy (December 25, 2015).

USA Today, "You've Heard of Evangelicals, But Who Are They?" http://usatoday30.usatoday.com/news/religion/story/2012-02-14/who-are-evangelicals/53095520/1 (December 25, 2015).

13 Islam

As a centuries-old global religion, Islam is multifaceted enough to be misunderstood, appealing enough to claim millions of devotees, and influential enough on the world stage to have both defenders and critics. It is the world's second largest religion (after Christianity), with 1.6 billion Muslims on six continents—almost a quarter of the planet's inhabitants. Most Muslims live not in the Middle East but in the Asia-Pacific region, which is home to nearly a billion adherents. In the Middle East/North Africa region, Muslims number over 300 million, but they constitute 93 percent of the region's population. The country with the largest Muslim population is Indonesia (approximately 209 million, or 87 percent of the population). Nearly 3.5 million Muslims live in North America, and many more live in Europe (43.5 million).[1]

The foundation of Islam is belief in one God, **Allah** (the same God revered by Jews and Christians), and in **Muhammad**, God's final prophet. As Islam's fundamental statement of faith says, "There is no God but Allah, and Muhammad is his messenger." Muslims are expected to live their lives so they become living witnesses to this creed. They affirm that Muhammad is the last in a long line of prophets, including Adam, Abraham, Moses, and Jesus—all figures in the Hebrew Bible and the New Testament. (Thus Muslims respectfully call Jews and Christians "the people of the book.") Muslims say that these prophets received revelations from God that became scripture but that the capstone of all these divine messages is God's revelation to Muhammad—Allah's final word to humankind preserved in the Muslim holy scriptures, the **Quran** (or Koran). Muslims believe in heaven, hell, angels, resurrection, God's guidance, and a final Day of Judgment. They hold that their ultimate fate after death depends on their submitting to the will of Allah in their earthly lives.

BEGINNINGS

Islam emerged in the Arabian peninsula in the seventh century CE. Zoroastrianism, Judaism, and Christianity were already well established in the Middle East, and knowledge of these traditions had spread to the Arabian city of Mecca, the birthplace of Muhammad. Monotheism was thus familiar to many, but the social and religious environment also included polytheism, idol worship, longstanding tribal values, and ideas brought by commercial traders.

According to tradition, Muhammad was born in 570 CE into the Arab tribe of the Quraysh. His father died before he was born, and his mother died when he was six years old, so he was

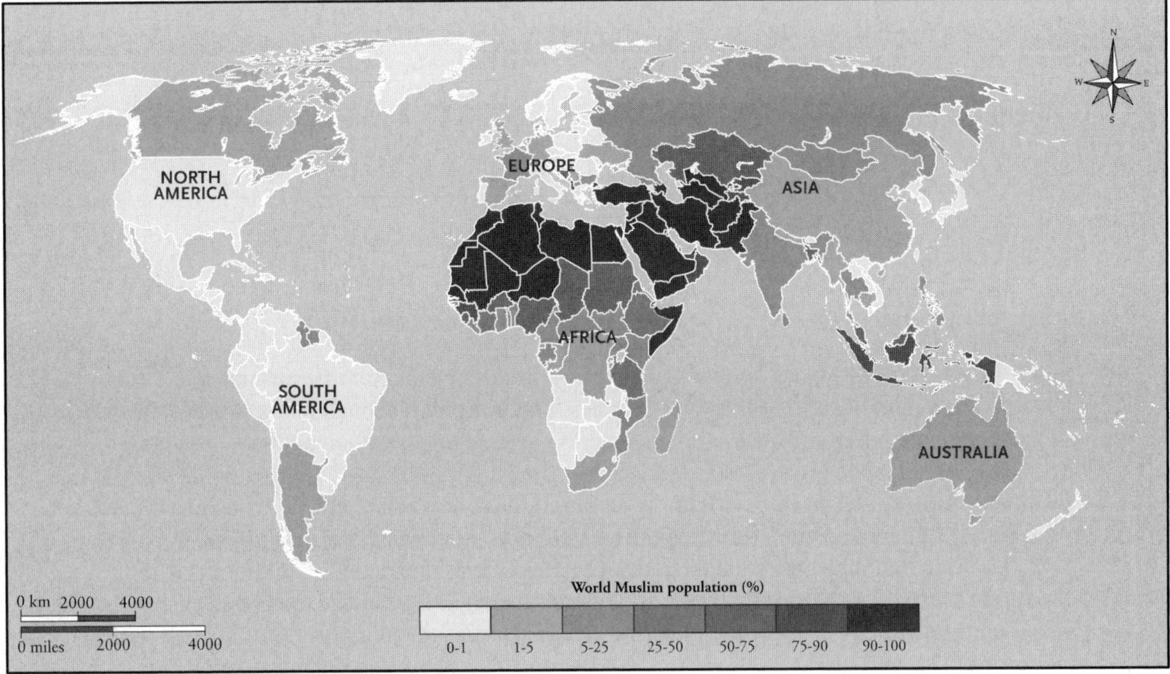

MAP 13.1 World Muslim population.

raised by his grandfather and uncle. It is said that when he was a young man he married the wealthy widow Khadija, who bore him several children. After she died, he is supposed to have taken several other wives.

Muslims believe that at age forty Muhammad retreated to a cave near Mecca to pray and meditate on the one true God. While he was praying, the angel Gabriel came to him and said, "O Muhammad, I am Gabriel, and you are the messenger of God." Gabriel commanded him to recite some sacred words:

> Read! In the name of your Lord who created: He created man from a clinging form [clot or early stage of an embryo]. Read! Your Lord is the Most Bountiful One who taught by [means of] the pen, who taught man what he did not know.[2]

But Muhammad was afraid and was reluctant to do as he was told because he was illiterate. Eventually he repeated the words dictated to him. This was Muhammad's first revelation from God, and the repeated words turned out to be the first revealed passages of the Quran, the first of many other verses that would be disclosed to him in several revelations over the next twenty-three years.

Muslims maintain that they are the spiritual heirs of Abraham, just as Christians and Jews are. Mohammad is not thought to have started a new religion but to have preached the old monotheistic faith of Abraham and the other biblical prophets—a faith that Christians and Jews had betrayed, straying from God's original message. Mohammad's mission, then, was to point people back to the true path.

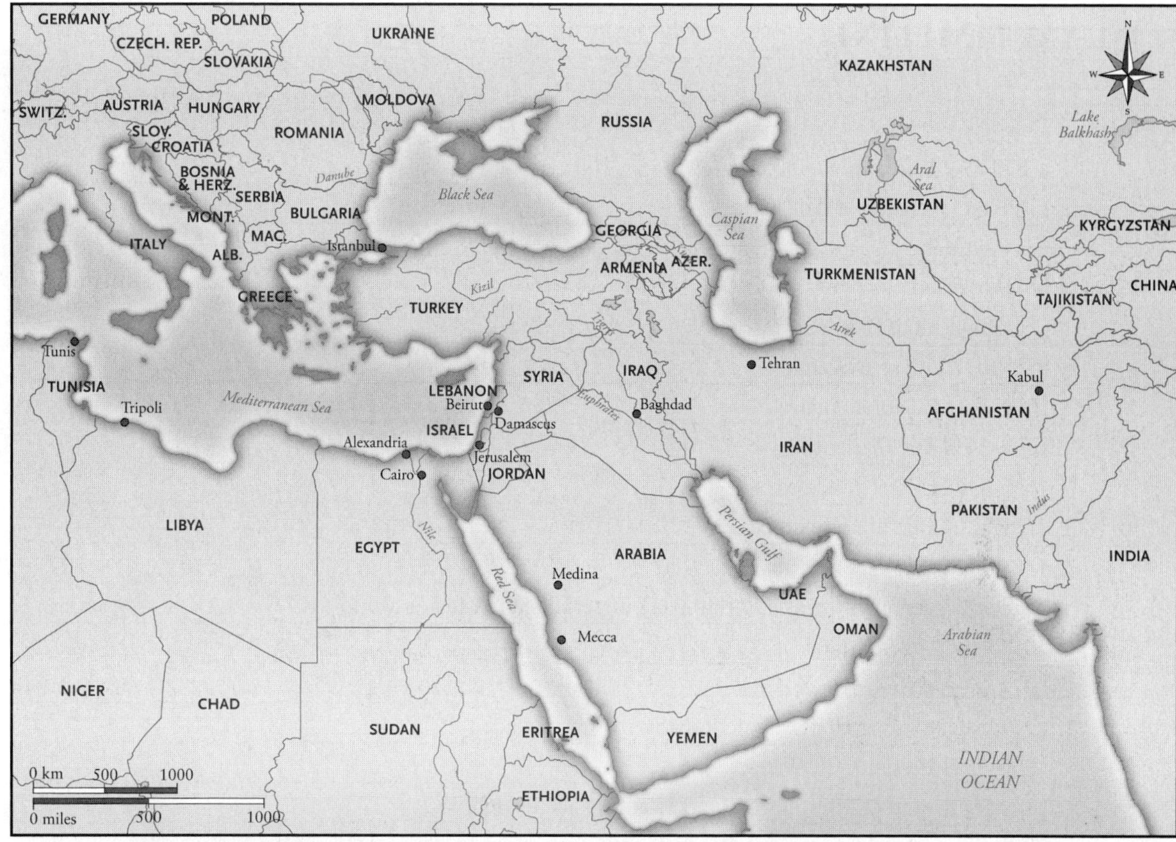

MAP 13.2 Significant sites in the history of Islam.

According to the traditional account, after Muhammad received additional revelations, he began to preach his message to the Meccans, many of whom rejected it as contrary to the prevailing polytheism. But many also became his followers—and thus were soon the objects of persecution at the hands of the nonbelievers. In 622, to escape the torments in Mecca, Muhammad and the Muslims moved north to Yathrib (later known as Medina) in a famous migration referred to as the *Hijra*. (The year 622 eventually became Year One in the Muslim calendar.) There Muhammad established a thriving Muslim community where he became not only its spiritual leader but also its political and social head.

Even after the *Hijra*, violent conflicts between the Muslims and the Meccans did not end. In 624 a band of Muslims defeated a whole army of Meccans in the battle of Badr, but the following year in the battle of Uhud, the Meccans prevailed. In 630 Muhammad marched on Mecca and forced it to surrender. He then destroyed the city's idols.

Muslims quickly became the dominant political and religious power throughout most of Arabia. The majority of the non-Muslim tribes on the Peninsula submitted to Muslim rule; some pagans willingly accepted Islam, but the others were told they must submit or be subject to second-class status or death. In less than a hundred years after the death of Muhammad in 632, his Muslim empire extended from southern Europe to the Middle East to Asia.

ISLAM TIMELINE

CE

c. 570–632 Life of Muhammad

610 First revelation of the Quran

633 Abu Bakr collects Quran into one volume.

661 Ali killed

786–809 Life of Harun al-Rashid

980–1037 Life of Avicenna

1058–1111 Life of al-Ghazali

1095–1453 The Crusades

1126–1198 Life of Averroes

1135–1204 Life of Maimonides

1281–1924 Ottoman Empire

Nineteenth century Advance of European imperialism in Muslim world

1967 Arab-Israeli War

1973 Second Arab-Israeli War

1979 Iranian Revolution; Islamic Republic of Iran founded

1990–1991 Persian Gulf War

1994 Jewish settler kills 29 worshippers at Mosque in Hebron.

2001, September 11 Attacks on World Trade Center by al-Qaeda and Osama bin Laden

2001 Pakistan becomes first Muslim nuclear power.

When Muhammad died, Muslims divided over who should succeed him—that is, who should be the **caliph**, a leader who, like Muhammad, has religious, political, and military authority. (The state governed by the caliph is called a **caliphate**.) Some insisted that succession should be hereditary and that Muhammad's cousin and son-in-law 'Ali should be the new leader (because Muhammad had no surviving sons). But many more followers thought the Muslim community as a whole should select a successor. This disagreement led to the fundamental split in Islam into the two groups we see today: the **Shi'a**, or Shi'ite (the minority favoring hereditary succession) and the **Sunni**, or Sunnite (the majority preferring succession by community consensus). The Shi'a make up 10 to 15 percent of all Muslims, the Sunni 85 to 90 percent. Today most Shi'a reside in Iran, Iraq, Pakistan, and India; the Sunni predominate in many other countries and have majorities in Saudi Arabia, Egypt, Jordan, Indonesia, and some African countries.

The Sunni and the Shi'a have many internal divisions or schools of thought that differ on doctrine and practice. There are also Muslim thinkers who have advocated reform, emphasized philosophical and rational speculation, focused on the legal aspects of Islam, or rejected rationalist views in favor of powerful personal experiences of God. **Sufism** is the best example of the latter. Sufis strive for a "vision of union and oneness" with God, a mystical revelation informed by the Quran and Muslim tradition.

One of Islam's most important thinkers is Ibn Sina, or Avicenna (980–1037 CE), a Persian philosopher and physician. He was a prodigy and polymath who made extraordinary contributions to both philosophy and science. He was born in present-day Uzbekistan (then Persia) and educated in mathematics, medicine, physics, and logic, purportedly mastering these subjects in his teens. By age sixteen he was a practicing physician, and by age twenty he had published an encyclopedia. In his life he wrote approximately two hundred books in both Arab and Persian, including the *Canon of Medicine* (a medical textbook used in the West for hundreds of years) and the philosophical works *Metaphysics*, *The Healing*, and *Deliverance*. He advanced important distinctions in ontology (the study of being, or existence), discovered useful relationships in logic, and made unique contributions to the field of medical diagnosis. In philosophy, Ibn Sina developed a systematic and comprehensive metaphysics—that is, a view of the fundamental nature of reality. Constructing this metaphysics was his greatest achievement: he combined his own interpretation of Aristotelian concepts with Neoplatonism and reconciled the whole with a version of Islamic theology. For him, there was no conflict between truth acquired through religion and truth arrived at through reason and argument; truth is truth wherever it is found. He is esteemed by Western readers for having devised a new argument for the existence of the soul. He also developed a sophisticated cosmological argument for the existence of God, one that Thomas Aquinas would use two hundred years later.

Another great thinker is Averroës, or Ibn Rushd (1126–1198). He was an eminent Islamic philosopher who wrote renowned commentaries on Aristotle and defended philosophy as a Quran-sanctioned method to reflect on God's (Allah's) design. He was born in Cordoba, studied science and Islamic law, became a judge in Seville, and finally died in Marrakesh, Morocco. He argues for the legitimacy of philosophy in *The Decisive Treatise* and for naturalism (the view that everything derives from the physical) in *Incoherence of the Incoherence*. In several works he departs from Muslim orthodoxy, a move that resulted, at one point, in his being persecuted by the authorities. He rejected ideas in Neoplatonism, took a skeptical view of Platonic Forms, and attacked Avicenna's cosmological argument. He also arrived at some non-Christian views, holding that the world is eternal (not created at a moment in time) and that all minds are one and eternal (as opposed to being individual immortal souls). He insists that if the Quran appears to contain contradictions, the discrepancies can be reconciled via a better grasp of philosophy.

PRACTICE

Muslims may disagree on many points of belief and practice, but they all accept the fundamental components of Muslim life: the **Five Pillars of Islam**. These are the essential

 A CLOSER LOOK

Countries with Large Numbers of Muslims

Country	Muslims	% of Population
Indonesia	204,847,000	88.1
India	177,286,000	14.6
Pakistan	178,097,000	96.4
Egypt	80,024,000	94.7
Nigeria	75,728,000	47.9
Algeria	34,936,806	98.2
Afghanistan	29,047,000	99.8
Iraq	31,108,000	98.9
Sudan	30,855,000	71.4
China	23,308,000	1.8
Ethiopia	28,721,000	33.8

Pew Research Center, "Table: Muslim Population by Country," January 27, 2011, http://www.pewforum.org/2011/01/27/table-muslim-population-by-country/ (December 27, 2015).

practices that unite Muslims in a worldwide community of the faithful and differentiate Muslims from all other religious adherents. The Five Pillars are as follows:

1. **The declaration of faith** (*Shahadah*). All Muslims must publically declare this basic belief: "There is no God but Allah, and Muhammad is his messenger." The first clause is an affirmation of the oneness of God and a repudiation of idolatry, which Muslims define as the act of associating God with any other being or thing. The second clause pledges complete acquiescence to God's will as expressed in God's message delivered through Muhammad.
2. **The daily prayer** (*Salat*). Pious Muslims pray five times a day at specific times—at dawn, noon, late afternoon, sundown, and evening. Prayers include recitation of verses of the Quran in Arab accompanied by specific movements and postures. To pray, Muslims face Mecca, Islam's holiest site.
3. **Almsgiving** (*Zakat*). Charitable giving is required of Muslims. The amount of the gift is set at 2.5 percent of a person's net worth annually, collected by religious or government officials and distributed to the poor, orphans, widows, and religious causes such as the building of mosques and hospitals.
4. **Fasting during Ramadan** (*Sawn*). Ramadan is the ninth month of the Islamic calendar and the time of year in which Muhammad is said to have received his first revelation. In the *sawn*, adult, able-bodied Muslims fast during the whole month of Ramadan in daytime, abstaining from food, drink, smoking, and sex. The fast is supposed to be

a time of reflection on Allah and religious obligations. Sunset, when the fast ends each day, is often a time of celebration, feasting, and family gatherings.

5. **Pilgrimage to Mecca** (*Hajj*). The **hajj** is an obligatory journey to Mecca to perform specified rituals in the Grand Mosque, especially the rites involving the holy *Ka'ba*. The Ka'ba is a large cubical monument located in the center of the Mosque's compound, said to have been built for Muhammad by Abraham. The *hajj* can be performed only during the last ten days of the lunar month of *Dhu'l-Hijja*. Muslims who are healthy enough and prosperous enough to travel to Mecca are required to perform the *hajj* at least once in a lifetime.

To these five pillars some Muslims add a sixth—the duty of **jihad**. The word means *to strive* or *to struggle*, and in Islam it usually refers to the inner struggle of a good Muslim to become a better person or to serve the Muslim community. Jihad can also mean warfare conducted in self-defense against aggressors who wish to attack or destroy Islam. But a few Muslims have taken *jihad* to mean a *holy war* of aggression. John Esposito explains:

> Jihad is a concept with multiple meanings, used and abused throughout Islamic history. Although it is not associated with the words *holy war* anywhere in the Quran, Muslim rulers, with the support of religious scholars and officials, have historically used the concept of armed jihad to legitimate wars of imperial expansion. . . .
>
> In recent years religious extremists and terrorists have insisted that jihad is a universal religious obligation and that all true Muslims must join the jihad to promote a global Islamic revolution. A radicalized minority have combined militancy with messianic visions to mobilize an "army of God" whose jihad is to "liberate" Muslims at home and abroad. They have engaged in acts of violence and terror in their attempts to topple Muslim governments and, like Osama bin Laden and others, engaged in a global jihad.[3]

FIGURE 13.1 The Ka'ba, the building in the center of the great mosque in Mecca, is greatly revered by Muslims. The structure is about 35 feet by 40 feet and 50 feet high.

BACKGROUND

Muslim Religious Attitudes

Scientific surveys suggest that Muslims mostly agree on the central tenets of Islam but differ substantially on many other aspects of the faith. In 2012 and 2013, two large surveys canvassed the opinions of tens of thousands of Muslims in dozens of countries with large Muslim populations. Here are some of the findings.

Statement of Belief	% of Country's Muslims Who Agree		
Religion is very important.	15% Albania	82% Iraq	69% U.S.
The Quran is to be taken literally, word for word.	90% Nigeria	74% Uganda	86% Mali
There is only one true interpretation of Islam.	78% Egypt	34% Morocco	37% U.S.
I have made a pilgrimage to Mecca.	28% Chad	20% Egypt	5% Turkey
Shari'a should be the official law in this country.	99% Afghanistan	12% Turkey	84% Pakistan
Shari'a has multiple interpretations.	70% Tajikistan	20% Tunisia	45% Indonesia
I pray five times a day.	90% Cameroon	4% Albania	83% Iraq

Pew Research Center, "The World's Muslims: Unity and Diversity," August 9, 2012; "The World's Muslims: Religion, Politics, and Society," April 30, 2013.

SCRIPTURES

The Quran is Islam's most sacred and authoritative scripture, the eternal words of Allah revealed to Muhammad in Arabic. Christians and Jews hold that their scriptures were authored by humans who were inspired by God. Muslims, on the other hand, consider the Quran to be God's words dictated directly to Muhammad. God, not Muhammad, is the author. Thus Muslims believe that copies of the Quran are embodiments of God's speech. Treating a physical copy of the Quran disrespectfully, then, is a grave offense, far more serious to Muslims than burning the Bible is to Christians and Jews. And since God spoke to Muhammad in Arabic, only a Quran in Arab is thought to be the true word of God; translations into other languages may be useful but are merely interpretations, a step removed from the real thing.

The Quran contains 114 chapters, or **suras**, with each chapter divided into verses, much as the Hebrew Bible or New Testament is. But unlike these texts, the Quran is not organized

FIGURE 13.2 The Holy Quran, the scripture of Islam, is thought by all Muslims to be the word of Allah, revealed to his prophet Muhammad.

as a sustained narrative or a series of narratives. Except for the first *sura*, it is laid out according to chapter length, not chronology, assembled from the longest *sura* to the shortest.

The traditional view is that at least part of the Quran was written down before Muhammad died and that a fully written version was not compiled and adopted until some time in the rule of the third caliph 'Uthman (reign, 644–656). Muslims consider this compilation the final, official text of the Quran. But some scholars claim that there were from the beginning several variant readings of the Quran and that these variants continue to raise questions about the authority of the official version.

The Quran includes sermons; stories and parables; legal and moral prescriptions; discussions of God's signs in creation; and calls for belief in the oneness of God, for devout worship, and for efforts to establish social justice. It deals with an array of social, political, and religious questions—prayer, fasting, warfare, marriage, divorce, inheritance, friends, enemies, repentance, idolatry, and more.

Another form of Islamic scripture—not quite as revered as the Quran but still considered authoritative—is the **hadith**, reports of the "words, deeds or silent approval" of Muhammad. For Muslims, the Prophet is neither a god nor the embodiment of a god but the perfect paragon of Muslim obedience and piety. He is thus the supreme example of how to live, and the *hadith* supply a detailed portrayal of the Prophet for Muslims to live up to.

Hadith anecdotes were conveyed orally for at least a hundred years before they were written down, and they continued to be collected for several more centuries after that. Along the way, scholars recognized that many *hadith* were probably more fable than fact, so they developed methods for weeding out the questionable from the genuine. Whether the scholars succeeded is a matter of dispute among contemporary investigators. In any case, most Muslims today regard the *hadith* as authentic and authoritative (although some *hadith* are regarded as more authoritative than others).

The Quran and the *hadith* are sources for a large part of Islamic law—that is, for **shari'a**, the principles, rules, and values that express God's will for humanity. Devout Muslims take the *shari'a* seriously and try to conduct their lives by its instructions. It is concerned with far

 BACKGROUND

Attitudes of American Muslims

Statement of Belief	% of U.S. Muslims Who Agree
Think of self as Muslim first, not some nationality	49%
Very/somewhat concerned about possible rise of Islamic extremism in the U.S.	60%
U.S. war on terrorism is not a sincere effort to stop terrorism in the world	41%
Suicide bombings against civilians to defend Islam are often/sometimes justified	8%
Suicide bombings against civilians to defend Islam can never be justified	81%
Very unfavorable view of al Qaeda	70%
Favorable view of al Qaeda	5%
Religion very important in my life	69%
Pray five times every day	48%

Pew Research Center, "Muslim American Survey," August 30, 2011.

more than what Westerners call the law; it includes regulations regarding worship, ritual, customs, family law, property law, crime, punishment, and commerce. But even though *shari'a* law is comprehensive, it is rarely applied across the board. In most countries where Islamic law is given a place in the legal system, only family law is applied. And most of the *shari'a* does not pertain to non-Muslims. Opinion polls show that acceptance of *shari'a* as official law varies from country to country. For example, only 12 percent of Turks want it, while 84 percent of Pakistanis do.

NOTES

1. Pew Research, "Global Religious Landscape," December 2012 (based on 2010 data), http://www.pewforum.org/2012/12/18/global-religious-landscape-muslim/, August 2014.
2. Quran 96:1–5, M. A. S. Abdel Haleem, trans. (Oxford: Oxford University Press, 2004).
3. John L. Esposito, *What Everyone Needs to Know About Islam* (New York: Oxford University Press, 2011), 134.

KEY TERMS

Allah God, the same deity worshipped by Christians and Jews.

caliph A supreme Muslim leader who has both religious and secular authority.

caliphate The state governed by a caliph.

Five Pillars of Islam The essential religious practices required of all Muslims.

hadith Reports of the "words, deeds or silent approval" of Muhammad.

hajj The obligatory journey to the sacred city of Mecca in Saudi Arabia to perform specified rituals in the Grand Mosque.

jihad *To strive* or *to struggle*; usually refers to the inner struggle of a good Muslim to become a better person or to serve the Muslim community. Also, warfare in self-defense, or holy war of aggression.

Muhammad The last prophet of Islam, who received the Quran from God.

Quran Muslim holy scripture revealed to Muhammad.

shari'a Islamic law; the principles, rules, and values that express God's will for humanity.

Shi'a The minority of Muslims who favor hereditary succession of the caliph.

Sufism A form of Islam that seeks powerful personal experiences of God.

Sunni The majority of Muslims who favor caliph succession by community consensus.

sura A chapter, or division, of the Quran.

READINGS

TEACHINGS

The Quran

The following *suras* cover a variety of subjects—creation, dietary laws, Jesus, treatment of polytheists (idolaters), the sin of idolatry, repentance, warnings to transgressors, and the Day of Judgment. Muslims repeat *sura* 1 daily in prayer.

The Quran, M. A. S. Abdel Haleem, trans. (Oxford: Oxford University Press, 2005), 3, 6–7, 16, 17, 20–28, 50–54, 62–63, 67–68, 75, 78–79, 116–119, 130–131, 136–137, 209–210, 347, 399–400, 429, 432, 434–435, 439.

1. THE OPENING

[1]In the name of God, the Lord of Mercy, the Giver of
Mercy! [2]Praise belongs to God, Lord of the Worlds,
the Lord of Mercy, the Giver of Mercy, [4]Master of
the Day of Judgement. [5]It is You we worship; it is
You we ask for help. [6]Guide us to the straight path:
[7]the path of those You have blessed, those who incur
no anger and who have not gone astray.

2. THE COW (CREATION)

[28]How can you ignore God when you were lifeless
and He gave you life, when He will cause you to die,
then resurrect you to be returned to Him? [29]It was He
who created all that is on the earth for you, then
turned to the sky and made the seven heavens; it is
He who has knowledge of all things.

[30][Prophet], when your Lord told the angels, 'I am
putting a successor on earth,' they said, 'How can
You put someone there who will cause damage and
bloodshed, when we celebrate Your praise and proclaim Your holiness?' but He said, 'I know things
you do not.' [31]He taught Adam all the names [of
things], then He showed them to the angels and said,
'Tell me the names of these if you truly [think you
can].' [32]They said, 'May You be glorified! We have
knowledge only of what You have taught us. You are
the All Knowing and All Wise.' [33]Then He said,
'Adam, tell them the names of these.' When he told
them their names, God said, Did I not tell you that I
know what is hidden in the heavens and the earth,
and that I know what you reveal and what you
conceal?'

[34]When We told the angels, 'Bow down before
Adam,' they all bowed. But not Iblis, who refused
and was arrogant: he was one of the disobedient.
[35]We said, 'Adam, live with your wife in this garden.
Both of you eat freely there as you will, but do not go
near this tree, or you will both become wrongdoers.'
[36]But Satan made them slip, and removed them from
the state they were in. We said, 'Get out, all of you!
You are each other's enemy. On earth you will have
a place to stay and livelihood for a time.' [37]Then
Adam received some words from his Lord and He
accepted his repentance: He is the Ever Relenting,
the Most Merciful. [38]We said, 'Get out, all of you!
But when guidance comes from Me, as it certainly
will, there will be no fear for those who follow My
guidance nor will they grieve—[39]those who disbelieve and deny Our messages shall be the inhabitants
of the Fire, and there they will remain.'

5. THE FEAST (FINAL REVELATION)

In the name of God, the Lord of Mercy, the Giver of
Mercy

[1]You who believe, fulfil your obligations. Livestock animals are lawful as food for you, with the
exception of what is about to be announced to you.
You are forbidden to kill game while you are on
pilgrimage—God commands what He will, [2]so, you
who believe, do not violate the sanctity of God's
rites, the Sacred Month, the offerings, their garlands,
nor those going to the Sacred House to seek the
bounty and pleasure of their Lord—but when you
have completed the rites of pilgrimage you may hunt.
Do not let your hatred for the people who barred you
from the Sacred Mosque induce you to break the
law: help one another to do what is right and good;
do not help one another towards sin and hostility. Be
mindful of God, for His punishment is severe.

[3]You are forbidden to eat carrion; blood; pig's
meat; any animal over which any name other than
God's has been invoked; any animal strangled, or
victim of a violent blow or a fall, or gored or savaged
by a beast of prey, unless you still slaughter it [in the
correct manner]; or anything sacrificed on idolatrous altars. You are also forbidden to allot shares
[of meat] by drawing marked arrows—a heinous
practice—today the disbelievers have lost all hope
that you will give up your religion. Do not fear them:
fear Me. Today I have perfected your religion for
you, completed My blessing upon you, and chosen as
your religion *Islam:* [total devotion to God]; but if

any of you is forced by hunger to eat forbidden food, with no intention of doing wrong, then God is most forgiving and merciful.

[4]They ask you, Prophet, what is lawful for them. Say, 'All good things are lawful for you.' [This includes] what you have taught your birds and beasts of prey to catch, teaching them as God has taught you, so eat what they catch for you, but first pronounce God's name over it. Be mindful of God: He is swift to take account. [5]Today all good things have been made lawful for you. The food of the People of the Book is lawful for you as your food is lawful for them. So are chaste, believing, women as well as chaste women of the people who were given the Scripture before you, as long as you have given them their bride-gifts and married them, not taking them as lovers or secret mistresses. The deeds of anyone who rejects faith will come to nothing, and in the Hereafter he will be one of the losers. . . .

5. THE FEAST (JESUS)

[109]On the Day when God assembles all the messengers and asks, 'What response did you receive?' they will say, 'We do not have that knowledge: You alone know things that cannot be seen.' [110]Then God will say, 'Jesus, son of Mary! Remember My favour to you and to your mother: how I strengthened you with the holy spirit, so that you spoke to people in your infancy and as a grown man; how I taught you the Scripture and wisdom, the Torah and the Gospel; how, by My leave, you fashioned the shape of a bird out of clay, breathed into it, and it became, by My leave, a bird; how, by My leave, you healed the blind person and the leper; how, by My leave, you brought the dead back to life; how I restrained the Children of Israel from [harming] you when you brought them clear signs, and those of them who disbelieved said, "This is clearly nothing but sorcery"; [111]and how I inspired the disciples to believe in Me and My messengers—they said, "We believe and bear witness that we devote ourselves [to God]."'

[112]When the disciples said, 'Jesus, son of Mary, can your Lord send down a feast to us from heaven?' he said, 'Beware of God if you are true believers.' [113]They said, 'We wish to eat from it; to have our hearts reassured; to know that you have told us the truth; and to be witnesses of it.' [114]Jesus, son of Mary, said, 'Lord, send down to us a feast from heaven so that we can have a festival—the first and last of us—and a sign from You. Provide for us: You are the best provider.' [115]God said, 'I will send it down to you, but anyone who disbelieves after this will be punished with a punishment that I will not inflict on anyone else in the world.'

[116] When God says, 'Jesus, son of Mary, did you say to people, "Take me and my mother as two gods alongside God"?' he will say, 'May You be exalted! I would never say what I had no right to say—if I had said such a thing You would have known it: You know all that is within me, though I do not know what is within You, You alone have full knowledge of things unseen—[117]I told them only what You commanded me to: "Worship God, my Lord and your Lord." I was a witness over them during my time among them. Ever since You took my soul, You alone have been the watcher over them: You are witness to all things [118]and if You punish them, they are Your servants; if You forgive them, You are the Almighty, the Wise.' [119]God will say, 'This is a Day when the truthful will benefit from their truthfulness. They will have Gardens graced with flowing streams, there to remain for ever. God is pleased with them and they with Him: that is the supreme triumph.' [120]Control of the heavens and earth and everything in them belongs to God: He has power over all things.

9. REPENTANCE

[1]A release by God and His Messenger from the treaty you [believers] made with the idolaters [is announced]—[2]you [idolaters] may move freely about the land for four months, but you should bear in mind both that you will not escape God, and that God will disgrace those who defy [Him]. [3]On the Day of the Great Pilgrimage [there will be] a proclamation from God and His Messenger to all people: 'God and His

Messenger are released from [treaty] obligations to the idolaters. It will be better for you [idolaters] if you repent; know that you cannot escape God if you turn away.' [Prophet], warn those who ignore [God] that they will have a painful punishment. [4]As for those who have honoured the treaty you made with them and who have not supported anyone against you: fulfil your agreement with them to the end of their term. God loves those who are mindful of Him.

[5]When the [four] forbidden months are over, wherever you encounter the idolaters, kill them, seize them, besiege them, wait for them at every lookout post; but if they turn [to God], maintain the prayer, and pay the prescribed alms, let them go on their way, for God is most forgiving and merciful. [6]If any one of the idolaters should seek your protection [Prophet], grant it to him so that he may hear the word of God, then take him to a place safe for him, for they are people with no knowledge [of it]. [7]How could there be a treaty with God and His Messenger for such idolaters? But as for those with whom you made a treaty at the Sacred Mosque, so long as they remain true to you, be true to them; God loves those who are mindful of Him. [8][How,] when, if they were to get the upper hand over you, they would not respect any tie with you, of kinship or of treaty? They please you with their tongues, but their hearts are against you and most of them are lawbreakers. [9]They have sold God's message for a trifling gain, and barred others from His path. How evil their actions are! [10]Where believers are concerned, they respect no tie of kinship or treaty. They are the ones who are committing aggression. [11]If they turn to God, keep up the prayer, and pay the prescribed alms, then they are your brothers in faith: We make the messages clear for people who are willing to learn. [12]But if they break their oath after having made an agreement with you, if they revile your religion, then fight the leaders of disbelief—oaths mean nothing to them—so that they may stop. [13]How could you not fight a people who have broken their oaths, who tried to drive the Messenger out, who attacked you first? Do you fear them? It is God you should fear if you are true believers. [14]Fight them: God will punish them at your hands, He will disgrace them, He will help you to conquer them, He will heal the believers' feelings [15]and remove the rage from their hearts. God turns to whoever He will in His mercy; God is all knowing and wise. [16]Do you think that you will be left untested without God identifying which of you will strive for His cause and take no supporters apart from God, His Messenger, and other believers? God is fully aware of all your actions.

[17]It is not right for the idolaters to tend God's places of worship while testifying to their own disbelief: the deeds of such people will come to nothing and they will abide in Hell. [18]The only ones who should tend God's places of worship are those who believe in God and the Last Day, who keep up the prayer, who pay the prescribed alms, and who fear no one but God: such people may hope to be among the rightly guided. [19]Do you consider giving water to pilgrims and tending the Sacred Mosque to be equal to the deeds of those who believe in God and the Last Day and who strive in God's path? They are not equal in God's eyes. God does not guide such benighted people. [20]Those who believe, who migrated and strove hard in God's way with their possessions and their persons, are in God's eyes much higher in rank; it is they who will triumph; [21]and their Lord gives them the good news of His mercy and pleasure, Gardens where they will have lasting bliss [22]and where they will remain for ever: truly, there is a tremendous reward with God.

[23]Believers, do not take your fathers and brothers as allies if they prefer disbelief to faith: those of you who do so are doing wrong. [24]Say [Prophet], 'If your fathers, sons, brothers, wives, tribes, the wealth you have acquired, the trade which you fear will decline, and the dwellings you love are dearer to you than God and His Messenger and the struggle in His cause, then wait until God brings about His punishment.' God does not guide those who break away. [25]God has helped you [believers] on many battlefields, even on the day of the Battle of Hunayn. You were well pleased with your large numbers, but they were of no use to you: the earth seemed to close in on you despite its spaciousness, and you turned tail and fled. [26]Then God sent His calm down to His Messenger and the believers, and He sent down invisible forces. He punished the disbelievers—this is what the disbelievers deserve—[27]but God turns in His mercy to whoever He will. God is most forgiving and merciful.

[28]Believers, those who ascribe partners to God are truly unclean: do not let them come near the Sacred Mosque after this year. If you are afraid you may become poor, [bear in mind that] God will enrich you out of His bounty if He pleases: God is all knowing and wise. [29]Fight those of the People of the Book who do not [truly] believe in God and the Last Day, who do not forbid what God and His Messenger have forbidden, who do not obey the rule of justice, until they pay the tax and agree to submit. [30]The Jews said, 'Ezra is the son of God,' and the Christians said, 'The Messiah is the son of God': they said this with their own mouths, repeating what earlier disbelievers had said. May God confound them! How far astray they have been led! [31]They take their rabbis and their monks as lords, as well as Christ, the son of Mary. But they were commanded to serve only one God: there is no god but Him; He is far above whatever they set up as His partners! [32]They try to extinguish God's light with their mouths, but God insists on bringing His light to its fullness, even if the disbelievers hate it. [33]It is He who has sent His Messenger with guidance and the religion of truth, to show that it is above all [other] religions, however much the idolaters may hate this. [34]Believers, many rabbis and monks wrongfully consume people's possessions and turn people away from God's path. [Prophet], tell those who hoard gold and silver instead of giving in God's cause that they will have a grievous punishment: [35]on the Day it is heated up in Hell's Fire and used to brand their foreheads, sides, and backs, they will be told, 'This is what you hoarded up for yourselves! Now feel the pain of what you hoarded!' . . .

10. JONAH (IDOLATRY)

[25]But God invites [everyone] to the Home of Peace, and guides whoever He will to a straight path. [26]Those who did well will have the best reward and more besides. Neither darkness nor shame will cover their faces: these are the companions in Paradise, and there they will remain. [27]As for those who did evil, each evil deed will be requited by its equal and humiliation will cover them—no one will protect them against God—as though their faces were covered with veils cut from the darkness of the night. These are the inmates of the Fire, and there they shall remain.

[28]On the Day We gather them all together, We shall say to those who associate partners with God, 'Stay in your place, you and your partner-gods.' Then We shall separate them, and their partner-gods will say, 'It was not us you worshipped—[29]God is witness enough between us and you—we had no idea that you worshipped us.' [30]Every soul will realize, then and there, what it did in the past. They will be returned to God, their rightful Lord, and their invented [gods] will desert them.

[31]Say [Prophet], 'Who provides for you from the sky and the earth? Who controls hearing and sight? Who brings forth the living from the dead and the dead from the living, and who governs everything?' They are sure to say, 'God.' Then say, 'So why do you not take heed of Him? [32]That is God, your Lord, the Truth. Apart from the Truth, what is there except error? So how is it that you are dissuaded?' [33]In this way, your Lord's word about those who defy [the Truth] has been proved—they do not believe. [34]Ask them, 'Can any of your partner-gods originate creation, then bring it back to life again in the end?' Say, 'It is God that originates creation, and then brings it back to life, so how can you be misled?' [35]Say, 'Can any of your partner-gods show the way to the Truth?' Say, 'God shows the way to the Truth. Is someone who shows the way to the Truth more worthy to be followed, or someone who cannot find the way unless he himself is shown? What is the matter with you? How do you judge?' [36]Most of them follow nothing but assumptions, but assumptions can be of no value at all against the Truth: God is well aware of what they do.

[37]Nor could this Qur'an have been devised by anyone other than God. It is a confirmation of what was revealed before it and an explanation of the Scripture—let there be no doubt about it—it is from the Lord of the Worlds. [38]Or do they say, 'He has devised it'? Say, 'Then produce a sura like it, and call on anyone you can beside God if you are telling the truth.' [39]But they are denying what they cannot comprehend—its prophecy has yet to be fulfilled for them.

In the same way, those before them refused to believe—see what was the end of those evildoers! . . .

11. HUD

In the name of God, the Lord of Mercy, the Giver of Mercy.

[1]*Alif Lam Ra*

[This is] a Scripture whose verses are perfected, then set out clearly, from One who is all wise, all aware. [2][Say, Prophet], 'Worship no one but God. I am sent to you from Him to warn and to give good news. [3]Ask your Lord for forgiveness, then turn back to Him. He will grant you wholesome enjoyment until an appointed time, and give His grace to everyone who has merit. But if you turn away, I fear you will have torment on a terrible Day: [4]it is to God that you will all return, and He has power over everything.'

[5]See how they [the disbelievers] wrap themselves up, to hide their feelings from Him. But even when they cover themselves with their clothes, He knows what they conceal and what they reveal: He knows well the innermost secrets of the heart. [6]There is not a creature that moves on earth whose provision is not His concern. He knows where it lives and its [final] resting place: it is all [there] in a clear record. [7]It is He who created the heavens and the earth in six Days—His rule extends over the waters too—so as to test which of you does best.

Yet [Prophet], if you say to them, 'You will be resurrected after death,' the disbelievers are sure to answer, 'This is clearly nothing but sorcery.' [8]If We defer their punishment for a determined time, they are sure to say, 'What is holding it back?' But on the Day it comes upon them, nothing will divert it from them; what they mocked will be all around them. [9]How desperate and ungrateful man becomes when We let him taste Our mercy and then withhold it! [10]And if We let him taste mercy after some harm has touched him, he is sure to say, 'Misfortune has gone away from me.' He becomes exultant and boastful. [11]Not so those who are steadfast and do good deeds: they will have forgiveness and a great reward.

[12]So [Prophet] are you going to abandon some part of what is revealed to you, and let your heart be oppressed by it, because they say, 'Why is no treasure sent down to him? Why has no angel come with him?'? You are only there to warn; it is God who is in charge of everything. [13]If they say, 'He has invented it himself,' say, 'Then produce ten invented suras like it, and call in whoever you can beside God, if you are truthful.' [14]If they do not answer you, then you will all know that it is sent down containing knowledge from God, and that there is no god but Him. Then will you submit to Him? [15]If any desire [only] the life of this world with all its finery, We shall repay them in full in this life for their deeds—they will be given no less [16]but such people will have nothing in the Hereafter but the Fire: their work here will be fruitless and their deeds futile. [17]Can they be compared to those who have clear proof from their Lord, recited by a witness from Him, and before it the Book of Moses, as a guide and mercy? These people believe in it, whereas those groups that deny its truth are promised the Fire. So have no doubt about it [Prophet]: it is the Truth from your Lord, though most people do not believe so.

17. THE NIGHT JOURNEY

[This sura *refers to what Muslims call "the Night Journey" when the angel Gabriel is said to have transported Muhammad to the temple in Jerusalem and then into heaven. The site from which he ascended is marked by the shrine known as the Dome of the Rock. Muhammad's trip to Jerusalem is part of the reason why the city is considered Islam's third most sacred city (the first and second most holy cities are Mecca and Medina).]*

In the name of God, the Lord of Mercy, the Giver of Mercy.

[1]Glory to Him who made His servant travel by night from the sacred place of worship to the furthest place of worship, whose surroundings We have blessed, to show him some of Our signs: He alone is the All Hearing, the All Seeing. [2]We also gave Moses

the Scripture, and made it a guide for the Children of Israel. 'Entrust yourselves to no one but Me, [3]you descendants of those We carried with Noah: he was truly a thankful servant.'

53. THE STAR

[This sura *is an affirmation of the divine source of Mahammad's revelation and of its trustworthiness as a message from God.]*

In the name of God, the Lord of Mercy, the Giver of Mercy.

[1]By the star when it sets! [2]Your companion has not strayed; he is not deluded; [3]he does not speak from his own desire. [4]The Qur'an is nothing less than a revelation that is sent to him. [5]It was taught to him by [an angel] with mighty powers [6]and great strength, who stood [7]on the highest horizon [8]and then approached—coming down [9]until he was two bow-lengths away or even closer—[10]and revealed God's servant what He revealed. [11][The Prophet's] own heart did not distort what he saw. [12]Are you going to dispute with him what he saw with his own eyes? [13]A second time he saw him: [14]by the lote tree beyond which none may pass [15]near the Garden of Restfulness, [16]when the tree was covered in nameless [splendour]. [17]His sight never wavered, nor was it too bold, [18]and he saw some of the greatest signs of his Lord.

75. THE RESURRECTION

*[*Sura *75 asserts that, contrary to what doubters might think, the Day of Resurrection will come, and the doubters and deniers will get what they deserve.]*

In the name of God, the Lord of Mercy, the Giver of Mercy.

[1]By the Day of Resurrection [2]and by the self-reproaching soul! [3]Does man think We shall not put his bones back together? [4]In fact, We can reshape his very fingertips. [5]Yet man wants to deny what is ahead of him: [6]he says, 'So, when will this Day of Resurrection be?'

[7]When eyes are dazzled [8]and the moon eclipsed, [9]when the sun and the moon are brought together, [10]on that Day man will say, 'Where can I escape?' [11]Truly, there is no refuge: [12]they will all return to your Lord on that Day. [13]On that Day, man will be told what he put first and what he put last. [14]Truly, man is a clear witness against himself, [15]despite all the excuses he may put forward.

[16][Prophet], do not rush your tongue in an attempt to hasten [your memorization of] the Revelation: [17]We shall make sure of its safe collection and recitation. [18]When We have recited it, repeat the recitation [19]and We shall make it clear.

[20]Truly you [people] love this fleeting world [21]and neglect the life to come. [22]On that Day there will be radiant faces, [23]looking towards their Lord, [24]and on that Day there will be the sad and despairing faces [25]of those who realize that a great calamity is about to befall them.

[26]Truly, when the soul reaches the collarbone; [27]when it is said, 'Could any charm-healer save him now?'; [28]when he knows it is the final parting; [29]when his legs are brought together: [30]on that day he will be driven towards your Lord. [31]He neither believed nor prayed, [32]but denied the truth and turned away, [33]walking back to his people with a conceited swagger.

[34]Closer and closer it comes to you. [35]Closer and closer still. [36]Does man think he will be left alone? [37]Was he not just a drop of spilt-out sperm, [38]which became a clinging form, which God shaped in due proportion, [39]fashioning from it the two sexes, male and female? [40]Does He who can do this not have the power to bring the dead back to life?

96. THE CLINGING FORM

[The first five lines of this sura *are from the beginning of the first revelation in which the angel Gabriel commands Muhammad to read. The rest of the* sura *warns against man's pride in thinking he is self-sufficient and can do without God.]*

In the name of God, the Lord of Mercy, the Giver of Mercy.

[1]Read! In the name of your Lord who created: [2]He created man from a clinging form. [3]Read! Your Lord is the Most Bountiful One [4]who taught by [means of] the pen, [5]who taught man what he did not know.

[6]But man exceeds all bounds [7]when he thinks he is self-sufficient: [8][Prophet], all will return to your Lord. [9]Have you seen the man who forbids [10][Our] servant to pray? [11]Have you seen whether he is rightly guided, [12]or encourages true piety? [13]Have you seen whether he denies the truth and turns away from it? [14]Does he not realize that God sees all? [15]No! If he does not stop, We shall drag him by his forehead —[16]his lying, sinful forehead. [17]Let him summon his comrades; [18]We shall summon the guards of Hell. [19]No! Do not obey him [Prophet]: bow down in worship and draw close.

97. THE NIGHT OF GLORY

[This sura *glorifies the night when Muhammad receives the first revelation of the Quran.]*

In the name of God, the Lord of Mercy, the Giver of Mercy.

[1]We sent it down on the Night of Glory. [2]What will explain to you what that Night of Glory is? [3]The Night of Glory is better than a thousand months; [4]on that night the angels and the Spirit descend again and again with their Lord's permission on every task; [5][there is] peace that night until the break of dawn.

100. THE CHARGING STEEDS

[In this sura *God declares that man is ungrateful, blind, and avaricious. God swears this by mighty charging steeds.]*

In the name of God, the Lord of Mercy, the Giver of Mercy.

[1]By the charging steeds that pant [2]and strike sparks with their hooves, [3]who make dawn raids, [4]raising a cloud of dust, [5]and plunging into the midst of the enemy, [6]man is ungrateful to his Lord—[7]and He is witness to this—[8]he is truly excessive in his love of wealth. [9]Does he not know that when the contents of graves burst forth, [10]when the secrets of hearts are uncovered, on that Day, [11]their Lord will be fully aware of them all?

102. STRIVING FOR MORE

[In sura *102 God denounces men who constantly strive for ever more wealth. On the Day of Resurrection, they will answer for their greed.]*

In the name of God, the Lord of Mercy, the Giver of Mercy.

[1]Striving for more distracts you [2]until you go into your graves. [3]No indeed! You will come to know. [4]No indeed! In the end you will come to know. [5]No indeed! If only you knew for certain. [6]You will most definitely see Hellfire, [7]you will see it with the eye of certainty. [8]On that Day, you will be asked about your pleasures.

103. THE DECLINING DAY

[Sura 103 is an exhortation to follow the way of salvation.]

In the name of God, the Lord of Mercy, the Giver of Mercy.

[1]By the declining day, [2]man is [deep] in loss, [3]except for those who believe, do good deeds, urge one another to the truth, and urge one another to steadfastness.

104. THE BACKBITER

[Sura *104 threatens the backbiter with Hell Fire.]*

In the name of God, the Lord of Mercy, the Giver of Mercy.

[1]Woe to every fault-finding backbiter [2]who amasses riches, counting them over, [3]thinking they will make him live for ever. [4]No indeed! He will be thrust into the Crusher! [5]What will explain to you what the Crusher is? [6]It is God's Fire, made to blaze, [7]which rises over people's hearts. [8]It closes in on them [9]in towering columns.

107. COMMON KINDNESSES

[Sura 107 declares that someone who denies the Judgment is selfish, heartless, and hypocritical.]

In the name of God, the Lord of Mercy, the Giver of Mercy.

[1][Prophet], have you considered the person who denies the Judgement? [2]It is he who pushes aside the orphan [3]and does not urge others to feed the needy. [4]So woe to those who pray [5]but are heedless of their prayer; [6]those who are all show [7]and forbid common kindnesses.

Hadith

These *hadith* are discourses on three themes: the nature of jihad, how Muhammad received the divine revelations, and the laws regarding divorce.

JIHAD

1 Abu Hurairah said, A man came to the Messenger of Allāh and said, Guide me to a deed which is equal to jihād. He said, "I do not find it." (Then) he said: "Is it in thy power that when the one engaged in jihād goes forth, thou shouldst enter thy mosque and stand in prayer and have no rest, and that thou shouldst fast and break it not?" He said, Who can do it? (Bukhari 56:1)

2 Abū Sa'īd al-Khudrī said, It was said, O Messenger of Allāh! Who is the most excellent of men? The Messenger of Allāh said, "The believer who strives hard in the way of Allāh with his person and his property." (Bukhari 56:2)

8 Ibn 'Abbās reported, The Messenger of Allāh wrote to the Cæsar inviting him to Islām, and sent his letter to him with Dihyah al-Kalbī, and the Messenger of Allāh ordered him to make it over to the Chief of Busrā that he might send it to the Caesar. (Bukhari 56:102)

9 Ibn 'Abbās reported, . . . And this (letter) ran as follows: "In the name of Allāh, the Beneficent, the Merciful. From Muhammad, the servant of Allāh and His Messenger, to Heraclius, the Chief of the Roman Empire. Peace be with him who follows the guidance. After this, I invite thee with invitation to Islām. Become a Muslim and thou wilt be in peace—Allāh will give thee a double reward; but if thou turnest away, on thee will be the sin of thy subjects. And, O followers of the Book! Come to an equitable

Chs. XXI in Maulana Muhammad Ali, trans., *A Manual of Hadith* (Lahore: Ahmadiyya, 1944).

proposition between us and you that we shall not serve any but Allāh, and that we shall not associate aught with Him, and that some of us shall not take others for lords besides Allāh; but if they turn back, then say: Bear witness that we are Muslims." (Bukhari 1:1)

10 Salamah said, I swore allegiance to the Prophet, then I turned to the shade of a tree. When the crowd diminished, he (the Prophet) said, "O Ibn al-Akwa'! Will thou not swear allegiance?" He said, "I said, I have already sworn allegiance, O Messenger of Allāh! He said, "And do it again." So I swore allegiance to him a second time. I (the reporter) said to him, O Abu Muslim! For what did you swear allegiance (to him) then? He said, For death. (Bukhari 56:110)

11 Abd Allāh ibn Abū Aufā reported, "The Messenger of Allāh said: And know that paradise is beneath the protection of the swords." (Bukhari 56:22)

12 Abū Hurairah said, I heard the Prophet say "By Him in Whose hand is my soul, were it not that there are men among the believers who cannot bear to remain behind me—and I do not find that on which to carry them—I would not remain behind an army that fights in the way of Allāh; and by Him in Whose hand is my soul. I love that I should be killed in the way of Allāh then brought to life, then killed again then brought to life, then killed again then brought to life, then killed again." (Bukhari 56:7)

13 Abū Hurairah said, The Messenger of Allāh said: "Whom do you count to be a martyr among you?" They said, O Messenger of Allāh! Whoever is killed in the way of Allāh is a martyr. He said: "In that case the martyrs of my community shall be very few—he who is killed in the way of Allāh is a martyr; he who dies a natural death in the way of Allāh is a martyr; he who dies of the plague (in the way of Allāh) is a martyr; he who dies of cholera (in the way of Allāh) is a martyr." (Muslim-Mishkat 18)

14 Anas said, On the day that battle was fought at Uhud, (some) people fled away from the Prophet. He said, And I saw 'Ā'ishah, daughter of Abu Bakr and Umm Sulaim, and they had both tucked up their garments, so that I could see the anklets on their shanks, and they were carrying skins (full of water) on their backs, and they poured water into the mouths of the people then they went back and filled them again, then came and poured them into the mouths of the people. (Bukhari 56:651)

16 'Abd Allāh reported, A woman was found among the killed in one of the battles of the Prophet, so the Messenger of Allāh forbade the killing of women and children.' (Bukhari 56:147)

17 Ibn 'Umar reported, The Messenger of Allāh said: 'I have been commanded that I should fight these people till they bear witness that there is no god but Allāh and keep up prayer and pay zakāt. When they do this, their blood and their property shall be safe with me except as Islām requires, and their reckoning is with Allāh." (Bukhari 2:16)

HOW DIVINE REVELATION CAME TO THE HOLY PROPHET

2 'Ā'ishah said: The first revelation that was granted to the Messenger of Allāh was the true dream in a state of sleep, so that he never dreamed a dream but the truth of it shone forth like the dawn of the morning. Then solitude became dear to him and he used to seclude himself in the cave of Hirā', and therein he devoted himself to Divine worship for several nights before he came back to his family and took provisions for this (retirement); then he would return to Khadījah and take (more) provisions for a similar (period), until the Truth came to him while he was in the cave of Hirā'; so the angel (Gabriel) came to him and said, Read. He (the Prophet) said, "I said I am not one who can read." And he continued: "Then he (the angel) took hold of me and he pressed me so hard that I could not bear it any more, and then he let me go and said, Read. I said, I am not one who can read. Then he took hold of me and pressed me a second time so hard that I could not bear it any more, then he let me go again and said, Read. I said, "I am not one who can read." (The Prophet) continued: "Then he took hold of me and pressed me hard for a third time, then he let me go and said, 'Read in the name of thy Lord Who created—He created man from a clot—Read and thy Lord is most Honourable.'" The Messenger of Allāh returned with this (message) while his heart trembled and he came to Khadījah, daughter of Khuwailid, and said, "Wrap me up, wrap me up," and she wrapped him up until the awe left him. Then he said to Khadījah, while he related to her what had happened: "I fear for myself." Khadījah said, Nay, By Allāh, Allāh will never bring thee to disgrace, for thou unitest the ties of relationship and bearest the burden of the weak and earnest for the destitute and honourest the guest and helpest in real distress.

Then Khadījah went with him until she brought him to Waraqah ibn Naufal ibn Asad ibn 'Abd al-'Uzzā, Khadījah's uncle's son, and he was a man who had become a Christian in the time of Ignorance, and he used to write the Hebrew script, and he wrote from the Gospel in Hebrew what it pleased Allāh that he should write, and he was a very old man who had turned blind. Khadījah said to him, O Uncle's son! Listen to thy brother's son. Waraqah said to him, My brother's son! What hast thou seen? So the Messenger of Allāh related to him what he had seen. Waraqah said to him, This is the angel Gabriel whom Allāh sent to Moses; would that I were a young man at this time—would that I were alive when thy people would expel thee! The Messenger of Allāh said, Would they expel me? He said, Yes; never has a man appeared with the like of that which thou hast brought but he has been held in enmity; and if thy time finds me (alive) I shall help thee with the fullest help. After that not much time had passed that Waraqah died, and the revelation broke off temporarily.

3 Jābir said, speaking of the temporary break in the revelation, (The Holy Prophet) said in his narrative: "Whilst I was walking along, I heard a voice from heaven and I raised up my eyes, and lo! the Angel that had appeared to me in Hirā' was sitting on a throne between heaven and earth and I was struck with awe on account of him and returned (home) and said, Wrap me up, wrap me up. Then Allāh revealed: 'O thou who art clothed! Arise and warn, And thy Lord do magnify, And thy garments do purify, And uncleanness do shun'." Then revelation became brisk and came in succession.

4 Ibn 'Abbās . . . said, The Messenger of Allāh used to exert himself hard in receiving Divine revelation and would on this account move his lips. . . . so Allāh revealed: "Move not thy tongue with it to make haste with it. Surely on Us devolves the collecting of it and the reciting of it." . . . So after this when Gabriel came to him the Messenger of Allāh would listen attentively, and when Gabriel departed, the Prophet recited as he (Gabriel) recited it.

5 'Ā'ishah reported that Hārith ibn Hishām asked the Messenger of Allāh, O Messenger of Allāh! How does revelation come to thee? The Messenger of Allāh said: "Sometimes it comes to me like the ringing of a bell and that is the hardest on me, then he departs from me and I retain in memory from him what he says; and sometimes the Angel comes to me in the likeness of a man and speaks to me and I retain in memory what he says." Ā'ishah said, And I saw him when revelation came down upon him on a severely cold day, then it departed from him and his forehead dripped with sweat.

6 Zaid ibn Thābit said, Allāh sent down revelation on His Messenger, and his thigh was upon my thigh and it began to make its weight felt to me so much so that I feared that my thigh might be crushed.

7 Safwān ibn Ya'lā reported that Ya'lā said to 'Umar, Show me the Prophet when revelation is sent down to him. So when the Prophet was in Ji'rānah and with him a number of his companions. . . . revelation came to him. Thereupon 'Umar made a sign to Ya'lā; so Ya'lā came and over the Messenger of Allāh was a garment with which he was covered and he entered his head under the garment), when (he saw that) the face of the Messenger of Allāh was red and he was snoring; then that condition departed from him.

8 'Ubādah ibn al-Sāmit said, The Prophet felt, when the revelation was sent down upon him, like one in grief and a change came over his face. And according to one report: He hung down his head, and his companions also hung down their heads, and when that state was over, he raised his head.

DIVORCE

1 Ibn 'Umar reported, The Prophet, said "With Allāh, the most detestable of all things permitted is divorce."

2 Thaubān said, The Messenger of Allāh said: "Whatever woman asks for divorce from her husband without any harm, the sweet odour of paradise shall be forbidden to her."

3 Ibn 'Abbās reported, The wife of Thābit Ibn Qais came to the Prophet and said, O Messenger of Allāh! I do not find fault in Thābit ibn Qais regarding his morals or faith, but I hate disbelief in Islām. The Messenger of Allāh said: "Wilt thou return to him his orchard?" She said, Yes. So the Messenger of Allāh, said (to Thābit): "Accept the orchard and divorce her."

4 Ibn 'Umar reported, He divorced his wife while she was menstruating. 'Umar mentioned this to the Messenger of Allāh, so the Messenger of Allāh became displeased on account of this and said: "He should take her back, then keep her until she is clean, then menstruates and (again) becomes clean, if it then appears to him that he should divorce her, he should divorce her while she is in a clean condition before he approaches her. This is the *'iddah* as Allāh has commanded it."

5 Ibn 'Abbās said, The (procedure of) divorce in the time of the Messenger of Allāh, in that of Abū Bakr and for two years in the caliphate of 'Umar ibn al-Khattāb, was that divorce uttered thrice (on one occasion) was considered as one divorce. Then 'Umar said, People have made haste in a matter in which there was moderation for them, so we may make it take effect with regard to them. So he made it take effect with regard to them.

6 Mahmūd ibn Labīd said, The Messenger of Allāh was informed about a man who divorced his wife, divorcing (her) three times together, so he stood up in displeasure and said: "Is the Book of Allāh being sported with while I am in your midst? "

7 Rukānah ibn 'Abd Yazīd reported, He divorced his wife Suhaimah thrice and informed the Prophet about it and said, I call Allāh to witness that I intended only a single (divorce). The Messenger of Allāh said "Dost thou call Allāh to witness that thou didst not intend but a single (divorce)?" He said, Yes, I call Allāh to witness that I did not intend but a single (divorce). So the Messenger of Allāh, returned her back to him, and he divorced her a second time in the time of 'Umar, and a third time in the time of 'Uthmān.

8 'Ali said, The 'Messenger of Allāh cursed the man who committed *halālah* and the one for whom *halālah* was committed.'

9 Mutarrif reported, 'Imrān was asked about a man who divorced his wife, then he had intercourse with her, and he did not call in witnesses on the occasion of the divorce, nor on taking her back. 'Imrān said, Thou divorcest against the Sunnah and takest back against the Sunnah; have witnesses on the occasion of her divorce and on taking her back.

10 'Ā'ishah said, The Messenger of Allāh gave us option; so we chose Allāh and His Messenger; this was not reckoned for us as anything.

11 Ibn al-Musayyab said. When a person is found missing while fighting, his wife shall wait for one year.

12 'Abd Allāh reported, A man from among the Ansār accused his wife of adultery; so the Prophet asked them both to take an oath, then he ordered them to be separated from each other.

13 Ibn 'Umar used to say, with respect to *ilā'* about which Allāh has spoken, It is not lawful for any one after the prescribed time (of four months) has passed away, except that he should either keep (the wife) in good fellowship or resolve upon divorce.

Sunni Beliefs (al-Ash'ari)

This is the first major statement of Islamic beliefs, developed by the Muslim theologian al-Ash'ari (d. 935) and later accepted as the creed of Sunni Muslims. Sunni Islam includes diverse sects and a variety of opinions on what Islam is. All Sunnis, however, believe in the acceptability of Muhammad's first four successors (Abu Bakr, Umar, Uthman, and Ali), chosen according to qualifications for leadership, not according to heredity as Shi'a Muslims prefer.

The sum of our doctrine is this, that we believe in God, His Angels, His Books, His Apostles, in all that has come from God, and what trustworthy men (*thiqat*) have reported from the Apostles of God; we oppose nothing thereof.

That God is One God, Single, One, Eternal; beside Him no God exists; He has taken to Himself no wife (*sahiba*), nor child (*walad*); and that Muhammad is His Servant (*abd*) and His Apostle. That Paradise and Hell are Verity and that the Hour (*as-sa'a*) will come without doubt, and God will arouse those that are in the graves. That God has settled Himself (*istawa*) upon His throne, as He has said, (Qur. 20: 4); "the Rahman has settled Himself upon His throne." That God has a countenance, as He has said, (Qur. 55: 27); "and the countenance of thy Lord will abide, full of majesty and glory;" and two hands, as He has said, (Qur. 5: 69); "much more! both His hands are spread out," and (Qur. 38: 75); "that which I have created with both My hands;" and two eyes, without asking how (*bila kayfa*), as He has said, (Qur. 54: 14'); "which swims forth under Our eyes." That whoever thinks that God's name is other than He, is in error. That God has Knowledge (*ilm*), as He has said, (Qur. 35: 12); "Not one woman becomes pregnant and brings forth, except by His knowledge." We maintain that God has Power (*qudra*), as He has said, (Qur. 41: 14); "and have they not seen that God who created them is stronger than they?" We maintain that God has Hearing (*sam*) and Seeing (*basar*) and do not deny it, as do the Mu'tazilites, Jahmites and Kharijites. We teach that God's Word (*kalam*) is uncreated, and that He has never created anything except by saying to it, "Be!" and it forthwith became, as He has said, (Qur, 16: 42); "Our speech to anything when We willed it was, 'Be' and it was." Nothing exists upon earth, be it good or bad, but that which, God wills; but all things are by God's Will (*mashya*). No one is able to do anything before God does it, neither is anyone independent of God, nor can he withdraw himself from God's Knowledge. There is no Creator but God. The works (*amals*) of creatures are created and predestined by God, as He said, (Qur. 37: 94); "and God has created you and what ye do." Man is able to create nothing; but they are created, as He has said, (Qur. 35: 31); "Is there any Creator except God?" and (Qur. 16: 17) "and is He who created like him who created not?" and (Qur. 52: 35); "were they created out of nothing, or are they the creators?" and such passages are many in the Qur'an. And God maintains the believers in obedience to Him, is gracious unto them, cares for them, reforms them, and guides them aright; but the unbelievers He leads astray, guides them not aright, vouchsafes them not Faith (*iman*), by His Grace, as the People of error and pride maintain.

For should He be gracious unto them and help them aright, then would they be pious, and should He guide them aright, then would they allow themselves to be guided aright, as He has said, (Qur. 7: 177); "whom God guideth aright, he allows himself to be guided aright, and whom He leads astray, they are the losers." God is able to help the unbelieving aright and to be gracious unto them, so that they shall

Sunni Creed, Sacred-texts.com.

become believing, but He wills that they shall be unbelieving as is known. For He has made them impervious to all help and sealed their hearts. Good and Evil happen according to the Destiny (*qada*) and Decree (*qadar*) of God for good and. evil, for the sweet and the bitter. We know that the misfortune that befalls us is not in order that we may go astray, and that the good fortune which befalls us is not in order that we may go aright. We have no control over that which is good or hurtful to us, except so far as God wills. We flee from our anxieties to God and commit at all times our distress and poverty to Him.

We teach that the Qur'an is God's Word, and that it is uncreated, and that whosoever says that it is created is an unbeliever (*kafir*).

We believe that God at the Day of Resurrection (*yawm al-qiyama*) will be visible to the eyes, as the moon is seen upon the night of the full moon; the believers will see Him, according to traditions which have come down from the Prophet. We teach that while the believers will see Him, the unbelievers will be separated from Him by a wall of division, as God has said, (Qur. 83: 15); "Surely not! They will be separated from their Lord, upon that Day." We teach that Moses besought God that he might see Him in this world; then God revealed Himself to the mountain and turned it into dust and taught Moses thereby that he could not see Him in this world (Qur. 7: 139).

We are of the opinion that we may not accuse anyone of unbelief (*kufr*), who prays towards Mecca, on account of sin committed by him, such as unchastity, theft, wine drinking, as the Kharijites believe, who judge that these thereby become unbelievers. We teach that whoever commits a great sin (*kabira*), or anything like it, holding it to be allowed, is an unbeliever, since he does not believe in its prohibition.

We teach that Islam is a wider idea than Faith (*iman*), so that not every Islam is Faith.

We believe that God turns the hearts upside down, and holds them between two of His fingers, that He lays the heavens upon a finger and the earth upon a finger, according to the tradition from the Prophet.

We believe that God will not leave in Hell any of those who confess His Unity (*muwahhid*) and hold fast to the Faith, and that there is no Hell for him whom the Prophet has by his witness appointed to Paradise. We hope for Paradise for sinners and fear on their account, that they will be punished in Hell.

We teach that God will release a few out of Hell, on account of Muhammad's intercession (*shafa'a*) after they have been scorched there.

We believe in the punishment of the grave. We believe that the Tank (*hawd*) and the Balance are Verities: that the Bridge *as-Sirat* is a Verity; that the Arousing (*ba'th*) after death is a Verity; that God will set up His creatures in a place (*mawqif*) and will hold a reckoning with the Believers.

We believe that Faith (*iman*) consists in word (*qawl*) and in work (*amal*) and that it increases and diminishes. We trust in the sound Traditions handed down from the Apostle of God, which trustworthy people (*thiqat*), just man from just man, up to the Apostle, have transmitted.

We hold by the love of the early Believers (*salaf*), whom God chose to be Companions to the Prophet, and we praise them with the praise with which God praised them, and we carry on their succession.

We assert that the Imam succeeding the Apostle of God was Abu Bakr; that God through him made the Religion (*din*) mighty, and caused him to conquer the Apostates (*murtadds*). The Muslims made him their Imam, just as Muhammad had made him Imam at prayers. Then followed [as legal Imam] Umar ibn al-Khattab; then Uthman ibn Affan; his murderers killed him out of wickedness and enmity; then Ali ibn Abi Talib. These are the Imams after the Apostle, and their Khalifate is that of the Prophetic office [*i.e.*, they are, though not prophets, successors of the Prophet].

We bear witness of Paradise for the Ten (*al-asharatu-l-mubashshara*), to whom the Apostle bore witness of it, and we carry on the succession of the other Companions of the Prophet and hold ourselves far from that which was in dispute between them.

We hold that the four Imams were in the true way, were rightly guided and excellent, so that no one equals them in excellence.

We hold as true the traditions which the People of Tradition (*naql*) have established, concerning the descent of God to the lowest heaven (*sama ad-dunya*), and that the Lord will say, "Is there a supplicant? Is there a seeker for forgiveness?" and the rest of that which they have handed down and established, contrary to that which the mistaken and misled opine.

We ground ourselves in our opposition on the Qur'an, the Sunna [example] of the Prophet, the agreement of the Muslims and what is in accordance therewith, but put forth no novelty (*bid'a*) not sanctioned by God, and opine of God nothing that we have not been taught.

We teach that God will come on the Day of Resurrection, as He has said, (Qur. 89: 23); "When the earth shall be turned to dust, and the Lord shall appear and the angels, rank on rank," and that God is near to His servants, in what way (*kayfa*) He wills, as He has said, (Qur. 50, 15); "and We are nearer to him than the artery in his neck;" and (Qur. 53: 8); "Then He approached and came near and was two bows' length distant or even nearer."

To our Religion (*din*) belongs further, that we on Fridays and on festival days pray behind every person, pious and profane—so are the conditions for congregational prayers, as it is handed down from Abd Allah ibn Umar that he prayed behind al-Hajjaj. To our Religion belongs the wiping (*mash*) of the inner boots (*khuffs*) upon a journey and at home, in contradiction to the deniers of this. We uphold the prayer for peace for the Imams of the Muslims, submission to their office, and maintain the error of those who hold it right to rise against them whenever there may be apparent in them a falling away from right. We are against armed rebellion against them and civil war.

We believe in the appearance of anti-Christ (*ad-Dajjal*) according to the tradition handed down from the Prophet; in the punishment of the grave, and in Munkar and Nakir and in their questions to the buried in their graves. We hold the tradition of the journey to heaven (*mi'raj*, Qur. 17) of Muhammad as true, and declare many of the visions in sleep to be true, and we say that there is an explanation for them. We uphold the alms for the dead of the Muslims and prayer for them, and believe that God will help them therewith. We hold as true that there are enchanters in the world, and that enchantment is and exists. We hold as a religious duty the prayer which is held over the dead of those who have prayed toward Mecca, whether they have been believers or godless; we uphold also their right of testation. We acknowledge that Paradise and Hell are created, and that whoever dies or is killed, dies or is killed at his appointed time (*ajal*); that the articles of sustenance (*rizq*) from God, with which He sustains His creatures, are permitted (*halal*) and forbidden (*haram*); that Satan makes evil suggestions to men, and puts them in doubt, and causes them to be possessed, contrary to that which the Mu'tazilites and the Jahmites maintain, as God said, (Qur. 2: 276); "Those who take usury will [at the Resurrection] stand there like one whom Satan causes to be possessed by madness," and (Qur. 114: 4 *ff.*); "I take my refuge in God, from the evil suggestion, from the stealthy one who makes suggestions in the hearts of men, by means of men and Jinn."

We affirm that God may distinguish the pious by signs which He manifests through them.

Our teaching concerning the little children of the polytheists (*mushriqs*) is this, that God will kindle a fire in the other world for them, and will say, "Run in there;"—as the tradition says.

We believe that God knows what men do and what they will to do, what happens and how that which does not happen, if it should happen, would happen.

We believe in the obedience of the Imams and in their counsel of the Muslims.

We consider right the separation from every inciter to innovation (*bid'a*) and the turning aside from the People of wandering desires (*ahl al-ahwa*).

Shi'a Beliefs (Ibn Babūya al-Sadūq)

Shi'a Muslims believe that the divine authority of Muhammad was passed to his legitimate hereditary successors beginning with Ali, the Prophet's son-in-law and cousin. They also contend that this line of succession was cut short by the murder of Ali and other rightful successors.

35. Our belief concerning the number of the prophets is that there have been one hundred and twenty-four thousand prophets and a like number of plenipotentiaries (*awṣīyā'*). Each prophet had a plenipotentiary to whom he gave instructions by the command of God. And concerning them we believe that they brought the truth from God and their word is the word of God, their command God's command, and obedience to them obedience to God. . . .

The leaders of the prophets are five (on whom all depends): Noah, Abraham, Moses, Jesus, and Muhammad. Muhammad is their leader . . . he confirmed the (other) apostles.

It is necessary to believe that God did not create anything more excellent than Muhammad and the Imāms. . . . After His prophet, the proofs of God for the people are the Twelve Imāms. . . .

We believe that the Proof of Allah in His earth and His viceregent (*khalīfa*) among His slaves in this age of ours is the Upholder (*al-Qā'im*) (of the laws of God), the Expected One, Muhammad ibn al-Ḥasan al-'Askarī (*i.e.*, the Twelfth *Imām*). He it is concerning whose name and descent the Prophet was informed by God, and he it is who WILL FILL THE EARTH WITH JUSTICE AND EQUITY JUST AS IT IS NOW FULL OF OPPRESSION AND WRONG. He it is whom God will make victorious over the whole world until from every place the call to prayer is heard and religion will belong entirely to God, exalted be He. . . .

Jesus, son of Mary, will descend upon the earth and pray behind him. We believe there can be no other *Qā'im* than him; he may live in the state of occultation (*ghayba*) (as long as he likes); were it the space of the existence of this world, there would be no *Qā'im* other than him.

36. Our belief concerning prophets, apostles, Imāms [in the special Shī'ī sense] and angels is that they are infallible (*ma'ṣūm*); . . . and do not commit any sin, minor or major . . . he who denies infallibility to them in any matter . . . is a *kāfir*, an infidel.

37. Our belief concerning those who exceed the bounds of belief, the *ghūlat* [such as those who ascribe divinity to 'Alī or the other *imāms.*—ED] and those who believe in delegation [*mufawwiḍa*: the belief that after creating Muhammad and 'Alī, God rested and delegated all the administration of His creation to their hands.—ED], is that they are *kuffār*, deniers of God. They are more wicked than the Jews, the Christians, the Fire Worshippers . . . or any heretics; none have belittled God more. . . .

Our belief concerning the Prophet is that he was poisoned (by Jews) during the expedition to Khaybar. The poison continued to be noxious and (shortening his life) until he died of its effects.

I. Imām: And the Prince of Believers ('Alī), on whom be peace, was murdered by . . . Ibn Muljam al-Murādī, may God curse him, and was buried in Ghārī.

II. Imām: Ḥasan ibn 'Alī, on whom be peace, was poisoned by his wife Ja'da bint Ash'ath of Kinda, may God curse (her and her father).

III. Imām: Ḥusayn ibn 'Alī was slain at Karbala. His murderer was Sinān ibn-Anas al-Nakhā'ī, may God curse him and his father.

Shaykh Saduq, A Shiite Creed, trans. Asaf A.A. Fyzee (London: Oxford University Press, 1942).

IV. Imām: 'Alī ibn Ḥusayn, the Sayyid Zayn al-'Abidīn, was poisoned by al-Walīd ibn 'Abd al-Mālik, God curse him.

V. Imām: Muhammad Bāqir ibn 'Alī was poisoned by Ibrahīm ibn al-Walīd, God curse him.

VI. Imām: Ja'far al-Sāḍiq was poisoned by Abū Ja'far al-Manśūr al-Dawanīqī, may God curse him.

VII. Imām: Mūsa al-Kāzim ibn Ja'far was poisoned by Harūn al-Rashīd, may God curse him.

VIII. Imām: 'Alī al-Riḍā ibn Mūsa was poisoned by Ma'mūn ibn Harūn al-Rashīd, may God curse him.

XI. Imām: Abū Ja'far Muhammad al-Tāqī ibn 'Alī was poisoned by al-Mu'tasim, may God curse him.

X. Imām: 'Alī al-Naqī ibn Muhammad was poisoned by Mutawakkil, may God curse him.

XI. Imām: Ḥasan al-'Askarī was poisoned by al-Mu'tamid, may God curse him. . . . And verily the Prophets and Imāms, on whom be peace, had informed (people) that they would be murdered. He who says that they were not has given them the lie and has imputed falsehood to God the Mighty and Glorious.

39. Our belief concerning *taqīya* (permissible dissimulation of one's true beliefs) is that it is obligatory, and he who forsakes it is in the same position as he who forsakes prayer. . . . Now until the time when the Imām al-Qā'im appears, *taqīya* is obligatory and it is not permissible to dispense with it. He who does . . . has verily gone out of the religion of God. And God has described the showing of friendship to unbelievers as being (possible only) in the state of *taqīya*.

And the Imām Ja'far said, "Mix with enemies openly but oppose them inwardly, so long as the authority is a matter of question." He also said, "Diplomacy (*al-ri'ā'*) with a true believer is a form of polytheism, but with a (hypocrite) in his own house, it is worship." And he said "He who prays with hypocrites (*i.e.*, Sunnīs), standing in the first row, it is as though he prayed with the Prophet standing in the first row." And he said, "Visit their sick and attend their funerals and pray in their mosques."

40. Our belief concerning the (ancestors of the Prophet, contrary to the Sunnīs) is that they were Muslims from Adam down to 'Abdallah, father of the Prophet. . . .

41. Our belief concerning the 'Alawīya (descendants of 'Alī) is that they are the progeny of the Messenger of God and devotion to them is obligatory (in) requital of his apostleship. . . .

The Sufi Path: Doorkeeper of the Heart

The following writings are by Rabi'a Al-Adawiyya (d. 801), a woman mystic in the Sufi tradition and a beloved saint in Islam. She was born into poverty, lived in Basra (now a city in Iraq), was enslaved at a young age, and was later freed by her master. She lived an ascetic life dominated, she said, by a passionate love of God, which she expressed in her poetry. She professed that her love of God was so all-consuming that "no space is left for loving—or hating—any but him." She taught that the sole motivation for worshipping God should be love, not the carrot-and-stick of hell and paradise. She achieved a rare status in Islam: a woman deemed the equal of men.

Rabi'a, in Charles Upton, trans., *Doorkeeper of the Heart: Versions of Rabi'a*, (Putney, VT: Threshold, 1988), 44, 49.

Your hope in my heart is the rarest treasure
Your Name on my tongue is the sweetest word
My choicest hours
Are the hours I spend with You —

O God, I can't live in this world
Without remembering You —
How can I endure the next world
Without seeing Your face?

I am a stranger in Your country
And lonely among Your worshippers:
This is the substance of my complaint. . . .

DREAM FABLE

I saw myself in a wide green garden, more beautiful than I could begin to understand. In this garden was a young girl. I said to her, "How *wonderful* this place is!"

"Would you like to see a place even more wonderful than this?" she asked.

"Oh yes," I answered. Then taking me by the hand, she led me on until we came to a magnificent palace, like nothing that was ever seen by human eyes. The young girl knocked on the door, and someone opened it. Immediately both of us were flooded with light.

God alone knows the inner meaning of the maidens we saw living there. Each one carried in her hand a serving-tray filled with light. The young girl asked the maidens where they were going, and they answered her, "We are looking for someone who was drowned in the sea, and so became a martyr. She never slept at night, not one wink! We are going to rub funeral spices on her body."

"Then rub some on my friend here," the young girl said.

"Once upon a time," said the maidens, "part of this spice and the fragrance of it clung to her body—but then she shied away." Quickly the young girl let go of my hand, turned, and said to me:

"Your prayers are your light;
Your devotion is your strength;
Sleep is the enemy of both.
Your life is the only opportunity that life can give you.
If you ignore it, if you waste it,
You will only turn into dust."

Then the young girl disappeared.

Al-Ghazali: The Classes of Seekers

Al-Ghazali (d. 1111), a renowned theologian and mystic, is another who took the Sufi path. While teaching Islamic law, he experienced a spiritual crisis that eventually led him into Sufi studies. He came to believe that the kind of reasoning favored by the philosophers cannot provide the wisdom that mystical experience can. Logic, however, could be applied fruitfully to codes of ethics. This excerpt is taken from his "Deliverance from Error," a guide to spirituality and the story of how he first encountered Sufism.

Al-Ghazali, *Deliverance from Error*, in W. Montgomery Watt, trans., *The Faith and Practice of Al-Ghazali* (Oxford: One World, 1953, 2000), 26–27, 56–58, 63–65.

When God by His grace and abundant generosity cured me of this disease, I came to regard the various seekers (after truth) as comprising four groups:—

1. the *Theologians* (*mutakallimun*), who claim that they are the exponents of thought and intellectual speculation;
2. the *Batiniyah*, who consider that they, as the party of 'authoritative instruction' (*ta'lim*), alone derive truth from the infallible imam;
3. the *Philosophers,* who regard themselves as the exponents of logic and demonstration;
4. the *Sufis or Mystics*, who claim that they alone enter into the 'presence' (of God), and possess vision and intuitive understanding.

I said within myself: 'The truth cannot lie outside these four classes. These are the people who tread the paths of the quest for truth. If the truth is not with them, no point remains in trying to apprehend the truth. There is certainly no point in trying to return to the level of naive and derivative belief (*taqlid*) once it has been left, since a condition of being at such a level is that one should not know one is there; when a man comes to know that, the glass of his naive beliefs is broken. This is a breakage which cannot be mended, a breakage not to be repaired by patching or by assembling of fragments. The glass must be melted once again in the furnace for a new start, and out of it another fresh vessel formed'.

I now hastened to follow out these four ways and investigate what these groups had achieved, commencing with the science of theology and then taking the way of philosophy, the 'authoritative instruction' of the Batiniyah, and the way of mysticism, in that order. . . .

When I had finished with these sciences, I next turned with set purpose to the method of mysticism (or Sufism). I knew that the complete mystic 'way' includes both intellectual belief and practical activity; the latter consists in getting rid of the obstacles in the self and in stripping off its base characteristics and vicious morals, so that the heart may attain to freedom from what is not God and to constant recollection of Him.

The intellectual belief was easier to me than the practical activity. I began to acquaint myself with their belief by reading their books, such as *The Food of the Hearts* by Abu Talib al-Makki (God have mercy upon him), the works of al-Harith al-Muhasibi, the various anecdotes about al-Junayd, ash-Shibli and Abu Yazid al-Bistami (may God sanctify their spirits), and other discourses of their leading men. I thus comprehended their fundamental teachings on the intellectual side, and progressed, as far as is possible by study and oral instruction, in the knowledge of mysticism. It became clear to me, however, that what is most distinctive of mysticism is something which cannot be apprehended by study, but only by immediate experiences (*dhawq*—literally 'tasting'), by ecstasy and by a moral change. What a difference there is between *knowing* the definition of health and satiety, together with their causes and presuppositions, and *being* healthy and satisfied! What a difference between being acquainted with the definition of drunkenness—namely, that it designates a state arising from the domination of the seat of the intellect by vapours arising from the stomach—and being drunk! Indeed, the drunken man while in that condition does not know the definition of drunkenness nor the scientific account of it he has not the very least scientific knowledge of it. The sober man, on the other hand, knows the definition of drunkenness and its basis, yet he is not drunk in the very least. Again the doctor, when he is himself ill, knows the definition and causes of health and the remedies which restore it, and yet is lacking in health. Similarly there is a difference between knowing the true nature and causes and conditions of the ascetic life and actually leading such a life and forsaking the world.

I apprehended clearly that the mystics were men who had real experiences, not men of words, and that I had already progressed as far as was possible by way of intellectual apprehension. What remained for me was not to be attained by oral instruction and study but only by immediate experience and by walking in the mystic way. . . .

I continued at this stage for the space of ten years, and during these periods of solitude there were revealed to me things innumerable and unfathomable. This much I shall say about that in order that others may be helped: I learnt with certainty that it is above all the mystics who walk on the road of God; their life is the best life, their method the soundest method, their character the purest character; indeed, were the intellect of the intellectuals and the learning of the learned and the scholarship of the scholars, who are versed in the profundities of revealed truth, brought together in the attempt to improve the life and character of the mystics, they would find no way of doing so; for to the mystics all movement and all rest, whether external or internal, brings illumination from the light of the lamp of prophetic revelation; and behind the light of prophetic revelation there is no other light on the face of the earth from which illumination may be received.

In general, then, how is a mystic 'way' (*tariqah*) described? The purity which is the first condition of it (as bodily purity is the prior condition of formal Worship for Muslims) is the purification of the heart completely from what is other than God most high; the key to it, which corresponds to the opening act of adoration in prayer, is the sinking of the heart completely in the recollection of God; and the end of it is complete absorption (*fana'*) in God. At least this is its end relatively to those first steps which almost come within the sphere of choice and personal responsibility; but in reality in the actual mystic 'way' it is the first step, what comes before it being, as it were, the ante-chamber for those who are journeying towards it.

With this first stage of the 'way' there begin the revelations and visions. The mystics in their waking state now behold angels and the spirits of the prophets; they hear these speaking to them and are instructed by them. Later, a higher state is reached; instead of beholding forms and figures, they come to stages in the 'way' which it is hard to describe in language; if a man attempts to express these, his words inevitably contain what is clearly erroneous.

In general what they manage to achieve is nearness to God; some, however, would conceive of this as 'inherence' (*hulul*), some as 'union' (*ittihad*), and some as 'connection' (*wusul*). All that is erroneous. In my book, *The Noblest Aim,* I have explained the nature of the error here. Yet he who has attained the mystic 'state' need do no more than say:

> "Of the things I do not remember, what was, was;
>
> Think it good; do not ask an account of it."
>
> (Ibn al-Mu'tazz)

In general the man to whom He has granted no immediate experience at all, apprehends no more of what prophetic revelation really is than the name. The miraculous graces given to the saints are in truth the beginnings of the prophets; and that was the first 'state' of the Messenger of God (peace be upon him) when he went out to Mount Hira', and was given up entirely to his Lord, and worshipped, so that the bedouin said, 'Muhammad loves his Lord passionately'.

Now this is a mystical 'state' which is realized in immediate experience by those who walk in the way leading to it. Those to whom it is not granted to have immediate experience can become assured of it by trial (contact with mystics or observation of them) and by hearsay, if they have sufficiently numerous opportunities of associating with mystics to understand that (ecstasy) with certainty by means of what accompanies the 'states'. Whoever sits in their company derives from them this faith; and none who sits in their company is pained.

PRACTICES

The Quran

Sura 2 is called "The Cow." The following two sections of it ("The Five Pillars" and "The Laws") give instructions on performing the five practices required of all Muslims and on observing particular laws, mostly those that concern marital issues.

2. THE COW (THE FIVE PILLARS)

[144]Many a time We have seen you [Prophet] turn your
face towards Heaven, so We are turning you towards
a prayer direction that pleases you. Turn your face in
the direction of the Sacred Mosque: wherever you
[believers] may be, turn your faces to it. Those who
were given the Scripture know with certainty that
this is the Truth from their Lord: God is not unaware
of what they do. [145]Yet even if you brought every
proof to those who were given the Scripture, they
would not follow your prayer direction, nor will you
follow theirs, nor indeed will any of them follow one
another's direction. If you [Prophet] were to follow
their desires, after the knowledge brought to you,
you would be doing wrong. [146]Those We gave Scripture know it as well as they know their own sons, but
some of them hide the truth that they know. [147]The
truth is from your Lord, so do not be one of those
who doubt. [148]Each community has its own direction
to which it turns: race to do good deeds and wherever
you are, God will bring you together. God has power
to do everything.

[149][Prophet], wherever you may have started out,
turn your face in the direction of the Sacred
Mosque—this is the truth from your Lord: He is not
unaware of what you do— [150]wherever you may have
started out, turn your face in the direction of the
Sacred Mosque; wherever any of you may be, turn
your faces towards it, so that people may have no
argument against you—except for the wrongdoers
among them: do not fear them; fear Me—and so that
I may perfect My favour on you and you may be
guided, [151]just as We have sent among you a Messenger of your own to recite Our revelations to you,
purify you and teach you the Scripture, wisdom, and
[other] things you did not know. [152]So remember Me;
I will remember you. Be thankful to Me, and never
ungrateful. . . .

[183]You who believe, fasting is prescribed for you,
as it was prescribed for those before you, so that you
may be mindful of God. [184]Fast for a specific number
of days, but if one of you is ill, or on a journey, on
other days later. For those who can fast only with
extreme difficulty, there is a way to compensate—
feed a needy person. But if anyone does good of his
own accord, it is better for him, and fasting is better
for you, if only you knew. [185]It was in the month of
Ramadan that the Qur'an was revealed as guidance
for mankind, clear messages giving guidance and
distinguishing between right and wrong. So any one
of you who is present that month should fast, and
anyone who is ill or on a journey should make up for
the lost days by fasting on other days later. God
wants ease for you, not hardship. He wants you to

The Qur'an, M.A.S. Abdel Haleem, trans., Sura 2 (The Cow) (Oxford: Oxford University Press, 2004), 16–28.

complete the prescribed period and to glorify Him for having guided you, so that you may be thankful. [186][Prophet], if My servants ask you about Me, I am near. I respond to those who call Me, so let them respond to Me, and believe in Me, so that they may be guided.

[187]You [believers] are permitted to lie with your wives during the night of the fast: they are [close] as garments to you, as you are to them. God was aware that you were betraying yourselves, so He turned to you in mercy and pardoned you: now you can lie with them—seek what God has ordained for you—eat and drink until the white thread of dawn becomes distinct from the black. Then fast until nightfall. Do not lie with them during the nights of your devotional retreat in the mosques: these are the bounds set by God, so do not go near them. In this way God makes His messages clear to people, that they may guard themselves against doing wrong. . . .

[195]Spend in God's cause: do not contribute to your destruction with your own hands, but do good, for God loves those who do good.

[196]Complete the pilgrimages, major and minor, for the sake of God. If you are prevented [from doing so], then [send] whatever offering for sacrifice you can afford, and do not shave your heads until the offering has reached the place of sacrifice. If any of you is ill, or has an ailment of the scalp, he should compensate by fasting, or feeding the poor, or offering sacrifice. When you are in safety, anyone wishing to take a break between the minor pilgrimage and the major one must make whatever offering he can afford. If he lacks the means, he should fast for three days during the pilgrimage, and seven days on his return, making ten days in all. This applies to those whose household is not near the Sacred Mosque. Always be mindful of God, and be aware that He is stern in His retribution.

[197]The pilgrimage takes place during the prescribed months. There should be no indecent speech, misbehaviour, or quarrelling for anyone undertaking the pilgrimage—whatever good you do, God is well aware of it. Provide well for yourselves: the best provision is to be mindful of God—always be mindful of Me, you who have understanding—[198]but it is no offence to seek some bounty from your Lord. When you surge down from Arafat remember God at the sacred place. Remember Him: He has guided you. Before that you were astray. [199]Surge down where the rest of the people do, and ask forgiveness of God: He is most forgiving and merciful. [200]When you have completed your rites, remember God as much as you remember your own fathers, or even more. There are some who pray, 'Our Lord, give us good in this world,' and they will have no share in the Hereafter; [201]others pray, 'Our Lord, give us good in this world and in the Hereafter, and protect us from the torment of the Fire.' [202]They will have the share they have worked for: God is swift in reckoning. . . .

2. THE COW (LAWS)

[219]They ask you [Prophet] about intoxicants and gambling: say, 'There is great sin in both, and some benefit for people: the sin is greater than the benefit.' They ask you what they should give: say, 'Give what you can spare.' In this way, God makes His messages clear to you, so that you may reflect [220]on this world and the next. They ask you about [the property of] orphans: say, 'It is good to set things right for them. If you combine their affairs with yours, remember they are your brothers and sisters: God knows those who spoil things and those who improve them. Had He so willed, He could have made you vulnerable too: He is almighty and wise.'

[221]Do not marry idolatresses until they believe: a believing slave woman is certainly better than an idolatress, even though she may please you. And do not give your women in marriage to idolaters until they believe: a believing slave is certainly better than an idolater, even though he may please you. Such people call [you] to the Fire, while God calls [you] to the Garden and forgiveness by His leave. He makes His messages clear to people, so that they may bear them in mind.

[222]They ask you [Prophet] about menstruation. Say, 'Menstruation is a painful condition, so keep away from women during it. Do not approach them until they are cleansed; when they are cleansed, you

may approach them as God has ordained.' God loves those who turn to Him, and He loves those who keep themselves clean. [223]Your wives are your fields, so go into your fields whichever way you like, and send [something good] ahead for yourselves. Be mindful of God: remember that you will meet Him.' [Prophet], give good news to the believers.

[224][Believers], do not allow your oaths in God's name to hinder you from doing good, being mindful of God and making peace between people. God hears and knows everything: [225]He will not call you to account for oaths you have uttered unintentionally, but He will call you to account for what you mean in your hearts. God is most forgiving and forbearing. [226]For those who swear that they will not approach their wives, there shall be a waiting period of four months: if they go back, remember God will be most forgiving and merciful, [227]but if they are determined to divorce, remember that God hears and knows all. [228]Divorced women must wait for three monthly periods before remarrying, and, if they really believe in God and the Last Day, it is not lawful for them to conceal what God has created in their wombs: their husbands would do better to take them back during this period, provided they wish to put things right. Wives have [rights] similar to their [obligations], according to what is recognized to be fair, and husbands have a degree [of right] over them: [both should remember that] God is almighty and wise.

[229]Divorce can happen twice, and [each time] wives either be kept on in an acceptable manner or released in a good way. It is not lawful for you to take back anything that you have given [your wives], except where both fear that they cannot maintain [the marriage] within the bounds set by God: if you [arbiters] suspect that the couple may not be able to do this, then there will be no blame on either of them if the woman opts to give something for her release. These are the bounds set by God: do not overstep them. It is those who overstep God's bounds who are doing wrong. [230]If a husband re-divorces his wife after the second divorce, she will not be lawful for him until she has taken another husband; if that one divorces her, there will be no blame if she and the first husband return to one another, provided they feel that they can keep within the bounds set by God. These are God's bounds, which He makes clear for those who know.

[231]When you divorce women and they have reached their set time, then either keep or release them in a fair manner. Do not hold on to them with intent to harm them and commit aggression: anyone who does this wrongs himself. Do not make a mockery of God's revelations; remember the favour He blessed you with, and the Scripture and wisdom He sent to teach you. Be mindful of God and know that He has full knowledge of everything. [232]When you divorce women and they have reached their set time, do not prevent them from remarrying their husbands if they both agree to do so in a fair manner. Let those of you who believe in God and the Last Day take this to heart: that is more wholesome and purer for you. God knows and you do not.

[233]Mothers suckle their children for two whole years, if they wish to complete the term, and clothing and maintenance must be borne by the father in a fair manner. No one should be burdened with more than they can bear: no mother shall be made to suffer harm on account of her child, nor any father on account of his. The same duty is incumbent on the father's heir. If, by mutual consent and consultation, the couple wish to wean [the child], they will not be blamed, nor will there be any blame if you wish to engage a wet nurse, provided you pay as agreed in a fair manner. Be mindful of God, knowing that He sees everything you do.

[234]If any of you die and leave widows, the widows should wait for four months and ten nights before remarrying. When they have completed this set time, you will not be blamed for anything they may reasonably choose to do with themselves. God is fully aware of what you do. [235]You will not be blamed whether you give a hint that you wish to marry these women, or keep it to yourselves—God knows that you intend to propose to them. Do not make a secret arrangement with them; speak to them honourably and do not confirm the marriage tie until the prescribed period reaches its end. Remember that God knows what is in your souls, so be mindful of Him. Remember that God is most forgiving and forbearing.

[236]You will not be blamed if you divorce women when you have not yet consummated the marriage

or fixed a bride-gift for them, but make fair provision for them, the rich according to his means and the poor according to his—this is a duty for those who do good. [237]If you divorce wives before consummating the marriage but after fixing a bride-gift for them, then give them half of what you had previously fixed, unless they waive [their right], or unless the one who holds the marriage tie waives [his right]. Waiving [your right] is nearer to godliness, so do not forget to be generous towards one another: God sees what you do. [238]Take care to do your prayers, praying in the best way, and stand before God in devotion. [239]If you are in danger, pray when you are out walking or riding; when you are safe again, remember God, for He has taught you what you did not know.

[240]If any of you die and leave widows, make a bequest for them: a year's maintenance and no expulsion from their homes [for that time]. But if they leave of their own accord, you will not be blamed for what they may reasonably choose to do with themselves: God is almighty and wise. [241]Divorced women shall also have such maintenance as is considered fair: this is a duty for those who are mindful of God. [242]In this way God makes His revelations clear to you, so that you may grow in understanding. . . .

Hadith: Charity (Zakat)

These hadith constitute a discourse on charity, or almsgiving, one of the five pillars of Islam. They explain the proper way to help the needy and thus fulfill the obligation of zakat under various circumstances.

1 Abū Mūsā reported, The Prophet said: "*Sadaqah* is incumbent on every Muslim." They (his companions) said, O Prophet of Allāh! And (what about him) who has not got (anything to give)? He said: "He should work with his hand and profit himself and give in charity." They said, If he has nothing (in spite of this). He said: "He should help the distressed one who is in need." They said, If he is unable to do this. He said: "He should do good deeds and refrain from doing evil—this is charity on his part." (Bukhari 24:31)

2 Abū Hurairah reported, The Prophet said: "On every bone of the fingers charity is incumbent every day: One assists a man in riding his beast or in lifting his provisions to the back of the animal, this is charity; and a good word and every step which one takes in walking over to prayer is charity; and showing the way (to another) is charity." (Bukhari 56:72)

3 Abū Hurairah reported, The Prophet said: "Removal from the way of that which is harmful is charity." (Bukhari 46:24)

4 Jābir said, The Messenger of Allāh said: "Every good deed is charity, and it is a good deed that thou meet thy brother with a cheerful countenance and that thou pour water from thy bucket into the vessel of thy brother." (*Musnad* of Ahmed Miskhat 6:6)

5 Abū Hurairah said, Then the Prophet said: "The man who exerts himself on behalf of the widow and the poor one is like the one who struggles in the way of Allāh, or the one who keeps awake in the night (for prayers) and fasts during the day." (Bukhari 69:1)

6 Abū Hurairah said, The Messenger of Allāh, "A prostitute was forgiven—she passed by a dog, panting with its tongue out, on the top of a well containing water, almost dying with thirst; so she took off

Maulana Muhammad Ali, trans., *A Manual of Hadith* (Lahore: Ahmadiyya, 1944).

her boot and tied it to her head-covering and drew forth water for it; she was forgiven on account of this." It was said: Is there a reward for us in (doing good to) the beasts? He said: "In every animal having a liver fresh with life there is a reward." (Bukhari and Muslim Miskat 6:6)

7 Abū Hurairah said on the authority of the Prophet (who said): "There is a man who gives a charity and he conceals it so much so that his left hand does not know what his right hand spends." (Bukhari 24:11)

8 Zubair reported, The Prophet said: "If one of you should take his rope and bring a bundle of fire-wood on his back and then sell it, with which Allāh should save his honour, it is better for him than that he should beg of people whether give him or do not give him." (Bukhari 24:50)

9 Fātimah bint Qais said, The Messenger of Allāh said: "In (one's) wealth there is a due besides the zakāt"; then he recited: "It is not righteousness that you turn your faces towards the East and the West." (Tirmidhi Miskat 6:6)

10 Ibn Abbās reported, The Prophet sent Mu'ādh to Yaman and said: "Invite them to bear witness that there is no god but Allāh and that I am the Messenger of Allāh; if they accept this, tell them that Allāh has made obligatory on them five prayers in every day and night; if they accept this, tell them that Allāh has made obligatory in their wealth a charity which is taken from the wealthy among them and given to the poor among them." (Bukhari 24:1)

17 Abū Hurairah said, When the Messenger of Allāh died and Abū Bakr became (his successor), and those of the Arabs who would disbelieve disbelieved, 'Umar said, How dost thou fight people (who profess Islām), and the Messenger of Allāh said "I have been commanded to continue fighting against people until they say, There is no god but Allāh; whoever says this will have his property and his life safe unless there is a due against him and his reckoning is with Allāh." (Abū Bakr) said, By Allāh! I shall fight those who make a difference between prayer and zakāt, for zakāt is a tax on property; By Allāh! if they withhold from me even a she-kid which they used to make over to the Messenger of Allāh, I shall fight against them for their withholding it." Umar said, By Allāh! Allāh opened the heart of Abū Bakr (to receive the truth), so I knew that it was true. (Bukhari 24:1)

CONTEMPORARY CHALLENGES

Reforming Islam

JOHN L. ESPOSITO

In this reading John L. Esposito, professor of religion and author of several books on Islam, discusses the need for, and obstacles to, reforming Islam to address the threat from religious extremists. "The struggle of Islam today," he says, "is between competing voices and

John L. Esposito, *Islam: The Straight Path* (New York: Oxford University Press, 2005), 266–271.

visions, between a dangerous and deadly minority, terrorists such as Osama bin Laden and al-Qaeda, and the vast majority of mainstream Muslims."

September 11 brought into sharp focus the threat from terrorist movements within the world of Islam. It accelerated the need to face critical issues of reform and more aggressively address the religious and political threat from religious extremists. However, reformers face formidable obstacles: the ultraconservatism of many (though not all) *ulama* (religious scholars and clergy); reform in the curriculum and training of religious scholars, leaders, and students; in particular, reform in those militant madrasas and universities that perpetuate a "theology of hate" and a jihadi culture; and the effective discrediting of militant jihadist ideas and ideologies. The obstacles to reform are compounded by the political and economic realities (repressive governments, failed economies, social injustice) of many parts of the Muslim world, conditions that create contexts conducive to the growth of extremist movements. The struggle (jihad) is religious, intellectual, spiritual, and moral. It must be a rapid and widespread program of Islamic renewal that not only builds on past reformers but also follows the lead of enlightened religious leaders and intellectuals today who more forcefully and more effectively engage in a wide-ranging process of reinterpretation (*ijtihad*) and reform (*islah*). In many ways, they face a period of reexamination, reformation, and renewal similar to the Protestant Reformation or Vatican II in Roman Catholicism. However, like the Reformation, it is a process not only of intellectual ferment and religious debate but also of religious and political unrest and violence.

The focus on extremists has often overshadowed the extent to which reformers have been active in reinterpreting Islam and promoting reform. There are many among the current generation of reformers who advocate a progressive Islam, one that is democratic, pluralistic, and tolerant.

The struggle of Islam today is between competing voices and visions, between a dangerous and deadly minority, terrorists such as Osama bin Laden and al-Qaeda, and the vast majority of mainstream Muslims. While the extremists grab the headlines and threaten Muslim as well as Western societies, the moderate mainstream, like most religious believers, pursue normal everyday lives and goals.

Moreover, for decades a group of reform-minded Muslims has articulated and sought to implement a progressive, constructive, modern Islamic framework in response to the realities of Muslim societies. As intellectual activists, these academics, lawyers, physicians, journalists, and religious scholars represent voices of reform from North Africa to Southeast Asia. They respond to the realities of many Muslim societies, the challenges of authoritarian regimes and secular elites, the dangers of religious extremism, and the need for fresh interpretations of Islam to counter the deadweight of well-meaning but often intransigent conservative religious scholars and leaders.

Contemporary reformers share a common commitment and framework for Islamic intellectual and moral revitalization and reform. They seek to identify and build upon a common ground of shared beliefs and values and engage in interreligious and intercivilizational dialogue. In contrast to others, many advocate change through the peaceful cultural and educational transformation of society, advocate gender equality and full citizenship rights for non-Muslims, and denounce the use of violence by militants. They call for government reforms to address political, social, and economic grievances. Many critique Western political and cultural hegemony. At the same time, the visions and ideologies of reformers often differ substantially as their ideas and activities are conditioned by and respond to differing cultural and political contexts and reflect diverse interpretations of religious texts and history.

In the Middle East journalists such as Fahmi Howeidi and lawyers and intellectuals such as Selim al Awa, Tareq al-Bishri, Kamal Aboul Magd, Heba Rauf Ezzat, and Abdol Karim Soroush have been prominent advocates of reform, whose message has had a global as well as regional impact. Distinguishing between unchanging principles and values and historically and culturally conditioned practices, they have addressed issues of banking (differentiating the Quran's condemnation of usury and acceptable forms of banking interest), advocated gender equality for Muslim women and full citizenship rights for non-Muslims, and supported democratization. These reformers emphasize change through the peaceful cultural and educational transformation of society rather than regime change. They denounce the use of violence by militants as contrary to Islamic teachings; call for government reforms to address political, social, and economic grievances; and are critical of Western political and cultural imperialism.

In Indonesia, diverse leaders such as Dr. Nurcholish Madjid, Dr. Amien Rais, and Abdurrahman Wahid have espoused a reformist Islam that speaks to Indonesia's multireligious and multiethnic society. However different, they all advocate a progressive Islam, one that is democratic, pluralistic, and tolerant. Their modern syntheses distinguish between unchanging religious doctrines or laws and those that can be altered to accommodate social change. Perhaps the most visible internationally has been Abdurrahman Wahid. Leader of the Nandatul Ulama (Renaissance of Religious Scholars), the largest (35 million members) Islamic organization in the world's largest Muslim country, he became the first democratically elected president in Indonesian history in October 1999.

In contrast to those who advocate the Islamization of Indonesian society, Wahid emphasizes the Indonesianization, or contextualization, of Islam with local culture. Bridging the worlds of traditional Islam and "modern" thought, Wahid espouses a cosmopolitan Islam, responsive to the demands of modern life and reflecting Indonesian Islam's diverse religious and ethnic history and communities. It is an inclusive religious, democratic, pluralistic force.

Wahid believes that contemporary Muslims are at a critical crossroads. Two choices, or paths, confront them: to pursue a traditional, static, legal-formalistic Islam or to reclaim and refashion a more dynamic cosmopolitan, universal, pluralistic worldview. He rejects the notion that Islam should form the basis for the nation-state's political or legal system, which he characterizes as a Middle Eastern tradition alien to Indonesia. Indonesian Muslims should apply a moderate, tolerant brand of Islam to their daily lives in a society where "a Muslim and a non-Muslim are the same," a state in which religion and politics are separate.

Rejecting legalistic formalism and fundamentalism as an aberration and a major obstacle to Islamic reform and to Islam's response to global change, Wahid affirms the right of all Muslims, both laity and religious scholars (*ulama*), to "perpetual reinterpretation" (*ijtihad*) of the Quran and tradition of the Prophet in light of "ever changing human situations."

In contrast to the past, when ideas and influence flowed one way, from Muslim countries to the West, today information, ideas, financial resources, and influence flow on a superhighway whose traffic travels in both directions. Indeed, given the more open religious, political, and intellectual climate in Europe and America, Muslim intellectuals and activists have increasingly had a significant impact on Islamic thought and activism through their training of a new generation at universities and through their writings, which often reflect fresh reinterpretations (*ijtihad*) of critical issues. It is a movement that encompasses diverse people, ideologies, institutions, and global communications. Two-way communication and exchange occur through scholars' and activists' travel, speaking engagements, publications, video and audio tapes, and increasingly in cyberspace. Muhammad Arkoun, an Algerian-born Sorbonne Professor, Rashid Ghannoushi, the leader of Tunisia's Ennahda (Renaissance Party), who lives in exile in London, Khurshid Ahmad, the founder of the Islamic Foundation in Leicester, Yusuf Islam, formerly Cat Stevens and a prominent Muslim spokesman, Tareq Ramadan, a Swiss academic and Egyptian-born grandson of Hasan al-Banna, Seyyed Hossein Nasr at George Washington University in Washington, D. C., Abdulaziz Sachedina of the University of Virginia, Mahmud Ayub of Temple University, and Sulayman Nyang of Howard University, who is based in Europe and America, all speak to Muslims overseas through their writings, their Muslim students, and their audio and video recordings. At the same time, diverse voices in the Muslim world such as Qatar's Yusuf Qardawi, Lebanon's Faysal Mawlawi and Muhammad Fadlallah, Turkey's Fetullah Gulen, and the emir of Pakistan's Jamaat-i-Islami have a similar presence and impact in Europe and America. The result is a process of reformation that addresses issues of faith and practice, religious leadership and authority, religious and political pluralism, tolerance, minority rights (Muslim and non-Muslim), and gender. European and American Muslim diaspora communities can have almost instant access to the fatwas of muftis throughout the Muslim world and can obtain answers to their own specific questions on internet sites that feature segments such as "Ask the Mufti."

Indeed, one of the clearest examples of the struggle for reform, its diverse voices, and the issues involved is the "war of the fatwas." The opinions of prominent religious scholars, or muftis, mainstream and extremist, are circulated and debated globally in the media and via the internet. Issues include terrorism and suicide bombings, organ transplants, marriage and divorce, abortion, polygamy, the veil (*hijab*), women in the home and workplace, banking interest and usury, Sunni–Shii and Muslim–non-Muslim relations, and citizenship and voting, especially that of Muslim minorities in America, Europe, and elsewhere.

In the post-September 11 world, not only Muslim extremists but also Islam itself have been targeted (under siege). While political leaders such as George W. Bush and Tony Blair have been careful to distinguish between the religion of Islam and the actions of Muslim extremists and a war against global terrorism and a war against Islam, many others have not. Leaders of the more militant wing of the American Christian Right such as Pat Robertson, Jerry Falwell, and Franklin Graham have denounced Islam as an evil religion and labeled Muhammad a terrorist and a pedophile. Right-wing political leaders and parties in Europe often blur the line between their Muslim citizens and residents and extremists and terrorists. Some have pressed for special legislation to profile and monitor Muslims and mosques and for revisions in immigration policy to block Muslim immigration or, as in Norway, have called for the banning of the religion of Islam itself.

The liberalism, pluralism, and tolerance of Western democracies in North America and Europe are also challenged. As they seek to wage a battle against global terrorists, they risk compromising their cherished principles and values, the religious freedom and civil liberties of their Muslim citizens and residents. The distinction between the "hijacking" of Islam by extremists and mainstream Islam remains critical. Osama bin Laden, al-Qaeda, and other extremist groups are no more representative of Islam than are Christians who have committed acts of terrorism in Northern Ireland, Bosnia, or America; Jewish fundamentalists who assassinated Israel's prime minister Yitzak Rabin or slaughtered Arab Muslims at prayer in a mosque in Hebron; or Hindu extremists who have killed Muslims and Christians in India.

In the twenty-first century, Islam remains the second-largest and fastest growing religion in the world. As in the past, so today, the faith and practice of Islam inform the lives of more than 1.3 billion Muslims and have a significant impact on Muslim societies and global politics. Muslims today are at a crossroads. The challenges are formidable: calls in many quarters for greater political participation and democratization; failed economies and educational systems; the impact of globalization; the growth and threat of religious extremism; the ongoing need for significant religious reform to address the challenges of contemporary Muslim communities and societies; and the fostering of pluralism and a modern understanding of tolerance based on mutual understanding and respect.

Generations of reformers, a minority within their communities, struggle today against powerful forces: (1) conservative religious establishments, with their medieval paradigms; (2) authoritarian regimes and political elites who often perceive reformers as a threat to the established order; and (3) extremists whose violence and terror threaten the safety and security of their own societies as well as the international community. Just as reform in Protestantism and Catholicism was a long process of not only theological debate but political and economic turmoil, in which religious persecution was not only between faiths or denominations but also within them, Muslim reformers often face similar challenges and threats. Thus, addressing these problems and issues will require self-sacrifice and decades of commitment by many devout and talented followers of the Straight Path of Islam.

Passages About Women: The Quran, Sura 4

Some of the attitudes toward women in Islam have been widely criticized. The following passage from the Quran, *sura* 4, *contains* some of the teachings that have been most controversial.

In the name of God, the Lord of Mercy, the Giver of Mercy.

[1]People, be mindful of your Lord, who created you from a single soul, and from it created its mate, and from the pair of them spread countless men and women far and wide; be mindful of God, in whose name you make requests of one another. Beware of severing the ties of kinship: God is always watching over you. [2]Give orphans their property, do not replace [their] good things with bad, and do not consume their property with your own—a great sin. [3]If you fear that you will not deal fairly with orphan girls, you may marry whichever [other] women seem good to you, two, three, or four. If you fear that you cannot be equitable [to them], then marry only one, or your slave(s): that is more likely to make you avoid bias. [4]Give women their bridal gift upon marriage, though if they are happy to give up some of it for you, you may enjoy it with a clear conscience.

[5]Do not entrust your property to the feeble-minded. God has made it a means of support for you: make provision for them from it, clothe them, and address them kindly. [6]Test orphans until they reach marriageable age; then, if you find they have sound judgement, hand over their property to them. Do not consume it hastily before they come of age: if the guardian is well off he should abstain from the orphan's property, and if he is poor he should use only what is fair. When you give them their property, call witnesses in; but God takes full account of everything you do.

[7]Men shall have a share in what their parents and closest relatives leave, and women shall have a share in what their parents and closest relatives leave, whether the legacy be small or large: this is ordained by God. [8]If other relatives, orphans, or needy people are present at the distribution, give them something too, and speak kindly to them. [9]Let those who would fear for the future of their own helpless children, if they were to die, show the same concern [for orphans]; let them be mindful of God and speak out for justice. [10]Those who consume the property of orphans unjustly are actually swallowing fire into their own bellies: they will burn in the blazing Flame.

[11]Concerning your children, God commands you that a son should have the equivalent share of two daughters. If there are only daughters, two or more should share two-thirds of the inheritance, if one, she should have half. Parents inherit a sixth each if the deceased leaves children; if he leaves no children and his parents are his sole heirs, his mother has a third, unless he has brothers, in which case she has a sixth. [In all cases, the distribution comes] after payment of any bequests or debts. You cannot know which of your parents or your children is more beneficial to you: this is a law from God, and He is all knowing, all wise. [12]You inherit half of what your wives leave, if they have no children; if they have children, you inherit a quarter. [In all cases, the distribution comes] after payment of any bequests or debts. If you have no children, your wives' share is a quarter; if you have children, your wives get an eighth. [In all cases, the distribution comes] after payment of any bequests or debts. If a man or a woman dies leaving no children or parents, but a single brother or sister, he or she should take one-sixth of the inheritance; if there are more siblings, they share one-third between them. [In all cases, the distribution comes] after payment of any bequests or debts, with no harm done to anyone: this is a commandment from God: God is all knowing and benign to all. [13]These are the bounds set by God: God will

The Qur'an, M.A.S. Abdel Haleem, trans., Sura 4 (Women) (Oxford: Oxford University Press, 2004), 50–54.

admit those who obey Him and His Messenger to Gardens graced with flowing streams, and there they will stay—that is the supreme triumph! [14]But those who disobey God and His Messenger and overstep His limits will be consigned by God to the Fire, and there they will stay—a humiliating torment awaits them!

[15]If any of your women commit a lewd act, call four witnesses from among you, then, if they testify to their guilt, keep the women at home until death comes to them or until God shows them another way. [16] If two men commit a lewd act, punish them both; if they repent and mend their ways, leave them alone—God is always ready to accept repentance, He is full of mercy. [17]But God only undertakes to accept repentance from those who do evil out of ignorance and soon afterwards repent: these are the ones God will forgive, He is all knowing, all wise. [18]It is not true repentance when people continue to do evil until death confronts them and then say, 'Now I repent,' nor when they die defiant: We have prepared a painful torment for these.

[19]You who believe, it is not lawful for you to inherit women against their will, nor should you treat your wives harshly, hoping to take back some of the bride-gift you gave them, unless they are guilty of something clearly outrageous. Live with them in accordance with what is fair and kind: if you dislike them, it may well be that you dislike something in which God has put much good. [20]If you wish to replace one wife with another, do not take any of her bride-gift back, even if you have given her a great amount of gold. [21]How could you take it when this is unjust and a blatant sin? How could you take it when you have lain with each other and they have taken a solemn pledge from you?

[22]Do not marry women that your fathers married—with the exception of what is past—this is indeed a shameful thing to do, loathsome and leading to evil. [23]You are forbidden to take as wives your mothers, daughters, sisters, paternal and maternal aunts, the daughters of brothers and daughters of sisters, your milk-mothers and milk-sisters, your wives' mothers, the stepdaughters in your care—those born of women with whom you have consummated marriage, if you have not consummated the marriage, then you will not be blamed—wives of your begotten sons, two sisters simultaneously—with the exception of what is past: God is most forgiving and merciful—[24]women already married, other than your slaves. God has ordained all this for you. Other women are lawful to you, so long as you seek them in marriage, with gifts from your property, looking for wedlock rather than fornication. If you wish to enjoy women through marriage, give them their bride-gift—this is obligatory—though if you should choose mutually, after fulfilling this obligation, to do otherwise [with the bride-gift], you will not be blamed: God is all knowing and all wise.

[25]If any of you does not have the means to marry a believing free woman, then marry a believing slave—God knows best [the depth of] your faith: you are [all] part of the same family —so marry them with their people's consent and their proper bride-gifts. [Make them] married women, not adulteresses or lovers. If they commit adultery when they are married, their punishment will be half that of free women. This is for those of you who fear that you will sin; it is better for you to practise self-restraint. God is most forgiving and merciful, [26]He wishes to make His laws clear to you and guide you to the righteous ways of those who went before you. He wishes to turn towards you in mercy—He is all knowing, all wise—[27]He wishes to turn towards you, but those who follow their lusts want you to go far astray. [28]God wishes to lighten your burden; man was created weak.

[29]You who believe, do not wrongfully consume each other's wealth but trade by mutual consent. Do not kill each other, for God is merciful to you. [30]If any of you does these things, out of hostility and injustice, We shall make him suffer Fire: that is easy for God. [31]But if you avoid the great sins you have been forbidden, We shall wipe out your minor misdeeds and let you in through the entrance of honour. [32]Do not covet what God has given to some of you more than others—men have the portion they have earned; and women the portion they have earned—you should rather ask God for some of His bounty: He has full knowledge of everything. [33]We have appointed heirs for everything that parents and close relatives leave behind, including those to whom you

have pledged your hands [in marriage], so give them their share: God is witness to everything.

[34]Husbands should take good care of their wives, with [the bounties] God has given to some more than others and with what they spend out of their own money. Righteous wives are devout and guard what God would have them guard in their husbands' absence. If you fear high-handedness from your wives, remind them [of the teachings of God], then ignore them when you go to bed, then hit them. If they obey you, you have no right to act against them: God is most high and great. [35]If you [believers] fear that a couple may break up, appoint one arbiter from his family and one from hers. Then, if the couple want to put things right, God will bring about a reconciliation between them: He is all knowing, all aware. . . .

[127]They ask you [Prophet] for a ruling about women. Say, 'God Himself gives you a ruling about them. You already have what has been recited to you in the Scripture about orphan girls [in your charge] from whom you withhold the prescribed shares [of their inheritance] and whom you wish to marry, and also about helpless children—God instructs you to treat orphans fairly: He is well aware of whatever good you do.'

[128]If a wife fears high-handedness or alienation from her husband, neither of them will be blamed if they come to a peaceful settlement, for peace is best. Although human souls are prone to selfishness, if you do good and are mindful of God, He is well aware of all that you do. [129]You will never be able to treat your wives with equal fairness, however much you may desire to do so, but do not ignore one wife altogether, leaving her suspended [between marriage and divorce]. If you make amends and remain conscious of God, He is most forgiving and merciful, [130]but if husband and wife do separate, God will provide for each out of His plenty: He is infinite in plenty, and all wise. [131]Everything in the heavens and the earth belongs to God. . . .

Women and the Quran: Problematic Verses

RUTH RODED

In this selection Ruth Roded examines the specific verses about women in the Quran that have drawn the most criticism. "This subject," she says, "has been and continues to be one of the central issues related to the status of women in Islamic Middle Eastern society."

Much of the Quran is difficult to understand because of obscure references as well as the traditional arrangement of chapters and verses in which unrelated passages are interspersed. As a result, philological analysis and additional information obtained from the Prophet's Companions were utilized to explain and amplify the meaning of the revealed text. In theory, this imprecision should enable alternate

Ruth Roded, ed., *Women in Islam and The Middle East* (London: I. B. Tauris, 2008), 27–31; translations by Marmaduke Pickthall, *The Meaning of the Glorious Koran* (New York: Dorset Press, n.d.).

readings of the legal and normative material in the Quran. In fact, classical exegetes created a mainstream Islamic interpretation of the Quran which was handed down from generation to generation. In the nineteenth and early twentieth century, Muslim scholars rejected the acquired wisdom as foreign and customary accretions and returned to the text of the Quran in search of true Islam. In recent years, there have been some modest attempts at feminist exegesis of certain passages of the Quran.

Only one woman is actually named in the Quran, but a large number of verses refer to women. These include exhortations addressed to 'the believing men and the believing women', revelations specific to women or to relations between men and women, and laws pertinent to marriage, divorce, inheritance, etc. According to one estimate, some 80 per cent of the legal material in the Quran refers to women.

It is interesting to note that according to Islamic tradition a number of women among the early believers had a role in the transmission of the text of the Quran. Aisha, the Prophet's favourite wife, heard passages of the Quran from the Prophet himself, ordered a full written copy to be prepared and corrected the scribe. Hafsa, daughter of the caliph Umar and widow of the Prophet, gave written pages of the Quran which she received from her father to the caliph Uthman. Uthman gathered the pages into a book and declared this text as the official version of the holy book. She also corrected a scribe who was writing a Quran. During the first four centuries of Islam, Uthman's text was only one of various versions of the Quran which were ascribed to Companions of the Prophet, the caliphs Umar and Ali, and widows of the Prophet—Aisha, Umm Salama and Hafsa. One of the Prophet's female Companions, Umm Waraqa, collected and recited the Quran and may have assisted Umar in assembling the text.

The first four excerpts below are the basis of the concept of *hijab* in the sense of the appropriate attire for Muslim women, their seclusion at home and the limitation of their contact with men who are not their kin. This subject has been and continues to be one of the central issues related to the status of women in Islamic Middle Eastern society.

Some specific questions arise from each of these verses. In The Light (*al-Nur*): 30-1, men and women are told to be modest. Is there a difference in the exhortations to the genders? What are women's adornment which should not be displayed? What sort of veils are referred to; what should they cover? Verses 32-3 and 53 of the chapter The Clans *(al-Ahzab)* refer to the wives of the Prophet. Should these regulations be inferred for all Muslim women? What is the definition of *hijab* in the context of the Quran? To whom is verse 59 addressed? What are the cloaks, also translated 'outer garments' (*jalabib, s.jilbab*)? Why should women 'draw them close round'?

The general questions which relate to all of the verses are: According to the text of the Quran, must a believing Muslim woman remain in her home? Must she be separated from men who are not her kin inside the house? What should she wear when she leaves the house? According to the Quran, what is Islamic dress? What should it cover? What may one reveal?

No less crucial are the classical, modernist and feminist interpretations of the opening phrase of verse 34, The Women, which the British Muslim Marmaduke Pickthall translated 'Men are in charge of women' (*al-rijal qawwamuna 'ala al-nisa'*). Classical exegesis explained this phrase as referring to the superiority of men over women in a number of religious, political and intellectual fields, and it was frequently quoted to justify the exclusion of women from positions of authority over men. The modernist Muslim translator and commentator A. Yusuf Ali renders the phrase: 'Men are the protectors and maintainers of women.' The Muslim feminist Azizah al-Hibri takes the definition of *qawwamun* one step further to the concept of moral guidance and caring.

Another thorny issue is the seeming recommendation in the Quran to 'scourge' disobedient wives. Within the framework of the ethical message of Islam classical Muslim scholars tried to protect women from undue violence from men but they did not question a man's right to use force to chastise his wife. Yusuf Ali builds on this tradition when he translates the verse: 'As to those women on whose part ye fear disloyalty and ill-conduct, admonish them (first), (next), refuse to share their beds, (and last) beat them (lightly);' If these three measures fail, Yusuf Ali adds, then a family council should be convened in accordance with the next verse (4:35) in order to work out the couple's problems. Verse 35 of 'The Women' is usually quoted by Muslims to offset husbands' almost unilateral right to divorce their wives in a simple and informal procedure as defined in Islamic law.

Women and the Shari'a

MALISE RUTHVEN

Malise Ruthven provides another view on women and Islamic law. He notes that traditionalists argue that Muhammad greatly improved the status of Arabian women in his day. Even so, he says, "there are particular [Quranic] verses which testify to the legal inferiority of women." These concern inheritance, plural wives, legal rules of evidence, and marriage.

As with other politically charged issues in contemporary Islam the debate surrounding the veil is fuelled by diverging upon an exemplary past. Traditionalists, most of them men, argue that the Prophet of Islam greatly improved the position of the Arabian women of his time, guaranteeing them basic rights in marriage that were denied to the women of the time of ignorance—the *jahiliya.* Makkan suras of the Quran refer with abhorrence to the custom of female infanticide and the neglect of widows and orphans. After Islam, women were given guaranteed rights of inheritance under the protective umbrella of the family. A woman's husband was obligated to provide for her and her children. Although polygyny (one man and a plurality of wives) was permitted the man was limited to four wives, each of whom had to be treated equally. No spiritual inequality is implied. The Quran explicitly addresses itself to females as well as males and morally women will be as answerable for their actions on the Day of Judgement as men.

That said, however, there are particular verses which testify to the legal inferiority of women. A sister shares only half the portion of her brothers under the Quranic laws of inheritance—the assumption being that her husband will maintain her. A husband may physically chastise a recalcitrant or disobedient wife as a final resort when other measures have failed. In certain legal proceedings a woman's testimony is only worth half that of a man: it is assumed that she will be unfamiliar with business matters and that she will need a friend to jog her memory. In the context of seventh-century Arabia these Quranic rubrics are not necessarily incompatible with the argument that Islam substantially improved the status of women, not least by improving their security in marriage and property. Modern feminists wishing to move beyond these positions, however, face a theological obstacle. As the unalterable speech of God the Quran is deemed to be non-negotiable: for the majority of Muslims, the spirit is firmly anchored in the letter. To argue that

Malise Ruthven, *Islam: A Very Short Introduction* (Oxford: Oxford University Press, 1997), 92–93, 95, 97–99.

modern conditions demand an end to the Quran's discriminatory provisions is to challenge the dogma that the text is fixed for eternity. Feminist writers are forced by the logic of their position to de-couple the text from the spirit in favour of a flexible doctrine that leads inevitably to the recontextualization of Islam's holy book. The issue of women's rights is inexorably caught up in the issue of modernism.

As modernists see it, the Quran was revealed at a specific time and in a specific social context. Their task is to reinterpret the spirit of its provisions in the light of modern realities. The difficulty facing modernists is that those who take the text at face value, refusing to deconstruct it to suit current social trends or fashions, are often closer to its original meaning and purpose. To take a well-known example, the verses allowing polygyny require that each wife be treated equally. Traditionalists interpreted equality in legalistic terms: the right of each wife to her own household, to equality of material provision. Modernists undermine the whole institution by adding an emotional and psychological dimension to the notion of equality, arguing that since no man can be expected to be equally emotionally involved with all his wives, polygyny is effectively ruled out.

Similar arguments are deployed by modernists to rationalize the draconian punishments against unfaithful wives or individuals accused of illicit sexual activity (*zina*). Under the strict Quranic rules of evidence, the crime of *zina* must be attested by four independent adult male witnesses to the act itself. Since in the nature of things such a provision is almost impossible to satisfy, according to this argument sexual propriety is satisfied in principle while intrusive social censoriousness is avoided. Thus Leila Badawi draws attention to legal interpretations that appear liberal by pre-modern standards: in the case of a deserted or widowed woman who becomes pregnant she may be protected by the legal fiction (*hila*) of the 'sleeping foetus', according to which a pregnancy can be accepted as lasting five or even seven years, while the child remains the legal heir of the dead or absent husband. An unmarried woman who becomes pregnant can resort to the fiction of the 'public bath'. Baths were traditionally opened on alternating days or hours for men and women, and a virgin, it was claimed, who visited the public baths after the men had just vacated them might inadvertently sit on a pool of semen thereby making herself pregnant.

If theory is sometimes harsher than practice in upholding marital fidelity, the converse can apply with regard to inheritance. In many Muslim lands women have been systematically denied their inheritance rights under Islamic law, either by family pressures or by legal devices such as the family *waqf* or trust. Marriage between first cousins, permitted under Islamic law, is often converted into a positive injunction, with girls obliged to marry their first cousins. The aim of such customs has been to keep property in the patriarchal family, countering the distributive effects of the laws of inheritance which allow women to inherit a portion of their parents' wealth.

Marriage in Islam is contractual, and given that contracts are negotiable, reformers and modernizers have argued that legal imbalances can be countered by specific contractual provisions, for instance, by following the example of the Prophet Muhammad's great-granddaughter Sukayna bint Hussein who stipulated that her husband remain monogamous. However not all the legal schools accept the woman's right to set the terms of the contract in this way and in any case her ability to do so is likely to be contingent on the power and status of her family. Just as in modern Pakistan it is not the women from upper-class families who suffer from harassment in the market, not least because they are driven around by male chauffeurs, so aristocratic women like Sukayna were spared the insecurities and indignities experienced by lower-class women.

Tolerating the Beliefs of Others

MICHAEL COOK

Michael Cook examines the verses in the Quran that seem to condone intolerance of other religious beliefs. He points out that some Islamic scholars want to interpret the Quran as requiring a much greater degree of tolerance than people might expect. But there are also Islamic fundamentalists who accept intolerance as legitimate Islamic policy.

In a modern Western society it is more or less axiomatic that other people's religious beliefs (though not, of course, all forms of religiously motivated behaviour) are to be tolerated, and perhaps even respected. Indeed it would be considered ill-mannered and parochial to refer to the religious views of others as *false* and one's own as *true*; for those fully educated into the elite culture of Western society, the very notion of absolute truth in matters of religion sounds hopelessly out of date. It is, however, a notion that was central to traditional Islam, as it was to traditional Christianity; and in recent centuries it has survived better in Islam.

The Quran has much to say about the treatment of false belief, but the traditional Muslim scholars saw the core of it in two verses. The first they dubbed 'the sword verse':

> Then, when the sacred months are drawn away, slay the polytheists wherever you find them, and take them, and confine them, and lie in wait for them at every place of ambush. But if they repent, and perform the prayer, and pay the alms, then let them go their way; God is All-forgiving, All-compassionate. (Q9:5)

In other words, you should kill the polytheists unless they convert. A 'polytheist' (*mushrik*) is anyone who makes anyone or anything a 'partner' (*shank*) with God; the term extends to Jews and Christians, indeed to all unbelievers. Such a prescription for dealing with people outside one's own religious community is considerably gentler than, for example, the stipulation in the Biblical law of war that 'of the cities of these people, which the Lord thy God doth give thee for an inheritance, thou shalt save alive nothing that breatheth' (Deut. 20:16). Yet it hardly meshes with a modern sensibility. Fortunately the second verse, dubbed 'the tribute verse', introduces a significant relaxation:

> Fight those who believe not in God and the Last Day and do not forbid what God and His Messenger have forbidden—such men as practise not the religion of truth, being of those who have been given the Book—until they pay the tribute out of hand and have been humbled. (Q9:29)

This is a bit opaque, but it clearly establishes a category of unbelievers who need not be fought once they accept a status which requires them to pay some kind of tax and endure some kind of humiliation. The scholars agreed that this category included the Jews and Christians (since both had been given 'the Book', that is to say the Bible), and they found reasons to extend it more widely. What we see here is not, of course, *respect* for false religion, but it clearly accords it conditional toleration. This offer of toleration was not, however, universal. At the very least it was agreed that the option was not available to pagan Arabs, though this hardly mattered in practice once that group had ceased to exist.

Despite their salience in the eyes of the scholars, these two verses do not represent the full range of

Michael Cook, *The Koran: A Very Short Introduction* (Oxford: Oxford University Press 2000), 33–36.

Koranic statements bearing on the question. Consider the following:

> No compulsion is there in religion. Rectitude has become clear from error. (Q2:256)

We can dub this the 'no compulsion' verse. It does not compromise the notion of absolute religious truth, but it strongly suggests that the true religion can nonetheless coexist with any and all forms of false religion. For the traditional scholars, as we will see later, such a declaration of unconditional—not to say indiscriminate—tolerance was an embarrassment; they had to find ways and means of getting it out of the way.

For modern-minded Muslims, by contrast, the verse is literally a godsend, scriptural proof that Islam is a religion of broad and general toleration. Thus when we turn to the commentary of 'Abduh and Rida, we find that the prime concern is to resist the allegation that Islam is a religion spread by the sword. The 'no compulsion' verse accordingly takes on the status of one of the 'great principles' and 'mighty pillars' of Islam. Qutb is in the same tradition. He sketches the background of Christian intolerance in late antiquity; then came Islam, and one of the first things it did was to announce this great principle of 'no compulsion'. Freedom of belief (note the Western turn of phrase) is fundamental to human rights, and it was Islam that first proclaimed this value.

Hawwa, representing a more recent vein of fundamentalism than Qutb, is notably less lyrical. In the relevant section of his commentary on the verse, he has nothing to say about great principles, freedom of belief, or human rights. Instead he begins by noting that all authorities are agreed that an Arab pagan has only the choice of Islam or the sword, whereas Jews and Christians also have the option of paying tribute; the standing of other religious communities, he remarks, has been a matter of some dispute. This, he says, is the basis on which Muslims have proceeded down the centuries, and in interpreting the 'no compulsion' verse this framework must be taken as given. The upshot is that we have been commanded to fight the unbelievers, but forbidden to compel them to convert except in the case of Arab pagans. At no point does Hawwa flinch at the idea that Islam is a religion of the sword.

The contrast between Hawwa and the other commentators we have drawn on reappears in connection with the tribute which non-Muslims are to pay according to the terms of Q9:29. Qutb refuses to discuss the details of the topic, stigmatizing it as one which has no practical relevance whatever given the current predicament of Islam. Maghniyya likewise regards talk of such tribute today as so much hot air; he further argues that the Koranic verse was in fact concerned solely with a particular historical context at the beginning of Islamic history—a time when the infidels of the Arabian peninsula constituted a dangerous anti-Muslim 'fifth column'. The Christians of Lebanon, he allows us to infer, need not live in fear of being confronted with renewed demands for tribute. Hawwa, by contrast, thinks that it is high time that the old practice of levying a tax on unbelievers was restored. His concession to the distemper of the times is a certain relaxation of the traditional rules. Non-Muslims living in an Islamic state will, of course, have to accept that Islam is the state religion, and that power will be in the hands of the Muslims. As non-Muslims, they will be required to pay a tax in lieu of military service. Should they wish to serve in the army rather than pay the tax, the Muslims will consider this request; but Hawwa is confident that in practice non-Muslims will prefer to be taxed. There is perhaps a further element of fundamentalist generosity implicit in this proposal: nothing has been said about humiliation.

STUDY QUESTIONS

1. What is the *Quran*? What is a *caliph*? What is a *caliphate*?
2. What are the doctrinal differences between the *Shi'a* and the *Sunni*?
3. According to tradition, how did Muhammad receive the Quran revelations?
4. How do Muslims view Muhammad? As a divine being? An immortal?
5. Who is Avicenna?

6. What are the *Five Pillars of Islam*?
7. How do Muslims regard the Quran? Do they view it the same way that Christians view the New Testament?
8. Do most American Muslims think that suicide bombings against civilians in the name of Allah are justified?
9. Do most American Muslims have a favorable or unfavorable view of al-Qaeda?
10. What is the *hadith*? What is *shari'a*?

FURTHER READING

Mahmoud M. Ayoub, "The Islamic Tradition," in William G. Oxtoby, ed., *World Religions: Western Traditions* (Ontario: Oxford University Press, 2002).

John Bowker, ed., *The Oxford Dictionary of World Religions* (Oxford: Oxford University Press, 1997).

Michael Cook, *The Koran: A Very Short Introduction* (Oxford: Oxford University Press, 2000).

Frederick M. Denny, *An Introduction to Islam* (Englewood Cliffs, NJ: Prentice Hall, 2010).

John L. Esposito, *The Oxford Dictionary of Islam* (Oxford: Oxford University Press, 2003).

Peter Heath, *Allegory and Philosophy in Avicenna (Ibn Sina)* (Philadelphia: University of Pennsylvania Press, 1992).

Irshad Manji, *The Trouble with Islam Today* (New York: St. Martin's, 2003).

John B. Noss, *A History of the World's Religions* (New York: Macmillan, 1994).

Ray C. Petry, ed., *A History of Christianity*, vol. 1 (Upper Saddle River, NJ: Prentice Hall, 1962).

Ruth Roded, ed., *Women in Islam and the Middle East: A Reader* (London: I. B. Tauris, 2008).

Malise Ruthven, *Islam: A Very Short Introduction* (Oxford: Oxford University Press, 2000).

Charles Upton, *Doorkeeper of the Heart: Versions of Rabi'a* (Putney, VT: Threshold Books, 1988).

W. Montgomery Watt, trans., *The Faith and Practice of Al-Ghazali* (Oxford: One World, 2000).

ONLINE

BBC, "Islam," http://www.bbc.co.uk/religion/religions/islam/ (December 26, 2015).

Islam and Islamic Studies Resources, http://islam.uga.edu/ (December 26, 2015).

Judaism-Islam, "Similarities Between Judaism and Islam," http://www.judaism-islam.com/ (December 26, 2015).

Pew Research Center, "The World's Muslims: Religion, Politics, and Society," http://www.pewforum.org/2013/04/30/the-worlds-muslims-religion-politics-society-overview/ (December 26, 2015).

14 New Religious Movements

The Western world is long past the days when religion dominated the state, when it defined society's controlling values, when it was the last word on questions that are now answered by science, and when it could admonish or punish anyone holding contrary views. The great monolith that was traditional faith began to crack in the Renaissance; its erosion accelerated after the Scientific Revolution; and modernity weakened its authority and credibility even further. In the modern era, traditional religious bodies—primarily Christian institutions—have been facing something they have not had to contend with for centuries: swift proliferation of new religious movements that are resilient and (in the traditional view) dangerous.

Many new religious movements that we see now began in the nineteenth century. The religion scholar J. Gordon Melton explains:

> By the beginning of the nineteenth century, new patterns of religious growth were evident. Periodically, the West convulsed with religious revivals as the churches, no longer always supported by state taxes, were forced to find ways to gain the voluntary support of the populace. Each wave of religious fervour, beginning with the well-known "Second Great Awakening" at the start of the nineteenth century, saw the birth of new alternative churches and religions. Older, minuscule groups often seized the opportunity of the revivals to jump into prominence. The "Second Great Awakening" in America launched the Methodists, Baptists, Disciples of Christ and Cumberland Presbyterians into the prominent position they attained during the rest of the century and initiated an era of prosperity for the Shakers. Later periods of revival saw the rise of Spiritualism, Latter-Day Saints, the Holiness Churches, New Thought, Christian Science and Pentecostalism.[1]

Some new religions, such as New Thought and Christian Science, drew inspiration from New England Transcendentalism and Ralph Waldo Emerson's fusion of idealism, pantheism, and mysticism. The beliefs and practices of other new faiths centered on occult or psychic phenomena. Spiritualism is one such religion, but there are many others that focused on reincarnation, astrology, UFO sightings, or channeling (communicating with spiritual beings or the deceased). Still others designed their faith around communal life (for example, the Shakers), the practice of magic (Wicca, Neo-pagans), Eastern religions (Hare Krishna and Transcendental Meditation), or ancient wisdom (Theosophy). New Age religions often combined many of these elements into a single worldview.

Several of these new religious movements are still with us, and they are not alone. In the last hundred years or so, thousands of new faiths have cropped up around the world. A large number of these have already disappeared, but many are still active and show no signs of withering.

Let's examine a few of the more durable religions along with their founding documents and sacred writings.

TIMELINE OF NEW RELIGIONS

1830 Beginning of the Church of Jesus Christ of Latter-day Saints (Mormonism)

1860s Founding of Baha'i Faith

1876 Beginning of the Christian Science movement

1881 Founding of the Watchtower Society (Jehovah's Witnesses)

1893 Parliament of the World's Religions in Chicago

1954 Beginning of Wicca and Scientology

1957 Maharishi Mahesh founds a center for Transcendental Meditation (TM).

1965 Founding of ISKCON (Hare Krishna Movement)

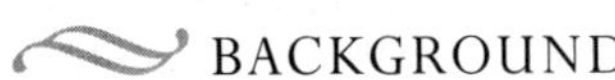 BACKGROUND

Religious and Paranormal Beliefs

82% of American adults believe in God.
60% believe in the devil.
76% believe in miracles.
23% believe in witches.
20% believe in reincarnation—that they were once another person.
26% believe in astrology.
72% believe in angels.
71% believe in the survival of the soul after death.

The Harris Poll, "What People Do and Do Not Believe," November 2009.

CHURCH OF JESUS CHRIST OF LATTER-DAY SAINTS

In 1830 in Fayette, New York, **Joseph Smith** (1805–1844) founded the Church of Jesus Christ of Latter-day Saints (called Mormons by outsiders). According to Smith, an angel named Moroni showed him where to find two gold plates that were inscribed with mysterious writing—text that turned out to be the words of God. Smith translated the plates (which were later lost), from which were derived the Latter-day Saints' holiest scriptures, the ***Book of Mormon***. The book recounts the history of the ancient lost tribes of Israel who migrated to America and of Christ who, after his resurrection, came to America later to restore true Christianity through the ministry of Joseph Smith. Smith and the Mormons were mistreated in several towns where they settled, and in one of them he was murdered by a mob. The majority of Mormons then put their trust in Brigham Young (1801–1877), who led them to the Salt Lake area in Utah where they took up permanent residence and built a new temple.

A CLOSER LOOK

U.S. Adherents of New Religious Movements

Religion	Total Adherents
Church of Jesus Christ of Latter-day Saints	6,144,582
Baha'i	171,449
Seventh-day Adventist	1,194,996
Jehovah's Witnesses	1,162,686
Spiritualist	426,000
Pagan	340,000

Association of Statisticians of American Religious Bodies, *Religious Congregations and Membership Study 2010,* "List of Religious Group Reported Numbers," 2010; National Council of Churches, Historic Archive CD; Yearbook of American and Canadian Churches; U.S. Census Bureau, "Self-Described Religious Identification of Adult Population: 1990, 2001, and 2008."

FIGURE 14.1 **The Temple of the Church of Jesus Christ of Latter-day Saints in Salt Lake City, Utah. It took about 40 years to build, from 1853 to 1893.**

The Latter-Day Saints consider the *Book of Mormon* a revelation as authoritative as the Bible, but they also revere two other books, *Doctrines and Covenants* (1835) and *The Pearl of Great Price* (1842).

CHRISTIAN SCIENCE

Christian Science (officially, the Church of Christ, Scientist) was founded in the 1870s by **Mary Baker Eddy** (1821–1910). As a young woman, she was in poor health for years, nearly an invalid, and she got no relief from conventional medicine. But in 1866 she claimed that she had been cured not through medicine but through faith. She went on to develop what she called "Christian Science," a new way of looking at the whole of reality. She declared that everything in the world that we think is material is actually spiritual. Everything is spiritual because everything is in God, who is himself entirely spiritual. The material world is thus an illusion; none of it is real, including human frailty, disease, sin, and mortality. If we have a true understanding of God's goodness and the spiritual nature of everything, health and happiness will ensue. She says that sin, sickness, and death seem real to us because of our

FIGURE 14.2 A portrait taken in 1886 of Mary Baker Eddy (1821–1910), the founder of the Christian Science faith.

fallacious beliefs, but through prayer and true spiritual knowledge we can vanquish these evils. Thus real healing does not require doctors, just proper "scientific" prayer.

For Christian Scientists, the Bible is scripture, and so is Eddy's most famous book, *Science and Health* (1875). (In later editions the words "*with Key to the Scriptures*" were added to the title.)

BAHA'I

In the 1860s Baha'i was founded in Iran by **Baha'u'llah** (1817–1892), who claimed that he was the latest manifestation of God, one of the many "Messengers of God" (or prophets) who had already appeared (in the form of Abraham, Buddha, Zarathustra, Jesus, Muhammad, and others) or would appear in the distant future. Baha'u'llah taught that there is one God, an all-good creator who is transcendent and unknowable except through his many manifestations. God is a unity, and the world should be the same—that is, all peoples should unite into one harmonious family. The goal of Baha'i, then, is one unified world, language, and government, all promoting the economic and legal equality of all people and the abolition of slavery, racism, and prejudice. The duty of Baha'is is to cultivate the values of unity in their personal lives and to work toward unity and peace in the world. Baha'i stresses monogamy, equality of the sexes, peaceful conflict resolution, and loyalty to legitimately established governments. It condemns extramarital sex, homosexual relationships, the use of alcohol, and political infighting.

Baha'i scriptures consist of the writings of the Messengers, the most revered being those of Baha'u'llah and a previous prophet known as the Bab (1819–1850). These writings are considered the most sacred and authoritative; writings of other Baha'i leaders are less so.

Baha'i is a tiny tradition, but it has nonetheless spread from Iran to every continent, including North America.

WICCA

As a form of modern witchcraft, **Wicca** is a nature religion that emphasizes sacred powers and divinities inherent in the natural world and in each person. Modern Wiccans bely the common stereotype of witches as maleficent Satan-worshippers who talk to demons, hold black masses, cast evil spells, and do other bad things with magic. (Recall that **magic** is the power to control events through supernatural or mysterious means.) Instead they hark back to the old pagan religions of pre-Christian times, worshipping nature gods or goddesses (or sometimes the God or the Goddess), all of which are thought to be manifestations of the divine energy that pervades everything and everyone in the universe. They do believe in magic but try to use it for good. (Most Wiccans subscribe to a code that forbids the use of magic to harm others.) Some Wiccans worship the Goddess and see the practice as a way to assert their freedom and equality in societies dominated by men.

Wicca has no scriptural texts, but it can claim several works that help to bring the religion to modern men and women. These include *Witchcraft Today* (1954) by Gerald B. Gardner; *The Gardnerian Book of Shadows* (1949), also by Gardner; *The Witch Cult in Western Europe* (1921) by Margaret Murray; and *Aradia or the Gospel of the Witches* (1899) by Charles G. Leland.

NOTE

1. J. Gordon Melton, "Modern Alternative Religions in the West," in John R. Hinnells, ed., *A New Handbook of Living Religions* (New York: Penguin, 1997), 595.

KEY TERMS

Baha'u'llah (1817–1892) Founder of Baha'i.

Book of Mormon The holiest scriptures of the Church of Jesus Christ of Latter-day Saints.

Mary Baker Eddy (1821–1910) Founder of the Church of Christ, Scientist.

magic The power to control events through supernatural or mysterious means.

Joseph Smith (1805–1844) Founder of the Church of Jesus Christ of Latter-day Saints (Mormons).

Wicca A nature religion that emphasizes sacred powers and divinities that are thought to be inherent in the natural world and in each person.

READINGS

CHURCH OF JESUS CHRIST OF LATTER-DAY SAINTS

Joseph Smith's Introduction to the Book of Mormon

THE BOOK OF MORMON
An Account Written by
THE HAND OF MORMON UPON PLATES
TAKEN FROM THE PLATES OF NEPHI

Wherefore, it is an abridgment of the record of the people of Nephi, and also of the Lamanites—Written to the Lamanites, who are a remnant of the house of Israel; and also to Jew and Gentile—Written by way of commandment, and also by the spirit of prophecy and of revelation—Written and sealed up, and hid up unto the Lord, that they might not be destroyed—To come forth by the gift and power of God unto the interpretation thereof—Sealed by the hand of

Moroni, and hid up unto the Lord, to come forth in due time by way of the Gentile—The interpretation thereof by the gift of God.

An abridgment taken from the Book of Ether also, which is a record of the people of Jared, who were scattered at the time the Lord confounded the language of the people, when they were building a tower to get to heaven—Which is to show unto the remnant of the House of Israel what great things the Lord hath done for their fathers; and that they may know the covenants of the Lord, that they are not cast off forever—And also to the convincing of the Jew and Gentile that JESUS is the CHRIST, the ETERNAL GOD, manifesting himself unto all nations—And now, if there are faults they are the mistakes of men; wherefore, condemn not the things of God, that ye may be found spotless at the judgment-seat of Christ.

TRANSLATED BY JOSEPH SMITH, JUN.

Christ Appearing in America

1 And now it came to pass that there were a great multitude gathered together, of the people of Nephi, round about the temple which was in the land Bountiful; and they were marveling and wondering one with another, and were showing one to another the great and marvelous change which had taken place.

2 And they were also conversing about this Jesus Christ, of whom the sign had been given concerning his death.

3 And it came to pass that while they were thus conversing one with another, they heard a voice as if it came out of heaven; and they cast their eyes round about, for they understood not the voice which they heard; and it was not a harsh voice, neither was it a loud voice; nevertheless, and notwithstanding it being a small voice it did pierce them that did hear to the center, insomuch that there was no part of their frame that it did not cause to quake; yea, it did pierce them to the very soul, and did cause their hearts to burn.

4 And it came to pass that again they heard the voice, and they understood it not.

5 And again the third time they did hear the voice, and did open their ears to hear it; and their eyes were towards the sound thereof; and they did look steadfastly towards heaven, from whence the sound came.

6 And behold, the third time they did understand the voice which they heard; and it said unto them:

7 Behold my Beloved Son, in whom I am well pleased, in whom I have glorified my name—hear ye him.

8 And it came to pass, as they understood they cast their eyes up again towards heaven; and behold, they saw a Man descending out of heaven; and he was clothed in a white robe; and he came down and stood in the midst of them; and the eyes of the whole multitude were turned upon him, and they durst not open their mouths, even one to another, and wist not what it meant, for they thought it was an angel that had appeared unto them.

Book of Mormon, 3 Nephi 11.1–15, 29–38, sacred-texts.com.

9 And it came to pass that he stretched forth his hand and spake unto the people, saying:

10 Behold, I am Jesus Christ, whom the prophets testified shall come into the world.

11 And behold, I am the light and the life of the world; and I have drunk out of that bitter cup which the Father hath given me, and have glorified the Father in taking upon me the sins of the world, in the which I have suffered the will of the Father in all things from the beginning.

12 And it came to pass that when Jesus had spoken these words the whole multitude fell to the earth; for they remembered that it had been prophesied among them that Christ should show himself unto them after his ascension into heaven.

13 And it came to pass that the Lord spake unto them saying:

14 Arise and come forth unto me, that ye may thrust your hands into my side, and also that ye may feel the prints of the nails in my hands and in my feet, that ye may know that I am the God of Israel, and the God of the whole earth, and have been slain for the sins of the world.

15 And it came to pass that the multitude went forth, and thrust their hands into his side, and did feel the prints of the nails in his hands and in his feet; and this they did do, going forth one by one until they had all gone forth, and did see with their eyes and did feel with their hands, and did know of a surety and did bear record, that it was he, of whom it was written by the prophets, that should come.

29 For verily, verily I say unto you, he that hath the spirit of contention is not of me, but is of the devil, who is the father of contention, and he stirreth up the hearts of men to contend with anger, one with another.

30 Behold, this is not my doctrine, to stir up the hearts of men with anger, one against another; but this is my doctrine, that such things should be done away.

31 Behold, verily, verily, I say unto you, I will declare unto you my doctrine.

32 And this is my doctrine, and it is the doctrine which the Father hath given unto me; and I bear record of the Father, and the Father beareth record of me, and the Holy Ghost beareth record of the Father and me; and I bear record that the Father commandeth all men, everywhere, to repent and believe in me.

33 And whoso believeth in me, and is baptized, the same shall be saved; and they are they who shall inherit the kingdom of God.

34 And whoso believeth not in me, and is not baptized, shall be damned.

35 Verily, verily, I say unto you, that this is my doctrine, and I bear record of it from the Father; and whoso believeth in me believeth in the Father also; and unto him will the Father bear record of me, for he will visit him with fire and with the Holy Ghost.

36 And thus will the Father bear record of me, and the Holy Ghost will bear record unto him of the Father and me; for the Father, and I, and the Holy Ghost are one.

37 And again I say unto you, ye must repent, and become as a little child, and be baptized in my name, or ye can in nowise receive these things.

38 And again I say unto you, ye must repent, and be baptized in my name, and become as a little child, or ye can in nowise inherit the kingdom of God.

Statement of Beliefs

1. We believe in God, the Eternal Father, and in His Son, Jesus Christ, and in the Holy Ghost.
2. We believe that men will be punished for their own sins, and not for Adam's transgression.
3. We believe that through the Atonement of Christ, all mankind may be saved, by obedience to the laws and ordinances of the Gospel.
4. We believe that the first principles and ordinances of the Gospel are: first, Faith in the Lord Jesus Christ; second, Repentance; third, Baptism by immersion for the remission of sins; fourth, Laying on of hands for the gift of the Holy Ghost.
5. We believe that a man must be called by God, by prophecy, and by the laying on of hands by those who are in authority, to preach the Gospel and administer in the ordinances thereof.
6. We believe in the same organization that existed in the Primitive Church, namely, apostles, prophets, pastors, teachers, evangelists, and so forth.
7. We believe in the gift of tongues, prophecy, revelation, visions, healing, interpretation of tongues, and so forth.
8. We believe the Bible to be the word of God as far as it is translated correctly; we also believe the Book of Mormon to be the word of God.
9. We believe all that God has revealed, all that He does now reveal, and we believe that He will yet reveal many great and important things pertaining to the Kingdom of God.
10. We believe in the literal gathering of Israel and in the restoration of the Ten Tribes; that Zion (the New Jerusalem) will be built upon the American continent; that Christ will reign personally upon the earth; and, that the earth will be renewed and receive its paradisiacal glory.
11. We claim the privilege of worshiping Almighty God according to the dictates of our own conscience, and allow all men the same privilege, let them worship how, where, or what they may.
12. We believe in being subject to kings, presidents, rulers, and magistrates, in obeying, honoring, and sustaining the law.
13. We believe in being honest, true, chaste, benevolent, virtuous, and in doing good to all men; indeed, we may say that we follow the admonition of Paul—We believe all things, we hope all things, we have endured many things, and hope to be able to endure all things. If there is anything virtuous, lovely, or of good report or praiseworthy, we seek after these things.—Joseph Smith.

The Pearl of Great Price, "Articles of Faith," 1–13, sacred-texts.com.

Vision and Conversion of Joseph Smith

1 Owing to the many reports which have been put in circulation by evil-disposed and designing persons, in relation to the rise and progress of the Church of Jesus Christ of Latter-day Saints, all of which have been designed by the authors thereof to militate against its character as a Church and its progress in the world, I have been induced to write this history, to disabuse the public mind, and put all inquirers after truth in possession of the facts, as they have transpired, in relation both to myself and the Church, so far as I have such facts in my possession.

2 In this history I shall present the various events in relation to this Church, in truth and righteousness, as they have transpired, or as they at present exist, being now [1838] the eighth year since the organization of the said Church.

3 I was born in the year of our Lord one thousand eight hundred and five, on the twenty-third day of December, in the town of Sharon, Windsor county, State of Vermont . . . My father, Joseph Smith, Sen., left the State of Vermont, and moved to Palmyra, Ontario (now Wayne) county, in the State of New York, when I was in my tenth year, or thereabouts. In about four years after my father's arrival in Palmyra, he moved with his family into Manchester in the same county of Ontario

5 Some time in the second year after our removal to Manchester, there was in the place where we lived an unusual excitement on the subject of religion. It commenced with the Methodists, but soon became general among all the sects in that region of country. Indeed, the whole district of country seemed affected by it, and great multitudes united themselves to the different religious parties, which created no small stir and division amongst the people, some crying, "Lo, here!" and others, "Lo, there!" Some were contending for the Methodist faith, some for the Presbyterian, and some for the Baptist.

6 For, notwithstanding the great love which the converts to these different faiths expressed at the time of their conversion, and the great zeal manifested by the respective clergy, who were active in getting up and promoting this extraordinary scene of religious feeling, in order to have everybody converted, as they were pleased to call it, let them join what sect they pleased; yet when the converts began to file off, some to one party and some to another, it was seen that the seemingly good feelings of both the priests and the converts were more pretended than real; for a scene of great confusion and bad feeling ensued, priest contending against priest, and convert against convert; so that all their good feelings one for another, if they ever had any, were entirely lost in a strife of words and a contest about opinions.

7 I was at this time in my fifteenth year. My father's family was proselyted to the Presbyterian faith, and four of them joined that church, namely, my mother, Lucy; my brothers Hyrum and Samuel Harrison; and my sister Sophronia.

8 During this time of great excitement my mind was called up to serious reflection and great uneasiness; but though my feelings were deep and often poignant, still I kept myself aloof from all these parties, though I attended their several meetings as often as occasion would permit. In process of time my mind became somewhat partial to the Methodist sect, and I felt some desire to be united with them; but so great were the confusion and strife among the different denominations, that it was impossible for a person young as I was, and so unacquainted with men and things, to come to any certain conclusion who was right and who was wrong.

9 My mind at times was greatly excited, the cry and tumult were so great and incessant. The Presbyterians were most decided against the Baptists and Methodists, and used all the powers of both reason

The Pearl of Great Price, "Joseph Smith—History," chs. 1–20, 22–23, 25–40, 42–47, 51–55, 59–72, sacred-texts.com.

and sophistry to prove their errors, or, at least, to make the people think they were in error. On the other hand, the Baptists and Methodists in their turn were equally zealous in endeavoring to establish their own tenets and disprove all others.

10 In the midst of this war of words and tumult of opinions, I often said to myself: What is to be done? Who of all these parties are right; or, are they all wrong together? If any one of them be right, which is it, and how shall I know it?

11 While I was laboring under the extreme difficulties caused by the contests of these parties of religionists, I was one day reading the Epistle of James, first chapter and fifth verse, which reads: *If any of you lack wisdom, let him ask of God, that giveth to all men liberally, and upbraideth not; and it shall be given him.*

12 Never did any passage of scripture come with more power to the heart of man than this did at this time to mine. It seemed to enter with great force into every feeling of my heart. I reflected on it again and again, knowing that if any person needed wisdom from God, I did; for how to act I did not know, and unless I could get more wisdom than I then had, I would never know; for the teachers of religion of the different sects understood the same passages of scripture so differently as to destroy all confidence in settling the question by an appeal to the Bible.

13 At length I came to the conclusion that I must either remain in darkness and confusion, or else I must do as James directs, that is, ask of God. I at length came to the determination to "ask of God," concluding that if he gave wisdom to them that lacked wisdom, and would give liberally, and not upbraid, I might venture.

14 So, in accordance with this, my determination to ask of God, I retired to the woods to make the attempt. It was on the morning of a beautiful, clear day, early in the spring of eighteen hundred and twenty. It was the first time in my life that I had made such an attempt, for amidst all my anxieties I had never as yet made the attempt to pray vocally.

15 After I had retired to the place where I had previously designed to go, having looked around me, and finding myself alone, I kneeled down and began to offer up the desires of my heart to God. I had scarcely done so, when immediately I was seized upon by some power which entirely overcame me, and had such an astonishing influence over me as to bind my tongue so that I could not speak. Thick darkness gathered around me, and it seemed to me for a time as if I were doomed to sudden destruction.

16 But, exerting all my powers to call upon God to deliver me out of the power of this enemy which had seized upon me, and at the very moment when I was ready to sink into despair and abandon myself to destruction, not to an imaginary ruin, but to the power of some actual being from the unseen world, who had such marvelous power as I had never before felt in any being, just at this moment of great alarm, I saw a pillar of light exactly over my head, above the brightness of the sun, which descended gradually until it fell upon me.

17 It no sooner appeared than I found myself delivered from the enemy which held me bound. When the light rested upon me I saw two Personages, whose brightness and glory defy all description, standing above me in the air. One of them spake unto me, calling me by name and said, pointing to the other, *This is My Beloved Son. Hear Him!*

18 My object in going to inquire of the Lord was to know which of all the sects was right, that I might know which to join. No sooner, therefore, did I get possession of myself, so as to be able to speak, than I asked the Personages who stood above me in the light, which of all the sects was right (for at this time it had never entered into my heart that all were wrong), and which I should join.

19 I was answered that I must join none of them, for they were all wrong; and the Personage who addressed me said that all their creeds were an abomination in his sight; that those professors were all corrupt; that: "they draw near to me with their lips, but their hearts are far from me, they teach for doctrines the commandments of men, having a form of godliness, but they deny the power thereof."

20 He again forbade me to join with any of them; and many other things did he say unto me, which I cannot write at this time. When I came to myself again, I found myself lying on my back, looking up into heaven. When the light had departed, I had no strength; but soon recovering in some degree, I went

home. And as I leaned up to the fireplace, mother inquired what the matter was. I replied, "Never mind, all is well, I am well enough off." I then said to my mother, "I have learned for myself that Presbyterianism is not true." It seems as though the adversary was aware, at a very early period of my life, that I was destined to prove a disturber and an annoyer of his kingdom; else why should the powers of darkness combine against me? Why the opposition and persecution that arose against me, almost in my infancy? . . .

22 I soon found, however, that my telling the story had excited a great deal of prejudice against me among professors of religion, and was the cause of great persecution, which continued to increase; and though I was an obscure boy, only between fourteen and fifteen years of age, and my circumstances in life such as to make a boy of no consequence in the world, yet men of high standing would take notice sufficient to excite the public mind against me, and create a bitter persecution; and this was common among all the sects, all united to persecute me.

23 It caused me serious reflection then, and often has since, how very strange it was that an obscure boy, of a little over fourteen years of age, and one, too, who was doomed to the necessity of obtaining a scanty maintenance by his daily labor, should be thought a character of sufficient importance to attract the attention of the great ones of the most popular sects of the day, and in a manner to create in them a spirit of the most bitter persecution and reviling. But strange or not, so it was, and it was often the cause of great sorrow to myself. . . .

25 So it was with me. I had actually seen a light, and in the midst of that light I saw two Personages, and they did in reality speak to me; and though I was hated and persecuted for saying that I had seen a vision, yet it was true; and while they were persecuting me, reviling me, and speaking all manner of evil against me falsely for so saying, I was led to say in my heart: Why persecute me for telling the truth? I have actually seen a vision; and who am I that I can withstand God, or why does the world think to make me deny what I have actually seen? For I had seen a vision; I knew it, and I knew that God knew it, and I could not deny it, neither dared I do it; at least I knew that by so doing I would offend God, and come under condemnation.

26 I had now got my mind satisfied so far as the sectarian world was concerned, that it was not my duty to join with any of them, but to continue as I was until further directed. I had found the testimony of James to be true, that a man who lacked wisdom might ask of God, and obtain, and not be upbraided.

27 I continued to pursue my common vocations in life until the twenty-first of September, one thousand eight hundred and twenty-three, all the time suffering severe persecution at the hands of all classes of men, both religious and irreligious, because I continued to affirm that I had seen a vision.

28 During the space of time which intervened between the time I had the vision and the year eighteen hundred and twenty-three, having been forbidden to join any of the religious sects of the day, and being of very tender years, and persecuted by those who ought to have been my friends and to have treated me kindly, and if they supposed me to be deluded to have endeavored in a proper and affectionate manner to have reclaimed me, I was left to all kinds of temptations; and, mingling with all kinds of society, I frequently fell into many foolish errors, and displayed the weakness of youth, and the foibles of human nature; which, I am sorry to say, led me into divers temptations, offensive in the sight of God. In making this confession, no one need suppose me guilty of any great or malignant sins. A disposition to commit such was never in my nature. But I was guilty of levity, and sometimes associated with jovial company, etc., not consistent with that character which ought to be maintained by one who was called of God as I had been. But this will not seem very strange to any one who recollects my youth, and is acquainted with my native cheery temperament.

29 In consequence of these things, I often felt condemned for my weakness and imperfections; when, on the evening of the above-mentioned twenty-first of September, after I had retired to my bed for the night, I betook myself to prayer and supplication to Almighty God for forgiveness of all my sins and follies, and also for a manifestation to me, that I might know of my state and standing before him; for I had

full confidence in obtaining a divine manifestation, as I previously had one.

30 While I was thus in the act of calling upon God, I discovered a light appearing in my room, which continued to increase until the room was lighter than at noonday, when immediately a personage appeared at my bedside, standing in the air, for his feet did not touch the floor.

31 He had on a loose robe of most exquisite whiteness. It was a whiteness beyond anything earthly I had ever seen; nor do I believe that any earthly thing could be made to appear so exceedingly white and brilliant. His hands were naked, and his arms also, a little above the wrist; so, also, were his feet naked, as were his legs, a little above the ankles. His head and neck were also bare. I could discover that he had no other clothing on but this robe, as it was open, so that I could see into his bosom.

32 Not only was his robe exceedingly white, but his whole person was glorious beyond description, and his countenance truly like lightning. The room was exceedingly light, but not so very bright as immediately around his person. When I first looked upon him, I was afraid; but the fear soon left me.

33 He called me by name, and said unto me that he was a messenger sent from the presence of God to me, and that his name was Moroni; that God had a work for me to do; and that my name should be had for good and evil among all nations, kindreds, and tongues, or that it should be both good and evil spoken of among all people.

34 He said there was a book deposited, written upon gold plates, giving an account of the former inhabitants of this continent, and the source from whence they sprang. He also said that the fulness of the everlasting Gospel was contained in it, as delivered by the Savior to the ancient inhabitants;

35 Also, that there were two stones in silver bows, and these stones, fastened to a breastplate, constituted what is called the Urim and Thummim, deposited with the plates; and the possession and use of these stones were what constituted "seers" in ancient or former times; and that God had prepared them for the purpose of translating the book.

36 After telling me these things, he commenced quoting the prophecies of the Old Testament. He first quoted part of the third chapter of Malachi; and he quoted also the fourth or last chapter of the same prophecy, though with a little variation from the way it reads in our Bibles. Instead of quoting the first verse as it reads in our books, he quoted it thus:

37 *For behold, the day cometh that shall burn as an oven, and all the proud, yea, and all that do wickedly shall burn as stubble; for they that come shall burn them, saith the Lord of Hosts, that it shall leave them neither root nor branch.*

38 And again, he quoted the fifth verse thus: *Behold, I will reveal unto you the Priesthood, by the hand of Elijah the prophet, before the coming of the great and dreadful day of the Lord.*

39 He also quoted the next verse differently: *And he shall plant in the hearts of the children the promises made to the fathers, and the hearts of the children shall turn to their fathers. If it were not so, the whole earth would be utterly wasted at his coming.*

40 In addition to these, he quoted the eleventh chapter of Isaiah, saying that it was about to be fulfilled. He quoted also the third chapter of Acts, twenty-second and twenty-third verses, precisely as they stand in our New Testament. He said that that prophet was Christ; but the day had not yet come when "they who would not hear his voice should be cut off from among the people," but soon would come. . . .

42 Again, he told me, that when I got those plates of which he had spoken, for the time that they should be obtained was not yet fulfilled, I should not show them to any person; neither the breastplate with the Urim and Thummim; only to those to whom I should be commanded to show them; if I did I should be destroyed. While he was conversing with me about the plates, the vision was opened to my mind that I could see the place where the plates were deposited, and that so clearly and distinctly that I knew the place again when I visited it.

43 After this communication, I saw the light in the room begin to gather immediately around the person of him who had been speaking to me, and it continued to do so until the room was again left dark, except just around him; when, instantly I saw, as it were, a conduit open right up into heaven, and he ascended till he entirely disappeared, and the room

was left as it had been before this heavenly light had made its appearance.

44 I lay musing on the singularity of the scene, and marveling greatly at what had been told to me by this extraordinary messenger; when, in the midst of my meditation, I suddenly discovered that my room was again beginning to get lighted, and in an instant, as it were, the same heavenly messenger was again by my bedside.

45 He commenced, and again related the very same things which he had done at his first visit, without the least variation; which having done, he informed me of great judgments which were coming upon the earth, with great desolations by famine, sword, and pestilence; and that these grievous judgments would come on the earth in this generation. Having related these things, he again ascended as he had done before.

46 By this time, so deep were the impressions made on my mind, that sleep had fled from my eyes, and I lay overwhelmed in astonishment at what I had both seen and heard. But what was my surprise when again I beheld the same messenger at my bedside, and heard him rehearse or repeat over again to me the same things as before; and added a caution to me, telling me that Satan would try to tempt me (in consequence of the indigent circumstances of my father's family), to get the plates for the purpose of getting rich. This he forbade me, saying that I must have no other object in view in getting the plates but to glorify God, and must not be influenced by any other motive than that of building his kingdom; otherwise I could not get them.

47 After this third visit, he again ascended into heaven as before, and I was again left to ponder on the strangeness of what I had just experienced; when almost immediately after the heavenly messenger had ascended from me for the third time, the cock crowed, and I found that day was approaching, so that our interviews must have occupied the whole of that night. . . .

51 Convenient to the village of Manchester, Ontario county, New York, stands a hill of considerable size, and the most elevated of any in the neighborhood. On the west side of this hill, not far from the top, under a stone of considerable size, lay the plates, deposited in a stone box. This stone was thick and rounding in the middle on the upper side, and thinner towards the edges, so that the middle part of it was visible above the ground, but the edge all around was covered with earth.

52 Having removed the earth, I obtained a lever, which I got fixed under the edge of the stone, and with a little exertion raised it up. I looked in, and there indeed did I behold the plates, the Urim and Thummim, and the breastplate, as stated by the messenger. The box in which they lay was formed by laying stones together in some kind of cement. In the bottom of the box were laid two stones crossways of the box, and on these stones lay the plates and the other things with them.

53 I made an attempt to take them out, but was forbidden by the messenger, and was again informed that the time for bringing them forth had not yet arrived, neither would it, until four years from that time; but he told me that I should come to that place precisely in one year from that time, and that he would there meet with me, and that I should continue to do so until the time should come for obtaining the plates.

54 Accordingly, as I had been commanded, I went at the end of each year, and at each time I found the same messenger there, and received instruction and intelligence from him at each of our interviews, respecting what the Lord was going to do, and how and in what manner his kingdom was to be conducted in the last days.

55 As my father's worldly circumstances were very limited, we were under the necessity of laboring with our hands, hiring out by day's work and otherwise, as we could get opportunity. Sometimes we were at home, and sometimes abroad, and by continuous labor were enabled to get a comfortable maintenance. . . .

59 At length the time arrived for obtaining the plates, the Urim and Thummim, and the breastplate. On the twenty-second day of September, one thousand eight hundred and twenty-seven, having gone as usual at the end of another year to the place where they were deposited, the same heavenly messenger delivered them up to me with this charge: that I should be responsible for them; that if I should let them go

carelessly, or through any neglect of mine, I should be cut off; but that if I would use all my endeavors to preserve them, until he, the messenger, should call for them, they should be protected.

60 I soon found out the reason why I had received such strict charges to keep them safe, and why it was that the messenger had said that when I had done what was required at my hand, he would call for them. For no sooner was it known that I had them, than the most strenuous exertions were used to get them from me. Every stratagem that could be invented was resorted to for that purpose. The persecution became more bitter and severe than before, and multitudes were on the alert continually to get them from me if possible. But by the wisdom of God, they remained safe in my hands, until I had accomplished by them what was required at my hand. When, according to arrangements, the messenger called for them, I delivered them up to him; and he has them in his charge until this day, being the second day of May, one thousand eight hundred and thirty-eight.

61 The excitement, however, still continued, and rumor with her thousand tongues was all the time employed in circulating falsehoods about my father's family, and about myself. If I were to relate a thousandth part of them, it would fill up volumes. The persecution, however, became so intolerable that I was under the necessity of leaving Manchester, and going with my wife to Susquehanna county, in the State of Pennsylvania. While preparing to start, being very poor, and the persecution so heavy upon us that there was no probability that we would ever be otherwise, in the midst of our afflictions we found a friend in a gentleman by the name of Martin Harris, who came to us and gave me fifty dollars to assist us on our journey. Mr. Harris was a resident of Palmyra township, Wayne county, in the State of New York, and a farmer of respectability.

62 By this timely aid was I enabled to reach the place of my destination in Pennsylvania; and immediately after my arrival there I commenced copying the characters off the plates. I copied a considerable number of them, and by means of the Urim and Thummim I translated some of them, which I did between the time I arrived at the house of my wife's father, in the month of December, and the February following.

63 Sometime in this month of February, the aforementioned Mr. Martin Harris came to our place, got the characters which I had drawn off the plates, and started with them to the city of New York. For what took place relative to him and the characters, I refer to his own account of the circumstances, as he related them to me after his return, which was as follows:

64 "I went to the city of New York, and presented the characters which had been translated, with the translation thereof, to Professor Charles Anthon, a gentleman celebrated for his literary attainments. Professor Anthon stated that the translation was correct, more so than any he had before seen translated from the Egyptian. I then showed him those which were not yet translated, and he said that they were Egyptian, Chaldaic, Assyriac, and Arabic; and he said they were true characters. He gave me a certificate, certifying to the people of Palmyra that they were true characters, and that the translation of such of them as had been translated was also correct. I took the certificate and put it into my pocket, and was just leaving the house, when Mr. Anthon called me back, and asked me how the young man found out that there were gold plates in the place where he found them. I answered that an angel of God had revealed it unto him.

65 "He then said to me, 'Let me see that certificate.' I accordingly took it out of my pocket and gave it to him, when he took it and tore it to pieces, saying that there was no such thing now as ministering of angels, and that if I would bring the plates to him he would translate them. I informed him that part of the plates were sealed, and that I was forbidden to bring them. He replied, 'I cannot read a sealed book.' I left him and went to Dr. Mitchell, who sanctioned what Professor Anthon had said respecting both the characters and the translation."

66 On the 5th day of April, 1829, Oliver Cowdery came to my house, until which time I had never seen him. He stated to me that having been teaching school in the neighborhood where my father resided, and my father being one of those who sent to the school, he went to board for a season at his house,

and while there the family related to him the circumstances of my having received the plates, and accordingly he had come to make inquiries of me.

67 Two days after the arrival of Mr. Cowdery (being the 7th of April) I commenced to translate the Book of Mormon, and he began to write for me.

68 We still continued the work of translation, when, in the ensuing month (May, 1829), we on a certain day went into the woods to pray and inquire of the Lord respecting baptism for the remission of sins, that we found mentioned in the translation of the plates. While we were thus employed, praying and calling upon the Lord, a messenger from heaven descended in a cloud of light, and having laid his hands upon us, he ordained us, saying:

69 *Upon you my fellow servants, in the name of Messiah, I confer the Priesthood of Aaron, which holds the keys of the ministering of angels, and of the gospel of repentance, and of baptism by immersion for the remission of sins; and this shall never be taken again from the earth until the sons of Levi do offer again an offering unto the Lord in righteousness.*

70 He said this Aaronic Priesthood had not the power of laying on hands for the gift of the Holy Ghost, but that this should be conferred on us hereafter; and he commanded us to go and be baptized, and gave us directions that I should baptize Oliver Cowdery, and that afterwards he should baptize me.

71 Accordingly we went and were baptized. I baptized him first, and afterwards he baptized me, after which I laid my hands upon his head and ordained him to the Aaronic Priesthood, and afterwards he laid his hands on me and ordained me to the same Priesthood, for so we were commanded.

72 The messenger who visited us on this occasion and conferred this Priesthood upon us, said that his name was John, the same that is called John the Baptist in the New Testament, and that he acted under the direction of Peter, James and John, who held the keys of the Priesthood of Melchizedek, which Priesthood, he said, would in due time be conferred on us, and that I should be called the first Elder of the Church, and he (Oliver Cowdery) the second. It was on the fifteenth day of May, 1829, that we were ordained under the hand of this messenger, and baptized. . . .

CHRISTIAN SCIENCE

Science and Health, Preface

MARY BAKER EDDY

To those leaning on the sustaining infinite, to-day is big with blessings. The wakeful shepherd beholds the first faint morning beams, ere cometh the full radiance of a risen day. So shone the pale star to the prophet shepherds; yet it traversed the night, and came where, in cradled obscurity, lay the Bethlehem babe, the human herald of Christ, Truth, who would make plain to benighted understanding the way of salvation through Christ Jesus, till across a night of error should dawn the morning beams and shine the guiding star of being. The Wise men were led to behold and to follow this daystar of divine Science, lighting the way to eternal harmony. The time for thinkers has come. Truth, independent of doctrines and time-honored systems, knocks at the portal of humanity. Contentment with the past and the cold conventionality of materialism are crumbling away. Ignorance of God is no longer the steppingstone to faith. The only guarantee of obedience is a right apprehension of Him whom to know aright is Life eternal. Though empires fall, "the Lord shall reign forever." A book introduces new thoughts, but it cannot make them speedily understood. It is the task of the sturdy pioneer to hew the tall oak and to cut the rough granite. Future ages must declare what the pioneer has accomplished.

Since the author's discovery of the might of Truth in the treatment of disease as well as of sin, her system has been fully tested and has not been found wanting; but to reach the heights of Christian Science, man must live in obedience to its divine Principle. To develop the full might of this Science, the discords of corporeal sense must yield to the harmony of spiritual sense, even as the science of music corrects false tones and gives sweet concord to sound.

Theology and physics teach that both Spirit and matter are real and good, whereas the fact is that Spirit is good and real, and matter is Spirit's opposite. The question, What is Truth, is answered by demonstration, by healing both disease and sin; and this demonstration shows that Christian healing confers the most health and makes the best men. On this basis Christian Science will have a fair fight. Sickness has been combated for centuries by doctors using material remedies; but the question arises, Is there less sickness because of these practitioners? A vigorous "No" is the response deducible from two connate facts,—the reputed longevity of the Antediluvians, and the rapid multiplication and increased violence of diseases since the flood.

In the author's work, *Retrospection and Introspection*, may be found a biographical sketch, narrating experiences which led her, in the year 1866, to the discovery of the system that she denominated Christian Science. As early as 1862 she began to

Mary Baker Eddy, *Science and Health with a Key to the Scriptures*, 1910.

write down and give to friends the results of her Scriptural study, for the Bible was her sole teacher; but these compositions were crude, the first steps of a child in the newly discovered world of Spirit.

She also began to jot down her thoughts on the main subject, but these jottings were only infantile lispings of Truth. A child drinks in the outward world through the eyes and rejoices in the draught. He is as sure of the world's existence as he is of his own; yet he cannot describe the world. He finds a few words, and with these he stammeringly attempts to convey his feeling. Later, the tongue voices the more definite thought, though still imperfectly. So was it with the author. As a certain poet says of himself, she "lisped in numbers, for the numbers came." Certain essays written at that early date are still in circulation among her first pupils; but they are feeble attempts to state the Principle and practice of Christian healing, and are not complete nor satisfactory expositions of Truth. To-day, though rejoicing in some progress, she still finds herself a willing disciple at the heavenly gate, waiting for the Mind of Christ.

Her first pamphlet on Christian Science was copyrighted in 1870; but it did not appear in print until 1876, as she had learned that this Science must be demonstrated by healing, before a work on the subject could be profitably studied. From 1867 until 1875, copies were, however, in friendly circulation.

Before writing this work, *Science and Health*, she made copious notes of Scriptural exposition, which have never been published. This was during the years 1867 and 1868. These efforts show her comparative ignorance of the stupendous Life-problem up to that time, and the degrees by which she came at length to its solution; but she values them as a parent may treasure the memorials of a child's growth, and she would not have them changed.

The first edition of *Science and Health* was published in 1875. Various books on mental healing have since been issued, most of them incorrect in theory and filled with plagiarisms from *Science and Health*. They regard the human mind as a healing agent, whereas this mind is not a factor in the Principle of Christian Science. A few books, however, which are based on this book, are useful.

The author has not compromised conscience to suit the general drift of thought, but has bluntly and honestly given the text of Truth. She has made no effort to embellish, elaborate, or treat in full detail so infinite a theme. By thousands of well-authenticated cases of healing, she and her students have proved the worth of her teachings. These cases for the most part have been abandoned as hopeless by regular medical attendants. Few invalids will turn to God till all physical supports have failed, because there is so little faith in His disposition and power to heal disease.

The divine Principle of healing is proved in the personal experience of any sincere seeker of Truth. Its purpose is good, and its practice is safer and more potent than that of any other sanitary method. The unbiased Christian thought is soonest touched by Truth, and convinced of it. Only those quarrel with her method who do not understand her meaning, or discerning the truth, come not to the light lest their works be reproved. No intellectual proficiency is requisite in the learner, but sound morals are most desirable.

Many imagine that the phenomena of physical healing in Christian Science present only a phase of the action of the human mind, which action in some unexplained way results in the cure of disease. On the contrary, Christian Science rationally explains that all other pathological methods are the fruits of human faith in matter, faith in the workings, not of Spirit, but of the fleshly mind which must yield to Science.

The physical healing of Christian Science results now, as in Jesus' time, from the operation of divine Principle, before which sin and disease lose their reality in human consciousness and disappear as naturally and as necessarily as darkness gives place to light and sin to reformation. Now, as then, these mighty works are not supernatural, but supremely natural. They are the sign of Immanuel, or "God with us," a divine influence ever present in human consciousness and repeating itself, coming now as was promised aforetime,

To preach deliverance to the captives [of sense],
And recovering of sight to the blind,
To set at liberty them that are bruised.

When God called the author to proclaim His Gospel to this age, there came also the charge to plant and water His vineyard.

The first school of Christian Science Mind-healing was started by the author with only one student in Lynn, Massachusetts, about the year 1867. In 1881, she opened the Massachusetts Metaphysical College in Boston, under the seal of the Commonwealth, a law relative to colleges having been passed, which enabled her to get this institution chartered for medical purposes. No charters were granted to Christian Scientists for such institutions after 1883, and up to that date, hers was the only College of this character which had been established in the United States, where Christian Science was first introduced.

During seven years over four thousand students were taught by the author in this College. Meanwhile she was pastor of the first established Church of Christ, Scientist; President of the first Christian Scientist Association, convening monthly; publisher of her own works; and (for a portion of this time) sole editor and publisher of the Christian Science Journal, the first periodical issued by Christian Scientists. She closed her College, October 29, 1889, in the height of its prosperity with a deep-lying conviction that the next two years of her life should be given to the preparation of the revision of SCIENCE AND HEALTH, which was published in 1891. She retained her charter, and as its President, reopened the College in 1899 as auxiliary to her church. Until June 10, 1907, she had never read this book throughout consecutively in order to elucidate her idealism.

In the spirit of Christ's charity, as one who "hopeth all things, endureth all things," and is joyful to bear consolation to the sorrowing and healing to the sick, she commits these pages to honest seekers for Truth.

Science and Health, Recapitulation

MARY BAKER EDDY

Question.—What is God? Answer.—God is incorporeal, divine, supreme, infinite Mind, Spirit, Soul, Principle, Life, Truth, Love.

Question.—Are these terms synonymous? Answer.—They are. They refer to one absolute God. They are also intended to express the nature, essence, and wholeness of Deity. The attributes of God are justice, mercy, wisdom, goodness, and so on.

Question.—Is there more than one God or Principle? Answer.—There is not. Principle and its idea is one, and this one is God, omnipotent, omniscient, and omnipresent Being, and His reflection is man and the universe. Omni is adopted from the Latin adjective signifying all. Hence God combines all-power or potency, all-science or true knowledge, all-presence. The varied manifestations of Christian Science indicate Mind, never matter, and have one Principle.

Question.—What are spirits and souls? Answer.—To human belief, they are personalities constituted of mind and matter, life and death, truth and error, good and evil; but these contrasting pairs of terms represent contraries, as Christian Science reveals, which neither dwell together nor assimilate. Truth is

Mary Baker Eddy, *Science and Health with Key to the Scriptures*, 1910.

immortal; error is mortal. Truth is limitless; error is limited. Truth is intelligent; error is non-intelligent. Moreover, Truth is real, and error is unreal. This last statement contains the point you will most reluctantly admit, although first and last it is the most important to understand.

The term souls or spirits is as improper as the term gods. Soul or Spirit signifies Deity and nothing else. There is no finite soul nor spirit. Soul or Spirit means only one Mind, and cannot be rendered in the plural. Heathen mythology and Jewish theology have perpetuated the fallacy that intelligence, soul, and life can be in matter; and idolatry and ritualism are the outcome of all man-made beliefs. The Science of Christianity comes with fan in hand to separate the chaff from the wheat. Science will declare God aright, and Christianity will demonstrate this declaration and its divine Principle, making mankind better physically, morally, and spiritually.

Question.—What are the demands of the Science of Soul? Answer.—The first demand of this Science is, "Thou shalt have no other gods before me." This me is Spirit. Therefore the command means this: Thou shalt have no intelligence, no life, no substance, no truth, no love, but that which is spiritual. The second is like unto it, "Thou shalt love thy neighbor as thyself." It should be thoroughly understood that all men have one Mind, one God and Father, one Life, Truth, and Love. Mankind will become perfect in proportion as this fact becomes apparent, war will cease and the true brotherhood of man will be established. Having no other gods, turning to no other but the one perfect Mind to guide him, man is the likeness of God, pure and eternal, having that Mind which was also in Christ.

Science reveals Spirit, Soul, as not in the body, and God as not in man but as reflected by man. The greater cannot be in the lesser. The belief that the greater can be in the lesser is an error that works ill. This is a leading point in the Science of Soul, that Principle is not in its idea. Spirit, Soul, is not confined in man, and is never in matter. We reason imperfectly from effect to cause, when we conclude that matter is the effect of Spirit; but a priori reasoning shows material existence to be enigmatical. Spirit gives the true mental idea. We cannot interpret Spirit, Mind, through matter. Matter neither sees, hears, nor feels.

Reasoning from cause to effect in the Science of Mind, we begin with Mind, which must be understood through the idea which expresses it and cannot be learned from its opposite, matter. Thus we arrive at Truth, or intelligence, which evolves its own unerring idea and never can be coordinate with human illusions. If Soul sinned, it would be mortal, for sin is mortality's self, because it kills itself. If Truth is immortal, error must be mortal, because error is unlike Truth. Because Soul is immortal, Soul cannot sin, for sin is not the eternal verity of being.

Question.—What is the scientific statement of being? Answer.—There is no life, truth, intelligence, nor substance in matter. All is infinite Mind and its infinite manifestation, for God is All-in-all. Spirit is immortal Truth; matter is mortal error. Spirit is the real and eternal; matter is the unreal and temporal. Spirit is God, and man is His image and likeness. Therefore man is not material; he is spiritual.

Question.—What is substance? Answer.—Substance is that which is eternal and incapable of discord and decay. Truth, Life, and Love are substance, as the Scriptures use this word in Hebrews: "The substance of things hoped for, the evidence of things not seen." Spirit, the synonym of Mind, Soul, or God, is the only real substance. The spiritual universe, including individual man, is a compound idea, reflecting the divine substance of Spirit.

Question.—What is Life? Answer.—Life is divine Principle, Mind, Soul, Spirit. Life is without beginning and without end. Eternity, not time, expresses the thought of Life, and time is no part of eternity. One ceases in proportion as the other is recognized. Time is finite; eternity is forever infinite. Life is neither in nor of matter. What is termed matter is unknown to Spirit, which includes in itself all substance and is Life eternal. Matter is a human concept. Life is divine Mind. Life is not limited. Death and finiteness are unknown to Life. If Life ever had a beginning, it would also have an ending.

Question.—What is intelligence? Answer.—Intelligence is omniscience, omnipresence, and omnipotence. It is the primal and eternal quality of infinite Mind, of the triune Principle,—Life, Truth, and Love,—named God.

Question.—What is Mind? Answer.—Mind is God. The exterminator of error is the great truth that God, good, is the only Mind, and that the supposititious opposite of infinite Mind—called devil or evil—is not Mind, is not Truth, but error, without intelligence or reality. There can be but one Mind, because there is but one God; and if mortals claimed no other Mind and accepted no other, sin would be unknown. We can have but one Mind, if that one is infinite. We bury the sense of infinitude, when we admit that, although God is infinite, evil has a place in this infinity, for evil can have no place, where all space is filled with God.

We lose the high signification of omnipotence, when after admitting that God, or good, is omnipresent and has all-power, we still believe there is another power, named evil. This belief that there is more than one mind is as pernicious to divine theology as are ancient mythology and pagan idolatry. With one Father, even God, the whole family of man would be brethren; and with one Mind and that God, or good, the brotherhood of man would consist of Love and Truth, and have unity of Principle and spiritual power which constitute divine Science. The supposed existence of more than one mind was the basic error of idolatry. This error assumed the loss of spiritual power, the loss of the spiritual presence of Life as infinite Truth without an unlikeness, and the loss of Love as ever present and universal.

Divine Science explains the abstract statement that there is one Mind by the following self-evident proposition: If God, or good, is real, then evil, the unlikeness of God, is unreal. And evil can only seem to be real by giving reality to the unreal. The children of God have but one Mind. How can good lapse into evil, when God, the Mind of man, never sins? The standard of perfection was originally God and man. Has God taken down His own standard, and has man fallen?

God is the creator of man, and, the divine Principle of man remaining perfect, the divine idea or reflection, man, remains perfect. Man is the expression of God's being. If there ever was a moment when man did not express the divine perfection, then there was a moment when man did not express God, and consequently a time when Deity was unexpressed—that is, without entity. If man has lost perfection, then he has lost his perfect Principle, the divine Mind. If man ever existed without this perfect Principle or Mind, then man's existence was a myth.

The relations of God and man, divine Principle and idea, are indestructible in Science; and Science knows no lapse from nor return to harmony, but holds the divine order or spiritual law, in which God and all that He creates are perfect and eternal, to have remained unchanged in its eternal history. . . .

Question.—What is error? Answer.—Error is a supposition that pleasure and pain, that intelligence, substance, life, are existent in matter. Error is neither Mind nor one of Mind's faculties. Error is the contradiction of Truth. Error is a belief without understanding. Error is unreal because untrue. It is that which seemeth to be and is not. If error were true, its truth would be error, and we should have a self-evident absurdity—namely, erroneous truth. Thus we should continue to lose the standard of Truth.

Question.—Is there no sin? Answer.—All reality is in God and His creation, harmonious and eternal. That which He creates is good, and He makes all that is made. Therefore the only reality of sin, sickness, or death is the awful fact that unrealities seem real to human, erring belief, until God strips off their disguise. They are not true, because they are not of God. We learn in Christian Science that all inharmony of mortal mind or body is illusion, possessing neither reality nor identity though seeming to be real and identical.

BAHA'I

Baha'u'llah and Basic Baha'i Teaching

The fundamental principle enunciated by that Baha'u'llah . . . is that religious truth is not absolute but relative, that Divine Revelation is a continuous and progressive process, that all the great religions of the world are divine in origin, that their basic principles are in complete harmony, that their aims and purposes are one and the same, that their teachings are but facets of one truth, that their functions are complementary, that they differ only in the nonessential aspects of their doctrines, and that their missions represent successive stages in the spiritual evolution of human society. . . .

His mission is to proclaim that the ages of the infancy and of the childhood of the human race are past, that the convulsions associated with the present stage of its adolescence are slowly and painfully preparing it to attain the stage of manhood, and are heralding the approach of that Age of Ages when swords will be beaten into plowshares, when the Kingdom promised by Jesus Christ will have been established, and the peace of the planet definitely and permanently ensured. Nor does Baha'u'llah claim finality for His own Revelation, but rather stipulates that a fuller measure of the truth He has been commissioned by the Almighty to vouchsafe to humanity, at so critical a juncture in its fortunes, must needs be disclosed at future stages in the constant and limitless evolution of mankind.

The Baha'i Faith upholds the unity of God, recognizes the unity of His Prophets, and inculcates the principle of the oneness and wholeness of the entire human race. It proclaims the necessity and the inevitability of the unification of mankind, asserts that it is gradually approaching, and claims that nothing short of the transmuting spirit of God, working through His chosen Mouthpiece in this day, can ultimately succeed in bringing it about. It, moreover, enjoins upon its followers the primary duty of an unfettered search after truth, condemns all manner of prejudice and superstition, declares the purpose of religion to be the promotion of amity and concord, proclaims its essential harmony with science, and recognizes it as the foremost agency for the pacification and the orderly progress of human society. . . .

Mirza Husayn-'Ali, surnamed Baha'u'llah (the Glory of God), a native of Mazindaran, Whose advent the Bab [Herald and Forerunner of Baha'u'llah] had foretold, . . . was imprisoned in Teheran, was banished, in 1852, from His native land to Baghdad, and thence to Constantinople and Adrianople, and finally to the prison city Akka, where He remained incarcerated for no less than twenty-four years, and in whose neighborhood He passed away in 1892. In the course of His banishment, and particularly in Adrianople and Akka, He formulated the laws and ordinances of His Dispensation, expounded, in over a hundred volumes, the principles of His Faith, proclaimed His Message to the kings and rulers of both the East and the West, both Christian and Muslim, addressed the Pope, the Caliph of Islam, the Chief Magistrates of the Republics of the American continent, the entire Christian sacerdotal order, the leaders of Shi'ite and Sunni Islam, and the high priests of the Zoroastrian religion. In these writings He proclaimed His Revelation, summoned those whom He addressed to heed His call and espouse His Faith,

Shoghi Effendi, *The Promised Day Is Come*, Preface, sacred-texts.com.

warned them of the consequences of their refusal, and denounced, in some cases, their arrogance and tyranny. . . .

The Faith which this order serves, safeguards and promotes is . . . essentially supernatural, supranational, entirely non-political, non-partisan, and diametrically opposed to any policy or school of thought that seeks to exalt any particular race, class or nation. It is free from any form of ecclesiasticism, has neither priesthood nor rituals, and is supported exclusively by voluntary contributions made by its avowed adherents. Though loyal to their respective governments, though imbued with the love of their own country, and anxious to promote at all times, its best interests, the followers of the Baha'i Faith, nevertheless, viewing mankind as one entity, and profoundly attached to its vital interests, will not hesitate to subordinate every particular interest, be it personal, regional or national, to the over-riding interests of the generality of mankind, knowing full well that in a world of interdependent peoples and nations the advantage of the part is best to be reached by the advantage of the whole, and that no lasting result can be achieved by any of the component parts if the general interests of the entity itself are neglected.

Baha'i Laws: Kitab-I-Aqdas

1 The first duty prescribed by God for His servants is the recognition of Him Who is the Dayspring of His Revelation and the Fountain of His laws, Who representeth the Godhead in both the Kingdom of His Cause and the world of creation. Whoso achieveth this duty hath attained unto all good; and whoso is deprived thereof hath gone astray, though he be the author of every righteous deed. It behoveth every one who reacheth this most sublime station, this summit of transcendent glory, to observe every ordinance of Him Who is the Desire of the world. These twin duties are inseparable. Neither is acceptable without the other. Thus hath it been decreed by Him Who is the Source of Divine inspiration.

2 They whom God hath endued with insight will readily recognize that the precepts laid down by God constitute the highest means for the maintenance of order in the world and the security of its peoples. He that turneth away from them is accounted among the abject and foolish. We, verily, have commanded you to refuse the dictates of your evil passions and corrupt desires, and not to transgress the bounds which the Pen of the Most High hath fixed, for these are the breath of life unto all created things. The seas of Divine wisdom and Divine utterance have risen under the breath of the breeze of the All-Merciful. Hasten to drink your fill, O men of understanding! They that have violated the Covenant of God by breaking His commandments, and have turned back on their heels, these have erred grievously in the sight of God, the All-Possessing, the Most High.

12 It hath been ordained that obligatory prayer is to be performed by each of you individually. Save in the Prayer for the Dead, the practice of congregational prayer hath been annulled. He, of a truth, is the Ordainer, the All-Wise.

13 God hath exempted women who are in their courses from obligatory prayer and fasting. Let them, instead, after performance of their ablutions, give praise unto God, repeating ninety-five times between the noon of one day and the next "Glorified be God, the Lord of Splendour and Beauty". Thus hath it

Baha'u'llah, *Kitab-I-Aqdas*, 1–2, 12–16, 30–45, 63–65, 149–150, sacred-texts.com.

been decreed in the Book, if ye be of them that comprehend.

14 When travelling, if ye should stop and rest in some safe spot, perform ye—men and women alike—a single prostration in place of each unsaid Obligatory Prayer, and while prostrating say "Glorified be God, the Lord of Might and Majesty, of Grace and Bounty". Whoso is unable to do this, let him say only "Glorified be God"; this shall assuredly suffice him. He is, of a truth, the all-sufficing, the ever-abiding, the forgiving, compassionate God. Upon completing your prostrations, seat yourselves cross-legged—men and women alike—and eighteen times repeat "Glorified be God, the Lord of the kingdoms of earth and heaven". Thus doth the Lord make plain the ways of truth and guidance, ways that lead to one way, which is this Straight Path. Render thanks unto God for this most gracious favour; offer praise unto Him for this bounty that hath encompassed the heavens and the earth; extol Him for this mercy that hath pervaded all creation.

15 Say: God hath made My hidden love the key to the Treasure; would that ye might perceive it! But for the key, the Treasure would to all eternity have remained concealed; would that ye might believe it! Say: This is the Source of Revelation, the Dawning-place of Splendour, Whose brightness hath illumined the horizons of the world. Would that ye might understand! This is, verily, that fixed Decree through which every irrevocable decree hath been established.

16 O Pen of the Most High! Say: O people of the world! We have enjoined upon you fasting during a brief period, and at its close have designated for you Naw-Ruz as a feast. Thus hath the Day-Star of Utterance shone forth above the horizon of the Book as decreed by Him Who is the Lord of the beginning and the end. Let the days in excess of the months be placed before the month of fasting. We have ordained that these, amid all nights and days, shall be the manifestations of the letter Ha, and thus they have not been bounded by the limits of the year and its months. It behoveth the people of Baha'i, throughout these days, to provide good cheer for themselves, their kindred and, beyond them, the poor and needy, and with joy and exultation to hail and glorify their Lord, to sing His praise and magnify His Name; and when they end—these days of giving that precede the season of restraint—let them enter upon the Fast. Thus hath it been ordained by Him Who is the Lord of all mankind. The traveller, the ailing, those who are with child or giving suck, are not bound by the Fast; they have been exempted by God as a token of His grace. He, verily, is the Almighty, the Most Generous.

30 The Lord hath ordained that in every city a House of Justice be established wherein shall gather counsellors to the number of Baha'i, and should it exceed this number it doth not matter. They should consider themselves as entering the Court of the presence of God, the Exalted, the Most High, and as beholding Him Who is the Unseen. It behoveth them to be the trusted ones of the Merciful among men and to regard themselves as the guardians appointed of God for all that dwell on earth. It is incumbent upon them to take counsel together and to have regard for the interests of the servants of God, for His sake, even as they regard their own interests, and to choose that which is meet and seemly. Thus hath the Lord your God commanded you. Beware lest ye put away that which is clearly revealed in His Tablet. Fear God, O ye that perceive.

31 O people of the world! Build ye houses of worship throughout the lands in the name of Him Who is the Lord of all religions. Make them as perfect as is possible in the world of being, and adorn them with that which befitteth them, not with images and effigies. Then, with radiance and joy, celebrate therein the praise of your Lord, the Most Compassionate. Verily, by His remembrance the eye is cheered and the heart is filled with light.

32 The Lord hath ordained that those of you who are able shall make pilgrimage to the sacred House, and from this He hath exempted women as a mercy on His part. He, of a truth, is the All-Bountiful, the Most Generous.

33 O people of Baha'i! It is incumbent upon each one of you to engage in some occupation—such as a craft, a trade or the like. We have exalted your engagement in such work to the rank of worship of the one true God. Reflect, O people, on the grace and blessings of your Lord, and yield Him thanks at

eventide and dawn. Waste not your hours in idleness and sloth, but occupy yourselves with what will profit you and others. Thus hath it been decreed in this Tablet from whose horizon hath shone the day-star of wisdom and utterance. The most despised of men in the sight of God are they who sit and beg. Hold ye fast unto the cord of means and place your trust in God, the Provider of all means.

34 The kissing of hands hath been forbidden in the Book. This practice is prohibited by God, the Lord of glory and command. To none is it permitted to seek absolution from another soul; let repentance be between yourselves and God. He, verily, is the Pardoner, the Bounteous, the Gracious, the One Who absolveth the repentant.

35 O ye servants of the Merciful One! Arise to serve the Cause of God, in such wise that the cares and sorrows caused by them that have disbelieved in the Dayspring of the Signs of God may not afflict you. At the time when the Promise was fulfilled and the Promised One made manifest, differences have appeared amongst the kindreds of the earth and each people hath followed its own fancy and idle imaginings.

36 Amongst the people is he who seateth himself amid the sandals by the door whilst coveting in his heart the seat of honour. Say: What manner of man art thou, O vain and heedless one, who wouldst appear as other than thou art? And among the people is he who layeth claim to inner knowledge, and still deeper knowledge concealed within this knowledge. Say: Thou speakest false! By God! What thou dost possess is naught but husks which We have left to thee as bones are left to dogs. By the righteousness of the one true God! Were anyone to wash the feet of all mankind, and were he to worship God in the forests, valleys, and mountains, upon high hills and lofty peaks, to leave no rock or tree, no clod of earth, but was a witness to his worship—yet, should the fragrance of My good pleasure not be inhaled from him, his works would never be acceptable unto God. Thus hath it been decreed by Him Who is the Lord of all. How many a man hath secluded himself in the climes of India, denied himself the things that God hath decreed as lawful, imposed upon himself austerities and mortifications, and hath not been remembered by God, the Revealer of Verses. Make not your deeds as snares wherewith to entrap the object of your aspiration, and deprive not yourselves of this Ultimate Objective for which have ever yearned all such as have drawn nigh unto God. Say: The very life of all deeds is My good pleasure, and all things depend upon Mine acceptance. Read ye the Tablets that ye may know what hath been purposed in the Books of God, the All-Glorious, the Ever-Bounteous. He who attaineth to My love hath title to a throne of gold, to sit thereon in honour over all the world; he who is deprived thereof, though he sit upon the dust, that dust would seek refuge with God, the Lord of all Religions.

37 Whoso layeth claim to a Revelation direct from God, ere the expiration of a full thousand years, such a man is assuredly a lying impostor. We pray God that He may graciously assist him to retract and repudiate such claim. Should he repent, God will, no doubt, forgive him. If, however, he persisteth in his error, God will, assuredly, send down one who will deal mercilessly with him. Terrible, indeed, is God in punishing! Whosoever interpreteth this verse otherwise than its obvious meaning is deprived of the Spirit of God and of His mercy which encompasseth all created things. Fear God, and follow not your idle fancies. Nay, rather, follow the bidding of your Lord, the Almighty, the All-Wise. Erelong shall clamorous voices be raised in most lands. Shun them, O My people, and follow not the iniquitous and evil-hearted. This is that of which We gave you forewarning when We were dwelling in Iraq, then later while in the Land of Mystery, and now from this Resplendent Spot.

38 Be not dismayed, O peoples of the world, when the day-star of My beauty is set, and the heaven of My tabernacle is concealed from your eyes. Arise to further My Cause, and to exalt My Word amongst men. We are with you at all times, and shall strengthen you through the power of truth. We are truly almighty. Whoso hath recognized Me will arise and serve Me with such determination that the powers of earth and heaven shall be unable to defeat his purpose.

39 The peoples of the world are fast asleep. Were they to wake from their slumber, they would hasten

with eagerness unto God, the All-Knowing, the All-Wise. They would cast away everything they possess, be it all the treasures of the earth, that their Lord may remember them to the extent of addressing to them but one word. Such is the instruction given you by Him Who holdeth the knowledge of things hidden, in a Tablet which the eye of creation hath not seen, and which is revealed to none except His own Self, the omnipotent Protector of all worlds. So bewildered are they in the drunkenness of their evil desires, that they are powerless to recognize the Lord of all being, Whose voice calleth aloud from every direction: "There is none other God but Me, the Mighty, the All-Wise."

40 Say: Rejoice not in the things ye possess; tonight they are yours, tomorrow others will possess them. Thus warneth you He Who is the All-Knowing, the All-Informed. Say: Can ye claim that what ye own is lasting or secure? Nay! By Myself, the All-Merciful, ye cannot, if ye be of them who judge fairly. The days of your life flee away as a breath of wind, and all your pomp and glory shall be folded up as were the pomp and glory of those gone before you. Reflect, O people! What hath become of your bygone days, your lost centuries? Happy the days that have been consecrated to the remembrance of God, and blessed the hours which have been spent in praise of Him Who is the All-Wise. By My life! Neither the pomp of the mighty, nor the wealth of the rich, nor even the ascendancy of the ungodly will endure. All will perish, at a word from Him. He, verily, is the All-Powerful, the All-Compelling, the Almighty. What advantage is there in the earthly things which men possess? That which shall profit them, they have utterly neglected. Erelong, they will awake from their slumber, and find themselves unable to obtain that which hath escaped them in the days of their Lord, the Almighty, the All-Praised. Did they but know it, they would renounce their all, that their names may be mentioned before His throne. They, verily, are accounted among the dead.

41 Amongst the people is he whose learning hath made him proud, and who hath been debarred thereby from recognizing My Name, the Self-Subsisting; who, when he heareth the tread of sandals following behind him, waxeth greater in his own esteem than Nimrod. Say: O rejected one! Where now is his abode? By God, it is the nethermost fire. Say: O concourse of divines! Hear ye not the shrill voice of My Most Exalted Pen? See ye not this Sun that shineth in refulgent splendour above the All-Glorious Horizon? For how long will ye worship the idols of your evil passions? Forsake your vain imaginings, and turn yourselves unto God, your Everlasting Lord.

42 Endowments dedicated to charity revert to God, the Revealer of Signs. None hath the right to dispose of them without leave from Him Who is the Dawning-place of Revelation. After Him, this authority shall pass to the Aghsan, and after them to the House of Justice—should it be established in the world by then—that they may use these endowments for the benefit of the Places which have been exalted in this Cause, and for whatsoever hath been enjoined upon them by Him Who is the God of might and power. Otherwise, the endowments shall revert to the people of Baha'i who speak not except by His leave and judge not save in accordance with what God hath decreed in this Tablet—lo, they are the champions of victory betwixt heaven and earth—that they may use them in the manner that hath been laid down in the Book by God, the Mighty, the Bountiful.

43 Lament not in your hours of trial, neither rejoice therein; seek ye the Middle Way which is the remembrance of Me in your afflictions and reflection over that which may befall you in future. Thus informeth you He Who is the Omniscient, He Who is aware.

44 Shave not your heads; God hath adorned them with hair, and in this there are signs from the Lord of creation to those who reflect upon the requirements of nature. He, verily, is the God of strength and wisdom. Notwithstanding, it is not seemly to let the hair pass beyond the limit of the ears. Thus hath it been decreed by Him Who is the Lord of all worlds.

45 Exile and imprisonment are decreed for the thief, and, on the third offence, place ye a mark upon his brow so that, thus identified, he may not be accepted in the cities of God and His countries. Beware lest, through compassion, ye neglect to carry out the statutes of the religion of God; do that which hath been bidden you by Him Who is compassionate and merciful. We school you with the rod of wisdom and

laws, like unto the father who educateth his son, and this for naught but the protection of your own selves and the elevation of your stations. By My life, were ye to discover what We have desired for you in revealing Our holy laws, ye would offer up your very souls for this sacred, this mighty, and most exalted Faith.

63 God hath prescribed matrimony unto you. Beware that ye take not unto yourselves more wives than two. Whoso contenteth himself with a single partner from among the maidservants of God, both he and she shall live in tranquillity. And he who would take into his service a maid may do so with propriety. Such is the ordinance which, in truth and justice, hath been recorded by the Pen of Revelation. Enter into wedlock, O people, that ye may bring forth one who will make mention of Me amid My servants. This is My bidding unto you; hold fast to it as an assistance to yourselves.

64 O people of the world! Follow not the promptings of the self, for it summoneth insistently to wickedness and lust; follow, rather, Him Who is the Possessor of all created things, Who biddeth you to show forth piety, and manifest the fear of God. He, verily, is independent of all His creatures. Take heed not to stir up mischief in the land after it hath been set in order. Whoso acteth in this way is not of Us, and We are quit of him. Such is the command which hath, through the power of truth, been made manifest from the heaven of Revelation.

65 It hath been laid down in the Bayan that marriage is dependent upon the consent of both parties. Desiring to establish love, unity and harmony amidst Our servants, We have conditioned it, once the couple's wish is known, upon the permission of their parents, lest enmity and rancour should arise amongst them. And in this We have yet other purposes. Thus hath Our commandment been ordained.

149 Recite ye the verses of God every morn and eventide. Whoso faileth to recite them hath not been faithful to the Covenant of God and His Testament, and whoso turneth away from these holy verses in this Day is of those who throughout eternity have turned away from God. Fear ye God, O My servants, one and all. Pride not yourselves on much reading of the verses or on a multitude of pious acts by night and day; for were a man to read a single verse with joy and radiance it would be better for him than to read with lassitude all the Holy Books of God, the Help in Peril, the Self-Subsisting. Read ye the sacred verses in such measure that ye be not overcome by languor and despondency. Lay not upon your souls that which will weary them and weigh them down, but rather what will lighten and uplift them, so that they may soar on the wings of the Divine verses towards the Dawning-place of His manifest signs; this will draw you nearer to God, did ye but comprehend.

150 Teach your children the verses revealed from the heaven of majesty and power, so that, in most melodious tones, they may recite the Tablets of the All-Merciful in the alcoves within the Mashriqu'l-Adhkars. Whoever hath been transported by the rapture born of adoration for My Name, the Most Compassionate, will recite the verses of God in such wise as to captivate the hearts of those yet wrapped in slumber. Well is it with him who hath quaffed the Mystic Wine of everlasting life from the utterance of his merciful Lord in My Name—a Name through which every lofty and majestic mountain hath been reduced to dust.

The Bab on Islam and Christianity

1 ALL praise be to God Who hath, through the power of Truth, sent down this Book unto His servant, that it may serve as a shining light for all mankind. . . . Verily this is none other than the sovereign Truth; it is the Path which God hath laid out for all that are in heaven and on earth. Let him then who will, take for himself the right path unto his Lord. Verily this is the true Faith of God, and sufficient witness are God and such as are endowed with the knowledge of the Book. This is indeed the eternal Truth which God, the Ancient of Days, hath revealed unto His omnipotent Word—He Who hath been raised up from the midst of the Burning Bush. This is the Mystery which hath been hidden from all that are in heaven and on earth, and in this wondrous Revelation it hath, in very truth, been set forth in the Mother Book by the hand of God, the Exalted. . . .
61 Verily, Christ is Our Word which We communicated unto Mary; and let no one say what the Christians term as 'the third of three', inasmuch as it would amount to slandering the Remembrance Who, as decreed in the Mother Book, is invested with supreme authority. Indeed God is but one God, and far be it from His glory that there should be aught else besides Him. All those who shall attain unto Him on the Day of Resurrection are but His servants, and God is, of a truth, a sufficient Protector. Verily I am none other but the servant of God and His Word, and none but the first one to bow down in supplication before God, the Most Exalted; and indeed God witnesseth all things.
62 O PEOPLE of the Qur'an! Ye are as nothing unless ye submit unto the Remembrance of God and unto this Book. If ye follow the Cause of God, We will forgive you your sins, and if ye turn aside from Our command, We will, in truth, condemn your souls in Our Book, unto the Most Great Fire. We, verily, do not deal unjustly with men, even to the extent of a speck on a date-stone.
63 O PEOPLES of the earth! Verily the resplendent Light of God hath appeared in your midst, invested with this unerring Book, that ye may be guided aright to the ways of peace and, by the leave of God, step out of the darkness into the light and onto this far-extended Path of Truth...

God hath, out of sheer nothingness and through the potency of His command, created the heavens and the earth and whatever lieth between them. He is single and peerless in His eternal unity with none to join partner with His holy Essence, nor is there any soul, except His Own Self, who can befittingly comprehend Him. . . .

O peoples of the earth! Verily His Remembrance is come to you from God after an interval during which there were no Messengers, that He may purge and purify you from uncleanliness in anticipation of the Day of the One true God; therefore seek ye whole-heartedly divine blessings from Him, inasmuch as We have, in truth, chosen Him to be the Witness and the Source of wisdom unto all that dwell on earth. . . .
68 Say, O peoples of the world! Do ye dispute with Me about God by virtue of the names which ye and your fathers have adopted for Him at the promptings of the Evil One? God hath indeed sent down this Book unto Me with truth that ye may be enabled to recognize the true names of God, inasmuch as ye have strayed in error far from the Truth. Verily We have taken a covenant from every created thing upon its coming into being concerning the Remembrance of God, and there shall be none to avert the binding command of God for the purification of mankind, as ordained in the Book which is written by the hand of the Bab.

Ali Muhammad Shirazi (The Bab), *Qayyumu'l-Asma'*, chs. 1, 62–63, 68, sacred-texts.com

World Peace

Whilst in the Prison of Akka, We revealed in the Crimson Book that which is conducive to the advancement of mankind and to the reconstruction of the world. The utterances set forth therein by the Pen of the Lord of creation include the following which constitute the fundamental principles for the administration of the affairs of men:

First: It is incumbent upon the ministers of the House of Justice to promote the Lesser Peace so that the people of the earth may be relieved from the burden of exorbitant expenditures. This matter is imperative and absolutely essential, inasmuch as hostilities and conflict lie at the root of affliction and calamity.

Second: Languages must be reduced to one common language to be taught in all the schools of the world.

Third: It behoveth man to adhere tenaciously unto that which will promote fellowship, kindliness and unity.

Fourth: Everyone, whether man or woman, should hand over to a trusted person a portion of what he or she earneth through trade, agriculture or other occupation, for the training and education of children, to be spent for this purpose with the knowledge of the Trustees of the House of Justice.

Fifth: Special regard must be paid to agriculture. Although it hath been mentioned in the fifth place, unquestionably it precedeth the others. Agriculture is highly developed in foreign lands, however in Persia it hath so far been grievously neglected. It is hoped that His Majesty the Shah—may God assist him by His grace—will turn his attention to this vital and important matter.

Were men to strictly observe that which the Pen of the Most High hath revealed in the Crimson Book, they could then well afford to dispense with the regulations which prevail in the world. Certain exhortations have repeatedly streamed forth from the Pen of the Most High that perchance the manifestations of power and the dawning-places of might may, sometime, be enabled to enforce them. Indeed, were sincere seekers to be found, every emanation of God's pervasive and irresistible Will would, for the sake of His love, be revealed. But where are to be found earnest seekers and inquiring minds? Whither are gone the equitable and the fair-minded? At present no day passeth without the fire of a fresh tyranny blazing fiercely, or the sword of a new aggression being unsheathed. Gracious God! The great and the noble in Persia glory in acts of such savagery that one is lost in amazement at the tales thereof.

Baha'u'llah, *Lawh-I-Dunya*, in *Tablets of Baha'u'llah Revealed after The Kitab-i-Aqdas*, sacred-texts.com.

WICCA

Drawing Down the Moon (1949)

High Priestess stands in front of Altar, assumes Goddess position (arms crossed). Magus, kneeling in front of her, draws pentacle on her body with Phallus-headed Wand, invokes, "I Invoke and beseech Thee, O mighty Mother of all life and fertility. By seed and root, by stem and bud, by leaf and flower and fruit, by Life and Love, do I invoke Thee to descend into the body of thy servant and High Priestess [name]." The Moon having been drawn down, i.e., link established, Magus and other men give Five-fold Kiss:

(kissing feet) "Blessed be thy feet, that have brought thee in these ways";

(kissing knees) "Blessed be thy knees, that shall kneel at the sacred altar";

(kissing womb) "Blessed be thy womb, without which we would not be";

(kissing breasts) "Blessed be thy breasts, formed in beauty and in strength";

(kissing lips) "Blessed be thy lips, that shall speak the sacred names."

Women all bow.

If there be an initiation, then at this time the Magus and the High Priestess in Goddess position (Arms Crossed) says the Charge while the Initiate stands outside the circle.

Gerald B. Gardner, *The Gardnerian Book of Shadows*, 1949, sacred-texts.com.

Power (1953)

Power is latent in the body and may be drawn out and used in various ways by the skilled. But unless confined in a circle it will be swiftly dissipated. Hence the importance of a properly constructed circle. Power seems to exude from the body via the skin and possibly from the orifices of the body; hence you should be properly prepared. The slightest dirt spoils everything, which shows the importance of thorough cleanliness. The attitude of mind has great effect, so only work with a spirit of reverence. A little wine taken and repeated during the ceremony, if necessary, helps to produce power. Other strong drinks or drugs may be used, but it is necessary to be very moderate, for if you are confused, even slightly, you

Gerald B. Gardner, *The Gardnerian Book of Shadows*, 1953, sacred-texts.com.

cannot control the power you evoke. The simplest way is by dancing and singing monotonous chants, slowly at first and gradually quickening the tempo until giddiness ensues. Then the calls may be used, or even wild and meaningless shrieking produces power. But this method inflames the mind and renders it difficult to control the power, though control may be gained through practice. The scourge is a far better way, for it stimulates and excites both body and soul, yet one easily retains control. The Great Rite is far the best. It releases enormous power, but the conditions and circumstances make it difficult for the mind to maintain control at first. It is again a matter of practice and the natural strength of the operator's will and, in a lesser degree, of those of his assistants. If, as of old, there were many trained assistants present and all wills properly attuned, wonders occurred. Sorcerers chiefly used the blood sacrifice; and while we hold this to be evil, we cannot deny that this method is very efficient. Power flashes forth from newly shed blood, instead of exuding slowly as by our method. The victim's terror and anguish add keenness, and even quite a small animal can yield enormous power. The great difficulty is in the human mind controlling the power of the lower animal mind. But sorcerers claim they have methods for effecting this and that the difficulty disappears the higher the animal used, and when the victim is human disappears entirely. (The practice is an abomination but it is so.) Priests know this well; and by their auto-da-fé, with the victims' pain and terror (the fires acting much the same as circles), obtained much power. Of old the Flagellants certainly evoked power, but through not being confined in a circle much was lost. The amount of power raised was so great and continuous that anyone with knowledge could direct and use it; and it is most probable that the classical and heathen sacrifices were used in the same way. There are whispers that when the human victim was a willing sacrifice, with his mind directed on the Great Work and with highly skilled assistants, wonders ensued but of this I would not speak.

STUDY QUESTIONS

1. Who is Mary Baker Eddy? Who is Joseph Smith?
2. What is the Christian Science perspective on reality?
3. Why does Mary Baker Eddy urge Christian Scientists to avoid conventional medicine?
4. According to the Mormon view, how did Joseph Smith come to possess the *Book of Mormon*?
5. Who is Baha'u'llah?
6. What is the ultimate goal of Baha'i?
7. What practices does Baha'i condemn?
8. What is Wicca?
9. How does modern Wicca differ from the stereotypical view of witches and witchcraft?

FURTHER READING

Margot Adler, *Drawing Down the Moon* (New York: Penguin, 2006).

Peter B. Clarke, ed., *Encyclopedia of New Religious Movements* (London: Routledge, 2006).

Charles S. Clifton, *Her Hidden Children: The Rise of Wicca and Paganism in America* (Guilford, CT: AltaMira Press, 2006).

Scott Cunningham, *Wicca: A Guide for the Solitary Practitioner* (Woodbury, MN: Llewellyn Publications, 1989).

Gerald B. Gardner, *The Gardnerian Book of Shadows* (Charleston, SC: Forgotten Books, 1953).

John R. Hinnells, ed., *A New Handbook of Living Religions* (New York: Penguin, 1997).

James R. Lewis, ed., *The Oxford Handbook of New Religions*, 2nd. ed. (New York: Oxford University Press, 2004).

James R. Lewis and Jesper Aagaard Petersen, ed., *Controversial New Religions* (New York: Oxford University Press, 2005).

Timothy Miller, *America's Alternative Religions* (Albany: State University of New York Press, 1995).

John B. Noss, *A History of the World's Religions* (New York: Macmillan, 1994).

Catherine Wessinger, ed., *Women's Leadership in Marginal Religions: New Roles Outside the Mainstream* (Chicago: University of Illinois Press, 1993).

ONLINE

The Baha'i Faith, http://www.bahai.org/ (December 31, 2015).

The Celtic Connection, "Wicca and Witchcraft," http://wicca.com/celtic/cc002.htm (December 31, 2015).

Christian Science, "What Is Christian Science?" http://christianscience.com/what-is-christian-science (December 31, 2015).

The Church of Jesus Christ of Latter-Day Saints, https://www.mormon.org/ (December 31, 2015).

Credits

CHAPTER 1

Page 2, Figure 1.1: Dan Howell/Shutterstock.com. **Page 4, Figure 1.2:** Evgenia Bolyukh/Shutterstock.com. **Page 6, Figure 1.3:** © Eye Ubiquitous/Alamy Stock Photo.

CHAPTER 2

Page 34, Figure 2.1: Everett Historical/Shutterstock.com. **Page 37, Figure 2.2:** Smithsonian Institution, National Anthropological Archives [1659-A].

CHAPTER 3

Page 84, Figure 3.1: Netfalls - Remy Musser/Shutterstock.com. **Page 86, Figure 3.2:** Rajesh Kumar Singh/The Associated Press.

CHAPTER 4

Page 136, Figure 4.1: © robertharding/Alamy Stock Photo. **Page 138, Figure 4.2:** © Frederic Soltan/Sygma/Corbis.

CHAPTER 5

Page 156, Figure 5.1: © The Trustees of the British Museum. **Page 166, Figure 5.2:** © British Library Board/Robana/Art Resource, NY.

CHAPTER 6

Page 209, Figure 6.1: Holger Mette. **Page 211, Figure 6.2:** Cornfield/Shutterstock.com.

CHAPTER 7

Page 233, Figure 7.1: XiXinXing/Shutterstock.com. **Page 236, Figure 7.2:** Brian Kinney/Shutterstock.com.

CHAPTER 8

Page 262, Figure 8.1: Foto Marburg/Art Resource, NY. **Page 266, Figure 8.2:** Luisa Puccini/Shutterstock.com.

CHAPTER 9

Page 289, Figure 9.1: Aleksandar Todorovic/Shutterstock.com. **Page 291, Figure 9.2:** Sean Pavone/Shutterstock.com.

CHAPTER 10

Page 304, Figure 10.1: suronin/Shutterstock.com. **Page 307, Figure 10.2:** Aleksandar Todorovic/Shutterstock.com.

CHAPTER 11

Page 327, Figure 11.1: Nicku/Shutterstock.com. **Page 329, Figure 11.2:** ruskpp/Shutterstock.com.

CHAPTER 12

Page 385, Figure 12.1: Nancy Bauer/Shutterstock.com. **Page 392, Figure 12.2:** Viacheslav Lopatin/Shutterstock.com.

CHAPTER 13

Page 439, Figure 13.1: Sufi/Shutterstock.com. **Page 441, Figure 13.2:** BEGY Production/Shutterstock.com.

CHAPTER 14

Page 483, Figure 14.1: Legacy Images/Shutterstock.com. **Page 484, Figure 14.2:** Copyright Bettmann/Corbis/AP Images.

Index